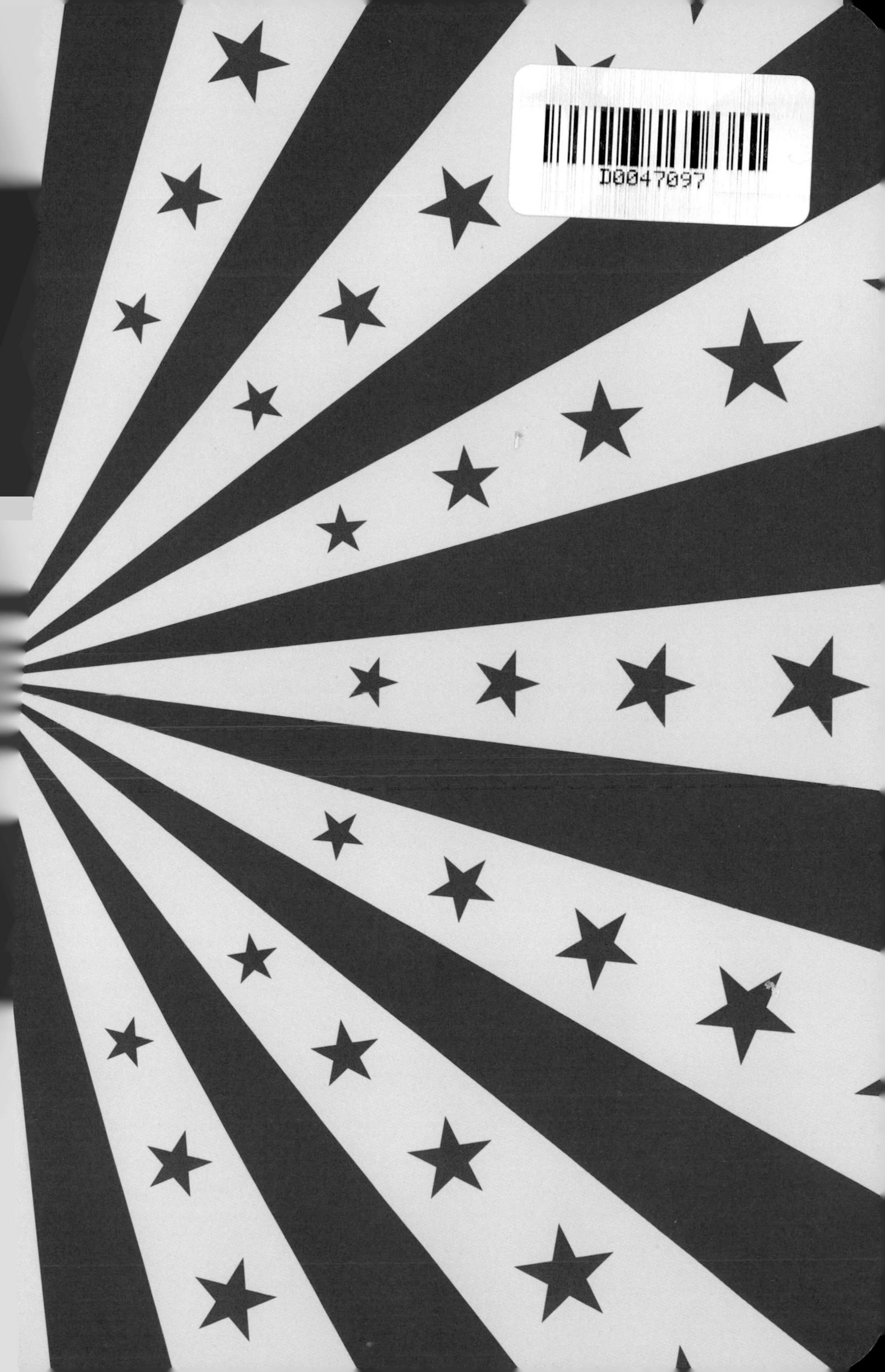
D0047097

Uncle John's No. 33 Greatest Know on Earth

Curiosities, Rarities & Amazing Oddities

By the Bathroom Readers' Institute

Portable Press

San Diego, California

PORTABLE PRESS

Portable Press / The Bathroom Readers' Institute
An imprint of Printers Row Publishing Group
10350 Barnes Canyon Road, Suite 100, San Diego, CA 92121
www.portablepress.com • mail@portablepress.com

Correspondence regarding the content of this book should be sent to Portable Press / The Bathroom Readers' Institute, Editorial Department, at the above address.

Publisher: Peter Norton • Associate Publisher: Ana Parker
Developmental Editor: Vicki Jaeger
Copy Editor: Dan Mansfield
Production Team: Jonathan Lopes, Rusty von Dyl, Julie Greene

Producer and Creator: Javna Brothers LLC

Interior, Illustrations, and Infographics Designer: Lidija Tomas
Cover and Endpaper Designer: Rosemary Rae

Cover, page i: tintin75/iStock/Getty Images Plus • Endpaper: tomozina/iStock/Getty Images Plus

Dedicated to Bo, Lou, Ivy, and Jean, B.R.I.T. (Bathroom Readers In Training)

"Humor keeps us alive. Humor and food. Don't forget food. You can go a week without laughing." –Joss Whedon

Library of Congress Control Number: 2020937287
ISBN: 978-1-64517-414-1

Printed in the United States of America

24 23 22 21 20   1 2 3 4 5

OUR "REGULAR" READERS RAVE!

I receive the *Bathroom Reader* every year as a Christmas gift from my mother-in-law. I can't tell you how much our family enjoys them.

—Susie D.

I have read many, many of your *Uncle John's Bathroom Readers* over the years, and have enjoyed them very much.

—Ken G.

My dad gave me a copy of *Absolutely Absorbing* when I went to college in 2000. And I just sent my daughter off to college with *Truth, Trivia, and the Pursuit of Factiness*!

—Janelle T.

Thank you for making these wonderful books. I read them every day and I learn so much from them. And they are super entertaining.

—Matthew W.

Your books bring my family lots of pleasure.

—Lou B.

Thanks to Uncle John, I always have something to talk about at parent socials. How else would I know about the government-funded study on the effectiveness of human urine fertilizer?

—Julie M.

Being home with the kids is a lot more bearable with a stack of *Bathroom Readers* around!

—Vince N.

You're everybody's uncle!

—Diego L.

I'm nearing the end of the book...and I'm eagerly awaiting the next one.

—Jon L.

My favorite Christmas present is the *Bathroom Reader*. I give one to myself every year.

—Mike C.

CONTENTS

Because the BRI understands your reading needs, we've divided the contents by length as well as subject.

Short—a quick read

Medium—2 to 3 pages

Long—for those extended visits, when something a little more involved is required

Medium

Long

FOOD FOR THOUGHT

Short

Medium

Long

FORGOTTEN HISTORY

Short

Medium

GOOD NEWS

Medium

INNOVATORS

Short

Medium

IT'S A WEIRD, WEIRD WORLD

Medium

* * *

A Clockwork Orange, Starring Mick Jagger

Anthony Burgess's 1961 novel *A Clockwork Orange* became a cult classic among England's disaffected youth—one of whom was the Rolling Stones' Mick Jagger. In 1968, it was announced that novelist Terry Southern would be adapting *Clockwork* for the screen, and Jagger wanted the lead role of gang leader Alex, who commits acts of "ultra-violence" around London. Many of Jagger's famous friends signed a petition and sent it to Southern (who was planning to cast someone else). But the project stalled until Stanley Kubrick took the helm, fresh off his sci-fi hit *2001: A Space Odyssey*. Kubrick adapted the screenplay and agreed to direct only if Malcolm McDowell was cast as Alex...and in 1971, *A Clockwork Orange* made McDowell a star.

Update: In 2017, that petition went to auction, where it was expected to sell for $25,000. Among the star-studded signers: all four Beatles. Their plan was for Jagger to star and for John, Paul, George, and Ringo to write and perform the music.

INTRODUCTION

Like most people, when I was a little kid I loved the circus. My favorite part: the sideshow. For me, all those bizarre characters and fascinating oddities relegated to the side of the main show *were* the main show. That started a lifelong love of all things weird, bizarre, and strange...right up to today.

I also really liked hearing the ringmaster's voice reverberating throughout the big top, kind of like this (ahem): "Ladies and gentleman, boys and girls, children of all ages! Welcome one and all to the 33rd edition of the *Bathroom Reader*:

UNCLE JOHN'S

GREATEST

KNOW

☆ ON EARTH ☆

And let's not forget the trapeze artists. I was mesmerized by how gracefully they flipped through the air from one to another. I even had a dream of flipping through the air like that myself. (That lasted all of 15 seconds.) Instead, here I am flipping through the manuscript of our latest masterpiece from the safety and comfort of my captain's chair.

It's a fun one to flip through, too—especially if you are fond of weirdos. You'll read about the man who holds the world record for "most pairs of underwear put on in one minute" (and the man who broke that record). Or the oddball artist whose work, *Nothing,* really was nothing (and it got an award). Or the singer who sued the actress for stealing a chicken named Doggie. Or the scientific study to determine why wombat poops are cube-shaped.

Not into weirdos? How about heroes—ordinary folks who commit brave acts of derring-do? Like the boy with a rare blood type who grew up to save countless lives, the scientist who brought us the songs of whales, the first woman to ski to the North Pole, the two boys who crossed the country alone on horseback, and the captains who evacuated lower Manhattan by boat on 9/11. And not just heroes, but goats! Yes, we actually have a page of goat facts...and another page of fart facts (both are way more interesting than you'd think).

That gets to the core of why we put on this circus year after year: to astound and amaze you with a menagerie of little-known facts you won't find anywhere else, all under one tent. As I often say, it's not just stuff you didn't know, it's stuff you didn't know you needed to know. You'll find out why every rainbow is unique to the person who is viewing it, how dress sizes are determined, what people eat for breakfast in other countries, and why you say "big, bad wolf" and not "bad, big wolf."

You're also in for a treat if you like origins, including the dune buggy, the beehive hairdo, telephone hold music, sports domes, Bigfoot, and the marine survival suit (which will introduce you to yet another hero who's saved countless lives).

And it wouldn't be a *Bathroom Reader* if we didn't lift the lid on some persistent myths and scams. Some examples: which popular "vegan" foods aren't really vegan, how third-party ticket brokers take advantage of you, how a clever public-relations campaign got everyone on the bacon bandwagon, and my personal favorite, the prankster who passed off "Hot Dog Water" as a real product...and people bought it.

Before we get this show started, let me take an opportunity to thank our hardworking cast of word jugglers, research acrobats, and behind-the-scenes roustabouts who, with seeming effortlessness, walk the tightrope between the profound and inane to surprise and delight you with great new things to know:

Gordon Javna
John Dollison
Jay Newman
Brian Boone
Thom Little
Kim Griswell
Gene Stone
J. Carroll
Lidija Tomas
Derek Fairbridge
Nitpicky Vicki
Dan the Man
Aunt Joan
Edward Kenton
Laurie Duncan
Michael Ford
Glenn Cunningham
Mary Gabriel
Drew Papanestor
Linda Fox
John Javna
Otis B. Driftwood
Eustace P. McGargle
Thomas Crapper

And finally, to you, dear reader, here's a heartfelt THANK YOU. It is because of your insatiable curiosity and continued support that this little trivia-book-series-that-could is still going strong after 33 years. Now it's time to settle into the comfort of your own seat—wherever it may be—and enjoy the wonder of it all.

And as always, Go with the Flow!

—Uncle John and the BRI Staff

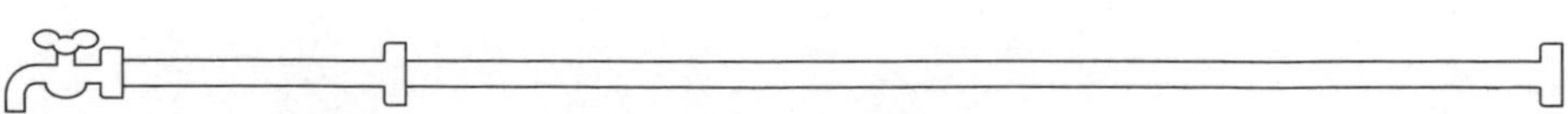

YOU'RE MY INSPIRATION

It's always interesting to find out where the architects of pop culture get their ideas. Some of these may surprise you.

THE JOKER: The Caped Crusader's archnemesis showed up in *Batman* No. 1, published in 1940. Comic book writers Bill Finger, Bob Kane, and Jerry Robinson drew their inspiration for the Joker from Gwynplaine, a tragic character who has been disfigured with a permanent grin in Victor Hugo's 1869 novel *The Man Who Laughs.* The basic look of the Joker—with his pale skin; haunting, maniacal smile; and swept-back hair—was based on Conrad Veidt's portrayal of Gwynplaine in the 1928 German silent film adaptation of Hugo's novel.

ELEVEN: The breakout character from the retro sci-fi show *Stranger Things,* which debuted on Netflix in 2016, is a mysterious girl who befriends a group of boys who try to help her. When Millie Bobby Brown was cast as Eleven, show creators Matt and Ross Duffer told her, "Basically, you're going to be an alien." And not just any alien, said Brown: "They told me that the performance that they wanted me to resemble was E.T." Both characters are uncertain of their surroundings, don't speak a lot, and must put their trust into kids. In a first-season episode, Eleven is dressed in a pink dress and blond wig similar to what E.T. wore in the 1982 film.

ARCHIE: Although hugely popular in the 1930s and '40s, the wholesome Andy Hardy movies starring teenaged Mickey Rooney aren't very well known today. But a character created to capitalize on that series has lived on. In 1941, a comic book publisher named John Goldwater collaborated with artist Bob Montana and writer Vic Bloom to come up with an Andy Hardy–like teenager that would attract the same fan base. The final Andy Hardy movie bombed in the 1950s, but Archie Andrews has endured, most recently in the hit syndicated series *Riverdale.*

THE FORCE: In 1963, filmmaker Arthur Lipsett spliced footage from the National Film Board of Canada to create an abstract short film called *21-87.* In one audio clip, cinematographer Roman Kroitor, while arguing that humans are more than mere machines, says, "Many people feel that in the contemplation of nature and in communication with other living things, they become aware of some kind of force, or something, behind this apparent mask which we see in front of us, and they call it God." *21-87* was hugely influential on *Star Wars* creator George Lucas, and he's confirmed that the Force, an "energy field...that binds the galaxy together," is "an echo of that phrase" from *21-87.*

FATBERGS AND COFFIN DODGERS

One type of news story that we at the BRI look forward to is the yearly list of new words that were added to the Merriam-Webster and Oxford English Dictionaries. Here are some of the latest.

Adorbs (adj.): short for “adorable”

Bawbag (n.): Scottish slang for “scrotum”

Bigsie (adj.): being or acting arrogant, pretentious, or conceited

Bottle Episode (n.): an episode of a TV series filmed on the cheap (“pulled out of the bottle like a genie”) using regular cast members and existing sets that require no additional preparation

Bougie (adj./n.): too concerned with status and material wealth (short for “bourgeois”)

Chicken-Licken/Chicken Littlin’ (n.): a person who panics easily and spreads fear and alarm to others

Chuggy (n.): a piece of chewing gum

Coffin Dodger (n.): someone seemingly close to death but who lives on and on; formerly applied to heavy smokers of advanced age

Fatberg (n.): a mass of fat and solid waste that collects in a sewer system (from “fat iceberg”)

Goldilocks (adj.): an orbital region around a sun where temperatures are neither too hot nor too cold to support life—in other words, just right

Garbage Time (n.): the final minutes of a game in which one team is so far ahead that the other team has no chance of winning and little-used players are given playing time

Salutogenesis (n.): measuring health according to well-being rather than by disease; a *Psychology Today* article called it “the best new word” of 2019

Hasbian (n.): a woman who no longer identifies as lesbian

Hophead (n.): a beer aficionado; first used in 1883 as slang for a drug addict, it has a less ominous definition today, thanks to the microbrewery craze

Marg (n.): short for margarita

Mocktail (n.): an alcohol-free cocktail

Pain Point (n.): a feature of a product or service that is annoying to customers

Purple (adj.): geographical areas with a roughly equal number of Democrats (blue) and Republicans (red)

Quillow (n.): a quilt that can be folded into a pocket to make a pillow

Schleppy (adj.): shabby, scruffy, or dowdy in appearance

Zoodle (n.): a long, thin strip of zucchini that resembles a noodle

THE TURNIP PRIZE

The Turner Prize is the most prestigious award that a visual artist in the United Kingdom can receive. The prize: £40,000. Far less prestigious is the Turnip Prize: a turnip nailed to a block of wood. You have a much better chance at winning a Turnip Prize. Here's how.

BED, BAR, AND BEYOND

The Turner Prize has been awarded annually since 1984. Early winners were mainly traditional artists in the same vein as namesake British painter J. M. W. Turner (1775–1851), known for his moody landscapes. Within a decade, however, more avant-garde conceptual artists were getting nominated. A 1999 finalist, for example, was Tracey Emin's *My Bed*—an unmade bed in a white room with garbage strewn around it.

Emin's controversial piece drew a lot of press and dominated the conversation at pubs throughout England, including one in Wedmore, Somerset, where it gave the bartender, Trevor Prideaux, an idea: "We thought, well, if *this* is art, then we can come up with better sh*t art than that. We called for people to send us...crap art using the least amount of effort possible. It started as a local thing but has gone international."

That means that anyone—including you—can enter a piece of "crap art" in the contest. Entries are accepted in person each November at the New Inn in Wedmore. Here's some advice: Even though Prideaux insists that minimal effort go into creating the actual artwork, the more clever and punny your title, the better your chances of winning. And a punny pseudonym doesn't hurt, either. To give you some inspiration, here are some of the more memorable Turnip Prize winners over the years.

Alfred the Grate: Alfred the Great ruled the Anglo-Saxons in the 890s. *Alfred the Grate* won the Turnip Prize in 1999. Artist David Stone's creation: two burned bread rolls on a cooking grate.

Take a Leaf out of My Chook: James Timms's winning entry for the 2003 Turnip Prize was a bunch of leaves stuffed into a raw chicken.

Dismal And: You've probably heard of the anonymous British street artist Banksy. Well, here's Mr. Bonksy of Bristol, who won the 2015 Turnip Prize for satirizing the satirist's *Dismaland.* Banksy's piece was a two-story replica of a decaying Cinderella's Castle; Mr. Bonsky created *Dismal And* by using a black marker to draw an ampersand (&) onto a piece of wood. To better convey the "dismal" theme, he drew a sad face in the top loop. "If you set your sights on the gutter and refuse to work hard," beamed Mr. Bonksy, "your dreams really can come true."

Birds Flew: Ian Osenthroat said he tried and failed to win a Turnip Prize several times,

maybe because he tried too hard. He finally won in 2005 with *Birds Flew,* a box of over-the-counter flu medicine sitting in a birds' nest that he found in his garage.

Torn Beef: "The work took no time at all to create," boasted Ian Lewis. "I fancied a corned beef sarnie [sandwich], got the tin out of the cupboard, and when trying to open the tin using the allotted key, instead of cutting around the top the key decided to go off in a different direction altogether and tore a big hole in the tin." Lewis ate the corned beef, submitted the empty can, and won the 2006 Turnip Prize.

Manhole Cover: Having some fun with a double entendre, Frank Van Bough won the 2009 Turnip Prize for presenting two pairs of men's underwear briefs, the kind with the little opening at the front. (Get it?)

Jamming with Muddy Waters: What do you get when you put some muddy water in a half-empty jar of jam...and then top it off with a bad pun? Jim Drew combined these three ingredients to win the 2011 Turnip Prize.

Play on Words: Percy Long-Prong's 2013 winning entry was a copy of William Shakespeare's *Macbeth* sitting atop *The Oxford Everyday Dictionary.* It's literally a play on words. At the awards ceremony, when Prideaux handed out the trophy, he said that the name Percy Long-Prong "will be remembered in art history for no time at all."

Tea P: In 2007, Bracey Vermin won a Turnip Prize for arranging a bunch of used wet tea bags in the shape of the letter "P." "I knew the moment I came up with the idea," she says, "the prize was in the bag."

Pulled Pork: Receiving our vote for the best pseudonym, 13-year-old Chris P. Bacon won in 2017 for a plastic toy tractor pulling a plastic toy pig. Her artist statement: "My inspiration came from my love of food."

Staple Diet: Another commentary on "society's troubled relationship with food" is 2015 finalist *Staple Diet.* The medium: a staple on a paper plate. The artist: Art Ist.

A Complete Waste of Thyme: An artist who goes by the name Canna B. Bothered was a 2019 finalist for spilling a jar of thyme onto a sheet of paper.

Nothing: Chloe Wilson won in 2001 for nothing. As in, she did nothing. She literally sent in nothing, called it *Nothing,* and won the Turnip Prize for it.

ONE LAST THING

Nearly every news story announcing the Turnip Prize, year after year, quotes the winner as saying something like, "In recent years I have unsuccessfully entered this competition, but my lack of effort has finally paid off!" Is this sloppy reporting, or are the winners having words put into their mouths by Trevor Prideaux? In the spirit of the Turnip Prize, we're not going to bother doing the research to find out. Meanwhile, in 2014, Tracey Emin's *My Bed* was sold to a private collector for $3 million.

At the height of the Cold War, U.S. President Ronald Reagan and Soviet General Secretary Mikhail Gorbachev agreed to team up in the event of an alien invasion.

OOPS!

Everyone makes outrageous blunders from time to time.
So go ahead and feel superior for a few minutes.

BIRD BRAIN CHALLENGE

Released in December 2018, Netflix's apocalyptic horror film *Bird Box* was a surprise hit. Sandra Bullock starred as a blindfolded mom who had to protect her two blindfolded children from monsters that provoke anyone who lays eyes on them to commit suicide. As the movie was breaking streaming records, a strange fad emerged: People filmed themselves doing mundane tasks while blindfolded and then posted the results online, using the hashtag #BirdBoxChallenge. Some challenges went way beyond the mundane, however, like the teenage girl who was driving her pickup truck on a busy road in Layton, Utah, and scared her passenger (a teenage boy) by pulling her beanie (wool cap) over her eyes and announcing, "It's the *Bird Box* challenge!" Then she veered into oncoming traffic and hit another car. Luckily, no one was seriously injured. Layton Police Lt. Travis Lyman said in a statement that the teen would be charged with reckless driving, and he echoed other law enforcement agencies from around the country with this plea to the public: "Honestly, I'm almost embarrassed to have to say, 'Don't drive with your eyes covered.' But, you know, apparently we do have to say that."

HIPSTER, KNOW THYSELF

In March 2019, the Massachusetts Institute of Technology (MIT) *Technology Review* reported on a recent Brandeis University study called "The Hipster Effect: Why Anti-conformists Always End Up Looking the Same." The MIT article included a stock photo of a typical hipster—complete with a beard, beanie, and flannel shirt. Beneath it was a caption: "Getty Images: Shot of a handsome young man in trendy winter attire against a wooden background." A few days after posting the article, MIT received the following e-mail:

> "You used a heavily edited Getty image of me for your recent bit of click-bait about why hipsters all look the same. It's a poorly written and insulting article and somewhat ironically about five years too late to be as desperately relevant as it is attempting to be. By using a tired cultural trope to try to spruce up an otherwise disturbing study. Your lack of basic journalistic ethics and both the manner in which you reported this uncredited nonsense and the slanderous unnecessary use of my picture without permission demands a response and I am of course pursuing legal action."

Gideon Lichfield, editor-in-chief of *Technology Review,* took the letter very seriously and contacted the stock photo agency. "Getty looked in their archive for the model release," reported Lichfield, "and came back to us with the surprising news: the model's name wasn't the name of our angry hipster-hater." When the protester was informed of his mistake, he replied, "Wow, I stand corrected, I guess." He went on to explain that his friends and family all thought it was him, and that he does wear a similar beard, hat, and shirt as the man in the photo. "It just proves the story we ran," remarked Lichfield. "Hipsters look so much alike that they can't even tell themselves apart from each other."

ANYONE SEEN A BOX OF GRENADES?

On May 1, 2018, the U.S. Air Force lost a 42-pound box of explosive grenade rounds after it tumbled out of the back of a Humvee somewhere along a six-mile stretch of gravel road connecting two North Dakota missile sites. More than 100 airmen searched the wooded route on foot, to no avail. (It didn't help that the ammo was stored in a camouflaged container.) It took the U.S. Air Force ten days to alert the public...a few hours after the local police did. Minot Air Force Base spokesman Lt. Col. Jamie Humphries offered a $5,000 reward for information leading to the box's safe return, and he reassured civilians that the explosives wouldn't work without an MK19 machine gun grenade launcher. He added that if you do happen to come across the container, don't touch it—especially if it's open: "Evacuate the area and call first responders." No word on whether the grenades were recovered, but two weeks later, a machine gun went missing from the same base. (Fortunately, it was not the kind of gun that can launch grenades.)

SHOCKING REQUEST

"I broke three bones in my left leg and one broke through the skin," wrote Tyler Uher in September 2019. "I have a slight fracture in my right hand and four minor breaks in my back. I also got a lot of burns from this. I will be out of work for at least eight weeks or more so anything helps. God bless." Despite the severity of Uher's injuries, many of the reactions to his GoFundMe page were less than supportive. "What in the name of God were you thinking?" read one comment. Another read, "It's your fault for doing this." Doing what? Uher was attending an Ohio University house party when he climbed to the top of an electricity pole. To the cheers of the partiers below, he chugged his beer, tossed the can away, and then for some inexplicable reason grabbed hold of an electrical wire. A bright flash lit up the night and then Uher went flying head over heels before plummeting 30 feet to the ground. He was unresponsive. After he was airlifted to a hospital, he was told to expect a long recovery and a mountain of medical bills. Uher's fundraiser originally asked for $100,000. After considerable mocking, the amount was reduced to $5,000. As of this writing it had only amassed $1,674. But not all the commenters were mean. One man, who donated $20, wrote, "Thanks for making me feel like less of an idiot."

And then for some inexplicable reason, he grabbed hold of an electrical wire.

ODD EGYPT

Strange facts about the land of the pharaohs.

FELINE FRIENDS: Cats were seen as protectors, and as living embodiments of the half-cat, half-human goddess Bastet, who protected the pharaoh. Cats owned by royalty and nobles were, in some cases, pampered even more than house cats are today: They wore golden collars and often ate off their owners' plates...*while* their owners were eating. When the cats died, many were embalmed and buried in special cat cemeteries, or in tombs with their owners. Killing a cat, even by accident, was punishable by death.

ALL IN THE FAMILY: Very few mummified fetuses or infants have been discovered in ancient Egyptian tombs, yet King Tutankhamun (1342–1325 B.C.) had two. They were his two daughters—his only known children. One was stillborn after five to six months of pregnancy; the other survived to full term but died either during or shortly after birth. Had this child lived, she would not have been healthy. Evidence suggests that she had spina bifida (incomplete closing of the spine), scoliosis (an irregularly curved spine), and Sprengel's deformity (one shoulder blade was higher than the other). These defects may have been due to inbreeding: Tutankhamun's parents were brother and sister, and he was married to his half-sister Ankhesenamun, with whom he fathered these children. King Tut's failure to produce an heir brought his family's dynasty—the Eighteenth Dynasty of Egypt—to an end.

HAVE A SEAT: King Tut was himself severely disabled, also probably because of inbreeding. His right foot was flat, his left foot was clubbed, and there is evidence that he too suffered from scoliosis. In paintings and statues, the boy king's clubfoot was never shown lest he'd seem weak. But unlike other pharaohs, paintings on the walls of his tomb depict him hunting birds and performing other activities while seated, as well as walking with the aid of a stick. To help him journey to the afterlife, he was buried with at least 130 of his walking sticks, some of which show signs of wear.

GO WITH THE FLOW: The ancient Egyptians' understanding of how the human body functioned was primitive, at best. Egyptian physicians believed the body functioned much like the Nile River. If the river was blocked from flowing, the crops growing along the fertile shoreline suffered. Therefore, it was necessary to keep the body's channels flowing as well. For this reason, great emphasis was placed on the use of laxatives—not just when patients were constipated, but any time they were feeling unwell for any reason. Headache? Laxatives. Sore back? Laxatives. These medicines (and many others) were administered using enemas. In the royal court, this was the job of a medical specialist called an *iri*, which translates as "shepherd of the anus."

KITCHEN CHEMISTRY

Let's see what's going on in the dairy aisle of the supermarket.

Butter: In its natural state, cow's milk is about 3.5 percent butterfat, in the form of microscopic globules encased in membranes made of lipoproteins. The membranes prevent the fat globules from clumping together. Butter is produced by agitating, or "churning," the milk. That damages the membranes around the butterfat globules, allowing them to clump together to form what are called "butter grains." The collected grains are then kneaded and pressed together to make butter. The butter you buy in a store is about 85 percent butterfat and 15 percent water.

Homogenized Milk: If you've ever seen a bottle of unhomogenized milk, you may have noticed that the cream in the milk floats to the top of the bottle. This creamy layer is the butterfat, and because it is a fat, it doesn't mix readily with the rest of the milk, which is water-based. (Kind of like vinegar-and-oil salad dressing.) The homogenization process breaks the fat globules down into smaller sizes that will mix more readily with the rest of the milk. This is done by forcing the milk through tiny holes under great pressure. Once the milk has been homogenized, or made uniform, the butterfat will no longer separate from the rest of the milk.

Pasteurized Milk: Cow's milk isn't just food for cows and people, it is also an excellent host for microorganisms. Beneficial microorganisms can be introduced to make sour cream, yogurt, and other products (see below), but harmful organisms, such as the bacteria that cause tuberculosis, can make raw milk deadly. For this reason, the U.S. Centers for Disease Control considers raw milk to be one of the world's most dangerous foods. Pasteurization is the process in which milk is heated to 161.5°F for 15 seconds to destroy any pathogens, rendering it safe to drink. The process is named for the French biologist Louis Pasteur, who in the 1880s showed that heat could be used to kill unwanted microbes in wine.

Sour Cream: Sour cream was traditionally made by skimming the cream from milk and letting it ferment at a warm temperature. The bacteria that formed thickened the cream and made it more acidic, giving sour cream its distinctive flavor. Today the same process is accomplished more quickly, and under controlled conditions, by adding acid-producing bacteria to the cream.

Yogurt: Unlike sour cream, which is made by fermenting the cream, yogurt is made by adding special bacteria called yogurt cultures to the milk, and letting it ferment. The yogurt cultures convert the lactose, or sugar, in the milk to lactic acid, which in turn acts on the proteins in the milk, thickening it and giving the yogurt its tart flavor.

In the market for a Rolls-Royce? You can order a new one in any of 44,000 different colors.

BAD CATS

Every few years, Hollywood comes out with a movie so bad that the most entertaining thing about it is the variety of creative ways critics come up with to tell us how bad it is. When it comes to Cats*—the ill-fated adaptation of Andrew Lloyd Webber's hit Broadway musical, rushed to release in December 2019 before the visual effects were even completed—the scathing reviews actually make us want to see it even more.*

"From the first shot—of just such a blue moon, distressingly fake, flanked by poufy cat-shaped clouds—to the last, *Cats* hurts the eyes and, yes, the ears, as nearly all the musical numbers, including 'Memory,' have been twisted into campy, awards-grubbing cameos for big-name stars in bad-CG cat drag."

—Peter Debruge, *Variety*

"*Cats* is both a horror and an endurance test, a dispatch from some neon-drenched netherworld where the ghastly is inextricable from the tedious."

—Justin Chang, *Los Angeles Times*

"The actual nightmare fuel occurs when human faces are put on tiny mice and Rockette-esque cockroaches."

—Brian Truitt, *USA TODAY*

"Describing the plot of Cats makes you feel like you're on bath salts. (Although not as much as does seeing it play out on screen.)"

—Isaac Feldberg, *Fortune* magazine

"Anyone who takes small children to this movie is setting them up for winged-monkey levels of night terrors."

—Ty Burr, *Boston Globe*

"Of course, cats don't actually speak. But neither do they sing their little feline hearts out or have oddly unsettling human breasts and faces that make them look like the winner of a Halloween costume contest as the Cowardly Lion."

—Michael O'Sullivan, *Washington Post*

"Eager cultists and the psychotropic-minded may lovingly feast on this *Cats* for years to come, and even children may feel they've learned a valuable lesson about the limits of the imagination. But for now (and to borrow its famed tagline, forever), this version is just a big swing and a hiss."

—Robert Abele, *The Wrap*

"To assess *Cats* as good or bad feels like the entirely wrong axis on which to see it. It is, with all affection, a monstrosity."

—Alison Willmore, *Vulture*

"I nearly succumbed to the temptation to insert feline-focused wordplay here–'purr-fectly dreadful' or 'a cinematic cat-astrophe.' But I haven't the energy, because the movie has sapped my strength."

—Linda Cook, *Quad-City Times*

Mixed message: As of 2017, the Kentucky Coal Mining Museum runs on solar power.

"Once seen, the only realistic way to fix *Cats* would be to spay it, or simply pretend it never happened. Because it's an all-time disaster—a rare and star-spangled calamity which will leave jaws littered across floors and agents unemployed."
—Tim Robey, *Telegraph*

"Virtually every homeless cat in the world could have been fed with the money Universal spent to make this film, and...there would still be enough left over to fund the animated version that Steven Spielberg pitched several years ago."
—Rohan Naahar, *Hindustan Times*

"After an hour of *Cats* I began to suspect the popcorn they fed us had been laced with a psychotropic drug. The only problem was that I wasn't actually enjoying myself."
—John McDonald, *Australian Financial Review*

"They sing(!), they teleport(?), they rub noses a lot; nobody ever seems to need a litter box."
—Leah Greenblatt, *Entertainment Weekly*

"You won't be able to look away, but you might wish you could forget the 'memory' of *Cats* by the movie's end."
—Corey Chichizola, *CinemaBlend*

"Jennifer Hudson...limps around hemorrhaging snot and looking either miserable or terrified, like she's been watching the dailies."
—David Rooney, *Hollywood Reporter*

"Neither human nor cat, they all look like laboratory mutants put through a Snapchat filter."
—John Nugent, *Empire*

"[Director Tom] Hooper's mistake is that he's tried to class up the joint. What a blunder! In feline terms, this is a movie without epic hairballs, without rear-end sniffing, without a deep, wounding scratch."
—Manohla Dargis, *New York Times*

"*Cats* feels like it's already on the way to becoming a new cult classic à la *The Rocky Horror Picture Show.* I can see it playing forever just so people can see it together and share the wonder, awe, and horror."
—Jessica Mason, *The Mary Sue*

* * *

James Corden (who played Bustopher Jones), on filming *Cats:* "We had one day, which was me, Taylor Swift, Rebel Wilson, Idris Elba, Sir Ian McKellen, and Judi Dench, all shooting a scene together. Now that in itself is quite extraordinary. Then when you add the layer of everybody pretending to be a cat, you really can't help but feel you're on some kind of hallucinogenic. You really think for a long time, 'Are we being punked? Is this real?' "

To date there have been two cosmonauts named Aleksandr Aleksandrov: one from the Soviet Union, and one from Bulgaria.

RESCUED FROM THE TRASH

Do you ever find yourself hemming and hawing when it comes to throwing something away? What if it's worth more than you realize? What if tossing it out will be the dumbest thing you ever did? These stories might persuade you to hold onto it for a little longer.

A FAMILY'S LIFE SAVINGS

Background: In August 2019, an unidentified man from Ashland, Oregon, became frantic after realizing that he'd mistakenly tossed a shoe box containing $23,000 into his blue recycling bin. He called the city's recycling service provider and was informed that the truck had already traveled five hours south to the Samoa Resource Recovery Center in Humboldt County, California. When the man called that facility, he was told not to get his hopes up. "We take quite a bit of material every day," manager Linda Wise told the *Press-Democrat*, "so the odds of finding that are not much better than a needle in a haystack." The center often gets frantic calls about mistakenly tossed-out items, but they're rarely ever rescued.
Rescued: Wise ordered that night's sorting crew to be on the lookout for a shoebox. Several hours later, just before dawn, workers spotted a tipped-over shoebox on the conveyer belt. When they went to check it, all the bills came tumbling out. Wise said that it's amazing the cash stayed in the unsecured shoebox for the entire ride over the mountains. The man was ecstatic when she called to tell him the news, and he wasn't the only one: "Everyone who was on the sorting line was beaming this morning."

SEVERAL SIGNED NBA SHOES

Background: The original Air Jordans weren't sold in stores. Nike debuted the shoes during Michael Jordan's rookie year in early 1984, when he was already being touted as one of the greatest basketball players of all time. Jordan wore those original black-toed shoes in five or so games. Then, after a loss to the Bucks in Milwaukee in February 1985, he signed the size-13 sneakers with the message "My Very Best" and gave them to a ball boy. The ball boy took them to Ron Tesmer, owner of Playmakers, a shoe store at Milwaukee's Capitol Court Mall. (Bucks ball boys and ball girls would routinely trade signed NBA shoes for a new pair at Playmakers.) Tesmer placed the Air Jordans in a plexiglass display along with other memorabilia, where they remained for more than a decade.

In 1997, Tesmer sold the store, but not the signed shoes—he put them all in a box and locked it in the basement storage room. He returned three years later only to find that the room had been cleared out. A year after that, the mall closed for good. "I had kind of written them off and didn't think they'd show up again," said Tesmer.

Dogs inhale through their nostrils and exhale through those little slits on the sides of their nostrils.

Rescued: Three years after that, as the shuttered mall was being demolished in 2001, a maintenance worker named Larry Awe was tasked with throwing out any items that had been left behind. Among the junk he discovered the box, and inside that box were several signed NBA shoes—including shoes from Larry Bird, Julius Erving, and Shaquille O'Neal. But the Holy Grail was the pair of Air Jordans. "This isn't going to the dump," Awe said.

He took the box home and kept it in his basement for nearly 20 years. Then, when his daughter was getting married, he gave the shoes to his future son-in-law, who decided to have them authenticated and valued. Experts confirmed that they were the real deal—one of only three pairs of original Air Jordans known to exist—and they're worth at least $20,000, perhaps much more. When Tesmer found out in 2019 that his shoe collection had been rescued from the trash, he attempted to stop the auction, claiming the shoes were rightfully his. What happened next is a mystery. The auction was scheduled for late February 2019, but the auction listing simply says "Not Sold."

A WORLD LEADER'S PERSONAL ITEMS

Background: After Queen Elizabeth II, the most famous Brit of the 20th century is probably Prime Minister Winston Churchill, who helped lead the Allies to victory in World War II. So if you owned a top hat that belonged to Churchill, as well as a box of his cigars and some personal letters, you might want to hold onto them. But for some reason—which remains a mystery—someone who actually *did* own these items threw them away in early 2019.

Rescued: "I've worked [at a garbage dump] for 15 years," David Rose told the *Telegraph*, "and I get to pull out whatever I like, mostly antiques." Rose said he has three sheds full of rescued treasures, but nothing like the Churchill collection that he brought to London for an episode of BBC's *Antiques Roadshow*. The appraisers were able to authenticate the collection thanks to the 200 letters that were stored with the top hat and cigars. The letters weren't written by Churchill himself, but by his personal cook. According to Rose, "She used to write to her son every day about the daily goings of Winston Churchill, what he was getting up to, how he was feeling and just interesting stuff about him." The collection has an estimated value of £10,000 ($13,000), but its worth goes beyond money; the content of the letters will provide historians with previously unknown aspects of Churchill's life. (If you're wondering at exactly which dump the items were found, don't ask Rose. He said he's keeping that detail to himself.)

A FAMOUS MOVIE MUSCLE CAR

Background: One of Hollywood's most memorable car chases took place in the

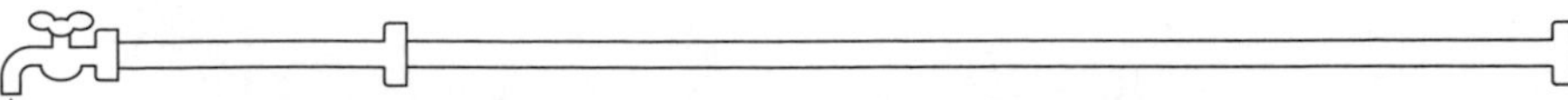

1968 crime thriller *Bullitt*, starring Steve McQueen as Lt. Frank Bullitt, who tears up the streets of San Francisco in a Highland Green Ford Mustang GT. Thanks in large part to that 10-minute sequence, the movie won an Oscar for Best Editing, and the muscle car became nearly as famous as McQueen.

The Ford Motor Company provided two fastback Mustangs for the film—a "hero car" used for close shots with McQueen, and a stunt car for all the jumps and chases. The hero car was purchased by a private buyer in 1974 for $6,000 and was kept in mint condition. It's still owned by the same family (who once declined to sell it to McQueen).

But what about the other car? After filming, Warner Bros. sold it to Max Balchowsky, the "wrenchman" in charge of keeping all the vehicles in working order during filming. The stunt car had taken such a beating that Balchowsky deemed it beyond repair. He sent it to a scrapyard to be crushed into a tiny cube.

Rescued: Nearly 50 years later, in 2017, a car collector named Hugo Sanchez purchased two "rotting away" Mustangs for $5,000 from the backyard of a house in Los Cabos, Baja, Mexico. He sent them both—a fastback and a coupe—to a restorer named Ralph Garcia. Ironically, their original plan was to combine parts from both cars to make a re-creation of "Eleanor," the Shelby Mustang from *Gone in 60 Seconds*. But there was something about the cream-colored 1968 fastback that caught Garcia's eye...so he halted the restoration and contacted Ford. After an investigation, it was determined that the vehicle identification number on the junk car matched the stunt car's VIN. And modifications made to the stunt car further proved that this was the real deal. Sanchez and Garcia took co-ownership of the "Bullitt" Mustang and restored it to its former glory.

How did such a hallowed piece of Hollywood history end up on the southern tip of Baja? No one knows for sure, but it's obvious that someone at that scrapyard saw something in the wrecked Mustang that Balchowsky hadn't.

A BEST-SELLING MANUSCRIPT

Background: In the early 1950s, an American minister named Norman Vincent Peale was writing a self-help book. He'd been reading it to his wife, Ruth, every night, but he wasn't happy with how it was coming out. She said she liked it; he thought she was just being nice. At one point Norman became so discouraged that he threw the book away and forbade Ruth from taking it out of the trash.

Rescued: Ruth complied with his demand, in that she didn't remove the manuscript from the trash. Instead, she took the entire trash can to her husband's publisher. *He* removed the manuscript and read it...and liked it as much as she did. The book went on to sell five million copies. Perhaps you've heard of it—it's called *The Power of Positive Thinking*.

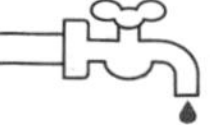

LET'S NAME IT NAMELESS COVE

Canada–home of poutine, pucks, and a preponderance of peculiar place names.

ONTARIO

Nottawa
Tiny
Pain Court
Crotch Lake
Happyland
Ball's Falls
Dorking
Pickle Lake
Moose Factory
Ethel
Dummer
Funnybone Lake
Pooh Lake

BRITISH COLUMBIA

Stoner
Salmon Arm
Clo-oose
Spuzzum
Likely
Ta Ta Creek
Hydraulic
Bella Bella
Blubber Bay
Fanny Bay
Poopoo Creek

MANITOBA

Flin Flon
Stupid Lake
Red Sucker Lake
Cranberry Portage
Pilot Mound

NEWFOUNDLAND AND LABRADOR

Happy Adventure
Cow Head
Bacon Cove
Heart's Desire
Herring Neck
Red Head Cove
Spread Eagle Bay
Come By Chance
Nameless Cove
Goobies
Dildo
Jerry's Nose
Ass Rock
Leading Tickles
Billy Butts Pond
Lawn
Tickle Cove
Pee Pee Island

NOVA SCOTIA

Joggins
Meat Cove
Lower Economy
Old Sweat
Sober Island
Mushaboom

PRINCE EDWARD ISLAND

Christopher Cross
Tignish
Lady Slipper
Crapaud

SASKATCHEWAN

Fertile
Radville
Big Beaver
Forget
Uranium City
Nut Mountain
Poor Man
Smuts
Xena
Climax
Eyebrow
Elbow

ALBERTA

Entrance
Cereal
Vulcan
Mirror
Dead Man's Flats
Seven Persons
Milk River
Head-Smashed-in Buffalo Jump
Little Smoky
Nojack
Westward Ho
Committee's Punch Bowl

YUKON

Snag
Brooks Brook
Mount Cockfield

More veggies are grown for cows than for people.

TRIVIA *TREK*

More than 50 years after Star Trek's *original run (1966–69), there have been eight spin-off series, 13 movies, and hundreds of novels and nonfiction books that dissect every aspect of this still-expanding universe. We've delved into these Trek-lopedias to bring you a few fascinating and obscure tidbits from the Final Frontier. Engage!*

Mr. Atoz: Played by legendary character actor Ian Wolfe, Mr. Atoz is a librarian in an episode of the original series called "All Our Yesterdays," which aired in season three. Plot: just before a supernova destroys his planet, Mr. Atoz sends Captain Kirk (William Shatner), Mr. Spock (Leonard Nimoy), and Dr. McCoy (DeForest Kelley) into that planet's past, where Spock reverts to being emotional and nearly kills McCoy. Just in case it's not obvious, the librarian's name is a play on "A to Z."

Stardate: "*Captain's log, stardate 42108.9.*" Do stardates actually mean anything? Not really. The original *Trek* scriptwriters' guide simply read, "Pick any combination of four numbers plus a percentage point." Continuity was required only within each episode. When *Star Trek: The Next Generation* (*TNG*) debuted in 1987, the stardate was revised to a five-digit number: "The first two digits...are always 41. The 4 stands for 24th century, the 1 indicates first season." According to one of the first *Trek* trivia books, 1976's *Star Trek Concordance,* creator Gene Roddenberry once explained that stardates are "a function of space as well as time, being influenced by a starship's position in the galaxy, its course and velocity."

The Agony Booth: Introduced in the original series episode "Mirror, Mirror," the Mirror Universe is just like ours, except the good guys are the bad guys. (You can tell because all the men have menacing facial hair.) "The agony booth," coldly states a bearded Mr. Spock, "is a most effective means of discipline." The windowed chamber flashes bright lights and makes horrible sounds while whoever's inside screams in agony. In addition, each Mirror Universe crewmember wears an "agonizer" on his belt. If he violates orders, he gets zapped with his own agonizer! The Mirror Universe and its agony devices have shown up in nearly every *Trek* incarnation since.

Dr. Arik Soong: *Star Trek: Enterprise* (2001–05) is about the first starship to carry that name, which embarked in the 2150s. Dr. Soong appears in three episodes of *Enterprise* as a scientist who was imprisoned for having revived the outlawed Eugenics program. (Back in the 1990s, that program created archvillain Khan Noonien Singh, a superhuman who centuries later will try to destroy the *Enterprise* in the original series, in the 1982 movie *Star Trek II: The Wrath of Khan,* and in the 2013 alternate-timeline reboot, *Star Trek: Into*

Darkness.) Arik Soong is also the grandfather of Noonian Soong, the cyberneticist who will create the androids Data, his evil twin brother Lore (*TNG*), and the "simpleton" B-4 (2002's *Star Trek: Nemesis*). Both Soongs and all three androids were played by Brent Spiner, who first put on the Data makeup in 1987 at age 38, and most recently wore it in 2020 for *Picard* at age 70.

I-Chaya: When Mr. Spock was a boy on Vulcan, he had a pet *sehlat* named I-Chaya. This fanged, bearlike creature was only mentioned in passing on the original series, and showed up on-screen in an episode of *Star Trek: The Animated Series* (*TAS*) called "Yesteryear," when Spock goes back in time to save his younger self from being killed by a lionlike Le-matya, which is too powerful for Spock's aging sehlat. Many fans consider *TAS*, which ran from 1973 to 1974, to be among the best *Trek* spin-offs, even though the episodes were only half an hour long. What makes it so good? For one thing, most of the cast returned to voice their roles. But as a cartoon, there were no budget constraints, allowing some of the best science-fiction writers of the day to let their imaginations run wild.

The Hengrauggi: In the 2009 reboot *Star Trek*—which saw young actors take over the original series roles in an alternate timeline—the Hengrauggi is a giant squidlike monster that tries to eat Captain Kirk (Chris Pine) on a frozen planet. There has been speculation that this is the same alien species that destroys New York in the 2008 horror film *Cloverfield*. J. J. Abrams, who produced both movies, won't verify that, but both do include the fictional soft drink Slusho, hinting that *Cloverfield* could actually be in the *Star Trek* universe (along with his TV shows *Alias* and *Lost*, which also feature Slusho).

The Maquis: This fierce band of freedom fighters—or terrorists, depending on whose side you're on—was inspired by French paramilitaries called *Les Maquis*, who fought Nazis in World War II. When *Star Trek* writers were developing *Star Trek: Voyager* in the early 1990s, they wanted their starship—which gets stranded on the other side of the galaxy—to include Federation officers and Maquis being forced to work together. Rather than waiting for *Voyager* to air to give the Maquis a backstory, the writers introduced them in several episodes of *TNG* and *DS9*.

"Wagon Train to the Stars": This was how World War II fighter pilot turned cop turned TV writer Gene Roddenberry pitched *Star Trek* to the networks in 1965. *Wagon Train* (1957–65) was a top-rated TV show that followed Old West pioneers as they made their way across a new frontier. Although *Star Trek*'s styles and tones have changed considerably over the years, that's still—in essence—what this franchise is all about: seeing what's out there.

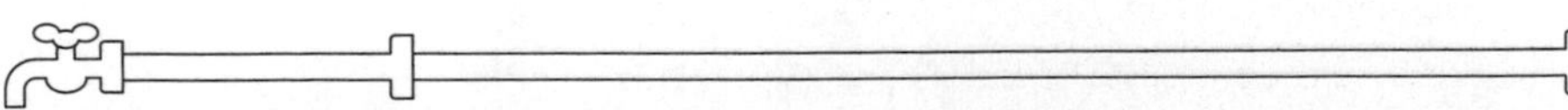

One day after Texas radio station KLUE banned Beatles records in 1966, it was hit by lightning.

THE LAZARUS PILL

Some of the most amazing medical advancements are the ones that are discovered by accident.

LOST...

In 1994, a 24-year-old South African man named Louis Viljoen was hit by a truck while riding his bicycle in a town east of Johannesburg. He suffered severe brain trauma, and doctors warned his mother, Sienie Engelbrecht, that he probably would not survive. Even if he did live, they didn't think he would ever regain consciousness.

But Viljoen did survive. He was treated at various hospitals until the doctors could do nothing more for him, then he was moved to a rehabilitation center, where he remained in what doctors call a "persistent vegetative state." One callous physician even referred to him as a "cabbage."

"His eyes were open but there was nothing there," Sienie Engelbrecht told the *Guardian* in 2006. "I visited him every day for five years and we would speak to him but there was no recognition, no communication, nothing."

Viljoen might have remained in that state for the rest of his life, were it not for the fact that sometimes late at night, he had spasms in his left arm that caused him to claw at his mattress. One of the nurses worried that the clawing might be a sign that he was restless and unable to sleep. She suggested to Engelbrecht that she ask the family doctor for a sleeping pill. The doctor prescribed the popular sleep aid Ambien (Zolpidem), which is sold in South Africa under the brand name Stilnox. Engelbrecht crushed one of the pills into powder, mixed it in a soda, and fed it to Viljoen in a bottle.

...AND FOUND

About 25 minutes passed; then Viljoen did something he hadn't been able to do since the accident. He made a noise. "Mmmm." He hadn't made a sound for five years, Engelbrecht said. "Then he turned his head in my direction. I said, 'Louis, can you hear me?' and he said, 'Yes.' I said, 'Say hello, Louis,' and he said, 'Hello, mummy.' I couldn't believe it! I just cried and cried." When the medication wore off, Viljoen drifted back into a vegetative state, only to improve when given Ambien again. But he made progress over time, and in addition to being able to speak, he learned how to feed himself. Some of his brain damage is permanent, and he will need to live in an assisted living facility for the rest of his life. He will also need to keep taking Ambien...but he's no longer trapped inside his own body. His is the first documented case of someone with severe brain damage being restored to consciousness by taking Ambien.

It was very rare for someone in a permanent vegetative state to show progress after such a long time, and Viljoen's case made a lot of headlines in South Africa. The attention prompted other South Africans to give Ambien to their loved ones in a similar condition. Some of these people made similar recoveries. Not all of them, but enough that in South Africa, Ambien has become known as the "Lazarus Pill" after the biblical character who was raised from the dead.

THE GOOD FIGHT

As word of the unexpected recovery of Viljoen and others like him continued to spread, similar cases began appearing in countries all over the world wherever Ambien was sold. A lot of this progress has been driven by the families of people with severe brain damage who give their loved ones Ambien against the advice of their physicians: When a 23-year-old Australian man named Sam Goddard suffered a series of strokes in 2010 that left him severely disabled and unable to communicate, his physicians refused to prescribe him Ambien...until his fiancée told the doctors a "huge big fat lie," as she puts it, and said that Goddard needed Ambien to sleep. Only then did he get the sleeping pill, and only then did he recover some of his motor skills and the ability to speak. As he explained to his fiancée, he'd been conscious for months, but was powerless to communicate this to anyone. Now, after 15 months in the hospital, he was well enough to return home.

He'd been conscious for months, but was powerless to communicate this to anyone.

SLEEP MODE

Cases like these have caused doctors to rethink what happens to a person's brain when they suffer a traumatic brain injury or a stroke. They used to believe that if brain tissue appeared inactive (dark) on brain scans following a stroke or a traumatic brain injury, that brain tissue was dead, and lost for good. But brain scans taken of people like Louis Viljoen and Sam Goddard show that Ambien stimulates some—but not all—of these dark areas to light up again. That means that some of the tissue that was thought to be dead was actually just dormant, and that Ambien somehow wakes it up again.

No one is sure how Ambien does this, and no one knows which brain-damaged patients will benefit from taking the drug and which ones will not. After Louis Viljoen regained consciousness and the ability to speak, his physician, Dr. Wally Nel, administered Ambien to 150 other patients with brain damage. He reported that up to 60 percent of the patients showed signs of improvement. Other studies have shown that the number of patients who benefit may be as low as 6 percent. But in the United States alone, there are an estimated 200,000 people living in a persistent vegetative state. Even if only 6 percent of them will benefit from taking Ambien, that could mean that for 12,000 people, consciousness and a better quality of life may be just a sleeping pill away.

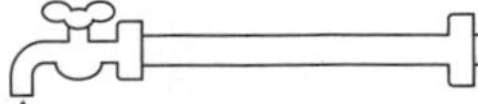

SILLY WORLD RECORDS

If it's your life's goal to be the holder of a silly world record but you don't know which one to go for, maybe one of these will spark inspiration. But beware: Once you attain your silly world record, you'll have to work pretty hard to keep it.

World Record: Spinning a basketball on the end of a toothbrush, while holding the toothbrush in your mouth

Details: According to the official rules, once you balance the basketball on the end of the toothbrush and give it a spin, you can't touch it. Sound difficult? It is. The first record—13.5 seconds—was set in 2012 by a Welshman named Tom "Conman" Connors. As with most of these records, it didn't stand for long. A few months later, Thaneshwar Guragai of Nepal kept his basketball spinning for 22.41 seconds. (Both men have amassed quite a "record collection": Connors owns 16 world records, and Guragai has 13, including an astonishing 444 basketball bounces in one minute.)

Guragai eventually reached 40 seconds with his spinning basketball, only to be bested by another record collector, Dipanshu Mishra of India, who spun his ball for 42.92 seconds. The current record holder: Sandeep Singh Kaila of British Columbia. In January 2019, he kept his basketball spinning on the end of a toothbrush for an amazing 1 minute, 8.15 seconds. "It took two years of very intense practice to get it," he told *Guinness World Records.* "I know records are made to be broken, so I have to keep practicing to stay number one."

World Record: Most blueberries held in the mouth for five seconds without breaking any

Details: David Rush of Idaho has amassed over 100 silly world records, including stacking 30 bars of wet soap on top of each other, and holding 100 lit candles in his mouth. To set the blueberry record, Rush had to best Dinesh Shivnath Upadhyaya of Mumbai, otherwise known as "Maximouth," who successfully fit 86 blueberries in his maw.

IN THE KNOW

The Guinness Book of World Records was born out of a 1954 argument over the fastest European game bird. (It's the golden plover...according to *Guinness.*)

According to the official rules set by Guinness, each blueberry must weigh more than 0.75 gram, and it cannot be crushed once inside the mouth. In June 2019, Rush laid out 150 blueberries on a picnic table and then methodically, strategically, placed each one into his ever-widening jaws. The more he got in there, the harder it became to keep his mouth open, or to keep from gagging—or worse, choking. After

blueberry 146, Rush knew that if he'd tried to stuff one more in there, they would all come out at once. So he stopped, and was able to hold all those blueberries in his mouth for the allotted five seconds. Then he carefully spit them out. Several blueberries were broken and therefore disqualified, but he still got the record. If you want to break it, you'll need to stuff at least 125 blueberries into your pie hole.

World Record: Longest eyelashes

Details: For women in many parts of the world, incredibly long eyelashes are considered a sign of beauty. Some women even get eyelash extensions, which are not allowed in this category for obvious reasons. The first record was set by Canadian Gillian Criminisi, whose longest lash measured 3.18 inches.

Beating that record by nearly two inches is You Jianxia from Shanghai, China. She was featured in the 2017 edition of *Guinness World Records* for her 4.9-inch-long eyelashes (that's almost as long as a pen). She said she first noticed that her eyelashes were growing long in 2013, and attributed the excessive growth to "being one with nature." Do her lashes ever get in the way? "They are a part of my body," she says, "so I never find them inconvenient." However, the medical website Health24 warns that "unusually long, dense lashes can be uncomfortable and affect your vision." Excessive growth is the result of a condition called eyelash trichomegaly, which "may occur in people who have lupus or are being treated for leukemia and AIDS, and is usually a side effect of medication." Another possible side effect: a world record.

World Record: Tallest mohawk

Details: The mohawk hairstyle is achieved by shaving both sides of the head, leaving a strip of hair on top that extends from front to back. The hairstyle—named for the Mohawk tribe, whose warriors sported the distinctive haircut—was popularized in the late 1970s by the punk rock scene and then made famous by Mr. T in the 1980s.

In 2008, a Nebraska punk rocker named Eric Hahn grew his "Hawk" (as he calls it) to 27 inches, setting the record. Not long after, Stefan Srocka of Germany grew his spiky mohawk to an impressive 31.5 inches. But neither of them stood a chance of holding the record after a Japanese designer named Kazuhiro Watanabe spent 15 years growing *his* mohawk. When he presented it to the folks at Guinness in New York City in 2013, it required three cans of hair spray to get the record-breaking hairdo to stand at a height of 3 feet, 8.6 inches. (Watanabe isn't very tall, so when his mohawk isn't rigid, it reaches down to his knees.)

World Record: Most people dressed up as Smurfs

Details: The Smurfs debuted as a Belgian comic book in the 1950s and peaked in the 1980s as an American cartoon, but they're still quite popular today.

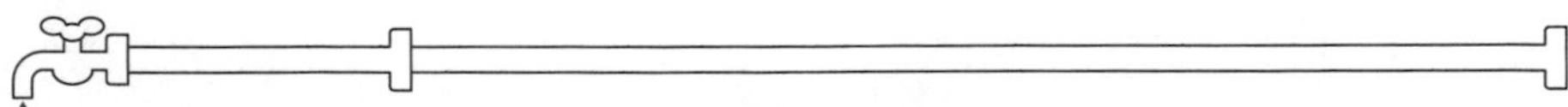

But would it want to? The human brain can store the memory equivalent of 300 years of TV shows.

The first world-record Smurf gathering took place in Wales in 2009, when 2,510 people dressed up as either Papa Smurf (with a long white beard, red pants, and red cap), a regular Smurf (white pants and a white cap), or Smurfette, with golden locks and a white dress.

Germans in the town of Lauchringen attempted to break the record in 2016, but not enough Smurfs showed up. A second attempt in February 2019 was much more successful, drawing 2,762 Smurfs. According to the rules, all exposed skin must be blue, or the entrant is disqualified. (A few attendees painted their entire upper bodies blue, but most simply wore blue shirts and painted their hands and faces.) The record-breaking Smurf army then paraded through town, singing and dancing to the cartoon's theme song. All who attended received an official Smurftificate.

World Record: Longest handshake

Details: There's a whole lotta shakin' going on in this category. "For the purpose of this record," says *Guinness*, "a handshake is a ritual in which two people grasp one of each other's like hands, accompanied by an up and down movement of the grasped hands." The first record was set in 2006 at 9 hours, 19 minutes. Two years later, two men from Hawaii, Kirk Williamson and Richard McCulley, upped the record to 10 hours. In 2009, two Minnesota high school students, Nathan Herzberg and Kyle Swanson, also shook hands for 10 hours. Not long after that, John-Clark Levin of New York and a friend shook hands for 10 hours, 10 minutes, and 10 seconds. Then two men from Sydney, Australia—Jack Tsonis and Lindsay Morrison—shook hands for 12 hours, 34 minutes, and 56 seconds. (Wrestler Hulk Hogan was on hand for that one.) That record stood for only a month. Beating them by nearly three hours, John-Clark Levin (again) and George Posner shook hands for 15 hours, 15 minutes, and 15 seconds. A month after that in California, Matthew Rosen and Joe Ackerman broke that record by 15 minutes. In 2011, two sets of handshakers—New Zealanders Alastair Galpin and Don Purdon, and Rohit and Santosh Timilsina of Nepal—shook hands for 33 hours and 3 minutes. That record was broken by Nepalese high school students Dinesh and Pawan Timilsina, whose handshake clocked in at 42 hours and 35 minutes.

In 2016, Matt Holmes, a Denver entrepreneur (who produces a video series called *Handshakin*), shook Juan Diaz de Leon's hand for 43 hours and 35 minutes. But did it count? According to the official rules, the handshakers are not allowed to separate at all—not even for bathroom breaks. But in an interview with the blog *Galvanize*, Holmes said, "The timer stopped at 46 hours, and after we deducted breaks we broke the record by one hour at 43 hours and 35 minutes." Breaks? Not allowed. So as of this writing, the official record for the longest handshake still belongs to Dinesh and Pawan Timilsina.

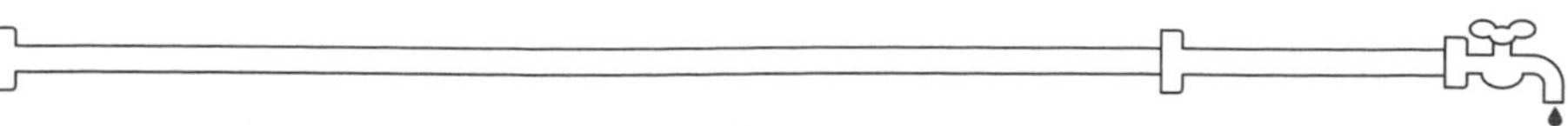

KNOW YOUR GOATS

World's first domesticated animals: goats, around 10,000 years ago. First livestock brought to the Americas: goats, brought by Columbus in 1493. Here are some more fascinating facts about the species Capra aegagrus.

Goat milk is more widely consumed across the world than cow's milk. It's higher in calcium and vitamin A than moo juice, and it's also naturally homogenized—which means it doesn't separate out into different layers. One more bonus: people who are lactose intolerant can drink goat's milk with no ill effects.

Young goats are called kids. Mother goats recognize their kids not by sight but from each young goat's distinctive call and scent.

A goat named Sgt. Bill was the mascot of the Canadian Expeditionary Force's 5th Infantry Battalion during World War I. He is credited for saving the lives of three soldiers by pushing them into a trench moments before a shell exploded next to where they were standing.

President Abraham Lincoln kept two pet goats (named Nanny and Nanko) in the White House. His young son Tad used them to pull him around in a little chariot.

The idea that goats will eat anything—including tin cans—is a myth. They're foragers who, as they poke around wherever they can with their highly sensitive lips, will eat just about any food source, but mostly plants.

Goats have rectangular pupils that provide vision almost all the way around—in the neighborhood of 340 degrees (out of 360)—which makes them aware of predators. But this unique setup means they're unable to move their eyes up and down. To look up at the sky or down at the ground, they have to move their entire head.

Adult goat names: a grown female goat is a *nanny* or a *doe*, a male goat is a *billy* or a *buck*, and a castrated male is a *wether*.

Like cows, goats have four stomachlike digestion chambers. The second, the rumen, holds up to five gallons of food and breaks down the cellulose in plants. That turns the rumen into a fermenter, which means a lot of gas is produced. Result: goats burp almost constantly.

Mountain goats aren't really goats—they're antelopes.

The Tennessee Stiff-leg, also known as a fainting goat, has a genetic trait called *myotonia*. The goat's neck and leg muscles completely stiffen when it senses danger...causing it to fall over. It looks like they're fainting, but they really don't—they're fully conscious during those seconds or minutes when the myotonia kicks in.

It's technically possible to win Monopoly in just four turns. How? Roll doubles, land on Boardwalk and Park Place,...

THE ADVENTURES OF "FLORIDA MAN"

In the previous edition of Uncle John's Bathroom Reader, *we included a sampling of real headlines that feature the phrase "Florida Man." They made us laugh so hard that we had to find more. And we did...but in true Uncle John's fashion, we also found out how this crazy meme got started.*

MAN OF THE HOUR

In 2013, Freddie Campion, an associate editor at GQ magazine, noticed that the state of Florida seemed to produce more than its fair share of oddball news items. He was a fan of the satirical "news" website *The Onion,* which publishes a lot of made-up news items under the headline "Area Man..." such as "Area Man Locked in Protracted Battle with Sweatshirt Neckhole" and "Area Man Nostalgic for Time When Ads Targeting Him Not as Sad."

Campion thought the real-life stories coming from Florida were just as entertaining as the fake stories in *The Onion,* so why not create some buzz around "Florida Man"? "I was just thinking: Florida's a crazy place. I don't really know what my reason was, beyond: This doesn't exist," he told the *Washington Post* in 2019, "so why don't I make it?"

Campion created the @_FloridaMan Twitter account, gave it the tagline "Real-life stories of the world's worst superhero," and whenever he came across an odd story with the words "Florida Man" in the headline, he posted a link on the Twitter account. Florida Man caught on: by 2019 the account had more than 400,000 followers...and Campion had begun to have second thoughts about the negative attention he was bringing to the people named in the news items, many of whom struggled with poverty, mental illness, drug problems, or all three. So he retired the account. But the idea lives on, and in March 2019 someone created "The Florida Man Challenge," in which people google their birthdates and the words "Florida Man" to see who can come up with the craziest headline. Here are some of the real news headlines we dug up.

NEWSMAKERS

February 21: "Florida Man Who Threw Toilet Through Glass Window of a Board of Education Building Arrested While Sitting on Another Toilet"

October 19: "Naked Florida Man Arrested for Beating Peeping Tom to Death. Police Say It Was Not in Self Defense"

July 30: "Florida Man Rode Horse During Attempted House Burglary, Deputies Say"

March 5: "Leaf-burning Florida Man Asks Cops, 'Did You Find All My Pot?'"

November 12: "Florida man driving 90 in a 55 zone 'needed to get home in a hurry because he was cheating on his wife' "

August 16: "Florida Man's Gun Goes Missing During Orgy"

January 7: "Florida Man Denies Syringes Found in Rectum Are His"

September 5: "Florida Man Goes Viral After Headbanging in a Force 5 Hurricane"

March 30: "Florida Man Accused of Attacking Mom When She Wouldn't Dress His Mannequin"

October 7: "Florida Man Arrested for Trying to Get Alligator Drunk"

July 18: "Deputies: Florida Man Held Wife's Lover at Gunpoint, Severed His Penis and Ran Away with It"

February 23: "Florida Man Steals $33,000 Worth of Rare Coins, Cashes Them in Coinstar Machine for $29.30"

February 28: "Florida Man Who Threatened Family with Coldplay Lyrics Ends Standoff after SWAT Promises Him Pizza"

January 6: "Florida Man Wearing 'Who Needs Drugs? No, Seriously, I Have Drugs' Shirt Arrested for Possession of Drugs"

August 16: "Florida Man, 55, Arrested at Walmart after 'Stuffing $7 Bottle of Wine Down Pants, Chugging It All in the Store Bathroom, and Trying to Leave' "

August 10: "Florida Man Gets Into Police Chase While on a First Date"

January 4: "Guards Let Florida Man Vape in Prison Because He Helped Them with Their Taxes"

December 25: "Florida Man Worried about Vampires Burns Down His House"

August 26: "Florida Man Gets 30 Months in Prison after Shooting Himself While Drinking"

October 16: "Florida Man on the Lam Arrested after Butt Dialing 911"

June 6: "Florida Man Charged with Pouring Ketchup on Girlfriend"

February 3: "Florida Man Who Had Sex with Dolphin Says It Seduced Him"

September 7: "Deputies: Florida Man Held Woman's Dog as Ransom for 'Sexual Favors' "

August 13: "Florida Man Accused of Killing Friend Asked iPhone's 'Siri' Where to Hide Body, Court Hears"

July 17: "Florida Man, 23, Arrested for 'Causing Car Crash, then Tasering Bystander at Accident Scene' "

August 21: "Trump-Shaped Ecstasy Pills Bring Charge for Florida Man"

April 30: "Florida Man Attacked [by squirrel] During Selfie with Squirrel"

Full name of Thing from *The Addams Family*: Thing T. Thing.

OUR FATHER, WHO ART IN THE ATTIC

The attic of a house in Amsterdam. A barn in Scotland. A long-forgotten building in Mexico. What do they have in common? They were clandestine houses of worship during times of religious persecution.

A PRIVATE HOUSE (Amsterdam, the Netherlands)

What It Contains: A Catholic church, hidden in the attic of a private house

Details: The Netherlands was ruled by Catholic Spain in the late 1500s, but the Dutch declared independence in 1581 and the Dutch Republic was officially recognized as an independent country in 1648. Roman Catholicism was outlawed from the start, and Calvinism, an austere branch of Protestantism founded by the French theologian John Calvin, became the state religion. Catholic churches were converted to Calvinist churches and Roman Catholics were driven underground, or in the case of a wealthy merchant named Jan Hartman, into his own attic: From 1661 to 1663, he converted the attic of his canal house at 40 Oudezijds Voorburgwal ("Old Front Wall") into a *schuilkerk,* or "clandestine church."

Entrance to the church was gained through a secret door hidden in the wall of Hartman's living room; from there, worshippers made their way up a wooden spiral staircase into the attic. Wealthy and prominent Catholics sat in pews on the main floor of the church; ordinary people stood around them or in the two galleries overhead. When packed to the rafters—literally—the church could accommodate 150 people. In its day, the secret church was known by the code name "Hart," for Hartman. But in time it came to be known as the Church of Our Lord in the Attic. It continued serving as a church even after the rights of Roman Catholics were restored in 1795, until the Church of St. Nicholas opened its doors nearby in 1887. The following year, the house reopened as a museum, one that still operates today and that still hosts Mass every Sunday. It is the second-oldest museum in the city and receives more than 85,000 visitors a year.

A HIDDEN BUILDING (Puebla, Mexico)

What It Contained: The Convent of Santa Monica

Details: The building, which sat in the center of a city block completely surrounded by houses, a church, and other buildings, served as the convent for the order of Augustinian Recollect nuns from the early 1680s until the mid-1850s. That's when

The duck-billed platypus has no stomach: its esophagus connects directly to its intestines.

reformers in the Mexican government began passing laws that stripped the Catholic Church of its property. Monasteries and convents were abolished, and the priests and nuns who lived in them were forced out into the world. That should have been what happened to the nuns at the Convent of Santa Monica, and for more than 70 years many people must have assumed that was what happened. After all that time, hardly anyone in Puebla even remembered that the building was there. Then in 1934, someone tipped off the police that it was still operational, and that access to the convent could be gained through the back wall of a boardinghouse, one of the buildings that surrounded the old convent. Police raided the boardinghouse and found nothing...at first: then someone moved a vase of flowers that hid a button on the back wall. The button was pushed, a panel opened, and the police found themselves staring into the face of a nun in full habit.

The police stormed the convent and found a dark maze of corridors and hidden chapels. Down a spiral staircase, they discovered 39 bare cells with narrow beds made from rough wooden planks. They also found priceless works of religious art, handcrafted lace, and embroidered robes. Fifty Augustinian nuns had been living undetected in the convent since the 1860s. A few trusted sympathizers in the outside world had been passing whatever goods the nuns needed through two secret doors: the one in the boardinghouse, and another in the back of the church. These two secret doors were the convent's only connection to the outside world.

So...did the Mexican authorities go easy on the nuns who'd stayed so carefully hidden for so long? No—after 250 years of continuous operation, the convent was shut down and the nuns evicted. Today the building serves as Puebla's Museum of Religious Art. The museum's collection consists largely of the priceless artwork and other artifacts seized from the nuns.

A LONG BARN (Tynet, Scotland)

What It Contains: St. Ninian's Catholic Church

Details: St. Ninian's Church was built at a time when religions other than the state religion were tolerated as long as they were hidden from public view. As in the Netherlands, Roman Catholicism was out of favor and Protestantism was ascendant. St. Ninian's was constructed in 1755 by a Father Godsman, who bought the original house from a poor woman and added onto it, giving the structure the appearance of a long barn: "an addition for sheep," the father claimed. The authorities knew it was a church, but because it didn't have a steeple, or a bell tower, or stained-glass windows, or anything else that might cause offense, it was ignored. It is the oldest surviving Roman Catholic Church built in Scotland after the Protestant Reformation.

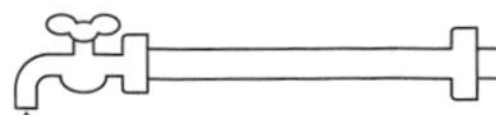

Good boy! Georgia's official state canine is "an adoptable dog."

THEY DREAMED IT

If you think people are only creative during their waking hours, you're dreaming.

DREAMER: Paul McCartney

STORY: During one "restless night" in 1968, McCartney had a dream about his mother, Mary McCartney, who'd died in 1956. "She came to me in the dream and it was as if she could see that I was troubled. And she sort of said to me, she said, 'Let it be.'" When he woke up, he immediately started writing "Let It Be," which begins with the lines "When I find myself in times of trouble / mother Mary comes to me / speaking words of wisdom, 'Let it be.'"

DREAMER: Stephenie Meyer

STORY: *Twilight*, Meyer's romantic saga of a vampire who falls in love with a small-town girl, was a publishing phenomenon in the early 2000s. Meyer had never written so much as a short story before she started work on it, the idea for which popped into her head while she slept. "It was two people in kind of a little circular meadow with really bright sunlight, and one of them was a beautiful, sparkly boy, and one was just a girl who was human and normal, and they were having this conversation," Meyer said in 2010. "The boy was a vampire, which is so bizarre that I'd be dreaming about vampires, and he was trying to explain how much he cared about her and yet at the same time how much he wanted to kill her." When she woke up, she jotted down every detail she could remember, but not because she thought it could be a book. "I just wanted to remember it." To date the *Twilight* series has sold more than 100 million copies.

DREAMER: Jack Nicklaus

STORY: By the end of 1973, the Golden Bear had won all four of golf's "majors": the U.S. Open (three times), the Masters (four times), the PGA Championship (three times), and the British Open (twice). But Nicklaus slumped in 1974—he lost tournament after tournament. One night, he dreamt that he was golfing, but he was holding the club slightly differently than how he did in real life...and he hit perfect shot after perfect shot. "When I came to the golf course yesterday morning, I tried it the way I did in my dream, and it worked," he told the *San Francisco Chronicle*. "I feel kind of foolish admitting it, but it really happened in a dream." He stuck with that swing for the rest of his career, which included six more wins at the majors.

In the Ottoman Empire, a *batman* was a unit of mass equivalent to 16 lb., 8 oz.

WEIRD AMERICAN COINS

Because change is good...and valuable.

UNIONS

Prior to statehood in 1850, California minted its own coins. After it joined the United States, California adopted U.S. currency, but there wasn't enough American paper money to circulate out to the far west, and the U.S. Mint wouldn't issue $50 or $100 coins. By 1877, the currency shortage was so bad that Congress considered issuing two new coins almost solely for California: a $100 coin called the Union, and a $50 coin called the Half Union. The measure failed and neither coin circulated, but two sample Unions and two sample Half Unions were produced, and surfaced with a coin collector in 1910.

BRASHER DOUBLOON

New York didn't ratify the United States Constitution until 1788. That meant that between 1787 and its official acceptance of American law—and coinage—it could issue its own coins. A New York goldsmith named Ephraim Brasher received a state contract to mint coins out of copper, but he decided to make gold coins instead. Bad idea. The state government rejected his coins...so he kept them. They surfaced over time, and seven are known to still exist. One, the first coin minted in the United States, sold in 2011 for over $7 million.

HALF DIMES

It's kind of odd that the nickel, or 5¢ piece, is worth half as much as a dime, but is physically almost twice as large. It wasn't always that way. From 1792 to 1873, among the most widely used coins was the half dime. Made of silver, they were worth half a dime, or five cents. When 5¢ pieces made of nickel alloy, or "nickels," came along in the 1860s, the half dime's time was up.

THREE-DOLLAR AND THREE-CENT COINS

You've heard of silver dollars and $2 bills, but did you know that for 35 years, the U.S. Mint made a $3 gold coin? At the time, the mint also circulated a $2.50 coin, so why the need for a $3 coin? To make buying stamps easier. In the 1850s, the U.S. Post Office lowered the cost of mailing a standard letter from 5¢ to 3¢. To encourage more stamp-buying, the government came up with a $3 coin to make buying 100 stamps simpler. The $3 coin was available—but not used much—between 1854 and 1889...until the price of mailing a letter went down to 2¢. (There were also 3¢ coins—good for one stamp each—jingling in Americans' pockets from 1851 to 1889.)

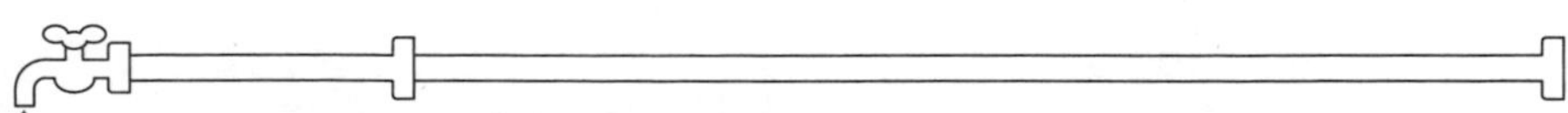

Aboard the Russian *Mir* space station (1986–2001), cosmonaut rations included vodka and cognac.

BULLION COINS

The most commonly used coins are alloys of various metals, but bullion coins are made entirely of precious metal. Four are currently produced in the United States, named for the image on each: the Silver Eagle ($1), the Gold Eagle ($5, $10, $25, and $50—the higher the denomination, the more gold it contains), the Gold Buffalo ($50), and the Platinum Eagle ($100). These are produced by the U.S. Mint, but they don't circulate, and can't even be obtained by buying them from the mint. A limited number of each are produced each year, and can be purchased from only a handful of authorized coin dealers. How much do they cost? Not face value, but rather the current value of the metal used to strike it, plus a small "coin production" fee.

STELLA

In the 1860s, well over a century before many European states joined together to use a cross-boundary currency called the euro, a few European nations formed the Latin Monetary Union. They established rules for producing gold and silver coins that were minted in different countries, but would be worth the same as one another. The United States almost joined the LMU and made a prototype gold coin in 1879 called the Stella (named for a design that included a *stella*, Latin for "star"), worth $4. Congress voted against joining the LMU, but the Stella was already in production. By the time production was halted, 425 of the coins had been made. (And the LMU fell apart in the aftermath of World War I.)

ALUMINUM PENNY

Copper prices were on the rise in the early 1970s, to the point where the U.S. Mint was barely breaking even on making pennies out of the metal—meaning it cost about 1¢ to make a 1¢ piece. The agency looked into making pennies out of other substances, including aluminum. A batch of silver-colored aluminum pennies—resembling the Lincoln-faced coin in every other way—were sent out to government officials in 1974 as samples, but the coins seemed flimsy and the idea was dropped. Only one example—the lone survivor of those struck as samples—is known to exist.

FRANKLIN DOLLAR

Just weeks after the signing of the Declaration of Independence and the official birth of the United States as a country, the newly formed federal government wanted to show the world it was for real by striking the first U.S. coins. Founding Father Benjamin Franklin came up with a design for a $1 coin. Circling the edge of the face are the words "Continental Currency" and "1776." In the middle of the design sits a sundial above the words "mind your business" and the Latin idiom *fugio*, which translates to "time flies." The coin was struck in pewter and brass, along with a handful in silver.

When e-mail was introduced in 1984, the customary signature was "Electronically yours."

MOUTHING OFF

TO QUOTE MYSELF...

Referring to yourself in the third person is called illeism. *Here are some prime examples.*

"Can you smell what The Rock is cooking?"

—The Rock

"More Americans are working. More have health insurance. Incomes are rising. Poverty is falling. Thanks, Obama."

—Barack Obama

"A Lothar Matthäus does not let himself be beaten by his body. A Lothar Matthäus decides on his fate himself."

—Lothar Matthäus

"If you had to leave your children with Bob Dole or Bill Clinton, I think you'd probably leave them with Bob Dole."

—Bob Dole

"DALÍ IS IMMORTAL AND WILL NOT DIE."

—Salvador Dalí

"WITHOUT THE FANS, FLOYD MAYWEATHER WOULDN'T BE WHERE HE'S AT TODAY."

—Floyd Mayweather

"You wouldn't even be hearing about immigration if it weren't for Donald Trump."

—Donald Trump

"I think that without sushi there would be no David Hasselhoff, because sushi is like the perfect way of describing the insides of David Hasselhoff. He is like a protein, clean and easy."

—David Hasselhoff

33'S COMPANY

In honor of Uncle John's 33rd annual edition, here are some fascinating facts with that special number.

Nuns. At the Convent of Las Descalzas Reales (the Royal Barefooted) in Madrid, the 33 nuns caretake the convent's 33 chapels.

Sports. Longest winning streak in NBA history: 33 games, by the 1971–72 Los Angeles Lakers.

Philosophy. A study of people over age 40 found that their happiest age was 33. Psychologist Donna Dawson says at 33, "innocence has been lost, but our sense of reality is mixed with a strong sense of hope."

Racing. Number of cars in the Indy 500: 33 (usually). The racing authorities calculated that a safe distance between cars positioned equally around a track is 400 feet, which allows 33 cars on the 2.5-mile speedway.

Adventure. Explorer Edmund Hillary was 33 years old when he and Nepalese climber Tenzing Norgay became the first people to summit Mount Everest. Hillary later became the third person to reach the South Pole and the first to achieve the exploration trifecta of visiting Earth's highest peak (Everest) and both the North and South Poles.

Religion. Islamic prayer beads are arranged in sets of 33 to help Muslims count during *dhikr*, or rituals in which they repeat prayers 33 times.

Freemasons. In Scottish Rite Freemasonry, members can reach any of 33 degrees, or ranks. To symbolize this, their headquarters in Washington, D.C., known as the House of the Temple, is surrounded by 33 columns, each one 33 feet high.

Bones. The human spine contains 33 vertebrae.

Heavy. A cinder block (they're actually made of concrete, not cinders) weighs 33 pounds. Think about your own weight in cinder blocks, and you might be surprised...or depressed.

History. Some historians believe Jesus was crucified on April 3, AD 33. Reason: the Bible says the Moon turned to "blood" after Jesus died, and the combination of a dust storm and a partial lunar eclipse that occurred that day likely made the Moon appear red.

Freight. In 1915, the cost of mailing a 33-pound package locally was 21¢. (Price to ship it 150 miles: 37¢.)

Disaster. In 2010, 33 miners were trapped in a collapsed mine in Chile. Once rescuers started drilling, it took 33 days to reach them. After a record-breaking 69 days underground, all 33 men were rescued alive on 10/13/10, which adds up to 33—and a happy ending.

R U IN CRISIS? TEXT 7-4-1-7-4-1

In its first seven years of operation, the Crisis Text Line has exchanged more than 140 million texts with teens and others in distress in the United States, Canada, and the UK.

GETTING INVOLVED

From 2003 to 2015, Nancy Lublin was the CEO of a nonprofit organization called DoSomething.org, which motivates young people to make positive change in their communities. The organization comes up with ideas for campaigns, such as donating food to food banks, and uses its website and social media platforms to encourage young people to get involved. Its voter registration drive, for example, registered more than 118,000 new voters in 2018 alone, and its "Teens for Jeans" campaign has donated more than a million pairs of lightly used jeans to homeless shelters in the United States.

If you're the parent of a teenager, you probably already know that their primary means of communicating with their friends is texting. (The average adolescent sends nearly 2,000 texts every month and communicates with their friends more frequently by text than by any other medium of communication, including e-mail, instant messaging, or even face-to-face.) This is how DoSomething communicates with teens, too. But as Lublin and others at the organization discovered, every time they sent out texts to promote one of DoSomething's campaigns, a few dozen kids would text back, not to talk about the campaign but to talk about problems they were having. Sometimes bullying at school was the issue; other times the texter might have been struggling with a drug problem, an eating disorder, or fighting with a boyfriend, a girlfriend, or a parent. When a texter wanted to talk about their problems, Lublin and her colleagues did whatever they could to help.

A CRY FOR HELP

Then in 2011, one of Lublin's employees, Stephanie Shih, received some disturbing texts from a young girl who revealed that she was being sexually abused. "He told me not to tell anyone," the girl explained. A few hours later the texter sent another message: "R U there?" Shih replied with a text asking the girl to identify the abuser. "It's my dad," she replied.

Shih texted contact information for an organization called Rape, Abuse & Incest National Network (RAINN), and encouraged the girl to reach out to them for help. But the girl said she was too afraid to call them. Shih assured her that contacting them

was "the right thing to do," but she never received another text from the girl. To this day, Shih has no idea if the girl ever got the help that she needed.

Shih printed out the text conversation and showed it to Lublin. It was so upsetting for both of them that a few days later they began working on an idea for a text-based counseling service for teenagers. The idea grew into the Crisis Text Line, a free, 24-hour text hotline that is available to anyone who wants to use it, not just teens. In 2015, Lublin stepped down from DoSomething to work at Crisis Text Line full time.

To contact Crisis Text Line, all a person has to do is text a message to the number 741741. Why was that number chosen? Because 7, 4, and 1 are the numbers on the left side of a cell phone's keypad, which makes it easy to remember. People who text messages to the number communicate in real time with trained volunteer counselors supervised by paid professionals.

GROWTH INDUSTRY

By 2020, Crisis Text Line had exchanged more than 140 million texts.

In August 2013, Crisis Text Line was quietly launched in two cities: El Paso, Texas, and Chicago, Illinois. Very little was done to promote it, but news spread quickly by word of mouth (well, word of text), and within four months the service was receiving texts from every area code in the United States, giving it a faster rate of growth than Facebook when it first launched. Growth remained strong in the years that followed; by 2020, Crisis Text Line had exchanged more than 140 million texts and had expanded to Canada and the UK, with plans in the works to spread to other countries in Europe as well as South Africa, Australia, and Central and South America.

BODY OF EVIDENCE

Because communication between Crisis Text Line counselors and users of the service is conducted entirely by text, computers can be used to analyze the words and syntax used in each of the millions of texts. This information is used to identify words, phrases, and even emojis that appear most frequently in the most serious cases. By using this method of "machine learning," as it's called, Crisis Text Line has identified more than 9,000 words or combinations of words that are predictors of the texter being at high risk of self-harm.

If an incoming text contains the words "numbs" and "sleeve," for example, analysis of the 140 million earlier texts has shown that there is a 99 percent chance that the texter is either cutting themselves right then or is thinking about doing it. Crisis Text Line's proprietary software will assign this texter the highest priority—"Code Orange"—and move them to the top of the list of incoming texts, so that they are assigned a counselor ahead of less urgent cases. On average, a Code Orange texter

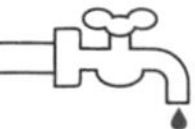

will have to wait just 39 seconds for a counselor to respond to the text, down from a two-minute wait a few years ago. The counselor will be prompted with the message, "99 percent match for cutting. Try asking one of these questions..."

COOLING OFF

The goal of these counseling sessions is to move the texters from "hot moments" to "cool moments," as Lublin puts it, by listening to the texter, working with them to explore solutions to their problem, and referring them to resources that are available in their own community. In about 1 percent of cases, the counselor will decide that the texter is at serious risk of self-harm or suicide, and will initiate what is called an "active rescue" by asking the texter for their address—"if you're texting a text line, you want help," Lublin explains—and calling the local police or 911. Over the years the service has gotten so good at identifying high-risk cases that 86 percent of suicidal cases are identified within the first couple of texts.

JUST YOU AND ME

Texting with a crisis counselor, rather than talking to them on the phone, may sound odd to anyone who isn't a teenager, but it does offer a number of advantages over calling. It's more private, since there's no risk of anyone overhearing your conversation. And you can text with counselors anywhere, anytime. Traffic at the Crisis Text Line spikes every weekday around noon, because teenagers text with counselors during lunchtime at school. As far as anyone else in the cafeteria can tell, the texter appears to be texting a friend. And the service is completely anonymous: because Crisis Text Line counselors interact with texters indirectly, through the text line's software, they don't even know the phone number of the person they are texting with.

AT EASE

Crisis Text Line may have started out as a service for teenagers, but it hasn't remained that way. Anyone can text the service, and over the years it has become popular with military veterans and even active-duty service members, among others. Vets and service members also volunteer as counselors, and they've become an important and valuable resource, Lublin says. "When we spike in volume and it becomes really hectic, it's the veterans who step up and say, 'We got this. We can do this.' They're amazing," she told the *Military Times* in 2016. "It's incredible to watch. They really are some of my favorite people."

To learn more about Crisis Text Line, turn to page 231.

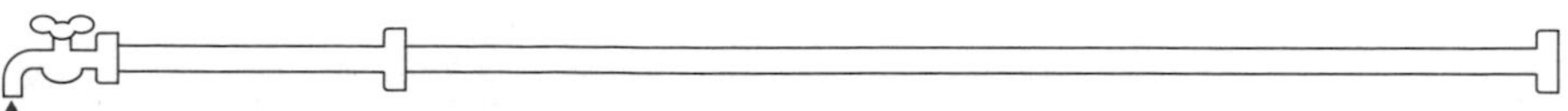

They need a law? In Indiana, it's illegal to tattoo a person's eyeballs.

IT'S IN THE CARDS

Even if you don't tell fortunes using tarot cards, they're certainly interesting to look at. How much do you know about them?

PLAYING WITH A FULL DECK

If you had to guess, which deck of cards would you say is older—ordinary playing cards or tarot cards? The artwork on tarot cards *looks* older, so it's reasonable to think that they may have been invented first. But if that's what you guessed, you're wrong. Decks of playing cards divided into four suits date back to around AD 1000 in Asia; they arrived in Europe sometime in the 1300s. Tarot cards only date to the late 1400s and are believed to have been invented in Italy. Surprisingly, they were originally used to play card games, including one called *tarocchi* that was similar to bridge. In France the game was called *tarot*, which is how the cards get their name. Telling fortunes with the cards didn't become popular until the late 1700s.

A standard deck of tarot cards contains 78 cards. Fifty-six of those are divided into four suits of 14 cards each, called the *minor arcana* (lesser secrets) cards. Each suit has 10 numbered cards plus king, queen, knight, and page/jack cards. The remaining 22 cards have no suits and are called the *major arcana* (greater secrets), or trump cards. The major arcana are numbered from 1 to 21; the 22nd card is the Fool and is not numbered.

TAKE YOUR PICK

The most widely used deck of tarot cards is known as the Rider-Waite deck. It was created by the British poet and mystic A. E. Waite using the artwork of a British artist named Pamela Colman Smith. The deck was first published by London printer William Rider & Son in 1909. It's the most popular deck of tarot cards ever produced. It is still sold today and has never gone out of print. When you picture tarot cards in your head, there's a good chance the images that come to mind are from the Rider-Waite deck.

IN THE KNOW

If you have an old Rider-Waite tarot deck lying around, hang on to it! In good condition, first-edition decks from 1909 with the included *Key to the Tarot* booklet can sell on eBay for close to $10,000.

Even if you don't use them to play tarochi or to predict the future, tarot cards can be an enjoyable and very collectible form of portable artwork. The style and variety of decks are almost endless, ranging from the weird and occult to the adorable and hilarious. Cats, dogs, pandas, gummy bears, zombies, motorcycles, rock and roll, you name it—there's probably a deck of tarot cards out there that features it. Here are some of our favorites:

The Fantod Pack Tarot. If you're a fan of the PBS series *Mystery!*, this deck may look familiar. Edward Gorey, the artist who provided the animated opening sequence for the show, designed a unique 20-card set of tarot cards in the 1960s called the Fantod Pack. (The word *fantod* means "a state or attack of uneasiness or unreasonableness.") The darkly comical outcomes that this deck can predict include hair loss, thwarted ambition, spasms, and shriveling. (Shriveling?) Also included with the Fantod Pack is a 32-page booklet of interpretations by Madame Groeda Weyrd (an anagram of Edward Gorey), who Gorey describes as the author of *The Future Speaks Through Entrails*. Gorey's illustrations feature characters such as the Child (a child-sized skeleton pulling a small black dog on a skateboard), the Limb (a bodyless prosthetic leg), the Plant (a dead lily), and the Waltzing Mouse, which portends "vertigo," "loss of jewelry," and "disorders of the large intestine." Fun for the entire family!

The Housewives Tarot. If June Cleaver from *Leave It to Beaver* read tarot, this would be her deck. It's packaged in a blue gingham-patterned "recipe box" (it actually does have a few recipe cards slipped between the tarot cards) and decorated with artwork that's evocative of 1950s magazine advertisements. "The Hanged Man" card shows a smiling aproned woman hanging her wash—and a miniature man—on a clothesline. The "Death" card features the image of a jar of "Salmonella" brand mayonnaise, "Judgment" shows a woman whose body is a fatty cut of steak standing on a bathroom scale, "The Devil" is a chocolate cake with legs, "The Star" is a woman displaying a prize-winning pie, and so on. The deck is "Guaranteed by the Housewife Occultists of America." Creator Paul Kepple also makes a deck of zombie-themed tarot cards.

The Banksy Tarot. These cards are inspired by the work of the mysterious British street artist (and self-described "art terrorist") Banksy...but they're not illustrated by him (or her). The deck was actually created by a Banksy admirer named Shilo Lewis, who calls herself an "artsy tarotist." Images in the deck include Yoda with his arm around E. T. ("Lovers"), Little Red Riding Hood ("The Fool"), Queen Elizabeth wearing a Nazi armband ("Judgement"), and a map of the world stenciled on a drainage ditch with South America and Africa going down the drain ("World"). The deck's four suits: Spray Cans (Swords), Buckets (Cups), Brushes (Wands), and Stencils (Pentacles).

Salvador Dalí's Tarot Deck. In the early 1970s, Albert Broccoli, producer of the James Bond films, hired the surrealist Spanish painter Salvador Dalí to create a custom set of tarot cards to be used as a prop in the upcoming 007 film *Live and Let Die*. The deck never appeared in the film. Why not? According to one story, Dalí wanted too much money, but Dalí himself claimed that Broccoli rejected the deck after Dalí put Sean Connery's face on the Emperor card. (*Live and Let Die* starred Roger Moore as Bond.) Whatever the case, Dalí liked the project and continued at it

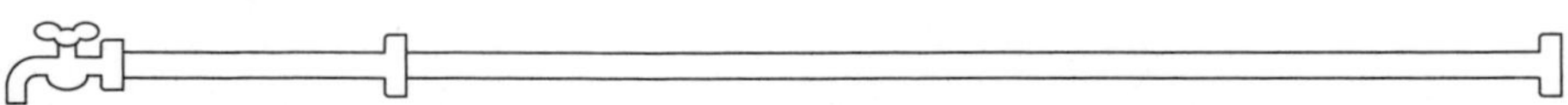

In addition to his Fabergé eggs, Peter Carl Fabergé made a single Fabergé potato.

off and on for another ten years, finally releasing the deck in 1984. Many of the 78 cards feature classic works of art, altered by Dalí. The artist himself appears as the Magician. (And the Emperor card does look like Sean Connery.)

The Brown Magick Oracle Deck. Artist Richie Brown says he created his 42-card deck for people who "need an outside source" to tell them what they already know. A friend's grandmother got the New Jersey artist hooked on "cartomancy"–divination using a card deck–and after practicing with other card decks, Brown used photos and pop-art images to create his own version of "grandma's deck." It's more of an oracle deck than a classic tarot deck, which means there are fewer rules about the images and how their meanings can be interpreted. In Brown's deck, a shiny green alien symbolizes "feeling like an outsider." Three pizza slices with sad faces represent "floating down the Lazy River on a raft hastily cobbled together from empty pizza boxes and energy drink cans that you found under the driver seat of your Honda Civic." Our favorite (of course): a pop-eyed pile of poop that symbolizes "satisfying relief."

Eight-bit Tarot. Remember the days (the 1970s and '80s) when video game graphics looked like they were made from square blocks? This deck of cards was created by an artist who wanted the illustrations to look like the video games he grew up with. Each image has the resolution of 88 by 152 pixels and uses only the colors that were available in the 8-bit Macintosh color palette. Available in full-size or pocket-size tarot decks.

African American Tarot. A deck lavishly illustrated with "scenes and imagery of African and Afro-American culture, animals, and art." The tarot themes add an element of fantasy that makes the imagery visually stunning. If you're a fan of the 2018 superhero film *Black Panther*, this is the deck for you.

Medieval Chihuahua Tarot. Creator Lynnette Monrean took photographs of her friends' chihuahuas, then photoshopped their heads onto medieval tarot-themed scenes to create the cards. The images are hilarious, and all the proceeds are donated to animal shelters. Also available: Medieval Cat Tarot.

Epicurean Tarot. Each card combines an image inspired by the classical Rider-Waite tarot deck with a tarot-themed recipe, such as the Fool's Caramelized Nuts, Three of Swords Broken Heart Fondue, the Knight of Cups' New England Clambake, and Five of Wands Buffalo Wings.

Gummy Bear Tarot. Another deck that draws inspiration from the Rider-Waite deck, but that replaces all of the people in the illustrations with gummy bears.

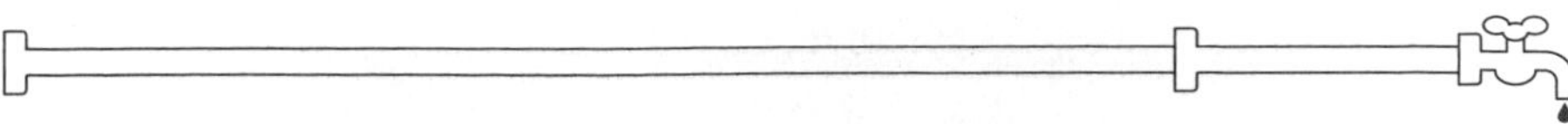

The tongue-eating louse is a parasite that eats a fish's tongue, then *becomes* the tongue.

POLICE BLUNDERS

These police officers are not having their best day on the job. Not by a long shot.

BAD COP, NO DONUT. Daniel Rushing of Orlando, Florida, often stops off on his way to work to buy a donut. One morning in 2015, he was pulled over by Cpl. Shelby Riggs-Hopkins for failing to come to a complete stop at a stop sign. Riggs-Hopkins noticed a "rock-like" substance on the floor that he suspected was meth. Rushing, 64, explained it was just a piece of his glazed donut. The officer didn't buy it and arrested Rushing. The substance was sent to the lab, where technicians quickly confirmed that it was indeed meth. Rushing spent ten hours behind bars before being released on a $2,500 bond...and when the substance was tested a second time, it came back as sugar. Rushing sued the police department, and in 2017 he was awarded a cash settlement of $37,500. But as of last report, the bogus charge still appears on his record, and whenever he applies for work, "People go online and see that you've been arrested," he complained to the *Orlando Sentinel*. For his part, Cpl. Riggs-Hopkins was given a formal reprimand.

BIG BROTHER, LITTLE BRAINS. A report in *Police Federation* magazine told of an embarrassing police chase that took place in Sussex, England, in 2012. A CCTV operator was monitoring cameras in an area that had been hit by several burglaries when he noticed a suspicious man walking on a sidewalk. He radioed the information to a plainclothes constable who was patrolling the area, and happened to be on that same street. While the operator kept the cameras trained on the suspect, the constable kept radioing his position. "You're right on his heels!" said the operator, and the chase intensified. According to the report, "Every time the man darted into another side alleyway, [the constable] was turning immediately into the same alleyway, but every time the CCTV operator asked what he could see, there was no trace." This went on for about 20 minutes until a sergeant walked into the monitoring room and immediately recognized the suspicious man...as the plainclothes officer. He'd been chasing himself the entire time. The sergeant reportedly "laughed hysterically."

BETTER SAFE THAN...WE ARE SO SORRY! In February 2017, officers at the Workington police station in Cumbria, England, noticed a suspicious car parked out front. Unable to locate the owner, they evacuated the building and surrounding area, called in the bomb squad, and—just to be safe—blew up the unattended vehicle. *Then* they located its owner. Turns out that earlier in the day, he'd become ill and was rushed to the hospital...and a police officer parked the man's car in front of the station. The explosion was blamed on an "internal communications error." The man was given an apology (and, we hope, a new car).

ASK THE EXPERTS: HAIRY QUESTIONS

Uncle John sought out the world's top trivia experts to find out the truth behind some questions that occurred to him...off the top of his head.

GREY DAY

Q: *Why does hair turn grey?*

A: "Grey (or white) is merely the base 'color' of hair. Pigment cells located at the base of each hair follicle produce the natural dominant color of our youth. However, as a person grows older and reaches middle age, more and more of these pigment cells die and color is lost from individual hairs. The result is that a person's hair gradually begins to show more and more grey. The whole process may take between 10 and 20 years—rarely does a person's entire collection of individual hairs go grey overnight." (From *Why Don't Penguins' Feet Freeze?*, published by *NewScientist*)

NOW HEAR THIS

Q: *Why does hair grow out of the ears of old men?*

A: "Vellus hair is short, thin, barely noticeable hair that covers most of a person's body during childhood. As people age, some of the vellus hair changes. During and after puberty, this hair can transform into thicker, darker hair known as terminal hair. This happens to a greater extent in men than in women, and by the time some men are old, the soft and downy vellus hair on and in their ears can become closer to what you'd expect to see on a werewolf. The leading theory to explain the hairy ears is prolonged exposure to testosterone. While the testosterone levels in old men usually drop, it is thought that the hormone may have a cumulative effect, so that as a man ages, the hair follicles are exposed to a greater overall amount of testosterone, and this encourages the growth of long black hairs." (From *Why Does Bright Light Make You Sneeze?*, by Andrew Thompson)

OFF THE DOME

Q: *What causes baldness?*

A: "Most men and women lose their hair as a result of genetic causes inherited from both the male and the female sides of the family. But since genes for baldness are so prevalent, that begs the question, what possible evolutionary advantage does baldness

provide? Sociobiologists Frank Muscarella and Michael Cunningham have discovered that women associate bald men with maturity, wisdom, and calmness. Muscarella and Cunningham suggest that some of our ape woman ancestors found these 'bald' qualities more attractive than the immature aggressiveness of younger, hairier apemen, and this could explain why baldness not only survived, but thrived." (From *Why? Answers to Everyday Scientific Questions,* by Joel Levy)

JUST DYE ALREADY

Q: *How does hair dye work?*

A: "For the most permanent dye, one that will not wash out, ammonia and strong hydrogen peroxide are used. The peroxide bleaches the hair so that dark hair can be dyed a lighter color. But the main reason for using the peroxide is because the dye is actually formed from small molecules that bind to the hair and then react with the ammonia and peroxide to form larger molecules that are locked into the hair strand." (From *Why Is Milk White? & 200 Other Curious Chemistry Questions,* by Alexa Coelho and Simon Quellen Field)

A STRAIGHT ANSWER

Q: *What makes hair curly or straight?*

A: "Research shows that the curvature of a strand depends on the nature of its follicle. When a follicle is asymmetrical, the hair that it produces is oval in shape and tends to curl. When it's symmetrical, the strand that emerges grows round and straight. A curly hair can also be described according to its composition and structure. A research team working for the cosmetics firm L'Oréal used electron microscopy to compare straight and curly hair fibers. The former were circular in cross section and symmetrical in structure. The latter, though, had an uneven distribution of a particular type of keratin, which accumulated near the inside edge of a curled hair, just beneath the curve." (From *Popular Science*)

CHEW ON THIS

Q: *How do you get gum out of hair without cutting it?*

A: "Find a jar of creamy style peanut butter or vegetable oil, such as olive oil. Cover the gum completely with peanut butter or oil using your fingers or an old toothbrush. With peanut butter, the oils in the product make the chewing gum base stiffer and less sticky. Wait a few minutes to allow the product to work. Remove the gum from the hair. Vegetable oil is especially useful when removing gum from eyebrows or eyelashes. Wash your child's hair as normal so your child does not smell like lunch." (From the American Academy of Dermatology)

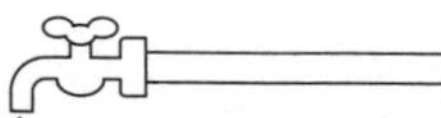

The number of Groundhog Days Bill Murray's character experiences in the film *Groundhog Day* has been estimated to be 12,403.

SPRECHEN SIE FART?

Farting is a universal language, which is to say that almost every language has some kind of phrase or idiom that evokes the very human need to break wind.

PHRASE: *Va pedo*
LANGUAGE: Spanish
LITERALLY: He's going to fart
MEANING: He's drunk

PHRASE: *Péter un cable*
LANGUAGE: French
LITERALLY: To break a cable or blow a fuse
MEANING: To fart

PHRASE: *Péter plus haut que son cul*
LANGUAGE: French
LITERALLY: To fart higher than one's own rear end
MEANING: To be arrogant

PHRASE: *Pjevaš kao da ti je slon prdnuo u uho*
LANGUAGE: Croatian
LITERALLY: You sing like an elephant farted in your ear
MEANING: You sing poorly

PHRASE: *Er drayt sich arum vie a fortz in russell*
LANGUAGE: Yiddish
LITERALLY: He wanders around like a fart in a barrel
MEANING: He's aimless

PHRASE: *Vivir en nube de pedos*
LANGUAGE: Argentine Spanish
LITERALLY: To live on a cloud of farts
MEANING: To be out of touch, delusional

PHRASE: *Duō tún pě ng pì'*
LANGUAGE: Mandarin Chinese
LITERALLY: Hold up the buttocks and praise a fart
MEANING: To use flattery to get what one wants

PHRASE: *Subo como pedo de buzo*
LANGUAGE: Argentine Spanish
LITERALLY: To rise like a diver's fart
MEANING: To scale the social ladder

PHRASE: *Ennen sian pieremää*
LANGUAGE: Finnish
LITERALLY: Before the pigs fart
MEANING: Extremely early in the morning

PHRASE: *Tuō kù zi fàng pì*
LANGUAGE: Mandarin Chinese
LITERALLY: Pulling down one's pants to fart
MEANING: Unnecessary

PHRASE: *Katosi kuin pieru saharassa*
LANGUAGE: Finnish
LITERALLY: Disappeared like a fart in the Sahara Desert
MEANING: To absolve oneself of all responsibility

PHRASE: *Itachi no saigoppeh*
LANGUAGE: Japanese
LITERALLY: The weasel's last fart
MEANING: A desperate act by a desperate person

PHRASE: *Jeden myslel, že si uprdne a posral se*
LANGUAGE: Czech
LITERALLY: He thought he would fart but instead he pooped himself
MEANING: The equivalent of "hindsight is 20/20"

PHRASE: *Lepkeing*
LANGUAGE: Hungarian
LITERALLY: Butterfly fart
MEANING: Easy or simple, no problem

Ohio's Cuyahoga River was so polluted that it caught fire about once every 8 years between 1868 and 1969.

WHO CONSUMES THE MOST...

One of the fun things about living in the Information Age is that people compile statistics about all kinds of odd things, including which countries eat the most of each kind of food.

...Beef. Is it really, as the commercials say, "what's for dinner"? It probably is in Uruguay, where the average person eats 124.2 pounds per year. (In the United States, the average is 79.3 pounds per year.)

...Meat. When all sources of animal flesh are considered and combined, the biggest meat-eaters are the United States and Australia. The average person in both countries eats about 220 pounds of meat a year, which works out to about 50 chickens.

...Bread. It's Turkey. Each person in that European/Asian bridge nation consumes a whopping 440 pounds of bread a year—that's more than a pound *every day.*

...Turkey. It's not Turkey—it's Israel. On average, an Israeli gobbles 28 pounds annually, far more than the 16.7 pounds the average American eats. (A lot of that Israeli turkey comes in the form of turkey pastrami.)

...Chocolate. Switzerland is famous for making chocolate, but the Swiss also consume more of it per capita than any other country. The average Swiss person eats 22 pounds a year. (That's about double of what the average American eats.)

...Candy. If you factor in all kinds of candy, Sweden takes the cake, er, candy bar. The average Swede scarfs down half a pound of candy every *week.* This stems from a cultural celebration of sweets, especially on *Lördagsgodis,* or "Saturday candy." Swedes tend to eschew candy during the week and go nuts on the weekend.

...Donuts. The deep-fried cakes are an important part of the cultural and economic fabric of Canada. The nation boasts five times more donut shops per capita than the United States, and Canadians eat more donuts than anybody else: about 27 per person per year.

...Sugar. It's not just an ingredient in sweets like chocolate, candy, donuts, baked goods, and sodas—it's also in all manner of processed foods, from breakfast cereals to spaghetti sauce. Americans lead the world in sugar consumption. Over the course of one year, the average American eats 126.4 grams (4.5 ounces) of sugar per day, or a total of around 100 pounds per year.

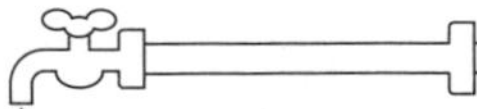

The "good" Samaritans of the Bible still exist. About 800 of them are living in Israel.

...Cheese. It's one entire course of a meal in France, the country that gave us such famous cheese varieties as Brie and Camembert. French people love cheese, and the per capita consumption rate is 57 pounds a year. That's the most in the world, but just barely more than second place—the residents of Iceland.

...Coffee. While coffee is grown in tropical, mountainous regions of North America, South America, and Africa, the country that actually *drinks* the most is Finland. On average, each Finn brews 21 pounds' worth of beans per year.

...Frozen pizza. It's Norway, where every man, woman, and child eats the equivalent of 11 pies per year. (Wisconsin is the U.S. state with the largest population of people with Norwegian descent, and it's also the #1 state for per capita frozen pizza consumption.)

...French fries. They were invented in Belgium, and they remain more popular there than any other place on Earth. A Belgian eats, on average, 165 pounds of fries a year.

...Carbonated drinks. Soft drinks—pop, soda, or whatever you want to call them—are more popular in Mexico than in any other country. If an average serving of soda is eight ounces, the average Mexican resident gulps down 632 of them a year.

...Spam. Introduced to Southeast Asia and Polynesia as a low-cost, shelf-stable meat product in World War II, the canned mystery meat (it's actually ham and pork shoulder) remains popular in that part of the world...but nowhere more than Guam, where the average resident eats the equivalent of 16 cans a year.

...Ice cream. It's New Zealand. The nation screams for ice cream, to the tune of 28.4 liters (7.5 gallons) per person, per year.

...Food. According to the UN's Food and Agricultural Organization, Austria eats more total calories than anyone else. The average Austrian packs away 3,800 calories a day, just edging out the average daily American intake of 3,750 calories.

...Beer. Ready to wash down all that trivia with a cold one? They apparently wash everything down with beer in the Czech Republic, which has a per capita beer consumption rate of 143.3 liters a year—about double what Americans drink.

Bonus: Which country has the most vegetarians per capita? India. The nation's Hindu, Buddhist, and Jain religions all advise nonviolence toward animals, or deliver an implicit instruction to avoid meat. Result: about 38 percent of India's billion-plus people are vegetarian, although most are lacto-vegetarians, meaning they'll eat dairy products.

MOUTHING OFF

DON'T!

Don't you just love it when people give you free advice?

"Don't spend time beating on a wall, hoping to transform it into a door."

—Coco Chanel

"DON'T CRY BECAUSE IT'S OVER, SMILE BECAUSE IT HAPPENED."

—Dr. Seuss

"DON'T WAIT. THE TIME WILL NEVER BE JUST RIGHT."

—Napoleon Hill

"Don't do things that kill you."

—John Bytheway

"Don't ever take a fence down until you know why it was put up."

—Robert Frost

"DON'T TRY TO LESSEN YOURSELF FOR THE WORLD; LET THE WORLD CATCH UP TO YOU."

—Beyoncé

"Don't count the days, make the days count."

—Muhammad Ali

"Don't feel stupid if you don't like what everyone else pretends to love."

—Emma Watson

"Don't try to make everyone happy; you can't. The only ones who try are clowns."

—Matshona Dhliwayo

"Don't let what you cannot do interfere with what you can do."

—John Wooden

"Don't let someone's words blind you from their behavior."

—Steve Maraboli

BOOKER, THALBERG & MACARTHUR

No, it's not a law firm. You've heard of these famous international prizes—now get to know their namesakes.

THE BOOKER PRIZE FOR FICTION

Description: The Booker Prize is awarded every year to the best novel written in English and published in the United Kingdom. It is one of literature's most prestigious awards. Winners include Salman Rushdie, for *Midnight's Children* (1981), Kazuo Ishiguro, for *The Remains of the Day* (1989), and Margaret Atwood, for *The Blind Assassin* (2000).

Named For: English brothers George and Richard Booker, who owned slaves and sugar plantations in British Guiana (now the nation of Guyana) in South America, as well as a shipping line based in Liverpool, in the 1830s. Their company later became known as Booker McConnell Ltd.

Story: By 1968, more than a century after its founding, Booker McConnell was a food wholesaling giant with warehouses all over the UK. Its chairman, Jock Campbell, heir to another British Guiana sugar fortune that merged with the Bookers', had spent his career reforming the firm, raising the pay and living standards of Booker McConnell's 60,000 workers in British Guiana and the West Indies, and diversifying out of the sugar trade. (He was made a member of the House of Lords for his work.)

One of the businesses Campbell, now Baron Campbell of Eskan, moved into was publishing. He bought companies that owned the rights to the works of famous authors, including Agatha Christie and Campbell's golfing buddy Ian Fleming. In 1969, Campbell founded the Booker-McConnell Prize. It kept that name until 2002, when Booker-McConnell ended its sponsorship and the Man Group, a business management company with its own history in the Caribbean sugar trade, stepped in as the new sponsor of the renamed Man Booker Prize. When the Man Group ended its sponsorship in 2019, Crankstart, a British charitable foundation, took over. "Crankstart Booker Prize" was probably a nonstarter; today it's simply known as the Booker Prize.

THE IRVING G. THALBERG MEMORIAL AWARD

Description: The award is a special trophy given by the Academy of Motion Picture Arts and Sciences to "creative producers whose bodies of work reflect a consistently high quality of motion picture production." It's awarded during the Academy Awards

ceremony, but it's not an Oscar statuette. It's a solid bronze bust of Thalberg set on a black marble base. Recipients have included Alfred Hitchcock (1967), Steven Spielberg (1986), Billy Wilder (1987), George Lucas (1991), Clint Eastwood (1994), and Francis Ford Coppola (2010).

Named For: Irving Grant Thalberg was a cofounder of the Metro-Goldwyn-Mayer film studio as well as the Hollywood wunderkind responsible for producing some of the finest films of Hollywood's golden age in the 1920s and '30s, including *The Jazz Singer, Mutiny on the Bounty, A Night at the Opera*, and *The Good Earth.*

Story: Thalberg had congenital heart problems at a time when heart surgery was in its infancy. Even after his first heart attack at the age of 25, there was little that doctors could do. Then in 1936, Thalberg contracted pneumonia after returning home from a vacation. With his weakened heart, he was unable to fight it off and he died at the age of 37. Though his health problems were no secret, his death at such an early age came as a tremendous shock. The following year, the Motion Picture Academy created the award to honor his memory.

THE MACARTHUR FELLOWS PROGRAM

Description: The MacArthur Fellows Program is a monetary prize awarded each year by the John D. and Catherine T. MacArthur Foundation to several "extraordinarily talented and creative individuals as an investment in their potential," says the foundation. About 30 fellows are named each year; each of them receives $625,000 and they are free to do whatever they want with the money. Past fellows include writer Cormac McCarthy (1981), jazz drummer Max Roach (1988), farmer Cheryl Rogowski (2004), and journalist Ta-Nehisi Coates (2015).

Named For: Philanthropists John D. and Catherine T. MacArthur, who made their fortune in insurance and Florida real estate.

Story: The couple started their foundation in 1970 as a place for their fortune to go when John MacArthur died, chiefly as a way to avoid paying estate taxes. When he did die in 1978, almost his entire estate—about $1 billion—went to that foundation. Over the next couple of years, MacArthur's son, Roderick, wrested control of the foundation's board from his father's cronies and started donating money to more liberal-minded ventures. In this spirit, the Fellows Program was founded in 1981. Better known today as the "MacArthur Genius Grant," the program has awarded its Fellowship prize to more than 940 people, ranging in age from 18 to 92, since its founding. In total, the John D. and Catherine T. MacArthur Foundation gives away more than $250 million every year.

* * *

"Only boring people get bored." —**Ruth Burke**

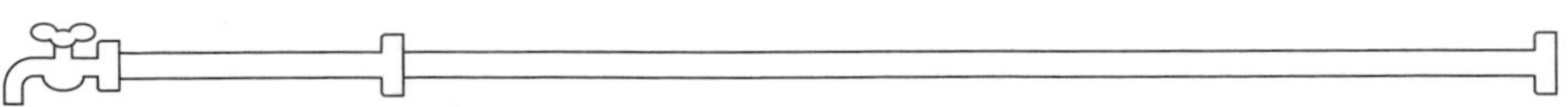

STRANGE LAWSUITS

These days, it seems like people will sue each other over practically anything. Here are some real-life examples of unusual legal battles.

THE PLAINTIFF: DeToya Moody of Decatur, Georgia

THE DEFENDANT: R. Henry, Inc., a local contracting company

THE LAWSUIT: In 2011, Moody drove to a Publix grocery store and parked her car on the road, behind a utility truck. When she exited her car, a bright orange ladder was extended above the sidewalk to a bank sign, where a worker was changing the letters. What occurred next was all captured on video surveillance footage. Moody walked underneath the ladder toward the store, then stopped and turned around to go back to her car, passing under the ladder a second time. She then walked to an ATM, passing under the ladder a third time. While she was using the ATM, the worker lowered the ladder, which was now spread across the sidewalk. Following safety procedures, he put cones on either side of the ladder. This time, as Moody went back to her car, she was texting on her phone. Result: she walked right into the ladder and fell onto the concrete. She was later diagnosed with "post-traumatic headaches and a mild concussion."

Moody hired personal injury lawyer Joseph Wilson, who filed a lawsuit against R. Henry, Inc. The contractor offered to settle the case for $5,000. Wilson countered with $75,000, which R. Henry declined, so they went to court. Now Wilson was seeking damages totaling $175,000.

THE VERDICT: Oddly, despite photo and phone record evidence, the jury found that Moody was only 8 percent liable for her injuries, and awarded her $161,000—92 percent of the $175,000 she was seeking. Her attorney told the Georgia legal journal the *Daily Report* that he wasn't sure how they came to that amount. He also said he was surprised that his client had actually won because he felt that R. Henry's defense team had made a good "common sense" argument that Moody "wasn't paying attention."

THE PLAINTIFF: A 70-year-old woman from Buenos Aires, Argentina, identified only as M. L.

THE DEFENDANT: M. L.'s ex-husband, identified as D. B.

THE LAWSUIT: Not long after M. L. earned a bachelor's degree in economics in the early 1980s, she married D. B. He wouldn't allow her to get a job, so she spent the next 27 years being a mom and housewife. Then, in 2009, he left her.

By the time they finalized their divorce two years later, M. L. had turned 60, the age when she would have started receiving retirement benefits if she'd spent the previous three decades in the workplace, rather than at home doing the cooking, cleaning, and all the other tasks that come with being a stay-at-home mom. Meanwhile, her advanced age and lack of experience made entering the job market nearly impossible. She was experiencing financial difficulties while her ex-husband was "living the good life." So M. L. sued him for lost wages.

THE VERDICT: "The economic dependence of wives on their husbands," said Judge Victoria Famá in the landmark ruling, "is one of the central mechanisms through which women are subordinated in society." She ruled in favor of M. L. and ordered the ex-husband to pay her eight million pesos ($173,000).

THE PLAINTIFF: David Hingst, 56, an engineer employed by Construction Engineering in Melbourne, Australia, in 2009

THE DEFENDANT: Greg Short, Hingst's supervisor at the firm

THE LAWSUIT: In 2017, Hingst sued "Mr. Stinky" (his nickname for his former boss) for bullying him...with farts. "I would be sitting with my face to the wall," Hingst told the reporters, "and he would come into the room, which was small and had no windows. He would fart behind me and walk away. He would do this five or six times a day." Hingst said he had to keep a bottle of spray deodorant at his desk. Then he had to move his workspace to another area farther away from Short. Then Hingst was "made redundant." (Translation: he was fired.) Hingst said the farting and subsequent firing led to "severe stress," so he sued for wrongful termination and harassment. He sought 1.8 million Australian dollars ($1.28 million).

Hingst sued "Mr. Stinky" (his nickname for his former boss) for bullying him... with farts.

The case made it all the way to the Supreme Court of Victoria. During the three-week trial, Hingst testified that Mr. Stinky and others were engaged in a prolonged bullying campaign designed to get him to quit his job. He said he also received threatening phone calls and was once called an "idiot," but the meat of this case revolved around whether flatulence could be considered bullying. In his defense, Short testified that he "may have done it once or twice, maybe," but he denied that he intentionally harassed the plaintiff.

THE VERDICT: Case dismissed—but not because Justice Rita Zammit didn't believe Hingst's story. She did. She just thought that Short's farts fell short of bullying. "Typical banter or mucking around," she called it. And she also agreed with Short's defense that Hingst's job loss was a "genuine redundancy" caused by the 2008 global financial crisis. Hingst pledged to appeal to Australia's highest court, but for now, the ruling seems to have given aggressive Aussie gas passers a free pass to pass gas at whomever they please.

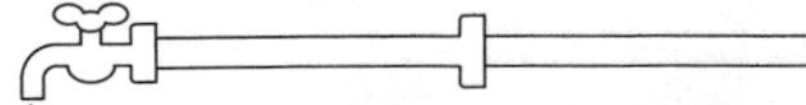

Name for that thin layer of black paint around a car's windshield: frit.

RESTAURANT SECRETS

We know that going out to eat is supposed to be a nice, relaxing treat... but after learning what really goes on behind the scenes at some eateries, you might prefer to stay home.

SPECIAL SECRET. In high-end restaurants, chefs use "daily specials" to highlight a limited quantity of local produce, or something that's deliciously in-season. But at most restaurants, daily specials are the way they get rid of ingredients of which there's a surplus...or that are about to go bad.

DIRTY SECRET. Sure, waitstaff and busboys wipe down tables after customers leave them, but is the rag clean? Probably not. That rag gets used all day, on all the tables, so it's actually collecting and spreading germs, not eliminating them. Another unclean spot: menus. Every customer who comes into the restaurant handles the menus, and when they do get a wipe-down, it's with the same rags that are used to wipe the tables.

JUICY SECRET. Waiters often differentiate between regular and diet soda with a lemon wedge rested on the rim of a glass of the diet drink. But did anybody wash that lemon? And it's been handled by who knows how many people before it made its way into your drink. So squirt the lemon juice into your soda, tea, or water if you must... but *don't* drop it into the drink.

PRACTICAL SECRET. It saves time and money to pre-make items, so that's standard operating procedure for lots of restaurants. One worker may spend an entire shift making side salads, which fill a fridge where waiters can pull them out and serve them immediately. How long they sit depends on how many are ordered, but it could be for up to three days. Similarly, large diner or breakfast-oriented chains like Denny's pre-make items they sell in huge quantities. Toast, bacon, and pancakes may be cooked in advance and then sent to a warming drawer.

PRICING SECRET. Ever notice that menus at nicer sit-down restaurants tend to exclude a dollar sign in front of the price of food items? That creates a subtle mental disconnect with money, encouraging customers to spend a bit more than they otherwise would have. (The same psychological trick is at play when only whole dollar amounts—such as "12"—are utilized instead of "11.99" or "11.95.")

FISHY SECRET. Restaurants may get fish delivered on various days of the week—but never on Sunday. So if you order fish on a Sunday, it's going to be at least a day old.

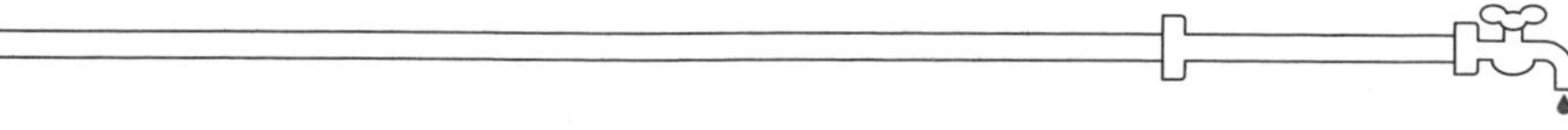

POINTED SECRET. Many high-end and chain restaurants carefully design their menu layout to maximize profits. Similar to the way newspapers put their biggest story in the most eye-catching spot—the top right of the front page—a menu will have the restaurant's most profitable selections in that very same spot. Other "cash cow" menu spots: the first and last items listed in a section, and in a two-page spread, just above center on the right-hand page.

SONIC SECRET. Music is an effective tool at building atmosphere and driving business. A study by the University of Leicester found that in restaurants where classical music was played as background music, customers spent more money. Reason: psychologically, it makes people feel wealthier and more willing to splurge a bit. So why do so many restaurants play loud rock music? That tends to move people out and along—eat, pay, leave...and make way for new customers.

INGREDIENT SECRET. Why does some restaurant food taste so much richer and more savory than it would if you made a similar item at home? Because restaurant chefs are very liberal with their use of butter and sugar. Butter adds flavor, an attractive shine, and eliminates food sticking to pans. Sugar adds shine and it cuts the bitterness of foods. Vegetable medleys and pizza dough might be treated with a pinch of sugar, as well. The same with kids' meals or kid-friendly items—they might be sweetened to satisfy young eaters' finicky palates.

OUTSOURCING SECRET. A fast-food restaurant's kitchen is a chaotic place, with up to a dozen people running around cooking, putting food in bags, and handing it off. Over the last decade, the process has become more automated, and many chains now employ the equivalent of a call center. When a customer pulls up and gives their order, it's taken by a person at a computer hundreds of miles away, who inputs it and sends it to the restaurant's kitchen monitors.

SICK SECRET. More than half of restaurant workers who responded to a 2015 poll said they routinely come into work—where they handle food—while sick. Restaurant jobs are generally relatively low paying, and employers don't offer sick days. If waiters and waitresses don't work, they don't get paid, so they clock in...even if they've got something easily transmittable to customers, such as a cold or a stomach bug.

CHECKMATE!

There are 10^{120}, or 10,000,000,000,000,000,000,000,000,000,000,000,000,000,000,000,000,000,000,000,000,000,000,000,000,000,000,000,000,000,000,000,000,000,000,000,000,000,000,000,000,000,000 possible moves in a game of chess.

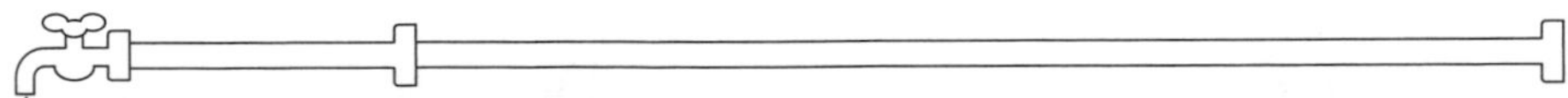

NICE STORIES

Every now and then we like to lock our inner cynics in a box and share some stories with happy endings.

A Humble Carpenter

When Dale Schroeder was coming of age in the 1950s, his family was so poor that he couldn't afford a college education. He learned carpentry and then spent the next 67 years working for the same company in Ames, Iowa. Then, not long before his death in 2005, Schroeder told a lawyer friend that he'd saved a lot of money over the decades, and that because he had no family to leave it to, "I'd like to help kids go to college." "How much are we talking, Dale?" asked the lawyer. "Just shy of three million." That was just enough money to pay the full tuitions of 33 small-town high school graduates who had the grades but not the funds to go to college. All that Schroeder asked in return: "Pay it forward." In 2019, those 33 students—none of whom had ever met their late benefactor—all gathered together to pay homage to him. The college graduates—including several doctors, teachers, and therapists—call themselves "Dale's kids."

A Christmas Miracle

There's that one house on every block that really goes for it during the holidays. In a Mulberry, Florida, neighborhood, that house belongs to Don Weaver. Since 2007, his Christmas light displays have been wowing people from near and far—no one more so than his 13-year-old neighbor, Kaitlyn De Jesus. The teenager, who is nonverbal autistic, never uttered more than one or two words at a time, and then only with visual and auditory prompts. Because Kaitlyn had been admiring the holiday display for most of her life, Weaver created a display of more than 200,000 lights in December 2019 and synched them to Kaitlyn's favorite songs. He made her a specially designed front-row seat to watch the light show and tap her toes to the music. It was a sweet gesture for a girl who doctors said would never talk in her life. Her mom, Marisabel Figueroa, had always held out hope that something would break her out of her shell. When she walked over to Mr. Weaver's driveway to see how her daughter was doing, all of a sudden, "Kaitlyn got up from the chair and started singing," Figueroa told *TODAY Parents*. Then she said, "Mom! Look at the blue lights. Look at the snowmen. Santa's coming!" Figueroa broke out in tears. "It was the first time she ever talked. If only Christmas could be around all year."

Life Line

Late one night in April 2018, several motorists called 911 to report a man standing on a highway overpass near Detroit, Michigan. He threatened to jump, so the highway

patrol called in crisis negotiators and closed the interstate in both directions. As the cars were being directed to surface streets, the police asked some truckers for a hand. They redirected 13 tractor-trailers to the bridge and instructed the drivers to park side by side beneath the overpass. Now, what would have been a 14-foot fall to the concrete below was only a 5-foot fall to the top of a trailer. Even with the trucks parked there, it took more than three hours for officers to convince the man to come down. He was taken to a hospital for evaluation and treatment. Afterward, a photo of all the trucks lined up under the overpass went viral. According to Lt. Mike Shaw, what the truckers did was special, but the real victory goes to the man on the bridge. "In that picture is somebody that was contemplating ending their own life. We want that to be the story—not what Michigan State Police did or what the truckers did, but that the person changed his own mind."

Kennedy's First Impression

A week before Christmas in 2019, Lauren Harper was driving in Greenville, South Carolina, when she saw a wrapped present sitting in the middle of a busy road. She jumped out and grabbed the gift. The tag said, "To Mom and Dad, from Kennedy." Harper took it home and posted a photo of the lost gift on her Facebook page, along with this caption:

> "This fell off a car on Woodruff Rd in front of Walmart tonight around 5:10pm. Hoping to find Kennedy so she can give her parents her gift! It got hit at least once but it feels like whatever it is still intact. Please share so Kennedy can message me!"

The post was shared more than 3,000 times, and it didn't take long before someone commented that the present looked like the ones that a local branch of La Petite Daycare sends home each Christmas. Conrad contacted the daycare center, and they confirmed that there was a lost gift, and that it was from Kennedy...but that she wouldn't be able to send a text because she's only three months old. The gift turned out to be a framed picture of the baby's footprint, and thanks to Harper it was delivered—intact—in time for Christmas. Here's the cool part, said Harper: "My mom still has a handprint poem from when I went to a La Petite in North Carolina probably 25 years ago. So, that was kind of special when I found out it was a footprint painting from a baby at La Petite."

Over the River and Through the Woods

In November 2019, Diana Chong and her husband and two daughters had just embarked on a road trip from Long Island, New York, to a Thanksgiving family reunion in Pennsylvania when they stopped at a bagel shop in the town of Middle Island. Chong went in, bought some bagels, got back into the passenger seat, and they

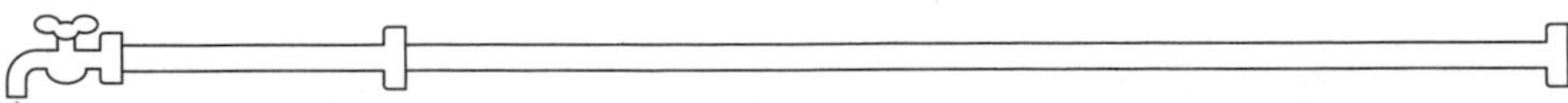

Detroit Red Wings hockey player Bob Probert spent so much time in his team's penalty box...

settled in for the four-hour drive. It was only when they got to their destination that Chong realized she'd left her key fob on the counter. The car could run without the fob, but it couldn't start. And they'd already turned it off. Suddenly stranded, "We were calling dealerships, we were calling locksmiths, we were calling AAA," Chong told CBS New York, but none of them could do anything on the weekend. So Chong called the bagel shop and asked the manager, Vinny Proscia, if the key fob was still there. It was. Then he said, "Why don't I just drive it to you?" Chong reminded him that it's nearly 200 miles away, but he insisted, even though he had to be back by 5:00 a.m. to open the store. Six hours later (due to the holiday traffic), Proscia arrived with the key fob. He was showered with hugs, gift cards, and coffee and treats before making the long drive home. On the way, he was pulled over for speeding, but the officer was so moved by Proscia's story that he let him off with a warning. After Chong shared the good deed with the press, the bagel shop enjoyed record business over the holidays. Best of all, the two families—strangers until that point—became friends. "People need to be kind to one another," said Chong, "and help each other out in this stressful world we live in."

Now Hear This

Medical complications following a premature birth left Scarlet Benjamin with severe hearing loss. For the first eleven months of her life, the baby's world was muffled. Then, in January 2019, she was fitted with her first hearing aid at Atlanta Hearing Associates in Milledgeville, Georgia. With her was her four-year-old sister, Halie, and her mother, Carol Dianne Benjamin, who filmed Scarlet's reaction: "Baby sister, baby sister," says Halie. Just then, Scarlet's confused expression changes to one of utter delight as she giggles uncontrollably at the sound of her sister's voice. Then, through tears, her mother says, "You can hear me!" Scarlet turns to look at Mom and laughs even louder. Scarlet's viral video was played by news outlets all over the world. Her mother called it one of the "absolute best days of our lives."

WEIRD JOB: EYEBALL DUSTER

Every year during winter break at the University of Iowa, Cindy Opitz, the Collections Manager at the Museum of Natural History, takes advantage of the empty hallways to carefully dust all the taxidermied eyes in the animal exhibits (she uses a cotton swab). It's more than just dust, she explains: "There's actually such a thing as glass disease. Dust attracts moisture from the air, which can destabilize the structure of the glass, causing cracking, crazing, or even weeping." One other advantage: "It's amazing, how simply cleaning dusty eyes can make a 100-year-old specimen look brand new."

ACRONYM-CRAZY

Acronyms are nicknames or abbreviations formed from the first letters of a series of words. Familiar examples: NATO, UNICEF, and FEMA. Here are some more that are funny, inappropriate, or just plain weird.

★ Iowa's Department of Elder Affairs handles issues important to older citizens, such as housing options, long-term care, and elder abuse. In 2009, the agency that caters to people in their final years changed its name to the Department on Aging, or **DOA**.

★ After the U.S.-led invasion of Iraq ousted dictator Saddam Hussein in 2003, the Coalition Provisional Authority put together a local defense force called the New Iraqi Corps. That had to be changed, however, when organizers realized that the acronym formed by the name, **NIC**, is an Arabic slang word that's the equivalent of English's f-word. (New name: Iraqi Armed Forces.)

★ The military action that led to Hussein's downfall was called Operation Iraqi Freedom, although some of President George W. Bush's political opponents thought the whole mission was a ruse to gain control of Iraq's valuable oil fields. That's why the invasion got the name Operation Iraqi Freedom instead of its original name, Operation Iraqi Liberation, or **OIL**.

★ Researchers at Washington University in St. Louis studying respiratory diseases developed a questionnaire to help diagnose rhinosinusitis, an inflammation of the nasal cavity and sinuses that results in a runny nose. The name of the questionnaire is the Sino-Nasal Outcome Test, or **SNOT**.

★ Dublin, Ireland, has a light rail network called the Dublin Area Rapid Transit. The Dallas, Texas, public transportation system is called Dallas Area Rapid Transit. Both organizations share the speedy acronym **DART**. Bonus: Dallas's is overseen by the DART Board. (Bull's-eye!)

★ Underwater researchers working at deep-sea observatories use a special tool to measure the water temperature and pressure. They place it into the openings of boreholes. The tool is called a circulation obviation retrofit kit, or **CORK**.

★ In Sir Arthur Conan Doyle's novels, detectives at Scotland Yard often consulted with the brilliant Sherlock Holmes to help them solve their toughest cases. Today, at the real-life Scotland Yard offices, the computer system is called the Home Office Linked Major Enquiry System, which spells out **HOLMES**.

★ How does nacho cheese sauce get that smooth and creamy consistency? That's from the additive sodium citrate. Coincidentally, the chemical formula to create sodium citrate is Na3C6H5O7—combining different volumes of sodium (Na), carbon (C), hydrogen (H), and oxygen (O)...or **NACHO**.

★ In 2000, conservative Alberta politician Stockwell Day formed a new moderate-to-right political party called the Canadian Conservative Reform Alliance Party. Immediately after the new endeavor was launched, Day changed it to the Canadian Reform Conservative Alliance when reporters pointed out that the party's name was **CCRAP**.

★ Do you sometimes sneeze when you walk out into bright sunlight? That's called the photic sneeze reflex. The more formal term is autosomal compelling helio-ophthalmic outburst syndrome, or **ACHOO syndrome**.

★ Located in Heifi, China, at the Institute of Plasma Physics stands an experimental energy reactor that uses the Sun and magnetic forces to generate fusion. The ultimate goal: creating some kind of artificial sun. The Sun rises in the east, and China is referred to as part of the Far East, so it's fitting then that the acronym for the Experimental Advanced Superconducting Tokamak is **EAST**. (In case you were wondering, a tokamak is a kind of magnetic confinement device that was developed to produce fusion power. The word itself is an acronym of Russian words that we can't pronounce.)

★ There's a trade organization for companies that sell merchandise to gift shops, and companies that operate gift shops: the Souvenir and Novelty Trade Association, or **SANTA** for short.

★ Are people who work on computers all day "nerds"? Two institutions that hire a lot of techies might think so. Cambridge, Massachusetts, is home to the Microsoft-funded New England Research and Development Center, but everybody calls it the **Microsoft NERD Center**. Across the Atlantic, Nintendo operates a facility in Paris where workers develop video game innovations. It's called Nintendo European Research and Development—another NERD.

★ There's a type of clinical depression that strikes sufferers in the darker and colder fall and winter months. It's a bit insensitive—but accurate—that psychiatrists named this condition seasonal affective disorder, or **SAD**.

★ There's a variant of SAD that affects people only during the warmest time of year, and that one is called summer-onset seasonal affective disorder...which is **SOSAD**.

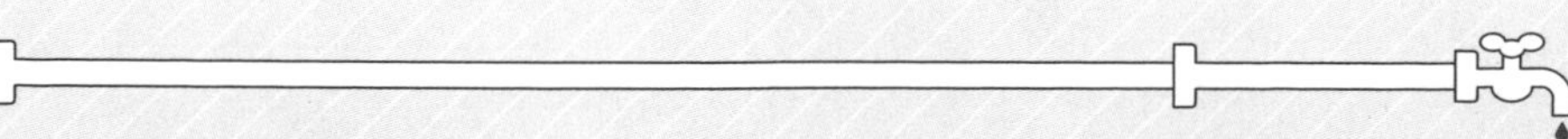

Total number of Walkmans sold by Sony since their introduction in 1979: 400 million.

THE IMMORTAL TARO TSUJIMOTO

He's one of the Buffalo Sabres' most famous hockey players, but you've never seen him play. In fact, no one has.

TOP SECRET

If you're the kind of devoted hockey fan who watches the National Hockey League's entry draft on TV, you might be surprised to learn how differently it was conducted in the 1970s. Today the NHL draft is open to the public and is conducted in a sports arena large enough to hold representatives of every team in the league, with plenty of seats for fans. If you can't attend in person, the draft is televised live; and if you're too busy to watch it on TV, you can receive updates in real time on Twitter and Facebook.

In 1974, things were completely different. That year, the NHL draft was conducted early, in secret, and entirely over the phone. There was no meeting to go to. It was done that way to prevent a two-year-old upstart rival hockey league called the World Hockey Association from poaching incoming players from the league. The NHL hoped to sign the players to contracts before the WHA even knew the draft had taken place.

CALL WAITING

The draft was run out of the office of the league's president, Clarence Campbell, in Montreal. Each round worked as follows: Campbell would call a team and ask for their draft pick, then he would call the next team and ask for their pick, and so on, until every team had been called. There were 13 teams in the NHL at that time, and every time Campbell called a team he had to read them the names of the players the other teams had just picked, so that the team he was calling could check those names off and select a draft pick from the names that remained.

IN THE KNOW

The first indoor hockey game ever: March 3, 1875, at the Victoria Skating Rink in Montreal, Canada. To reduce the risk of broken windows and injured spectators, the players decided to use a flat square block of wood, or "puck," instead of the usual lacrosse ball. Rubber pucks soon followed. They remained square in shape into the 1880s.

Once a team manager gave Campbell the name of their draft pick, there was nothing to do but wait around until he called again, about an hour later, to get their next draft pick. It was an incredibly tedious process, and it dragged on for three days. By round 10 on the second day, George "Punch" Imlach, the general manager of the

Des Moines, Iowa, and Munich, Germany, both translate as "of the monks" in English.

Buffalo Sabres, was going crazy. He had already picked all the players he thought he needed or was ever likely to use. The players that remained to be drafted were so far down the list that most were probably never going to make the team. Imlach wanted to get back to work, but the draft went on and on.

PAYBACK

The situation became so frustrating that Paul Wieland, the team's head of public relations and a man with a reputation for pulling pranks, said, "Why don't we draft someone that doesn't exist?" Imlach liked the idea, so while they sat around that hour waiting for Campbell to call for the Sabres' 11th-round draft pick, he and Wieland invented a fictional hockey player.

"Why don't we draft someone that doesn't exist?"

They decided that the player would be from Japan, to make it harder for the NHL to verify that he really existed. In those days, NHL teams recruited players almost exclusively from the United States and Canada, but they were just starting to send scouts to other parts of the world in search of undiscovered talent. It made sense that the Sabres might have sent a scout overseas to recruit players from Japanese teams, and only the Sabres knew for sure that they had not done so.

Taro is a popular man's name in Japan, and back when Wieland was in college, he'd often driven past the Tsujimoto Grocery store on Route 16, south of Buffalo. So "Taro Tsujimoto" it was. They decided to say that he played hockey for the Tokyo Katanas, a team that didn't exist. (A *katana*, like a sabre, is a type of sword.) Since the team wasn't real, that made it much harder for the NHL to double-check the pick. In those pre-Internet days, you couldn't just google for information the way people do today.

When Clarence Campbell called to get the name of the Sabres' 11th-round draft pick, Imlach told him, "Buffalo selects Taro Tsujimoto from the Tokyo Katanas," and spelled out the name for the NHL president. Campbell accepted the information without question and moved on to the next call. What made the prank all the more funny to Imlach and Wieland was that they knew Campbell was going to have to spell out Tsujimoto's name letter by letter in each of his phone calls to the twelve other teams. "It's not like it was Brown or Jones or something. It just slowed the draft down even more," Wieland told an interviewer in 2014.

ALL IN

When the draft was over, other members of the Sabres organization joined in the fun and kept the ruse going for weeks. They made Tsujimoto a team jersey, put his name on one of the stalls in the locker room, and included his name in the team's press materials. When reporters asked where Tsujimoto was and when he was coming to

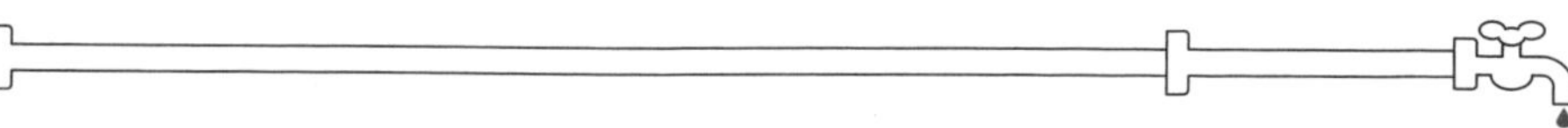

Buffalo, the press office made up stories about him training in the Himalayas.

The Sabres kept at it right up until players started reporting to training camp; then they admitted that Tsujimoto didn't exist. That didn't go over well with Clarence Campbell, but there wasn't a whole lot that he or any other league officials could do about it. The NHL struck Tsujimoto, and "draft pick #183," from the draft roster as an "invalid claim," and left it at that. A few years later, the World Hockey Association folded, and drafting by telephone became a thing of the past. In 1980, the NHL draft became a public event, and four years later it was televised for the first time.

TARO CARDS

The NHL may have crossed Tsujimoto off of their list, but the Sabres' faithful weren't about to let a little thing like nonexistence spoil the fun. Fans started showing up for games wearing homemade jerseys and signs, many of them with the number 74 for the year he was drafted. For years afterward, whenever the Sabres were down a lot of goals late in the game, the fans would chant, "We want Taro! We want Taro!" A fake biography was published, and so was a book about the hoax itself. In 2011, Tsujimoto received the ultimate honor: being made into a hockey trading card. (It featured a photo of an unidentified Asian man playing hockey, wearing a jersey similar to the Sabres'.)

Nearly 50 years after the 1974 NHL draft, Tsujimoto lives on: He's still listed in the Sabres' press materials as one of the team's 1974 picks, and he has Facebook and Twitter accounts with posts that purport to be written by him. Fans still wear his #74 jerseys to games and wave homemade Taro signs from the stands. Who knows? The player who never lived may never die either, at least not as long as the Buffalo Sabres are around to keep his memory alive. "He's one of my favorite people in the world," Paul Wieland says. "I'm telling you, Taro lives!"

* * *

COOKING WITH SHERRY

If you've ever cooked with "cooking sherry," you might know that it is regular sherry (fortified wine) with salt added. Why would anyone add salt to sherry? Cooking has nothing to do with it. The salt was added to get around Prohibition, which banned the production, importation, transportation, and sale of alcoholic beverages from 1920 to 1933. But the ban only applied to alcohol that was drinkable, and sherry producers realized that if they added enough salt to their product to make it undrinkable, they could continue to sell it. Prohibition ended in 1933...so why does cooking sherry still have salt in it? So that it can be sold in grocery stores that don't have liquor licenses.

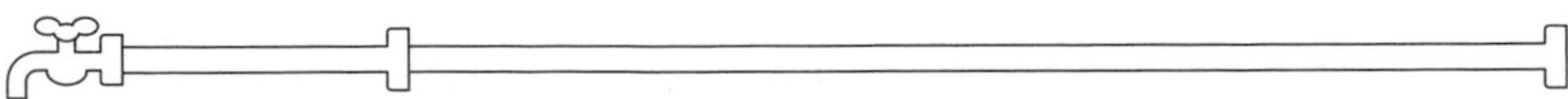

THE PRESIDENT'S GRANDCHILDREN

Some family trees, it turns out, have deeper roots than others. Much deeper. *Don't believe it? Have a look at this family tree, which traces its roots back to a U.S. president.*

POP QUIZ

If you had to guess the earliest U.S. president who still has living grandchildren, who would you pick? Franklin D. Roosevelt, the 32nd president, who held office from 1933 to 1945? Or maybe his predecessor, Herbert Hoover, the 31st president (1929–33)? Perhaps Hoover's predecessors, Calvin Coolidge, the 30th president (1923–29), or Warren G. Harding, the 29th (1921–23)?

These are all reasonable guesses...but if you picked any of them, you were way off. The correct answer is John Tyler, the *tenth* president of the United States, who was born in 1790 and held office from 1841 to 1845. As of February 2020, he had two grandchildren still living: Leon Gardiner Tyler Jr., born in 1924, and Harrison Ruffin Tyler, born in 1928.

HIS ACCIDENCY

Perhaps Tyler's biggest claim to fame is that he was the first vice president to succeed a president who died in office. He became president after William Henry Harrison died just 32 days into his first term in 1841. The United States Constitution was unclear as to whether the vice president inherited the *office* of the presidency or just the president's "powers and duties," without the title. Tyler set a decisive precedent by taking the oath of office as soon as he learned Harrison had died, then delivering an inaugural address, and finally, moving quickly into the White House.

Tyler also had the rare distinction of being expelled from his own political party, the Whigs, while president, following a dispute over banking policy. And he's the president who orchestrated the annexation of Texas, which had declared independence from Mexico in 1836. He signed the annexation bill into law three days before leaving office in 1845.

FAMILY MEN

For the purposes of this story, however, Tyler's most important claim to fame is that he was the first president to marry in office, following the death of his first wife, Letitia Christian Tyler, in 1842. Two years later, President Tyler, now 54, married

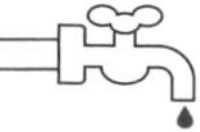

He fathered more children than any other president—15.

Julia Gardiner, who was 24. Tyler had already fathered eight children with his first wife, seven of whom lived to adulthood. After he remarried, he had seven more children with Gardiner. That's another of Tyler's claims to fame: He fathered more children than any other president—15.

LIKE FATHER, LIKE SON

One of President Tyler's children by Julia Gardiner was a son named Lyon Gardiner Tyler, who was born in 1853 when Tyler was 63. Like his father, Lyon Gardiner Tyler married twice and fathered children late in life. He had three children with his first wife, Anne Baker Tucker, who died in 1921. Two years later, the 70-year-old Tyler married 35-year-old Sue Ruffin and had three sons with her. The youngest son died in infancy, but Tyler's other two sons were still alive in 2020. Lyon Gardiner Tyler Jr. was born in 1924 when Tyler was 71, and Harrison Ruffin Tyler was born in 1928 when Tyler was 75.

Lyon Gardiner Tyler Jr., 96, is living in Tennessee and said to be in poor health; Harrison Tyler, 92, is doing better and still living at his grandfather's Sherwood Forest Plantation in Virginia, which has been in the family since Tyler bought it in 1842. The house is open to public tours. If you ever stop by for a visit, there's a good chance that members of the Tyler family, including Harrison, will be there to greet you. He doesn't get around as well as he used to, but he's hanging in there. As he told a CBS News reporter in 2017, "I'm still here."

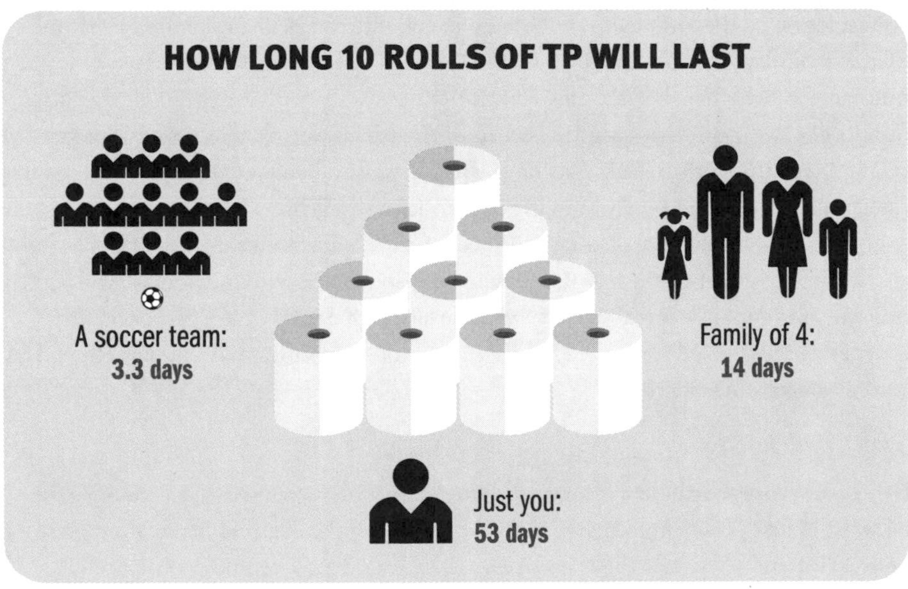

STRANGE DEATHS

Will the end of your life be interesting enough to warrant mention in a Bathroom Reader?

THE LAST LAUGH

In April 2019, a 60-year-old British comedian known as Ian Cognito (real name: Paul Barbieri) arrived at the Atic bar in Bicester to perform his stand-up routine. Cognito told club owner Andrew Bird that he wasn't feeling well that evening, but he'd do his best. Bird later told reporters that the set got off to a great start, as Cognito joked about being sick and even about having a stroke. A few minutes later, he sat down in a chair and stopped talking. Then he collapsed. "Everyone in the crowd, me included, thought he was joking," said Bird. Not only was Cognito not joking, he wasn't breathing. A nurse ran to the stage to try and revive him, but he'd died on the spot.

BURDEN OF PROOF

In 2017, Jordan Easton was at a friend's house in northeastern England, bragging about his "stab-proof" vest. It turns out the vest wasn't stab-proof, which he discovered while trying to prove it was, by stabbing himself in the chest with a kitchen knife. Easton, 22, was rushed to the hospital, but he didn't make it. (The coroner ruled it death by "misadventure.")

DON'T EAT THAT! (PT. 1)

A Chinese vlogger known as Sun came up with a bizarre way to gain followers on his various social media accounts: He made a spinning wheel (like on a game show) with categories that included eggs, vinegar, insects, lizards, beer, and liquor. He'd give the wheel a spin, and whatever it landed on, he would eat or drink. In 2019, during what turned out to be his final performance, Sun consumed a copious amount of alcohol, several mealworms, some poisonous centipedes, and a gecko. Shortly after eating the menagerie—all of which were alive at the time—Sun collapsed and landed off camera. The livestream continued; Sun was later found dead on the floor of his apartment.

SAY CHEESE

In May 2015, Anna Ursu, a "selfie-obsessed" teenager from Romania, attempted to snap a pic of herself on top of a parked train. While lying on her back, she held her phone above her and lifted one of her legs in the air...not realizing there were 27,000 volts of electricity hovering around the cable. The shock actually caused Ursu to burst into flames. She did not survive.

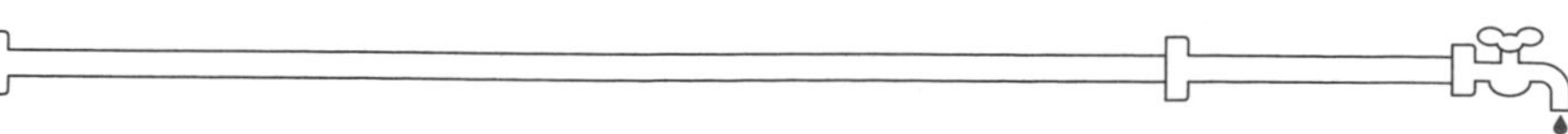

DON'T EAT THAT! (PT. 2)

Thirty-four-year-old David Dowell of Queensland, Australia, described in press reports as "happy-go-lucky," was at a Christmas party in 2018 when he was dared to eat a live Asian house gecko that someone had found outside. Most lizards will run away when you approach, but this one was very sluggish and easy to catch. Dowell took the dare and ate the reptile. The next day, he felt bad, and even worse the day after that. So he went to the hospital where, according to the news reports, "He began vomiting green bile, his urine turned black, and his stomach was so bloated he looked six months pregnant." Ten days after eating the gecko, Dowell died. Doctors first suspected that he'd contracted salmonella poisoning, but it's more likely he was done in by parasitic tapeworms called *Spirometra* that were already growing in the lizard when Dowell ate it, which would explain why the gecko was so sluggish.

SCAVENGER HUNT

In 2019, Brandon and Jennifer Husband were riding their motorcycle on a Kansas highway when a large vulture flew out of a ditch and struck Brandon in the head. He lost control of the bike and crashed into a barbed-wire fence. Neither of them were wearing helmets, and neither survived.

A BAD SIGN

In 2009, Mark and Diane Durre of Chambers, Nebraska, drove their Ford pickup truck to a Taco Bell on Interstate 80 in order to meet a couple to whom they were going to sell a puppy. They parked in the prearranged meeting spot under the 75-foot-tall Taco Bell sign, but before the meeting could take place, tragedy struck. Strong wind gusts—later estimated at around 40 mph—put so much strain on the sign that the pole broke about 15 feet above the ground. The large sign came crashing down and landed right on the Durres' truck. Amazingly, Mark's only injury was a broken finger, and the puppy was unharmed...but Diane wasn't as lucky. She took the brunt of the hit and was pronounced dead at the scene.

HEADING OUT

In 2008, Gerald Mellin decided to end his life in what police later described as a "manner most unusual." The wealthy Welsh businessman was mired in debt, and he blamed his troubles on his estranged ex-wife. Wanting to leave her with nothing, Mellin, 54, canceled his life insurance policy, and then tied one end of a rope around a tree and the other end around his neck. Then he got into his convertible Aston Martin and sped off. According to *Wales Online*, "Officers found his headless body on the leather driving seat of the car with his head on the back seat."

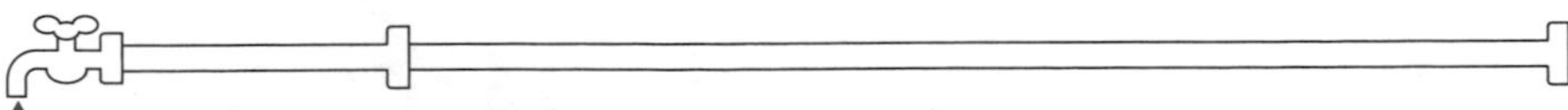

HUMAN SCIENCE

Here's a look at some of the more interesting and entertaining recent studies in science and medicine.

KNIFE TRICK: In his 1998 book *Shadows in the Sun*, anthropologist Wade Davis relates a tale told to him by an Inuit man named Olayuk Narqitarvik. Narqitarvik claimed that his grandfather, desperate and without any tools, once shaped his frozen poop into a crude knife and used it to butcher a dog. Davis was skeptical. He thought of the story as "a classic case of people having some fun with a visiting tourist/ anthropologist." But another anthropologist, Metin Eren, wanted to test the veracity of the claim the only way possible: by fashioning poop knives and using them to cut meat. All week he ate an Arctic diet: high in protein and fatty acids, with occasional produce and carbs. He collected his excrement for days, froze it, and recruited a team for the (fun) task of shaping it into knives. Some used knife molds, others molded it "by hand." (Narqitarvik claimed the knife was sharpened with "a spray of saliva," but Eren, mercifully, did not ask that of his team.) Then the scientists filed the knives to make them sharp and tested them on a pig carcass. Alas, the knives failed to slice the meat and just left nasty streaks across it. For good measure, the team also tried the experiment using the poop of someone who ate a Western diet, but again they crapped out. Eren's conclusion: "This idea that a person made a knife out of their own frozen feces—experimentally, it is not supported."

LET'S DANCE: At the Centre for Interdisciplinary Music Research in Finland, people dance for science. How they dance, researchers theorized, could reveal their current mood and personality traits, such as how extroverted, neurotic, or empathetic they are. The study: they told 73 participants to dance however they wanted to while listening to eight genres—pop, blues, jazz, country, dance/electronica, metal, rap, and reggae. As the dancers rocked out to Duran Duran's pop song "Want You More!" and the rap song "It's Like That" by Run-DMC and Jason Nevins, motion-capture technology recorded their moves. Then a computer program assessed the movements of their head, shoulders, sternum, wrists, hips, knees, and other body parts. It was supposed to identify what genre of music each person had boogied to based on their moves. But the computer guessed with less than 25 percent accuracy.

However, the computer did identify something the scientists didn't expect: 94 percent of the time, it correctly determined which person was dancing, no matter what the genre. It turns out that whether you're swinging to jazz or boot-scootin' to country, your moves are similar—and identifiable. The study, which is aptly titled "Dance to Your Own Drum," was conducted by Dr. Emily Carlson. She wants to investigate further, wondering "whether our movement signatures stay the same across our life span, whether we can detect differences between cultures based on these movement signatures, and how well humans are able to recognize individuals from their dance movements."

PRACTICE MAKES PERFECT: 3-D printers are revolutionizing the medical field with intricate models that can be made quickly, cheaply, and accurately. This is one of the technological advancements that made it possible for Cleveland Clinic surgeons to perform the country's first total face transplant in 2017. Patient Katie Stubblefield, 21, survived a self-inflicted gunshot wound to her face from a suicide attempt when she was a teenager, and was left terribly disfigured. She had no nose and was unable to see, speak, or eat. After three years of planning and preparation, Stubblefield's doctors were ready when a suitable female donor died in 2017. There was no room for error in one of the most complicated surgeries ever attempted: Working against the clock, experts printed detailed 3-D models of both the patient's and donor's skulls, and used the models and virtual-reality technology to rehearse the surgeries until they felt they were ready to proceed with the real thing. Then, in a 31-hour procedure, a team of 11 surgeons removed both faces and attached the donor's face to Stubblefield's head, reconnecting its muscles, nerves, and capillaries. The surgery was a success. Stubblefield regained the ability to eat, talk, and breathe through her nose, and her vision is improving. It's thanks in large part to printing technology that such a difficult surgery could even be attempted in the first place.

HAVE A HEART: In the future it may be possible to use 3-D printers to create actual functioning organs. The research is already underway: In 2019, scientists at Tel Aviv University used a 3-D printer to create a miniature artificial heart using "ink" made of collagen and other biological molecules extracted from the fat cells of human donors. The heart is tiny—about the size of a rabbit's, but it has the anatomical structure of an actual heart. Now the scientists are trying to "teach" it how to pump. "The cells...can currently contract, but we need them to work together," lead scientist Professor Tal Dvir told the Israeli newspaper *Haaretz*. "Our hope is that we will succeed and prove our method's efficacy and usefulness." If the team can get the heart to pump, the next step is to test similar hearts in animals and eventually, if all goes well, develop artificial hearts for human patients using their own cells, to reduce the risk of organ rejection. "This is the first time anyone anywhere has successfully engineered and printed an entire heart complete with cells, blood vessels, ventricles and chambers," Dvir says.

* * *

"If I cannot do great things, I can do small things in a great way."

—Martin Luther King Jr.

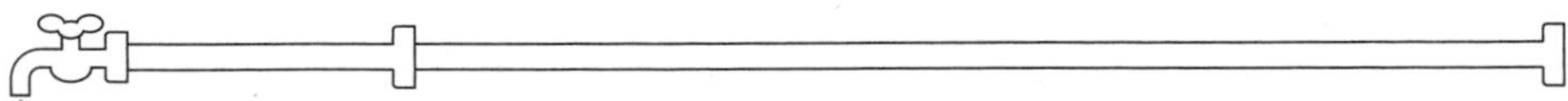

Salisbury steak was invented by Dr. James Salisbury in the 1890s to treat anemia and gout.

REACH FOR THE SKY

Every time somebody builds a really tall structure, someone else says, "We can top that." Here's a look at the tallest buildings in history...and their successors.

2560 BC The Great Pyramid of Giza is completed. Of all the pyramids for which ancient Egypt is known, none are taller than this. The first *really* giant structure on the planet, the limestone-and-granite pyramid stands 280 cubits high—in modern measurements, 481 feet tall. It will be the world's tallest structure for the next 3,800 years.

AD 1311 After 126 years of construction, the Lincoln Cathedral in Lincolnshire, England, is completed and, at 524 feet, claims the title of world's tallest building. With its extensive stone carvings, vaulted arches, flying buttresses, and pointed spires, it is one of the finest examples of Gothic architecture in Europe.

1549 The spire of the Lincoln Cathedral collapses, instantly turning that structure into the world's *second*-tallest building. The 495-foot-tall Saint Mary's Church, built in the late 1200s in Stralsund, Germany, becomes the de facto titleholder. Like Lincoln Cathedral, the architectural style is Gothic, but unlike Lincoln Cathedral, which is made of stone, Saint Mary's is made of brick.

1569 The main tower of St. Pierre's Cathedral, a monumental stone Gothic church in Beauvais, France, reaches a mighty 502 feet tall, just seven feet more than Saint Mary's Church. The building is never fully completed: construction, which started in 1225, is interrupted by fires, structural failings, sieges, and conflicts such as the Hundred Years' War. The spire and bell tower collapse in 1573, restoring the "world's tallest" honors to Saint Mary's Church.

1647 A lightning storm sets part of Saint Mary's Gothic steeple afire, burning the tower to the ground. (It was later replaced with a Baroque dome, but 100 feet shorter.) The tallest building is now the 466-foot-tall Strasbourg Cathedral, completed in 1439, on the French-German border. It's visible from the Vosges Mountains, more than 60 miles away, which is also the source of the sandstone used in the building of the cathedral, and is why it has a slightly pink color.

1874 The Church of St. Nicholas in Hamburg was built as a simple wooden chapel in 1195, replaced with a brick building in the 1300s, and destroyed by fire in 1842. The church is rebuilt in the style of a Gothic cathedral and reopens in 1874. At 482 feet tall, it becomes the tallest building in the world.

1876 Massive construction projects take hold in Europe and the United States, and there's something of a race to build each one a little bigger than the previous "world's tallest structure." The Rouen Cathedral in Normandy, France, is completed in this year, and stands 495 feet tall. It's built on the site of a church that existed in the late 300s, was destroyed during a Viking raid in the 800s, and was then slowly rebuilt over the centuries.

1880 Next comes the Cologne Cathedral, at 516 feet. It's the largest Gothic-style church in Europe, and boasts the largest facade of any church on the planet. It will remain the largest Gothic church and, in fact, the largest religious building in the world.

1884 The Washington Monument in Washington, D.C., juts into the sky 555 feet high. The design—an obelisk—evokes ancient Egyptian architecture, and is intended to signify that America is as important and powerful as that iconic civilization once was.

1889 Built for the World's Fair in Paris, the Eiffel Tower becomes one of the most famous buildings on the planet and a universally recognized symbol of France. It also enjoys a few decades as the tallest structure on Earth, at 984 feet. (It was scheduled for demolition after the fair, but the French government decided to use it as a radio tower during World War I.)

1930 The Chrysler Building opens in New York City. Not only is the sleek Art Deco skyscraper the first man-made structure to top 1,000 feet (it measures 1,046 feet, including the spire), but it's also the world's tallest building...for less than a year.

1931 Eleven months later, another New York skyscraper completes construction, and steals the right to be called the world's tallest building. That structure is the Empire State Building, measuring 1,250 feet. The 2,760,000-square-foot office building is built on the site of New York's original Waldorf-Astoria Hotel, and is designed to include a special feature at its very top—a docking station for dirigibles. It was never used.

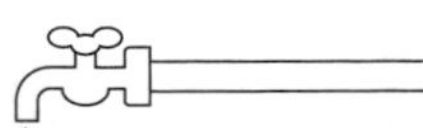

Air New Zealand cuts down on waste by serving coffee in edible biscotti "cups."

1972 Another Manhattan skyscraper overtakes the Empire State Building: the World Trade Center's North Tower, at 1,368 feet. Its sibling building, the South Tower, stands 6 feet shorter upon completion. The Twin Towers rank as the tallest buildings in skyscraper-loaded Manhattan until their destruction on September 11, 2001.

1973 The 1,450-foot, 110-floor Sears Tower goes up in Chicago. The developer—Sears, Roebuck & Co.—wanted to build it taller, but the Federal Aviation Administration limited the height to protect air traffic. It consists of nine individual "tubes," each essentially a separate building, bundled together. This architectural innovation proves to be a more efficient and less costly way to build, and will be the way most future supertall buildings are constructed.

IN THE KNOW

Not on this list: the Tokyo Tower of Babel. Proposed in 1992, it was envisioned by architects as a 33,000-foot structure that could house tens of millions of people, which would easily make it the tallest building in history. The idea was scrapped after planners realized it would cost $19 trillion and take 150 years to complete.

1998 The 25-year reign of the Sears Tower as the tallest building—and the reign of Europe and the Americas as home of the tallest structures—ends with the opening of the 1,483-foot-tall Petronas Towers in Kuala Lumpur, Malaysia, named for the government-owned oil company that's based there.

2004 Taipei 101 (the Taipei World Financial Center) in Taipei, Taiwan, is emblematic of the 21st-century Far East construction boom. At 1,671 feet, it is the tallest building ever. Not only a record-setter for height, it also set a new speed record for elevators. Its main car, which travels from the 5th floor to the 89th floor, makes the 2,000-foot trip in just 37 seconds.

2009 The Burj Khalifa, a sleek, spire-topped skyscraper in the wealthy city of Dubai, United Arab Emirates, becomes the first building over 2,000 feet tall. Actually, it's 2,722 feet tall—more than two Chrysler Buildings stacked on top of each other. It was designed by Skidmore, Owings & Merrill, the same architectural firm responsible for the Sears Tower in Chicago, and employed the same "bundled tube" construction technique.

* * *

"The end of the human race will be that it will eventually die of civilization."

—Ralph Waldo Emerson

One more thing to like about seals: they have retractable nipples.

WORD ORIGINS

Ever wonder where certain words came from? Here are the interesting stories behind some of them.

SYPHILIS

Meaning: A degenerative venereal disease

Origin: "The term 'syphilis' was introduced by Girolamo Fracastoro, a poet and medical personality in Verona. His work *Syphilis sive Morbus Gallicus* (1530) encompasses three books and presents a character named Syphilus, who was a shepherd leading the flocks of King Alcihtous, a character from Greek mythology. In Fracastoro's tale, Syphilus, mad at Apollo for consuming the springs that fed the shepherd's flocks, vowed not to worship Apollo but his king. Apollo gets offended and curses people with a hideous disease named syphilis, after the shepherd's name." (From *Journal of Medicine and Life*)

CLUE

Meaning: A leading hint

Origin: "This word originates from Greek mythology. Theseus, the Greek hero, used a ball of thread to find his way out of the labyrinth after he killed the Minotaur of Crete. And after the story was told in medieval England—where the word for a ball of thread was 'clew'—a guide to the solution of any problem became known as a *clew* or *clue.*" (From *Word Origins,* by Dhirendra Verma)

LICORICE

Meaning: A sweet, spicy candy

Origin: "The most common meaning of licorice is the sweet black chewy stuff used in various forms of confectionery. However, it also refers to a plant common to Europe and Asia, the root of which is the source of the distinctive flavoring, and it is in this that the origins of the word lie. In the Anglo-French used by the descendants of the Norman conquerors of England, the root was called *lycorys.* This was derived from the late Latin *liquiritia,* which came from Greek *glukhurrhiza,* from *gklukus,* meaning 'sweet' and *rhiza,* meaning 'root.' " (From *Dictionary of Word and Phrase Origins,* by Martin Manser)

PAMPHLET

Meaning: A folded-over piece of paper or small booklet bearing information

Origin: "These little flyers have one love poem to thank for their name—'Pamphilus de amore,' or 'a poem about love.' While written in Latin, this poem is believed to be of

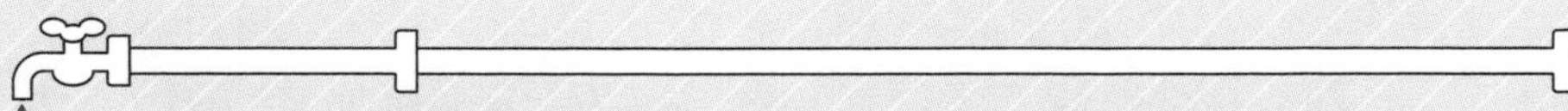

French origin, and the poet behind it seems to be something of a mystery. Nevertheless, the poem was insanely popular in the Middle Ages. It was printed out on little bits of paper and passed around, so everyone could read it. Imagine a very old, nowhere near-as-funny meme. This poem's name was shortened to just 'Pamphilus' and eventually became the name we all call these little informational pieces of paper: pamphlets." (From *The Origin of Names, Words and Everything in Between,* by Patrick Foote)

MUSCLE

Meaning: The body tissue that makes movement possible
Origin: "It turns out that *muscle* comes from the French word *musculus,* which in turn comes from the Latin *musculus,* meaning 'mouse.' 'Mouse'? Yes, 'mouse.' Lift up your sleeve and expose your bicep. Now flex your muscle. Watch your bicep closely. It kind of looks like something is moving around, doesn't it? It almost looks like a little mouse running around there under your skin." (From *Hot for Words,* by Marina Orlova)

CLOWN

Meaning: A performer specializing in broad physical comedy
Origin: "Associated today with circuses and children's nightmares, 'clowns' once referred to people who lived out in the country. For example, if you've read Shakespeare, you'll find his works are populated with 'clowns.' When you first encountered the Bard in high school, you might have pictured...well, clowns, in makeup, with bulbous oversized shoes. After all, Shakespeare's 'clowns' did offer what passed in those days for comic relief. In fact, the 'joke' was that 'clowns' were people from the sticks, and therefore backward, compared to urbane city dwellers like Shakespeare." (From *The Unexpected Evolution of Language,* by Justin Cord Hayes)

FEISTY

Meaning: Lively and bold
Origin: "The word *feisty* began its career as the West Germanic term *first,* meaning 'to break wind.' It entered English in the mid-15th century as the verb and a noun that meant 'breaking wind' and stayed that way for a while. In the 16th century, people in England started describing certain dogs as *fisting hounds.* These were invariably small lapdogs, and you can imagine that when one broke wind, it wouldn't be pleasant. Eventually *fist* became associated with these small dogs themselves, and when the word crossed the Atlantic, the pronunciation changed so that it rhymed with *heist.* The meaning also broadened to refer to any dog that barked constantly, and eventually the spelling settled on *feist.* By the end of the 19th century, folks were describing any such people as *feisty.*" (From *The Complete Idiot's Guide to Weird Word Origins,* by Paul McFedries)

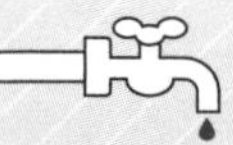

Harrison Ford has survived two plane crashes and one near-miss.

OM NOM NOM

As George Bernard Shaw observed, "There is no love sincerer than the love of food."

"A balanced diet is a cookie in each hand."
—Barbara Johnson

"Whoever thought a tiny candy bar should be called fun size was a moron."
—Glenn Beck

"My personal motto is 'Eat clean to stay fit, have a burger to stay sane.'"
—Gigi Hadid

"Now, have I ever been tempted to break into a Krispy Kreme donut store in the middle of the night? Oh, yeah."
—Mike Huckabee

"Chocolate covered peanuts, chocolate covered raisins, chocolate covered pretzels...Chocolate. So afraid to be alone."
—Dana Gould

"I love French stuff. Mmmm, French fries."
—Denis Leary

"Life is a combination of magic and pasta."
—Federico Fellini

"The world is split into two halves: the bacon, and the bacon eaters."
—Nick Offerman

"Life is too short to miss out on the beautiful things, like a double cheeseburger."
—Channing Tatum

"I must be part rabbit; I never get bored with raw carrots."
—Marilyn Monroe

"Never underestimate how much assistance, how much satisfaction, how much comfort, how much soul and transcendence there might be in a well-made taco and a cold bottle of beer."
—Tom Robbins

"A slice of pie without cheese is like a kiss without a squeeze."
—Stephen King

"Life is mostly pain and struggle; the rest is love and deep dish pizza."
—Benedict Smith

"We all like chicken."
—Malcolm X

JUST PLANE WEIRD

Are you reading this on a plane? Do yourself a favor and turn to another page before reading any further. Save this article for when you're back on solid ground.

PICTURE THIS

In March 2018, the British carrier easyJet suspended two pilots for goofing off in the cockpit and making Snapchat videos on their cell phones when they should have been focused on their job: flying their Airbus A320 from Paris to Madrid. In one video, the copilot, not named in news reports, "dances" in his seat with a cartoon owl generated by the messaging app; in another, Captain Michel Castellucci mugs for the camera with a cartoon bear's ears, nose, and mouth superimposed over his face. In none of the images does either pilot appear to be paying much attention to the aircraft, or to the flight controls. The incident came to light after Castellucci posted the images on his Facebook and Instagram accounts. He deleted both accounts as soon as he realized he was in trouble...but not soon enough to save his job. He was fired by the airline, and his copilot resigned. "Whilst at no point was the safety of the passengers compromised," easyJet said in a statement, "this falls well short of the high standards easyJet expects of its pilots."

BOY TROUBLE

Two pilots with the Algerian carrier Air Algerie hit some career turbulence in 2018, after they allowed a 10-year-old orphan boy to take control of their airplane during the filming of a news story about a children's charity. On the flight from Algiers to Setif, in eastern Algeria, the boy is shown sitting in the captain's seat as he adjusts the plane's power settings and the altimeter while the captain explains to viewers that the boy really is adjusting the controls on the aircraft, not just pretending. That, not surprisingly, is against Algerian law. The documentary aired on TV on July 26; on July 29, the pilots were suspended. The captain was later arrested for "permitting a child into the cockpit and permitting the child to control the aircraft in flight."

The boy is shown sitting in the captain's seat as he adjusts the plane's power settings.

AIR APPARENT

In July 2018, an Air China flight from Hong Kong to Dailan, in northeast China, lost cabin pressure and had to make an emergency descent, dropping 25,000 feet in ten minutes, while terrified passengers breathed from the emergency oxygen masks that dropped from the ceiling. An investigation found that the incident was triggered when the copilot wanted to smoke an e-cigarette in the cockpit. To prevent his smoke from wafting back to the passenger compartment, he tried to switch off the air recycling fans...but accidently flipped the wrong switch and turned off the air conditioner instead, "resulting in insufficient oxygen in the cabin and an altitude warning," said a spokesperson for China's Civil Aviation Administration. Air China fired both the captain and copilot and recommended that their pilot's licenses be revoked. "I'm not physically hurt, but the psychological impact lingers," one passenger told CNN following the incident. "When I close my eyes, I see the oxygen masks dangling in front of me."

TAKING A STAND

Two pilots with India's largest airline, IndiGo, were grounded for two months in 2019 after they flew from Hyderabad to Vijaywada knowing that a piece of ground equipment was still attached to the tail of their ATR 27 aircraft. The equipment, called a tail stand or tail prop, is attached during loading of passengers and cargo to prevent the plane from tipping backward and the tail striking the ground. It's supposed to be removed before takeoff (and the pilots are supposed to verify that it has been removed), but this time it wasn't, and they didn't. "The flight crew was informed immediately after takeoff by the Air Traffic Controller regarding departure of the aircraft with the tail prop attached. However, the crew continued to its destination instead of returning to Hyderabad. This could have caused structural damage to the aircraft during flight," India's Directorate General of Civil Aviation concluded in a report. "Both pilots...admitted that landing back in Hyderabad would have been a better decision."

BIRD BRAIN

In February 2019, British Airways suspended one of its training pilots, Russell Williams, not because of anything he did while flying an aircraft or training other pilots, but because of "offensive behavior" on the job. Specifically, in 2015 he e-mailed a pornographic image of a man and a chicken, with the caption "It's Friday. Shag some birds this weekend" to five other British Airways pilots. ("Bird" is British slang for a woman, and "shag" means, well, figure it out for yourself.) "I accept that these e-mails, while sent some time ago, were ill-judged and unprofessional," Williams said in a statement following his suspension.

* * *

"Advice is what we ask for when we already know the answer but wish we didn't."

—Erica Jong

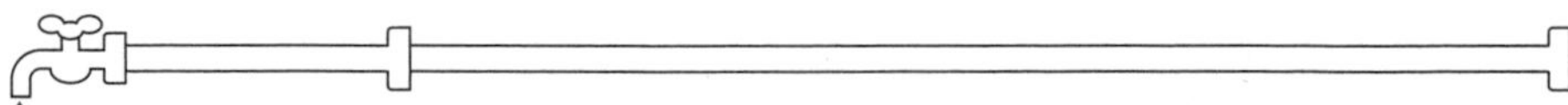

By any other name: In Malaysia, tater tots are known as "popcorn hash."

THE DIFFERENCE BETWEEN...

And now Uncle John helps you navigate life's subtle nuances. For example, do you know the difference between...

APPLE JUICE AND APPLE CIDER? Cider is what you get when you remove all the liquid from pressed apples. Sometimes it's given a quick filtering before bottling to remove some pulp, naturally occurring yeasts, and other solid materials. But most of that stuff is usually left in there. Apple juice is cider that's been processed to remove the sediment and then pasteurized for a longer shelf life.

AN OCEAN AND A SEA? Geographically speaking, both are large bodies of saltwater. Seas are smaller than oceans; they are partially landlocked, but they feed into an ocean. The Bering Sea is part of the Pacific Ocean, for example, and the Mediterranean Sea in Europe makes its way to the Atlantic Ocean via the Strait of Gibraltar.

CROWS AND RAVENS? Both are *corvids*—members of the Corvidae family—and both are large, black birds with similarly shaped heads and beaks. But ravens are much larger and they hang out in pairs; crows go around in groups. Another difference: crows have fan-shaped tails, while ravens' tails are triangular. They have different calls, too. A crow says "caw," whereas a raven makes more of a low croak.

ALLIGATORS AND CROCODILES? To tell them apart, look at the snout (but not too closely). An alligator's snout is wide and U-shaped. A crocodile's snout is narrow, pointed, and V-shaped. If you see either of these in the wild, it's more likely to be a crocodile; there are 13 species of crocs living on several continents. There are, however, only two species of alligators—the endangered Chinese alligator and the American alligator, which lives in the southeastern United States.

GRAY AND GREY? Remember those gourmet mustard commercials where one Rolls-Royce pulls up next to another Rolls-Royce, a window rolls down, and a pompous-sounding British man asks, "Pardon me, but do you have any Grey Poupon?" If he were American, he would have asked for "Gray Poupon," and that's the difference: The original spelling of "grey" comes from the UK; it was later Americanized to "gray."

CONCRETE AND CEMENT? Cement is just another name for powdered limestone (with a little bit of clay). And it's actually an ingredient in concrete. Mix cement with water, sand, and gravel, and you've got the building material known as concrete.

ALE AND LAGER? Generally speaking, ales are thick, heavily flavored beers, as opposed to lagers—crisp, thin, and light. (Craft beers such as porters, stouts, and IPAs are ales, and Budweiser and Corona are lagers.) The difference between the two depends on the type of yeast used in the brewing process. Ales use yeast that ferments on the top of the batch, brewed in warm water. Lager is made with cold-fermented, bottom-feeding yeast, which also means it takes longer to brew.

JAIL AND PRISON? Usually under the jurisdiction of a city or county, a jail is a temporary detention facility where suspects are held overnight after being arrested. But they can be held there indefinitely if they are unable to post bail, or if they are deemed dangerous or a flight risk. Then they will be kept in jail until their trial date. If convicted and sentenced to prison, the felon is taken to prison—a larger, more permanent facility located far from major population centers.

A GEEK AND A NERD? While both terms are used to describe socially maladjusted or awkward individuals, they aren't the same thing. Geeks are smart, studious, and obsessive about their intellectual pursuits and passions. Nerds, on the other hand, are obsessed with stuff they like, sometimes to the detriment of their social awareness. A tech billionaire is more likely to be a geek, while someone with a collection of *Star Wars* toys (still in the original packaging) is a nerd.

SNOW AND SLEET? Both begin as falling precipitation, and both require temperatures that are cold enough to freeze water. Snow forms in water inside clouds that are already below freezing. As the snow falls, it will remain snow if the air stays at or just below freezing. But if the air between the clouds and the ground warms up, the snow will melt into rain. Then, if the rain then travels through pockets of cold air and refreezes, it turns into little icy pellets called sleet.

A BANK AND A CREDIT UNION? Banks are for-profit institutions, whereas credit unions are not-for-profit. That's why you are a "customer" of a bank but an "owner" or "member" of a credit union. Members get to vote for a credit union's board of directors, and any profits go into keeping interest rates low and serving the community. Banks' profits go directly to the shareholders.

A DIVORCE AND AN ANNULMENT? You can't get divorced if you were never really married in the first place. That's where an annulment comes in. A divorce legally ends a marriage that was entered into willingly and considered valid under the law. But sometimes marriages are ruled invalid for reasons such as bigamy, coercion, or if one or both parties were intoxicated. In that case, a court would issue an annulment. Like a divorce, an annulment dissolves the union, but from a legal standpoint, it acts as if the ill-fated marriage never happened at all.

Kanye North and South are parliamentary districts in Botswana (but Kanye West isn't).

THE MAN WITH THE GOLDEN ARM

Donating blood can save lives, but few of us who do so have the opportunity to save this many lives.

TOUCH AND GO

In 1951, a critically ill Australian boy named James Harrison had to undergo surgery to remove one of his lungs. The difficult procedure lasted several hours, and the 14-year-old nearly died. He required 13 units—nearly 3.5 gallons—of blood transfusions before doctors could get his bleeding under control. Then he spent three months recovering in the hospital before he was well enough to go home.

While he was in the hospital, James's father explained to him that his life had been saved in part by 13 people he would never know—the people who had donated the blood that kept him alive. Inspired by their example, James decided that, when he was old enough, he would become a blood donor. He made his first donation soon after turning 18 in late 1954.

SOMEONE SPECIAL

For more than a decade, James was just another ordinary blood donor. Then in the late 1960s, he was contacted by scientists who were working on a treatment for a blood condition called Rh disease, or hemolytic disease of the fetus and newborn (HDFN), which killed thousands of babies in Australia each year. The disease occurs when a mother's blood lacks a protein called Rh, making her blood "Rh negative," and her unborn child's blood does have the protein, because it has inherited the "Rh positive" gene from the father. If the mother's body sees the baby's Rh positive blood as a foreign body, it will produce antibodies in an attempt to destroy the baby's blood supply. This can harm the baby or, in severe cases, it can cause death. Seventeen percent of all babies born in Australia were Rh positive, born to mothers who were Rh negative.

The scientists had discovered that injecting the mother with a medication containing an antibody found in human blood could prevent her body from attacking her unborn child's blood supply. Only problem: the antibody is very rare. Fewer than 200 Australians were believed to produce the antibody at all, and only a handful of these produced it in large quantities. The researchers scoured blood bank records looking for donors capable of producing the elusive antibody, and one stood out as being able to produce it in large quantities: James Harrison. (Ironically, scientists believe he may have developed his prodigious ability to produce the antibody after he was accidentally given the wrong kind of blood during one of the transfusions he received when he was 14.)

FREQUENT FLYER

When he donated whole blood, Harrison was limited to one donation every three months, which was about how long it took for his body to replace the donated blood. But when he was asked to become the first donor in the program to create a treatment for HDFN, he switched from donating blood to donating just the blood plasma, the yellowish liquid component of blood that carries the blood cells. Plasma can be donated every two to three weeks, so he began doing just that. The first Rh negative mother to receive what would become known as "anti-D" immunoglobulin, created from the rare antibodies taken from Harrison's blood plasma, was treated at Sydney's Royal Prince Alfred Hospital in 1967.

GOLD STANDARD

Harrison continued donating blood plasma every couple of weeks for another 51 years. He'd still be donating blood today, were it not for the fact that when he reached the age of 81, the Australian Red Cross decided that the risks to his own health from the regular plasma donations had become too great and they stopped accepting his plasma. "The Man with the Golden Arm," as he was dubbed by the press, made his 1,173rd—and final—donation on May 11, 2018. (All but 10 of the 1,173 donations were taken from Harrison's right arm; he says it hurts more when they draw blood from his left arm.) In all that time—from 1967 to 2018—17 percent of all expectant Australian mothers received injections of anti-D immunoglobulin, with every single dose containing antibodies that were taken from Harrison's blood. His antibodies are credited with saving the lives of more than two million babies—including Harrison's own grandson—who would have died had their mothers not been treated with the injections.

His antibodies are credited with saving the lives of more than two million babies—including Harrison's own grandson.

Harrison must have eaten plenty of Red Cross cookies in all those years of donating plasma, but one thing he says he's never done, not even once, while donating blood or plasma, is look at the needle as it's being inserted into his arm. Harrison hates needles. "I look at the nurses, the ceiling, the spots on the wall, anything but the needle," he told the *Sydney Morning Herald* in 2018. "It's too macabre, I think, watching yourself get stuck with the needle."

Nyet! 200,000 people get trapped in elevators in Russia each year.

GROANERS

For a terrible joke to be funny, it needs to hurt a bit as well. Like these.

Q: What did the drummer name his twin daughters?
A: Anna 1, Anna 2.

A guy walks into a pet shop and says, "I'd like to buy a fly." The clerk replies, "We don't sell flies here." The guy says, "There's one in the window."

Brutus: "Hey, Julius, how many salads did you eat?"
Caesar: "Et two, Brute."

Q: How was the Roman Empire divided up?
A: With a pair of Caesars.

A horse walks into a bar and the bartender says, "Why the long face?" The horse says, "Because I'm an alcoholic and it's destroying my life."

A plateau is the highest form of flattery.

Q: Who invented fractions?
A: Henry the 1/8th.

If I had a quarter for every time I failed a math test, I'd have $4.15 by now.

Q: Why do birds fly south for the winter?
A: It's much easier than walking.

Two birds are on a perch, and one says, "Do you smell fish?"

Q: How do taco trucks keep warm in winter?
A: They use chicken fajitas.

Q: How can you tell a male chromosome from a female chromosome?
A: Pull down its genes.

I got fired from my stagehand job, but I left without making a scene.

We had a few more jokes about being unemployed, but none of them work.

Q: What's blue and not very heavy?
A: Light blue.

I was just given a raise at the crematorium! Now I'm the top urner.

Dogs can't operate MRI machines, but cats can.

I love my GPS. I'd be lost without it.

Jokes about Peter Pan never get old.

Q: What do you call a hen looking at a veggie garden?
A: Chicken Caesar salad.

I tried to stop the rumor about the melted butter, but it was spreading too fast.

Q: What do you call a bear with no teeth?
A: A gummy bear.

I was caught cheating at a tongue-twister tournament. The judge is sure to give me a really tough sentence.

Q: What did the one nut say when it was chasing the other nut?
A: I'm a cashew.

You know the worst part about getting fired from my job as a guillotine operator? No severance package.

Old MacDonald had some really bad Scrabble tiles: e-i-e-i-o.

Sometimes I fill up a bun with ham and pineapple. That's Hawaii roll.

Sometimes I get down on my knees, slowly lean forward as I tuck in my head, and then, using my forearms for leverage, propel myself over and onto my knees again. That's how I roll.

THESE KIDS TODAY

According to a 2017 column in the Daily Mail*, "Millennials are lazy and think basic tasks are beneath them." To keep things in perspective, here are some other grumpy geezers from ages past complaining about the same thing.*

"When I was young, we were taught to be discreet and respectful of elders, but the present youth are exceedingly wise and impatient of restraint."

—Hesiod, 8th century BC

"We defy anyone who goes about with his eyes open to deny that there is, as never before, an attitude on the part of young folk which is best described as grossly thoughtless, rude, and utterly selfish."

—*Hull Daily Mail*, 1925

"Never has youth been exposed to such dangers of both perversion and arrest as in our own land and day."

—*The Psychology of Adolescence*, 1904

"We have fallen upon evil times and the world has waxed very old and wicked. Politics are very corrupt. Children are no longer respectful to their parents."

—King Naram-Sin, 3800 BC

"What really distinguishes this generation from those before it is that it's the first generation in American history to live so well and complain so bitterly about it."

—*Washington Post*, 1993

"The free access which many young people have to romances, novels, and plays has poisoned the mind and corrupted the morals of many a promising youth; and prevented others from improving their minds in useful knowledge."

—Reverend Enos Hitchcock, 1790

"Probably there is no period in history in which young people have given such emphatic utterance to a tendency to reject that which is old and to wish for that which is new."

—*Portsmouth Evening News*, 1936

"The beardless youth...does not foresee what is useful, squandering his money."

—Horace, 1st century BC

"Modern fashions seem to keep on growing more and more debased."

—Yoshida Kenkō, circa 1330

"Whither are the manly vigor and athletic appearance of our forefathers flown? Can these be their legitimate heirs? Surely, no; a race of self-admiring, emaciated fribbles can never have descended in a direct line from the heroes of Potiers and Agincourt."

—*Town and Country* magazine, 1771

The Adak National Forest, on the Aleutian island of Adak, contains just 33 trees.

WHEN WORLDS COLLIDE

Humans and animals occupying the same space at the same time...with memorable results.

YOU HAVE OCTOPUS ON YOUR FACE

Did you know that octopuses are venomous? Neither did Jamie Bisceglia. Nor did she know that octopuses have sharp beaks that they use to deliver that venom. In August 2019, the Fox Island, Washington, woman was on a boat during a fishing derby when a friend on a neighboring boat suggested she put an octopus (caught by another angler) on her face so that he could take a picture for a photo contest. Bisceglia agreed. Bad move. At first the octopus felt "squishy" and "fun" on her face. But then came the beak and the venom and the suckers on the tentacles that wouldn't let go. Knowing she couldn't just yank the barbed beak away, Bisceglia waited for several agonizing minutes until the octopus loosened its grip enough for her to fling it onto the deck. Her face bled for a half hour, and as the days went by, her symptoms got worse: "My eyes were swollen, I couldn't see very well," she explained. "Underneath my chin was a large pus pocket, and then the left side of my face was completely paralyzed." Next thing she knew, Bisceglia was in the hospital receiving a heavy dose of antibiotics. Doctors told her it could take months to fully recover, and she'll have a scar for life. No word on whether her friend won the photo contest, but Bisceglia said the octopus, which she took home and cooked, was delicious.

A SURFER WALKS INTO A BAR

In July 2019, a professional surfer named Frank O'Rourke was riding the waves in Jacksonville Beach, Florida, when a shark took a bite out of his arm and knocked him off his board. Lifeguards administered first aid, and then told the wounded surfer to go to the hospital to get his arm stitched up. But O'Rourke had other ideas. "He immediately went to the bar," his friend RJ Berger told local news station News4JAX, "because he was like, 'Hey, I got bit by a shark!' And people were like, 'Hey, I'll buy you drinks!'"

HITCHCOCKIAN

A pair of herring gulls built a nest on the roof of Roy and Brenda Pickard's home on the English coast in May 2019. A few weeks later, two of the chicks fell out and landed in the canopy over the elderly couple's front door. The gulls left the chicks there, and then refused to allow Roy or Brenda to get anywhere near them. Roy

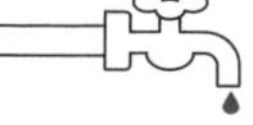

discovered that the hard way when one of the angry birds attacked him and punctured his skull, requiring a trip to the hospital. "If that bird had hit me in the face instead of the back of the head," he said, "I dread to think how seriously injured I would have been." They tried calling several animal organizations to remove the birds, only to be told it's against the law to disturb a protected species during nesting season. Result: neither of the Pickards could go in or out their front door for six days.

IN THE KNOW

Recent studies have concluded that increased human activity is turning some diurnal (daytime active) animals into night owls. One of the most affected went from spending 19 percent of its time awake at night to 95 percent. Native to Indonesia, this now-nocturnal species is *Helarctos malayanus*, commonly known as the sun bear.

KARMA?

A squirrel met an untimely end in 2016 when it darted across a path and jammed itself into the spokes of a bicycle being ridden by Howard Brookins Jr., alderman for Chicago's 21st Ward. Brookins went flying over the handlebars and landed on his head, fracturing his skull and losing a few teeth. The politician later told the *Chicago Tribune* that this was more than a freak accident: "I can think of no other reason for this squirrel's actions than that it was like a suicide bomber, getting revenge." Revenge for what? The alderman had recently been complaining about "aggressive squirrels" at city council meetings: "We are spending too much money on replacing garbage carts because the squirrels continue to eat through them!" Does that mean the animal was actually trying to send Brookins a message? No, of course not; that would be crazy. And yet...

HOOVED

Here are three interesting facts about the wild horses that live on Maryland's Assateague Island: 1) they most likely arrived there three centuries ago via a shipwreck; 2) there are about 300 of them on the island; and 3) you should never try to pet one. An unidentified tourist did just that when one of the horses wandered onto a crowded beach in 2019. The horse responded with a swift kick to the man's Speedo. Only one of them walked away.

BAD KITTY!

Dee Gallant was hiking with her dog in a forest outside of Duncan, British Columbia, when she saw a mountain lion staring her down from about 50 feet away. Murphy (the dog) didn't even notice it. Gallant, apparently believing the big cat was just checking her out from a safe distance, started recording the encounter on her

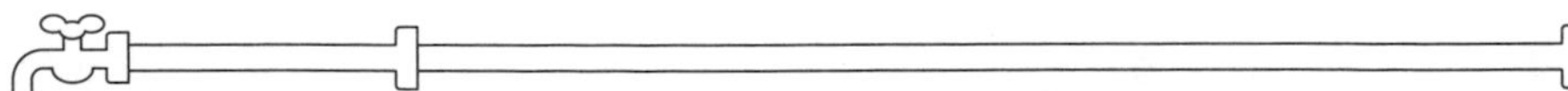

The Coca-Cola recipe isn't patented. Why not?
To do so would require revealing the formula. (And patents expire.)

phone. But then the predator lowered its shoulders and slowly started approaching her. "Bad kitty!" she yelled. "Get out of here!" The mountain lion ignored her and kept advancing. And Murphy *still* didn't know the cat was there. Thinking quickly, Gallant scrolled through her music library, looking for the "noisiest thing on my phone," hoping it would scare away the cat. The song she chose: "Don't Tread on Me" by Metallica. "As soon as the first notes blared out, it ran into the bush," and Gallant and Murphy (who finally noticed the predator) quickly hightailed it out of there.

Bonus: Gallant told her story to the press, and it made its way to Metallica front man James Hetfield, who was so amused that he gave Gallant a call. "He was just an absolutely wonderful guy," she beamed, "very down to earth."

GRAB AND GO

In May 2017, a group of tourists in Richmond, British Columbia, were gathered on a dock watching a sea lion swimming in the calm water. At one point, a little girl in a white dress (name not released) stood up. The large animal sprung out of the water, startling everyone, before sinking below the surface again. A moment later, the girl sat back down on the edge of the dock. Bad idea. The sea lion poked out its head, grabbed the girl's dress in its mouth, and yanked her into the water at an alarming speed. It let her go soon after, and she was rescued by one of the adults in the group. The girl was later treated with antibiotics as a precaution, but she was otherwise okay (physically, anyway). Explaining the animal's behavior, Andrew Trites of the Marine Mammal Research Unit at the University of British Columbia told *Live Science* that the tourists were "unintentionally teasing" the sea lion by extending their hands but not offering anything. "The animal was expecting food," Trites said. Once it realized she wasn't a snack, it let her go.

SOLE SURVIVOR

An English fishing tradition says that when you catch a Dover sole, you give it a kiss. In 2017, Sam Quilliam, a 28-year-old fisherman from Bournemouth, caught a six-inch-long Dover and attempted to follow the tradition, but just as he was about to kiss the fish on the mouth, it wiggled out of his hands and leapt right down his throat. The fisherman started choking, and his panicked friends were unable to dislodge the fish from his windpipe. By the time an ambulance arrived, Quilliam was in cardiac arrest. With time running out, a paramedic was able to remove the Dover with a pair of forceps. Quilliam made a full recovery; the fish did not.

* * *

"A fish may love a bird, but where would they live?"

–Drew Barrymore

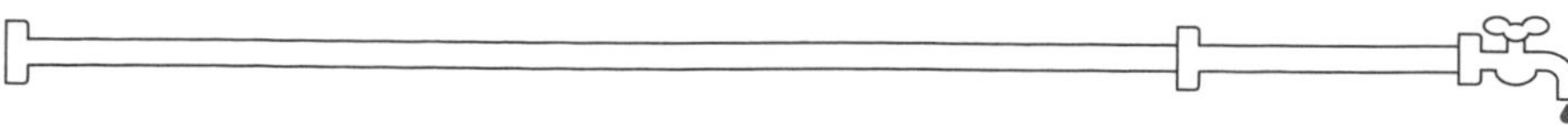

THE TRIPLE CROWN

Okay, you won the big match or the big race. Now can you do it two more times at events of equal or greater stature? If so, you've just won a "triple crown"...like these folks.

HORSE RACING

The most famous triple crown is the one for U.S. thoroughbred horse racing. Only 13 horses have won it, coming in first in the Kentucky Derby, Preakness Stakes, and Belmont Stakes, all of which are raced in a single two-month period. The last horse to do it: Justify (2018).

BASEBALL (BATTING)

In Major League Baseball's 150-year history, only 14 hitters finished a season leading their league in batting average, home runs, and runs batted in. Rogers Hornsby and Ted Williams each achieved this feat twice. When Miguel Cabrera of the Detroit Tigers accomplished it in 2012, he was the first since Carl Yastrzemski in 1967.

BASEBALL (PITCHING)

There's also a title for pitchers who lead their league in games won, strikeouts, and earned run average in a single season. In 2011, Clayton Kershaw of the Los Angeles Dodgers did it in the National League and Justin Verlander of the Detroit Tigers did it in the American League.

GOLF

The triple crown of men's golf is rare. It includes same-year wins for two major tournaments—the U.S. Open and the British Open—and also for the relatively minor Canadian Open. Only two guys have ever done it: Lee Trevino in 1971 and Tiger Woods in 2000.

AUTO RACING

The triple crown of motorsport is an unofficial accomplishment. A driver achieves it when they win three of the hardest auto races on the world stage, each of a different style. The component races are Formula One's Monaco Grand Prix, endurance racing's 24 Hours of Le Mans, and IndyCar's Indianapolis 500. British driver Graham Hill is the sole person ever to win this crown.

TENNIS

To achieve the triple crown of tennis, a player must win the singles, doubles, and mixed doubles sectors of a single "Grand Slam" tournament. That means playing nonstop, near-perfect tennis for two weeks. A few dozen players have done it, although the last time was in 1987 by Martina Navratilova at the U.S. Open. Impressively, Doris Hart achieved a triple crown at Wimbledon in 1951, winning all three final matches over the course of a single day.

BASKETBALL

Another unofficial title, the triple crown of basketball, is said to be won by any individual players who have won an NCAA national title, an Olympic gold medal, and an NBA championship. Just seven players have ever done it, including Magic Johnson and Michael Jordan.

HIKING

There are three major extra-long trails in the United States to test a hiker's true mettle: the Continental Divide Trail, which stretches 3,100 miles through the Rocky Mountains; the 2,184-mile Appalachian Trail in the eastern United States; and the Pacific Crest Trail, which covers 2,654 miles and goes through the Sierra Nevada and Cascades mountain ranges. Only about 400 hikers have been certified by the American Long Distance Hiking Association to have completed all three.

SURFING

The final three events of the professional surfing season in November and December each occur at major surfing hotbeds on the Hawaiian island of Oahu. The surfer who is judged to have performed the best across all three competitions wins the Triple Crown of Surfing (technically the Vans Triple Crown of Surfing, as the shoe company owns the branding rights). The events are the Hawaiian Pro at Haleiwa Ali'i Beach Park, the World Cup of Surfing at Sunset Beach, and the Pipeline Masters at Ehukai Beach Park.

ACTING

A triple crown of acting? Yes, and about two dozen actors have achieved it, having won all three of the major American acting awards: an Emmy Award (for television), an Academy Award (for film), and a Tony Award (for staged works on Broadway). Those who have done it include Maggie Smith, Al Pacino, Jessica Lange, and Viola Davis.

...in the range are named for members of an actual executive committee.

DEAD NEWS

We have a folder in our files simply marked "Death." Let's see what we can dig up.

Not Another HEPA

Wouldn't it be great to spend eternity at a Disney theme park? Unfortunately for the folks at Disney, a lot of people feel that way. In fact, the problem of families spreading their loved ones' ashes at Disneyland and Disney World (most popular spot: the Haunted Mansion) has become so rampant that there's a special employee code for it: "HEPA Cleanup." HEPA refers to the industrial-strength filter required to vacuum up human remains. What happens to all the tiny cremains that the vacuum can't suck up? The dustlike particles become airborne and float around the park unseen...until they come to rest on your hot dog.

Have You Heard about Death?

The Kid Mai Death Café (*kid mai* means "think new") in Bangkok, Thailand, is a macabre outdoor café that opened in 2018. The theme is "death awareness." After you've been seated at a table, you're fed a "last meal" (black cookies and death-themed coffee drinks). Then you're invited to lie down in a coffin—with the lid securely closed—for three minutes. The idea, explains owner Veeranut Rojanaprapa, is for customers to experience the sensation of death so they'll start living better lives. (The restaurant is actually his PhD thesis project.) He told *CNN Travel:* "Our Lord Buddha...said when one thinks and is aware of his death, he will decrease the 'me' inside his mind and he will decrease greed and decrease anger." Does the coffin do what it purports to do? Maybe. "When the lid closes," says Rojanaprapa, "customers realize that eventually they cannot take anything with them."

Well, If You're Going to Get Technical...

Under the erroneous assumption that a corpse counts as a "person" when driving in the carpool lane, a Las Vegas hearse driver tried to shave a few minutes off his commute. A state trooper pulled the hearse over and gave the driver (not named in press reports) a warning. A Nevada Highway Patrol spokesperson used the incident as a "teachable moment," tweeting the clarification that only "living, breathing people count for the HOV lane."

Show-off

A 27-year-old Pennsylvania woman named Angel Stewart wanted, as she later testified in court, to "gross out" her friends. And being a funeral director, she had the means to do it: She simply snapped and shared pictures of corpses being prepared for burial. Some photos featured open chest cavities; one featured a body covered in maggots.

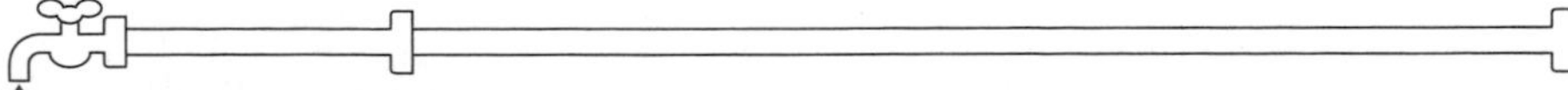

Queen guitarist Brian May has a PhD in astrophysics. He also designs sports bras.

Thanks to an anonymous tip (presumably from a grossed-out friend), police seized Stewart's phone and discovered her grisly photo album. When the relatives of the dearly departed found out, they were horrified: "It wasn't just photos," said one. "It was my mom." Stewart was charged with 16 counts of corpse abuse and sentenced to 10 years' probation.

Ashes to Ink

In 1996, Marvel comic book writer Mark Gruenwald's life was tragically cut short at age 43 due to a heart attack. Per his last wishes, his cremains were mixed in with the ink for the first printing of the paperback compilation of *Squadron Supreme.* So if you happen to have one of the first printings, you also have a bit of Mark.

Ouch

The Dani people, a tribe in the central highlands of western New Guinea, believe that the pain of grief associated with the death of a relative must be felt physically. They perform a funeral ritual called *Ikipalin*, in which a grieving woman will have her fingertip chopped off. The procedure begins by tightly tying a string around the top half of the finger to cut off the circulation, and then leaving it for about half an hour. Then a family member uses a stone blade to quickly amputate the fingertip. The wound is cauterized to stop the bleeding, and the fingertip is dried and then burned in a ritual to ward off the restless spirits of the dead. It's uncertain for how long the Dani have been practicing *Ikipalin*, or why it's only the women who lose digits. Although the ritual has been officially banned, it's rumored that some families still do it.

Carrion My Wayward Sons

One of the world's oldest religions still practiced today is Zoroastrianism. It's been around since at least the fifth century BC, and there are approximately 100,000 practitioners worldwide, mostly in Iran and India. Among the religion's core beliefs is that, upon death, the body is contaminated by a "corpse demon" known as *nasu.* If the body is buried or cremated, then this demon will pollute the two most sacred elements, earth and fire. To prevent that from happening, Zoroastrians place their dead atop a structure called a *Dakhma*, a Persian word that translates to "Tower of Silence." After a funeral, *nusessalars*—special caretakers who are the only ones allowed to enter these structures—place the body on the platform, made of three concentric circles, which slope down to a pit in the center. Deceased men are placed on the outer ring, then women, then children. Nature then takes its course as vultures and other scavengers eat the flesh and the sun slowly bleaches the bones left behind. Over time, the decaying matter collects in the pit, where it disintegrates until the remains are small enough to pass down a drain and through filters made of coal and sand. Then the pure, clean water harmlessly drains away.

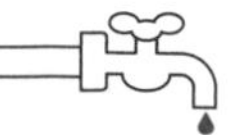

THE QUOTABLE DIAMOND DAVE

Through both his time as the front man of Van Halen and his solo career, David Lee Roth was as much a clever wit as he was a rock star.

"I USED TO JOG, BUT THE ICE CUBES KEPT FALLING OUT OF MY GLASS."

"It's not whether you win or lose, it's how good you looked doing it."

"The world is run by people who never feel well."

"I would just like to say that after all these years of heavy drinking, bright lights and late nights, I still don't need glasses. I drink right out of the bottle."

"It doesn't get better, it doesn't get worse, but it sure gets a lot different."

"My pop would tell me, 'Kid, don't be humble. You're not that good.'"

"YOU'RE NOT A ROCK STAR UNTIL YOU CAN SPELL 'SUBPOENA.'"

"If all the world's a stage, I want better lighting."

"We've all got our self-destructive bad habits, the trick is to find four or five you personally like the best and just do those all the time."

"I'm not conceited. Conceit is a fault and I have no faults."

THE DUNE BUGGY MAN

People have been stripping down old cars and fixing them up to drive on the beach since the 1940s, if not earlier. But it wasn't until the late 1960s that one man turned the hobby into a craze.

BEACH BUM

Bruce Meyers was a thirtysomething World War II veteran living in Newport Beach, California, in the early 1960s. After coming home from the war, he spent a lot of time in art school studying portrait painting. But he made his living building sailboats out of fiberglass. The material had been around since the 1940s, and people had only recently begun making boats with it. Meyers was one of only a few people who knew how to do it.

When he wasn't making boats or hanging out on the beach, Meyers made fiberglass surfboards for his friends. He also liked to tinker with cars, and he was a fan of "sand buggies," stripped-down jalopies that car buffs liked to race on the beach. The cars' doors, door frames, fenders, hoods, trunk lids, body panels, and even the windows, windshields, and roof were removed out of necessity—ordinary cars were too heavy. They were prone to sinking in the soft sand, so sand buggy builders removed everything they could down to the bare steel chassis to lose as much weight as possible, then replaced standard tires with big, fat "balloon" tires that had better traction in the sand. With so many parts removed, the sand buggies were little more than oversized go-karts: They were ugly, kind of like the automotive equivalent of skeletons, but they got the job done...to a degree.

They were ugly, kind of like the automotive equivalent of skeletons.

In those days most sand buggies were made from big American cars from the 1950s or earlier. Even when stripped down, they were still pretty heavy. They could race around on flat sand, such as along a beach, but relatively few were true dune buggies, able to race up and down the sides of steep sand dunes without getting stuck.

MADE IN GERMANY

Meyers thought a sand buggy made from a smaller, lighter vehicle would perform better and could be a true dune buggy. In the mid-1960s, one car in particular was the obvious choice for such a project: the Volkswagen Beetle, one of the smallest, lightest, and most simply constructed cars on the market. VW "Bugs," as they were popularly known, had begun trickling into the United States in the late 1940s. By the 1960s, they were the best-selling imported car in America, and their sales climbed

Until the late 1400s, "girl" meant "child." Male babies were "knave girls" and females were "gay girls."

every year. There were lots of cheap used Beetles around to work with, and lots of parts from wrecked Beetles in junkyards.

Other people had already begun making sand buggies out of VW Beetles. It was easy to do, because they were constructed in a way that allowed the owner to remove the car's entire body—passenger compartment, engine compartment, trunk, hood, and all four fenders—in a single piece, simply by removing several bolts and lifting the body off the chassis. And for people who didn't want to scrounge up parts for their VW dune buggies one by one, there was a company in Los Angeles that sold kits containing all the parts that were needed.

Meyers was not impressed with the homemade VW sand buggies, or with the ones made from kits: "I hated the looks of all of them," he remembered. "I liked their function, but I didn't like their looks." As a professionally trained artist, he valued the aesthetics of a vehicle as much as anything else, perhaps more so. As a builder of fiberglass boats, he had the skills to do something about it. He set to work building a VW-based dune buggy with a fiberglass body.

KEEPING IT SIMPLE

After experimenting with more complicated designs, Meyers settled on the idea of fabricating the entire body out of a single piece of fiberglass, much like the boat hulls he used to build. The only other fiberglass parts needed would be the front trunk lid, and the dash panel that would hold the speedometer and other gauges. That was it. There would be no doors, no side or rear windows, and no roof other than a removable fabric top.

Installing the dune buggy body onto a stripped-down VW Beetle chassis would be as simple as lifting it onto the chassis and bolting it into place. (The only tricky part was shortening the VW chassis, or "pan," by 14½ inches, but that was something that a welder could do in a couple of hours if the dune buggy builder didn't have the skills.) Once the body was bolted down, all a person had to do was install the front windshield, seats, headlights, and other mechanical parts, and the dune buggy was ready to roll.

CUTE AS A BUG

Back when he was in art school, Meyers spent a lot of time drawing human figures and making them appear as if they were in motion. He put this training to use when designing the look of his dune buggy. He wanted it to have "a strong feeling of adventure, [so] that it looked as though it was going to go somewhere and be fun," he said.

The design he came up with, a short, curvy, flowing fiberglass body with oversized

What's Chen Siyuan's special talent? She can write with both hands and both feet at the same time, in Chinese and English.

tires and bug-eyed headlights mounted on the hood, looked almost cartoonish, like something that Mickey Mouse or Donald Duck might drive. That was no accident: Meyers was a fan of Disney cartoons and he loved the whimsical appearance of the cars that the characters drove. He did his best to emulate the look. "I wanted a design that would make you smile," he told *AutoWeek* magazine. "I added all the line and feminine form and Mickey Mouse adventure I could." Even when his dune buggy was parked, it looked like it was moving. And unlike nearly every other dune buggy around, it looked like an actual motor vehicle, instead of just an ugly, cobbled-together assemblage of random junkyard auto parts.

IN THE KNOW

VW Beetles first became available to consumers after WWII, and by the early 1970s, more than 15 million had sold. They were so well-built that they were nearly airtight and could float. When VW featured this in a TV ad in 1973, a skeptical TV reporter drove a VW Beetle into Beetle Creek, Wisconsin, expecting it to sink. It didn't. VW used a photo of the reporter floating in his VW in its next print ad. Slogan: "It definitely floats, but not indefinitely."

Drive over to page 184 for part II of the story.

GARBAGE AND YOU

If you're average, this year you will produce 2,157 pounds of garbage. According to the EPA, 1,606 pounds will go into the landfill (the weight of a cow), while only 551 pounds are recycled (the weight of a large pig).

Those tiny, sealed plastic cups of coffee creamer have a name: milkettes.

CARE FOR A BOWL OF DUNK-A-BALLS?

The breakfast cereal market is crowded and competitive, so manufacturers have to come up with clever names for their new products. Here's a bowlful of real cereal names that went far beyond clever...all the way to unappetizing.

Antioxidant Indulgence

Yogurt Burst

Huskies

Granola Planks

Vector Meal Replacement

Great Grains Digestive Blend

Tigger and Pooh

Twinkles

Krumbles

Size 8

Wackies

Uncle Sam Cereal

Surprize

Mud & Bugs

Bugs N' Mud

Sugar Corn-fetti

Good Morenings

Purple Bam!

OKs

Xtreme Fun Blast-ems

Eat My Shorts

Halfsies

Freakies

Klondike Pete's Crunchy Nuggets

Dinky Donuts

Norman

Millenios

Body Buddies

Dunk-A-Balls

Chicken & Waffles

Sea Creature Berries

Mystery Crunch

Kream Krunch

Rippled Wheat Breakfast Food

Orange Quangaroos

PB&J

Ship Shake Cap'n Crunch Liquid Cereal

Holy Crap

Diamond Shreddies

"oho!"

Prophet's Pastry Pops

Green Slime Cereal

BoneWise

Fingos

Korn-Kinks

Popeye Cocoa Blasts

Egg-O-See

Dinersaurs

Sugar Smacks

Great Goodstuff

Graham Bumpers

Drinket

Cinna-mum-m-m

Grins & Smiles & Giggles & Laughs

Blasted Shreds

Sanitarium Corn Flakes

Corn Crackos

Cookie Doughn't You Want Some

Rice Bubbles

Mr. Wonderfull's Surprise

Magic Puffs

Crunchy Loggs

IRONIC, ISN'T IT?

There's nothing like a good dose of irony to put the problems of day-to-day life into proper perspective.

Meow-rony

In 2007, Andrew Lloyd Webber, composer of the musical *Cats*, was nearly finished writing another musical (the sequel to *Phantom of the Opera*), but the entire score was accidentally deleted when his cat stepped on his computer.

Ironic Ad Break

- "Science helps build a new India," went a hopeful-turned-ironic Union Carbide ad campaign in 1962. Twenty-two years later, science did just the opposite at Union Carbide's pesticide plant in the city of Bhopal, where a gas leak caused a massive explosion that exposed half a million people to a toxic cloud of methyl isocyanate gas. Several nearby towns were evacuated and up to 15,000 people perished. Today, the factory in this "new India" is still standing, but it's off limits because the air is still too poisonous.
- In 2015, higher-ups at the TV channel France 3 wanted to prove to viewers that they weren't sexist, so they produced a 40-second commercial that takes place in an unoccupied house: The oven is smoking, the iron is burning a shirt, and the toilet seat is up—all while the song "Where Are the Women?" plays. The answer pops up on-screen: "On France 3...where the majority of our presenters are female." They quickly pulled the ad after receiving a barrage of complaints that the commercial's message—if women don't clean, then no one will—was *overtly* sexist, putting a lot more scrutiny on the station's alleged misogyny than if it had simply stayed quiet.

Irony of the Deep

In 2019, Jordan's military sank some decommissioned equipment in the Red Sea to provide an artificial reef for sea life. In addition to a troop carrier, an anti-aircraft battery, and a combat helicopter, there were several tanks. They are now actual, literal "fish tanks."

Firony Trucks

- In 2019, a fire department in Abilene, Texas, got a brand-new $350,000 pumper truck. A month later, a mechanic was giving it a test drive when something "popped" and a tire caught fire, quickly engulfing the fire truck in flames. It was a total loss.

- Firefighters battling flames in a field near Rue de Hamm, Luxembourg, parked much too close to the wind-fueled blaze. Before they knew it, their fire truck was on fire, and they had to run away. Then the truck exploded, making the fire even harder to put out. Thankfully, the firefighters were able to extinguish the blaze before it could cause any substantial damage (other than to the fire truck).

Help Wanted: Irony

Amazon's "Talent Acquisition" page (the section of its website used to recruit employees) once included a photo of a man named Jordan Guffman talking to two women on the company's campus. The caption read, "At Amazon, we pursue excellence in talent acquisition." A few years later, Guffmann came across the website and the photo, and tweeted about its irony: The day it was taken, he explained, "I went to Amazon for a job interview that I did NOT get." Shortly after Guffman's tweet went viral (he's since become a successful tech guru), Amazon replaced the photo with a picture of someone who (we presume) actually works there.

Grounded Irony

Two of American Airlines' top lawyers were preparing to fly to a meeting with union representatives during a bitter dispute in which American accused mechanics of "sabotaging the performance" of the airline, leading to delays and cancellations. But the two lawyers never made it to the meeting. Reason: their flight was canceled.

Throwing Fuel on the Irony

A homeowner in Springfield, Massachusetts, was burning a brush pile in 2019 when the flames caught his gas can on fire. Thinking quickly, he threw the gas can into his aboveground swimming pool. Good idea, right? Wrong. The fuel spread out over the surface, setting the entire pool on fire. Spraying water on the water made the fire worse, so firefighters had to use foam to put it out.

Environy

- On a topsy-turvy weather day in January 2018, it was colder in Jacksonville, Florida (high: 41°F), than it was in Anchorage, Alaska (high: 49°F).
- In 2018, President Donald Trump's administration reversed an Obama-era ban on oil drilling in the Arctic. Reason for the ban: to slow rising temperatures in the region. The reversal allowed a Texas oil company to finally begin construction of a man-made island five miles off the Alaska coast. Per the original plan, dump trucks would transport the gravel to the new island over a seasonal ice road. But the project had to be expanded from one year to two. Reason: due to rising temperatures, the annual ice season had become nearly two months shorter than it was when the oil company's plans were first drawn up.

Why does milk come in 1 percent, 2 percent, but not 3 percent?
Because whole milk is 3.25 percent fat.

THE TOWN WITH TOO MUCH TOILET PAPER

Have you ever had too much of a good thing?
You've got company.

ON A ROLL

In 2006, municipal officials in the tiny Bavarian town of Fuchstal (about 50 miles from Munich, in southern Germany) tried to save on expenses by buying toilet paper in bulk. But thanks to a clerical error, they purchased far more toilet paper than the town of 4,000 people needed, something they only realized when the first of *two* truckloads arrived. The administrators managed to get the second truckload canceled, but they still had to do something with the $6,600 worth of toilet paper—thousands of rolls—that had been delivered by the first truck.

Giving the excess toilet paper away free to the townspeople didn't work, because nobody wanted it. The paper was a cheap, gray, single-ply paper that turned yellow and brittle when exposed to sunlight. Throwing it all away was out of the question, so town officials set up a committee of four people and put them in charge of storing the toilet paper in every nook and cranny in every public building in town. Shelves, drawers, cabinets, basements, and attics were stuffed with the rolls. "In primary schools, the secondary school, with us in the town hall, the toilet paper was hidden in the storage rooms everywhere," Fuchstal's mayor, Erwin Karg, told reporters. Bit by bit, roll by roll, the toilet paper was taken from storage and put to use in the town's public restrooms. Years passed.

WINDING DOWN

Finally, *12 years* after the toilet paper arrived, the very last roll was used up. How did the town officials celebrate? By placing an order for *more* toilet paper—only this time a much smaller order, for much nicer paper: white instead of gray, and two-ply instead of one-ply. How are the town employees adjusting to the fancy new rolls? "It'll probably take me another twelve years to get used to it," Mayor Karg says.

TALK TO THE HAND

Humans communicate using much more than words. We use signs and gestures, and many of them are universally understood. Here's how they originated.

CHEF'S KISS

Description: Thumb and forefinger pinched together, then kissed, then pulled away from the mouth quickly

Meaning: "Delicious!"

Origin: A cliché sometimes associated with cartoonish images of Italian chefs (with big mustaches and big chef's hats), this gesture really did originate in Italy. There, it's called *al bacio,* which translates as "as good as a kiss," but is used colloquially to mean "perfect." Italian culture blossomed in the United States after World War II, when thousands of servicemen who served in Italy brought it back with them...including *al bacio.* Kraft used images of Italian chefs making the gesture in ads for ravioli and spaghetti kits. By the time the Swedish Chef did it on *The Muppet Show* in the 1970s, it was a well-known gesture and understood to be something all chefs did to denote the quality of their food.

HANG LOOSE

Description: The three middle fingers fold down into the palm of the hand, and the pinky and thumb are outstretched

Meaning: "Be cool, don't stress, no worries!"

Origin: In Hawaii, where it's very common, the gesture is called the "shaka," and it's an expression of sharing positive feelings with others. Local lore says it started in the early 1940s at the massive Kahuku Sugar Mill outside of Honolulu. A man named Hamana Kalili worked in the plant, feeding sugarcane into industrial rollers that squeezed out juice. One day his hand got caught in the machinery, and his index, middle, and ring fingers were ripped clean off. No longer able to handle the sugarcane, Kalili was transferred by his bosses to a job as a security guard on the company's train that shuttled workers to and from the plant. As people came and went, Kalili would wave at them with his two-fingered hand. Over time, imitating the way his hand looked grew into a homegrown Honolulu greeting.

DEVIL HORNS

Description: The middle and ring fingers are tucked into the palm, held down by the thumb. The upward-facing pinkie and forefinger resemble horns.

Meaning: First it was "Protect us from evil," then "Hail Satan," then "This rocks!"

Origin: The idea of an "evil eye," or that a watchful universe will curse the envious, occurs throughout several cultures. In ancient Rome, people thought they could hold back the evil eye by making a powerful gesture: forming a fist, but extending the pinkie and index finger. It looks like horns, and so in Rome and other Italian places, the gesture became known as *corna*, or "horns." It was introduced to heavy metal, a genre of music that loves to flirt with the evil and demonic, in the late 1960s by Coven, one of the first heavy metal bands. On the back cover of its first album, *Witchcraft Destroys Minds & Reaps Souls,* lead singer Jinx Dawson flashes the gesture, clearly implying homage to the devil (borne out by their songs' lyrics). Over time, fans of hard rock and heavy metal bands (like Coven) began to mimic the gesture as a sign of appreciation at concerts, where it means less "Hail Satan!" and more "This rocks!"

I LOVE YOU

Description: Like the devil horns, but the thumb is extended

Meaning: "I love you!"

Origin: The shape the hand takes looks like a stylized combination of the letters I, L, and Y. The pinkie is the I, the forefinger and outstretched thumb form the L (for love), and the pinkie and thumb make a y (for you), hence "I love you." This is the actual sign for "I love you" in American Sign Language, and it made its way into the mainstream.

V FOR VICTORY

Description: The index and middle fingers extend upward, forming a "V" shape

Meaning: "We're victorious!"

Origin: During World War II, former Belgian minister of justice Victor de Laveleye served as director of BBC Radio's French-language Belgian broadcasts. During a January 1941 program, de Laveleye suggested that a good way for Belgians to build morale and stay positive during wartime would be to flash a "V" with their fingers—the first letter of the French word *victoire,* or "victory." De Laveleye believed it would unnerve the Nazis: "The occupier, by seeing this sign, always the same, infinitely repeated, would understand that he is surrounded, encircled by an immense crowd of citizens eagerly awaiting his first moment of weakness, watching for his first failure." Graffitied "V"s started showing up in Belgium, then in other French-speaking areas that heard the BBC French broadcasts, including the Netherlands and northern France. By July 1941, it was so widespread and understood that English prime minister Winston Churchill started using it when photographed or after speeches.

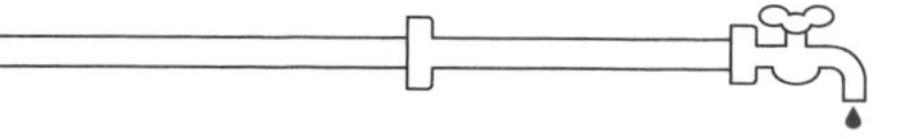

If the Moon didn't exist, an Earth day would be about six hours long.

TERRIBLE TYPOS

The lesson here is simple: prooofread.

NEITHER EDISON NOR EINSTEIN

Here's a famous Thomas Edison quote: "Genius is one percent inspiration and ninety-nine percent perspiration." In 2015, Swedish clothing retailer H&M sold a T-shirt on its website featuring that quote—printed in big block letters—with one glaring goof: "Genious is one percent inspiration and ninety-nine percent perspiration." After the ironic misspelling went viral, H&M quickly pulled the shirt from stores (before Uncle John was able to buy one).

SLICK CONDITIONS

Tulsa, Oklahoma, doesn't get a lot of snow. That still doesn't excuse the tasteless (but funny) typo that Fox23 News displayed on-screen for several long minutes during a 2012 "Winter Blast." The graphic shared several helpful tips for "DRIVING ON SNOT AND ICE."

SEEING RED

The editors of the *Comox Valley Record* apologized for an unfortunate typo that made the small British Columbia newspaper the laughingstock of the Internet in November 2019. In a full-page ad for the upcoming Christmas Parade, one of the advertised activities was "Pictures With Satan." (We're pretty sure they meant Santa.) Despite the incessant mocking—"That editor did a hell of a job!"—or perhaps because of it, event organizers credited the typo with making the parade a huge success. One resident even showed up dressed as the devil himself and posed for photos. According to reports, "Satan raised $136 for the local food bank."

BE GOOD, OR ELSE...

Another Canadian Christmas promotion gone bad comes courtesy of the Metro Supermarket chain. A store placard announced that, for $250, you can purchase a "Christmas Bag of Threats."

THE IRISH ARE LANDING!

In 2019, to celebrate 50 years since humans landed on the Moon, the Republic of Ireland issued a commemorative postage stamp honoring four astronauts with Irish ancestry. The caption read, "The 50th Anniversary of the First Moon Landing." Beneath it was the same phrase in Gaelic: "*Cothrom 50 Bliain na Chead Tuirlingthe ar an nGaelach.*" Oops. The Gaelic word for "moon" is *gealach*, not *nGaelach*...which means "Irish." Result: the translation celebrates the "50th Anniversary of the First Irish Landing." The government issued an apology and reissued a corrected set of stamps.

THIRD I BLIND

Do you happen to have one of the Australian $50 banknotes that was released in 2019? If so, look closely at the "micro-text" in the background, behind the portrait of Edith Cowan, Australia's first female member of parliament. An excerpt from her first speech is repeated over and over: "It is a great responsibilty to be the only woman here." Notice the goof? The typesetters left out the final "i" in "responsibility." Making it even more embarrassing, the printing was billed as "new and improved" to prevent counterfeiting. The Australian mint printed 46 million $50 banknotes before the error was discovered.

A TEACHABLE MOMENT

During Black History Month in 2017, the U.S. Secretary of Education, Betsy DeVos, sent out the following tweet:

> "Education must not simply teach work—it must teach life." —W.E.B. DeBois

Not long after, the NAACP, which was cofounded by the man DeVos quoted, replied with another quotation from the civil rights icon...along with the correct spelling of his surname:

> "In the Days of Loose & Careless Logic, We Must Teach Thinkers to THINK."
> —William Edward Burghardt DU Bois

TRASH TALK

No one noticed the goof until after 10,000 trash bins had been deposited around the city of Prichard, Alabama. Printed in large, white letters on both sides of the large, gray bins was the proud slogan, "Crossroads of Mobile Country." Only it was supposed to say "Mobile *County.*" When pressed for an explanation, the mayor blamed the public works department. (No one from public works could be reached for comment.) But the mayor did say that the typo wasn't embarrassing enough to warrant replacing all those bins.

YOU MUST BE OKING

How do you not notice the "J" missing from "Jingle Bells"? That mystery had Australian holiday shoppers flummoxed in December 2019. The wrapping paper with the glaring typo—printed in festive lettering inside festive circles—was sold at Kmart stores across the country. The retail giant offered no xplanation.

MILLITARY SPENDING

In 2011, Aussie soldiers dispatched to the Middle East were issued uniforms emblazoned with the words "Royal Australlian Navy" (with an extra "l" in "Australian"). The navy's excuse caused as much criticism as the goof itself: The Tasmania company responsible for the uniforms outsourced them to a factory in Hong Kong...and no one in the home office had bothered to proofread them.

THE CHUCK NORRIS BRIDGE

A naming contest can be a great publicity stunt—it gets the public involved and it's free. It's been used successfully to name products, sports teams, arenas, and much more. But thanks to the Internet, where all it takes is a few keystrokes and a click to enter, naming contests quickly turn into pranking contests. Here are a few examples.

CONTEST: In the mid-2000s, "Chuck Norris facts" became a hugely popular Internet fad. People would invent and share trivia items that spoke to the masculinity and toughness of the *Delta Force* and *Walker, Texas Ranger* star. (For example, "Chuck Norris can kill two stones with one bird," and "Chuck Norris makes onions cry.") In 2012, as the craze was reaching its peak, the city of Bratislava, Slovakia, held an online vote to name a new pedestrian and cycling bridge. Someone suggested "The Chuck Norris Bridge," and two months later it was by far the #1 choice, with 12,000 votes.

RESULT: The Bratislava City Council refused to name their bridge after an American actor. They went with the #2 selection, "Freedom Cycling Bridge," even though it received just 457 votes.

CONTEST: The town council of Oldham, a town seven miles northeast of Manchester, England, issued a Twitter request to give an official name to a newly purchased gritter—a heavy-duty piece of machinery that spreads sand and salt over icy roads. A facetious suggestion easily took home the most votes: Gritsy Bitsy Teeny Weeny Yellow Anti Slip-Machiney.

RESULT: The Oldham City Council rejected "Gritsy Bitsy," but wound up using another funny suggestion: Nicole Saltslinger. That's a pun on the name of Pussycat Dolls singer and *The Masked Singer* judge Nicole Scherzinger.

CONTEST: Austin, Texas, with a thriving music scene, the annual South by Southwest Music Festival, and the long-running PBS performance show Austin City Limits, is one of the world's music capitals. So it's only fitting that somebody would try to give the Texas capital's new solid waste processing center a musically themed name. In 2011, the local government asked the Internet for suggestions, and someone submitted "The Fred Durst Society of the Humanities and the Arts." Who's Fred Durst? The lead singer of late 1990s rap-rock band Limp Bizkit. (In

other words, they were comparing Durst's music to the substance that's processed at solid waste processing centers.)

RESULT: The suggestion got a lot of traction and support, amassing 30,000 votes. Amazingly, even Durst tweeted out his approval of the name. But the city decided against enacting the popular choice, and went with "Austin Resource Recovery."

CONTEST: In 2012, Mountain Dew executives announced plans for a new flavor: green apple. But they did not yet have a name for the product, so they put it to the Internet to suggest one in a campaign called "Dub the Dew." While some legitimate ideas came in, the leaderboard on Mountain Dew's website of the top 10 vote-getters quickly became overloaded with joke ideas. Among them: "Soda," "Diabeetus," and "Soylent Green." (The others are too offensive to print.)

RESULT: Mountain Dew quickly called off the promotion and took down all "Dub the Dew" materials. It launched the soda in 2013 as a product available only at Pizza Hut, and called it "Mountain Dew Electric Apple."

CONTEST: The environmental advocacy organization Greenpeace wanted to raise the awareness of the plight of humpback whales in 2007, but in a fun way. So they invited the world to name a whale that they were tracking as it migrated to the Antarctic Ocean. More than 11,000 people submitted names, and 150,000 voted, and when it was all said and done, the winning entry was... Mr. Splashy Pants. And it wasn't even close, winning with 78 percent of the vote. (Second place: Humphrey, with just 3 percent.)

The winning entry was... Mr. Splashy Pants.

RESULT: Greenpeace actually honored the winning entry, bestowing the name on the whale in all of its press materials.

CONTEST: Rory Fitzpatrick is the very definition of a "journeyman" professional athlete. By the start of the 2006–2007 season, he was playing with his fifth hockey team in a decade-long career that wasn't exactly illustrious—he'd scored just nine goals and 18 assists in his career. When fan voting for the NHL All-Star Game opened in 2007, Fitzpatrick's stat line consisted of a single assist, and he'd missed a month of play due to injury. Nevertheless, a New York man named Steve Schmid thought Fitzpatrick should be rewarded for his service and launched a website called VoteForRory.com, aiming to get the veteran player onto the all-star roster. The campaign went viral, and Fitzpatrick initially received a whopping 428,800 votes, enough to earn a spot as a starter.

RESULT: Fans of other players ultimately came through with *their* votes and, despite the vigorous support he'd received, Fitzpatrick finished third in the vote for defensemen, shutting him out of a spot in the 2007 NHL All-Star Game.

CONTEST: Similar to breath-freshening strips, Sheets Energy Strips are thin wafers of a plasticlike material that dissolves on the tongue, providing a small, quick boost of caffeine. In 2012, the makers of Sheets teamed up with Walmart for a promotion: The Walmart store that got the most "likes" on its individual Facebook page would receive a visit and a mini concert from Sheets' spokesman, the rapper/singer Pitbull. David Thorpe, a writer with a large social media following, set out to sabotage the campaign, and encouraged his fans and readers to go like the Facebook page associated with the most remote Walmart in the entire United States—the one in Kodiak, Alaska.

RESULT: Guess who won a visit from Pitbull? Kodiak, with 60,000 "likes." (Kodiak Island's population: only 6,100.) Sheets informed the singer that he'd have to make a trip up to Alaska because the contest had been rigged, but Pitbull was a good sport and made the trip to Kodiak.

CONTEST: In 2012, pop music superstar Taylor Swift, along with corporate sponsors Papa John's Pizza and the textbook distributor Chegg, held a contest to award a special prize to a lucky school: Swift would show up at whichever institution won the most votes on Facebook. Some pranksters on the online communities 4chan and Reddit were better organized than the students at those schools, and they overwhelmed the online vote. The winning school: Boston's Horace Mann School for the Deaf. (The point of the prank, in case you didn't get it, was that Swift would have to play for an audience of people who couldn't hear her music.)

RESULT: Horace Mann was ultimately disqualified because of the way the contest had been hijacked, but Swift personally rewarded the students of the school. She made a $10,000 donation to Horace Mann—matched by Papa John's, Chegg, Cover Girl, and American Greetings for a total of $50,000—and gifted every student a ticket to one of her concerts (which they wouldn't be able to hear).

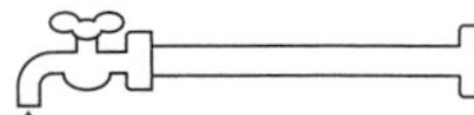

STRANGE CRIME

Some true crime stories are tough to categorize. They're just...strange. (Shameless plug: for more bizarre crime stories like these, check out Portable Press's Strange Crime.*)*

MAKE YOURSELF AT HOME

Two weeks after Timothy Smith and his fiancée moved into their dream house in Gresham, Oregon, in July 2019, they arrived home to find that some odd objects had been left on their car—including a bottle of cider, a laptop computer, and several knives. When they took the stuff inside, they found somebody's vape pen on the kitchen table. Smith, 24, looked around and discovered more odd things: there was a hole in the bedroom wall, the bathroom mirror had been removed, his hats were in the bathtub, and someone else's clothes were on the washing machine. Then he found the hatch to the crawl space open. Peering inside, he saw a cat that did not belong to him wearing a cashmere shirt that belonged to his pet Chihuahua. Smith quickly shut the door, and decided to call the cops and let them take over.

Later, as the nervous couple waited out front, officers emerged with a man named Ryan Bishop, who was wearing a "hooded onesie adorned with hearts and snowflakes" that belonged to Smith's fiancée. According to *OregonLive,* Bishop, 38, had also "made himself coffee, ate a cupcake, drank beer from the fridge, smoked their marijuana, and played video games in the garage." Hypodermic drug needles were also found in the garage. "I don't hate the guy," Smith said, "and I guess if there is anything I hope people take away from this it's that if you're looking for help, then seek it, because there's nothing else you can do for yourself in that situation."

THE ROBOTIC ARM OF THE LAW

A "very violent man" named Brock Ray Bunge was wanted for armed robbery and murder in September 2016, and the cops chased him into a desert just outside of Los Angeles. Armed with a rifle and protected by the dark of night, Bunge hid behind a berm beneath some bushes and used wire fencing to build himself a little barricade. A standoff ensued. After more than six hours, cautious deputies decided to send in a robot to get a clear view of the suspect. The $300,000 robot—which is mainly used to defuse bombs—rolled into the makeshift bunker and approached Bunge from behind. The robot's night-vision camera revealed that the perp was lying on his stomach, looking out at the SWAT vehicles...and his shotgun was on the ground at his feet. When Bunge didn't react to the robot's presence, deputies hatched a plan: they flew a helicopter low over the hideout and yelled through the loudspeaker, creating a cacophonous diversion

Billionaire Warren Buffett prefers to pay in cash. He carries about $400 in his wallet.

as the robot grabbed Bunge's rifle with its robotic arm and quietly rolled back out of there. A few minutes later, it returned and started to remove the fencing. Bunge went to grab his gun...which was gone. He was apprehended without incident and later sentenced to 97 years in prison.

ME LOVE COOKIE

A man wearing a Cookie Monster T-shirt walked into a Forest Grove, Oregon, convenience store, ate half a bag of cookies, and then left without paying for them. "This entry was brought to you by the letters C and T, and the number 3, as in Citation for Theft 3," read a *Sesame Street*–style Facebook post from police the next day. They didn't have to work too hard to catch the "Cookie Monster bandit." He showed up at the station later that day and confessed that he had "indeed taken a cookie from the convenience store." He claimed the entire thing was a misunderstanding.

DOYOUTHINKHESAURUS

Police in Plymouth, Devon, England, were hot on the trail of a fleeing T. rex late one night in July 2019. The eight-foot dinosaur—actually an intoxicated man in an inflatable suit—waddled along for a while, until the cops finally ran over him. Just kidding. They apprehended him peacefully. "You wonder how they became extinct, don't you?" quipped one policeman.

TOYING WITH THE COPS

In 2019, Megan Holman led police on a low-speed chase on the neighborhood streets of Wahalla, South Carolina. Holman, 25, was driving a child-sized Power Wheels toy truck. Max speed: 5 mph. Officers pulled her over about a mile from her house and gave her a sobriety test, which she failed. Interestingly, she wasn't given a DUI because she wasn't actually operating a motor vehicle. So the cops settled for a charge of public intoxication instead. When asked what drove her to drive a toy truck down the road, Holman said she "wanted to be a professional wrestler like her father and this was how to do it."

* * *

MYTH-NOMER

When couples get married in a church, they almost never "walk down the aisle." The central passage that runs from the entrance to the altar is actually called the *nave*. The aisles are the *side* passages.

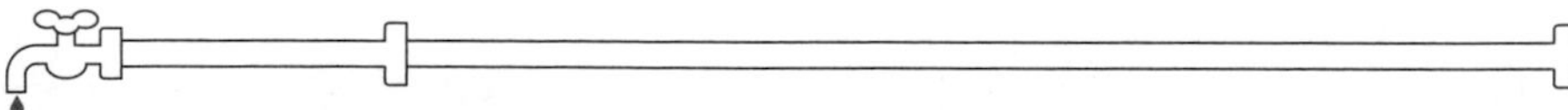

UNCLE JOHN'S PAGE OF LISTS

Top tidbits from our bottomless files.

Pythagoras's Cycle of Life

1. Birth
2. Growth
3. Decay
4. Death
5. Absorption
6. Metamorphosis

9 Styles Derived from Hip-hop

1. Boom bap
2. Crunk
3. Horrorcore
4. Hyphy
5. Neurohop
6. Mumble rap
7. Illbient
8. Trvxrap
9. Turntablism

6 Official Languages of the United Nations

1. Arabic
2. Chinese
3. English
4. French
5. Russian
6. Spanish

11 Oddly Named *Dungeons & Dragons* Devils

1. Adramalech
2. Baalphegor
3. Bileth
4. Cozbinaer
5. Erac's Cousin
6. Hag Countess
7. Morax
8. Phongor
9. Zagum
10. Zariel
11. Zepar

13 Diners in Da Vinci's *The Last Supper*

1. Bartholomew
2. James Minor
3. Andrew
4. Judas
5. Peter
6. John
7. Jesus
8. Thomas
9. James Major
10. Philip
11. Matthew
12. Thaddeus (Jude)
13. Simon

5 Fastest Fish

1. Black marlin: 80 mph
2. Sailfish: 68 mph
3. Swordfish: 60 mph
4. Yellowfin tuna: 47 mph
5. Shortfin mako shark: 45 mph

3 Alliterative Animal Groupings

1. A gaggle of geese
2. A covert of coots
3. A husk of hares

7 Basic CPR Steps

1. Recognize the emergency (tap on the shoulder and shout, "Are you okay?")
2. Activate EMS (call 911).
3. Check for breathing.
4. Compressions: Provide 30 compressions.
5. Airway: Open the victim's airway.
6. Breathing: Give two breaths.
7. Continue steps 4, 5, and 6 until help arrives.

HIGH-TECH UNDERWEAR

Better living through underwear technology? You be the judge.

 LAMBS "FARADAY CAGE" BOXER BRIEFS

What They Do: Prevent your cell phone from frying your "junk" (supposedly)

How They Work: Even when you're not using your cell phone, if it's on, it's constantly signaling or "pinging" nearby cell towers to check for incoming calls, e-mails, etc. There's no scientific evidence that these or any other cell phone emissions are bad for your health, but many people do carry their cell phones in their pants pockets, mere inches from their private parts. For those who do worry that the signals may be harmful to their reproductive health, the Lambs underwear company has created radiation-blocking underpants. "Our tightly-woven mesh of silver fibers (conductive fibers) creates an electromagnetic shield," also known as a Faraday cage. When a cell phone signal strikes the silver mesh, "the radiation induces a displacement of electrons inside the conductive material, and reflects off the shield. Thus your privates are totally safe from electromagnetic fields!"

ACABADA CBD-INFUSED SPORTS BRAS

What They Are: Sports bras containing *cannabidiol*, or CBD, one of the active ingredients in marijuana (but not *tetrahydrocannabinol*, or THC, the ingredient that gets you high)

How They Work: CBD has been credited with helping to ease a host of medical complaints including pain, anxiety, depression, insomnia, and inflammation—though to date the evidence to support these claims is largely anecdotal. And the jury's also out on whether CBD can be readily absorbed through the skin into the bloodstream. But that hasn't stopped Acabada from trying to capitalize on the CBD craze: Its sports bras are made from "high-performance fabrics that are strategically infused with up to 25 grams of zero-THC, lab-certified, 99.9% pure CBD," using "a cutting-edge technology known as micro-encapsulation," says the company. "These micro-capsules are then embedded into the multilayers of the fibers," and the CBD-infused fabrics are "placed throughout the garment to align with your major muscle groups." Acabada claims the microcapsules are tough enough to last through 40 washing machine cycles, yet somehow are able to release therapeutic doses of CBD into the skin every time the wearer works out. (And if you believe that, maybe you should cut back on the wacky tobacky.)

More bottled water is sold each year in the U.S. than all brands of sodas combined.

SIENTE EL JUEGO ("FEEL THE GAME") PANTIES

What They Are: Panties that "stimulate" the wearer's interest in World Cup soccer... by stimulating the wearer *during* World Cup soccer

How They Work: Are you familiar with the term "football widow"? There's a similar phenomenon in Mexico during World Cup soccer. Vicky Form, a Mexican lingerie company, claims that "every year, four million couples separate because of fútbol" when the male is interested in the World Cup but the female is not. The company says it has created a pair of women's undies that address the problem by letting the wearer "feel the passion of the game" via a vibrating panel in the garment. According to Vicky Form, the panel is "linked to a robot that interprets the action and transforms it into vibrations in real time" whenever a goal is scored. The more action there is on the field, the more action (so to speak) there is in the panties.

To date, the technology exists only as a prototype; Vicky Form says it will bring the vibrating soccer skivvies to market only "if there is enough demand" for the product. Judging from the nearly universal revulsion that greeted the prototype when it was unveiled in 2018—"disgusting," "degrading," "pathetic," and "stupid" were typical responses on social media—Feel the Game panties probably won't be hitting store shelves anytime soon.

KNOCK OUT! PANTIES

What They Are: Odor-absorbing panties

How They Work: The underwear is made with fabric containing *hydroxypropyl beta cyclodextrin* (HP-beta-CD), the same odor-trapping ingredient as Febreze odor eliminator. The HP-beta-CD molecules trap odorous molecules within its molecular structure, making the smells harder to detect. Stay-at-home mom Angela Newnam got the idea for the panties in 2009 after learning about a line of hunting gear called No Trace that hunters used to mask their scent while hunting deer. Newnam incorporated the same technology into her line of underwear and sold 20,000 pairs her first year in business. The panties are good for at least 40 washes before the HP-beta-CD loses its effectiveness.

* * *

LOCATION, LOCATION, LOCATION

Europe and Asia are both part of the same landmass, so why are they considered two separate continents? Blame the ancient Greeks. They believed that Greece, on one side of the Aegean Sea, was on a different landmass than Anatolia (modern-day Turkey) on the other side of the Aegean. They were wrong—it's not.

The famous "Welcome to Fabulous Las Vegas" sign is actually in Paradise, Nevada. So is most of the Las Vegas Strip.

FAMOUS FOR 15 MINUTES: THE HUGGING BABIES

Most people find their 15 minutes of fame as adults, or, less frequently, as kids. Brielle and Kyrie Jackson of Worcester, Massachusetts, found theirs within days of being born.

EARLY BIRDS

In October 1995, a Massachusetts woman named Heidi Jackson went into labor prematurely and delivered twin girls twelve weeks early. The tiny girls, named Kyrie and Brielle, weighed about 2 pounds apiece. (Full-term babies, by comparison, weigh from 5.5 to 8 pounds at birth.) The girls' health was extremely precarious; they had very little body fat and struggled to stay warm. They were placed in separate incubators in the hospital's neonatal intensive care unit (NICU).

The doctors cautioned Jackson and her husband, Paul, that the weeks ahead might be difficult for one or both of the twins. That prediction turned out to be true: while Kyrie made steady progress, Brielle did not. She gained little weight and had regular crying fits that interfered with her breathing, giving her skin a bluish tinge from lack of oxygen and causing her vital signs to become erratic. Nothing the doctors, nurses, or Brielle's parents did seemed to comfort the tiny baby—not swaddling her in blankets, holding her, or suctioning her nose to make breathing easier. The crying fits continued.

DOUBLING UP

Because premature babies are so fragile, it was standard practice in the 1990s to isolate them in individual incubators to reduce the risk of viruses and infections spreading from one baby to another. This was certainly the case when a mother gave birth to a single baby, but Brielle was a twin. One of the NICU nurses, a woman named Gayle Kasparian, wondered if Brielle might be more comfortable if she were placed in the same incubator with her sister. She asked the Jacksons for permission to move Brielle into Kyrie's incubator, and they agreed.

REACHING OUT

Kasparian carefully laid Brielle in the incubator alongside Kyrie. As soon as Kyrie sensed that Brielle was there, she reached out with her left arm and placed it over Brielle's shoulder in a sort of hug. "It happened very quickly," Paul Jackson

remembered. "They really couldn't move that much but it was a bit of a squirm and the arm kind of just went up."

As soon as Brielle felt her sister's touch, she began to improve. "When I put Brielle in with her sister, it was amazing. She immediately calmed down. Her heart rate stabilized, and her color changed," Kasparian told the Worcester *Telegram & Gazette* in 2013. Brielle made steady progress from that day forward, just like her sister. After about two months in the NICU, both babies were healthy enough to go home.

WORTH A THOUSAND WORDS

What makes Kyrie and Brielle different from just about every other set of "preemie" twins who've spent time in a NICU unit is that on the day that Brielle was placed in the incubator next to her sister, the photo editor of the Worcester *Telegram & Gazette,* Chris Christo, happened to be in the NICU taking pictures for a news story. He was standing right there when Kyrie reached out to Brielle, and he took a photograph of what would become known as "the rescuing hug." The photo was published in the *Telegraph & Gazette,* then picked up by the wire services. Soon it was running in newspapers all over the country, as well as in *Life, Reader's Digest,* and other national magazines. In time, the image of one tiny twin embracing the other would become a common sight framed and hanging on the walls of medical offices everywhere.

> **IN THE KNOW**
>
> The first incubator for premature babies was invented in 1880 by a French obstetrician, Etienne Stéphane Tarnier, after he saw an incubator for exotic bird eggs at the Paris Zoo. Tarnier's first incubator consisted of a wooden box with a glass lid, heated by hot water in a bottom tank. Within three years, his incubators lowered the infant mortality rate at his hospital by 28 percent.

How fast did the picture spread, and how popular was it? By the time two months had passed, and Kyrie and Brielle were healthy enough to leave the NICU and go home, the photo had already generated so much buzz—and so many people were calling the Jacksons at home to learn more about it—that they had to change their phone number.

MAGIC TOUCH

And as the photo spread around the world, so too did the story behind it: how something as simple as the touch of a tiny infant had accomplished something that all the medical equipment in the NICU and all the doctors and nurses with all their training and expertise had been unable to do—restore another tiny infant to health. As far as anyone knows, Kyrie and Brielle were the very first infants at their hospital, the Medical Center of Central Massachusetts, to be placed in the same incubator

together. But they wouldn't be the last. The NICU nurses began placing babies together whenever they had a difficult case, and on countless occasions they saw the same improvement in health that they had seen in Brielle.

The story of "the rescuing hug," as it became known, helped to spark a revolution in neonatal care as doctors and nurses everywhere began placing premature babies together whenever they thought it might do some good. Today the practice is commonplace, thanks in large part to the picture of Kyrie and Brielle.

HOLDING ON

The World Wide Web was still in its infancy when Kyrie and Brielle were born in 1995, but the picture and story of the rescuing hug soon started circulating on the Internet. They still do today. Uncle John only learned of the story in 2018, when the photo of the twins popped up on his Facebook feed.

Today Kyrie and Brielle are in their 20s, and while they both lead private lives, they still get contacted by news organizations eager for an update on what they are doing. At last report, both had graduated from college and were pursuing masters' degrees. Kyrie lives in New Mexico and Brielle lives in Nevada.

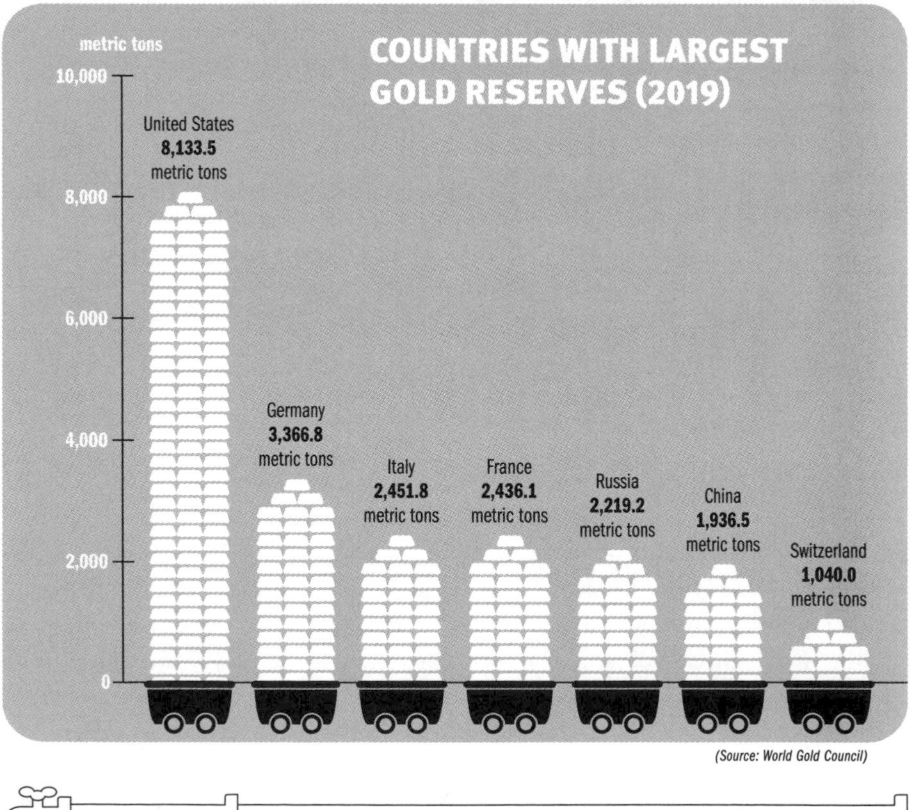

COUNTRIES WITH LARGEST GOLD RESERVES (2019)

metric tons
10,000
8,000
6,000
4,000
2,000
0

United States **8,133.5** metric tons
Germany **3,366.8** metric tons
Italy **2,451.8** metric tons
France **2,436.1** metric tons
Russia **2,219.2** metric tons
China **1,936.5** metric tons
Switzerland **1,040.0** metric tons

(Source: World Gold Council)

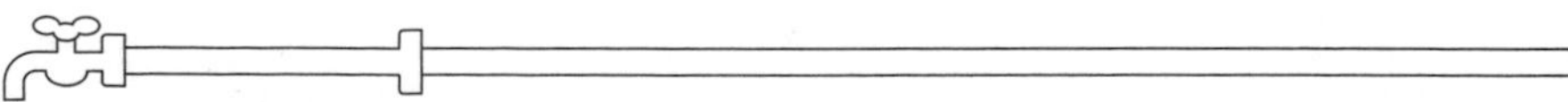

THE ORIGIN OF CHEWBACCA

A long time in ago in a decade far, far away (the 1970s), Star Wars *took the galaxy by storm. One of the biggest reasons stood about eight feet tall and had a whole lot of fur. Here's the inside story behind a beloved pop-culture icon.*

A PILLAR OF SOCIETY

"I don't think there's another *Star Wars* character that's able to spread happiness quite like Chewie," said Peter Mayhew, who played the Wookiee for nearly 40 years. "He's quite unique in that way." He may be right: According to *Guinness Book of World Records,* the most popular Facebook live video of all time—topping 160 million views—is 2016's "Chewbacca Mom," a clip of a woman who puts on a growling Chewie mask and can't stop laughing. Even a YouTube video of a can sliding across a table that *sounds like* Chewie went viral. And *Entertainment Weekly* named the Wookiee copilot the fourth-greatest sidekick of all time (behind George Costanza, Robin, and *The Tonight Show*'s Ed McMahon).

The reasons for the character's success are as varied as the people who brought him to life—from the writer who created him, to the team that designed and built him and gave him a voice, to the actor who became him. Here's how the Wookiee was put together.

THE BORROWER

After directing the 1973 sleeper hit *American Graffiti,* George Lucas wanted to make a film that re-created for modern audiences the thrill he'd had as a kid watching science-fiction films like *Flash Gordon* and *The Forbidden Planet.* To create *Star Wars,* Lucas borrowed elements not just from space movies but from Akira Kurosawa's *The Hidden Fortress,* J. R. R. Tolkien's *The Lord of the Rings,* and L. Frank Baum's *The Wonderful Wizard of Oz.* He was also inspired by real life—the Imperial troopers were Nazis, the Jedi were samurai, and Chewbacca was his dog. "I had a large dog named Indiana, an Alaskan malamute," Lucas recalled. "When he sat in the car, he was bigger than I was. That's where I said, 'That would be a fun character for *Star Wars.*' " (Lucas would use the name "Indiana" for his archaeologist in *Raiders of the Lost Ark.*)

But Lucas's original concept for the Wookiees was quite different from what ended up on-screen. The first incarnation was closer to what eventually became the Ewoks in 1983's *Return of the Jedi.* "[Wookiees] weren't technical at all, they were primitive," Lucas

explained. His shooting script ended up way too long, "so I realized I had to cut the Wookiees out of the end of the [first] movie; I decided to save one and make him the copilot. That's really how Chewbacca ended up with his starring role."

NAMING THE ALIEN

Chewbacca wasn't the only character to undergo major changes during the writing process. In early drafts of *Star Wars* (which Lucas originally called *Journal of the Whills*), Luke "Starkiller" was a 60-year-old general, and Han Solo was a green-skinned alien. There was a narrator character named Chuiee that Lucas scrapped...but he kept the name, respelled as "Chewie." Chewbacca's full name was inspired by the Russian word for "dog"–*собака*–pronounced "sobaka."

"I think I just ran over a Wookey."

Lucas already had the word "Wookiee" in his arsenal; he was just looking for the right way to use it. Back in 1970, while recording additional dialogue for Lucas's dystopian sci-fi film *THX-1138*, a radio DJ named Terry McGovern was dubbing in the voice from a police band radio, and ad-libbed the line "I think I just ran over a Wookey." (The movie featured furry, dwarflike creatures running amok.) McGovern explained to Lucas that the ad-lib was a way to "stick it" to a friend of his named Ralph Wookey: "I thought he'd get a kick out of hearing his name in a film," said McGovern.

SOOTHING THE SAVAGE BEAST

Finding the character's look and personality wasn't as simple. In 1975, about two years into writing *Star Wars*, Lucas described Chewbacca as a "barbarian prince from the jungle planet of Yavin." (His home planet was later changed to Kashyyyk, but Yavin stayed in the film as the location of the secret Rebel Base.) And this incarnation of Chewie was not intended to "spread happiness." Here's a description from an early draft of the script:

> Ben is standing next to Chewbacca, an eight-foot-tall savage-looking creature resembling a huge grey bushbaby monkey with fierce baboon-like fangs. His large blue eyes dominate a fur-covered face and soften his otherwise awesome appearance. Over his matted, furry body he wears two chrome bandoliers, and little else. He is a two-hundred-year-old Wookiee and a sight to behold.

Star Wars conceptual artist Ralph McQuarrie—who came up with such iconic imagery as Darth Vader's helmet and the two droids—was having trouble with Chewbacca's look. Drawing on the words "savage" and "bushbaby monkey," he painted a menacing gray beast with short fur, huge teeth, buggy eyes, and pointy ears. Meanwhile, Lucas was rewriting the character as more of a friendly protector for Han Solo, so he needed a creature that was a lot less scary.

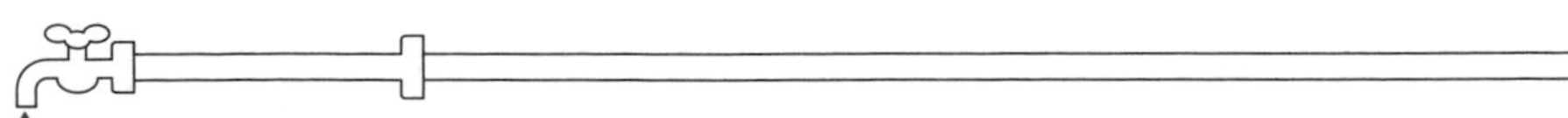

THE UNCREDITED COLLABORATOR

Then, sometime in early 1976, Lucas showed McQuarrie an image of a furry beast that looked very similar to what Chewbacca would eventually become. McQuarrie used *that* image to create the look that ended up getting approved, and is very close to the Chewbacca we know today. For years afterward, McQuarrie said in interviews that the painting Lucas had shown him was "from the 1930s," but it was actually the July 1975 cover illustration of the sci-fi magazine *Analog* for a novelette called "And Seven Times Never Kill Man" by George R. R. Martin (later of *Game of Thrones* fame). That cover was painted by legendary sci-fi artist John Schoenherr, best known for his cover of Frank Herbert's *Dune.* (One difference: Schoenherr's furry beast had six breasts.)

According to author Michael Heilemann in *Kitbashed: The Origins of Star Wars,* "It's interesting to note that Lucas rarely talks about bushbaby Chewie, perhaps because he knows that if he starts down that road, he might have to try and bridge the gap from that to the post-Schoenherr Chewie, which he can't do without admitting that it was essentially borrowed wholesale." In 2010, the year Schoenherr died, his son Ian wrote on his blog, "What troubles me—and has troubled my family and many of my father's friends in the Science Fiction world since 1977—is that [John Schoenherr] was the unwitting, uncredited, and uncompensated 'collaborator' in this creative endeavor."

SEEKING ONE GIANT

"Borrowed" or not, they'd found Chewie's look. Now Lucas had to find an actor who could play an eight-foot-tall Wookiee. According to co-star Mark Hamill (Luke Skywalker), the first actor they considered was 6' 9" Ted Cassidy, best known as Lurch on *The Addams Family.* There was a problem with Cassidy, though: He was American, and the movie was being filmed in England. As Hamill tells it, "The British government said, 'If you've got a mask on, you have to cast an English person.'" That's why every masked character in *Star Wars*—including Chewbacca, Darth Vader, C-3PO, and R2-D2—was played by an Englishman. With Cassidy out, Lucas approached British bodybuilder David Prowse, who recalled:

> When we were introduced, Lucas, who remembered me from Stanley Kubrick's seminal 1971 film *A Clockwork Orange,* offered me two roles. The first was a character called Chewbacca. I said: "What the hell is Chewbacca?" and he told me it was a hairy gorilla on the side of the good guys. Well, all I could think about was three months in a gorilla suit, so I said, "What's the other part?" And he said it was the big villain of the film, so I chose that because people always remember the bad guy.

Now they had a Darth Vader, but they still needed a Chewbacca.

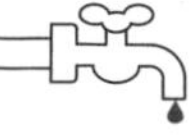

...A: 1) Alaska, 2) Alaska, 3) Alaska—because the Aleutian Islands cross the International Date Line. Hawaii is the southernmost state.

A STAND-UP GUY

Born in London in 1944, Peter Mayhew was diagnosed with gigantism when he was eight years old, but he actually suffered from Marfan syndrome, a genetic disorder that can cause sufferers to have disproportionately long arms and legs. Fearing the boy's height could eventually exceed eight feet, doctors blasted his pituitary gland with X-rays. It worked...kind of. Mayhew topped out at about 7' 3".

The soft-spoken giant studied engineering in school, but he was working as an orderly at King's College Hospital in 1975 when a reporter profiled him for a story about people with really big feet. Mayhew's photo was seen by the producers of Ray Harryhausen's *Sinbad and the Eye of the Tiger*, who hired him to play the Minoton, an 8½-foot-tall metallic minotaur. Afterward, Fox executives asked Mayhew if he'd be interested in more acting work, to which he replied, "Yes, please." But he went back to work at the hospital and didn't hear anything for nine months. Then he received a call from Fox that they were looking for "somebody big" for a new science-fiction movie being filmed near London.

Mayhew recalled that he was sitting on a couch when George Lucas and producer Gary Kurtz walked into the room to meet him: "So naturally, what do I do? I was raised in England, so as soon as someone comes in through the door, I stand up. George literally turned to Gary and said, 'I think we found him.' "

With the actor and the look in place, they had to figure out how to build a Wookiee from the ground up. Easy, right? Wrong. *Part II is on page 236.*

* * *

VOTE VERMIN!

A Massachusetts man who goes by the name Vermin Supreme has run in several state and national elections since the 1980s, most recently for president in 2020. If you think the world's weird now, imagine what it could be like if President Supreme (he always wears a boot on his head) ever got to deliver on these actual campaign promises:

- Give every American a free pony.
- Convert to a "pony-based economy."
- Legalize human meat.
- Make crime against the law.
- Harness zombie power using the latest in hamster-wheel technology.
- Mandatory dental hygiene.
- Travel back in time and kill Adolf Hitler.
- Give all sick people a bus ticket to Canada.
- Gradually dismantle the government.

During the 30 years NASA's space shuttle program was operational, it averaged about one mission every 11 weeks.

WEIRD ANIMAL NEWS

This year's menagerie of weirdness features poop that is square, dogs that are blue, and some noisy birds that have dangling, wormlike wattles.

Biting the Tongs that Feed You

An Australian snake owner named Aaron Rouse thought he'd come up with a safe new method to feed his pet python, Winston. In May 2015, Rouse picked up Winston's food in a pair of metal salad tongs and put the tongs up to the snake's mouth. Then Winston bit off more than he could chew—namely, the tongs. Rouse couldn't get the reptile to release them, and before he knew it, the tongs were nowhere to be seen...but they could be felt inside the middle of the snake. Rouse took Winston to a local university, where a veterinarian had to cut an incision into the python's belly to remove the tongs.

Little Dog Blue

Citizens and officials in Mumbai, India, became concerned in August 2017 after reports came in that bright blue dogs were running around an industrial neighborhood. Amid fears of a dangerous pollutant, an investigation was launched. The culprit turned out to be dyes released by a detergent factory. There was a wire fence around the area to keep people out, but several stray dogs had found a way in and were cooling themselves off in the blue wastewater pool. Officials reassured residents that the dyes are not harmful. Not long after, heavy rains washed the blue out of those dogs' fur.

Roll the Dice

Here's something only a scientist would say: "We opened those intestines like it was Christmas." The scientist, David Hu of Georgia Tech, was attempting to answer the age-old question: Why is wombat poop cube-shaped? Even though the anus of this Australian marsupial is as round as a human's, its pellets come out square-shaped. Why and how this occurs remained a mystery until Hu and his fellow researchers presented their findings in November 2018. The "why" part is because wombats use their pellet piles to mark territory, and cubes are less likely to roll away. The animals actually stack their poops to make the piles even higher. To figure out the "how" part, the researchers compared the intestines of pigs to wombats (that were hit by cars).

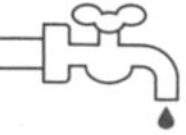

Their findings: "In wombats, the feces changed from a liquid-like state into a solid state in the last 25% of the intestines—but then in the final 8% a varied elasticity of the walls meant the poop would take shape as separated cubes." Lead researcher Patricia Yang told *Science News*, "I have never seen anything this weird in biology." She also said that the discovery may have implications beyond wombats: "We currently have only two methods to manufacture a cube: We mold it, or we cut it. Now we have this third method."

Dog Gone

It's an interesting fact about newborn mammals that they all kind of look alike, no matter what the species. It's not until they start to grow that their distinctive features begin to emerge. That may explain why a farmer in China's Yunnan province didn't realize that the two "puppies" he thought he'd purchased—to raise into watchdogs—were an entirely different species. It took him two years to figure this out. By that point the farmer had nearly gone broke trying to feed the furry beasts, which were much larger than dogs, and had developed a taste for live chickens. So what were they? Bears. The farmer finally realized this while attending a local wildlife protection exhibition that included Asian black bears. Unfortunately, because the bears had been raised by a human, they couldn't be released into the wild. But they were taken—together—to a wildlife rehabilitation center.

WHAT?

Which bird is the loudest? The white bellbird. The male of this Amazon rainforest species has a deafening mating call—recorded at 125 decibels. And he doesn't just do it from the top of a tree. He'll scream it directly into a female's face from point-blank range. That's equivalent to standing a few inches away from a speaker at a rock concert or next to a jet during takeoff. The female (which doesn't have any vocalizations herself) then decides if the male is loud and proud enough to warrant mating. According to researcher Jeff Podos of the University of Massachusetts, when the bird couples perch together, "the males sing only their loudest songs. Not only that, they swivel dramatically during these songs, so as to blast the song's final note directly at the females." The males can achieve this volume thanks to extra-strong abdominal muscles and very short bursts that don't require much air intake. The result is something that sounds otherworldly. Adding to the bird's weirdness: the males have long, wormlike wattles that dangle from their beaks. As Podos says, "They just seem alien."

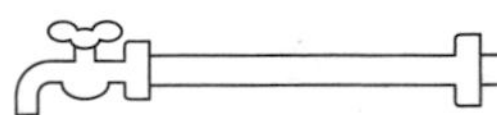

HISTORY'S TOY BOX

It seems like every year there's one hot toy that every kid in the neighborhood just has to have. Here are the most popular playthings of every year, for the past 60 years. How many of these do you remember?

1960
Etch-A-Sketch

1961
Chatty Cathy

1962
Matchbox cars

1963
Easy-Bake Oven

1964
G.I. Joe action figures

1965
Operation game

1966
Twister game

1967
Lite Brite

1968
Hot Wheels

1969
Astronaut Snoopy

1970
The first Nerf ball

1971
Weebles

1972
Big Wheel

1973
Evel Knievel Stunt Cycle

1974
Magna Doodle

1975
Pet Rock

1976
Stretch Armstrong action figures

1977–78
Star Wars action figures

1979
Atari VCS video game console

1980
Rubik's Cube

1981
Smurfs toys

1982
Masters of the Universe action figures

1983
Cabbage Patch Kids

1984
Transformers

1985
Care Bears

1986
Teddy Ruxpin talking teddy bear

1987–88
Nintendo Entertainment System

1989
Nintendo Game Boy

1990
Teenage Mutant Ninja Turtles action figures

1991
Super Nintendo Entertainment System

1992
Troll dolls

1993
Talkboy personal tape recorder

1994
Mighty Morphin Power Rangers action figures

1995
Pogs

1996
Tickle Me Elmo doll

1997
Tamagotchi (an electronic "virtual pet")

1998
Furby dolls

1999
Pokémon cards

2000
Razor scooters

2001
Bratz dolls

2002
Rapunzel Barbie

2003
Electronic Hulk Hands

2004
Robosapien robot

2005
Webkinz dolls

2006
Nintendo Wii video game console

2007
Nintendo DS handheld video game

2008
Bakugan Battle Brawlers (plastic marbles with tiny figures inside)

2009
ZhuZhu Pets (robotic hamsters)

2010
Zoobies

2011
Let's Rock Elmo doll

2012
Nintendo Wii U video game console

2013
Big Hugs Elmo doll

2014
Elsa from *Frozen* doll

2015
BB-8 robotic toy from *Star Wars*

2016
Hatchimals dolls

2017
Sony PlayStation 4 video game console

2018
WowWee Pinkfong Baby Shark Official Song Puppet

* * *

"If Barbie is so popular, why do you have to buy her friends?" –**Steven Wright**

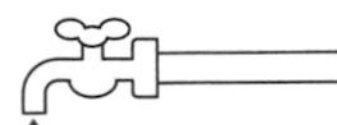

RANDOM ORIGINS

Once again, the BRI asks—and answers—the question: Where does all this stuff come from?

RED DELICIOUS APPLES

In the early 1870s, Jesse Hiatt noticed a different kind of apple tree growing on his Iowa farm—probably a hybrid of two other varieties. Since he knew he hadn't planted this seedling, he decided to cut it down. But it grew back...and again he cut it down. Eventually, he figured that such a persistent plant deserved a shot at life, so he let it grow. Good move. He called it the Hawkeye apple, and in 1894 introduced it to the marketplace by winning a competition held by the Stark Brothers Nursery. The original Hawkeye had red and yellow stripes, and was so sweet that company president C. M. Stark declared it the best apple he'd ever tasted. Stark bought the rights to the Hawkeye from Hiatt, and in 1914, he renamed it the Red Delicious because after 40 years of growth, the red stripes completely dominated the yellow (and it *was* delicious). By the 1950s, Red Delicious apples—which have both the color and the shape that one thinks of when they think of an apple—represented 90 percent of all apples grown in the United States.

DOG BONES

Until the 1860s, dogs ate whatever they could scrounge or whatever table scraps their masters gave them. And before they ate dog food—canned or kibble—they ate dog biscuits, the first commercially available dog food. On a trip to London in 1860 to sell lightning rods, an electrician from Ohio named James Spratt witnessed a pack of stray dogs near the docks eating what a sailor had thrown to them: leftover hardtack—dry, crunchy biscuits that last forever and were standard sailor fare because hardtack can last for months at sea. That gave Spratt the idea to come up with a hardtack-style biscuit specially formulated for ideal dog nutrition. Later that year, he created Spratt's Patent Meat Fibrine Dog Cakes, made from grains, vegetables, and dried beef gelatin. They were too expensive for most dog owners—a 50-pound bag cost about what the average blue-collar worker made in a day—so Spratt focused on sales to wealthy English landowners. (An early ad for the biscuits boasted a testimonial from a wealthy baron who claimed that his greyhound, Royal Mary, won all her races because of a diet consisting solely of Spratt's Dog Cakes.) By the turn of the century, Spratt's Dog Cakes were available (and popular) in the United States. But amazingly, in all this time, nobody had thought to make dog food in the shape of something that would appeal to dogs: bones. Carleton Ellis (inventor of paint remover, polyester, and margarine) introduced that innovation in 1907, along with adding surplus milk he'd purchased cheaply from a local slaughterhouse. Ellis sold the rights to his idea to the

Democratic California congressman Raul Ruiz's competitor in the 2020 election: a Republican named... Raul Ruiz. (The Republican Ruiz later dropped out after suffering two heart attacks in one month.)

F. H. Bennett Biscuit Company, which launched Milk-Bones in 1908. They remained nutritional until after World War II, when the Milk-Bone became a dog treat, loaded with extra fat and calories.

HOLD MUSIC

Have you ever been stuck on hold waiting to talk to customer service ("your call is very important to us") and found yourself humming along to the smooth jazz or soft rock that plays while you wait? Music on hold is everywhere today, but its creation was a complete accident. In 1962, a factory owner named Alfred Levy was trying to figure out why the quality of phone calls in and out of his building was subpar, and why some were even getting dropped. He discovered that the line was damaged, and that a loose wire was touching the steel frame of the office building next door. That metal-on-metal contact was turning the entire office building into a giant radio receiver. Whenever callers were placed on hold, the music from a local radio station (amplified by a random radio playing in somebody's office) would appear. Levy realized that this was all a pretty great idea, and in 1966, he patented music on hold, ensuring the proliferation of low-fi easy-listening music for generations to come.

REFEREE SHIRTS

In the early 1900s—football's early years—referees typically wore white dress shirts, often accompanied with a bow tie. Reason: a well-dressed man was immediately understood to be someone with authority, especially among a field of guys in mud-covered athletic wear. The problem was that football players' uniforms were also often white. At a game in Arizona in 1920, a white-uniformed quarterback passed the ball off to referee Lloyd Olds, mistaking him for one of the running backs. Olds realized this scenario was likely to happen more and more as football's popularity grew, so he asked George Moe, a friend who ran a sporting goods store, to make him a shirt that was easily seen, but wouldn't look like any team's uniform. Olds wore Moe's design—a black-and-white-striped shirt—in 1921. The crowd booed Olds (since they could better see the ref, it was easier to boo him), but he continued to wear the shirt, and soon the idea spread to other referees.

CHIROPRACTIC MEDICINE

A man named D. D. Palmer is regarded as the "father of chiropractic medicine." In the late 19th century, he devised the principles that still guide the alternative medical practice of back-cracking today, but he claimed he wasn't the inventor. He said he "received chiropractic" from Dr. Jim Atkinson, whom he met at the Mississippi Valley Spiritualists Camp in the late 1800s...at a séance. Palmer claimed he learned everything he knew from the *spirit* of Dr. Atkinson, who had died 50 years earlier.

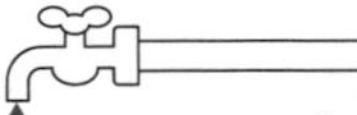

In ancient Egypt, mummified cats were buried with mummified mice, so they'd have something to play with.

JUDGE NOT...

Just because judges are supposed *to hold themselves to a higher standard doesn't mean they're always up for it. Here are a few who fell short of the mark.*

FAMILY COURT

Defendant: Tommy D. Phillips II, a Dunkirk, Indiana, City Court judge

Case: In August 2016, Judge Phillips was meeting with Dunkirk Police Chief Dane Mumbower (who also happens to be his nephew) to "discuss several issues of conflict between the police department and the city court," according to a sheriff's report. When the meeting turned heated, the judge lunged at his nephew and shoved him, "knocking (Mumbower) back into the wall and causing him pain and discomfort and knocking him off balance." Witnesses outside the room reported hearing "a large amount of shouting...and banging noises" coming from the room.

Outcome: Judge Phillips was charged with felony battery against a public safety official, which could have landed him in prison for up to 30 months. The Indiana Supreme Court suspended him from the bench pending resolution of the charges. Later, in a deal with prosecutors, Phillips resigned his judgeship, pled guilty to a single misdemeanor charge, and was given a one-year suspended sentence plus 100 hours of community service. While on probation, he was not allowed to have any contact with his nephew, the police chief. (He was also banned from the bench for life, but he got to keep his other job: teaching middle school.)

NO DEPOSIT, NO RETURN

Defendant: Timothy M. Dougherty, a Pennsylvania District Court judge

Case: One of the district court's responsibilities is tallying up the fines, restitution, court costs, and other payments made to the court, and depositing them in the bank at the end of each day. Judge Dougherty took it upon himself to make the daily deposits personally, or at least he *said* he was making the deposits. But when discrepancies were found in the court's bank account in 2016, a forensic audit led to Dougherty being charged with stealing more than $15,000. (Dougherty was also the treasurer of the Wyomissing Volunteer Fire Company; an investigation into their finances found that he had stolen more than $97,000 from them as well.) When asked what he did with all the money, Dougherty answered that he spent it on "life," but not on anything "exciting" like "drugs or prostitutes."

Outcome: In May 2016, Dougherty was charged with nine felony counts relating to the thefts. He resigned from the bench, forfeited his pension, and in a deal with prosecutors, pled guilty to two felony counts. He was sentenced to 6 to 23 months in prison, plus five years' probation.

HIGH COURT

Defendant: Hillary H. Green, a Harris County, Texas, justice of the peace from 2007 to 2018

Case: If you think your love life is bad, consider Judge Green's. Both her ex-husband and her ex-boyfriend accused her of illegal conduct and conduct unbecoming a judge, including using marijuana, ecstasy, and cocaine; abusing prescription drugs; exchanging sexually explicit texts with a bailiff from the bench; buying drugs from the same bailiff; and hiring call girls with her boyfriend so that they could engage in "three-ways." (As justice of the peace, Green oversaw low-level drug possession cases involving minors in her court.)

Outcome: Judge Green admitted to the State Commission on Judicial Conduct that she had smoked marijuana, taken ecstasy, abused prescription cough medicine, sexted with the bailiff, and bought prescription cough syrup from him, but she denied using cocaine or hiring prostitutes with her ex-boyfriend. She also contended that most of the allegations were "exaggerated, untrue, or stem from bitter ex-lovers." But she admitted to enough misconduct for the Texas Supreme Court to suspend her without pay in July 2017, pending a trial to remove her from the bench permanently. Harris resigned from the bench in March 2018, about a month before the trial was set to begin, citing "family issues." Her attorney told the *Houston Chronicle* that her resignation was "totally unrelated to the charges which she continues to deny and contest."

COURT FIGHT

Defendants: Clark County, Indiana, judges Andrew Adams and Bradley Jacobs; and Crawford County judge Sabrina R. Bell

Case: In April 2019, the three judges were at a hotel in Indianapolis the night before a judicial conference. They began drinking at the hotel, and then at 12:30 a.m., adjourned to a local bar, where they continued drinking until 3:00 a.m. Thoroughly sloshed, they next went to a nearby strip club, but it was closed, so they walked to a White Castle to get something to eat. The three judges were standing in the parking lot when two men, Brandon Kaiser and Alfredo Vasquez, drove past in an SUV and shouted something inappropriate at Judge Bell. She responded by giving the men the finger. Kaiser and Vasquez parked their vehicle and engaged in a verbal confrontation

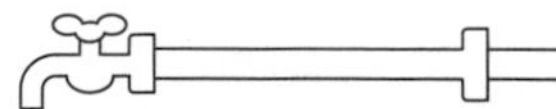

There's a full-size replica of the Greek Parthenon in Nashville, Tennessee. (It's an art museum.)

with the three judges that soon turned physical, ending only when Kaiser pulled out a gun and shot Judge Adams once in the stomach and Judge Jacobs twice in the chest. He and Vasquez fled but were later apprehended. Judge Adams and Judge Jacobs survived the shooting.

Outcome: Kaiser was charged with 14 crimes—including eight felonies—and was scheduled to go to trial in January 2020. Alfredo Vasquez was sentenced to 180 days of home detention plus 12 months' probation for misdemeanor battery and for violating his probation.

Judge Adams was charged with six counts of felony battery and one count of disorderly conduct for his part in the fight, but no criminal charges were filed against Judges Jacobs or Bell. In September 2019, Judge Adams pled guilty to a single misdemeanor count of battery and was given a suspended sentence of one year in jail.

Criminal charges are one thing; conduct unbecoming a judge is another. The Indiana Supreme Court found all three judges guilty of judicial misconduct "by appearing in public in an intoxicated state and behaving in an injudicious manner" that "gravely undermined public trust in the dignity and decency of the entire Indiana judiciary." The court suspended Adams without pay for 60 days, and suspended Judges Jacobs and Bell without pay for 30 days.

TRAFFIC COURT

Defendant: William Pearson, a judge on Arkansas' 5th Judicial District Circuit Court

Case: One evening in January 2017, Judge Pearson was driving down State Highway 109 near Clarksville when he came upon a sobriety checkpoint. Rather than stop, he blew through the checkpoint—narrowly missing three police officers as he did—and then led police on a chase that ended when he was blocked by a police car and could go no further. When pulled from his vehicle, he was unable to stand; when asked how much he'd had to drink, he slurred, "None of your business."

Outcome: Pearson was arrested on charges of drunk driving, refusal to submit to a sobriety test, reckless driving, and fleeing the police, which is a felony. He pled guilty to misdemeanor drunk driving and reckless driving and received a six-month suspended sentence, plus five days in jail. He was also ordered to pay $1,020 in fines and court costs, plus $1,829.24 in restitution for the damage to the police car that pulled him over. After a brief suspension, he returned to the bench. "I make no excuses for my actions," he said in a prepared statement. "I simply should have known better not to drink and drive intoxicated. The shame and embarrassment is mine."

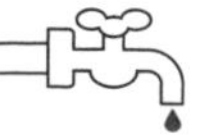

LIFE IN 1933

In honor of this, the 33rd annual edition of Uncle John's Bathroom Reader, *here's a look back to what daily life was like in 1933. (The Great Depression was underway, so you probably wouldn't have purchased anything as extravagant as a trivia book.)*

IN THE KITCHEN

- A five-pound bag of apples: **19¢**
- A one-pound slab of bacon: **13¢** (Want it sliced? That cost about **30¢**.)
- A loaf of sliced bread (a product introduced just two years earlier): **8¢**
- A dozen eggs: **15¢**
- A pound of brown sugar: **5¢**
- A bunch of carrots: **7¢**
- A pound of potatoes: **1¢**
- A one-pound package of peanut brittle: **15¢**
- A can of corn: **3¢**
- A five-pound bag of cornmeal: **10¢**
- A 25-pound bag of Gold Medal Flour: **65¢**
- A one-pound package of frankfurters (hot dogs): **10¢**
- 10 pounds of dried navy beans: **24¢**
- A 10-pound bag of sugar: **47¢**
- A pound of ground beef: **15¢**
- A one-pound can of 8 O'Clock Coffee (grocery chain A&P's store brand): **19¢**
- A packet of Jell-O: **7¢**
- A box of Kellogg's Bran Flakes: **10¢**
- A can of evaporated milk: **8¢**
- A bag of six grapefruits: **25¢**
- A pound of butter: **24¢**
- A pound of oleo, a butter substitute: **10¢**
- When Prohibition was repealed in late 1933, a quart of beer cost about **50¢**

HOME GOODS

- A pair of galoshes: **$1.69**
- Light bulbs: **3 for 25¢**
- A sewing machine: **$23.95**
- An electric iron: **$8.95**
- An electric percolator: **$3.50**
- A compact radio ("compact" meant it could sit on a table, rather than on the floor): **$69.50**
- A new refrigerator: **$99.50**
- A flannel nightgown: **75¢**
- A first-class postage stamp: **3¢**
- A 20-pill bottle of Ju-Van Diet Pills (amphetamines): **$1.00**
- A pint-sized bottle of cod liver oil, an all-purpose (and foul-tasting) medicine: **44¢**

In 2014, a bit of white noise from a Taylor Swift album was downloaded so much it topped the Canadian music chart.

ON THE ROAD

- A used 1923 Ford Model-T car: about **$275**
- A brand-new car, on average: **$605**
- A gallon of gas to put in either car: **15¢**
- Firestone tire: **$4.05**

SALARIES

- Average weekly salary for a factory worker: **$17**
- Average weekly salary for a doctor: **$61**

BOOKS

- The best-selling titles of the year were *Anthony Adverse* by Hervey Allen, *As the Earth Turns* by Gladys Hasty Carroll, and *Ann Vickers* by Sinclair Lewis.

RADIO

- *The Lone Ranger* begins its 21-year run, and *The Romance of Helen Trent* starts its 27-year run.

MUSIC

- Elsewhere on the dial, listeners would have heard the biggest hits of the year: Ethel Waters's "Stormy Weather," Duke Ellington's "Sophisticated Lady," and Bing Crosby's "Shadow Waltz."

MOVIES

- Some of the biggest box office hits include the original *King Kong*, the musical *42nd Street*, and the Academy Award winner for Best Picture, *Cavalcade*.

SPORTS

- Babe Ruth hits the first home run in the first MLB All-Star game, the New York Giants win their fourth World Series title (over the Washington Senators), Primo Carnera knocks out Jack Sharkey in the sixth round to be named heavyweight boxing champion of the world, and Broker's Tip wins the Kentucky Derby.

VITALS

- Life expectancy of an average American was 61.7 years for men and 65.1 for women. The population of the United States (which comprised 48 states at the time) was 125.6 million.

BANNED ALBUM COVERS

Before streaming services, CDs, and mp3s, most people bought music on long-playing record albums (or what we call "vinyl" today). And before you listened to an album, you got to look at the cover art—an important marketing tool that reflects the music inside...if it wasn't so offensive that it was rejected by the record label first.

Artist: The Beatles
Album: *Yesterday and Today* (1966)

Details: This album isn't really an album—it's a compilation of songs that Capitol Records didn't include on the North American releases of *Rubber Soul* and *Revolver,* along with some other tracks. When the label asked the Beatles to submit some ideas for the cover, they sent in a picture of the group taken earlier that year as part of a planned triptych called *A Somnambulant Adventure,* by photographer Robert Whitaker. The photo depicted the Beatles, all grinning widely and wearing butcher smocks, covered in raw meat and dismembered parts of baby dolls. The image unnerved Capitol Records executives, but Paul McCartney said the picture of butchered kids was the band's comment on the Vietnam War. Capitol had to let a band as powerful (and lucrative) as the Beatles have their way and reportedly printed 750,000 copies of the "butcher cover" before its June 15, 1966, release date. They sent out advance copies to record stores...most of which refused to stock an album with such a gruesome cover. And so, on June 14, just one day before the LP's on-sale date, Capitol Records enacted "Operation Retrieve" and recalled the covers. It reissued *Yesterday and Today* in a sleeve featuring a generic shot of the band sitting around a steamer trunk. Some of the records were put into totally new sleeves while others had the new cover pasted over the butcher cover, which plenty of Beatlemaniacs peeled off to reveal the original beneath. Still, a few intact "first state" covers got out. In mint condition, one can be worth as much as $125,000 today.

Artist: Lynyrd Skynyrd
Album: *Street Survivors* (1977)

Details: The Southern rock band that gave the world "Free Bird" embarked on its "Tour of the Survivors" on October 13, 1977, to promote its album *Street Survivors,* set for release on October 17. After the fifth concert of the tour, in Greenville, South Carolina, the band chartered a small plane to fly to its next stop, Baton Rouge, Louisiana. Two-thirds of the way through the flight, the plane ran out of

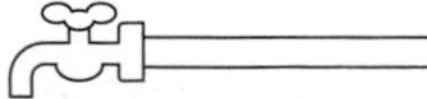

fuel. The pilots attempted an emergency landing on a small airstrip in Mississippi but overshot the runway, and crashed into a forest. Upon impact, both pilots died, as did lead singer Ronnie Van Zant, guitarist Steve Gaines, backup singer Cassie Gaines, and assistant road manager Dean Kilpatrick. At the band's request, their record label, MCA Records, pulled *Street Survivors* from stores. Reason: the cover art was just too ghoulish—it featured a portrait of the band, surrounded by flames. The record was re-released, but with a different cover—a different picture from the same photo shoot...and without the flames.

Artist: The Rolling Stones
Album: *Beggars Banquet* (1968)

Details: The Stones frequently seemed to be pushing the envelope in the 1960s with controversial songs like "Satisfaction," "Sympathy for the Devil," and "Let's Spend the Night Together." In 1968, they went too far as far as their label, Decca Records, was concerned. For their album *Beggars Banquet,* they hired graphic designer Tom Wilkes to make a cover out of a picture by photographer Barry Feinstein. Decca rejected it. Reason: the photo was of a graffiti-strewn bathroom, and company execs thought it was tasteless, bordering on scandalous. Decca and the Stones argued for months, delaying the release of the album, before finally settling on a cover that was almost the opposite of the "toilet" design—a plain off-white sleeve that looked like an elegant invitation, with the words "Rolling Stones," "*Beggars Banquet,*" and "R.S.V.P." written in formal script.

Company execs thought it was tasteless, bordering on scandalous.

Artist: Guns N' Roses
Album: *Appetite for Destruction* (1987)

Details: Guns N' Roses' debut album, *Appetite for Destruction,* sold 18 million copies, the most ever for a first LP. The cover art became so familiar that the band adopted it as its official logo: a Celtic cross adorned with five skulls, each representing a different band member. It all worked out for GNR, but only after they were forced to abandon their initial cover idea. The group wanted to license the 1978 painting by artist Robert Williams that gave the record its name—*Appetite for Destruction.* It depicts a robot (with a bear trap for a head) standing next to a distressed semi-nude woman lying on the street. The robot appears to have assaulted the woman, but it's about to get what's coming to it courtesy of the giant alien beast soaring through the sky above, as it shoots off bloody skulls. It's pretty extreme, and even Williams saw trouble, urging the band to look through his portfolio to choose a less offensive image. But Guns N' Roses was adamant...until several chain stores advised Geffen Records that they wouldn't carry the album as is. Artist Billy White Jr. quickly came up with the cross/skulls concept, and Williams's painting was moved to the inside cover.

Artist: Bon Jovi
Album: *Slippery When Wet* (1986)

Details: The hair metal band got the name for this album from a Vancouver strip club they frequented. It featured dancers showering on stage, with a sign nearby to warn strippers and guests that the floor was "slippery when wet." For an album cover to match the title, the band selected a photo of a young female model wearing a torn, wet T-shirt emblazoned with the words "Slippery When Wet." There's no nudity, but the photo is pretty sexy, so Mercury Records refused to allow the album to ship to stores, fearing that major retail chains would balk at the suggestive cover art. Just weeks before the album's release date, the band approved a new cover: a wet plastic garbage bag with the words "Slippery When Wet" traced into the moisture.

Artist: Roxy Music
Album: *Country Life* (1974)

Details: England's Roxy Music was among the most successful "art rock" bands of the 1970s, adding synthesizers, oboes, and violins to the usual rock lineup of guitars and drums (along with the crooning vocals of lead singer Bryan Ferry). In 1974, the band released its fourth album, *Country Life,* full of songs about romance and lust written by Ferry. While writing lyrics in Portugal, Ferry went out to a bar one night and met two Roxy Music fans from Germany, Constanze Karoli and Eveline Grunwald. He talked them into posing for the *Country Life* cover (named after an English lifestyle magazine), and photographer Eric Boman captured the sexual nature of the songs by snapping them wearing skimpy, transparent lingerie while standing in front of a bush. The band's American label, Atco, refused to print the cover on the grounds that it was too explicit. The album hit stores in the United States with a different cover—the models were excised from the picture, leaving a photograph of just a bush.

* * *

"Map out your future, but do it in pencil." —**Jon Bon Jovi**

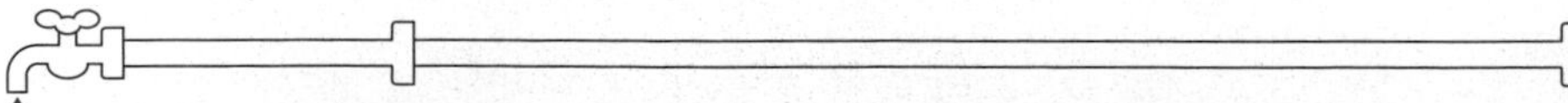

WHAT'S FOR BREAKFAST?

Millions of North Americans start their day with pancakes, cereal, or bacon and eggs. Here are some traditional breakfasts in other countries.

Silog *(The Philippines)*
Garlic fried rice served with eggs and some kind of meat, such as sausage, cured beef, or milkfish

Idli sambar *(Southern India)*
Balls made from fermented rice and lentils, simmered in lentil stew

Uttapam *(Central India)*
A thick rice and lentil pancake topped with vegetables and chutney

Asagohan *(Japan)*
Steamed rice, miso soup, and pickled vegetables

Kaya toast *(Singapore)*
Toast topped with coconut jam and a soft-boiled egg

Banitsa *(Bulgaria)*
A layered pastry of eggs and cheese between filo sheets, then baked, served with yogurt

Katogo *(Uganda)*
Peeled green bananas cooked in a stew made up of beef, nut paste, and organ meat

Laverbread *(Wales)*
Bread made out of oatmeal and boiled seaweed paste, often fried with bacon and cockles

Tartines *(France)*
Bread, either a sweet one like brioche, or a baguette, served with butter and jam

Arepas *(Colombia)*
Cornmeal cakes topped with cheese, meat, or eggs

Ackee *(Jamaica)*
A fruit that takes on a scrambled egg-like texture when cooked, and it's traditionally served with cured fish and a stewed green called callaloo

Loco moco *(Hawaii)*
A hamburger patty (or a slab of Spam) and eggs served over rice and topped with brown gravy

Menemen *(Turkey)*
A casserole-like dish made of eggs, tomatoes, green peppers, olive oil, and feta cheese

Kasha *(Russia)*
Buckwheat porridge

Muesli *(Switzerland)*
Raw rolled oats mixed with other grains, fruit, seeds, nuts, and served with yogurt

Htamin jaw *(Myanmar)*
Fried rice and boiled peas

In 1908, the Russian team was 12 days late to the London Olympics because they were still using the Julian calendar.

Shakshuska *(Israel)*
Eggs poached in a chunky tomato-and-pepper sauce

Ampesi *(Ghana)*
A stew made from fish, boiled yams, plantains, cassava, and spinach gravy

Buber ayam *(Indonesia)*
Congee topped with shredded chicken, eggs, breadsticks, and soybeans

Bake and saltfish *(Guyana)*
Fried bread dough and salt-preserved whitefish, respectively

Lablabi *(Tunisia)*
A garlic, cumin, and chickpea soup served atop crusty bread

Kanapki *(Poland)*
An open-faced sandwich of buttered bread topped with eggs or slices of meat

Youtiao *(Mainland China)*
Deep-fried breadsticks, often served with congee (rice pudding)

Gallo pinto *(Costa Rica)*
Rice, beans, and mixed vegetables topped with eggs and served with a caramelized plantain

Full English breakfast *(England)*
A skillet-fried feast of bacon, sausage, eggs, black pudding, baked beans, tomatoes, and mushrooms, also called a "fry up"

Brekkie *(Australia)*
A fry up

Pão de Queijo *(Brazil)*
It translates to "bread cheese" – baked cheesy bread balls

Porridge *(New Zealand)*
Porridge

GOING BACK FOR SECONDS

In J. R. R. Tolkien's *The Hobbit*, the titular creatures are so food-obsessed that they eat many more than three meals a day, including something called "second breakfast." That's a real thing. It's a traditional part of the culture in parts of Germany and Austria. In Germany, it's known as *zweites frühstück* (literally "second breakfast"), but in the region of Bavaria, it's called *brotzeit* ("bread time"), and in Austria, *gabelfrühstück* ("breakfast with a fork"). First breakfast is eaten early, but then second breakfast occurs between 10:00 and 11:00 a.m. In some cities, it's customary to just have a pastry, while in others—particularly in Munich—the traditional foods are pretzels, a soft sausage called *weisswurst*, and beer.

The name Jessica was invented by Shakespeare. It makes its first appearance in *The Merchant of Venice*.

FOR ONE NIGHT ONLY!

Plenty of weird concepts make it to the Broadway stage, like singing cats or a rapping Alexander Hamilton. Those odd ideas became long-running smash hits. These are not those. These Broadway shows lasted for just one performance.

Idol: The Musical (2007)

Story: At the peak of the popularity of Fox TV's *American Idol,* producer and writer Todd Ellis staged this musical, making fun of the show and its tens of millions of fans. The musical's press release labeled *Idol* devotees an "outrageous and delusional fan base," thus alienating a huge potential audience before the show even debuted. But the show wasn't really about *American Idol* at all. It takes place in a town in Ohio, where nine high school seniors—including a piano prodigy, a wannabe exotic dancer, and a goth voodoo practitioner—all belong to the same obsessive fan club devoted to former *American Idol* contestant Clay Aiken. (Songs include "Quakin' for Aiken" and "Burnin' Hunk of Clay.") When Aiken announces he'll be touring through the town, they all strive to win a contest to be the singer's opening act, which, it is later revealed, was just a hoax. Nine days before the scheduled opening on August 12, 2007, organizers announced that they'd replaced the entire cast. Despite having less than two weeks to get their act together, the new cast pulled off the opening night performance...which turned out to be the show's final performance, too.

Review: "The canned music, tinfoil set, and garish lighting were just three more elements working against this sinking ship." —*CurtainUp*

Cleavage (1982)

Story: When a troupe called the Sheffield Ensemble Theatre presented this musical in Biloxi, Mississippi, in 1979, *Cleavage* was embraced as a provocative, envelope-pushing hit. It consisted of vignettes about people of several different ages falling in love and exploring their sexual identities. (Songs included "Living in Sin," a drag number called "Boys Will Be Girls," and a lengthy comic sequence about same-sex relations in the Marines.) It caused such a sensation that backers brought the show to Broadway for a debut in 1982. One problem: what was seen as wild and progressive in Mississippi was ho-hum in the more libertine New York City. It played to a half-empty Playhouse Theatre on its first and only night. (Writers Buddy and David Sheffield lived to work again—the former became the head writer on the sketch comedy show *In Living Color* and the latter cowrote the Eddie Murphy comedy *Coming to America.*)

What do bells, boots, bones, and balls have in common?
They're all McDonald's Chicken McNugget shapes.

 *Dance a Little Closer* (1983)

Story: In 1936, Robert E. Sherwood won a Pulitzer Prize for *Idiot's Delight,* a play about a group of strangers trapped in a hotel as a world war breaks out. That was the basis for the musical *Dance a Little Closer,* adapted by Alan Jay Lerner, whose previous credits included *Camelot* and *My Fair Lady,* and songwriter Charles Strouse, whose previous credits included *Bye Bye Birdie* and *Annie.* With a team like that, what could go wrong? Plenty. Lerner and Strouse updated the story to be set on the eve of nuclear annihilation, with a cast of characters that included a pair of American singers who once dated, and a diplomat who was obviously based on Henry Kissinger. Critics thought the show didn't quite know what it wanted to be—it was a little bit anti-war satire, but also a romantic comedy, and a political thriller. Audiences didn't like it either—it closed after one night. It's the last work Lerner ever finished.

IN THE KNOW

Not on this list: Broadway musical comedy *Carnival in Flanders,* which closed in 1953 after six performances. Critics panned almost everything about the show...except the actress Dolores Gray, who won the Tony Award for Best Performance by a Leading Actress in a Musical. That makes *Carnival in Flanders* the shortest-running Broadway show to win a major Tony.

Review: "A huge, extravagant mishmash that seems to have taken on a rampaging, self-destructive life of its own." —*New York Times*

 *Infidel Caesar* (1962)

Story: Most if not all Broadway shows stage anywhere from a few to dozens of "previews." These don't count toward an official performance count because the production is still considered a work in progress, with the writer, director, actors, and designers still tinkering with various elements, based on audience reaction, until they lock everything in for the show's true opening night. Theater critics aren't even allowed to publish their reviews of a preview. Even shows that only last through their opening nights go through weeks of preview performances to get things right (apparently to no avail). But *Infidel Caesar* holds the dubious record of shortest time ever on Broadway: It never made it to its real opening night, lasting for just one preview performance. The play is a reworking of William Shakespeare's *Julius Caesar,* set in early 1960s Cuba during the Fidel Castro regime. Caesar becomes Castro, Marc Antony becomes his brother and top advisor Raúl Castro. Almost all of Shakespeare's dialogue is left intact, although the American-born actors labored through it with thick, overdone Spanish accents.

Review: "It ranks with the most pretentious and ludicrous productions ever to insult the intelligence of New York theater-goers." —*Columbia Spectator*

MYTH-CONCEPTIONS

"Common knowledge" is frequently wrong. Here are some examples of things that many people believe...but, according to our sources, just aren't true.

MYTH: When the Great Depression began with the stock market crash of October 1929, dozens of broke investors jumped to their deaths from Wall Street skyscrapers.
TRUTH: On the day of the plunge, a visiting German scientist *fell* out of a 16th-floor window of the Savoy Plaza Hotel near Central Park, and it was reported along with all the other bad financial news. The two events became so linked in the public consciousness that an often-seen protest sign following the Great Recession of 2007 read "Jump, you [censored]."

MYTH: Your stomach rumbles because you're hungry.
TRUTH: Known medically as *borborygmi*, those noises aren't coming from your stomach, nor do they necessarily indicate hunger. Your small and large intestines are hollow groupings of muscles that expand and contract to move the food along *after* it has left your stomach—which is much higher than you might realize, just below your nipples. (Bet you just looked down.) The rumbling comes from intestinal muscles contorting and squeezing secreted fluids and swallowed air. The acoustics depend on the ratio of solids, fluids, and gases.

MYTH: The first American gold rush started when gold was discovered in California in 1849.
TRUTH: Fifty years earlier, in 1799, a 12-year-old boy found a 17-pound gold nugget in Cabarrus County, North Carolina. Within a year, more than 30,000 prospectors had flooded the state.

MYTH: Saying "God bless you" after a sneeze is a throwback to the days when people feared that the soul could escape in the sneeze.
TRUTH: They were actually afraid of catching the plague, which ravaged Europe in the sixth century. There was no effective medical treatment, so Catholics heeded Pope Gregory's order to say a prayer of "God bless you" after someone sneezed to keep the plague in check.

MYTH: Buddha was overweight.
TRUTH: The spiritual icon who became known as the Buddha was born Siddhartha Gautama, and lived in India in the fifth and fourth centuries BC. He was not fat—he was thin for most of his life. Somewhere along the way, he became mixed up with a

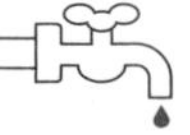

10th-century Chinese folk hero and Buddhist leader named Budai. It's Budai—not Siddhartha—who is depicted in all those chubby Buddha statues.

MYTH: Ernest Hemingway, known for his straightforward prose, made a bet that he could write a short story consisting of just six words. He won: "For sale. Baby shoes. Never worn."
TRUTH: Various versions of this anecdote have been bandied about since a 1910 *Spokane Press* article was headlined "Tragedy of Baby's Death is Revealed in Sale of Clothes." The first writer to attach it to Hemingway (known for *The Sun Also Rises* and *The Old Man and the Sea*) was sci-fi author Arthur C. Clarke in 1992. The myth was solidified four years later when John deGroot included it in his one-man play about Hemingway called *Papa.* deGroot defended his portrayal but did admit, "Whether these things actually happened is something we'll never know truly."

MYTH: Yellow underarm stains in clothes are caused by sweat.
TRUTH: Most antiperspirants contain aluminum—the active ingredient that covers up body odor. When aluminum reacts chemically to the proteins in sweat, it turns the sweat yellow...along with your shirt.

MYTH: Jesus Christ was a carpenter.
TRUTH: The Gospels are the part of the New Testament that tell the story of Jesus's life. Originally written in Greek, when the text was translated to other languages, the word for "home builder" was mistranslated as "carpenter." In Jesus's homeland of Judea, buildings were constructed almost entirely of stone, so it's far more likely that he was a stonemason.

MYTH: Black Friday, the day after Thanksgiving, is so named because the high volume of Christmas shopping puts so many stores into profitable territory for the year, or "in the black."
TRUTH: Philadelphia police started calling it Black Friday in the late 1950s because the annual Army–Navy college football game was held there, which meant they'd have to work overtime and deal with the thousands of rabid sports fans in addition to throngs of suburban Christmas shoppers invading the city for the holiday weekend.

MYTH: The rainforests are the "lungs of the Earth," providing most of its breathable oxygen.
TRUTH: About 50 percent of the planet's oxygen supply is generated by phytoplankton, one-celled organisms that live on the ocean floor.

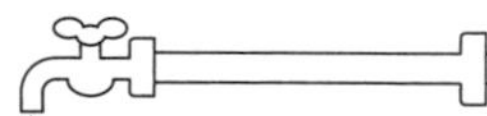

Spit take: Dairy cows produce five times more saliva each day than they do milk.

POP ART? TRY *POT* ART

Here's a look at two famous pieces of art that not only draw inspiration from plumbing fixtures, they actually were *plumbing fixtures.*

FOUNTAIN (1917)

What It Is: A urinal—northing more, nothing less—signed by the artist

Artist: Marcel Duchamp

Background: As an obscure young French artist in the early 1900s, Duchamp grew to reject art that only aimed to please the eye—something he called "retinal art"—in favor of art whose purpose was to stimulate the mind. One way he did this was by developing the concept of "ready-made" art created from found objects. When an artist selected an ordinary object and reoriented it, named it, and signed it, he argued that the ordinary object became art.

Duchamp chose his objects not because they were remarkably beautiful or even ugly, but because they gave him a feeling of indifference. His ready-made pieces included a snow shovel (which he titled *In Advance of the Broken Arm*), a dog-grooming comb (*Comb*), and a coat rack (*Trap*). These pieces challenged the notion of what is art, both among his contemporaries and among the general public. Whether people agreed or disagreed with this idea—and they still argue about it today—Duchamp achieved his goal of getting people to think about art.

Objet d'Art: His most famous ready-made was *Fountain*, made from a urinal he purchased at a plumbing supply house. Duchamp chose it, he later explained, because it was an object "that had the least chance of being liked. A urinal—very few people think there is anything wonderful about a urinal." Duchamp reoriented the urinal 90 degrees, so that the side that mounted vertically on the wall was now horizontal and facing the floor. He signed it "R. Mutt 1917," and other than that, did not alter it physically at all. It was, and remained, an ordinary urinal.

In 1917, Duchamp tried to enter *Fountain* in an exhibit hosted by the Society of Independent Artists, on whose board he served, without identifying himself as the creator of the work. The society refused to exhibit it, on the grounds that it was not art. Duchamp resigned from the group.

The original *Fountain* is long gone: It's believed that one of Duchamp's colleagues tossed it out soon after the 1917 exhibition. (It was *just a urinal*, after all, and Duchamp was not well known, so why not throw it out?) But a photograph of the

piece survived, and so did the idea behind it. As the years passed, *Fountain*'s reputation grew, and Duchamp's along with it. By the 1960s, art historians considered it to be one of the most influential pieces of art created in the 20th century. Duchamp, who, ironically, had long since abandoned the art world in favor of competitive chess, was now seen as an artist on par with Pablo Picasso and Andy Warhol.

AMERICA (2016)

What It Is: A solid gold, fully functioning toilet

Artist: Maurizio Cattelan

Background: One of the drawbacks of creating a work of art like *Fountain* is the risk that smart-alecky "performance artists" will try to add to, improve, or simply comment on the work by using the plumbing fixture for its original intended purpose. This was the case with Marcel Duchamp's *Fountain*: Though the original urinal was tossed out, the work grew in stature in the 1950s and '60s, and Duchamp commissioned 16 different replicas of the original, which were exhibited in museums all over the world. To date there have been at least five documented attempts to pee into the replica *Fountains*, four of which were successful. (If you ever visit a museum that has one of the replicas on display, don't be surprised if it's protected behind a glass enclosure.)

When Maurizio Cattelan, an Italian artist known for satirical works of art that also contain biting social commentary, came up with the idea for his solid gold toilet, he decided not to protect the piece but to make such human "interactions" a central part of the work. He approached the staff of the Guggenheim Museum in New York City about his idea, and they agreed to cooperate.

The toilets were disassembled, and the pieces were used to create molds into which molten gold could be poured.

Objet d'Art: The Guggenheim shipped two of their restroom toilets to Cattelan in Florence, Italy. There, the toilets were disassembled, and the pieces were used to create molds into which molten gold could be poured to create exact duplicates of the toilet parts. Then the gold parts were assembled into a single, functioning solid gold toilet, which was shipped back to the Guggenheim Museum, where a plumber installed the toilet in a small, single-person restroom.

Once testing and troubleshooting of the gold toilet was complete, the restroom was reopened to the public in September 2016. Unlike with Marcel Duchamp's *Fountain*, using the golden toilet for its intended purpose *was* the point: "This notion of having a very intimate, private experience with a work of art, and a work of art that speaks dramatically about its own value, is fascinating on many levels," said a spokesperson for the Guggenheim. "It's an extraordinary opportunity to spend time completely alone with a work of art by a leading contemporary artist." Or as Cattelan

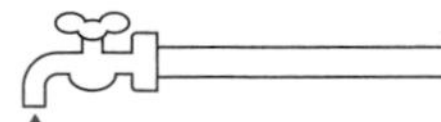

himself put it, the golden toilet was "one percent art for the ninety-nine percent."

Speaking of the 1 percent, when the Trump White House asked to borrow one of the Guggenheim's paintings by Vincent van Gogh so that it could be displayed in the Executive Mansion, the museum replied that the painting was "not available," and offered to lend *America* in its place. Though Trump is well known for his love of gilt-edged furniture and decor, the White House turned down the offer.

Audience Participation: In all, it's estimated that more than 100,000 visitors to the Guggenheim used the golden toilet while it was on display. One such "end user" was Adam Gabbatt, a reporter for the UK's *Guardian* newspaper. "I can confirm that it works," he told his readers. "The bright bowl glimmered under the bathroom's harsh fluorescent light, while the 18-carat gold seat looked sparkly and inviting. The surface proved forgiving on the rear of the thigh and once the procedure was complete, the flush worked like a charm. The golden toilet was able to handle solids."

If you were hoping to take Cattelan's pot of gold for a test drive but haven't done so already, you missed your chance. In 2019, the Guggenheim loaned the toilet to Blenheim Palace, an English World Heritage Site that was hosting an exhibit of Cattelan's works. Within days of being installed in a water closet, the toilet was stolen in a brazen overnight burglary, and has not been seen since. It's likely that the toilet has since been melted down, and the gold sold. Though he's well known as an art world prankster, Cattelan says he had nothing to do with the burglary. Not that he minds too much: "I always liked heist films, and finally I'm in one of them," he says. The crime remains unsolved.

SYNECDOCHES

What's a synecdoche? It's a figure of speech in which a part of something is used synonymously for the entire thing. Example: "wheels." You may refer to your vehicle by the four things that touch the ground and spin around, but the wheels are only part of the car, not the whole car. Here are some more common synecdoches.

A bite. You don't literally "get a bite to eat"—you get an entire meal.

Silverware. Flatware...which may or may not be made of silver.

Blue hairs and gray beards. These are features of elderly people that are used to refer to elderly people in general.

Keys. The one, playable part of the piano, used to refer to the entire piano.

Ivories. Because piano keys used to be surfaced with strips of ivory, the phrase "tickling the ivories" meant touching the piano keyboard, thereby playing the entire instrument.

Paper. When someone says they're reading "the paper," they mean they're reading the news—the paper is just the medium upon which the news is printed.

Threads. Clothing, because clothes are made of threads.

Plastic. Referring to credit cards, which are generally made of plastic.

Mouths. "Hungry mouths to feed" refers to a family of dependents... mouths and all.

Boots. As in "boots on the ground"—troops or soldiers, who wear boots.

Lead. Bullets, because bullets are commonly constructed from this material.

Heads. A hundred "head of cattle" means 100 cows, not 100 cow heads.

Glasses. It really just means the lens part of a pair of spectacles, but we call them glasses. (And lenses aren't usually made of glass anymore.)

Stick. A car that uses a manual transmission—with a gear-shifting stick—may be called by this name.

Hands. "All hands on deck" requires the full bodies of a crew of sailors, not just their hands.

Blade. The sharp part of a sword is often used interchangeably with the sword itself.

Capitol Hill. Reporters use it to refer to the activities of the legislative branch of the U.S. government—the Senate or the House of Representatives, which convene on Capitol Hill.

ABCs. Kids learn the whole alphabet, not just the first three letters.

THE SAGA OF "CATCH 'EM ALIVE JACK"

When we think of tough guys, we think of boxers, gangsters, or maybe a Clint Eastwood character. But this cowboy would have put them all to shame. Here's the little-known story of one of the bravest, hardiest guys on the range.

YOUNG COWBOY

Born in Texas in 1876, Jack Abernathy grew up on the rough frontier. His father was a Confederate soldier who was taken prisoner during the Civil War. His mother had been widowed by a Confederate soldier and was raising six kids. Then the new couple had five more. The youngest of eleven children, Jack was self-reliant early on. At six years old, he began sneaking out of his house with his older brother...to work. At a rowdy saloon in Sweetwater, Texas, Jack played piano until midnight while his brother accompanied him on violin and accordion. Each was paid a hefty $13 per shift to entertain cowboys who didn't make that much in two weeks. When Jack turned nine, he became a cowboy. He helped with cattle drives, branded farm animals, and patrolled the ranch with his .38 six-shooter. (A .45 was too heavy for him.) As a teenager, he became a lead cowboy—the one who broke in wild horses, the most dangerous job on the ranch. And he successfully saddled more than 300 of them.

In 1894, when Abernathy was 18, he got married to a music teacher named Jessie Pearl. During the dramatic event, he pulled his gun on porters who tried to stop them on behalf of her angry family. The new husband worked as a piano and organ salesman until they could afford to buy cattle. Then as homesteaders, the couple resettled in Oklahoma, where they (and their young kids) lived in a piano crate until Abernathy could build a dugout home.

WOLF HUNTING

Living on the frontier, Abernathy soon realized he had a lucrative talent. Using a novel (and bizarre) method he'd discovered as a teenager, he could protect ranchers' livestock from wolves and coyotes. When a wolf lunged at his greyhound dog, he tried to punch the wolf, but accidentally jammed his hand into its throat. Quickly, he grabbed its lower jaw with that hand before it could bite him...but they were stuck. Eventually a companion helped Abernathy release his arm and tie up the creature. It weighed an astounding 130 pounds—more than Abernathy himself. At a time when shooting wolves on sight was the norm, Abernathy was able to subdue them with his bare hands, earning him the name "Catch 'Em Alive Jack."

Charging $50 apiece, the cowboy captured and sold more than a thousand wolves to zoos, parks, and breeders. Abernathy was fit for wrangling wildlife, having been described as "not more than 5 foot 2, but built like an ox, with muscles like steel." Though he tried to teach others his technique, they were always too scared to reach behind the teeth and ended up with mangled hands.

A COUPLE OF ROUGH RIDERS

His exploits caught the attention of President Theodore Roosevelt, himself a naturalist and an adventurer, and the commander in chief arranged to join Abernathy on a wolf hunt in 1905. The first time Abernathy leaped off his horse and shoved his fist into a wolf's mouth, President Roosevelt rushed to his side to shake hands with him. By now, Abernathy had perfected his technique. He recalled, "I shoved my left thumb into the wolf's mouth, prying the jaws apart. Then I grabbed the jaw with my left hand, freeing my right. I then reached up with my right, shaking hands with the President." The president was thoroughly impressed, calling it "as remarkable an exhibition of pluck and skill as I have ever seen." In turn, Abernathy was awed that Roosevelt could keep up with him while chasing wolves on horseback.

"I shoved my left thumb into the wolf's mouth, prying the jaws apart."

The two became fast friends, and with a companion like President Roosevelt, Abernathy met many powerful people: Alexander Graham Bell, financiers Andrew Carnegie and John Jacob Astor, and writers Mark Twain and Jack London. Recognizing Abernathy's sense of justice and integrity, in 1906 the president appointed the 30-year-old Abernathy as a U.S. marshal—the youngest ever. Soon after, Jessie Pearl tragically died of illness, just as Roosevelt's young wife had. It gave the two men even more in common and left Abernathy a single father of four girls and two boys.

FIERCE LAWMAN

With help from relatives, Abernathy raised his kids while serving as marshal of the Western District of the Oklahoma Territory. He battled whiskey smugglers and gunmen, survived shootouts and murder attempts, and put 782 criminals behind bars. He earned a huge $5,000 salary (more than $100,000 today), but also made enemies.

In 1909, his two young sons (fearless like their father) traveled alone through outlaw territory. They were followed by bandits, including a cattle rustler whose friend had been shot by Abernathy. Using the lead tip of a bullet as a pencil, the rustler wrote a note to the lawman that said, "I don't like one hair on your head, but I do like the stuff that is in these kids. We shadowed them through the worst part of New Mexico to see that they were not harmed by sheepherders, mean men, or animals." His sons' grit may have saved their lives. Instead of being alarmed, Abernathy was pleased, saying, "It just goes to show you there's good in all men. He'd have killed me at the drop of a hat, but he was honorable to protect my innocent boys."

Abernathy resigned as marshal in 1910 and became a U.S. Secret Service agent. He also served briefly in Mexico's secret service, guarding the president, Francisco Madero. When Abernathy moved back to Texas in 1919, he became a wildcatter, drilling exploratory oil wells in hopes of finding a gusher. He made good money—but lost it during the Great Depression. He also almost lost his life (again). In a drilling accident, Abernathy was so badly injured that a doctor pronounced him dead. The oilman was being transported to the mortuary when he suddenly began breathing. Eventually, he recovered.

The man who seemed able to survive anything died of natural causes in 1941. He was 65 years old. History professor Jon T. Coleman sums up Abernathy's life this way: "Uttering phrases like 'I am a goner for keeps' and 'Hands up, Keller!,' Jack Abernathy could lay claim to an exquisite dime novel identity: he was a singing, gun-toting cowboy/lawman who busted broncs, settled wildernesses, and drilled gushers." But perhaps Abernathy's greatest legacy was his two young sons, who made national headlines demonstrating that they were every bit as rugged and independent as their father.

To read about the amazing adventures of Abernathy's sons, gallop over to page 377.

* * *

OOPS!

A day after undergoing oral surgery in November 2019, TV traffic reporter Nick Vasos was overmedicated and dehydrated, so he couldn't make it to his shift at Fox 4 in Kansas City, Missouri. After texting his supervisor and not receiving a reply, he decided to send her an e-mail informing her of his predicament. "That was a mistake," Vasos later admitted. In his grogginess, he'd forgotten the station's e-mail protocols had recently changed, so he typed in "news@" and then his boss's name—which is what he was accustomed to doing—but he didn't notice that the address had autocorrected to "news@Nexstar.com." So instead of only going to his immediate supervisor, Vasos's sick note arrived in the inbox of every employee in the Nexstar Media Group, which runs 200 stations across the United States. Almost instantly, his inbox began filling with well wishes—most of them in jest—from his thousands of coworkers. Mock memorials were set up online, and Vasos was even offered a Las Vegas vacation from Nexstar's Nevada affiliate. Things really got interesting when the hashtag #PrayersforNick started trending on Twitter. Confusion briefly ensued as to who this Nick fellow was and why everyone was praying for him. Afterward, Vasos tweeted, "Sorry to @RealNickCage @nickjonas @NickCannon @NickLachey @nickcarter fans. #PrayersForNick"

MODERN WISDOM

Famous folks and their random thoughts on life.

"Whatever you want to do, do it now. There are only so many tomorrows."

—Michael Landon

"You can be childlike without being childish."

—Christopher Meloni

"Everyone says love hurts, but that is not true. Loneliness hurts. Rejection hurts. Losing someone hurts. Envy hurts. Everyone gets these things confused with love, but in reality love is the only thing in this world that covers up all pain and makes someone feel wonderful again."

—Meša Selimović

"The greatest enemy of knowledge is not ignorance; it is the illusion of knowledge."

—Stephen Hawking

"It's amazing what you can get if you quietly, clearly, and authoritatively demand it."

—Meryl Streep

"It's the friends you can call up at 4 a.m. that matter."

—Marlene Dietrich

MOUTHING OFF

"You are the CEO of your life. Some people need to be hired and some need to be fired."

—Robert Downey Jr.

"WINNING IS NOT ALWAYS THE BAROMETER OF GETTING BETTER."

—Tiger Woods

"Larger-than-life characters make up about .01 percent of the world's population."

—Tom Hanks

"The hardest years in life are those between ten and seventy."

—Helen Hayes

"Wanting to be someone else is a waste of who you are."

—Kurt Cobain

"Knowledge is power. And you need power in this world. You need as many advantages as you can get."

—Ellen DeGeneres

"All endings are also beginnings. We just don't know it at the time."

—Mitch Albom

"You can only become truly accomplished at something you love. Don't make money your goal. Instead, pursue the things you love doing, and then do them so well that people can't take their eyes off you."

—Maya Angelou

THIRTY-THREE YEARS

Since this is Uncle John's 33rd Bathroom Reader, we thought it would be interesting to look at some major world events that occurred in years ending in 33.

AD 33 The court of Roman governor Pontius Pilate orders the death by crucifixion of Jesus of Nazareth. The charge: treason against the Roman Empire, for claiming to be "king of the Jews" and the son of God. The crucifixion occurs at a place called Golgotha, just outside of Jerusalem.

133 Roman tribune (an elected official) Tiberius Gracchus deposes another tribune, Marcus Octavius, to prevent him from voting on a government bill that would take land illegally held by the rich and give it to its rightful, less wealthy owners. This leads to a riot in which 300 people die, including Tiberius, who is bludgeoned to death with the leg of a bench during the melee.

233 Roman emperor Severus Alexander returns home to Rome to celebrate his victory in Persia the previous year...although his forces had actually been defeated by the armies of Sassanian emperor Ardashir I.

333 Roman emperor Constantine orders his troops out of Britain. Within a few decades, the centuries-long Roman occupation of Britain will end. Constantine also orders Roman soldiers to abandon their posts on Hadrian's Wall, a defensive fortress and Roman border post in northern Britain.

433 According to Irish folklore, Patrick—the future St. Patrick—defies High King Laoire and celebrates Easter by burning a ritual Paschal fire on the Hill of Slane in County Meath (northeastern Ireland). It is during this ceremony that Patrick introduces Christianity to Ireland, demonstrating the Holy Trinity with the three-leafed shamrock.

533 Ignoring his advisors' pleas, Justinian I, emperor of the Eastern Roman Empire (Byzantium), launches a quest to take back North Africa from the brutal Vandal hordes. Under the command of Belisarius, hundreds of Byzantine ships with nearly 40,000 troops leave the capital of Constantinople and arrive in Carthage (now Tunisia) after three months of preparation and travel. By the end of the year, and after many bloody victories (for both sides), Belisarius expels the Vandals from Africa.

633 A year prior, Abu Bakr became the first caliph, or spiritual leader, of Islam. (He was the father-in-law of Islam's prophet Muhammad, and one of the faith's first converts.) By 633, Islam has spread so far through the Arabian Peninsula that Abu Bakr has full authority over the region, leading to Islam becoming the dominant religion of Persia and most of the rest of the Middle East.

733 Emperor Leo III creates a major split between his Eastern Roman Empire and the Catholic Church by annexing (stealing) papal territories in Calabria (southern Italy) and Sicily.

833 The Arab-Byzantine War, in which the Muslim conquests of Asia butted up against the Eastern Roman Empire (Byzantium), comes to a halt when Byzantine emperor Theophilos agrees to an armistice plan that sends 100,000 gold coins to the ruling Abbasid Caliph in exchange for the release of 7,000 Byzantine prisoners of war.

933 At this time in history, Italy is a constituent part of the Holy Roman Empire, ruled by a king, Hugh of Provence. In this year, he sends a delegation to Rome to depose its ruler, Alberic II, who had seized power in 932 by deposing its previous ruler...Hugh of Provence (who also happens to be his stepfather). The coup fails. Roman militias beat back the invasion, sending Hugh into retreat.

1033 While many European religious scholars held that the end of the world would come in the year 1000, it didn't, and several sects (particularly in France) looked forward to the year 1033 as the true date of the apocalypse. Why 1033? It marked 1,000 years since the crucifixion of Jesus. While some events of 1033 are recorded as omens—a famine that ravages the region of Gaul, for example—the world continues to turn.

1133 As Europe's dominant religion, the Roman Catholic Church holds tremendous power, including the authority to resolve land disputes. In this year, Pope Innocent II issues a papal bull (an official, legally binding decree) giving the island of Sardinia and half of the island of Corsica to the powerful, seafaring Republic of Pisa (in the Tuscan region of Italy). Pisa will be defeated by rival Genoa in 1284, lose Sardinia to Spanish forces in 1324, and be sold to Florence in 1402.

1233 Genghis Khan's Mongol forces complete a major part of their conquest of China, capturing the ruling Jin Dynasty's capital city of Kaifeng in early 1233, following months of siege. In December, the Mongols (without Genghis Khan, who died in 1227), will start the siege of Caizhou, the final battle between Mongols and the Jin, which ends the Jin Dynasty.

Tom Hanks checks into hotels using the aliases "Harry Lauder" and "Johnny Madrid."

1333 In the northern England town of Berwick-upon-Tweed, the Battle of Halidon Hill is fought on July 19, one of the last and most decisive battles in the Wars of Scottish Independence. English archers under the command of King Edward III overwhelm the freedom fighters, killing more than 500 knights in a single day. Control of Berwick-upon-Tweed reverts to England. The war continues for another 24 years; Scotland emerges as an independent kingdom.

1433 After seven successful "treasure voyages," the powerful Ming Dynasty of China disbands its navy for reasons unknown and pulls the massive fleet out of the Indian Ocean. This creates a power vacuum in the region, which leads to an increase in exploration and commercial traffic from European nations.

1533 Two years into his third expedition into Peru, Spanish conquistador Francisco Pizarro destroys the Incan Empire. Pizarro executes Incan king Atahualpa in July 1533 and subsequently conquers the Incan capital city of Cuzco.

1633 An inquisition led by the Roman Catholic Church forces Italian astronomer Galileo Galilei to recant and deny his scientific observation that the Earth revolves around the Sun. Reason: it was contrary to Church teachings. (The Church would eventually apologize and admit that it was wrong...but not until 1992.)

1733 Great Britain passes the Molasses Act, levying heavy taxes in the American colonies on sugar, molasses, and rum imported from any territory not under English rule. It was designed to establish a monopoly for sugarcane plantations in the British West Indies and to exclude producers from French territories. Because it greatly increases the price of molasses (and rum, which is distilled from molasses), the new law is unpopular with colonists, and one of the English tax laws that would eventually lead to the American Revolution.

1833 The British Parliament passes the Slavery Abolition Act, ending the practice of forced labor in its colonies around the world. More than 700,000 enslaved people are granted their freedom.

1933 German president Paul von Hindenburg appoints Nazi Party leader Adolf Hitler to the position of chancellor. Just four weeks later, Hitler's forces set fire to the Reichstag, the German parliament building. Within months, Hitler withdraws Germany from the peacekeeping League of Nations and usurps complete control of the government, setting the stage for World War II.

Last time elephants were used in war: 1987.

OOPS! ARCHAEOLOGY EDITION

Everybody makes mistakes. Some people make big mistakes.

OFF THE WALL

In March 1992, seventy members of a French Protestant youth group called the *Eclaireurs* ("Those Who Show the Way") volunteered to clean graffiti off the walls of a cave in the south of France. The youngsters set to work scraping the walls with wire brushes...until someone noticed that some of the graffiti seemed older than the rest. How much older? About 15,000 years. The overenthusiastic kids had destroyed bison paintings that had decorated the cave walls since the Stone Age. Rene Gachet, the region's director of cultural affairs, described the incident as "Absolutely stupid!" A spokesperson for the *Eclaireurs* expressed regret at the error but was also "indignant that the actions of well-meaning youths should be called into question."

CLEARING THE TABLE

In 2015, contractors were hired to install a concrete picnic table in a park in the town of Cristovo de Cea, Spain. When the contractors arrived at the site, they saw a collection of granite slabs that they assumed were part of an old, broken picnic table. So they smashed the slabs, cleared them from the site, then poured a new slab of concrete and set the picnic table in the slab. It wasn't until after they finished that they learned the old stones weren't an old picnic table, they were markers for a 6,000-year-old Neolithic tomb, now completely destroyed, its burial chamber filled with concrete. "Sometimes accidents happen," archaeologist Juan Barceló told reporters after learning of the blunder. "I am sure that such disasters happen in many other countries but have not been published."

WHAT THE HILL?

In 2013, a construction company building a road in northern Belize began excavating a hillside to use as fill for the road. Only problem: the "hillside" was actually the buried ruins of a 2,300-year-old Mayan pyramid, one of the largest in Belize. By the time the work was finished, 70 percent of the pyramid had been reduced to gravel. The director of the company, Danny Grijalva, was later found guilty of willful destruction of an ancient monument and fined the equivalent of $3,000. He apologized for the destruction and promised to "work with the government to ensure that it would not happen again."

BOOBY HATCHES AND JOLLYBOATS

One of Uncle John's favorite writers is studying to be a merchant marine, and brought us this list of fascinating (and colorful) nautical lingo.

Topsides: The section of a ship's hull that's above the waterline.

Allision: A collision with a large and (easily avoidable) fixed object, such as a bridge, where the ship is presumed to be at fault.

Dolphin: A vertical post rising out of the water offshore; often used as a place for ships to tie up.

Booby hatch: A sliding hatch or cover on a ship's deck.

Lizard: A small rope that's attached to a larger rope to hold it in position.

Asylum harbor: Any harbor that provides shelter from a storm.

Binnacle: The stand that a ship's compass is mounted on.

Bird farm: An aircraft carrier.

Binnacle list: The list of crew members too sick to report for duty, kept near the binnacle.

Reefer: A refrigerated container on a ship, used to transport frozen food.

Donkeyman: A ship's engineer in charge of maintaining a piece of machinery other than the main engine.

Bumboat: A private ship that goes around selling goods to other ships at anchor.

Jollyboat: The boat that ferries sailors from their ship (when anchored offshore) into shore.

Bitt: A pair of vertical posts mounted on the ship's deck, used to secure ropes to.

Bitter end: The end of the rope that is tied around the bitt.

Chunderbox: A toilet.

Jonah: A crew member said to be cursed with bad luck that endangers other crew members as well as the ship itself.

Monkey's fist: A large knot tied at one end of a rope to add weight, so that the rope can be thrown more easily. It's tied in a way that makes it look kind of like a small fist or paw.

Thunderbox: A toilet hung over the rear or stern of a ship.

Blue Peter: A flag consisting of a white square surrounded by a blue border—the signal for the letter P. It's hoisted to signal to crew members ashore that a ship is ready to set sail.

Ro-ro: Short for "roll on, roll off," it's a ship that transports automobiles—they are driven on and driven off.

HIDDEN IN PLAIN SIGHT

These true stories might make you take a second look at some of those odd items sitting around your house.

THAT'LL BE A TENNER

The Find: A 26-carat diamond ring

Hidden: At some point, most likely in the late 19th century (although no one knows for sure), this massive diamond was cut and set onto a mount. Whoever owned the ring, and how they lost it, is also unknown. But somehow it ended up at West Middlesex Hospital in London in the 1980s at a "car boot sale." (A boot sale is a British kind of flea market in which people gather in a parking lot to sell stuff from the *boots,* or trunks, of their cars.) A young woman paid £10 for the diamond ring, thinking it was costume jewelry. According to press reports, "The stone was set in a 'filthy mount,' " but the woman (name withheld from reports) cleaned the ring and then wore it nearly every day for the next 30 years, not even bothering to remove it for chores or shopping.

In Plain Sight: In early 2017, she decided to see what, if anything, the ring was worth. The jeweler she brought it to reportedly gave it one look and told her it was almost certainly a real diamond. The Gemological Institute of America later confirmed its authenticity—an astonishing 26.27 carats. Named the "Tenner" diamond—after how much she paid for it—it went up for auction later that year. Conservative estimates valued it at about £350,000...but it brought in nearly twice that, at £656,750 ($850,000).

UNLUCKY RABBIT

The Find: One of Disney's first cartoons

Hidden: In 1927, when Walt Disney was just an up-and-coming animator, he and another cartoonist, Ub Iwerks, co-created Oswald the Lucky Rabbit. Then, due to an intellectual property dispute with Universal Studios, Disney lost all rights to Oswald. (That's why he created Mickey Mouse.) By that time, 26 Oswald shorts had been made, but because the rabbit's ownership was in limbo, most of the Oswald cartoons were lost. Longtime Disney animator Dave Bossert reported this fact in his 2017 book *Oswald the Lucky Rabbit: The Search for the Lost Disney Cartoons.* He wrote about a 16-mm cartoon called "Neck & Neck" that was among seven of the original Oswald cartoons thought to be lost forever.

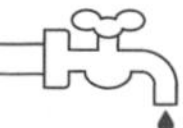

What do Australia, Italy, and the U.S. have in common?
They celebrate Mother's Day on the same day (second Sunday in May).

In Plain Sight: In 2018, Yasushi Watanabe, an 84-year-old Japanese animation historian—and huge Disney fan—was reading Bossert's book...and immediately started looking through his cartoon collection. He pulled out a 16-mm reel that was labeled, in Japanese, "*Mickey Manga Spide*" ("Mickey Cartoon Speedy"). Watanabe watched it, and saw that it wasn't Mickey Mouse. It was Oswald the Lucky Rabbit in "Neck & Neck." He had purchased the reel in Osaka, Japan—for less than $5 in today's money—when he was a kid in the 1930s. For more than 70 years, he'd owned one of the rarest, most sought-after cartoons in the world and didn't even know it. At last report, the cartoon was being kept safe at a film archive in Japan.

GREASE COLLECTOR

The Find: A painting by 13th-century artist Cimabue

Hidden: Only 11 of Cimabue's paintings are known to exist. In 1280, the influential Italian artist (real name: Cenni di Pepo) painted eight small works—about 8 by 10 inches each—that depicted Jesus's crucifixion. One of them, called *Christ Mocked,* was thought to be lost forever.

In Plain Sight: In 2018, while an elderly French woman was preparing to sell her house, an appraiser asked her about the small painting hanging in the kitchen above her hot plate. She said she didn't remember where or when she got it, and that she thought it was a depiction of a Greek religious icon. Suspecting that the painting could be something very special, the appraiser brought it to an art specialist named Jerome Montcouquil, who later told CNN, "It didn't take long for us to see that it was an artwork by Cimabue. He's a father of painting, so we know his work very well." Despite the fact that *Christ Mocked* had been collecting grease in the woman's kitchen (and who knows what else it endured over the past 700 years), it's in very good condition. The painting went on the block—the first of Cimabue's works ever to do so—and sold for an astonishing 24.2 million Euros ($26.8 million).

A DOORSTOP OLDER THAN EARTH

The Find: A 22-pound meteorite

Hidden: In 1988, a man (unnamed in press reports) purchased a farm in Edmore, Michigan. When he asked about a small boulder that was holding a barn door open, he was told it was a "space rock" that the original owners witnessed fall from the sky one night in the 1930s. The story went that when they searched their land the next morning, they found the still-warm, metallic object in a small crater. The new homeowner must not have thought much of the story, because the rock remained a doorstop for the next 30 years.

By the time the last woolly mammoths died out in 1650 BC, the Great Pyramid at Giza was already 1,000 years old.

In Plain Sight: In January 2018, a meteor lit up the skies over Detroit, and several people reported finding small meteorites the next day. When the homeowner found out that some of the small shards were selling for thousands of dollars each, he suddenly became curious about that old doorstop. So he took it to Central Michigan University and showed it to geology professor Dr. Mona Sirbescu. "I could tell right away that this was something special," she said. Made of 85 percent iron and 15 percent nickel (a combination that is rare on Earth), the 22.5-pound meteorite is the sixth-largest ever found in the state. "It's the most valuable specimen I have ever held in my life, monetarily and scientifically," she added. The monetary part is estimated at $100,000. The scientific part: "Just think: what I was holding is a piece of the early solar system that literally fell into our hands."

MINTY FRESH

The Find: A 4,000-year-old pot

Hidden: In around 1900 B.C. in what is now Afghanistan, a potter made a small clay vessel and decorated it with a drawing of an antelope. The potter was a member of the Indus Valley Harappan civilization, an advanced Bronze Age society that thrived from 5,300 to 3,300 years ago in southern Asia. Researchers have uncovered sculptures, jewelry, toys, figurines, and other artifacts there, made from wood, stone, clay, and bronze.

In 2013, Karl Martin purchased the clay pot at a car boot sale in Derbyshire, England, for £4. He knew the pot was old, but he had no idea how old—or else he wouldn't have used it as a toothbrush holder for the next five years. "It even ended up getting a few toothpaste marks on it," he admitted. It just so happened that Martin worked at an auction house, and while he's well versed in British history, his knowledge of the Age of Antiquity is limited.

In Plain Sight: In 2018, Martin was at the auction house helping a colleague unload some Indus Valley artifacts and thought they looked a lot like his toothbrush holder. He brought his pot to work the next day, where antiquities expert James Brenchley confirmed that it was a 4,000-year-old "genuine antiquity from Afghanistan" and it was in remarkably good condition (despite the toothpaste). Martin auctioned the pot, which sold for £80 (about $105), not as much as he was hoping for but still a tidy profit. "How it ended up at a South Derbyshire car boot sale, I'll never know."

IN THE KNOW

World's most expensive painting: *Salvator Mundi* ("Savior of the World"), painted by Leonardo da Vinci circa 1500. It depicts Jesus in Renaissance clothing, crossing his fingers with one hand, and holding a glass orb in the other. In 2017, a Saudi prince bought it for $450 million.

DUMB CROOKS

Here's proof that crime doesn't pay.

CLEAR AND PRESENT DUH

One afternoon in April 2018, Kerry Hammond Jr., 22, was captured on a surveillance camera walking around in a GameStop store in St. Marys, Georgia. Later that night, a masked burglar was captured on that same surveillance camera. The burglar had the same build as Hammond, the same tattoo on his right arm, and he was wearing the same blue shirt and khaki pants. That evidence alone would have been enough to tie Hammond to the crime, but the cops didn't need it. Reason: Hammond's "mask" consisted of the plastic wrapper from a case of bottled water. It's not known what he thought the mask would hide, but his face showed up clear as day in the surveillance footage.

WIGGING OUT

A man got on a plane in Bogotá, Colombia, and flew to Spain. But when he arrived, Spanish police noticed something odd about his hair: It was very large. Suspicious, they detained the man and removed what press reports later described as an "oversized hairpiece." Inside the toupee: more than $30,000 worth of cocaine. "There is no limit to the inventiveness of drug traffickers trying to mock our controls," said a police spokesperson.

POSITIVELY STUPID

"Let me get this straight," said Judge Frank Fregiato, who was more than a bit bewildered. "To avoid the positive test with your *own* urine, you used *someone else's* urine, which also turned out to be positive?" Kiana Wallace, 24, who was on probation for drug possession, nodded yes. "That's bizarre," said the judge...and then sentenced her to 18 months in prison.

ONLINE TUTORIAL

A Facebook post captioned "Today's lesson how to remove a GPS tracking bracelet without stopping the circuit...encase anyone was curious" landed Dustin W. Burns in jail. The 33-year-old Springfield, Missouri, man was on parole after violating a restraining order, and he apparently thought his tutorial would be untraceable because he didn't include his face in the video. However, a quick scroll of the Facebook page on which the post appeared made it clear to investigators that not only was Burns the same man in video, but that he'd recently taken a vacation to Oregon—sans ankle bracelet—where he shared a selfie on a cannabis farm with the caption "Dream come true!" Burns was arrested shortly after posting the video.

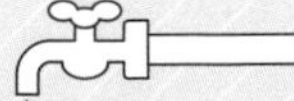

COME SAIL AWAY

"The fun isn't stopping anytime soon," wrote Paul LaMarche, 67, on his sailboating website. But it did stop...very soon. For several years, LaMarche had been collecting disability payments for conditions that included "debilitating headaches daily" and being unable to "lift, pull, or carry heavy items." Yet somehow the Seattle, Washington, man was able to run a successful sailboating business, and—as he demonstrated on a Seattle tourism video—he was pretty good at doing "paddleboard yoga." Investigators from the Justice Department caught up with the fraudster in 2018 after he'd collected more than $177,000 in disability payments, which he had to pay back in full. LaMarche was later sentenced to nine months in prison (where he'll have plenty of time to practice yoga).

TRAFFIC JAMMER

In 2017, 67-year-old Timothy Hill of North Yorkshire, England, installed a laser jammer in his white Range Rover. Hill wanted to thwart the speed traffic camera that police often parked on the side of the highway. The ploy worked; the jammer blocked the speed gun. But Hill did himself no favors by "flipping off" the camera every time he sped past it. A police spokesperson told *Metro News*, "If you want to attract our attention, repeatedly gesturing at police cameras with your middle finger while you're driving a distinctive car fitted with a laser jammer is an excellent way to do it." When police tracked down Hill, they couldn't charge him with speeding, but they did arrest him for interfering with law enforcement and making rude gestures. His middle finger got him eight months behind bars.

NEED A LYFT?

One night in February 2019, just after bedtime, a 28-year-old Maywood, New Jersey, man named Nicholas Maziot broke into an unoccupied home. At least he thought it was unoccupied. (That's not the dumb part.) Turns out someone was in the home, sleeping. Awoken by the sounds of someone breaking through their back door, they called the police. When Maziot realized someone was home, he escaped onto the roof, and then jumped down and ran away. By the time the police arrived, he was hiding in a nearby backyard. Lacking an escape vehicle of his own, he used a ride-sharing app on his phone to hire a Lyft. (Amazingly, that's still not the dumb part.) A few minutes later, a car pulled up out front. Maziot snuck out of the yard, walked up to the car and asked, "Are you my Lyft driver?" (That's the dumb part.) After realizing that most Lyft drivers don't wear police uniforms, Maziot tried to get away, but Officer Brian Rubio quickly got out of his unmarked police car and detained him. Meanwhile, the Lyft driver, who showed up at the same time as the cops, had to find a new fare.

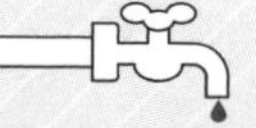

It takes 7 times as much force to bite through a finger as it does a carrot.

WE KNOW NUT-THING!

A true nut, botanically speaking, is the fruit of a plant, having a hard, woody shell that contains one or two seeds. The seed sprouts only after the pod falls from the plant, and the shell decays and softens. Examples: chestnuts, hazelnuts, and filberts. But the word "nut" is also used for "culinary nuts"—nutlike foods, such as peanuts, cashews, pistachios, and pine nuts. It's enough to drive you nuts! Here are some you've probably never heard of (but might want to try).

CANDLENUT: These not-true nuts grow on bushy medium-sized trees, cultivated in Southeast Asia for at least 4,000 years, and probably much longer. Candlenuts grow in large round pods up to 2½ inches in diameter. They look like large, bumpy macadamia nuts, and they have a creamy, soapy texture when raw. They are used in a variety of foods across Southeast Asia and on many Pacific islands, most notably in sauces (crushed). Candlenuts have a bitter taste, are mildly toxic when eaten raw (not recommended!), and have an almondlike flavor when cooked. In Hawaii—where candlenuts are called *kukui*—they're used to make the condiment *inamona*—a common ingredient in the popular dish *poke*. Ancient Hawaiians also used them for...candles. When lit, the candlenut's oily flesh provided light, and burned for about 15 minutes.

MONKEY PUZZLE NUT: The monkey puzzle tree is an evergreen native to lower regions of the Andes mountains in Chile and Argentina. They produce round, coconut-sized cones that hold approximately 200 narrow, pointy seeds, each about 1½ inches long. Inside those seeds: an edible kernel, similar to a pine nut, only much larger. They've been harvested by local peoples for centuries, and are eaten raw, boiled, or toasted. When ground, they're used as a kind of flour (and to make an alcoholic beverage). The flavor of the nuts (when cooked) has been described as a cross between sweet corn and chestnut.

BONUS: There are no monkeys in the region, so why the name? It came from a comment made around 1850 by a man who saw one of the trees in a garden in England. Because of the tree's characteristic configuration—they have very straight, tall, branchless trunks, with branches emanating only from the very top of the tree—the man remarked that "it would puzzle a monkey to climb that," and the name stuck.

MALABAR CHESTNUT: A culinary nut that grows on a tree native to tropical wetlands in Central and South America. The large podlike fruit—they're shaped a bit like large avocados—will burst open in the autumn to reveal 10 to 25 light brown seeds, about ½–¾ inch in diameter. These are Malabar chestnuts, also known as saba nuts, monguba nuts, pumpo nuts, and Guiana peanuts. The flesh is creamy and white, and they can be eaten raw, fried, roasted, and ground up to make a hot nutty drink. The flavor is similar to European chestnuts or macadamia nuts.

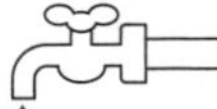

BONUS: Where in Central or South America is Malabar? Nowhere. Malabar chestnuts got their name after being exported around the world, and becoming especially popular on the Malabar Coast of southwest India.

BEECHNUT: You're probably familiar with beech trees: They're tall, stoutly trunked trees with smooth, silver-gray bark, and are common in the United States. But have you ever eaten their nuts? They grow in small, spine-covered pods, just an inch or so long, that fall from the trees in the autumn. Each pod contains a hard, dark brown, three-sided shell that holds one or two small, pointy nuts, ½ inch long. Beechnuts are true nuts, and have been a favorite food for foragers in North America, Europe, and Asia for millennia. You can eat them right off the ground and out of the shell, or you can gather them up, take them home, and eat them raw or roasted in a salad. The flavor is described as slightly sweet but bitter. (Roasting reduces the bitterness.) **BONUS:** If you encounter a beech tree in spring, not autumn, experts suggest you pick a few of the young leaves—they make a delicate and tasty salad green.

YEHEB NUT: These reddish-brown seeds—about the size of marbles—grow one to four in a pod on the shrublike yeheb tree, found in very dry desert regions of northeastern Africa. They are edible, but they have a sour taste when eaten raw, so they're commonly eaten only after being either roasted or boiled, and then dried. The flavor is similar to cashews or chestnuts. These extremely nutritious nuts have been eaten by desert-dwelling peoples in Somalia and Ethiopia for centuries, and are still an important food source to nomadic groups and their animals. Bad news: the native habitat has been reduced in recent years and the wild population has dramatically decreased. Result: the yeheb tree is currently classified as endangered.

MORE NUT FACTS TO DRIVE YOU NUTS:

- Many culinary nuts are actually *drupes*—fleshy fruit that contain hard stones or pits with a seed inside. Drupes include fruits such as cherries, peaches, and apricots, and culinary nuts such as cashews, almonds, and pistachios.
- More nuts you may know nut-thing about: the breadnut—found from Mexico to South America, and eaten raw, roasted, or ground into flour; the *karuka* nut—a staple in Papua New Guinea for millennia, found in fruit clusters that can hold more than 1,000 nuts; and the tiger nut—known to have been eaten by ancient Egyptians more than 7,000 years ago, and although it looks and tastes like a nut, it grows underground, and is actually a tuber (like a sweet potato).
- Mongongo nuts, native to southern Africa, grow inside fruit, and are the size and shape of chicken eggs. They are harvested off the ground after the fruit falls from the tree, or from elephant dung. Elephants eat mongongos for the fruit; they cannot digest the hard-shelled nuts inside them. So nut nuts can pick mongongos out of the dung, crack them open—and voilà!—tasty poop nuts!

WELCOME TO LJUBLJANA

Uncle John likes to brag that he knows the names of all the world capitals, so we came up with this quiz to test him. He got four right. Can you do better? *Answers are on page 405.*

1) Moldova
2) Fiji
3) Botswana
4) Myanmar
5) Uganda
6) Suriname
7) Kazakhstan
8) Cyprus
9) Belize
10) Laos
11) Kiribati
12) Zimbabwe
13) Uzbekistan
14) Tanzania
15) Papua New Guinea
16) Slovenia
17) Kosovo
18) Cote D'Ivoire
19) Bhutan
20) Guinea
21) Estonia
22) Barbados
23) Sierra Leone
24) Mongolia
25) Kyrgyzstan
26) Liechtenstein

a. Paramaribo
b. Conakry
c. Harare
d. Gaborone
e. Ulaanbaatar
f. Freetown
g. Kampala
h. Chisinau
i. Yamoussoukro
j. Nicosia
k. Ljubljana
l. Suva
m. Dodoma
n. Nur-Sultan
o. Tallinn
p. Vientiane
q. Naypyitaw
r. Vaduz
s. Thimphu
t. Bridgetown
u. South Tarawa
v. Port Moresby
w. Belmopan
x. Pristina
y. Tashkent
z. Bishkek

THE ROBOTS ARE COMING (FOR YOUR JOB)

As artificial intelligence technology grows more sophisticated with each passing year, more and more aspects of daily life are becoming robotized. How far are we from robots replacing us at work? Closer than you might think.

★ Human employees—or "people" as they're sometimes called—are expensive. Workers' wages, plus things like health benefits and 401K matching, cut into a company's profits. What's the alternative? Robots, machines, and automation. The cost of installing robotic arms to replace humans on an assembly line may be high initially, but in the long run those bots will pay for themselves because they don't get salaries or benefits, nor do they require training or need to take days off, nor can they be poached by a competitor.

★ In 1961, the General Motors assembly line at the Inland Fisher Guide Plant in New Jersey activated Unimate, the country's first industrial robot. Today, half of all robots in the United States are used to build cars, and comprise about 10 percent of the manufacturing workforce. That percentage is growing. According to a study by Bank of America, robots will perform about half of all U.S. manufacturing jobs by the end of the 2020s, displacing as many as 20 million workers. The same Bank of America study found that half of *all* jobs available in the late 2010s could be taken on by automation in a decade's time.

★ The infiltration of robots into the workplace has been relatively minimal. So far. About 600,000 jobs have been permanently lost to automation, but the rise in robot tech combined with a decreasing price tag may soon lead to robot overload. An MIT study says that there are currently about two industrial robots for every 1,000 human workers. By 2025, that number will triple. That equates to somewhere between 2 million and 3.5 million human jobs lost.

★ While robots can most easily be programmed to perform repetitive and even dangerous work, they're making inroads in many job sectors. The McKinsey Global Institute reported in 2018 that 30 percent of the global workforce could lose their jobs to automation by 2030. That's about 800 million jobs worldwide, and it includes jobs that aren't made up of rote or routine tasks, such as retail, law, finance, and journalism.

★ Which jobs do experts think will be mechanized? Any that require a specific set of physical or problem-solving skills...and can be programmed into a robot—tour

guides, bakers, pharmacy technicians, telemarketers, accountants, mortgage processors, toll-booth operators, paralegals, soldiers, astronauts, babysitters, bank tellers, retail stockers, construction workers, farmers, and even models.

★ Particularly at risk: taxi and delivery drivers, whose jobs are threatened by autonomous robotic vehicles. Studies show that five million driving jobs will be eliminated by 2025.

★ While the word "robot" conjures an image of a metallic humanoid clomping around, it can also be applied to an algorithm programmed into a computer to perform complex data analysis. The financial sector has already made the transition. In 2000, Goldman Sachs' New York trading office employed 500 stock traders. Today is uses only three—the other 497 have been replaced by algorithms.

★ Industrial and manufacturing facilities were the first to start replacing humans with machines, and the fast-food sector is likely the next. Chains like Wendy's and McDonald's have already introduced self-serving kiosks at hundreds of locations, to say nothing of apps that allow customers to order from their phones. That's a kind of automation that reduces the need for cashiers. Even in the fast-food kitchen, automation technology has cut the number of employees needed in half. By 2024, as many as 80,000 fast-food jobs could be gone forever.

★ But not *everybody* is going to lose their job to a robot in the next few years. Analysts believe that while robotic technology is very sophisticated, it can't replicate (or at least it can't *yet* replicate) distinctly human traits such as empathy, intuition, social cues, and case-by-case judgment. The jobs most likely to *resist* the robot uprising: firefighters, clergy, teachers, coaches, artists, cosmetologists, and social workers.

★ Robots are an increasingly useful tool in medicine, but they won't replace doctors or nurses anytime soon. Studies show that people prefer a flesh-and-blood human when they're in a vulnerable position...such as in a hospital.

BARTENDERS are also at risk of losing their jobs to robots. After all, robotic arms and dispensing machines can be programmed to do relatively simple tasks like mix and pour drinks on command. A robotics company called Makr Shakr produces a line of machine bartenders called Toni. The company feels so bad about the fact that its products could eventually replace bartenders that it started a giveaway program in December 2019. Makr Shakr selects one employed human bartender every month and gives them $1,000 in a sort of "sorry about eventually replacing you" gesture.

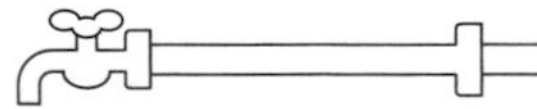

In France, French toast is called *pain perdu*—"lost bread."

WEIRD SCIENCE

Here are some of the most unusual scientific studies—some new, some aged to odd perfection—that we've come across over the years.

THROUGH THICK AND THIN: In 2004, Edward Cussler, a chemical engineering professor at the University of Minnesota, and his student Brian Gettelfinger dumped 300 kilograms (about 660 pounds) of an edible thickening agent called guar gum into the school's swimming pool, which made the water about twice as thick. Why'd they do that? To find out whether swimming in syrup is easier or more difficult than swimming in water. Sixteen volunteers, some competitive swimmers and some recreational swimmers, swam laps in ordinary water, and then swam in water with the guar gum added. "It looked like snot," reported Professor Cussler. "I don't know how to describe it any more poetically." The swimmers were timed in each pool and the two times were compared. Finding: the swimmers' speeds varied no more than 4 percent, and neither water nor syrup produced consistently better times. The thicker water created more "viscous drag" on the swimmers, but the swimmers generated more forward force with each stroke, and the two effects canceled each other out.

THE STING: To determine where on the body a bee sting would hurt the most, in 2014, a Cornell University graduate student named Michael Smith went back to basics...and let honeybees sting him in 25 areas all over his body. He was stung about 200 times in total, and he ranked the pain of each sting on a scale of 1 to 10. Then he compared the stings on each of the 25 body parts. His conclusions: The most painful place to be stung: the nostril, followed by the upper lip and the shaft of the penis. "A sting to the nostril is so painful," he said, "it's like a whole body experience."

THE WRITING ON THE WALL: In the early 1950s, sexologist Alfred Kinsey studied graffiti written in public restrooms, hoping it would provide insight into the suppressed sexual desires of men and women. Messages written in women's rooms were analyzed and compared to graffiti written in men's rooms. Kinsey's conclusions: 86 percent of men's messages were explicitly erotic in nature, while only 25 percent of women's messages were. Most of the female messages referred to love in nonerotic terms.

THIGHS OR BREASTS?: In the mid-1960s, two researchers at Penn State University wanted to know what parts of the female turkey stimulated male turkey mating behavior. They started out with an intact, taxidermied female to get the male turkeys' interest, then removed the female's body parts one by one to see if the males were still interested. They kept at it until all they had left was the female's head and neck on a stick, which they presented to the males. Then they presented the female's body

with the head removed and compared the responses. Their findings: "Male turkeys presented a body without the head displayed [sexual behavior] but did not mount. Presenting the head alone released display behavior followed by 'mounting' and copulatory movements immediately posterior to the head." The researchers concluded that it was the neck more than the head that stimulated the male, because that's the only part of the female's body that's visible during copulation.

TRAPPED: Pitcher plants, like Venus flytraps, are carnivorous. They trap insects and other invertebrates with deep, pitcher-shaped leaves filled with a fluid "bait" that attracts prey: Insects climb down into the pitcher to drink the fluid and can't get back out. They either starve to death or drown in the fluid, then are broken down by digestive enzymes in the fluid and absorbed by the plant. In 2019, biologists at the University of Guelph in Ontario, Canada, peeked inside dozens of pitcher plants in a bog and made a shocking discovery: Pitcher plants also regularly "eat" vertebrates, which scientists had previously assumed was rare and accidental. It turns out the plants digested a lot of baby salamanders. Of the 144 pitcher plants studied, 20 percent had caught at least one. The team estimates that these silent predators are killing up to 5 percent of the baby salamander population there.

SOUR NOTES: People can get distracted by music, but can mosquitoes? That was the question Malaysian researchers were asking when they played "Scary Monsters and Nice Sprites," a Grammy Award–winning song from the electronic music artist Skrillex, for a species of mosquito that carries yellow and dengue fever. The music was played in ten-minute intervals; their behavior was compared to a second group of mosquitoes that were not exposed to music. Among the researchers' conclusions: "The occurrence of blood feeding activity was lower when music was being played" and "adults exposed to music copulated far less often than their counterparts kept in an environment where there was no music." But as one disease control expert warns, "There's no way that you could use this level of noise to repel mosquitoes—unless you happen to be at a music festival."

BLACK COFFEE, BLACK SOULS: In a 2015 study that examined correlations between taste preferences and antisocial personality traits, researchers at the University of Innsbruck, Austria, surveyed nearly 1,000 people and had them fill out questionnaires that asked about their food and drink preferences. The participants were also asked questions relating to narcissism, psychopathy, Machiavellianism, and other antisocial traits. The researchers' findings: tastes for bitter foods (black coffee, beer, celery, and radishes) were "positively associated" with malevolent personality traits in general, and everyday sadism in particular. People who preferred sweet-tasting foods did not show the same associations.

The Chrysler Turbine Car (1963–64) could run on gasoline, kerosene, jet fuel, peanut oil, tequila, or perfume. Only 55 cars were made.

GOVERN-MENTAL

We've been writing about strange politicians since the 1980s...and they keep getting stranger.

LIFE IMITATES ART: In 2019, a software engineer named Francis Tseng was researching agricultural tariffs on the USDA's website. While looking through a list of the nation's trade partners, he came across a country that left him, as he later told *Reuters,* "very confused." It was Wakanda, the fictional sub-Saharan African country where Marvel superhero Black Panther lives. At first, Tseng thought he "misremembered" the name. Yet there it was—Wakanda—complete with a list of exports to the United States, including "ducks, donkeys, and dairy cows." A USDA official later explained that Black Panther's homeland was "added to the list by accident during a staff test" and has since been removed.

RECOUNT RECONSIDERATION: In 2017, Wisconsin governor Scott Walker signed a law that allowed a candidate to request a recount only if they're behind by less than 1 percent of the vote. (The bill was in response to a third-party presidential candidate's demand for a recount after she lost by 99 percent of the vote.) A year later, Governor Walker lost a reelection bid by what appeared to be just a few thousand votes. "The fight is not over," said his lieutenant governor at an election night rally. "We must ensure every valid vote in the state of Wisconsin is counted." But when the final tallies came in, Walker had lost by 1.2 percent of the vote. So, prohibited by law from demanding a recount, Walker had to concede the election.

SORRY, WRONG LETTER: In April 2018, an official letter from the Trump White House was posted on Twitter. It had been sent to the parents of a teenager who had earned the rank of Eagle Scout. That's a common practice. But whoever was in charge of sending out the letters goofed. It began with, "I appreciate you taking the time to send me your thoughts and suggestions." The rest of the letter praised the recently deceased former First Lady Barbara Bush. Not a word about Eagle Scouts. (It's a good bet that somewhere out there was a Barbara Bush fan who received a congratulatory letter for becoming an Eagle Scout.)

YOU SAY TOMATO; I SAY TORONTO: It began life as a typical pothole. As it grew out from the curb on Poplar Plains Road, a residential street in Toronto, neighbors began referring to it as "the crater." Before long, it was two feet deep and as wide as a car. A city crew showed up and placed orange cones around the crater, but then...nothing. For months. Because the pothole wasn't blocking the primary flow of traffic, it wasn't a priority. Calling and complaining had no effect, so a few neighbors decided to fill the crater with potting soil and turn it into a tomato garden. By summer, the plants had grown so large that big tomato cages had to be placed around them. That's when word about the garden started to make it to Reddit, then to Twitter, and then to news outlets around the world. All of a sudden, the crater became a priority. Not to worry, said Toronto mayor John Tory, "We have successfully begun the process of transferring the tomatoes to a community garden so they will survive." He also promised to have the crater filled in. It wasn't the first time something like this has occurred. According to a 2015 report by Mashable.com, "A mystery vandal known as 'Wanksy' has been getting the city of Bury, England, to fix potholes by painting massive penises around them."

HOW TO WIN AT LOSING: This bizarre election outcome is the result of a "quirk in the city charter" of Fall River, Massachusetts, which allows a politician to run in a recall election even if he or she is the one being recalled. That's exactly what embattled Mayor Jasiel F. Correia II did. The 27-year-old Democrat, who'd recently been reelected to a second term, was arrested in 2018 for stealing more than $230,000 from investors in a company that he'd owned prior to his time in office. Defiantly maintaining his innocence, Mayor Correia refused to resign, setting in motion a recall election for March 2019. At the ballot box, a majority voted to recall Correia. The next item was to choose his replacement. And the winner, besting four other candidates with 35 percent of the vote, was none other than Correia himself. Result: even though he was ousted, he was able to succeed himself and stay on as mayor. But the road ahead would be difficult as the embattled mayor faced several indictments, an arrest (for extorting legal cannabis vendors), further recall efforts, and multiple calls to resign. He ran for reelection in November 2019...and lost in a landslide.

MY, WHAT A BIG FOOT YOU HAVE: Most state congressional races go under the national radar, unless something really bizarre emerges. That's what happened in Virginia in 2018 when it was revealed that one of the candidates was into (if you're under 18, cover your eyes now) "Bigfoot erotica." The row began when Democratic candidate Leslie Cockburn tweeted that her Republican opponent, Denver Riggleman, has been "exposed as a devotee" of that particular genre. Riggleman promptly denied accusations that he wrote anything salacious about Sasquatch. He did, however, admit that he posted an "eyebrow-raising" cartoon of a naked Sasquatch with his naughty bits covered by a black "censored bar." Riggleman described the cartoon as "a 14-year practical joke between me and my military buddies." He said he doesn't believe in Bigfoot but has been fascinated by the topic ever since he was a kid. "I didn't know there was Bigfoot erotica," he added, "even with all my Bigfoot studies. I thought this was such a joke that nobody would ever be dumb enough to think that this was real, but I guess her campaign did." Cockburn's camp countered that Riggleman was currently writing a book with the working title *The Mating Habits of Bigfoot and Why Women Want Him.* It didn't hurt: Riggleman won.

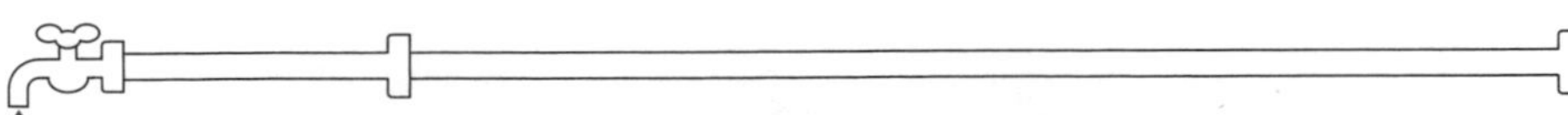

Ray Charles anonymously started and funded a charity to pay for cochlear implants for deaf people.

VIDEO TREASURE: *DINNER FOR ONE*

It's one of the most popular holiday shows in the world, yet few Americans have ever seen it.

LET'S EAT

In 1962, a German television host named Peter Frankenfeld traveled to England with a producer named Heinz Dunkhase to look for fresh material that they could take back home to German television viewers. While passing through Blackpool, a seaside resort town in the northwest of England, they visited a comedy club and took in a performance of a one-act play called *Dinner for One,* starring comedian Freddie Frinton and actress May Warden. The two had been performing in the play together since 1945.

Dinner for One is the story of Miss Sophie, an upper-class English spinster (played by Warden) who is hosting a New Year's Eve dinner party that is also a celebration of her 90th birthday. Her dinner guests are four of her closest friends: Sir Toby, Admiral von Schneider, Mr. Pomeroy, and Mr. Winterbottom. But there's a catch: none of Miss Sophie's dinner guests is actually present at the dinner party, because she has outlived them all. The last of the four died 25 years earlier, and Miss Sophie has dined alone on her birthday ever since. For all those years she has relied upon her long-suffering butler, James (Freddie Finton), to stand in for each of the four missing dinner guests, imitating each of their voices and gestures in turn.

HERE'S TO YOU

Each time Miss Sophie toasts one of her dinner guests, James drinks for them. That's a lot of drinking, because the meal has four courses and Miss Sophie toasts each of her four absent guests during each of the four courses—meaning that James must consume 16 servings of alcohol before the dinner is over. He does so reluctantly: "The same procedure as last year, Miss Sophie?" he asks each time before serving the alcohol. "The same procedure as *every* year, James," she replies each time. James dutifully downs one drink after another, becoming progressively more drunk after each toast. By the time dinner is over, he can barely stand, and his voice is so slurred that he is at times incoherent.

Dinner for One is a cute play, and both Frankenfeld and Dunkhase thought that German audiences would like it. They arranged for Frinton and Warden to come to

Germany and perform the play in a theater in front of a live audience in Hamburg in July 1963. The performance was filmed and then broadcast on Peter Frankenfeld's show on Germany's NDR public television station.

FILLING IN

German TV programs aren't like American programs in the sense that they don't always end exactly on the hour or the half hour. Quite often they end early, and that means that something has to be inserted into the schedule to fill in the remaining time. The filmed version of *Dinner for One,* or *Der 90 Geburtstag (The 90th Birthday),* as it's known in Germany, was just under 18 minutes long, which made it a convenient and entertaining candidate for use as filler. It received quite a lot of airplay over the next several years, and its popularity began to grow.

Then in 1972 it was aired on New Year's Eve at 7:40 to fill in a gap between two other shows. And perhaps because it was a play about a New Year's Eve dinner, this time it really clicked, receiving such a large audience that NDR decided to air it again in the same time slot on New Year's Eve 1973. It has been airing on New Year's Eve each year ever since, not just on NDR but on a number of other German TV stations as well. And not just in one time slot: some stations begin airing it in the morning around 10:30 a.m., then show it several more times during the day until just before midnight. It's estimated that more than half of the entire population of Germany will watch *Dinner for One* at least once before ringing in the new year, something that's all the more impressive when you consider that the play was filmed in black and white and in *English,* not German. In the 1980s and 1990s, the play held the Guinness World Record for being the most frequently repeated television program ever.

THE SAME PROCEDURE AS EVERY YEAR

Dinner for One has become such a regular part of the holidays that "the same procedure as every year" has become a popular buzz phrase, one that appears frequently in conversation and even in news headlines. Trying to keep up with James as he downs toast after toast is a popular New Year's Eve drinking game. And if you plan to eat out in Germany on New Year's Eve, there's a good chance that you'll be able to find a restaurant that serves the same four-course meal as in *Dinner for One*: mulligatawny soup, haddock, chicken and fruit; paired with the same drinks each

IN THE KNOW

Mulligatawny is a soup that originated in southern India and became popular in England. The name comes from the Tamil words *milagu* ("pepper") and *tanni* ("water"). It's made with spicy curry, onions, and stock.

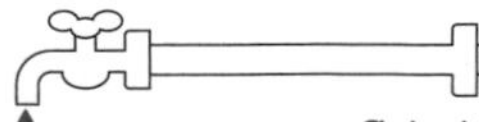

Coincidence? The longest-running daytime drama, *Guiding Light,* and the longest-running prime-time sitcom, *The Simpsons,* are both set in Springfield.

course: dry sherry, white wine, champagne, and port. If you happen to be flying into, out of, or around Germany on December 31, you don't need to worry, because the German airlines show *Dinner for One* as an in-flight screening so that none of their customers will miss out on what has become a beloved holiday tradition.

Trying to keep up with James as he downs toast after toast is a popular New Year's Eve drinking game.

HERE, THERE, (NEARLY) EVERYWHERE

Over the years, *Dinner for One* mania has spread well beyond Germany's borders. Today it airs all over northern Europe and Scandinavia, as well as in Australia and South Africa. Oddly enough, it never aired in the UK, not even once, until 2018, when it finally aired on British TV on New Year's Eve. Neither Freddie Frinton nor May Warden were alive to see it, though. Frinton died in 1968 when he was only 59, and Warden died in 1978 at the age of 87. But Frinton's widow Nora and his daughter Madeline were able to watch *Dinner for One* at a special screening at the Zeitgeist German pub in London. For the first time in more than half a century, they were able to enjoy a live audience reacting to Frinton and May's performances. "It's amazing that so many people still laugh so much," Nora told the BBC. "You know, it's unbelievable, actually, so many years after, [that people are] still talking about it."

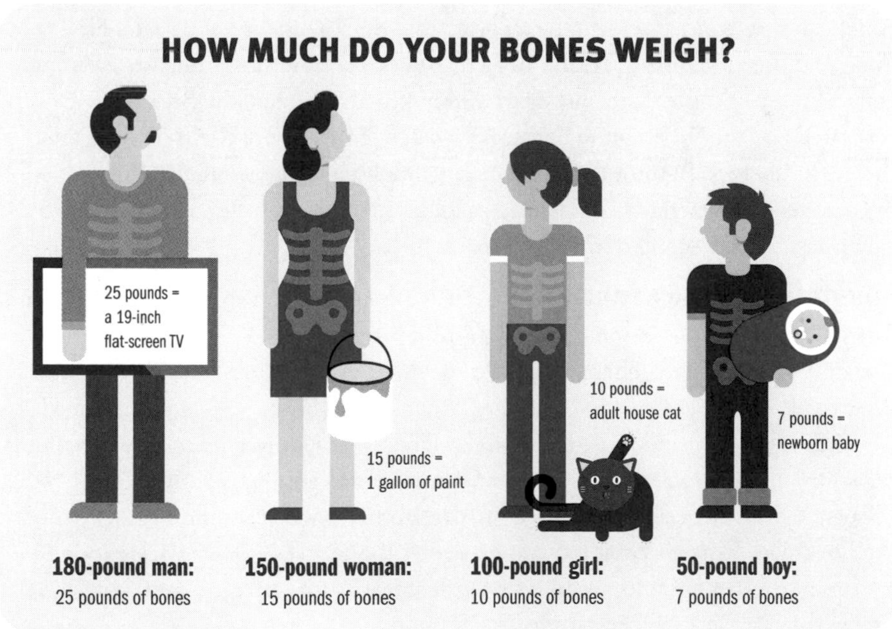

EXPANSION HALTED

Cities hit the big time when they snag a pro sports team, but all too often they shoot a Hail Mary and strike out.

MIFFED IN MEMPHIS: In the early 1970s, the NFL, having recently expanded to include ten AFL teams when the two leagues merged in 1970, decided to create two more new teams. The five finalists for the franchises: Seattle, Tampa, Phoenix, Honolulu, and Memphis. While the first two did get teams (and the St. Louis Cardinals would move to Phoenix in 1988), Honolulu and Memphis got left out. Honolulu was ruled out because the extra time and expense of travel would have wreaked havoc on the league. But Memphis got another shot at it when the NFL expanded again in the mid-'90s. This time, the potential owners even had uniforms designed and picked a team name... and the city was overlooked again, losing to Charlotte and Jacksonville. The name they picked probably didn't help. The owners—who also managed the estate of local hero Elvis Presley—had planned to call their team the Memphis Hound Dogs.

NO GO IN BUFFALO: Major League Baseball underwent its biggest expansion to date in 1969, adding four new teams—two for the American League and two for the National League. The AL got the Kansas City Royals and the Seattle Pilots, and the NL added the San Diego Padres and a team in Buffalo. Buffalo? No. Actually, the second NL team was the Montreal Expos, but the *New York Daily News* and a number of other American newspapers accidentally reported that the finalist city of Buffalo, New York, had been awarded the team. In fact, both of the other 1969 finalists eventually got a team: the Seattle Pilots moved to Milwaukee and became the Brewers just a year later, and the Washington Senators moved to Dallas–Fort Worth and became the Texas Rangers. But not Buffalo. The city didn't make it past the final round of consideration when MLB expanded again in 1993, nor did they make the 1998 expansion. And they still don't have a major league team.

HOUSTON? THEY HAD A PROBLEM: The NBA announced an expansion from 14 teams to 18 for the 1970–71 season, adding four teams in the cities of Cleveland, Buffalo, Portland, and Houston. Those teams became the Cleveland Cavaliers, Buffalo Braves (now the Los Angeles Clippers), and the Portland Trailblazers. The Houston squad would have played its home games on the campus of the University of Houston, but six weeks after their selection as an expansion team was announced, they folded. What happened? The ownership group, led by Alan Rothenberg, a lawyer for the owner of the Los Angeles Lakers, couldn't scrape together the $750,000 down payment on its $3.7 million NBA entrance fee in time for the March 1970 college player draft. Silver lining: the San Diego Rockets moved to Houston just in time for the 1971–72 season.

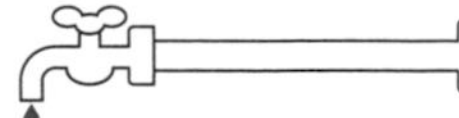

Number of people serving life sentences in England and Wales (combined) in 2019: 70. The United States: more than 50,000.

NATURAL GAS REPORT

Whether we like it or not, flatulence is a natural part of life. So, naturally, it's going to make headlines once in a while.

CABIN FEVER

In February 2018, a Transavia Airlines flight from Dubai to Amsterdam in the Netherlands had to make an emergency landing in Vienna, Austria. Mechanical problems? A bird sucked into an engine? Hardly: when a gassy older passenger continued to fart loudly even after two younger men seated near him asked him to stop, the young men became so unruly that the pilot reported the incident as "passengers on the rampage" and asked for permission to land at the nearest airport. Vienna police pulled the two young men off the flight, along with two young women seated in the same row. (The two women are suing the airline; they say they don't know the men and had nothing to do with the disturbance.) All four passengers have been banned from Transavia Airlines for life. What about the farting passenger? He was allowed to remain on the plane, which continued on to Amsterdam without further incident.

BLADE RUNNER

In November 2018, police were called to the Dollar General store in Dania Beach, Florida, following an armed standoff between a man and a woman in the checkout line. The incident began when Shanetta Wilson, 37, let one rip, and a man behind her in line, John Walker, made a nasty comment that was "in reference to the defendant farting loudly," the police noted in their report. Wilson's response: she pulled a knife on Walker, threatened to "gut" him, and then "pulled back her right hand with the knife as if she was going to attack the victim." By the time police arrived, Wilson had fled the scene, but she was located a short time later and arrested. She was booked on one felony count of aggravated assault with a deadly weapon (without intent to kill). At last report, she was out on $2,500 bail and awaiting trial.

SNIFFED OUT

In July 2019, officers with the Clay County Sheriff's Office and the Liberty City, Missouri, Police Department attempted to arrest a suspect on an outstanding warrant for possession of a controlled substance. But when they arrived at the man's address to arrest him, he was nowhere to be found. Had he fled the scene...or was he hiding? The officers got their answer when the suspect let out a loud fart while they were searching for him. "If you've got a felony warrant for your arrest, the cops are

There are more nerve connections in your brain (500 trillion) than there are stars in the Milky Way (200 billion).

looking for you and you pass gas so loud it gives up your hiding spot," the Sheriff's Office tweeted triumphantly after the man was taken into custody, "you're definitely having a 💩 day."

WRONG ANSWER

In November 2017, police in Kansas City, Missouri, pulled over a motor vehicle during a routine traffic stop. One of the passengers in the car was 25-year-old Sean Sykes Jr., a convicted felon. When police searched the vehicle, they found a backpack containing drugs and two handguns, one of which had been reported stolen out of a car a few days earlier. Sykes was taken into custody but was uncooperative when subjected to further questioning: When a detective asked him for his address, Sykes "leaned to one side of his chair and released a loud fart before answering with his address," the detective noted in his report. "Mr. Sykes continued to be flatulent and I ended the interview." So did Sykes fart his way to freedom? No. A *second* traffic stop while he was out on bail led to more charges, and he eventually pled guilty to possessing drugs with intent to sell, and using a firearm in furtherance of a drug crime. In June 2019, he was sentenced to 10 years, 11 months in prison.

GAS BAG

In March 2019, authorities in the Welsh village of Bedwas brought Detective Constable Claire Fitzpatrick, 44, before a police disciplinary board on charges of 25 instances of unprofessional behavior during the last six months of 2017 alone. Among the charges: verbally abusing members of the public; bullying, cursing, and propositioning her subordinates; quizzing colleagues on their sex lives; and volunteering details of her own. But what likely earned Fitzpatrick countless headlines as well as the tabloid designation "Britain's rudest female police officer" was her penchant for "openly breaking wind in front of other officers and giving the inappropriate and offensive explanation 'Rather out than in!' " Fitzpatrick was remorseful at her hearing, telling the disciplinary board that while she considered her foul language and sex talk to be part of the police station's "culture of banter," the disciplinary proceedings "made me realize how much I need to change. How much I need to be a better person." Too late. She was fired after 22 years on the force.

* * *

A WORD WITH A CHECKERED PAST

"Plaid" comes from the Scottish word *plaide*, which means "blanket." For centuries, Scots wore woolen blankets woven in checkered patterns as warm outer garments. In time it was the patterns, not the blankets, that came to be known as plaid.

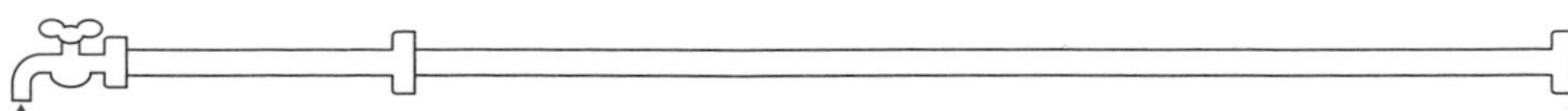

According to the Sword Swallowers Association International, you're not a real sword swallower...

STRANGE CELEBRITY LAWSUITS

We're back with one of our regular features: unusual legal battles involving famous people.

THE PLAINTIFF: Kristina Karo, 27, a Ukrainian-born pop singer living in Los Angeles
THE DEFENDANT: Mila Kunis, 33, a Ukrainian-born actress known for *That '70s Show* and *Bad Moms*
THE LAWSUIT: In 2015, Karo announced that she was suing Kunis for stealing her pet chicken. According to the up-and-coming singer, the two girls were "inseparable" in their village in Berezhnytsia, Soviet Ukraine. Mila would visit Kristina's farm every day to play with their favorite chicken, named Doggie. But then one day Doggie disappeared. Karo said that Kunis confessed to the crime, saying, "Kristina, you can have any other chicken as a pet, you have a whole chicken farm."

Losing her beloved Doggie left Karo an "emotional wreck," and when she arrived in Los Angeles years later, the mere presence of Kunis, who also lived there, "brought back all the bad memories" and forced her back into therapy. In an amazing coincidence, Karo announced the $5,000 lawsuit—for emotional distress and therapy bills—at the same time she was debuting the video to her new song "Give Me Green Card," in which she dances provocatively in an American flag bikini at various L.A. locations (including, for some reason, a Home Depot parking lot).

Kunis said she doesn't even know the singer, and the math doesn't add up because Karo was just a baby when Kunis was seven. "I was like, 'Which chicken did I steal?' because I was obviously in the village when I stole these chickens. So I apologize to this woman who was maybe or maybe not a month old."
THE VERDICT: "There is only one judge and that is God," said Karo, while announcing that she was dropping her lawsuit against Kunis. "I pray for her soul and the soul of Doggie, that he has found peace finally in chicken heaven."

Kunis's response: "I would like to launch a counter $5,000 lawsuit for making me sit there and watch your music video. My body hurts. My eyes hurt, they're burning. That requires money." (The video topped 750,000 views.)

THE PLAINTIFF: Alfonso Ribeiro, who played Carlton Banks on the 1990s sitcom *Fresh Prince of Bel-Air*
THE DEFENDANT: Epic Games, maker of the video game *Fortnite*
THE LAWSUIT: *Fortnite* was already the most popular multiplayer game in the world in January 2018, when Epic offered players a dance move "emote" (an action or symbol

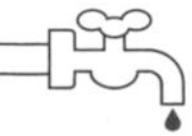

that expresses an emotion, available via an in-game purchase) called "Fresh." "Fresh" is almost identical to "the Carlton Dance," the awkwardly funny 1980s dance move that was Ribeiro's signature move on *Fresh Prince.* The Carlton Dance became a pop culture staple (especially at weddings), so it's not surprising that Ribeiro is protective of it. He concluded his winning season of *Dancing with the Stars* by doing it as the crowd danced along.

Turns out Carlton, er, Ribeiro, wasn't the only one whose likeness had been appropriated by Epic: *Fortnite* players could also buy the signature dance moves of rapper 2 Milly (Terrence Ferguson), rapper BlocBoy JB (James Lee Baker), and an Instagram star known as the "Backpack Kid" (Russell Horning). None of these people are mentioned in the game, nor were any of them asked for their permission.

In December 2018, the *Fresh Prince* actor became the first public figure to sue the video game giant. "Epic cannot profit from its intentional misappropriation of Ribeiro's original content and likeness," read the complaint. The other three public figures filed similar suits, and then a viral video star known as "Orange Shirt Kid" sued Epic (technically, his mom did)—even though he originally submitted his stiff dance routine to *Fortnite* as part of a contest.

The lawsuits got even stranger in February 2019 when a hacker claiming to represent one of the rappers sent fraudulent e-mails to the U.S. Copyright Office demanding that "our copyright claims [are] to be terminated/dismissed because they were false/baseless." It's unclear who sent the e-mails but the FBI was alerted, and all the while, *Fortnite* was garnering a ton of free publicity.

THE VERDICT: In early 2019, the celebrity plaintiffs dropped their suits...temporarily. Why temporarily? Because none of them had actually copyrighted their signature dance moves, so their lawyers said they would refile when—and if—their clients were able to successfully trademark their signature moves. If so, a judge ruled that they would be allowed to sue Epic retroactively. But later that year, Ribeiro's copyright was denied on the grounds that the Carlton Dance "consists of three dance movements," so "it is not a work of choreography and is thus not protected under copyright law." Not helping Ribeiro's claim was a 2015 *Variety* interview in which he said the dance was inspired by "Courtney Cox in the Bruce Springsteen video 'Dancing in the Dark'...or in Eddie Murphy's 'Delirious' video, 'The White Man Dance,' as he called it." The other litigants ran into similar copyright-claim issues. As of last report, the *Fortnite* dancing lawsuits were on "pause."

THE PLAINTIFF: Minnie Driver, 44, a British-born actress known best for *Good Will Hunting,* who moved next door to the Perelmutters

THE DEFENDANT: Daniel Perelmutter, described in press reports as "a 74-year army vet and heart transplant survivor" who lives with his elderly wife Mary Lou in Los Angeles

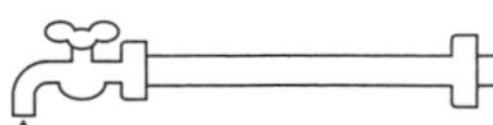

THE LAWSUIT: In 2014, Driver purchased a three-bedroom, $2.5 million home at the top of a long driveway in a fancy neighborhood not far from the famous Hollywood sign. She shared the driveway with three other neighbors, including Perelmutter. Things began cordial enough. Driver asked if it would be okay to put a gate in the driveway to deter peeping paparazzi. Perelmutter agreed because he didn't use that driveway. (He had another one.) But things soured the following year when Perelmutter started construction of a new home in his backyard. To make room for a wall, he narrowed the shared driveway by six feet. Driver was so angry about it (and the noise and trucks) that she retaliated by changing the gate code so that his workers couldn't enter the yard.

Then it got really nasty. Driver told reporters that Perelmutter "blew smoke in her son's face and made misogynistic comments." After police broke up a verbal altercation between the two neighbors, Driver filed a restraining order, and then a lawsuit against Perelmutter, claiming he told workers to leave mounds of dirt blocking her driveway.

THE VERDICT: Driver won. Perelmutter was ordered to remove the wall, perform community service, pay a $1,000 fine, and pay Driver's attorney fees of $200,000. The next time they saw each other, Perelmutter claims Driver said she was "glad he got [censored]" and that she hopes he "loses everything." Would Perelmutter let this stand? See the next entry.

THE PLAINTIFF: Daniel Perelmutter

THE DEFENDANT: Minnie Driver

THE LAWSUIT: In 2016, not long after Driver won her lawsuit against Perelmutter (see the previous entry), he sued her right back, claiming that her changing of the gate code cost him $100,000 in work delays. "She has made my life a living hell," he told reporters. "I've had a heart transplant, 14 back surgeries and a knee replacement, and Minnie Driver isn't helping my health."

Among Perelmutter's other accusations: Driver pelted his new house with baby food jars full of black paint, threatened to have his workers deported, and tried to run him over in her car. Driver denied everything, claiming it was *he* who leaped in front of *her*. Perelmutter, who walks with a cane, responded, "Look at me. I'm handicapped—I wish I could leap!" Driver's lawyer called the suit "frivolous," saying, "Daniel Perelmutter has been the bane of his neighbors for years."

THE VERDICT: At the pretrial hearing in superior court, both parties arrived with an armada of attorneys. Judge Rita Miller expressed her disappointment: "The heart of this case is who's richer than who, I guess." Shortly before the trial began—surprise!—the warring neighbors settled out of court. It's unclear who came out on top, only that "money changed hands."

* * *

"Too much money ain't enough money." —**Lil Wayne**

Cat owners are less likely to be churchgoers than people who don't own cats.

HISTORY'S FORGOTTEN WOMEN

You've heard the proverb, "Behind every great man there is a great woman." It's time for these great women to get the credit they deserve.

FIRST LADY OF THE ARCTIC

Historians are still debating whether the Arctic explorer Robert Peary really made it to the North Pole in 1909, but for decades he was the one who got the credit. Less remembered today is his wife Josephine Diebitsch Peary, who accompanied him on six of his eight Arctic expeditions (but not to the North Pole). During the Pearys' 1891 expedition to Greenland, Robert Peary was badly injured aboard the sailing ship *Kite* when the ship's tiller, used to steer the ship, moved suddenly and struck Peary in his leg, breaking both bones between the knee and ankle. It took him six months to recover. During that time, Josephine added caring for her husband to her other responsibilities, which included hunting deer and trapping foxes, cooking for the expedition (mock-turtle soup, broiled breasts of eider duck, and plum-duff with brandy sauce were all on the menu), and assisting Inuit women with making clothing and sleeping bags out of animal skins. That expedition proved that Greenland was, in fact, an island. Two years later on another expedition, Josephine gave birth to a daughter, Marie Ahnighito, in the Arctic. In so doing she became famous in her own right: The press dubbed her the "First Lady of the Arctic," and her daughter the "Snow Baby." True to her devotion to her husband's endeavors, she used her newfound celebrity to raise money to fund their future Arctic expeditions by writing books, hosting fund-raisers, and touring the country giving lectures.

SOLO SKIING TO THE NORTH POLE

There's *no* debate as to whether explorer Helen Thayer of New Zealand made it to the (magnetic) North Pole. She did it in 1987, solo, on skis, at the age of 50. She pulled her own sled and was accompanied only by her dog, a black husky named Charlie. Thayer was the first woman to make the trip alone without being resupplied along the way. She attempted the journey after training for two years, which included spending several weeks living with Inuits on Resolute Bay in the Canadian Arctic. They taught her traditional survival skills, including how to protect herself against polar bears. "It was only after I had lived with the [Inuit] and learned all I could that I made my final decision as to whether I should go or not," she says. "And if I'd had any doubts that I could handle it, I wouldn't have gone." In

Q: Finland and North Korea are almost 4,200 miles apart. How many countries are there between them? A: One—Russia.

1992, Thayer made the trip again, this time with her husband, Bill; they were the first married couple ever to reach the magnetic North Pole on foot, without being resupplied.

THE CALIFORNIA GOLD RUSH

Most folks thought the shiny nugget James Marshall found near Sutter's Mill was nothing but "fool's gold." Jennie Wimmer knew better. She was Marshall's camp cook, and having grown up in the gold-filled hills of north Georgia—and having panned for gold herself—she was the only one in camp who'd actually seen the precious metal in its raw form. "This is gold," Wimmer said when Marshall showed her that first nugget, and she knew how to prove it. Fool's gold would break apart and dissolve if thrown into a pot of caustic lye. Gold would not. So Jennie tossed the nugget into her kettle while she was making lye soap. "If it is gold, it will be gold when it comes out," she promised. The nugget passed Jennie's test, and the California gold rush was on.

BUILDING THE BROOKLYN BRIDGE

Washington Roebling is the person who went down in history as the builder of the Brooklyn Bridge, the world's longest suspension bridge when it opened in 1883. But his wife, Emily, deserves much of the credit. The project suffered a setback in 1872 when Washington Roebling, the chief engineer, fell ill with caisson disease, also known as decompression sickness or "the bends." The condition is caused by spending too much time in the pressurized underwater chambers (caissons) that were used to build the foundations for the bridge's two towers. The high pressure inside the chambers kept the water out, allowing workers on the river bottom to dig down to solid bedrock. What no one understood at the time was that if people didn't depressurize slowly after leaving these chambers, they could fall ill from the effects of sudden decompression. This is what shattered Roebling's health, leaving him partially blind, deaf, mute, paralyzed, and unable to return to the job site. Emily Roebling stepped in and for more than ten years served as the go-between for her husband and the engineers, workmen, and suppliers on the site, while also caring for her husband. In the process, she learned so much about engineering and bridge building that she became the de facto chief engineer of the project. In 1872, she lobbied public officials to let her husband keep his job. Thanks to her efforts, the bridge was completed in 1883, and Washington Roebling was still listed as chief engineer.

* * *

"Confidence is 10 percent hard work and 90 percent delusion."

—Tina Fey

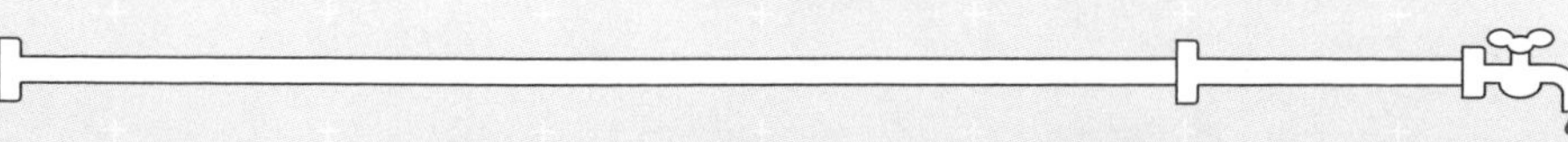

ABLAUT REDUPLICATION

And now for some little-known rules of English you didn't know you knew.

Zagging and Zigging: Try saying "chat-chit" out loud. Feels weird, doesn't it? Almost as weird as popping a "Tac-Tic" into your mouth. But it is *chit-chat* and *Tic-Tac*—and *zigzag, wigwam, flim-flam, shim-sham, dilly-dally,* and *this-and-that.* Why is "i" always before "a"? Because of *ablaut reduplication.* In linguistics, reduplication is a form of alliteration in which two words in a phrase differ only slightly, as in *nitty-gritty.* With ablaut reduplication, it's the vowel sound that changes. And the short "i" will always come first. You wouldn't say "hop-hip" or "flop-flip," would you? How did this even become a rule? And why do we all just seem to do it instinctively? No one knows for sure. It might have something to do with how the human tongue naturally forms sounds. It's just easier to say "Big Bad Wolf" than "Bad Big Wolf"...which could explain why the Big Bad Wolf breaks the next rule.

A Big, Great, Weird Language: When *The Lord of the Rings* author J. R. R. Tolkien was a boy, he wrote a story about a "green, great dragon." As Tolkien later recalled, "My mother pointed out that one could not say 'a green great dragon,' but had to say 'a great green dragon.' I wondered why, and still do." The reason, according to linguist Mark Forsyth in his book *The Elements of Eloquence,* is a little-known rule concerning the order of adjectives. They must go "opinion-size-age-shape-color-origin-material-purpose noun." That means *Uncle John's Great Big Bathroom Reader* might not have sold over a million copies if we'd called it *Uncle John's Big Great Bathroom Reader.* If we really went for it, it could have been *Uncle John's Great Big All-New Rectangular Red American-made Soft-cover Make-You-Smarter Bathroom Reader.* Back to the Big Bad Wolf—the name breaks this rule because ablaut reduplication takes precedence over the order of adjectives.

Nothing to ſneeze At: Ever notice how many nose-y words start with "sn"? There's sneeze, sniff, sniffle, snoot, snooty, snore, snort, and snot. They were formed via onomatopoeia—phonetic spellings of sounds. But your nose doesn't really make an "sn" sound, so what gives? About a millennium ago in Old English, "sneeze" was spelled *fneosan* and pronounced with the "fn" sound—which sounds more like an actual sneeze. (Try it.) Back then, a lowercase "s" at the beginning of a word looked like this: ſ. Etymologists are unsure exactly how—most likely because people were spelling it both *fneosan* and *ſneosan*—but it entered Middle English as *nesen.* In the 17th century, it entered Modern English as sneeze—one of several "fn" words whose "f" and was replaced by an "s."

THE FISHERMAN'S FRIEND

Here's the story of how the untimely death of one man's grandfather spurred him to create something that saved hundreds of lives—and continues to do so today.

THE NEWCOMER

In 1954, a 25-year-old Norwegian man named Gunnar Guddal immigrated to the United States and settled in South Dakota, where he found work as a farmhand. He soon moved to Alaska, where he worked as a woodland firefighter, and then in 1956 moved to Ballard, Washington, where he set up his own business as an importer of marine electronics and fishing gear.

Guddal was an inveterate tinkerer, and spent a lot of time trying to invent new products that would be useful in the fishing and maritime industries. One such invention was inspired by the memory of his grandfather, a fisherman who had died at sea in the frigid waters off the coast of Norway. Cause of death: hypothermia, brought on when he fell off the boat and the cold water caused his body temperature to drop so low that he succumbed within a few minutes of entering the water. Guddal thought that if he could build a suit that kept the seawater out and a person's body heat in, it might give fishermen and mariners a fighting chance at surviving long enough for rescue crews to arrive and pull them from the water.

SEEING RED

The suit that Guddal came up with was made from neoprene, a synthetic material similar to rubber that was water resistant and a good insulator, and it floated. He devised a suit with integrated gloves, boots, and a hood to maximize heat retention. The wearer climbed into the suit by means of a watertight zipper that ran from the neck to the waist; when the wearer pulled on the hood and closed the zipper, the suit kept out the water and retained enough body heat to keep the wearer alive in frigid waters for 12 hours or longer. Bonus: the neoprene material Guddal used to make the suit was bright fluorescent orange, which made the wearer much easier to spot if they were floating in the sea.

THAT SINKING FEELING

Guddal's firm began selling his "immersion suits," as they would become known, in 1969. To increase interest in the new product, he demonstrated them on the docks where the fishermen kept their boats, and he gave some of the suits away free in the hope that this would spur sales to other fishermen. He also demonstrated the suits at trade shows, where he or his daughter floated in a wading pool to show how they worked.

None of these efforts had much of an impact on sales. Immersion suits were expensive, and fishermen were notoriously tight with their money. They were a fatalistic bunch as well, used to the idea that they might die at sea. If such a thing had to happen, the thinking went, it was better to die from the cold in a few minutes than to don one of Guddal's suits and linger for days before finally dying from thirst with no fresh water to drink.

LAW SUIT

It wasn't until 1991 that sales of the immersion suits began to take off, and then only because the U.S. Coast Guard issued a new regulation requiring fishing boats and other vessels to carry a suit for every member of the crew. Soon thousands of the suits were stowed aboard ships in U.S. waters. (They were nicknamed "Gumby suits" because they made the wearer look like Gumby, a popular character on *The Gumby Show,* an animated children's program.) And just as Guddal had hoped, the suits began to save lives. After more than 20 years of trying and failing to interest fishermen and the maritime industry in his lifesaving suits, Guddal, by now in his 60s, began to experience the pleasure of receiving letters and even occasional visits from the people his invention had saved. One woman, who survived for nine hours in Alaskan waters and then ten days ashore on a remote beach before being rescued, sent Guddal a Christmas card every year for the rest of his life. In all, it's estimated that his suits have saved hundreds of lives since they were mandated in 1991, and the number will only grow.

They were nicknamed "Gumby suits."

Guddal never patented his invention, which meant that other businesses were free to create and market their own immersion suits. But the competition has helped to keep the suits affordable, and has spurred innovations that made them even more effective at saving lives. One immersion suit, introduced in 2014, features a snorkel-like breathing apparatus that circulates warm, exhaled air back into the suit, keeping the wearer warm for 24 hours or more.

* * *

MYTH-CONCEPTION

MYTH: The Sun is yellow.

TRUTH: The Sun emits pure white light, which is all the colors of the spectrum combined. When sunlight passes through the atmosphere, some of those colors are absorbed by particulates, making the Sun appear darker. As it gets lower in the sky, its light must pass through several hundred miles of atmosphere—first appearing as yellow, then orange, and then red before disappearing.

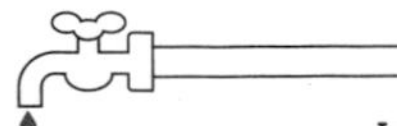

In 2014, three towns banded together as the "Trinity of Tedium": Boring, Oregon; Dull, Scotland; and Bland, Australia.

HOME AWAY FROM HOME

People leave their native lands for any number of reasons—seeking a better life or fleeing political strife, for example. They often resettle together in new places, forming new communities and laying down roots. Here's where some of those people ended up.

Ethiopians

Addis Ababa, the capital and largest city in Ethiopia, has the world's largest concentration of Ethiopians, with a population of about 3.3 million. But outside the country, the most Ethiopians and people of Ethiopian descent live in Washington, D.C. Not all are well-documented, though—estimates range from around 100,000 to as many as 250,000.

Japanese

Outside of Japan, where the vast majority of its 127 million citizens are Japanese, the most people of Japanese descent live in Brazil. There are about 1.5 million Japanese-Brazilians. (Brazil is becoming a true melting pot. It's also home to the most African people outside of Africa and Syrians outside of the Middle East.)

Vietnamese

Hundreds of thousands of Vietnamese natives fled their country during and after the Vietnam War, and more settled in Southern California than in any other place. Today, about 184,000 Vietnamese-Americans live in Orange County, comprising around 6 percent of that county's population.

Cambodians

Cambodians left their country en masse in the 1970s, hoping to escape the reign of terror, torture, and death wrought by Pol Pot's Khmer Rouge regime. The United States is home to about 320,000 Cambodian-Americans today, of which 118,000 live in California. The highest concentration is in the town of Long Beach, California, where 20,000 Cambodians and their descendants reside.

Palestinians

As the ongoing conflict with Israel has left them without a permanent political state, Palestinians have dispersed throughout the Middle East. More than three million reside in Jordan—double the number that live in Israel. Outside of the Middle East, the largest Palestinian community is in Chile, home to about half a million.

IN THE KNOW

When a large population leaves its ancestral homeland involuntarily (often due to war or desperate economic conditions) and resettles elsewhere, it is known as a *diaspora*. The United States is home to many diasporas, including Italian, Irish, and Jewish refugees in the late 19th and early 20th centuries. More recent arrivals: Salvadorans (2.1 million), Colombians (1 million), and Bangladeshis (280,000).

Francophone Canadians

Canada is officially a bilingual nation—the country's languages of record are English and French, although only about 20 percent of Canadians speak French fluently. The majority of French speakers live in Quebec, where 95 percent of residents speak French as either their first or second language. Apart from Quebec, the most Canadian French-speakers live in the province of New Brunswick—a third of its more than 775,000 people speak *la langue française.*

Icelanders

What country is home to more people with an Icelandic background than any other (except Iceland)? It's Canada. Around 2,000 Icelandic-Canadians live in Gimli, Manitoba. That's about a third of the small town's population.

Welsh speakers

Welsh isn't a widely spoken language...even in Wales. Less than 20 percent of its three million people—about 580,000 people—can speak it. The second-most Welsh speakers—110,000—live in neighboring England. Apart from the British Isles, the most people who can speak Welsh live in the Chubut province in southern Argentina. Welsh people emigrated to the area in the 19th century, and today about 5,000 people there still speak the old language.

Americans

Americans—meaning people born in the United States—have migrated in large numbers all over the world. Around 900,000 expat Americans live in Mexico, the majority of them of Mexican descent. Another 750,000 Americans now live in Canada, and 800,000 reside in Europe (of those, two-thirds can be found in Italy, Germany, France, and England). In Asia, India is home to the largest collection of people born in the United States—around 700,000 in all.

* * *

A DUMB JOKE

What's the difference between boogers and broccoli? Kids won't eat broccoli.

A WHALE OF A TALE

The first "hydrophones," microphones that listen for sounds underwater, were invented to detect enemy submarines in wartime. But that wasn't all they heard...

THE EAVESDROPPER

Frank Watlington was an engineer assigned to the U.S. Navy's top-secret Sound Fixing and Ranging (SOFAR) station on St. David's Island, Bermuda, in the late 1950s. Those were some of the darkest days of the Cold War between the United States and the USSR, and the SOFAR station's mission was to listen for sounds made by Russian submarines that might be lurking off the eastern coast of the United States. In Watlington's office, an audio terminal was connected by an undersea cable to a *hydrophone* (an underwater microphone) on the ocean floor some 30 miles out to sea; the hydrophone was capable of picking up sounds from hundreds of miles away. Using the terminal, Watlington could listen to whatever sounds the hydrophone picked up. He also had a tape recorder, and anytime the hydrophone picked up something interesting, he turned on the tape recorder and recorded the sound.

Many of the sounds detected by the hydrophone were human in origin, such as ship and submarine noises, but others clearly were not. Every winter, the hydrophone picked up strange sighs, rumbling, groans, mumbles, clicks, and other mysterious sounds from the deep. Another U.S. Navy listening station in Hawaii reported hearing similar noise as early as 1952, but no one there knew what had made them, either.

Watlington made a tape containing just those sounds—so that he wouldn't reveal the top-secret nature of his work—and played it to anyone in Bermuda who he thought might be able to tell him what had made them. It didn't take him long to find an answer: "The story that I've heard is that he played it for some fishermen, and they said, 'Oh, those are whales,'" Watlington's grandson, Dan Ruetenik, told CBS News in 2013. Sailors had been hearing the noises for centuries, and they believed that the sounds were made by the ghosts of fellow sailors who had drowned. The Bermuda fishermen knew the sounds were made by whales because when the whales are close enough to a fishing vessel, if the engine isn't running, the sounds can be heard through the hull of a ship. This explanation made sense to Watlington, because winter was the time of year that humpback whales could be seen in the waters off Bermuda.

UNHEARD OF

The sounds made by whales are so familiar today that it's difficult to understand just how unfamiliar they were in the late 1950s. Very few people on Earth even realized that whales made noises, let alone heard them. Hardly anyone *could* have heard them: Watlington's tapes of whale sounds are apparently the first recordings of whale noises

ever made, so if you weren't out at sea on a very quiet ship standing right next to the hull as a whale happened to swim by, you would never have had an opportunity to hear the sounds.

Though he was fascinated by the noises, Watlington kept his recordings a secret once he knew what they were, because he was afraid that whalers might be inspired to use hydrophones to track whales from hundreds of miles away. The whaling industry was killing too many whales already: In recent decades, technological advances like motorized whaling ships and exploding harpoons had sent the annual harvest soaring to some 30,000 whales killed each year. Many species, including blue whales, right whales, sperm whales, and humpback whales, were sliding ever closer to extinction. It wasn't clear how much longer many of these species would be able to hold out. Watlington continued to record the whale sounds, but he told almost no one what he was doing.

THE VISITOR

Watlington kept his secret until 1967, when a biologist named Roger Payne came to Bermuda to study humpback whales. He was introduced to Watlington, who took Payne out on his research vessel to watch the humpbacks up close. While they were out at sea, Watlington said to Payne, "You know they make sounds, don't you?" This was news to Payne—he'd only recently switched to studying whales after spending years studying owls, bats, and moths. Watlington took Payne belowdecks to where he had a tape recorder set up. "[Watlington] gave me some earphones and said, 'Listen to this,' " Payne remembered. "It was the most astonishing, extraordinary thing I'd ever heard in the wild."

Payne asked Watlington if he could take some of the tapes back home with him to New York, and Watlington agreed. Back home, Payne played the whale tapes for hours on end. "I would just leave it on—just going again and again and again. And after a long while of listening to this, I suddenly realized, 'My God, this thing is repeating itself,' " he told National Public Radio in 2014. The whales were *singing.* Not in a human sense, but in the animal sense: "A regular sequence of repeated sounds such as the calls made by birds, frogs, and crickets."

JUST THE THING

When Payne switched from studying owls, bats, and moths to studying whales, he did so because, like Watlington, he understood that whales were heading for extinction, and he wanted to do something about it. He thought that one good way to accomplish this would be to get people to think differently about whales, or at least get them to think about whales at all. In the past, the giant creatures had been misunderstood and largely ignored. "I felt that unless people got interested in whales, there was no hope of saving them, and I realized that I might be able to help change that," he told the Library

Harvard University, founded in 1636, is older than calculus (1684). Cambridge University (1209) is older than the Aztec Empire (1345).

of Congress in 2017. But he didn't know *how* he was going to do it...until he heard Watlington's recordings. "When I realized that whales sing, I thought, 'My God! This is just what is needed to get the world interested in whales.' "

"My God! This is just what is needed to get the world interested in whales."

NOW HEAR THIS

Payne spent the next two years traveling around the country playing the tapes for anyone who would listen, and giving talks on the plight of the whales before any organization that would host him. Then in 1970, he took two of Watlington's best whale recordings and two that he and his wife Katy had recorded on a sailboat and released them in the form of a record album called *Songs of the Humpback Whale,* complete with a 48-page booklet that described the songs and explained the plight of the whales.

Payne had high hopes for the album, but nothing like it had ever been released before, and nobody knew how well it would sell, or whether it would sell at all. They needn't have worried: The original release of *Songs of the Humpback Whale* sold more than 100,000 copies—more than any nature sound recording had ever sold. (In January 1979, *National Geographic* magazine included a "flexi-disc" recording of some of the whale songs in all 25 language editions of the magazine, more than 10.5 million copies in all, making it the single largest press run of any album of recorded music in the history of the recording industry.)

TAKING ACTION

More importantly, *Songs of the Humpback Whale* really did help to change the public's attitude toward whales. Where once they had been barely noticed "swimming bags of blubber" with little apparent value other than as the source of raw materials used to make soap, lipstick, margarine, and cat food, the album helped people to see them as intelligent, endangered creatures worthy of preservation.

The organization Greenpeace, which got its start in the late 1960s protesting nuclear weapons testing in Alaska (which it succeeded in stopping), adopted whale conservation as its next campaign after some of its organizers listened to *Songs of the Humpback Whale* at a meeting in Vancouver, British Columbia, in the early 1970s. "That was the first time any of us heard those recordings," Rex Weyler, a former director of Greenpeace, told National Public Radio in 2014, "and it certainly was a huge factor in convincing us that the whales were an intelligent species."

As other environmental organizations joined the "Save the Whales" movement, public pressure on the whaling industry began to build. Finally, in 1982, the International Whaling Commission, which was established in 1946 to regulate the whaling industry, buckled to pressure from its member nations and adopted

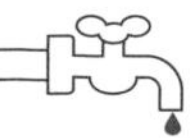

a worldwide ban on commercial whaling that came into force in 1986. Not every country agreed to abide by the moratorium: Norway, Iceland, and Japan are notable exceptions, but the moratorium reduced the number of whales killed each year from 30,000 to between 3,000 and 4,000.

ON THE MEND

As of 2020, the moratorium is still in effect, and whale numbers are increasing, though some species of whales have rebounded more quickly than others. Blue whale and gray whale populations have increased, but they're still considered critically endangered. Humpback whales, by contrast, are one of the success stories: After dropping from an estimated population of 1.5 million at the start of the 19th century to as few as 7,000 whales the year the moratorium went into effect, the population has rebounded to some 80,000 whales, prompting the International Union for the Conservation of Nature to move humpbacks from the "vulnerable" category to "least concern."

Fifty years after *Songs of the Humpback Whale* was released, it's still racking up sales and remains the best-selling nature recording of all time. If you've never listened to the album but you've seen the 1986 film *Star Trek IV: The Voyage Home,* you've heard some of the tracks from the album, because they were used in the whale scenes.

Some of the tracks from *Songs of the Humpback Whale* were among the first animal sounds to leave the solar system in 2012, because they were included with other animal and nature sound recordings on a golden record placed aboard the *Voyager 1* spacecraft when it launched in 1977. (*Voyager 1* crossed into interstellar space on August 25, 2012.) Thanks to the popularity of the album and the whale conservation movement that it helped launch, if aliens ever do encounter *Voyager 1* and decide to travel to Earth to get a look at the animals whose sounds were placed aboard the spacecraft, there's at least a chance that the humpback whales will still be around for them to visit.

* * *

ON THE LEVEL

Technically speaking, there's no such thing as "sea level," because the level of the seas and oceans is constantly changing, thanks to the changing tide and numerous other factors. The way sea level is calculated at a given place is to measure the level of the sea or ocean at high and low tide over many months or even years, and then calculate an average or "mean" sea level. When people refer to "sea level," what they really mean is "mean sea level."

After Prince's death in 2016, Pantone honored him with a new color called Love Symbol #2. (It's a shade of purple.)

HUH?

Are these quotes ironic wisdom...or double-talk?

"I am the wisest man alive, for I know one thing, and that is that I know nothing."

—Socrates

"Sometimes I'm confused by what I think is really obvious. But what I think is really obvious obviously isn't obvious."

—Michael Stipe

"Good judgment comes from experience, and experience comes from bad judgment."

—Barry LePatner

"Never have children, only grandchildren."

—Gore Vidal

"Give me a couple of years, and I'll make her an overnight success."

—Samuel Goldwyn

"TO BE WITHOUT SOME OF THE THINGS YOU WANT IS AN INDISPENSABLE PART OF HAPPINESS."

—Bertrand Russell

"Reality exists in the human mind, and nowhere else."

—George Orwell

"I quote others only in order the better to express myself."

—Michel de Montaigne

"TO DO TWO THINGS AT ONCE IS TO DO NEITHER."

—Publilius Syrus

"It is never too late to be what you might have been."

—George Eliot

THE DUNE BUGGY MAN, PART II

Can you imagine what it's like to come up with an innovative product, and then have illegal knockoffs of your product drive you out of business? Here's part II of the story. *(Part I is on page 89.)*

ONE BY ONE

It took Bruce Meyers a year and a half to finish building his first dune buggy; it finally hit the sand in the summer of 1964. And just as he'd hoped, it was a true dune buggy, able to race up and down the sand dunes with ease and leaving larger, heavier dune buggies in the dust. (Well, sand.) But Meyers didn't know what to name his new vehicle, and neither did his wife, Shirley, who worked in the advertising department at *Road & Track* magazine. She asked her coworkers at the magazine to help come up with a name for the stubby little car. More than 30 people made suggestions, including four who suggested they call it the Manx, after the bobtailed housecats that originated on the Isle of Man. And that's what they named it: the Meyers Manx.

Once his dune buggy was complete, Meyers started building fiberglass bodies and selling them in kit form to his friends, so that they could build their own Manxes. He didn't expect to build more than ten kits a year. And for the first few years, that was all he sold. But then in April 1967, *Car and Driver* magazine put the Meyers Manx on the cover with the caption "You Can Build This Fun Car for $635!"

"Once that article hit, we had 350 orders almost overnight," Meyers told *Car and Driver* in 2006. He started hiring staff and ramping up production until he was building 25 kits a week.

THE SINCEREST FORM OF FLATTERY

The Meyers Manx was arguably the first dune buggy with personality and a beauty all its own, and it sparked a dune buggy craze. Elvis Presley drove one in the 1968 film *Live a Little, Love a Little,* and Steve McQueen drove one the same year in *The Thomas Crown Affair.* The fad was helped along by the fact that used VW Beetles were plentiful and cheap. They could be bought for as little as $50, and turned into a Meyers Manx for under $1,000. Volkswagen Beetles were popular all over the world, and as the dune buggy craze took hold, so too did interest in Meyers Manx dune buggies.

But one of the drawbacks of creating a design as simple as Meyers's was that it was also easy to copy. Being made from fiberglass only made the problem worse: Fiberglass parts are made by creating a mold, then lining the mold with glass fibers—hence the name—and pouring resin into the mold to harden or "cure" the mixture into the exact shape of the mold. Anyone could buy a single Meyers Manx kit, use it to construct a mold, and then use the mold to make fiberglass body parts identical to the ones made by Meyers himself. People started doing just that—lots of people. So many imitators sprung up that not only did Meyers struggle to win new customers, he started losing what business he did have to the knockoffs. "They were all over the place," he later told one reporter. "They were all over England and *everywhere.*"

IN THE KNOW

In March 2019, Volkswagen introduced an electric dune buggy concept car called the I.D. Buggy that drew inspiration from the Meyers Manx. At last report, the I.D. Buggy was still just a one-off that VW has no plans to bring to market. But that's also what VW said about its retro-styled electric minivan concept car, the I.D. Buzz, when it debuted in 2017. A few months later, the company announced that it would begin selling the Buzz in 2022.

The problem got worse when Meyers sued one of his biggest competitors for infringing on his dune buggy patent. The judge not only decided in favor of the competitor, he ruled that Meyers's patent was invalid, which meant that now anyone was free to copy his design. And there was nothing he could do to stop them.

WRECKED

Meyers tried to keep ahead of the competition by coming up with new designs for dune buggies and other vehicles, but none of these kits sold as well as the original Meyers Manx. All they did was eat up his rapidly dwindling capital. His sales fell from 25 kits a week to 20, then to 15, and they kept dropping. Finally, in 1970, he threw in the towel. "We just gave it up and backed out of it and went away broke with our tails between our legs," he told an interviewer.

The company staggered on for a few more months without him, then shut its doors in 1971. No official count is available, but by the time the dune buggy craze wound down in the late 1970s, it's estimated that as many as 250,000 Meyers Manx–inspired dune buggies had been built around the world. Only about 5,000 of these were built from kits made by Bruce Meyers's company. All of the others were rip-offs.

TAKING A BREAK

The experience of having his design stolen and his business destroyed left Meyers so bitter that he abandoned dune buggies entirely and moved on to other things. In the years that followed, he invented the first fiberglass hot tub, made bedliners for pickup trucks, and even created a children's bed shaped like a race car. He also

restored old cars, and for a time, he worked for a company that turned ordinary cars into convertibles.

It wasn't until 1994 that he dipped a toe back into the dune buggy world by accepting an invitation to attend a Volkswagen dune buggy rally in France. Just as he feared, there were lots of Meyers Manx knockoffs at the rally. But more importantly, there were many people there who knew who he was, and who appreciated the role he'd played in bringing dune buggies to the world. Their adulation inspired Meyers to start a dune buggy club back home in California, which he used to see if people would be interested in buying new dune buggy kits.

Many people who joined the club were owners of Meyers Manx knockoffs who were eager to trade up to the genuine article; that inspired Meyers to announce the production of a limited edition of 100 new "Classic Manx" kits in 2000. When those sold out in a single month, he jumped back into the dune buggy kit business full-time. As of 2020, he's 94 years old going on 17, and still selling dune buggy kits. The Classic Manx is still available, and there are four brand-new models to choose from. But they don't cost $695 anymore—prices range from $2,400 to $13,000, depending on models and options, and you'll still have to find an old Volkswagen Beetle to put them on.

As of 2020, he's 94 years old going on 17, and still selling dune buggy kits.

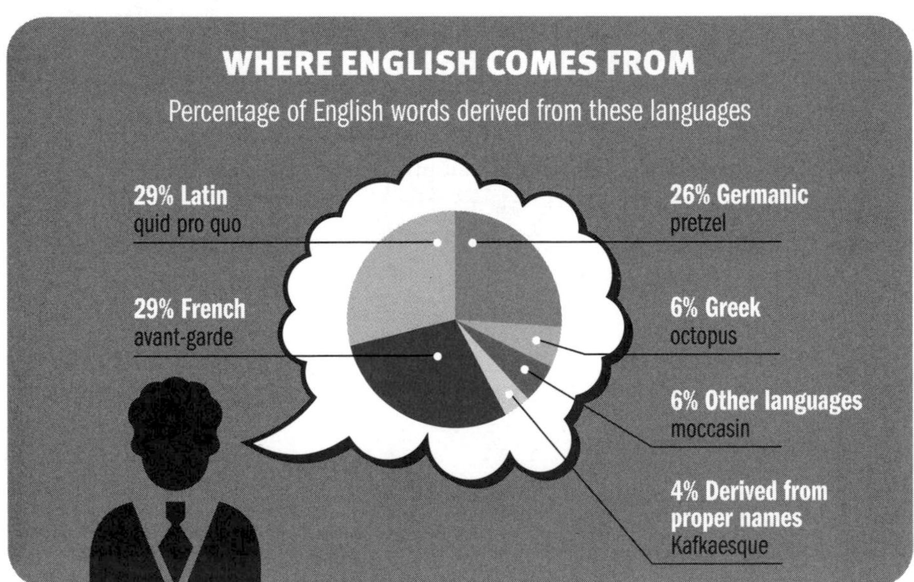

PORTMANTEAU, INC.

When two big entities merge, what do you call the new company? One idea: you come up with a new name that merges the names of the old companies. Here are some company names you probably didn't know were other names mashed together.

- In 1929, Margarine **Unie** (Dutch for "Margarine Union"), a Netherlands-based producer of several brands of faux butter, including Blue Band, Rama, and Vitello, merged with the British company **Lever** Brothers, manufacturer of Lifebuoy Soap, to form a new company that would become a massive multinational corporation, owning such brands as Dove Soap, Birds Eye, Good Humor, Ragú, Cutex, Vaseline, Hellmann's, Ben & Jerry's, and Axe...**Unilever**.

- In 1967, New York–based First National City Bank reorganized as **Citi**corp—and became an umbrella corporation for a number of varied businesses, mostly banking and financial concerns. In 1998, it merged with another financial company, Travelers **Group**, to form what is now one of the largest banks in the United States, **Citigroup.**

- Farmers often enter into co-op agreements. Sort of like forming a large corporation, it allows small, regional businesses to sell and distribute products to a larger territory. In 1964, about 100,000 French dairy farmers formed a co-op to sell their products across the country. A year later, two of those co-op participants, the yogurt-focused **Yo**la and Co**plait**, merged to become a larger yogurt producer called **Yoplait**. It slowly grew to become the largest yogurt company in the world, and in 2011 General Mills purchased a controlling interest and made it a division of the international food company.

- What's the opposite of a merger? The closest thing is when the federal government breaks up a company that it rules has an unfair monopoly on an industry. That's what happened to John D. Rockefeller's Standard Oil in 1911. Standard Oil was one of the first U.S.-based international companies and the biggest oil refiner in the world, but the U.S. Supreme Court ordered it to split up into more than 30 smaller and regional oil providers, among them Standard Oil of New Jersey, Standard Oil of Iowa, and the South **Penn** Oil Company. With the oil and petroleum markets opened up to the competition, other companies could more easily join the industry. In 1953, future president George H.W. Bush used part of his family's fortune to help start a Texas-based company called Zapata **Oil**. After less than a decade in operation, South Penn purchased Zapata and rebranded itself as **Pennzoil**, the same name as its signature product, a line of motor oils.

- In 1884, six gas companies—New York, Manhattan, Harlem, Metropolitan, Knickerbocker, and Municipal—merged into one big company called **Con**solidated Gas. (In those days, "gas" was manufactured from coal, and used primarily for street lighting.) In the early 20th century, Consolidated acquired the first and biggest of the more than 30 electricity companies in the northeastern U.S.: the New York **Ed**ison Company (founded in 1882 as the Edison Illuminating Company by inventor Thomas Edison). In 1936, the Consolidated Gas Company wanted to reflect the fact that it offered both gas and electricity, and changed its name to Consolidated Edison, or **ConEd**.

- In 1839, Rhode Island textile magnate Oliver Chace started the Valley Falls Company, operating several textile mills on the Blackstone River. Ninety years later, it merged with its Massachusetts-based competitor, the Berkshire Cotton Manufacturing Company, and the new entity was called **Berkshire** Fine Spinning Associates. Then in the 1950s, yet another New England textile firm, the **Hathaway** Manufacturing Company, merged with Berkshire to create a massive textile conglomerate called **Berkshire Hathaway**, employing as many as 12,000 people. With the textile industry in decline in the late 1950s and early 1960s, the company started shutting down mills, and rising-star investor Warren Buffett started buying large quantities of the company stock. By 1964, he owned a controlling interest in the failing company, and by 1967, he was using it as an umbrella corporation for his various holdings, including insurance and real estate. The last textile mill in the company closed down in 1985.

- Hollywood movie studio **Twentieth Century** Pictures was founded in 1933 by Joseph Schenck and Darryl F. Zanuck, after they left their respective employers, United Artists and Warner Bros. The new studio retained relations with United Artists, which distributed the company's films to theaters, until a disagreement between Zanuck and the UA board led him to work out deals with other distributors. In 1935, Twentieth Century found the deal it wanted, buying the bankrupt **Fox** Film, established as a silent movie producer by William Fox in 1915. The new company, **Twentieth Century Fox**, became one of the biggest moviemaking entities in history. In 2019, the company was purchased by the Walt Disney Corporation, which renamed its newly acquired division Twentieth Century Pictures, dropping the "Fox" that had been part of its name for nearly a century.

IN THE KNOW

The name of the African country of Tanzania is a portmanteau. Established as a nation in 1964, before that time it was two separate, sovereign nations: **Tan**ganyika and **Zan**zibar.

LUCKY FINDS

Ever stumble upon something valuable? It's an incredible feeling. Here's the latest installment of one of the BRI's regular features.

LUCKY WAS WITH HIM

The Find: A 1.35-pound gold nugget

Where It Was Found: On a walk

The Story: In 2019, a man (who wished to remain anonymous) took his dog, Lucky, for a walk somewhere (he wouldn't say exactly where) outside the city of Bendigo, about two hours north of Melbourne, Australia. Joining him were his two daughters, and it's a good thing they did. "I actually walked right past it," he later told the *Bendigo Advertiser*, "but my daughter pretty much kicked it as she was walking. She then goes, 'Dad, is this gold?'" He replied, "I think it might be." Unable to find a jeweler, they brought the fist-sized chunk to a grocery store deli to weigh it, and it topped 20 ounces. Experts have since confirmed the nugget's authenticity. "We've come on some tough times," the dad said, "so it couldn't be better timing." He said the family discussed keeping their lucky find, but they ultimately decided to sell it. Estimated value: $24,000.

HIGH SCORE

The Find: A rare video game still in its original packaging

Where It Was Found: In a box in an attic

The Story: On Mother's Day in 2019, Scott Amos of Reno, Nevada, was visiting his childhood home in Humboldt County, California, to finally get his stuff out of his mom's attic. While he was going through the boxes, he came across a JCPenney shopping bag. Inside it was a Nintendo video game called *Kid Icarus* that Amos didn't even remember owning. Judging by the December 1988 receipt, it was most likely a Christmas present that never got wrapped. Nor had it been opened, which makes this lucky find a huge deal. According to gaming expert Valarie McLeckie, *Kid Icarus* is a highly sought-after cult classic, and there are fewer than 10 known unopened copies in existence: "To find a sealed copy 'in the wild,' so to speak, not to mention one in such a nice condition, is both an unusual and rather historic occurrence." Amos put the video game—which originally cost $38.45—up for auction, and sold it for $9,000. He used the windfall to take his family to Disney World.

ALL'S WHALE THAT ENDS WHALE

The Find: A 14-pound chunk of ambergris (aka whale vomit)

Where It Was Found: On a beach

The Story: Jumrus Thiachot was down on his luck. The 55-year-old Thai fisherman was only making about 400 baht ($13) a day, and had very little money to his name. Then, one day in early 2019, Jumrus was walking on the beach and found a yellow lump of...something in the sand. He thought the waxy substance might be ambergris. Made in the belly of a sperm whale, only a tiny amount of it is needed to make a fragrance last longer. That makes this "floating gold" highly desirable in the perfume industry. But because ambergris is so rare, Jumrus wasn't getting his hopes up. He took a few slivers of it to be tested, but the tests were inconclusive. Unsure of what to do next, Jumrus stored the lump in his shed and got back to his life.

Nearly a year passed. Jumrus "needed to know the truth," so he contacted the provincial governor, who brought an expert to the fisherman's house. Result: the substance was determined to be at least 80 percent ambergris, with an estimated value of $320,000. "Now that I know it is real whale vomit, I will sell it," he said.

ON THE MONEY

The Find: A horde of historic gold coins

Where It Was Found: In a field in Northern Ireland

The Story: Paul Raynard is a lighting engineer from West Yorkshire, England. In his spare time, he's a "detectorist"—someone who hunts for treasure with a metal detector. But it wasn't treasures he was hunting for in November 2019. Raynard was vacationing in Ballycastle, Northern Ireland, when his friend, Michael Gwynne, asked for help finding a lost wedding ring in a field. After an hour and a half of searching with Raynard's high-end metal detector, all they found were a horseshoe and a five-pence coin. Still no ring.

Then Raynard's detector started beeping, and he started digging. About a foot below the soil, he pulled the first coin out, then another, and then another. "There's millions!" he shouted to Gwynne. All told, they pulled 84 gold coins out of the ground. Some of them dated back to the 1500s, including a rare King Henry VIII coin worth over $6,000. They brought their unburied treasure to Ulster Museum in Belfast, where it was estimated to be worth £100,000 ($125,000). Experts have called it the biggest horde of gold coins ever found in Ireland. "It's something I have dreamed of finding since I was a kid," said Raynard (who never did find the wedding ring).

For more detectorist lucky finds, sweep over to page 273.

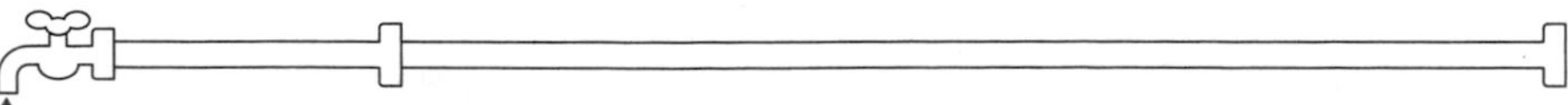

UNDERWEAR IN THE NEWS

Nearly everybody wears underwear, but hardly anyone makes headlines because of it.

END RUN

In May 2019, officials at Colorado State University announced that they would not allow the school's annual "Undie Run" to take place that year. During the run, which takes place at dusk on the last Friday before spring semester finals, students blow off steam by stripping down to their skivvies and running around on campus. But that year, Dean of Students Jody Donovan put her foot down, saying that the Undie Run takes place "in an atmosphere of public intoxication and behavior that risks personal injury and sexual misconduct," and that in the past, non-students had participated, but "only to take photographs and videos," and to "keep those images for their personal use or post it online." So did the school succeed in putting the kibosh on the Undie Run? Hardly, but they did put a dent in it: 1,300 students participated in the run, down from 3,000 to 5,000 in earlier years. For now, at least, the tradition lives on.

FOLLOW THE YELLOW BRA ROAD

In January 2019, police in Portage, Indiana, engaged in a high-speed pursuit of a woman suspected of shoplifting underwear from the local Kohl's department store. The suspect, a 32-year-old woman named Holly Sansone, wasn't hard to follow, because she tossed bras and panties out of the car as she drove. The police finally got her to stop by placing spike strips on State Highway 49, puncturing her two right tires and causing her to crash into the highway shoulder. Sansone, who had still more stolen underwear in her car, was taken into custody without further incident. (She was later found to be wearing two pairs of shoplifted underwear with the security tags still on them.) After pleading guilty to one count of resisting arrest with the use of a motor vehicle, the other charges against her were dropped and she was sentenced to 90 days in jail plus probation.

The suspect wasn't hard to follow, because she tossed bras and panties out of the car as she drove.

PANT LOAD

In January 2019, a drug-sniffing dog named Jake had to be rushed to the veterinarian after getting a snootful of contraband while assessing underpants worn by a passenger preparing to board a cruise ship in Port Canaveral, Florida. Police say the passenger, a 33-year-old Montana man named Leslie Bennett, had hidden a bag of ecstasy pills,

"possibly crushed," in his boxer shorts. When Jake sniffed at Bennett's skivvies, he inhaled so much ecstasy that he had a seizure and lost motor control. Deputies, fearing that Jake might have inhaled opioids, administered the anti-overdose drug Narcan on the spot. Then they took him to the vet. Jake made a speedy recovery and is back at work sniffing for drugs; Bennett pled no contest to two counts of drug possession and was sentenced to probation.

OPEN HOUSE

Police in San Mateo, California, are looking for a man they believe stole every one of a homeowner's push-up bras while touring her home during a real estate open house in March 2019. A video camera set up in the living room shows a slender man, who identified himself to the real estate agent as "James," walking out of camera range toward the woman's bedroom. When he walks back into the living room, plainly visible is "a noticeable bulge around his abdomen that wasn't there when he initially entered the home," San Mateo police said in a statement. Earlier in the video, the real estate agent, who is not named in news reports, steps out of the front door and closes it behind him, leaving the suspect to wander around unescorted inside the home. The real estate agent says he usually leaves the front door open so that he can keep an eye on people touring the home, but in this case the homeowners asked him to keep the door closed so that their cat wouldn't get out. No word on whether the bras were recovered.

POLICE PROTEST

Croydon, New Hampshire, a town of about 750 people, had its own police department until February 2020, when the town government decided to abolish the department and rely on the state police to enforce the law. Croydon police chief Richard Lee, who worked part-time as the department's only employee, was let go without notice after nearly 20 years on the job. He did not take the news lightly: When told during the town meeting to hand in his gun and his uniform "immediately," he complied immediately—by stripping down to his underwear on the spot. "I gave them my uniform shirt. I gave them my turtleneck. I gave them my ballistic vest. I sat down in the chair, took off my boots, took off my pants, put those in the chair, put my boots back on, and walked out the door," he told Fox News. When the startled town officials told Lee he could leave his uniform on and turn it in another day, he refused. "This is what they demanded of me, and this is what I'm doing," he told them before walking out the door into a snowstorm. He trudged his way homeward in his underwear in the 26°F weather and got about a mile before his wife picked him up.

Added together, the asteroids in the asteroid belt weigh about 4% of what the Moon weighs.

MEASUREMENTS AND WHAT THEY MEAN

Life sure is complicated. Every day we're inundated with all manners of measurements, sizes, and figures. Some of them make sense (for example, a pair of pants with a 38-inch waist actually does have a 38-inch waist), but the following measurements have some explaining to do.

VISION

If your optometrist says you have 20/20 vision, it doesn't mean you have "perfect" vision. What it does mean is that you can see an object clearly at 20 feet away that someone with normal vision can see at that distance. This measure of eyesight is called "visual acuity," the ability to see a sharp edge as a line, as opposed to a blur. So, if you're looking at the Snellen eye chart, developed by Dutch eye doctor Herman Snellen in the 1860s, and you can clearly read the letters on line 8, you are considered 20/20. (That line is usually "DEFPOTEC" if you want to cheat.) However, if the only letter you can clearly read is that giant "E" at the top of the chart, you are 20/200 – which means someone with normal vision could see that letter E clearly from 200 feet away. It also means you need some really thick glasses.

TEXT SIZE

If you do any sort of work on a computer, you probably play around with font or point sizes. The standard, readable size for a business letter is 12-point; any smaller and it's harder to read, but you can fit more on a page. But what *is* a point? It's 1⁄72 inch, so a 12-point letter stands ⅙ inch tall. This goes back to the days of physical typesetting on giant printing presses, when metal plates for individual letters had to be substituted to make different print sizes. (Fun fact: *Uncle John's Bathroom Reader* publishes in 10-point type.)

CALORIES

When you are "counting calories," what exactly are you counting? Energy. That's all calories are–tiny units of energy. One calorie (also called a "large calorie," the kind used to measure food energy) is the amount of energy required to raise the temperature of 1 kilogram of water by 1 degree Celsius. Today, food packagers can determine calorie counts by simply looking up each individual ingredient in a calorie database–which is the product of decades of scientists burning food in laboratories. They'd placed the food inside a "bomb calorimeter," a sealed chamber surrounded by a second chamber filled with water. Then, as the food burned, the

scientists would observe the rise in water temperature to determine the amount of calories. If you're an average American, the U.S. Food and Drug Administration recommends you consume about 2,000 calories each day to fuel your activities.

DRESS SIZES

Determining dress sizes is complicated and imprecise. Clothing manufacturers combine several body measurements—bust, waist, and hip—to come up with a simple 8 or 10 dress size. In U.S. measurements, a size 6 dress is currently made for a woman with a 34-inch bust, a 26.5-inch waist, and 37-inch hips. A size 10, meanwhile, is ideally suited to a woman with a 38-inch bust, 31-inch waist, and 41-inch hips. But by the time you're reading this, those numbers might have changed. Why? There are no government standards for determining dress sizes, and there haven't been for decades. As recently as a century ago, most women's clothes were made at home. If there were sizes, they usually corresponded to age. In the 1930s, the U.S. Department of Agriculture set the first standard dress sizes, but their sample size of women was too small, leading to so many inconsistent sizes that in 1958, the National Bureau of Standards set tighter guidelines. As time went on, dress manufacturers simply ignored those, preferring instead to use "vanity sizing," a sneaky tactic designed to make women feel thinner and therefore more likely to buy a dress. That's why a size 12 woman in the 1960s would be considered as size 6 today, or how a seemingly impossible size 0 garment can exist at all. For the record, a size 0 is a 28-inch bust, 19-inch waist, and 31-inch hips. In 2001, that would have been considered a size 2.

HAT SIZE

At least dress sizes use whole numbers, unlike hat sizes, which use fractions. But even though it seems baffling and complicated, using fractions is much more accurate. A hat with a size of 7¾ should fit comfortably on an adult whose head has a circumference of 7.75 inches. In the United States, hats are sized by the quarter inch, usually ranging in size from 6¾ up to 8. (Adult heads almost all sit within the same small window of circumference.)

SHOE SIZE

The shoe size you wear—8, 9, 10, etc.—doesn't equate with the length of your foot in inches, although that is a determining factor. To gauge shoe size, first measure the longest part of the foot (in inches), then multiply that figure by 3 and subtract 24. So if a man's foot is 11.5 inches long, shoe size can determined by the algebraic equation $S = 3F - 24$. ("S" is shoe size and "F" is the length of the foot.) Answer: he wears a 10½ shoe. Also, it's different for men and women. Men's feet are, on the whole, larger than women's. Rule of thumb: a woman's shoe size is a man's shoe size plus 1.5. For example, a women's size 9 equals a men's size 7½.

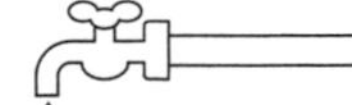

THE WORLD'S SLOWEST RACE

If you've ever wanted to experience a car race like no other, pay a visit to Granby, Canada, the next time the Défi-Vision race is running.

RUFF STUFF

The Mira Foundation is an organization in Quebec that provides trained service dogs free of charge to people with visual or physical disabilities, or who have autism. Raising and training the dogs costs a lot of money, and one of the ways the Mira Foundation raises the funds is with its annual *Défi-Vision,* or "Challenge Vision," auto race, which it created in 1987. The Mira Foundation proudly calls it "the slowest race in the world." Why so slow? Because all of the race car drivers are blind or visually impaired.

The event is held at the Autodrome Granby, in Granby, Quebec, one of the largest oval dirt racetracks in Canada. The cars are donated by junkyards, and mechanics volunteer their time to tune up the cars and get them in good running order. The names and logos of sponsors who contribute money to the Défi-Vision race are plastered all over the cars, which makes the otherwise sedate sedans and minivans look a little more like race cars.

COPILOTS

Each driver is paired with a "navigator," usually a journalist, politician, or celebrity, who acts as the eyes for the driver, shouting directions at them from the passenger's seat and telling them when to stop, go, back up, or turn left or right. That's all the navigators are allowed to do: Touching the steering wheel or any other controls is against the rules. And because some of the drivers do have limited vision, such as the ability to see shapes or distinguish between light and dark, the visors of all the drivers' crash helmets are covered with black electrical tape so that no one has an unfair advantage.

The rules of the race are fairly straightforward: The drivers aren't allowed to drive faster than 35 kilometers per hour (about 22 mph), and the first team to circle the track ten times wins the race. (The track is 1/2 mile, so ten laps is five miles.) No one is allowed to exit their vehicles until after the race has ended. In a typical year more than 30 cars will be in the race, so because there are so many cars on the track and the cars drive as slowly as they do, it can take 20 minutes or longer for the winning car to make it across the finish line.

As many as 10,000 spectators turn out to watch the race. As soon as it starts, the cars go off in every direction; there's a lot of stopping, starting, sudden turns, and one

Why is a crocodile's stomach more acidic than any other vertebrate's? So that it can dissolve hooves, bones, and horns.

bottleneck after another as the cars bunch up on the track. There are also plenty of collisions: At times the event can seem more like bumper cars than a road race. As the race progresses, the dirt track becomes more of an obstacle course, with pieces of cars falling off and some cars becoming too damaged to go any farther. And yet in all the years the Défi-Vision race has been held, there have been no serious injuries.

For the drivers who've always been blind, this is perhaps the only chance they'll ever get to experience what driving a car feels like. Before this, they could have had only the vaguest sense of what steering wheels, gas and brake pedals, and stick shifts are, and how they're used to control a car. For drivers who lost their sight as adults, driving a car again is a trip down memory lane and a chance to use a skill they haven't been able to in a long time. Just as importantly, the race gives the sighted navigators a sense of what being blind is like.

ROAD WARRIORS

Writer Ryan Knighton, 35, drove in his first Défi-Vision race in 2008. He was born with normal vision but began to lose it in his late teens, something he didn't realize until he started having car accidents. When he had his vision tested, he was diagnosed with a degenerative eye disease called *retinitis pigmentosa* and had to give up driving. Over the next decade he went completely blind; by the time he entered the Défi-Vision race, he hadn't driven a car in 17 years. "My hands sweated something awful for the first three laps, and I felt the thrill of being in control," he told *Esquire* magazine. "I also felt desperately out of control...When you're blind, you want to bump into things to know where you are."

Knighton's navigator was another writer named Pasha Malla, 30. For Malla, the challenge was tailoring his instructions to Knighton's responses: "Once we were around the first bend, we began to establish better communication. A calm 'left' suggested a gentle turn," he said, "while 'LEFTLEFTLEFT!' meant we were inches from hitting a damned tractor inexplicably parked in the infield. 'Stop,' regardless of how calmly I said it, resulted in Ryan slamming on the brakes as violently as possible, often giggling."

EVERYBODY WINS!

In addition to giving both drivers and navigators an exhilarating experience they'll never forget, the race raises a ton of money from ticket sales and corporate sponsorships—more than $2 million so far—every penny of which goes into providing trained service animals to disabled people. In a typical year, Mira will train 200 service dogs and place them with their owners. To date, more than 3,500 blind, disabled, and autistic people have been given dogs free of charge. Just as the race does for the drivers, the dogs give their owners a measure of independence they likely would not have been able to experience otherwise.

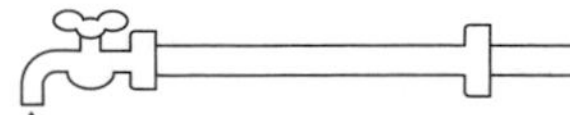

APARKALYPSE NOW

In the 2010s, America's national parks and outdoor recreation areas saw a huge uptick in visitors—with far-reaching effects. Longtime BRI writer (and veteran nature photographer) Jay Newman wanted to know why this is happening and what we can do to help keep nature natural. Here's what he found.

THE ZOMBIES OF ZION

The Narrows, located in Utah's Zion National Park, is where the Virgin River cuts through Zion Canyon. The water is shallow (most of this trail is actually *in* the river), the river is only 20 or 30 feet wide, and the steep walls of the gorge are up to 1,000 feet high. It is considered one of the most incredible and unique hikes in the United States. Want to hike it? Be forewarned: On nearly any day of the year, you will be surrounded by literally hundreds of other hikers—all of you trudging through the murky, knee-deep water. It begins to feel less like a walk in the park and more like a horde of zombies... who stop often to take selfies. It's gotten so crowded there that you can no longer drive to the trailhead anymore; you have to leave your car outside the national park and take a shuttle bus crammed full of other soon-to-be zombies. If you go, plan on hiking at least two to three miles up the river before the horde starts to thin out.

LOVING NATURE TO DEATH

These same kinds of crowds have been taking over Yosemite, Yellowstone, and dozens more. In 2016, nearly 331 million people visited a national park—that's more than the entire U.S. population (323 million in 2016). This isn't what the federal government had in mind in 1916 when it founded the U.S. National Park Service (NPS) to set aside special places and "leave them unimpaired for the enjoyment of future generations." They weren't prepared for this generation.

Making matters worse, this overuse and abuse is spilling over to the national forests and wilderness areas *around* the parks—not to mention the small towns and, until recently, little-known swimming holes, waterfalls, hot springs, secluded beaches, and even public flower farms. It's happening in wilderness areas all over the world, but the American West has been hit especially hard. For example, Horseshoe Bend, a scenic overlook of the Colorado River in Arizona's Glen Canyon National Recreation Area, saw the number of visitors increase from a few thousand per year in 2000 to 4,000 people *per day* in 2017. The facilities at these remote places weren't designed for this kind of onslaught, and the damage to the infrastructure and the environment has been swift and severe.

President Calvin Coolidge's favorite prank:
He'd press a buzzer to summon his bodyguards, then hide under his desk.

THE NOT-SO-GREAT RECESSION

How did this happen? If you asked most people that question, they'd probably blame social media influencers and the "selfie generation." While those do play a big part, it really began with the Great Recession, the worldwide economic downturn following the collapse of the U.S. real estate market in 2007. Unemployment rates rose to nearly 10 percent, and those who kept their jobs saw wages stagnate while the costs of rent, groceries, and fuel steadily rose. Airfares skyrocketed at the same time employers were cutting back. People were stressed out and needed a vacation...and no one could afford one.

The recession technically ended in June 2009, but for years afterward, wages remained flat and airfares weren't getting any cheaper. In 2020, for a family of four to fly to a California Disney vacation, including lodging and a rental car, it would cost around $5,000—nearly double pre-recession prices. But if Mom and Dad could convince the kids to spend a long weekend camping in a national park—or in lodgings nearby—that vacation would cost a fraction of what Mickey Mouse would have charged. So they went to Yellowstone.

How did they choose that particular park?

OUTSIDE INFLUENCERS

"Social media is the No. 1 driver," Maschelle Zia told the *Denver Post* in 2018. She manages the Horseshoe Bend overlook, which now draws in 1.5 million visitors a year. "People don't come here for solitude. They are looking for the iconic photo." In the social media era, an iconic photo is one that amasses thousands of likes and shares on such social media sites as Facebook, Pinterest, Tumblr, Twitter, and others. In Horseshoe Bend's case, that iconic photo is a pair of bare feet dangling high above the bendy blue river.

The main culprit: Instagram, a photo-sharing site launched in 2010 that gave rise to the role of the "influencer." If you're not familiar with influencers, the most popular ones are A-list celebrities, but there are countless other "micro influencers"—regular people turned Internet celebrities—who are paid as "brand ambassadors" by companies. They're also paid by hotels, restaurants, and resorts to post photos from their stay and "geotag" the locations.

MARCH OF THE TRIPODS

A picture may be worth a thousand words, but it could lead to a million footsteps. Anyone with a smartphone—which is nearly everyone these days—can post photos from a hiking trail because more and more parks are getting Wi-Fi. What better way to make your coworkers jealous than by posting your own feet-dangling selfie at Horseshoe Bend?

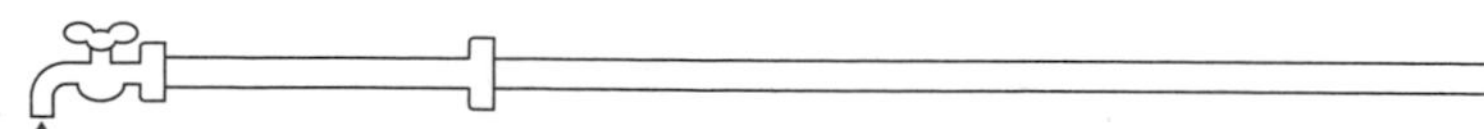

In the UK, it's illegal to drive a car through a puddle intending to splash pedestrians.

But it's more than just smartphones and selfies. Interest in outdoor photography—both amateur and professional—has grown exponentially since the rise of digital cameras in the early 2000s. While always a presence at the parks, shutterbugs have all but taken over some of the most "gotta-have" spots. Mesa Arch at Utah's Canyonlands National Park is especially problematic because only about a dozen photographers can fit side by side to get a decent view of the site's quintessential sunrise image, in which the underside of the arch glows like molten lava. For that one moment at dawn, it looks like a scene from another world. The NPS describes it as "a perfect trail for beginners, families with small children or light hikers, and one of Canyonlands' most iconic vistas." That, wrote pro photographer Don Smith, leads to situations like this one that occurred at a workshop he conducted there in 2017. In addition to his group, "serious photographers arrived a couple hours prior to sunrise. To make matters worse, two buses of tourists descended upon the Arch 10 minutes prior to sunrise. As the sun began to crest, one man grabbed one of my Workshop participants by the arm and said 'MOVE,' as he edged in with his iPhone for a shot." Skirmishes like this are playing out at other spots:

- On most days at Utah's Delicate Arch, from before sunrise to past sunset, dozens of landscape photographers vie with tourists for position on the large sandstone slab.
- A strikingly photogenic (and fragile) Arizona sandstone formation called the Wave has no marked trails, so hikers must find their way across the desert. But due to overcrowding, only 20 hikers are allowed in each day, and they have to win a lottery to get there. In 2017, more than 160,000 people applied.
- Arizona's Upper Antelope Canyon isn't much wider than a hallway. After a 2011 photograph of a sunlit shaft of dust called "The Phantom" sold for a record $6.5 million, an onslaught of photographers—with tripods—overran the slot canyon, posing a huge problem for the tourists who had to tiptoe around them. The NPS began offering photographer-only tours...and then canceled them in 2020 due to "negative feedback from attendees." (Sample review: "I didn't pay 200 bucks just to get rushed through!") Result: No tripods are allowed in Upper Antelope Canyon...at all.

FANTASY VS. REALITY

Instagram has had another effect on outdoor photography. The social media app was originally known for its array of creative filters that could make any smartphone pic look like a party scene, or an old sepia photo, or a Monet painting, and so on. As landscape photography began to connect with the Instagram generation, a new kind of hyper-real nature photograph emerged, one that is equal parts photography and digital art.

For most of landscape photography's history—a field popularized by Ansel Adams at many of these same national parks in the mid-20th century—the challenge was to portray an accurate representation of a pristine scene in optimal conditions. Today's digital darkroom comes with filters that allow photographers to add elements such as a more dramatic sky or a larger moon. Whereas an Ansel Adams waterfall photograph would look pretty much like a waterfall, a 21st-century Instagram-ographer photo of that waterfall would have the same basic composition, but the falls may have become turquoise and luminous, bathed in an ethereal glow beneath the technicolor core of the Milky Way. Another big difference from Adams: today's Instagram-ographer isn't behind the camera; he's likely to be standing *in* the shot at the base of the waterfall ("to give it scale"), posed dramatically on a patch of moss, shining his flashlight beam at the starry sky.

In their attempts to outdo each other, these "outdoor influencers" (a term that showed up in 2016) have collectively created a new genre of clichéd photos. In addition to "Man Standing at Base of Waterfall," there's "Feet Sticking Out of Tent," "Pretty Girl Lying in Lavender," "Pretty Girl in Hat From Behind," "Rugged Man on Outcrop Over Gorge," and dozens more.

IN THE KNOW

Deep Thoughts: America's **deepest lake** is Oregon's Crater Lake (1,943 feet). The **deepest gorge**, at 7,993 feet, is Hells Canyon, in Oregon and Idaho. New Mexico's Carlsbad Caverns is the nation's **deepest cave** (1,593 feet), and the **deepest spot** above ground is Badwater Basin in Death Valley National Park, which is 282 feet below sea level.

TAG! YOU'RE IT!

Aesthetics aside, these photographs are having a huge impact on nature, due to the thousands of outdoor influencers who post these kinds of photos every single day. Many of them have more than 100,000 followers, and nearly every post includes geotags to the locations. Commonly called tagging, the practice was originally used by serious adventurers to share secret locations with each other, but tagging locations on social media now lets everyone in on it. That waterfall photographer may post his photo to his Instagram page, his Facebook page, and then to one or more regional Facebook groups. Forty percent of Earth's population—more than three billion people—uses social media, which means that any one of these posts can potentially reach millions of people. And the photo of the "natural" world that they're seeing has all the crowds cropped out and the "fairytale filter" set to max.

THE SECRET IS OUT

Secret Beach boasts one of the most spectacular views of rock formations (called "sea stacks") on the Oregon Coast. But there's no trailhead there, nor is there a

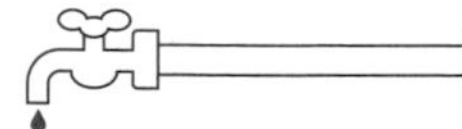

proper trail—just a steep decline through the forest down to the beach. There's no parking lot, either—just a small, rutted clearing off of busy Highway 101. That's why it was known by locals as Secret Beach: You had to know someone who knew about it to get directions. Today, that small clearing is often crammed with the cars of people who clicked on detailed directions they found in articles from magazines and websites, including one from OregonLive.com titled "10 Low-tide Treasures on the Oregon Coast." As traditional print media wanes, these outlets rely on social media to keep them afloat. And they're not just trying to get you out into nature. They need you to click on their links...and an enticingly named place called "Secret Beach" is very clickworthy.

AD NAUSEUM

Tourism boards and parks departments have also been doing their best to get more people out to the wilderness. Ad campaigns utilize TV, magazines, guerrilla marketing, professional photography, and social media influencers. Colorado's award-winning "Come to Life" campaign, named the most effective in the country in 2018, "generated significant incremental travel," according to the Colorado Tourism Office, "driving more than 2.66 million influenced trips to Colorado with a total impact of $4.45 billion." The good news is that it brought jobs and revenue to the state—and an 81 percent increase in park revenue from 2014 to 2019—but it also brought larger crowds to wild places.

Even car commercials have played a part. Companies like Subaru, Toyota, and Jeep have cashed in on the stay-local traveling trend by marketing their mid-size, all-wheel-drive, fuel-efficient "adventure" models as an inexpensive way to reach incredible places. A young couple drives their Outback from one vista to another, where there's always a pretty sunset and there are never any other people.

What do you get when you put all of these factors together? Long lines just to drive into the busier parks (that you *can* drive into), limited parking when you're in there, and visitors from all walks of life walking over each other. There's more trash, more crime, more accidents, more selfie-takers, more tripods, more grumpy kids who are still mad they couldn't go to Disneyland, and more signs like this one at the top of the Angels Landing Trail in Zion: "Toilets have reached capacity—closed due to extreme use."

This crisis affects more than the experience—the creatures of the forest are none too pleased, not to mention the environment. Turn to page 344 for some more horror stories from the great outdoors.

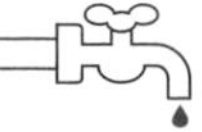

...First legal Internet purchase: in 1984, a grandmother in the UK used a phone-based service on her TV to buy margarine, eggs, and cornflakes.

OTHER SYRUPS

Do you put syrup on your pancakes? No, not maple syrup. Let's try something a little more unusual, such as...

Birch Syrup: It's like maple syrup—except that it's made from birch trees. It's most popular in far northern locations, where birch trees are most abundant—especially Alaska and the far north of Canada, Europe, and Russia. It's not as sweet as maple syrup, and it has what is described as a savory, minerally flavor. It's most often used for sauces, glazes (especially for salmon and other fish dishes), and as a flavoring for drinks, including beer.

Cider Syrup: Also known as apple molasses, cider syrup is a thick, dark honey-colored syrup made from apple cider. It has a sweet, fruity flavor—with a tart edge—and has been made in New England states since colonial times. It can be used in a variety of recipes, including as a sweetener for dessert dishes, a glaze for pork recipes, or just as a syrup for pancakes, waffles, or ice cream.

Date Honey: Also known as date syrup and date nectar, date honey is extracted from boiled and mashed dates. Food historians believe it was first developed in Iran (or perhaps Iraq) thousands of years ago, later becoming popular throughout the Middle East and North Africa, all regions where date palm trees are numerous. In Arabic, date honey is called *rubb,* and in Hebrew it's *silan.*

Yacón Syrup: The yacón is a plant in the daisy family found in South America's Andes mountains, and the plant's large, juicy, crunchy, sweet tuberous roots have been eaten, both raw and cooked, by Andean peoples for millennia. Just in the last 20 years or so, the yacón became known for its purported health benefits—especially for people with diabetes and digestive disorders—and has since become increasingly popular around the world as a produce item, as well as in syrup form. Yacón syrup is promoted primarily as a sweetener replacement for sugar.

Kuromitsu: Meaning "black honey" in Japanese, kuromitsu is syrup made from *kurozato*—"black sugar"—an unrefined brown sugar found only on a group of islands in the Japanese prefecture of Okinawa, where it has been made since the 17th century. Kuromitsu is immensely popular in Japan today, as a sweetener in many packaged products, and also as a syrup to pour over toast, yogurt, pancakes, ice cream, or in tea.

Falernum: This very flavorful, citrusy syrup used almost exclusively as an ingredient in alcoholic beverages—mostly tropical rum-based cocktails such as the zombie

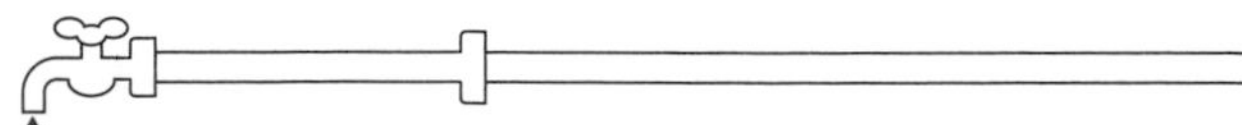

and mai tai. It was first developed in the 18th or 19th century somewhere in the Caribbean, most likely on the island of Barbados. Recipes for falernum have varied over time, and from region to region, but today it's usually made from cane sugar, ginger, almond, lime, lime zest, and cloves. You can buy falernum in stores or online—in both nonalcoholic and alcoholic form—but it is also easily made from scratch. (You can find lots of recipes online.)

Sugar Beet Syrup: A favorite breakfast in the Rhineland region of western Germany is bread, butter, and *zuckerrübensirup*—"sugar beet syrup"—a dark syrup made from sugar beets. (Sugar beets are related to red-colored beets, but are white in color and contain much more sugar.)

Petimezi: Grapes aren't just for wine—they're for syrup, too! This one, made from boiled, skinned, and mashed grapes, has been a favorite in regions around the Mediterranean Sea for centuries. (The oldest record of it goes back to the fifth century BC and the ancient Greeks.) You can still find it in supermarkets in Greece today, under the name petimezi (and pekmez in Turkey). Among the many ways it's enjoyed: as a breakfast dish, with tahini on toast. (Bonus: Mix grape syrup, water, and rose water, add crushed ice, top with some golden raisins and pine nuts, and stir. That's *jallab*, a popular drink in Syria and Lebanon. Cheers!)

* * *

THE HIGH COST OF BEING BATMAN

In 2017, the website MoneySupermarket.com tallied up how much it would cost to be Batman as depicted in *The Dark Night*. Here's their estimate:

- Batsuit (padded, insulated, armored, fireproof, bulletproof, comfortable to wear for long periods; cowl and memory-cloth batcape included): $1,058,600
- "The Tumbler" (Batmobile): $18,000,000
- "Batpod" (Batcycle): $1,500,000
- "The Bat" (Batplane): $60,000,000
- Wayne Manor and subterranean Batcave: $600,000,000
- Wayne Manor Annual Operating Costs: $37,000
- Estate Manager's Annual Salary: $150,000
- Alfred the Butler's Annual Salary: $80,000
- Special Training and Education for Bruce Wayne: $1,713,610
- Bat Gadgets $213,610
- Bat Weapons: $10,000

Total Bat-Cost: $682,450,750

WHERE'D EVERYBODY GO?

We tend to take toilets for granted. But it's really a marvel of science and engineering that we can simply do our business, push a lever, and whoosh, it's gone without a trace, replaced with a bowl of fresh, clean water. It wasn't always so simple, though, as this timeline of the history of toilets should make clear.

4000 BC Archaeologists have discovered water pipes dating to this time, which flow from the remnants of buildings into the Indus River in India. It is assumed that some kind of container for human waste was attached, but all that remains are the pipes.

3000 BC Found among the ruins of a Scottish settlement called Skara Brae that dates to this time is a stone hut with a drain extending through a wall and out of the building. Again, it's assumed that there was some kind of thing that someone sat on attached, but whatever it was, it's lost to history.

1700 BC Within the Palace of Knossos on the Greek island of Crete is an early toilet used by royalty. It consists of a pan made of hardened clay (with a wooden seat) that connects to terra-cotta pipes, which carry the waste out of the castle.

1200 BC A popular proto-toilet used by wealthy Egyptians is a sand-filled container into which a person does their business, and is then emptied by slaves. (It's essentially a cat litter box...for people.)

500 BC to AD 450 In the heyday of ancient Rome, plumbing is a big deal. Along with 220 miles of gravity-powered aqueducts and pipes that kept fresh water flowing into homes, public baths offer bench-style toilets that whisked waste away via those same water channels.

1100s Portchester Castle, located on Portsmouth Harbour in southern England, is retrofitted (by monks) with stone chutes. Occupants do their business into a chute, and the waste is carried away by the coastal sea.

1200s The "hole in the wall" concept extends to other castles in England. Called a *garderobe,* it consists of little more than a stone seat with a hole going out the side of a castle. Whatever went through the hole emptied directly into a moat...which made the moat all the more fearsome.

1300s A few *privies,* or "houses of easement," are installed on streets in London—basically a pit that a person sat over to do their business. They

Myth-nomer: The Pacific Ocean's Ring of Fire (an area with many volcanoes) is actually horseshoe-shaped.

were overburdened, to say the least—by the end of the 1300s, London had a ratio of about one privy for every 2,000 people. And it was some unlucky person's job to scoop it out. That low-paid position is called a *gong farmer.* ("Gong" is a derivative of the Old English word *gang,* which meant "going.")

1400s For those who can't go out of the side of a castle or down the street, there is the *chamber pot.* It's exactly what it sounds like—kept in a bedroom (or "chamber"), it's a ceramic pot into which one empties their bladder or bowels...and then empties directly into the streets.

1500s Outhouses begin to spread across Europe. More or less chambers for chamber pots—or a privy that accommodates one person at a time—they're small buildings unattached to the rest of the house that offer a place to sit privately and relieve oneself. Like a privy, it's situated over a dug-out pit. Shoveling out its contents is still the job of the gong farmer.

1596 Sir John Harrington, Queen Elizabeth I's godson, gives Her Majesty a special gift—the first flushing toilet. (He makes two: one for the queen and one for himself.) It consists of little more than a stone seat, a bowl, and a cistern of water (for flushing) propped up behind the seat.

Late 1600s The chamber pot earns the nickname "Bourdaloue," after a popular but long-winded French minister named Louis Bourdaloue. His sermons were reportedly so long that people brought their chamber pots with them to relieve themselves without missing a word. (Bourdaloue's name may be the origin of *loo,* a slang term for toilet.)

1775 The first modern-day toilet is devised by Scottish inventor Alexander Cumming. His design improved on Harrington's flushable model, adding an "S" trap—an S-shaped pipe that left some water in the bowl part of the toilet. That bit of water prevents malodorous gases from getting back into the house.

1778 London plumber Joseph Bramah works for a company installing Cumming's toilets (or "water closets"), and notices that the water inside freezes when the temperature drops. So he replaces the toilet's sliding valve (also invented by Cumming) with a hinged flap, which seals the bottom of the bowl from the rest of the plumbing and prevents freezing. He goes into business for himself manufacturing toilets, and this becomes the standard design of the commode—found almost exclusively in the homes of the wealthy or in fancy hotels—for more than a century.

Billie Holiday's other claim to fame: she was Billy Crystal's babysitter.

1850s Various styles of flush toilets are widespread in Europe and the United States, but most rural communities continue to use the tried-and-true outhouse.

1880 While he's not the inventor of the toilet as is commonly believed, Thomas Crapper was, in fact, a plumber who worked in London. He installed toilets in English royal family residences, and in this year, he opens the first toilet showroom.

1891 Crapper patents the valve-and-siphon toilet. Still widely used today, it allows a flushed toilet bowl to fill with water, and when it's full, a weighted ballcock in the toilet tank automatically stops the flow of water. This becomes the dominant toilet style of the 20th century.

1966 A copper shortage leads to the development of plastic piping systems for toilets.

1986 Japan introduces sensor-enabled toilets. They sense when a person is finished and self-flush, no longer requiring the person to push a lever.

1992 The U.S. Congress passes the Energy Policy Act, requiring all toilets to use only 1.6 gallons of water per flush, which is about half of what we used to use.

2010s While toilets continue to grow more high-tech in the West and in Japan, the developing world lags far behind. According to the World Health Organization, more than two billion people lack access to modern toilets with running water and the sanitation they provide. Throughout Asia and Africa, ancient latrine-style waste management is still the standard, and this can lead to infestations of ground and drinking water with fecal-based pathogens that cause deadly diseases like cholera and dysentery. Some philanthropists, including Microsoft founder Bill Gates, are working with scientists on this issue. Through his foundation, Gates has pledged more than $400 million to improve toilets in the developing world, and in 2018 he spoke at the Reinvented Toilet Expo, where inventors showed off a new generation of toilets that safely dispose of germ-laden waste using little or no water.

* * *

A BATHROOM JOKE

How do you tell a boy tuna from a girl tuna? Watch and see which can they use.

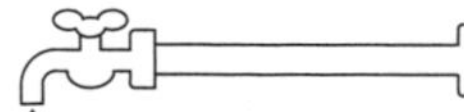

**Medieval holiday on the Christian calendar:
Feast of the Ass (January 14), honoring the Bible's donkeys.**

STRANGE DEATHS

When you gotta go, you gotta go, and some people shed this mortal coil in very bizarre ways.

TWISTED

One night in October 2019, paramedics in Oxford, Indiana, responded to a 911 call at the home of local sheriff Don Munson. He was fine...and so were the 140 snakes that lived on the premises. Munson's house, it turns out, was a de facto snake and reptile preserve, open to the public, and 36-year-old Laura Hurst was a frequent visitor. She dropped in a couple of times a week to check up on the 20 snakes she'd contributed to Munson's collection. When Munson arrived home on that night, he discovered Hurst, unresponsive due to the eight-foot-long reticulated python that was wrapped around her neck. Paramedics were unable to save her.

RISE AND FALL

Catherine Shaw, a 23-year-old yoga teacher from England, hiked up a volcano outside San Juan La Laguna, Guatemala, before dawn one day in March 2019...and never returned. She was missing for six days before authorities discovered her dog, alive but cold, and then Shaw's dead body, naked and badly bruised. Months later, an inquest and extensive interviews with Shaw's family put together the circumstances of the woman's death. It wasn't murder—Shaw was a nudist, and investigators and her parents believe she hiked up the volcano, taking off articles of clothing as she went, intending to watch the sunrise in the buff. Because she'd been fasting for a few days before the hike, it's likely that she was in a weakened state when she slipped off a peak and tumbled to her death.

MISHANDLED

Prosecutor Addelaid Ferreira-Watt was arguing a robbery case in the Umzimkhulu Regional Court (in the KwaZulu-Natal province of South Africa) in November 2019. The defendants were accused of stealing a shotgun in the nearby town of Ixopo. During the trial, the gun in question was brought into the courtroom to be entered into evidence. The court officer who brought it in, however, fumbled the firearm...and dropped it. Not only was the officer in charge of transporting the gun, he was supposed to ensure that it wasn't loaded before it became evidence. He failed at both tasks. When he dropped the gun, it discharged, sending a bullet into the hip of Ferreira-Watt. She was immediately transported to a local hospital, but did not survive the gunshot.

The court officer who brought it in, however, fumbled the firearm...and dropped it.

Supermarket chicken has twice the fat and two-thirds the protein that it did 30 years ago.

A CAR ACCIDENT

One day in December 2019, 21-year-old Michael Kosanovich was walking through the South Jamaica neighborhood of Queens, New York, when he stopped to look at a red 2002 Lexus IS 300 that was for sale. He was standing behind the Lexus, and in front of the car parked directly behind it (oddly, another 2002 Lexus IS 300, only it was gray). Then, according to a police report, the gray Lexus sprang to life—the ignition turned on by a remote-start feature—and owing to some glitch, it lurched forward, pinning Kosanovich between the two cars. Passers-by rushed to the man's aid and pushed the car off of him, only for the gray Lexus to once again roll forward and trap Kosanovich again. Paramedics freed him and took him to a local hospital, where he died from internal injuries the next day.

IT WORKED TOO WELL

On the night of Thanksgiving 2019, police in Van Buren, Maine, rushed to the home of 65-year-old Ronald Cyr, responding to a 911 call reporting a shooting in the residence. When police arrived, they discovered that it was Cyr who'd been shot. And he'd done it himself, although it was an accident. He had rigged up a booby trap at the front door—anyone making an unauthorized entrance would be automatically shot with a handgun. Police discovered so many other booby traps on the premises that they had to call in the state bomb squad to safely search the house. Cyr later died from his injuries, before he could tell authorities why he'd set up so many traps, or exactly how he'd shot himself.

LICKED TO DEATH

The academic periodical *European Journal of Case Reports in Internal Medicine* published a paper in 2019 about the curious death of a man in Germany. Doctors placed the blame squarely on the man's dog. Fatal bite on a major artery? Mauled to death? Nope. The man contracted a fatal infection when his dog licked him. After three days of high fever and difficulty breathing (he thought he had the flu), the man sought medical treatment. He was admitted to a hospital, and as his condition worsened, doctors struggled for four days to diagnose the problem. A test finally revealed the presence of a virulent bacteria called *Capnocytophaga canimorsus.* It's commonly found in dogs, but can be devastating for humans. In the few cases of humans having contracted it, the infection was acquired via a dog bite—never before had a simple lick spread the contagion. Unfortunately, it was too late for the dog owner. The infection spread rapidly through his body and killed him just 16 days after his dog licked him.

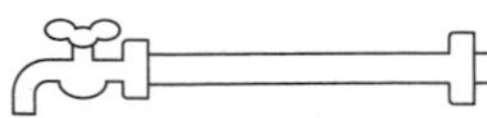

You got a problem with that? In New Jersey, November 17 is Danny DeVito Day.

BET YOU DIDN'T KNOW THAT...

We didn't call this book The Greatest Know on Earth *for nothing!*

...there's actually a difference between coffins and caskets: coffins are six-sided, with "shoulders," and are tapered from the shoulders down; caskets are four-sided and rectangular.

...the unit of measurement for the speed of a computer mouse is known as a mickey.

...Will Smith's real first name is not William—it's Willard.

...the name of the old, bearded sorcerer in Walt Disney's 1940 film *Fantasia* is Yen Sid—which is "Disney" spelled backward.

...the involuntary act of yawning and stretching that you (and your dog and cat) do upon waking up or when very sleepy is called *pandiculation.*

...the official bird of Redondo Beach, California, is the Goodyear Blimp.

...the longest TV commercial ever aired was a 14-hour ad for Old Spice aftershave, which aired in São Paulo, Brazil, on December 8, 2018. (It starred *Brooklyn 99* actor Terry Crews.)

...there's a court above the U.S. Supreme Court. It's a basketball court. (It's on the fifth floor of the Supreme Court Building. The courtroom is on the second.)

...*Playboy* magazine has been available in Braille editions since 1970.

...the device they use to measure your feet in shoe stores is called a Brannock Device. (It was invented by Charles Brannock.)

...the cosmetics company Max Factor is named after a real person: Maksymilian Faktorowicz, a Polish beautician who emigrated to the United States in 1904.

...a prearranged fight between two people is called a duel. If it's between three people, it's a *truel.*

...McDonald's once offered bubble gum–flavored broccoli at its restaurants.

...the book that holds the record for being the book most often stolen from public libraries: *Guinness World Records.*

Oops! The cover image of a 2004 European Union statistical handbook accidentally left off Wales.

THE FURTHER ADVENTURES OF "FLORIDA MAN"

More fun, true-to-life headlines that pop up when people google their birthdate and the words "Florida Man." (Part I of the story is on page 25.)

NOVEMBER 29

"Florida Man, Woman Arrested for Practicing Dentistry Without a License on a Bus"

JULY 8

"VIDEO: Florida Man Crash Lands onto Roof of Car and then Walks Away"

JUNE 26

"Florida Man Accused in Flamingo's Death Fatally Struck by Pickup Truck"

MAY 9

"Florida Man Gets Life for Slaying He Blamed on Sleepwalking"

DECEMBER 24

"Florida Man Who Wanted to 'Time Travel' Crashes Car Through a Strip Mall"

FEBRUARY 8

"Florida Man Charged with Assault with a Deadly Weapon after Throwing Alligator Through Wendy's Drive-Thru Window"

OCTOBER 6

"Florida Man Wears 'F*ck the Police' Shirt to Court, Wins Case"

September 14

"Florida Man Missing Since 1997 Found at the Bottom of a Pond Thanks to Google Earth"

JULY 5

"Florida Man 'Impersonating a Police Officer' Is Arrested after Pulling over a Real Cop and Warning Him to 'Slow Down'"

JUNE 25

"Florida Man Jailed for Eviscerating His Dad's Body"

MARCH 11

"Florida Man Charged with 'Intentionally' Pressure Washing His Neighbor"

JANUARY 21

"Florida Man, Woman Run Over by Patrol Car While Lying in Road to Watch Eclipse"

JULY 30

"FLORIDA MAN ACCUSED OF PULLING GUN ON WOMAN WHO REFUSED TO TRY HIS VAPE PEN AT MCDONALD'S"

NOVEMBER 11

"Florida Man on Probation Burglarizes Probation Office, Police Say"

APRIL 25

"72-year-old Florida Man Stabs Nephew for Taking Too Long on the Toilet"

AUGUST 21

"Botched Home Castration Sees Florida Man Arrested"

AUGUST 7

"Florida Man in Coma after Wheelchair Struck by Lightning"

JANUARY 28

"Florida Man Learns the Hard Way He Stole Laxatives, Not Opioids"

JULY 3

"DNA from Tooth in Florida Man's Foot Solves 25-year-old Shark Bite Mystery"

NOVEMBER 1

"Donald Trump Is Officially a Florida Man"

MARCH 30

"Florida Man Suspected of Using Private Plane to Draw Giant Radar Penis"

NOVEMBER 6

"Florida Man Has Screwdriver Surgically Removed from Rectum"

BRAINTEASERS

You'll have to put on your thinking cap for these cranial conundrums. If you get stumped, the answers are on page 405.

- **PALINDROMIC MINUTE:** Two examples of a palindromic minute on a digital clock are 5:45 and 6:36 (they read the same forward and backward). The time elapsed between them is 51 minutes. What two palindromic minutes have the shortest time between them? And which two have the longest?
- **ONE TALENTED WORD:** What word reads the same forward, backward, right side up, and upside down?
- **SPEAKING OF TIME:** If John gave 15 cents to Brian and 10 cents to Jay, what time is it?
- **RIDING THE BUS:** There are 22 passengers on a bus. If 15 get off at the first stop and 4 get on, and 4 get off at the second stop and 15 get on, how many people are on the bus?
- **WHERE THE WIND BLOWS:** There are apples on some apple trees. A strong gust of wind comes through. Afterward, there are neither apples on the trees nor apples on the ground. How can this be?
- **REFRESHING MURDER MYSTERY:** Two friends are drinking iced tea, and one of them is very thirsty, so he drinks three glasses in quick succession. The other one isn't so thirsty and takes his time finishing his drink. Just then, the waiter says, "Both of your glasses have been poisoned!" Then the guy who drank only one died, while the guy who drank three was just fine. Why?
- **THE ADDING TIMES:** If you add 2 + 2 or multiply 2 × 2, both equal 4. This fun math trick will also work for a set of three numbers. What are they?
- **EXACT CHANGE:** This classic brainteaser still stumps people today: A candy bar and a jawbreaker cost a total of $1.10. The candy bar costs a dollar more than the jawbreaker. How much does the jawbreaker cost?
- **TO THE NINES:** If you had to write the numbers 900 to 999 on a piece of paper, how many times would you write the number 9? There are two acceptable answers.
- **TECH TALK:** Why is a brayed coin like a bunch of mixed-up ones and zeros?
- **OUT TO SEA:** Two crewmen are standing on opposite sides of a ship. One is facing east, and the other is facing west, but they can see each other just fine. How?
- **ROLL CALL:** Aria has six daughters named Dottie, Rebecca, Mindy, Faith, Sonia, and Laurie. Will her final daughter be named Tabitha, Tessa, or Tina?

DOME, SWEET DOME

The domed stadium is a distinctly American contribution to architecture. They were built beginning in the 1960s as pro baseball and football teams expanded into hotter and colder climates, where players and the fans who came to see them needed protection from the elements. Here are the stories of some of the most famous and quirkiest domes...some still standing, some not.

ASTRODOME: The opening of the Houston Astrodome in 1965 set off the sports dome craze. The world's first completely indoor stadium—and home of baseball's Houston Colt .45s (later renamed the Astros)—was a tourist attraction, billed as the "Eighth Wonder of the World." It was also the first sports facility to use artificial turf—appropriately, AstroTurf—because with no access to sunlight, real grass could not be cultivated. But anyone who played in the Astrodome (it was also home to two football teams: the NFL's Houston Oilers and the USFL's Houston Gamblers) felt the effects of AstroTurf. It was harder than grass, which made balls travel faster and bounce higher, and it was hard on athletes' legs, leading to fatigue and injury. The Gamblers folded in 1985, the Oilers moved to Tennessee in 1996, and the Astros moved to the brand-new Minute Maid Park in 2000. The last major event in the Astrodome, the Houston Livestock Show and Rodeo, also moved to that venue, leaving the Astrodome virtually unused after 2003. In 2005, the stadium was occupied temporarily when it was used to house evacuees from New Orleans after Hurricane Katrina. An inspection in 2008 revealed so many building code violations that admission is now restricted to authorized maintenance teams. Meanwhile, the Houston city council refuses to demolish it, on the grounds that the implosion (or explosion) required would also harm the surrounding neighborhoods.

KINGDOME: The King County Multipurpose Domed Stadium, or just the Kingdome as it was commonly known, opened in Seattle in 1976 to house two professional sports teams: the NFL's Seattle Seahawks and baseball's Seattle Mariners. After four years of construction, builders discovered that the roof leaked...two months before the first football game was scheduled to be played. Those leaks and many others were patched in various ways over the years, with no solution proving to be a permanent fix. In 1993, King County officials decided to strip off the roof's coating and replace it with a more water-resilient one. They tried to pressure-wash the coating off. That didn't work. So they to tried get it off by sandblasting it. That didn't work either—but it did result in even more leaks. By that time, there was so much water ponding on the roof that in July 1994, four 26-pound ceiling tiles fell into the stands during the Mariners' pregame warm-ups. Had the tiles fallen 30 minutes later, after the gates

... due to "excessive alcohol use." That's about 1 in 10 deaths among working-age adults. More than half of those deaths are from binge drinking.

opened to fans, someone likely would've been injured (or worse). After further repairs failed to fix the problem, King County imploded the Kingdome in 2000.

METRODOME: The Hubert H. Humphrey Metrodome opened its doors in Minneapolis in 1982, with tenants including baseball's Minnesota Twins and football's Minnesota Vikings. The ceiling of the dome over the playing field was painted a stark white—pretty much the same shade of white as a high-hit baseball. Countless fielders lost track of the ball while looking up to the ceiling to track it, resulting in plenty of errors and base hits by opponents that should have been easy outs. But that ceiling wasn't entirely white. In one prominent spot where several tiles met, the dark gaps between white tiles accidentally formed the unmistakable shape of a swastika. All those problems fell away in late 2010. On December 11, a TV crew preparing for the next day's Vikings game spotted leaks in the roof, and rain and snow seeping in from a huge winter storm. A work crew was dispatched to the roof to remove the 17 inches of accumulated snow...but high winds prevented the workers from removing it, at which point the roof sagged in the middle under the weight. Around 5:00 a.m. that morning it collapsed, tearing open three panels and sending all that snow and ice right into the Metrodome. It cost $18 million to repair the roof for the two more years it stayed open. The Metrodome was demolished in 2014.

TROPICANA FIELD: St. Petersburg, Florida, constructed a domed stadium in 1990. It was built to house a Major League Baseball franchise...which the area didn't actually have. Organizers built what was initially called the Florida Suncoast Dome in order to attract either an expansion team or an existing one. The San Francisco Giants, Chicago White Sox, Detroit Tigers, and Seattle Mariners all got up the hopes of Florida baseball fans by publicly toying with the idea of a move, but all ultimately stayed put. After many false starts, Major League Baseball finally did grant a team to the area, and scheduled it to start play in 1998. That means the sports dome sat without a baseball team for eight long years until the Tampa Bay Devil Rays showed up. (From 1993 to 1996, the NHL's Tampa Bay Lightning took up residence in the way-too-big-for-hockey facility, and renamed it the ThunderDome.) One of Tropicana Field's unique features is its catwalks, four ring-shaped, dome-supporting metal bridges near the ceiling. It's extremely common for hitters to knock a ball into a catwalk, which can send it in unpredictable directions. Major League Baseball developed rules pertaining specifically to the catwalks at the "Trop": If a ball hits either of the two lower catwalks, it remains in play. If it hits one of the two higher catwalks, it's either a home run or a foul ball, depending on where it strikes the catwalk. The Rays and fans will have to deal with the Trop for a bit longer—the team is contracted to play in the stadium until 2027.

BEN KUROKI'S WAR

Here's the story of one of the most unlikely heroes of World War II. Not because he wasn't brave, but because it was so unlikely that he'd ever get a chance to fight.

THE SAME...BUT DIFFERENT

Ben Kuroki was 24 years old and living on his parents' potato farm in Hershey, Nebraska, in 1941. When Japan bombed Pearl Harbor on December 7 of that year, bringing the United States into World War II, Kuroki's response was the same as a lot of other Nebraska men: He wanted to join in the fight and serve his country. His father encouraged both Ben and his younger brother, Fred, to enlist in the military, telling them, "This is your country. Go ahead and fight for it." But when the brothers went to the recruiting office in nearby North Platte and signed up to join the U.S. Army, they never heard anything back. "We passed our physicals and everything, and we just waited and waited and never received any word, and we realized we were getting the runaround," Kuroki told an interviewer in 2007.

Unlike so many of the friends they'd grown up with in Nebraska, Kuroki and his brother were Japanese American, and *nisei*—the sons of Japanese immigrants. That's why the army didn't want them. The recruiter in North Platte didn't know what to do with a Japanese American who wanted to enlist. But Kuroki didn't give up. When he heard on the radio that the Army Air Corps (the predecessor of the U.S. Air Force) was recruiting people in Grand Island, Nebraska, a town 150 miles away, he decided to try again. He called Grand Island and asked the recruiting sergeant if his Japanese ancestry would be a problem. "Heck no," the recruiter answered, "I get two bucks for everyone I sign up." Kuroki and his brother made the 150-mile trip and enlisted in the Army Air Corps. They were among the very first Japanese Americans to join the military after Pearl Harbor. In all, four Kuroki brothers served in the military during World War II.

GROUNDED

Ben and Fred were sent to basic training at Sheppard Field, near Wichita Falls, Texas. Fred wanted to become a navigator on an aircrew, but he was assigned to a ditch-digging unit of the engineering corps "with no explanation," Ben Kuroki remembered. Ben wanted to be trained as a gunner on a bomber, but he was sent to clerk-typist training in Colorado, and then assigned to the 409th Squadron of the 93rd Bombardment Group. He fought repeated attempts to drop him from his squadron's roster, and when it moved to England, he went along...as a clerk typist. Then, when the need for gunners on aircrews became acute, Kuroki volunteered for gunnery school and was accepted.

TAKING FLIGHT

In December 1942, Kuroki was assigned to the crew of a B-24 bomber as a turret gunner. Serving aboard a B-24 was a dangerous job—so dangerous that the bomber crews were required to complete only one 25-mission tour of duty before they could transfer to less hazardous duties. Many airmen were killed before their 25 missions were up.

Kuroki served his 25 missions in bombing runs over Nazi-occupied Europe and North Africa, and he saw his fair share of danger: On one bombing run over North Africa in February 1943, his plane ran out of fuel and crash-landed in Spanish Morocco. The entire flight team was captured by the Spanish. Kuroki tried to escape but was recaptured; three months later he and his crew were released. They returned to England and rejoined the war effort, and three months after that, they were part of a giant raid to bomb Romanian oil fields at Ploesti. On that August day, 53 of 176 bombers were shot down, including seven of nine planes in Kuroki's squadron. Only his plane and one other in the squadron returned. More than 300 airmen lost their lives.

The courage that Kuroki demonstrated under fire earned him the respect of his crewmates and the nickname "Most Honorable Son," which they painted on the fuselage of the bomber next to Kuroki's turret. "I didn't have any problems once I started flying missions," he remembered. "We all flew together as a family...For the first time since Pearl Harbor, I felt that I belonged."

When his 25 missions were up, Kuroki volunteered for another full tour of 25 missions in honor of his brother Fred, who was still stateside and unable to fight overseas. The Army Air Corps physicians cleared him for another tour, but for just five missions, bringing his total to 30.

On his 30th and final bombing mission over Europe and North Africa, Kuroki was nearly killed when antiaircraft flak struck the plexiglass dome of his gun turret, shattering it. He was spared only because he happened to duck down to talk to the radio officer just as the flak hit the turret. For his service in the European theater, Kuroki was awarded two Distinguished Flying Crosses, and also acclaimed as the "first nisei hero of the war."

PUBLIC RELATIONS

With his service as a bomber over, Kuroki returned home to the United States, where he was sent on a speaking tour of three internment camps that held Japanese Americans who had been forcibly relocated from the west coast of the United States in the name of "national security." Times had changed since Kuroki had tried to enlist in the military in 1941. Not long after he and his brother joined the Army Air Corps, the War Department had formalized its policy regarding *nisei* who wanted to

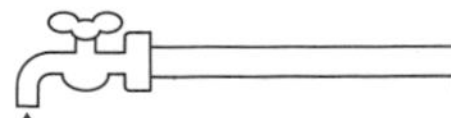

enlist and ordered that in the future they be classified as "undraftable enemy aliens," even though they were American citizens by birth. By 1943, however, the military had reversed the policy and had begun accepting *nisei* into the armed forces, including those who'd been interned in the camps. Kuroki was sent to the camps in order to encourage these young men to join the war effort.

Because Kuroki's family lived in Nebraska, they hadn't been interned. He knew little about the camps, and his first visit to one came as a shock: "It was a strange thing," he told an interviewer in 2006. "I was really shocked because the armed guards were wearing the same uniforms I was wearing. I was quite shocked to see my own people in these internment camps." His message to the *nisei* received a rocky reception. Many young men in the camps were angry that the same government that had imprisoned their families was now asking them to fight in the war. Some were inspired by Kuroki's talk, and more than 1,000 young men in the camps enlisted. But as many as 18,000 others refused to serve, at least not until their families were released from the camps and had their civil liberties restored. The military eventually resorted to drafting young men straight out of the camps and arresting anyone who resisted.

The military eventually resorted to drafting young men straight out of the camps and arresting anyone who resisted.

CALL OF DUTY

Kuroki was back home in Nebraska when he learned that his best childhood friend, Gordy Jorgenson, had been killed in action fighting the Japanese in the Solomon Islands, leaving a widow and infant son. This loss, plus an incident in Denver, Colorado, when another U.S. serviceman refused to share a taxi with him because he was a "Jap" (Kuroki was in full uniform), motivated him to try and get back into the war by volunteering to serve on a bomber crew in the Pacific. Under ordinary circumstances this would have been impossible, because the War Department had a rule forbidding Japanese Americans from serving as aircrew anywhere in the Pacific theater. Government officials weren't sure Japanese Americans would remain loyal to the United States if they were sent into battle against Japanese soldiers. (It had no similar qualms about sending German Americans to fight in Germany, or Italian Americans to fight in Italy.)

But Kuroki was determined to get back into the fight. On his speaking tour, he'd given a speech in San Francisco at the Commonwealth Club, and there he made a lot of influential friends, including the editor of the *San Francisco Chronicle,* a former president of Stanford University, and others. They lobbied Secretary of War Henry Stimson on his behalf. After reviewing the case, Stimson lauded Kuroki's "splendid record" of wartime service and granted him an exemption to the War Department's rule. He was assigned to the crew of a B-29 bomber, which was named the *Honorable*

Sad Saki in his honor. Kuroki became the only Japanese American in the entire war to participate in bombing raids over Japan.

ON TO VICTORY

Just as he had in Europe, Kuroki completed 25 bombing missions, then volunteered for more. He was approved to fly five, but he only completed three before the war ended. In all, Kuroki flew 58 combat missions during the war, and he earned his third Distinguished Flying Cross, plus other honors, for his service in the Pacific. One medal he didn't earn: the Purple Heart, awarded to soldiers injured or killed in action. In those 58 dangerous missions, he had barely suffered a scratch. His only serious injury came just days before the end of the war, when he was attacked by a knife-wielding friend after they had been drinking together. Kuroki was recovering in the hospital with 24 stitches to his scalp when the first atomic bomb was dropped on Hiroshima. Three days later the second atomic bomb was dropped on Nagasaki, and six days after that Japan surrendered unconditionally.

ONE LAST MISSION

After the war ended, Kuroki embarked on what he called his "59th mission," touring the country and speaking about the importance of racial tolerance. During a stop in Idaho, he met a Japanese American university student named Shige Tanabe and fell in love. They married in August 1946, and the two moved to Lincoln, Nebraska, where Kuroki earned a degree in journalism at the University of Nebraska on the G.I. Bill. He led a pretty quiet life after that, raising three daughters and working at newspapers in Nebraska, Michigan, and California. He retired in 1984 after serving as news editor of the *Ventura County Star-Free Press.*

Kuroki made headlines again in the late 1980s, when some of the veterans he'd served with lobbied the military to award him the Distinguished Service Medal, not just for his impressive record of combat, but also for the battles he fought to overcome discrimination that would have kept him from fighting in the first place. After a years-long campaign, Kuroki was awarded the medal at a ceremony in Lincoln, Nebraska, on August 12, 2005. "Receiving this medal so many decades after the fact is truly incredible," he told the audience at the award ceremony. "I had to fight like hell for the right to fight for my own country, and now I feel completely vindicated." He died in Camarillo, California, in 2015 at the age of 98.

* * *

"The people who are crazy enough to think they can change the world are the ones who do."

—Steve Jobs

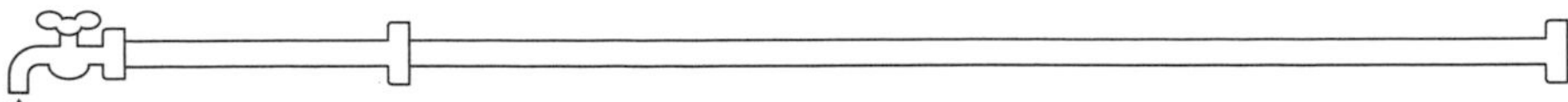

In ancient Athens, only the 300 richest citizens had to pay taxes.

CAKE-TASTROPHES

These true stories of cakes that went wrong might make you want to comfort yourself with a nice piece of cake.

DON'T TOUCH IT

Alexandra Schroeder of Lansing, Michigan, spent two months planning her daughter's fifth birthday party in 2019, and she went all-out—renting an entire bakery for $370. Included in the price: a unicorn cake with a shiny, golden horn that, from the look of its photo on the order form, would be professionally made. But when the cake was finally unveiled at the party, according to one news agency, "it had a decidedly more phallic horn than expected." Schroeder told a local TV reporter that it "came out in a shape that was so embarrassing. It had fingerprints on it and was not gold." After Schroeder went to the press with her story, the bakery owners countered that the partygoers made a huge mess. Then there was a dispute over whether the balance was paid in full, which the parties said "would be settled through litigation."

ASHES TO HASHISH

After a funeral in Germany, it's customary for the mourners to gather at a restaurant for coffee and cake. One such post-funeral party that took place in the town of Wiethagen took a very strange turn. When the restaurant worker went to get the cake out of the back, she inadvertently grabbed another cake—one that was infused with hashish—that her 18-year-old daughter had baked for another occasion. So, how did the funeral after-party go? According to an Associated Press report, "Thirteen people experienced nausea and dizziness and needed medical treatment."

MMM...CAKE?

In June 2109, a Pasadena, Texas, mom named Marsy Flores went to Walmart to pick up the two-tiered cake she'd ordered for her daughter Lea Nava's graduation, but there was no cake—someone had lost her order. The hour of the party was fast approaching, so the manager told Flores to pick any cake she wanted from the display case. She chose a smaller blue one (the school colors), and the bakery staff added a cap and gown and a photo of Lea to it. Crisis averted...or so they thought. Later, at the party, "I went to cut the cake," Flores told local news station KPRC, "and it was not budging." Upon closer inspection, the revelers discovered that beneath the icing, the cake was made of Styrofoam. "This is my baby," said Flores with tears in her eyes, "and she was graduating, so it was very important to me." When reporters

reached out to Walmart, the retail giant responded: "Incident was a result of a misunderstanding. The matter has been resolved. The customer was given a [$60] gift card for her inconvenience." "Inconvenience" is not how Flores would describe it: "They can't replace the moment that we lost."

THE GREAT BRITISH CAKE DROP

Controversy clouded a November 2019 episode of the British cooking show *Junior Bake Off.* In the "Technical Challenge," each of the kid contestants had to bake eight identical "English madeleines, evenly coated in jam, covered in coconut with a single crowning cherry on top." When the alloted hour was up and the children were bringing their plates up to the judging table, eleven-year-old George joked, "Here's where I drop them." A few seconds later, right after ten-year-old Ollie put his own plate on the table and ran back to his station, he brushed past George...whose cakes went flying and the plate shattered on the floor. "Oh no!" he cried. George's fellow contestants, including Ollie, quickly helped him pick up the cakes (apparently beating the five-second rule because the judges still tasted one). Afterward, George remarked, "My career as a juggler is over." But many home viewers weren't convinced it was an innocent mistake, and an intense debate raged on Twitter that night. One tweeter was sure that Ollie "knocked them out of his hand!" Another defended Ollie, saying, "To be fair, George wasn't looking where he was going." Because other kids were blocking the view of the incident from the camera, the footage doesn't make it clear exactly whose fault it was. But in the end, it didn't matter because neither kid's cakes tasted good enough to advance to the next round.

SIZE MATTERS

In December 2017, two brothers (names not released) in their 20s from Moundville, Alabama, were each going to have a piece of cheesecake. So far, so good. But when the older brother cut the cake and presented it to his sibling, he was holding a butcher knife. The younger brother later told police that he "felt threatened" by the knife. Exactly what happened next, and why a butcher knife was used to cut cheesecake, isn't exactly clear from news reports. But an argument ensued over the size of the piece that the older brother presented, specifically whether it was "big enough for a grown (expletive) man." With the matter in dispute, fists flew (but no butcher knives). Someone called the cops and the older brother was arrested on domestic violence charges. He denied that he'd punched his brother, telling officers that "he only patted the victim on the face and head like a dog." It's unclear whether either brother got to eat their cheesecake.

Why did ABBA wear such cheesy costumes in the 1970s?
They were tax-deductible. (Regular clothes weren't.)

FARTS IN THE NEWS

Here's news about windy conditions that didn't qualify for the weather report.

THE SWEET SMELL OF SUCCESS

After the Los Angeles Lakers played the Oklahoma City Thunder on the latter's home court in November 2019, each team's biggest star—LeBron James and Chris Paul—went out to dinner together at the Mohogany Prime Steakhouse. A group of fans waited outside for the two NBA stars to leave the restaurant, and when they did, one member of the group ran over to James to ask for his autograph while a friend stayed on the other side of the parking lot to record the moment for posterity. They got posterity all right: Instead of signing the autograph or declining verbally, James lifted a leg and farted so loudly that the camera phone 20 feet away picked it up. Then James and Paul drove off.

HE SAID, SHE SAID

Who are worse farters—men or women? According to a 1998 study at the University of New South Wales in Australia, men fart far more often than women. On average, men pass gas 12.7 times per day, while women toot a mere 7.1 times. But this battle of the sexes isn't decided yet. Although men fart more, women's farts actually smell worse. According to gastroenterologist Dr. Michael Levitt, the world's preeminent flatulence researcher (really), everybody has a different gut flora profile. Our digestive systems all have the same types of microbes that process food, and we all emit gas as a byproduct, which builds up and travels out of the stomach and exits via the rear-end. But a woman's microbes, by and large, produce higher concentrations of hydrogen sulfide—one of the foulest-smelling compounds in a fart.

BEST IN SHOW

Indian singer Yatin Sangoi, 48, was watching a movie with his family one night when inspiration struck...or seeped out. "I farted in the middle of watching a movie with my family and one of them laughed," Sangoi told reporters, "and said that if there was a contest, I would've won." So Sangoi went ahead and started a contest. In September 2019, he organized "What the Fart" at a bar in Surat, India—the country's first ever farting contest. Prizes of up to 15,000 rupees (about $210) went to winners in categories

whose farts were judged (by Sangoi) to be the loudest, longest, and most "musical." Sure, the idea of a fart contest is funny, but it comes from a good place, deep inside. "I want to normalize the process of farting," Sangoi said. "Even doctors will tell you that farting is one of the healthiest human body functions."

HIS CUP RUNNETH OVER

In November 2019, California congressman Eric Swalwell, a member of the House Intelligence Committee, appeared on the MSNBC show *Hardball with Chris Matthews* in a remote interview from the Capitol Building, to discuss developments in the impeachment hearings of President Donald Trump. "So far the evidence is uncontradicted that the president used taxpayer dollars to ask the Ukrainians to help him cheat...[pause]...an election." Reason for the pause: he was interrupted by the loud sound of what seemed to be flatulence. The *Hardball* clip went viral, and Swalwell went into denial mode. "It was not me!!!!!" he texted Buzzfeed. "Ha. And I didn't hear it when I was speaking," he added (even though he paused during the time of the presumed fart). *Hardball* later came to Swalwell's defense. The show's representative tweeted that the "fart" noise actually came from their studio: It was host Chris Matthews's coffee mug "scraping across the desk."

IN THE KNOW

After Christianity took hold in Europe, a medieval writer (his name is lost to history) invented a Roman god of flatulence named Crepitus Ventris, which translates from Latin as "intestinal noise." That bit of satire made it into history books for hundreds of years as an example of an actual god Romans worshipped.

THE AIR UP THERE

Dr. Lilian Gogo represents a part of the large city of Nairobi in the Kenyan legislature, and she's also a member of the lawmaking body's Committee on Transport, Public Works, and Housing. It's there in September 2019 where Gogo opened an issue for debate: passing a law to ban farting on airplanes. "There is one irritant that is often ignored, and this is the level of farting within the aircraft," Gogo said. "There are passengers who literally irritate fellow passengers by passing bad smells and uncomfortable farts." While many of Gogo's colleagues agreed that farts on planes smell very bad, they were skeptical about how much a law could ever be enforced. Gogo called for "special training" of flight attendants, and that they should provide "bicarbonate of soda to passengers after meals and drinks have been served."

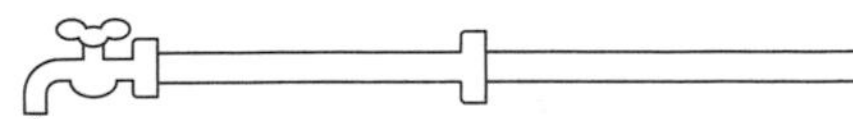

WRESTLE MANIACS

Some people love pro wrestling for the action, other people (including us) watch it for the entertaining characters, costumes, and storylines. Here are some of our favorites.

Kerwin White (2005). Played by Chavo Guerrero Jr., third-generation member of a famous Mexican-American lucha libre wrestling family. The Kerwin character was a Waspy white conservative Republican. Guerrero bleached his hair blond to play the role, dressed in a preppy polo shirt with a sweater tied around his neck, and made his entrances driving a golf cart. His tagline: "If it's not White, it's not right."

The Boogeyman (2005–19). The Boogeyman smashed alarm clocks over his head, recited creepy nursery rhymes, and ate live worms. When he defeated his opponents, he stuffed worms in their mouths and spit in their faces. In some matches he fought alongside a little person named Little Boogeyman.

Mordecai (2004). A religious fanatic with white hair and beard, dressed in a white wizard robe and carrying a shepherd's crook shaped like a cross. When Mordecai wasn't beating the sin out of his opponents, he condemned his fans for their sins and led them in prayer.

Sister Angelica and Mother Smucker (1997). Two male wrestlers who dressed up in nuns' habits and fought in the ring as the Flying Nuns, in a nod to the 1960s TV show of the same name. After a few appearances as nuns, the wrestlers reverted back to their more popular identities, Mosh (Charles Warrington) and Thrasher (Glenn Ruth), aka the Headbangers.

Perry Saturn (1990–2013). The wrestler, whose real name is Perry Satullo, played a character made mentally ill by a concussion suffered in the ring. His madness peaked in 2001, when he left his girlfriend for a mop named Moppy; the affair ended when the girlfriend fed Moppy into a woodchipper.

Phantasio (1995). A wrestler played by amateur magician Harry Del Rios, Phantasio wore mime makeup and performed magic tricks in and out of the ring. His specialty: pulling the underwear of referees and opponents right out from under their clothes.

Xanta Klaus (1995). Santa Claus's evil brother. He lived at the South Pole, wore a red and black Santa suit and beard, and stole presents from good boys and girls.

Papa Shango (1992–93). A voodoo witch doctor with skull makeup, top hat, and bone necklace. Shango carried a smoking skull into the ring and cast spells on his opponents before his fights. His most famous spell: getting the Ultimate Warrior to projectile vomit split pea soup onto the ring physician.

The word "swims" is an *ambigram*—it reads the same upside down as right side up.

MAKING A SPLASH

It's not always clear why some baby names become popular and others don't. But there is one name whose origin is clear...and we have Hollywood to thank for it.

SOMETHING TO SEE

If you're ever sitting at home and you can't find something to watch on TV, you might consider giving the 1984 romantic comedy *Splash* a look. Directed by Ron Howard and starring Tom Hanks, Daryl Hannah, John Candy, and Eugene Levy, it's the story of a man named Allen Bauer (Hanks) who falls in love with a mysterious woman (Hannah) who turns out to be a mermaid. *Splash* was a box office and a critical success, and it helped to launch the film careers of all of its stars.

Splash also made a mark on American popular culture in a way that is still being felt nearly 40 years later. This is thanks to the scene in the film where Allen asks the mermaid her name while they're standing in an electronics store. She replies that she can't pronounce it in English, and when he tells her to pronounce it in her own mermaid language, she lets out a dolphin-like screech that shatters nearly every TV in the store. That name won't do, so as they're walking down a street in Manhattan, Allen proposes several names for her like Joanie, Hilary, Linda, and Kim, none of which attract her interest. Then he pauses and asks, "Where are we?" He looks up at a street sign, and sees that they're on Madison Avenue. "Madison," he says.

"Madison!" the mermaid replies. "I like Madison."

"Well, Madison's not a name," Allen says. Then he relents: "Well, all right. Okay, fine. Madison it is. Good thing we weren't on 149th Street."

NO-MENCLATURE

At the time the movie was filmed, Allen was correct: Madison was definitely not a girl's name. According to the Social Security Administration, not a single girl born in the United States in 1983, the year before *Splash* hit the silver screen, was given the name Madison. Only 23 boys were. It was virtually unheard of for a girl to be named Madison, and that was why the screenwriters picked it: It was a ridiculous answer, and obviously not a girl's name. The line was intended to get laughs, and to communicate the mermaid's innocence. She was so naive, so unfamiliar with the human world that she actually believed Madison was a girl's name. Ha-ha-ha!

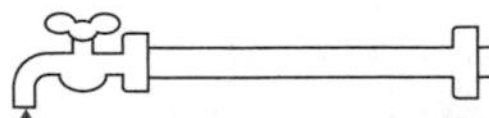

Watch your step! When a horse is born, its sharp hooves are covered in a protective gel called "deciduous hoof capsule."

BABY BOOM

Turns out, however, that Madison the mermaid had the last laugh, because in the years that followed, parents did begin naming their girls Madison. Not many at first: in 1985, the first full year after *Splash* played in theaters, only 300 girls were named Madison. But the name did have a nice ring to it, and a nice nickname—"Maddie." The numbers grew steadily from one year to the next.

When the kids who grew up watching *Splash* hit their childbearing years, the name really began to take off. In 1994, the tenth anniversary of the film, Madison was the 51st most popular girl's name in the country, beating out old favorites like Erica, Shannon, and Kelly. The following year, it was the 29th most popular, and in 1999 it was the seventh most popular. And still it kept climbing, reaching third place in 2000, and peaking at second place in 2001 and 2002. (Emily was #1 both years.)

Madison has been going strong ever since. As of 2018, it's still the 29th most popular name selected for baby girls in America. "It's funny because...the whole point of me choosing that name was because it [was such a] silly name," Daryl Hannah told Yahoo News in 2014. "No one really saw it as a first name and that was the joke. And now, of course, it's not funny at all. It's just like, 'Oh what a beautiful name!' It was funny at the time and now it's not even ironic."

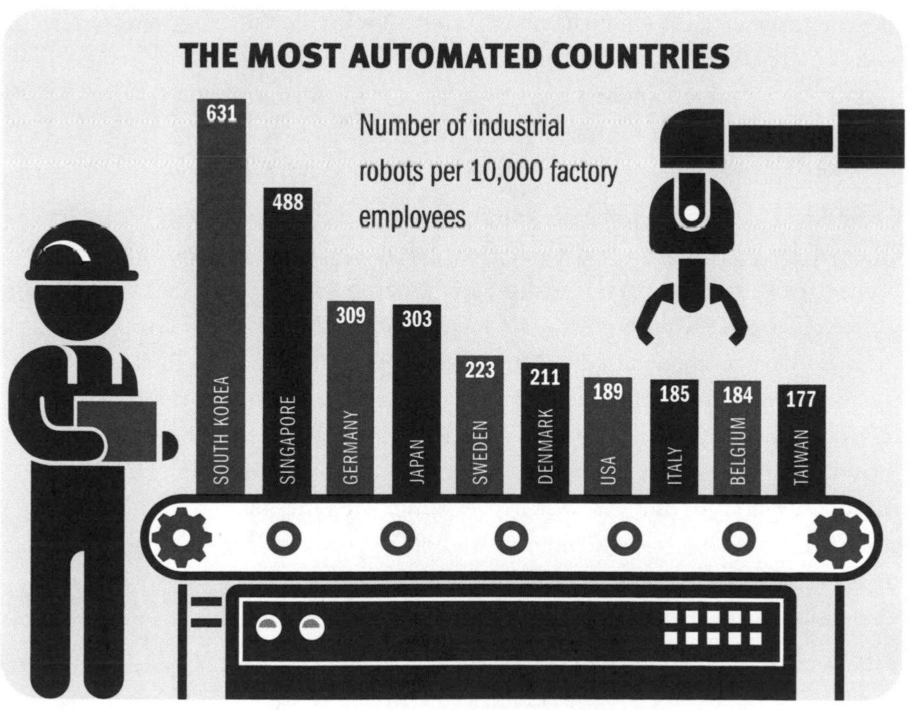

WATCHE$

On a recent trip to upstate New York, Uncle John met Gene Stone, a Bathroom Reader *fan who also happens to be a writer...and a watch collector. He contributed this article. (Want to learn more about the topic? Check out Gene's book* The Watch.*)*

BACKGROUND

Ask someone to name a high-end watch brand, and they'll probably say "Rolex." And for good reason. Rolex is one of the world's most prestigious watch manufacturers. (Little-known fact: Rolex is actually a not-for-profit company, owned by the Hans Wilsdorf Foundation, a private charitable organization.) But let's say you're at a very fancy party, and the guests are talking about their fancy wristwatches. You'd like to sound knowledgeable, but you've never heard of the brands being mentioned.

The fact is, there are many brands that produce more complicated, more expensive, and more beautiful watches than any of Rolex's offerings. (Another interesting fact: when referring to watches, the word "complicated" refers to the functions a watch has besides the standard hour, minute, and second hands, such as the date, moon phase indicator, chronograph function, *sonnerie* [chime], perpetual calendar, or a *tourbillon*—a tiny rotating cage that contains major parts of the movement, designed to eliminate timing errors. A tourbillon on a high-end watch can add, say, $100,000 to the sticker price.)

So if you want to impress a horophile, here are the brands to know. Want to *really* impress them? Consider buying one. But remember that some will set you back more than you'd spend on a car. Or, in some cases, a house. Or a small country.

CARTIER. This brand is primarily known for another business—jewelry (Piaget and Chopard are also excellent watch and jewelry establishments). But this company has been a trendsetter in high-end watches since it was founded in 1847 by Louis-Francois Cartier. One of the company's most influential designs is now over a century old: the tank watch, fashioned in the shape of World War I tank tracks. Cartier has often used movements made by Jaeger-LeCoultre, Vacheron, and Audemars Piguet, but its styling has always been individual and much copied by other brands. The line includes (besides tank watches) dress watches, sports watches, and unique designs that often appear for only one year. The expense here varies more than most brands—although you can easily spend more than $100,000, you can also get a Cartier for under $3,000. Former First Lady Michelle Obama and actor Angelina Jolie wear a Cartier tank. So did President John F. Kennedy.

AUDEMARS PIGUET. Founded in Switzerland by two watchmakers—Jules Audemars and Edward Piguet—in 1875, this brand created a limited number of complicated

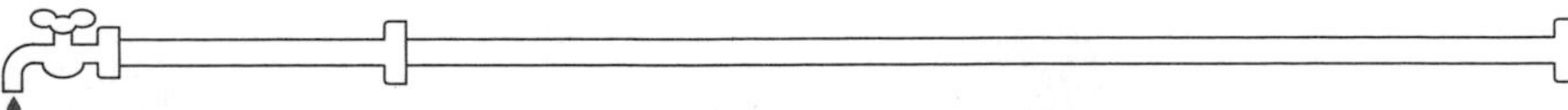

high-end watches for many years. AP nearly went out of business during the Depression, and then hit hard times again in the 1960s, but its fortunes were resuscitated in 1972 by its introduction of the Royal Oak, the first sports watch to be made of stainless steel and one of the most successful launches in watch history. The company, still family-owned and employing many family descendants, now sells a complete line of beautifully designed and crafted watches alongside the Royal Oak, which now comes in a variety of sizes and metals. It takes about $15,000 to buy AP's least expensive model. James Corden wears a Royal Oak while doing "Carpool Karaoke"; basketball star LeBron James wears a Royal Oak Offshore (among his many other watches). Arnold Schwarzenegger, Serena Williams, Tom Cruise, and Kim Kardashian also own APs.

PATEK PHILIPPE. Patek is probably *the* most prestigious brand of watches. The company was founded in 1839 by Polish watchmaker Count Antoni Norbert de Prawdzic (he changed his name to Patek when he became a Swiss citizen) and French watchmaker Adrien Philippe. It's known for its highly complicated watches, its dress watches, and its sports watches, all of which tend to appreciate mightily in value. The least expensive model costs around $20,000; the most expensive costs over $1,000,000. Patek's best-known and best-selling line is the Calatrava, first introduced in 1932. The CEO of Toyota wears a Calatrava. John Lennon wore a Patek, as did Charlotte Brontë, Albert Einstein, Leo Tolstoy, Pyotr Tchaikovsky, Pablo Picasso, Clark Gable, the 14th Dalai Lama, and Pope Leo XIII.

A. LANGE & SÖHNE. Patek's rival for top of the line, this brand was established in 1845 in Germany and for generations produced excellent timepieces under the aegis of the Lange family. But after its factories were bombed in World War II, the company was taken over by the East German government and merged into a state-owned watch manufacturer and nationalized in 1948. Then, after the German reunification in 1990, Walter Lange, the founder's great-grandson, restored the company, which has since achieved renown for its upscale dress watches and chronographs (a combination watch and stopwatch). Entry-level Lange & Söhne watches begin in the $20,000 range. Among the brand's fans: Tsar Alexander II of Russia, singer Ed Sheeran, actor Brad Pitt, and President Bill Clinton.

VACHERON CONSTANTIN. Making luxury watches since 1755, Vacheron is the world's oldest continually active watch manufacturer. The company barely made it through the Great Depression, but reemerged as a trailblazer in artfully styled watches, using its own in-house enamel artisans, engravers, and gem setters. The company's Reference 57260 pocket watch from 2015 is considered the most complicated watch ever made. (It has 57 complications.) That one would cost an astronomical sum to buy, but low-end models start at around (only) $10,000. These watches tend to do very well in the vintage market:

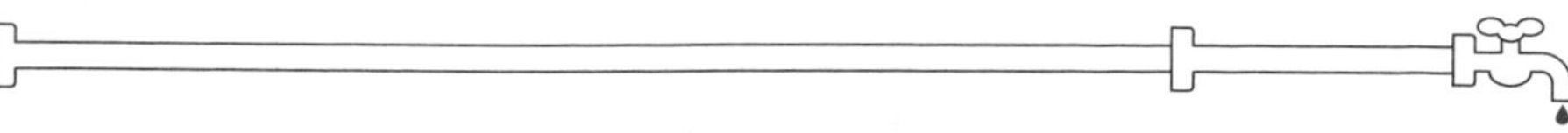

Amount of money John Lennon left to his oldest son, Julian, in his will: $0.

you can invest in an older Vacheron for as little as $2,000. Actors Elizabeth Taylor and Marlon Brando owned Vacherons, as did Diana, Princess of Wales, author Henry James, and John D. Rockefeller when he was the richest person in modern history.

JAEGER-LECOULTRE. This company, founded in 1833 by Antoine LeCoultre in Switzerland (Edmond Jaeger did not join up until 1937), is known for its many innovations, from the Atmos clock that runs on changing air temperature to its creation of the world's smallest mechanical movements. It is best known, however, for its Reverso models: watches that turn on an axis to either reveal a blank or skeletonized rear side—or even another dial keeping its own time. Invented in 1931 to help stop polo players from breaking their watches during a match, Reversos are a major part of this company's sales, but JLC also offers many other lines, and is one of the few companies that produces its own movements, cases, dials, hands, and bracelets. Highly regarded within the industry, JLC is often referred to as the watchmaker's watchmaker. You can get a new JLC for under $10,000. Or, of course, you can spend a great deal more. The CEO of Citibank wears a JLC Master Perpetual Calendar. Other owners, past and present, include aviator Amelia Earhart, President Lyndon Johnson, and entertainers from Charlie Chaplin to Jay-Z.

IWC. The International Watch Company is the only major European watch brand founded by an American—specifically, Florentine Ariosto Jones, in 1868. However, the flamboyantly named founder was unable to keep the company afloat, and IWC ended up in Swiss hands for many generations before eventually becoming part of the behemoth Richemont Group in 2000. Known for a wide variety of models, its most famous lines are its pilot watches (the Mark X lines), and its Portuguese models, which are oversized and very dressy. You can get a new IWC for under $10,000. Actors Dev Patel and Dwayne Johnson have been spotted wearing one. Actor Chris Evans (he plays Captain America in Marvel movies) is an IWC brand ambassador.

BREGUET. Possibly the greatest watchmaker of all was Abraham-Louis Breguet (1747–1823), whose many inventions have made the modern wristwatch possible. His watches were the Rolexes of their day: Everyone from author Alexandre Dumas to Marie Antoinette sought out and bought Breguets. Today the line is highly stylized with hand-engraved silver plate over gold dials and glowing cases with reeded edges. But Breguet also makes chronographs, used by the French Air Force in the 1950s, and a full range of sport watches. Spend anywhere between $10,000 and $500,000 and you can get a Breguet (and a lot of horophile approval). Napoléon Bonaparte, Serge Rachmaninoff, Winston Churchill, and Queen Victoria are just a few of the many titans of history who wore Breguets. More recently, Ben Affleck wore a Breguet Tradition Fusee Tourbillon in *Batman v Superman: Dawn of Justice.* You can pick one of those up for a mere $175,000.

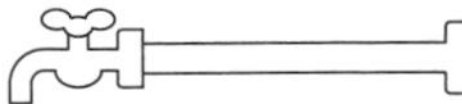

THE RUFF RIDER

Some people love to ride the bus, other people say it's for the dogs. Here's a dog who couldn't agree more.

THE BIG CITY

Eclipse is a black Labrador–bull mastiff mix who was living in rural western Washington. In 2012, when she was six months old, she and her owner, Jeff Young, moved to the big city—Seattle. They found a place to live in the city's Belltown neighborhood, not too far from the Space Needle. Living in the city was quite an adjustment for Eclipse: Instead of lots of dog-friendly open spaces like there'd been in the country, downtown Seattle had asphalt, sidewalks, and a dog park at Third Avenue and Bell Street, five stops from their home on the city's Metro Transit bus line. Luckily for Eclipse and Young, Metro Transit encouraged riders to bring their dogs with them on the bus.

NOW YOU SEE HER...NOW YOU DON'T

Young and Eclipse went to the dog park several times a week, so often that riding the bus became a habit. How much of a habit? One day in 2015, after they'd been living in Seattle for about two years, Young was waiting for the bus while chatting with friends and smoking a cigarette. When the bus arrived, Young hadn't finished his cigarette, so he decided to wait for the next bus to come along. The first bus left without him...and only then did he realize that Eclipse was nowhere to be found. Where could she have disappeared to so quickly? Only one place: the bus. So Young caught the next one and rode it to the dog park, hoping 1) that he was correct in assuming that Eclipse had gotten on the bus; and 2) that the dog had gotten off at the right stop.

GOOD GIRL!

Sure enough, when the bus pulled up next to the dog park, Eclipse was there, waiting for him. That was Eclipse's first trip to the dog park all by herself, but it wouldn't be the last. Sometimes when she was really eager to get to the dog park and Young was busy with something else, she'd go on her own and Young would catch up with her later. Other times Eclipse just went on her own, then when she was ready, She got on the return bus and came home. She even learned how to use the crosswalk: She waits

The oldest beer recipe, written on a Sumerian tablet, is a poem dating to 1800 BC.

at the curb until everyone else crosses the street (when the "WALK" sign flashes), then she crosses with them and waits at the bus stop for the bus that takes her home.

One day in January 2015, a local radio host named Miles Montgomery happened to get on the bus when Eclipse was riding alone. "She didn't appear to have an owner," he recounted. "The dog gets off at the dog park. I just look out the window and I'm like, 'Did that just happen?'" Montgomery mentioned the story on the air; then the local ABC-TV affiliate, KOMO Channel 4, reported the story on the evening news. That got the network's attention, and they ran stories on *World News Tonight* and *Nightline*. CNN did a story as well, and soon Eclipse was a genuine media phenomenon with her own Facebook page, Twitter account, and a children's book titled *Dog on Board: The True Story of Eclipse, the Bus-Riding Dog*. She even has a fan club whose members call themselves "Ecliptomaniacs."

"The dog gets off at the dog park. I just look out the window and I'm like, 'Did that just happen?'"

STAY!

So, with all of her newfound celebrity, did some wet blanket at Metro Transit spoil the fun by telling Young that Eclipse can't ride the bus alone anymore? Nope—quite the opposite, in fact. Metro made Eclipse the star of a "Bus Doggy Dog" hip-hop video promoting the agency's trip planning app, and gave her a bus pass of her own.

As of 2020, Eclipse is eight years old, fit and healthy, and still taking the bus to the dog park nearly every day. She's become an unofficial ambassador for the dog-friendly city, and, according to Young, she's also the Seattle Seahawks' "number-one self-appointed unofficial four-legged mascot." (He's a big Seahawks fan.) Eclipse is still making new friends all the time. How does Young know they're new friends? "Probably once a week I get a phone call: 'Hi, I have your dog Eclipse here at Third and Bell,' " he says. "I have to tell them, 'No. She's fine. She knows what she's doing.' "

* * *

UNCLE JOHN'S STALL OF FAME

Honoree: Yuri Gagarin, Russian cosmonaut, first person to go to space

Notable Achievement: Launching a preflight tradition that continues to this day

Details: After being driven out to the launch pad on April 12, 1961, Gagarin had to make a quick "pit stop" on his way to the rocket. So he peed on a bus tire. Ever since then, after cosmonauts are driven to the launch site, they honor the Soviet hero's memory by peeing on the bus tire. (Men do it the classic way; women bring it in a jar and splash it on the tire.)

R U IN CRISIS, PART II: FACTS AND FIGURES

On page 34, we told you the story of the Crisis Text Line, which has analyzed more than 140 million texts from people contacting the service. Here's some of what the analysis has revealed.

- More texters contact the Crisis Text Line to talk about depression or sadness than any other topic. Second most common topic: relationships. Anxiety and suicidal thoughts are #3 and #4.
- Texters to the Crisis Text Line who struggle with eating disorders are more likely to contact the service on Monday than on any other day of the week.
- A male texter is 2.5 times more likely than a female texter to talk about gender and sexual identity issues.
- One in five texters over the age of 55 is contacting the Crisis Text Line to talk about loneliness or isolation.
- Odds that a texter will bring up the subject of parents or parenting: 1 in 5. If a texter is a parent, they're 2.7 times more likely to talk about their finances than a texter without kids.
- Texters over the age of 25 are most likely to use the Crisis Text Line early in the morning; texters under 25 tend to text in late at night.
- Middle-of-the-night texts tend to peak in June and July, when young people don't have to get up early for school the next morning.
- 65 percent of texters say they're telling their crisis counselor something they've never told anyone else before.
- Texts from LGBTQ+ texters tend to surge in the summer, possibly because college-age texters are back home from college and staying with unaccepting families.
- 20 percent of the texts received by the Crisis Text Line come from areas of the country with the lowest per capita income.
- Six of the ten states that have the most people texting about substance abuse are Midwestern states.
- Native Americans make up 1.3 percent of the U.S. population, but are 6 percent of the people who text the Crisis Text Line. They're most likely to text from Arkansas, Oklahoma, Montana, and South Dakota.
- Texters under the age of 18 are more likely to be non-white than white.

- African Americans make up 13 percent of the U.S. population...and 12 percent of the people who text the Crisis Text Line.
- 40 percent of texts from people under the age of 13 that mention self-harm will contain the words "scared" and "alone."
- College-age users of the Crisis Text Line are most likely to use the service in April, when they're dealing with midterm, final exam, and graduation stress. Texts from people who report feeling suicidal also tend to peak in April and May.
- Texts dealing with anxiety peak every morning between 8:00 a.m. and 11:00 a.m., and again at 11:00 p.m. Texts from people who are depressed tend to peak at 8:00 p.m., and people who are at risk of self-harm are most likely to text around 4:00 a.m. People dealing with substance abuse are most likely to text at 5 a.m.
- If a texter is age 13 or under, they're three times more likely to talk about bullying and twice as likely to talk about gender and sexual identity than someone over the age of 13.
- Texts dealing with eating and body image are most likely to be sent at the beginning of the week. Lonely texters tend to reach out on Sunday and Monday nights, and are more likely to be from Florida and Mississippi than any other state.
- If a person mentions social media in their text, they are three times more likely to be texting out of concern for the well-being of another person than they are about themselves. If a person is 55 or older, they're twice as likely as a younger person to contact the Crisis Text Line because they're worried about someone else. Texts from people concerned about others are more likely to come from Colorado, Vermont, and Montana than from other states.
- Conversations about suicide tend to peak on Sunday nights and are at the lowest on Fridays and Saturdays. They're also more common in the spring than any other time of year.
- The most anxiety-related texts are received on Wednesdays. Texts dealing with bullying are most common on Tuesdays and Wednesdays.
- Texters who are 65 or older are twice as likely to text about grief than texters who are younger than 65; texts concerning grief tend to peak during the month of December.
- Text conversations mentioning the military community (active service members and veterans) climb between 7:00 a.m. and noon, and usually peak around 9:00 a.m. They're also more common on Tuesdays, Fridays, and Saturdays than on other days of the week. Service members and vets are more likely to text from South Carolina, Hawaii, and Alabama than from any other state.

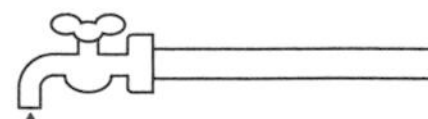

Typhoid fever occurs when the bacteria that causes salmonella invades the bloodstream.

IT'S A BAD DEAL

Some bargains seem too good to be true...because they are.

PAYDAY LOANS

President Ronald Reagan's administration did away with a lot of bank regulations in the 1980s. That led to big banks taking over the financial landscape, absorbing or pushing out smaller regional and community banks. And some of those small hometown banks tended to offer modest, short-term loans to familiar customers; the big banks never did because they couldn't make enough money on it (versus, say, a 30-year mortgage on a home). When those tiny banks died out in the 1980s, check-cashing or payday loan companies picked up the slack. They offer loans in the form of an advance on salary for people living paycheck to paycheck. Let's say someone with a bank balance of $4 gets a flat tire three days before payday. If they go to a check-cashing place, they can get an advance on their upcoming paycheck to meet that unexpected expense. By 2010, payday loans was a $46 billion industry. Why? Because the interest rates they charge on those short-term loans can be astoundingly high—anywhere from 20 to 1,000 percent. That means a loan of $100 could end up costing as much as $1,000. Payday loan businesses fall into the category of "predatory lending" and are illegal in 14 states and Washington, D.C.

LIGHT BULBS

Do you still use old-fashioned, incandescent light bulbs? That technology has remained largely unchanged for a century. They're not as readily available as they used to be, but you can still get them for about $1 apiece. The other bulbs on the market today are the newer, energy-efficient LED lights. Cost of a single LED bulb: $8.00! An incandescent bulb is far cheaper, isn't it? Not really. Incandescents last a maximum of 1,200 hours, and over the course of around 25 years, you'd have to change it 21 times and you'd burn through $180 of electricity. The LED bulb lasts for as long as 25,000 hours, and in those same 25 years, would consume just $30 worth of power.

DISCOUNT DESIGNER CLOTHES

Discount retail chains like TJ Maxx, Ross, Burlington Coat Factory, and (in Canada) Winners all advertise themselves as places to find fancy clothes from name-brand designers at deep discounts. Sure enough, if you sort through the racks, you're likely to find items made by companies like Ralph Lauren, Nautica, Kate Spade, and

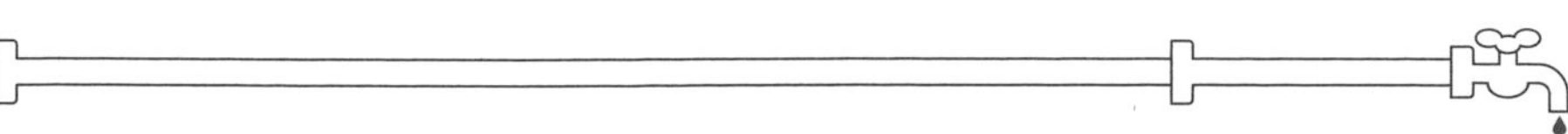

Nike at low prices. That price tag says that TJ Maxx is charging just $14.95 for that Tommy Hilfiger shirt, which has a "suggested retail price" of $90, and the consumer assumes that's what it would cost in a department store. But in reality, that $14.95 TJ Maxx shirt never cost $90 and was never available at Bloomingdale's. Major fashion companies produce less expensive clothing lines specifically for the discount chains.

WINNING A CAR ON A GAME SHOW

When a game show contestant wins a brand-new car, it's certainly the thrill of a lifetime for the individual (and great TV for the rest of us). But once the cameras stop rolling and the celebration ends, the contestant has to sign some forms and write some checks. As far as the Internal Revenue Service is concerned, prizes won on game shows qualify as taxable income...which means the winner of the new car has to pay taxes on it. In other words, that free car is far from free. On *The Price Is Right*, for example, participants are required to take ownership of their prizes immediately, and thus pay taxes on it immediately. Let's say they win a $30,000 SUV. If they want to take it home, they'll have to fork over around $5,000 in taxes. That "free" car actually cost them $5,000. And if they can't afford the upfront cost right then and there, they don't get to take it home.

LIQUIDATION SALES

Generally, when large stores or chains go kaput, they'll stay open for a few more weeks to hold a "Going Out of Business!" or "Everything Must Go!" sale. Are they trying to squeeze a few more bucks out of consumers so they can pay down their mounting debts? Not really. The people in charge have already washed their hands of the situation. Often, those "Last Days" sales aren't run by the store itself, but rather by a liquidation company. That's a business that buys up a store's assets and then sells them off, as quickly as possible, in the store's old location. Because all of the merchandise (and fixtures) now belong to this new company, they can charge whatever they like...and they do, frequently marking up prices—and even bringing in stock from other stores—to maximize profits.

* * *

A BAD JOKE

Q: What do Cedric the Entertainer, Attila the Hun, and Felix the Cat have in common?

A: The same middle name.

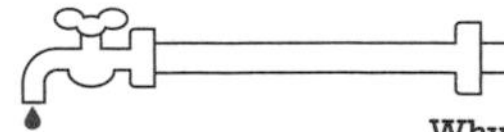

LOST IN TRANSLATION

If you had to write an ad in a foreign language, using loosely translated words that you hope are correct, how do you think it would turn out? Probably a lot like these real Web ads that foreign-language speakers attempted to write in English. (Some of these might hurt your brain.)

Satisfaction guarantee from a Chinese seller:
"What a charming people brings you is not only the trust, but also the kindness!! We have not met about 90% of our customers, who just pay us first and then we deliver the goods."

From a tool factory that sells ratchet wrenches:
"New product & handle or Funny tools will be developed by 3D design every year."

In an eBay posting for a motorcycle mask:
"Function: dustproof windproof sand, high-quality materials plus perfect workmanship, but also you breathe comfortable and healthy new air. Moisture perspiration effect is very good, reduce the movement of breathing position of the hot side, Material fit the skin very comfortable, so you better enjoy the transport launch."

From a description of a child's alarm clock on eBay:
"Natural sound alarm clock, colorful color clock, look like an alien machine warehouse oh, super magical."

Shipping information for a toy described as "Multivariant Combatteam Juncle":
"The trade is cross-border and Airmail is cheapest post way, so it'll take along time for delivery. If you don't want to wait so long time, please pay the Express fee or don't buy it.
We don't Responsible for your Customs duty.
We believe good communication can thrive good relationships."

From a craigslist ad for a battery-operated trash can:
"Conventional Garbage can in use will make a lot of noise, how our kitchen trash can use slow down technology, you can rest assured that you can use, do not worry about disturbing the rest of the family. Can be used in all places where we can use it. It's big, beautiful and the price is right. Even in your kid's cabin, I think it's all right to put one."

Is this a description of a toy ball for cats, or a beautiful poem?
"Sound knot pet cat toy
Soft thorns do not hurt the cat
Spherical design, cats play with handy
Beautiful colors, falling in
love with one eye"

THE ORIGIN OF CHEWBACCA: BODY BUILDING

Taking the Wookiee from page to screen turned out to be one of the most difficult parts of making Star Wars*...but also one of the most successful.* *(Part I is on page 111.)*

Special Effects

Determined to utilize the best filmmakers in the business, George Lucas hired renowned creature designer Stuart Freeborn to oversee Chewbacca's creation. Freeborn's greatest achievement (until *Star Wars*) was the "Dawn of Man" sequence in Stanley Kubrick's *2001: A Space Odyssey* (1969) that features prehistoric apes freaking out about a mysterious black monolith. According to Hollywood lore, Freeborn wasn't nominated for a Costume Design Oscar because Academy voters thought the apes were real. They weren't—they were actors inside very convincing ape suits, and Lucas wanted that same level of realism for the look of *Star Wars*. Freeborn ended up designing many of the saga's most memorable aliens. In fact, you've already seen his face—part of it, anyway: Freeborn combined his own mouth and nose with Albert Einstein's eyes to create Yoda.

Coming to Life

"Chewbacca was a fascinating one," said Freeborn, "because he had to look nice, though he could be very ferocious when he wanted to be. I kept pulling the nose out and pushing it back. It was difficult, because we were trying to do a combination of a monkey, a dog, and a cat. I really wanted it to be cat-like more than anything else, but we were trying to conform to that combination."

The hardest part was getting the mouth to work. To achieve that, Freeborn combined puppetry and animatronics to devise a simple system of cables and toggles that connected the actor's lips to the mask's lips. Whenever Peter Mayhew opened his mouth, it activated cables that opened Chewbacca's mouth. One side had slightly shorter cables, giving Chewie his trademark snarl. (One of Lucas's biggest regrets with *Star Wars* was that he wasn't able to put that same level of sophistication into any of the other alien masks.) Freeborn's simple mechanism worked so well that later Chewbacca technicians couldn't improve upon it. "Complicated is great, but simple is genius," said creature designer Tom Spina, who was hired to create a working Chewbacca costume in 2017. "Stuart devised simple ways to achieve amazingly lifelike results."

What do you call a grandfather clock that's shorter than 6'?
A grandmother clock. If it's shorter than 5'2", it's a granddaughter clock.

Hair and Makeup

In *Star Wars,* Princess Leia dismisses Chewbacca as a "walking carpet," but the costume was actually made more like a wig than a carpet. The team tasked with building Chewbacca—which included Freeborn's wife Kay—tested several different kinds of fur, wool, and hair, before finally settling on knotted yak hair and rabbit fur over a mohair base (mohair is the silk of the Angora goat). The fur was originally intended to be gray, but Lucas decided on alternating layers of red and brown fur to help Chewie stand out from the black-and-white spaceship interiors. Using a fiberglass mold of Mayhew's head, they created a snug-fitting mask that had padding on top, bringing Chewbacca's height to a full eight feet.

IN THE KNOW

Few *Star Wars* actors boast more "geek cred" than 4'4" Deep Roy: He was a stand-in for Yoda in *The Empire Strikes Back*, played flute player Droopy McCool in *Return of the Jedi*, played every Oompa-Loompa in the 2005 remake of *Charlie and the Chocolate Factory*, played a guard in *Transformers: Revenge of the Fallen*, and played Scotty's alien sidekick Keenser in the *Star Trek* reboot movies.

Meanwhile, the art department crafted sets of Chewie's canine teeth, his bandolier, and his signature bowcaster weapon. According to Wookieepedia, the official *Star Wars* wiki page, this half-rifle, half-crossbow is "more powerful and accurate than blasters, firing a metal quarrel encased in plasma energy." In real life, Chewie's bandolier and bowcaster were the work of John Mollo, a military historian who had no knowledge of science fiction when Lucas hired him to design the costumes for the Rebels, the Jedi Knights, Darth Vader, and the Empire. (Mollo won an Oscar for the costumes in *Star Wars* and, later, one for his work on *Gandhi*.)

I, Chewbacca

Within an hour of being hired for the role, 32-year-old Peter Mayhew was getting fitted for his Chewbacca costume, which was still being designed. With nothing to base his character on except some rough notes and drawings, Mayhew realized he had to do some independent research...so he went to the zoo. He spent long hours studying bears, lions, and gorillas—as he described it, "the growling variety." He tried to mimic how they move, how they use their eyes, and how they vocalize. He worked with mime performers to come up with Chewbacca's distinctive gait.

But Mayhew didn't really inhabit the Wookiee until he was inside the full costume for the first time. "I put that mask on, and Chewie transformed me. I transformed. The attitude was different. The walk was different. Chewie 'turned on.' Do the scenes, come back, take the mask off, and Peter was back."

The Wookiee Has No Pants

Filming *Star Wars* almost gave George Lucas a nervous breakdown. The 32-year-old director had never worked on a movie this big, and the older British crew, believing it to be a "rubbish children's film," fought Lucas at every turn. Many of the older actors, especially Alec Guinness (Obi-Wan Kenobi), were embarrassed to be in it. The younger actors were treating it like a vacation. And nervous 20th Century Fox executives started sending what every director dreads: notes. Mark Hamill remembered looking over Lucas's shoulder at one note that requested, "Can't they put pants on the Wookiee?" To placate the execs, Hamill said the prop department made a pair of "Wookiee lederhosen," which Lucas refused to use. (Lucas actually had to take a few days off from filming to recover from stress and exhaustion.)

All of Mayhew's filming for *Star Wars* took place at Elstree Studios near London. The completed Chewbacca costume looked convincing, but it was very hot and heavy. It's unknown how many were made for the film; if you ask Mayhew's costars, not enough. (Rumor had it that the Chewie costume was at its stinkiest while they were shooting the trash compactor scene on the Death Star.) Although he wore a leotard underneath to absorb the sweat, it could only do so much. When Mayhew sweated profusely, his eyes would detach from the mask, which stopped everything while Chewie's face was put back together.

Interestingly, Chewbacca has actual lines in the script, which Mayhew said from behind the mask (only to be overdubbed with animal noises). For example, in one scene, after Obi-Wan Kenobi leaves the room, the Wookiee lets out a growl. However, as is shown in a rare behind-the-scenes clip (on YouTube), Mayhew said in his proper British accent, "That old man's mad," to which Han Solo replies, "You said it, Chewie."

We'll Fix It in Post

"Most of the crew thought that the film was a bit odd," said John Mollo. "We doubted that it would ever be shown." Mayhew wasn't sure, either. Once filming was completed, he returned to his hospital job, not really expecting to play the Wookiee ever again. Unbeknownst to him, there was some bona fide movie magic taking place in California. The technical wizards at Industrial Light and Magic, which Lucas had created specifically for *Star Wars*, were constructing and filming the groundbreaking space-battle sequences. Composer John Williams was writing what would become one of the best-known scores in movie history. And sound designer Ben Burtt was working with Lucas to figure out what all these alien worlds sounded like. Still in film school when he was hired for *Star Wars*, Burtt came up with the lightsaber's distinctive hum, Darth Vader's menacing breathing, and R2-D2's beeps and whistles. But Chewbacca's voice was his first assignment, and it turned out to be the toughest, taking more than a year to get right.

GRRWWWARGG RRAWWAWGGR HERRNNGGHHH!

(Translation: Part III is on page 304.)

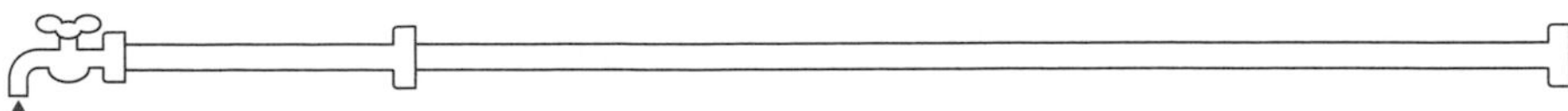

LIST IN SPACE

This is Ground Control to Uncle John. Can you hear me, Uncle John? Can you... ...here am I sitting on my tin can, reading random tidbits from the final frontier.

13 LUNAR "SEAS"

1. Sea of Knowledge

2. Sea of Cold

3. Sea of Showers

4. Sea of Cleverness

5. Sea of the Edge

6. Sea of Moscow

7. Sea of Nectar

8. Sea of Clouds

9. Sea of Serenity

10. Sea of Tranquility

11. Sea of Waves

12. Sea of Vapors

13. Sea of Alexander von Humboldt

4 MAIN COMPONENTS OF THE ORIGINAL DARTH VADER COSTUME

1. Black clerical robes

2. Motorcycle suit

3. Gas mask

4. German military helmet

12 ALLEGED ALIEN RACES

1. Grays (or Greys)

2. Plejaren (previously known as Pleiadeans)

3. Venusians

4. Tall Whites

5. Agarthans

6. Reptilians and Reptiloids

7. Blue Avians

8. Lemurians

9. Arcturians

10. Lyran

11. Mantis

12. Zeta Reticulans

8 RANDOM OBJECTS LAUNCHED INTO SPACE

1. Artifacts from the Jamestown English settlement

2. James Doohan's ashes (Scotty from *Star Trek*)

3. Luke Skywalker's original lightsaber

4. Amelia Earhart's watch

5. Parts from the Wright brothers' *Flyer*

6. Tesla Roadster

7. Wheel of Gruyère cheese

8. Disco ball

7 BRIGHTEST OBJECTS IN EARTH'S SKY

1. Sun

2. Moon

3. Venus

4. Jupiter

5. Mars

6. Mercury

7. Sirius (binary star system)

5 NASA MARS ROBOTS

1. Sojourner (1997)

2. Spirit (2004)

3. Opportunity (2003)

4. Curiosity (2011)

5. Perseverance (2020)

7 STARS OF THE BIG DIPPER (URSA MAJOR)

1. Alioth

2. Dubhe

3. Merak

4. Alkaid

5. Phecda

6. Megrez

7. Mizar

The Grateful Dead sponsored the 1992 Lithuanian Olympic men's basketball team. (They won the bronze medal.)

3 ASTRONOMY THEORIES

1. Big Bang: About 13.77 billion years ago, the universe expanded from a very high-density and high-temperature state.

2. Hubble's Law: Objects observed in deep space are moving away from Earth because the universe is expanding.

3. Rainbow Gravity: Different wavelengths of light experience different gravity levels and are separated in the same way that a prism splits white light into the rainbow.

5 FIRST WOMEN IN SPACE BY NATIONALITY

1. Valentina Tereshkova (Russian, 1963)

2. Sally Ride (American, 1983)

3. Roberta Bondar (Canadian, 1992)

4. Chiaki Mukai (Japanese, 1994)

5. Liu Yang (Chinese, 2012)

7 ANCIENT OBSERVATORIES IN THE UK

1. Ballochroy: Three standing stones in Scotland that predict the summer solstice

2. Boscawen-Un: Bronze Age stone circle in Cornwall

3. Bryn Celli Ddu: "The Mound in the Dark Grove," a prehistoric tomb in Wales

4. Callanish Stones: Neolithic standing stones placed in a cruciform pattern in Scotland

5. Maeshowe: Chambered cairn in Scotland, built circa 2800 BC

6. Stonehenge: A ring of standing stones, each approximately 13 feet high, built in Wiltshire (in southern England) around 3000 BC

7. Woodhenge: A timber circle monument two miles from Stonehenge that wasn't discovered until a plane flew over it in the 1920s

13 SPACEY SONGS

1. "Space Oddity" (David Bowie)

2. "Rocket Man" (Elton John)

3. "Astronomy Domine" (Pink Floyd)

4. "Tranquility Base Hotel & Casino" (Arctic Monkeys)

5. "Mothership Connection (Star Child)" (Parliament)

6. "Intergalactic" (Beastie Boys)

7. "Orion" (Jethro Tull)

8. "Ballrooms of Mars" (T. Rex)

9. "Lift Off" (Jay-Z & Kanye West featuring Beyoncé)

10. "E.T.I. (Extra Terrestrial Intelligence)" (Blue Öyster Cult)

11. "Satellite 15... the Final Frontier" (Iron Maiden)

12. "Third Stone from the Sun" (The Jimi Hendrix Experience)

13. "The Day that Lassie Went to the Moon" (Camper Van Beethoven)

David Bowie's only #1 album: *Blackstar*, released the day after he died in 2016.

WEIRD CANADA

O Canada: where the health care is free, the french fries are smothered in gravy and cheese, and the news stories are really, really odd.

FRENCH KISS-OFF

Canada is a bilingual nation by law—legally, all federal government documents and signage must be presented in both English and French. While only about 17 percent of the country is fluent in both languages, French is the dominant language in the province of Quebec, to the point where the government eschews *anything* English. In 2019, a woman named Émilie Dubois applied for permanent residency in Quebec. She's about as French as can be: She was born and raised in France, French is her first language, and she received her entire education in French, up through the doctorate program at Quebec City's Laval University. But provincial authorities still deemed her not sufficiently fluent in French. Reason: one small section of her thesis on cellular biology was written in English—because she'd written that part for an English-language scholarly journal—and they denied her residency application. (The decision was later overturned on appeal.)

LET'S DUEL IT

The Criminal Code of Canada is more than 1,200 pages long and dates back to the late 1800s. In 2017, the Canadian parliament passed a sweeping justice bill that eliminated laws found to be "obsolete, redundant, or already ruled as unconstitutional." This makes certain practices, which haven't been monitored for decades, technically legal in Canada now. Example: "crime comics"—comic books depicting grisly crimes—were outlawed after causing a moral panic in the 1950s. But they're fine now. Other newly legal activities: pretending to use witchcraft or sorcery, and engaging in a duel. (The last death-by-duel in Canada occurred in 1833.)

CURB APPALL

January 26, 1993, is a date that figures prominently in the life of Winnipeg man Calvin Hawley. That's the day he brought his second son home from the hospital. It's also the day he noticed that a city snowplow had knocked out a huge chunk of the curb in front of his house. After the spring thaw, Hawley called the city to request a repair. Nobody came. So he kept calling every few months to register a complaint...for years. Every time he called, he was told that somebody would come out to repair that curb, but no one ever arrived. In 2017, Hawley woke up to the sound of a road crew on his street...but they were fixing a less-damaged section of curb across the street. Finally, in 2019, he was given an official complaint number, and

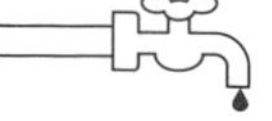

when he went online to check it, he found a concrete repair date: the curb would be fixed by June 26, 2037.

WHAT A WAY TO START THE DAY

Lots of restaurants have a "secret menu," a list of special food and drink items that fans pass around the Internet. There's a secret menu for Tim Hortons, the huge chain of coffee-and-donut shops. (There are more than 4,300 Tim Hortons in Canada.) The chain was started in Hamilton, Ontario, in 1964 by hockey star Tim Horton, and millions of Canadians stop by each morning for a "double-double"—coffee with two creams and two sugars. In 2019, news of a secret menu item at Tim Hortons went viral: a Gretter, named for another hockey legend, Wayne Gretzky, who wore the number 99 throughout his storied career. A Gretter at Tim Hortons is a coffee with nine creams and nine sugars. Calorie count: about 960.

A Gretter at Tim Hortons is a coffee with nine creams and nine sugars. Calorie count: about 960.

PHOTO FINISH

In 2017, a Toronto man named Noah Maloney really wanted actor Jason Segel (*The Muppets, How I Met Your Mother*) to eat a picture of him. (Why? Why not.) In an effort to force Segel's hand, Maloney started eating a photo of Segel every single day. We know this because he made a YouTube video each time he ate the picture, which he'd sometimes just chew up and eat, blend into a shake, or eat with a pickle. On one occasion, he dunked the photo in a glass of beer and then drank the beer. The photo formed into a dense, wet ball that became lodged in Maloney's throat. "It was stuck and there was 15 seconds where I came to terms with the fact that that was how I would go. Jason Segel would have killed me," he told reporters. But then he removed it...and ate it anyway. Maloney's experiment lasted three months, and ended after he consumed his 100th photo of Jason Segel...who never did eat a picture of Maloney.

* * *

POTATOES IN THE NEWS

In 2018, Jason Stiber of Connecticut got a ticket for distracted driving. He insisted that he wasn't on the phone—he was eating a McDonald's hash brown...but neither the cop nor the judge believed him, and he was fined $300. Stiber hired a high-priced lawyer, who showed up to the trial armed with phone logs and a hash brown wrapper that he illustrated *could* look like a phone screen. The judge ruled in Stiber's favor—not because she believed his story, but because the officer couldn't prove otherwise—and dismissed the ticket. Legal fee: more than $1,000. "It was probably the most expensive hash brown in history," said the lawyer, "but it was worth it."

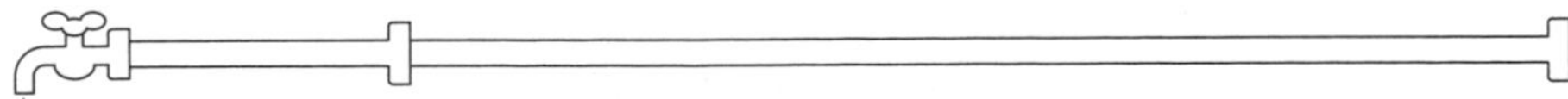

HOW THEY MAKE HOT DOGS

The phrase "how the sausage is made" is usually used to refer to something done behind the scenes that you probably don't want to see because it makes the end product less appealing. Really? We like knowing how the sausage—or in this case, the hot dogs—are made.

1. The meat used in hot dogs—beef, pork, or chicken—is a combination of meatpacking and processing leftovers. After steaks, pork chops, and other popular cuts of meat are carved out, what's left is then ground up into pea-sized chunks resembling hamburger. Which parts of the animal do the leftovers come from? The UN Food and Agriculture Organization defines these meat sources as "lower-grade muscle trimmings, fatty tissues, head meat, animal feet, animal skin, blood, liver, and other edible slaughter byproducts," or just "trimmings" for short. In the United States, hot dogs that contain such cuts list "byproducts" on the label if organ meats are involved, and "variety meats" if raw, straight-off-the-bone muscle is used.

2. "Mechanically separated meat" is the euphemistic term for meat derived by pressing pork or chicken bones at high pressure through a sieve to get every last morsel of flesh. That's added to the trimmings.

3. Under FDA guidelines, up to 3.5 percent of a hot dog can consist of "non-meat binders and extenders." That's a fancy term for "fillers"—usually dry milk powder and a mix of starches like flour, oatmeal, and bread crumbs. (Another 2 percent of the total weight can be made from soy protein). This is all added to the ground meat mixture.

4. Also added: sodium phosphate, a type of salt that provides salty flavor and also keeps the meat-and-filler mixture from drying out.

5. Spices are mixed in to flavor the meat, including onion powder, garlic powder, and mustard powder, along with preservatives to prevent bacteria from growing, and a small amount of corn syrup to provide a hint of sweetness and to improve the gummy mouthfeel of the meat and spices.

6. After the meat and other ingredients are mixed together in a giant vat, water is sprayed into the mix. Then it's all blended.

7. Then *more* water is slowly added to make the mixture as juicy as can be. (Per FDA requirements, a hot dog cannot be more than 10 percent water.) It's all stirred up and blended once more until it's a slurry—a thick, smooth puree of meat that's almost entirely devoid of air.

8. Cellulose tubing rolls are placed into a stuffing machine. The meat slurry is then shot at high pressure and speed into those tubes, and the machine twists the ends closed.

9. Long chains of the casing-encased hot dogs are left to hang on racks and are then sent to an oven to cook, at which time liquid smoke is introduced to add flavor.

10. The hot dogs are drenched in cold salt water to chill them before packaging.

11. The casings are then steamed off and peeled away.

12. The finished hot dogs are packaged, boxed, and sent off to stores (where they're sold in packs of ten next to hot dog buns that are sold in packs of eight).

* * *

SURVIVAL STORY

During a January 2019 snowstorm, Christopher Larue was driving his Ford pickup truck (he was towing a tractor on a trailer) over "Dead Man's Corner," a steep, windy pass on Highway 12 in Washington's Cascade Mountains. All of a sudden there was an oncoming car in Larue's lane, so he swerved into a snowbank and broke through the guardrail...and went over a cliff. The truck and trailer fell at least 200 feet before hitting the side of the cliff and cartwheeling the rest of the way down. When Larue, 42, came to in the smashed truck, he was about 700 feet below the road. Amazingly, he only had some bruises and a split lip. "That truck saved my life," he later said. Wearing only "cowboy boots, pants, and a Carhartt jacket," Larue started hiking down to the valley. That night, the temperature plummeted to below zero. (He should have stayed with his truck.) At around 3:00 a.m., a transportation worker saw the hole in the snowbank and called the police. Hours later, a trooper named Sgt. Brian Mulvaney rappelled all the way down to the wrecked truck and followed the footprints into the canyon until he caught up to Larue, who was huddling beneath a cedar tree. They hiked three more miles until finally reaching a road the next day. At last report, the trailer and tractor were never found, and the other driver was never identified.

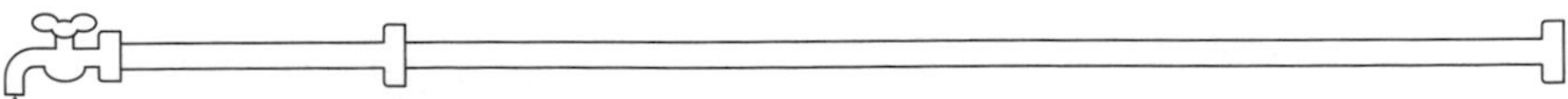

POT SHOTS

It stands to reason that when a country like the United States has more guns (393 million) than people (327 million), gun-related mishaps are going to happen, and some of them are going to happen in the bathroom.

GUN OWNER: Aldo Mercedes Tobal, 36, a convicted drug smuggler living on the island of St. Thomas, U.S. Virgin Islands

POT SHOT: One evening in January 2018, Tobal was partying at Mi Bloque VI, a disco on St. Thomas, with a handgun tucked into the waistband of his pants. At some point he took a bathroom break, which necessitated removing the gun from his pants. When he finished his business and tried to put the handgun back, it discharged, narrowly missing him but striking another patron in the foot.

AFTERMATH: Tobal was charged with third-degree assault. At last report he was out on $25,000 bail, awaiting trial. Because possessing the handgun violated the terms of his parole, he also faced the possibility of returning to prison to serve the last two years of his 10-year sentence for smuggling 185 pounds of cocaine into Puerto Rico in 2004.

GUN OWNER: Sean Simpson, 43, a high school science teacher and survivor of the mass shooting at Marjory Stoneman Douglas High School in Parkland, Florida, in February 2018

POT SHOT: After a 19-year-old former student murdered 14 students and three staff members in the school shooting, Simpson, who holds a concealed weapons permit, was one of only a few members of the faculty who publicly voiced support for arming teachers as an additional line of defense. But two months later, in April 2018, he became an argument *against* his own cause when he visited the Deerfield Beach Pier and left his Glock 9mm handgun in a restroom stall after using the bathroom.

Simpson realized his mistake within five minutes and returned to the restroom to retrieve the handgun. But before he could get there, an intoxicated homeless man named Joseph Spataro, 69, found the gun and fired it "to find out if it was loaded," according to the police report. No one was injured; the bullet lodged in a concrete wall of the restroom and Simpson wrestled the gun away from Spataro before he could cause any more harm.

AFTERMATH: Spataro was charged with trespassing and with firing a weapon while intoxicated. He served nine days in jail and was fined $371. Sean Simpson was charged with failing to safely store a firearm, a second-degree misdemeanor,

James Bond actor Roger Moore had hoplophobia—a fear of guns.

and released on $250 bail. The charges were later dropped when he completed a misdemeanor diversion program that required him to take a concealed weapons training course. School authorities are not expected to take any action against him; he still teaches science at Stoneman Douglas High School.

GUN OWNER: Thomas Frankenberry, a former New York City Police Department officer living in Florida

POT SHOT: In October 2016, Frankenberry was using the restroom in a Chick-fil-A restaurant in Surfside, South Carolina. As he stood up and was exiting the restroom stall, the SIG Sauer P320 handgun he was carrying as a (legal) concealed weapon in the waistband of his pants suddenly discharged, firing a 9mm bullet that entered his right hip and passed through his upper thigh before lodging in his kneecap.

AFTERMATH: Frankenberry claims the gun discharged without him touching the trigger or any other part of the gun, and in 2019 he sued the gunmaker for $10 million. He claims the gun is defective and the company's advertising about the gun's safety features is misleading...and he may have a point: Back when the San Francisco Police Department issued the SIG Sauer P320 as its primary weapon, it recorded 29 cases of accidental discharges between 2005 and 2011, an average of one incident every 2½ months. (As of 2019, the bullet is still lodged in Frankenberry's kneecap.)

GUN OWNER: Chief Deanna Cantrell of the San Luis Obispo Police Department in California

POT (NOT): In July 2019, Chief Cantrell went to grab a bite at the nearby El Pollo Loco restaurant on her lunch break. While she was there, she went to use the restroom. She says she removed her Glock 42, still in its holster, and set it down next to her. But when she exited the restroom, she forgot to take her gun with her. It took her more than 20 minutes before she realized she'd left her gun in the restroom, and by the time she went back to get it, it was gone. Later that afternoon she publicly admitted the goof and apologized for her "irresponsible and careless" actions. "I talk about transparency and therefore want to be as transparent as possible," she said. "I inadvertently left my firearm in a public restroom and it has not been recovered."

But when she exited the restroom, she forgot to take her gun with her.

Surveillance video recorded by the restaurant's security cameras identified a likely suspect, a man who was the next person to use the restroom after Cantrell.

The images were released to the public that afternoon and aired on local TV news. Two days later, the man in the video, 30-year-old Skeeter Carlos Mangan, turned himself in to police and surrendered the weapon.

AFTERMATH: Chief Cantrell forfeited $1,600 in salary and had to undergo firearm safety training. She was also required to have a "personal discussion" with police department staff about "lessons learned" from the incident, but she got to keep her job. Mangan could have been charged with misdemeanor theft or possession of stolen property for taking the handgun, but the district attorney declined to press charges, saying that doing so would not have been "in the interest of justice."

GUN OWNER: Mark J. Bird, 69, a professor emeritus at the College of Southern Nevada in Las Vegas

POT SHOT: Professor Bird's incident was no accident. In August 2018, he locked himself in an empty campus restroom, taped a $100 bill to the mirror along with a note that read "for the janitor," and then pulled out a .22-caliber Cobra Derringer and shot himself in the left forearm. Why'd he do it? According to the police report, "Bird stated that...the main reason why he shot himself was due to the fact that he is upset with the way President Trump was running our country...[and] to promote better gun control...He believed that by shooting himself he was able to effectively deliver the message he intended to deliver." (No word on whether the janitor got to keep the $100 bill.)

AFTERMATH: Bird was jailed on $50,000 bail. He faced felony charges of firing a handgun in a prohibited building, carrying a weapon without a permit, and one gross misdemeanor count of possessing a dangerous weapon on public property. But after agreeing to a plea deal, he was sentenced to probation. He was a professor *emeritus* at the time of the shooting, which means that he was semi-retired and not teaching courses. Given what happened, it's difficult to imagine he'll ever be allowed to teach at the College of Southern Nevada again.

* * *

3 FAMOUS REFUGEES

1. Actress Mila Kunis, whose Jewish family left Soviet Ukraine to escape religious persecution
2. Singer Freddie Mercury, whose family fled the 1964 Zanzibar Revolution
3. Secretary of State Madeleine Albright, whose family left Czechoslovakia in 1939 to escape the Nazis. In 1997, she became the highest-ranking woman in U.S. government history.

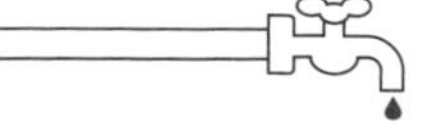

Eew! In 2020, Washington state legalized "human composting" as a form of burial.

FIGHT OR FLIGHT? TRY FIGHT *IN* FLIGHT

Air travel (at least in coach class) has become so cramped and unpleasant that inevitably—and understandably—scuffles may break out from time to time. But in the cockpit?

GOBSMACKED

In January 2018, a Jet Airways flight en route from London to Mumbai was left without anyone in the cockpit to fly the plane—twice—after the pilot and copilot (not named in news reports) got into an argument that turned physical. When the copilot, a male, slapped the female captain, she left the cockpit in tears and refused to return, despite the copilot's repeated requests over the intercom that she do so. Finally, the copilot "abandoned the controls to retrieve the captain, leaving the cockpit empty," *Forbes* magazine reported. When the captain left the cockpit a second time a few minutes later, the copilot again followed, trying to coax her back. This time, the flight attendants—along with several passengers, who had become aware of the quarreling—expressed panicked concern for everyone's safety...and the pilots returned to the cockpit for the duration of the flight. Jet Airways later fired both the captain and the copilot, and India's Directorate General of Civil Aviation was considering stripping the copilot's aviation license permanently, because he was the one who left the cockpit with no one at the controls, behavior the Directorate said was "unheard of and calls for extreme action."

FOOD FIGHT

In July 2018, the captain and copilot of an Iraqi Airways flight from Mashhad, Iran, to Baghdad, Iraq, got into an in-flight brawl so violent that it damaged the cockpit and had to be broken up by security guards. According to the copilot, who was not named in news reports, the fight began when the captain "forbade an air hostess from bringing me a meal tray, under the pretext that I hadn't asked him for authorization," he explained in a letter to airline management. After the captain received his own meal, he "hit and insulted the (copilot), prompting the arrival of a security agent." The fight was broken up, only to resume once the plane landed in Baghdad. "The pilot again hit and insulted me. I had to defend myself," the copilot wrote. Afterward, the Iraqi Ministry of Transportation suspended both pilots. In a statement, it said the pilots "will have no chance of escaping harsh penalties, and will face the worst and most severe punishments, the least of which is denial of flight for life."

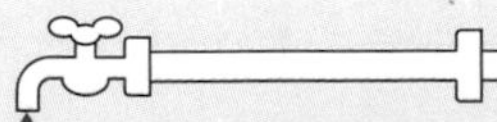

MORE HUMAN SCIENCE

If these recent studies are any indication, the future of humanity is going to get even weirder.

AS THE WORM TURNS: In a paper published in the July 2019 edition of the scientific journal *Cell Reports*, an international team of scientists reported that they had succeeded in extending the life of the C. *elegans* roundworm fivefold. Why does it matter? C. *elegans*, it turns out, is ideal for studies on human aging. The millimeter-long worm has many genes similar to human genes. And because it lives for only a few weeks, researchers can observe the effects of different genetic and environmental factors over its life span, and apply the findings to humans. Companies are already testing drugs that alter a cellular pathway in humans to potentially make them live longer, healthier lives. For this study, scientists genetically altered two of the worm's pathways. While they expected to increase the worm's life span by about 130 percent, they were shocked when it jumped 500 percent. C. *elegans* lived the human equivalent of 500 years. Calling the discovery "really wild," lead author Jarod Rollins noted, "The effect isn't one plus one equals two, it's one plus one equals five. Our findings demonstrate that nothing in nature exists in a vacuum." He said the research could one day help humans live longer, healthier lives.

THE HARD TRUTH: A small study for the Netflix documentary *The Game Changers* (2018) found that three male athletes who ate a vegan meal had stronger sexual responses than when they ate meat. We know because the subjects wore rings around their penises that tracked their erections while they slept. On the first night, they consumed a meat burrito. The second night, they ate a vegan burrito, after which their erections were 8 percent stronger and lasted three to five times longer. One possible explanation: plant-based diets, which are typically low in saturated fat and cholesterol, lead to better blood flow in the body. Better circulation is thought to improve sexual function. In contrast, excessive cholesterol levels, which can come from eating too much saturated fat in meats, has been linked to erectile dysfunction. "The harder your heart has to work to pump blood to your organs and everywhere else, the less actually makes it to the penis," explains urologist Seth Cohen. Only three men participated in the experiment, and a direct link between vegan diet and sexual performance hasn't been proven. More studies, with bigger (ahem) sample sizes will need to be conducted before urologists start telling their patients to lay off the meat and cheese.

Male athletes who ate a vegan meal had stronger sexual responses than when they ate meat.

NOTHING TO SNEEZE AT: Have you ever tried to stifle a sneeze? You might want to think twice before doing it again. In 2018, three ear, nose, and throat physicians with the University Hospitals of Leicester, United Kingdom, reported the case of a 34-year-old Englishman who'd held his nose and mouth shut to suppress a sneeze. First he heard his throat pop. Then he felt pain and had difficulty swallowing and speaking. Soon physicians discovered air bubbles leaking from his windpipe into his neck. How? A hole had ripped open in his throat, a reaction that's known as "spontaneous perforation of the pharynx." The man was hospitalized and tube-fed for a week. Afterward the ENTs warned, "Halting a sneeze via blocking nostrils and mouth is a dangerous maneuver and should be avoided." A sneeze can blast air at 100 mph, and the pressure that builds from blocking one can burst blood vessels, rupture eardrums, collapse your lungs, or even cause an aneurysm. Fortunately, the patient healed fully, but it took him two months.

WHEN FOOD IS DEADLY: Food allergies are harrowing, especially in children, who suffer them more commonly than adults do. Even food particles in the air can kick off a potentially deadly reaction in some people. The treatment, called oral immunotherapy, is no picnic either. The patient must visit an allergist regularly to ingest tiny doses of the offending food. Then the amount is gradually increased—even if it triggers a reaction. Besides causing discomfort, the therapy can take a year and requires eating the allergen every day. In 2019, though, Stanford University researchers tested an alternative treatment. They injected an antibody called *etokimab* into patients. Preliminary findings show that 73 percent of participants with a severe peanut allergy could eat the equivalent of a peanut two weeks later...without any reaction. Also, the antibody might be useful for other food allergies, which could make 32 million Americans with food allergies eat—and rest—easier.

GRAY'S ANATOMY: In a study published in the journal *Nature* in January 2020, Harvard biologist Dr. Ya-Chieh Hsu wanted to see if it was true that stress can cause hair to turn prematurely gray. She and her colleagues conducted a study that caused mice stress in three different ways: mild pain, psychological stress, and restricted movement. Just as in humans, stressors triggered the release of the neurotransmitter norepinephrine, which increases heartbeat and blood pressure. The team showed that the flood of norepinephrine damaged the mice's hair follicles. Within days, the fur lost its pigment and turned gray, then white. And the researchers found that the toll that stress takes on hair follicles is permanent. "After just a few days, all of the pigment-regenerating stem cells were lost," Hsu explained. "Once they're gone, you can't regenerate pigment." On the flip side, the study paves the way for exciting new research. "Understanding how our tissues change under stress," Hsu says, "is the first critical step towards eventual treatment that can halt or revert the detrimental impact of stress."

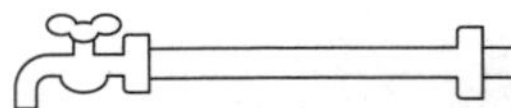

Type of fish used in McDonald's Filet-O-Fish: hoki, also known as the blue grenadier.

YOU DON'T KNOW SHIRT

Every morning you put on a shirt or a sweater, but do you ever think, "Why is this sweater called a cardigan?" or "Why does this T-shirt have a pocket?" or "Who invented the hoodie?" We do.

Blouse: *Blouse* is a term for a loose-fitting, light, buttoned shirt. It used to refer to both women's and men's shirts—and some people still use it that way—but it has come to refer only to women's shirts. The English word "blouse" was borrowed from the French *blouse,* referring to a peasant's smock, in the early 19th century.

Sweater: A knitted or crocheted overgarment, intended for cool weather. Modern sweaters originated with hand-knitted wool garments made by women for their fisherman husbands on Britain's Channel Islands in the 15th century, but they didn't become widely popular among the public until the first half of the 20th century. In the UK, Australia, and some English-speaking Commonwealth countries, sweaters are called *jumpers.* Bonus fact: the term *jersey*—now mostly used for the top of a sports team's uniform—was originally the name of a type of knitted sweater, first made on Jersey, one of the British Channel Islands.

Cardigan: A button-up sweater or, more precisely, an open-front, collarless, knitted garment, using buttons or zippers for closure. Famous cardigans: the one Fred Rogers wore every day on the PBS children's show *Mister Rogers' Neighborhood,* and the heavier, patterned one worn by Jeff Bridges's character "the Dude" in *The Big Lebowski.* (Both had zippers, not buttons. Now you know.) It was named for Major General James Brudenell, the 7th Earl of Cardigan, who supposedly wore a sleeveless version of the garment while leading the Charge of the Light Brigade during the Crimean War in 1854.

T-shirt: T-shirts first appeared in the late 19th century; crew necks were added in the 1930s. But T's were only worn under heavier garments. To be seen in public wearing a T-shirt was like being seen walking around in your underwear. That is, until 1951, when 26-year-old Hollywood heartthrob Marlon Brando sported a tight-fitting T in the film *A Streetcar Named Desire.* All of a sudden, the T-shirt epitomized cool. Later that decade, the pocket-T debuted. Why a pocket? To hold a pack of cigarettes. (Bonus fact: it's T-shirt—not t-shirt—because it's shape like a capital "T," not a lowercase "t.")

Halter Top: A sleeveless top held up by a strap that is tied around the back of the neck. (*Halter strap* is the term for the neck strap that gives this shirt its name. *Halter* comes from the German *halter,* meaning "holder," referring to the way the strap "holds" the shirt up, as in the German *büstenhalter,* for "bust holder"—the German word for "bra.")

The famous James Bond theme music was originally written for a musical called *A House for Mr. Biswas.*

Polo Shirt: Polo shirts are basically T-shirts with a collar and a three-button opening at the neckline. They originated in the late 1800s, as shirts made by British clothiers for players of the modern game of polo. (Polo originated in India.) In the 1920s, French tennis star René Lacoste got tired of wearing the stiff, long-sleeved shirts that were the norm for players, and designed his own shirt—which was pretty close to a modern polo shirt, only made out of a more breathable cotton pique knit. Lacoste's nickname: "the Crocodile." So he put a crocodile emblem on his shirt. When he retired in the early 1930s, he started a clothing line, called simply Lacoste, around that shirt—and the company and the crocodile polo shirt (or tennis shirt) are still popular today.

Sweatshirt: A long-sleeved pullover shirt, developed to wear while playing or practicing sports. It's called a sweatshirt because the body of the shirt was meant to absorb sweat. It was invented in the 1920s by American sportswear maker Russell Athletic as a less-itchy alternative to wool. The Champion sportswear company, based in Rochester, New York, made the first hooded sweatshirt. They introduced it (in pullover form) in the 1930s as warm wear for people working outdoors in upstate New York.

Tank Top: The sleeveless shirt with narrow shoulder straps and large armholes is commonly used as an undershirt but also as a shirt by itself. Why "tank top"? Because of the shirt's resemblance to the top of tank suits—one-piece bathing suits for women that were popular in the 1920s. (Swimming pools were called swimming "tanks.") Other common names for this garment include *muscle shirt* and, in British Commonwealth countries, *singlet.*

Tube Top: A sleeveless, strapless, tube-shaped women's upper garment that fits tight around the chest, employing elastic bands around both the top and bottom of the garment to keep it from falling down. The style originated as the top of two-piece swimwear in the 1940s, and evolved into the tube top shirt that became popular in the 1970s. (A *bandeau,* French for "band" or "strip," is similar to a tube top, but is usually shorter, and is commonly associated with swimwear.)

Oxford Button-Down Shirt: A men's long-sleeve, casual dress shirt with two breast pockets and "button-down" collars—meaning the collars can be buttoned to the front of the shirt—and, most important, made from Oxford cloth, a cotton fabric made in a basketweave pattern, giving the shirts their heavy feel and texture. And neither the shirt nor the fabric are from Oxford. The fabric was first designed in Scottish fabric mills in the 19th century, and named after Oxford University in England. The button-down aspect of the shirt came in the 1890s, when John E. Brooks—grandson of the founder of Brooks Brothers, an American menswear company—noticed that polo players used pins to hold their collars down so they wouldn't flap up and down while they galloped—and the rest is button-down history.

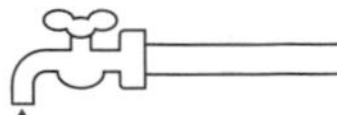

SAMMY SEYMOUR'S FIRST TRIP AWAY FROM HOME

In 1865, a five-year-old country boy made his first trip from Easton, Maryland, into Washington, D.C. It was a trip he'd never forget.

TRAVELING IN COACH

In April 1865, a Maryland farmer and estate overseer named George Seymour had to make a trip into Washington, D.C. with his employer, a Mr. Goldsboro. When Goldsboro's wife learned about the trip, she asked if she could go along, and whether she could take Seymour's five-year-old son (and her godson), Sammy, along with them. Sammy had never been to a city before, and Mrs. Goldsboro thought it would be fun and educational to show him the capital while the men conducted their business. Mr. Goldsboro agreed, and Sammy's nurse, Sarah Cook, accompanied them on the trip as well.

If you had to travel from eastern Maryland into Washington, D.C., today, most likely you'd go by car. If you didn't hit a lot of traffic, you could make the trip in less than two hours. Things were different in 1865: The party traveled in Mr. Goldsboro's horse-drawn coach and had to cross the Chesapeake Bay by steamboat instead of going over a bridge. It took them a couple of days to make the journey, and it wasn't until late afternoon on April 14 that the coach pulled up in front of what five-year-old Sammy described as "the biggest house I'd ever seen...like a thousand farmhouses all pushed together." Sammy's father explained that the giant building was their hotel.

ARMY DAYS

The big hotel wasn't the only thing that made an impression on Sammy that afternoon. As they made their way into the city, it seemed to him that everyone he saw was carrying a gun, "and every gun seemed to be pointed at me," he remembered. He was trembling when they arrived at the hotel and was so scared of getting out of the coach that he used a rip in his shirt as an excuse to stay put right where he was. As his nurse, Sarah, tried to close the rip with a safety pin, Sammy suddenly felt a sharp pain in his side. He thought one of the scary men with the guns was responsible. "I've been shot! I've been shot!" he screamed. It was just the safety pin; the nurse had accidently jabbed him while fastening it to his shirt. After the adults explained to Sammy that the men with guns were soldiers celebrating the end of the Civil War

following the surrender of General Robert E. Lee five days earlier, Sammy was finally persuaded to leave the coach and go into the hotel.

THE SURPRISE

After freshening up in their hotel rooms, the party went to dinner. Mrs. Goldsboro told Sammy that she had a surprise for him: Later that evening she was taking him and his nurse to see a play called *Our American Cousin,* and President Lincoln would be there. Sammy had never been to a play before, and didn't know what one was. "I thought a play would be a game like tag and I liked the idea," he remembered.

That night at Ford's Theatre, Mrs. Goldsboro pointed to a balcony draped in flags and said, "See those flags, Sammy? That's where President Lincoln will sit." Lincoln, his wife Mary Todd Lincoln, and their two guests did not arrive until after the play had started. As they took their seats in the presidential box, the actors onstage paused for a moment while the orchestra played "Hail to the Chief," and the full house of some 1,700 theatergoers gave Lincoln a standing ovation. Mrs. Goldsboro lifted Sammy up so that he could see Lincoln clearly: "He was a tall, stern-looking man," Seymour later recalled. "I guess I thought he looked stern because of his whiskers, because he was smiling and waving to the crowd."

THE MOMENT

As Sammy became engrossed in the comedic plot of *Our American Cousin,* he began to shed the nervousness he'd felt since arriving in the city. His newfound calm didn't last long, though, as he recounted to biographer Frances Spatz Leighton many years later:

> "All of a sudden, a shot rang out...and someone in the president's box screamed. I saw Lincoln slumped forward in his seat. People started milling around and I thought there'd been another accident when one man seemed to tumble over the balcony rail and land on the stage."

The man who tumbled out of the president's box was Lincoln's assassin, John Wilkes Booth, but Sammy didn't know that. His first instinct was to ask Mrs. Goldsboro if they could go and "help the poor man who fell down." But Booth was quickly back on his feet, and after reportedly shouting "*Sic semper tyrannis!*" ("Thus always to tyrants"), he limped across the stage and fled through a side exit into an alley where his horse was waiting. Booth rode off into the night and remained at large for 12 days, until he was discovered hiding in a barn on a farm in Virginia and was surrounded. When Booth refused to come out of the barn, it was set on fire; he was shot and killed as he tried to escape out the back door armed with a pistol and a rifle.

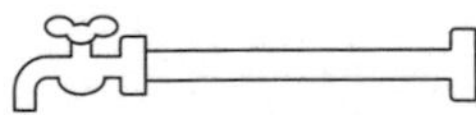

MEMORIES

Sammy Seymour was one of the youngest—if not *the* youngest—people in Ford's Theatre that fateful night. He lived into his 90s, and in his later years he was the last living eyewitness to Lincoln's killing. "I sometimes still relive the horror of Lincoln's assassination, dozing in my rocker as an old codger like me is bound to do," he told Frances Spatz Leighton in 1954.

Seymour lived to see the television age, and in February 1956, the 96-year-old was a guest on the CBS panel show *I've Got a Secret,* in which three celebrity contestants competed to be the first person to guess his secret. A video clip of his appearance on the show can be seen on YouTube.

"You witnessed something to do with Abraham Lincoln. Was this a pleasant thing?" celebrity contestant Jane Meadows asks him. "Not very pleasant, I don't think. I was scared to death over it," Seymour replies, after which Meadows correctly guesses that he witnessed Lincoln's assassination. Seymour was in poor health when he appeared on the show; he died two months later on April 12, 1956, just two days shy of the 91st anniversary of Lincoln's assassination.

IN THE KNOW

Last surviving Civil War veteran on either side of the war: Albert Henry Woolson, who became a drummer boy in the Union Army in 1864 at the age of 14. His regiment was assigned to defend Chattanooga, Tennessee, in case Confederate general John Hood tried to retake the city. He didn't, and Woolson never saw combat. He died in 1956 at the age of 106.

* * *

A CLASSIC BRAINTEASER

The old Duke's butler, Felix, has gone blind, but the Duke has kept him on out of sympathy. Though Felix can no longer see, he has become surprisingly efficient at his job. One day the Duke asks Felix to go to his sock drawer and bring him a pair of matching socks; the color doesn't matter, as long as the socks match. The Duke's sock drawer contains twenty black socks and twenty white socks. What's the smallest number of socks that Felix can bring to the Duke and be sure he has a matching pair?

ANSWER: Three. If the first sock Felix chooses is black, and the second sock he chooses is black, he has a matching pair. If the second sock he chooses is white, the third sock he chooses will be either black or white, making a matching pair.

Mangoes are so closely related to cashews that people allergic to one are often allergic to the other.

MOUTHING OFF

IN MY TIME OF DYING

What is death? We're all going to find out... but here's how some great minds have thought of it.

"THE FIRST BREATH IS THE BEGINNING OF DEATH."

—Thomas Fuller

"To the well-organized mind, death is but the next great adventure."

—J. K. Rowling

"It's inspirational to see someone who is dying smile."

—Arlen Specter

"One should die proudly when it is no longer possible to live proudly."

—Friedrich Nietzsche

"I'm not afraid of death because I don't believe in it. It's just getting out of one car, and into another."

—John Lennon

"Life should not be a journey to the grave with the intention of arriving safely in a pretty and well preserved body, but rather to skid in broadside in a cloud of smoke, thoroughly used up, totally worn out, and loudly proclaiming, 'Wow! What a ride!' "

—Hunter S. Thompson

"Death commences too early—almost before you're half-acquainted with life, you meet the other."

—Tennessee Williams

"Almost everything—all external expectations, all pride, all fear of embarrassment or failure—these things just fall away in the face of death, leaving only what is truly important."

—Steve Jobs

"No one is actually dead until the ripples they cause in the world die away."

—Terry Pratchett

"The fear of death follows from the fear of life. A man who lives fully is prepared to die at any time."

—Mark Twain

"Dying is a wild night and a new road."

—Emily Dickinson

"DEATH IS NOT THE OPPOSITE OF LIFE, BUT A PART OF IT."

—Haruki Murakami

"DEATH IS NOTHING... TO DIE, TO SLEEP, TO PASS INTO NOTHINGNESS, WHAT DOES IT MATTER? EVERYTHING IS AN ILLUSION."

—Mata Hari

"We all die. The goal isn't to live forever, the goal is to create something that will."

—Chuck Palahniuk

"They say you die twice. One time when you stop breathing and a second time, a bit later on, when somebody says your name for the last time."

—Banksy

"Of all escape mechanisms, death is the most efficient."

—H. L. Mencken

"The darkness of death is like the evening twilight; it makes all objects appear more lovely."

—Jean Paul

"THE FEAR OF DEATH IS THE MOST UNJUSTIFIED OF ALL FEARS, FOR THERE'S NO RISK OF ACCIDENT FOR SOMEONE WHO'S DEAD."

—Albert Einstein

RECORD CLUB CONFIDENTIAL

Uncle John still remembers the thrill off getting 10 free compact discs in the mail from a record club...and the pain of having to buy new albums at above retail price for a year or two afterward. Here's a look at how those clubs made their money.

THEY BANKED ON FORGETFULNESS. Clubs like Columbia House and BMG operated on a principle called "negative option billing." You signed up for a membership and they sent you monthly shipments of something–an album of the month in this case–unless you sent back a postcard telling them not to send it. Each month, millions of subscribers would forget to send in the postcard, receive the album, and then neglect to send that back, too. Then Columbia House charged them full price for the album.

YOU STILL HAD TO PAY FULL PRICE. A stipulation of membership was that subscribers had to buy a certain number of albums at full price over a certain time frame, usually two or three years. Columbia House made up for the lost income from giving away CDs by jacking up the price of these albums well above the retail price. In the mid-'90s, when a CD at a record store cost about $13, Columbia House charged as much as $18.

THE ALBUMS WERE VERY CONVINCING BOOTLEGS. The albums the clubs sold were not always the same albums sold in music stores. Instead, the clubs would rent the master tapes of popular albums and press their own copies. (They'd re-create album art and CD liner notes, too, although sometimes the booklets found in the record club versions weren't as thick or detailed.) This gambit, which was essentially legalized bootlegging, cost about half as much as it would have to buy the albums wholesale.

THEY PAID LOWER ROYALTIES. Columbia House and BMG paid music publishers only 75 percent of the standard royalty rate. When Columbia House was called out for this in the early 2000s, its lawyers argued that since publishers cashed those checks, that it was an implicit agreement to the discounted royalty rate.

THE FREE ALBUMS DIDN'T COST THEM MUCH. The famous "signing bonus" of joining a record club: up to a dozen records, tapes, or CDs that cost nothing (not counting the cost of shipping). Under some arcane laws about musician royalties, the clubs didn't have to pay royalties to performers or songwriters for music they didn't charge for. (It makes sense: If a singer gets a 5 percent royalty on an album and the album was sold for $0.00, their cut is...zero.)

DO THE MATH. A free album cost Columbia House or BMG about $1.50. A full price album cost about $3. If a subscriber claimed 10 free albums and then bought six at full club price, they paid $108. The 10 free albums cost the record club $10.50, and the full-price ones around $18, which adds up to about $79 profit for the company.

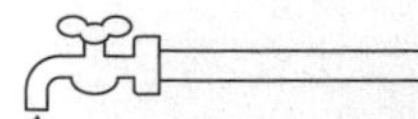

UNCLE JOHN'S STALL OF FAME

We're always amazed by the creative ways people get involved with bathrooms, toilets, toilet paper, etc. To honor them, we've created Uncle John's Stall of Fame.

HONOREE: Thitibodee Rungteerwaattananon, a Thai artist

NOTABLE ACHIEVEMENT: Promoting Thai art—and protesting the Western art world—in a way that had never been done before

TRUE STORY: In 2006, Rungteerwaattananon visited the Tate Modern gallery in London. While there, he saw many works by Western artists he'd studied in art school...but none by any Thai artists. The Tate collection seemed to ignore Thailand's contribution to the art world entirely. That got him thinking about the Western-centric nature of art institutions. "Many Thai artists would probably like to see their works exhibited alongside those of Van Gogh or Picasso," he told the *Bangkok Post.* But they weren't.

Rungteerwaattananon started a guerrilla campaign to get the work of Thai artists into the Tate: He ran ads in several publications in Thailand inviting artists to send examples of their work to him by mail in London. After he received works from more than a dozen Thai artists, he and several associates smuggled them into the Tate Modern and set them up in the mens' room, along with captions and explanatory texts, as if they were an officially sanctioned exhibit. The "Thai Message" exhibition, as he called it, made quite a statement about neglected Thai artists, but it didn't last long. The works remained up for a few days, until the museum's management realized they were there, and took them down.

Update: More than a decade later, Rungteerwaattananon is still at it. He has exhibited his Thai Message shows in museum restrooms in Jogjakarta, Indonesia; Sydney, Australia; as well as in Bangkok and other cities in Thailand. "Historically, many artworks came straight out of the bathroom. I'm bringing artworks back inside that space," he says.

HONOREES: Brian and Maria Schulz, of Ocean Township, New Jersey

NOTABLE ACHIEVEMENT: Tying the knot...right next to the pot

TRUE STORY: In January 2018, Brian and Maria were at the Monmouth County Courthouse and minutes away from being married when Brian's phone rang. It was

his mother, calling from the ladies' room, where she was having a severe asthma attack. Brian ran to be by her side. "She was not looking well. Her face was very pale, and she was profusely sweating," he told the *New York Post*.

Officer Leonard Maxfield from the Monmouth County Sheriff's Office was on hand administering oxygen to Mrs. Schulz; he advised against moving her from the restroom for the time being. But Brian and Maria had to get married *right now*. If not, they'd have to cancel their court appointment and wait another 45 days for another marriage license to be processed. "Since the Sheriff's Officers were concerned about the mom and did not want her moving from the ladies' room, Maxfield kicked his thinking into high gear—why not get married in the ladies' room?" the Sheriff's Office said in a statement posted on Facebook.

Judge Katie Gummer agreed to the change of venue and married the couple in the ladies' room.

Judge Katie Gummer agreed to the change of venue and married the couple in the ladies' room in front of Mrs. Schulz and other witnesses who crowded in. How did Brian Schulz feel about being married in a bathroom? "It really doesn't bother me at all. It's not embarrassing," he told the *Post*. "I don't think it means any less than somebody that got married in a church or on a beach or in Jamaica."

HONOREE: Zoe Morrison, 36, a British woman who writes a blog called EcoThriftyLiving.com

NOTABLE ACHIEVEMENT: Finding an Eco Thrifty alternative to toilet paper

TRUE STORY: Morrison quit her job as an internal auditor after her second child was born, but she wanted to find ways to save money to make up for the fact that she was no longer bringing home a salary, and she wanted to help the environment in the process. She bought eggs from a local farm, grew mint and chamomile to make her own herbal teas, and switched out her shampoo and conditioner for much cheaper olive oil soap. When she decided to cut back on the 300 rolls of toilet paper her family uses each year, she looked around the house for alternatives and settled on...*squirt guns*.

"We have a few of them that normally barely get used, so I fished them out of the back of a cupboard," she writes on her blog. "They don't use up much water and a small one can be carried around with you. We had them already, so I am now making better use of what we have." These and other small changes allowed Morrison to trim more than $14,000 from her family's yearly expenses, and she has posted all of her tips on her blog. "To start with, people thought a lot of what I was doing was a bit weird," she told the *Argus* newspaper in 2019, "but there's been a real tide change in the environment at the same time."

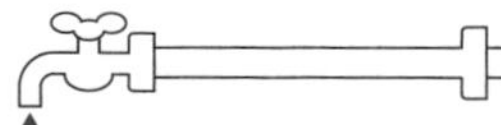

Cubicle Lubicle was lubricant sold in the '80s to speed up Rubik's Cube solving times.

WEIRD ANIMAL NEWS

This just in: Animals are weird. (So are people.)

Ant Misbehavin'

It was a clear summer day in July 2019, and no one expected rain, but that's exactly what was showing up on radar screens over the south of England. "It doesn't quite match what rainfall looks like," said BBC weatherman Simon King, who described the readings as "eerie." Then came the reports of what was causing the anomaly: black garden ants. A massive swarm of the flying insects was so thick that weather satellites had interpreted it as a rainstorm. Locals call the annual event "Flying Ant Day" (even though it lasts for a few weeks). Thanks to an extra hot and humid summer, the 2019 swarm was especially thick. What were all those ants doing? Mating. The queens release pheromones that attract the males. Once the mating frenzy is over, the males all die, and the queens go back underground to lay their eggs.

Rodent of Unusual Size

In 2019, two little girls were taking a walk in the German town of Bensheim when they came across a plump sewer rat stuck in a small opening in a manhole cover. The girls went for help, and before long a multi-agency rescue effort was underway. Meanwhile, a photo of the stuck rat—with a pathetic look on its face—was posted to the department's Facebook page and immediately went viral. All of a sudden, hundreds of well-wishers from all over the world were watching the action unfold in real time, with many offering words of support, such as, "Awwww poor thing is like 'Heeeeelp meeee. I'm stuck.' " More than half a dozen firefighters and animal control experts joined in the rescue effort, which took 25 minutes. They had to remove the steel cover and grease the rat's underside. Then, using a device called a fixation rod, they were able to pop the animal free. "The rat had quite a lot of winter fat and got stuck on its hips," said rescuer Michael Sehr. The oversized rat was then released in a nearby park, and the rescuers were lauded for their dedication to saving an animal that most people would be revolted by.

Money Hungry

In June 2018, an ATM at the State Bank of India suddenly stopped working. According to press reports, "When technicians finally opened the machine to have a look inside, they found between 1.2 and 1.3 million shredded rupees...and a dead rat." The money totaled about $18,000, and, like the rat, it was a total loss.

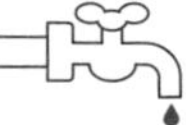

POLITICS AT THE POINT OF A GUN

Have you heard the saying "War is the continuation of politics by other means"? Here are a few examples of American politicians who weren't above using gunplay to get what they wanted.

WILLIAM W. "BILLY" COTTRELL
Mayor of Cedar Key, Florida, 1889

The tiny island town of Cedar Key, 130 miles north of Tampa on Florida's Gulf Coast, was a sleepy community when Cottrell, a Democrat, was elected mayor. It didn't stay sleepy for long, thanks to the fact that Mayor Cottrell was a mean drunk. And he was drunk most of the time. Tales of his misdeeds abound: holding some women at gunpoint while they were trying to do their shopping, forcing an African American man to beat a telegraph operator senseless, firing a shot at the lighthouse keeper while both men were dining at the same restaurant, and killing his own brother-in-law.

Cottrell got away with murder—literally—thanks to his political connections. (His father was a state senator.) And the townspeople were too frightened to fight back against someone so unpredictable and violent. That began to change in 1890, when a new customs collector named J. H. Pinkerton arrived in town. The customs collector was a federal appointee, and Cottrell, who moonlighted in the (subordinate) position of customs inspector, had hoped to be promoted to the job of customs collector himself. Instead, Pinkerton fired him. When Cottrell told him to leave town, and then ordered the town marshal to shoot him if he didn't, Pinkerton wired President Benjamin Harrison, who dispatched the gunboat *McLane* to Cedar Key to restore the federal government's authority. As soon as the ship arrived, it began firing blank rounds at the town. Cottrell fled and began making his way north, with federal marshals and crew members of the *McLane* hot on his trail. He got as far as Montgomery, Alabama, where, drunk again, he challenged the police chief to a duel. Rather than agree, the chief pulled out a shotgun and killed Cottrell with two blasts, one to the torso and one to the head, something the *New York World* hailed as "a bloody ending of a bloodthirsty monster."

CALEB POWERS
Kentucky Secretary of State, 1899

In 1899, Powers, a Republican, was elected Kentucky's secretary of state. That election went smoothly, but the election for the state's governor did not. The

Republican candidate, William S. Taylor, was declared the winner; the Democratic Party challenged the results on grounds of voter fraud, and ultimately succeeded in overturning the result of the election in favor of Taylor's Democratic opponent, William Goebel. The Republicans did not go quietly: Powers recruited a militia of as many as a thousand armed "mountain men" and had them surround the state capitol in Frankfort to keep Governor Taylor in office.

On the morning of January 30, 1900, as Goebel, accompanied by two bodyguards, tried to enter the state capitol, several shots rang out. Goebel had been struck in the chest. The shots were later determined to have been fired from a window in Powers's office in the capitol. Powers, conveniently, was in another county that day.

Goebel took the oath of office on his deathbed on January 31 and died from his wounds three days later. He remains the only U.S. state governor to be assassinated while in office. Powers, widely believed to be the mastermind of the plot to kill Goebel, was convicted of being an accessory to murder. But the court system in Kentucky proved to be just as crooked as the political system. His conviction was overturned and he was tried three more times, resulting in two convictions (both overturned) and a hung jury. He was pardoned by Republican governor Augustus Willson in 1908; by then he had spent a total of eight years in prison. He later served eight years in the U.S. House of Representatives, and for the rest of his life bragged that he had spent as much time in Congress as he had behind bars.

MIKE MARTIN
Texas House of Representatives, 1981–82

Martin, a Republican, isn't remembered so much for how he came into office (by unseating a Democrat), or what he did while he was in office (almost nothing; *Texas Monthly* magazine named him one of the "Ten Worst Legislators" of 1981), but for how he went out of office: with a BANG! On July 21, 1981, someone fired a shotgun at the 29-year-old Martin as he was exiting his car, blasting big holes in the door and striking his left elbow with buckshot. At first Martin told police he had no idea who shot him or why. Later, he claimed he'd been shot by a member of the "Guardian Angels of the Underworld," a satanic cult he was investigating. Then his cousin, Charles Goff, admitted that he was the one who'd fired the shot, and had done so at Martin's request, to generate sympathy for the politician as he prepared a long-shot bid for a seat in the Texas Senate. Goff says Martin promised him cash and a state job in exchange for pulling the trigger. When the plot was exposed, Martin fled the capital. He was later located at his mother's farmhouse, where Texas Rangers found him hiding in a stereo cabinet. Martin resigned his house seat, pled guilty to misdemeanor perjury, and paid a $2,000 fine. The *Dallas Times Herald* called Martin's shooting the most bizarre event in the 135 years of Texas statehood.

MR. TELEVISION

"Uncle Miltie" is largely forgotten today, but in the late 1940s and early 1950s, comedian Milton Berle, host of the variety show Texaco Star Theatre, *was TV's first superstar.*

BITING THE BULLET

Do you remember how much you paid for your last TV? Do you even own one anymore, or do you just watch shows on your laptop or your phone? If you do own a TV, odds are it cost you less than $1,000. Maybe even less than $200.

Now imagine paying $4,000 for a TV. And not a wide-screen, ultra-HDTV with stereo surround sound. Imagine spending that much on a tiny black-and-white set—one with a 12-inch screen and a single mono speaker. That's the kind of set that was available when people bought their very first TVs in the late 1940s and early 1950s. And the price of those black-and-white TVs—around $400—is the equivalent of $4,300 in today's dollars.

Many consumers were understandably reluctant to pay that kind of money for something they'd never owned before, something that they'd always gotten along just fine without. What finally prompted them to take the plunge? For millions of Americans, the reason they spent all that money on their first TVs was so that they could watch Milton Berle on *Texaco Star Theatre.*

DÉJÀ VIEW

If you watch late-night talk shows like *The Tonight Show* or *The Late Show with Stephen Colbert,* you're familiar with the basic format of *Texaco Star Theatre.* Berle opened the show, usually dressed as a woman, or as a Roman gladiator, or wearing some other ridiculous costume. He'd act out a short comic sketch or tell jokes for a few minutes, then introduce the variety acts that filled out the rest of the show. It was a pretty simple formula—essentially vaudeville acts presented on television—but Berle's manic, physical style of comedy, combined with his rapid-fire jokes, brilliant ad-libbing, and his willingness to do anything (and wear anything) to get a laugh, was a perfect fit for the new medium. He was electrifying, and people raced out by the millions to buy their first TVs so they wouldn't miss out on the fun.

On the day Milton Berle hosted *Texaco Star Theatre* for the first time in 1948, fewer than four million households owned televisions. By 1956, the year the show ended, more than 34 million households had TVs, and Berle is credited with creating most of the demand. *Texaco Star Theatre* was a ratings juggernaut: At the peak of its popularity in the early 1950s, as many as 97 percent of American households with a TV tuned in on Tuesday night at 8:00 p.m. to watch the show.

Telegraph inventor Samuel Morse was a talented art forger who painted himself a copy of the *Mona Lisa*.

Texaco Star Theatre is long gone; it's been off the air for more than 60 years. So is Milton Berle, who continued performing into his 90s and died in 2002 at the age of 93. But even though they're old fashioned and corny, his jokes live on, circulating around the Internet. Here are a few of our favorites.

- "My wife always starts the day with a smile and gets it over with."
- **"A friend of mine has no fear. When he got sick he told his doctor, 'I don't have any money, but I'll pay you out of the malpractice suit.'"**
- "After returning from a hunting trip, a man told his friend, 'On the last night I was surprised by a giant bear. It gestured to me that it wanted my gun.' 'Did you give it to him?' 'I did. And then he pointed it right at me.' 'What did you do then?' 'What else could I do? I married his daughter.'"
- **"Once on a hunting trip I fired twenty shots at a deer and missed every time. Finally the deer came over to me, gave me a dollar, and said, 'Here, pal, I don't want to see you go hungry.'"**
- "Some hotels have towels that are so soft and fluffy, you can hardly get your suitcase closed."
- **"Two drunks staggered into the lion's cage at the zoo. The lion roared, and one drunk said, 'I'm getting out of here!' 'Not me,' the other one said. 'I'm staying for the movie.'"**
- "A friend of mine just joined Alcoholics Anonymous. He still drinks, but under an assumed name."
- **"Have you heard the one about the woman who had water on the knee? She got rid of it by wearing pumps."**
- "A little girl was crying and yelling at her mother because she backed the car over her doll. Her mother said, 'Don't come crying to me. I told you not to leave it on the porch.'"
- **"I never go to a dentist who's had his office soundproofed."**
- "An American couple is on vacation in Germany. While they're shopping for souvenirs, the wife sneezes and the shopkeeper says, 'Gesundheit!' 'Thank God,' the husband says. 'Somebody who speaks English.'"

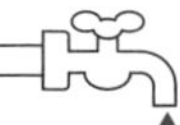

- **"A man is away on a business trip when he gets a call from the town mortician. The man's wife has died, and the mortician wants to know, 'Should I embalm, cremate, or bury her?' The man says, 'All three. Let's not take any chances.' "**
- "The other day I asked a salesman in a suit store to show me something cheap. He said, 'Look in the mirror.' "
- **"The town idiot was elected dogcatcher. He knew he was supposed to catch the dogs. But doing what?"**
- "My bookie told me the horse I bet on would win in a walk. Unfortunately, the other horses ran!"
- **"A guy I know agreed to dog-sit for a friend's very large dog. 'Just don't aggravate him,' the owner told him. 'How will I know when he's aggravated?' 'You'll know by the whoosh of air through where your crotch used to be.' "**
- "You know your kid is growing up when he stops asking you where he came from and won't tell you where he's going."
- **"I have only one concern when I go to the hospital. I want to be sure the doctors didn't go to the same school as the cooks."**
- "When I was a kid we had the laziest rooster. He never crowed. He'd wait for the rooster next door to crow, and he'd just nod."
- **"A man shows his friend a ring with a huge diamond in it and explains that it's a birthday present for his wife. 'I thought she wanted a Mercedes,' the friend says. 'I know,' the man says, 'but where can you buy a fake Mercedes?' "**
- "Always guard your rear end in the hospital. You're in enema territory!"
- **"How can you tell when an elephant is about to charge? He takes out his credit card."**
- "What do you call a cat after he's four days old? Five days old."
- **"My neighbor came home to find his wife in bed with his best friend. Upset, he said to his friend, 'Al, I have to, but you?' "**
- "My greatest fear is that I'll be in line behind Mother Teresa at the Pearly Gates, and I'll hear Saint Peter tell her, 'You didn't do enough.' "

THE MOTORCYCLE QUEEN OF MIAMI

Have you wanted to do something new or outrageous only to be told, "You can't"? It happens to everyone. But some people are driven to do it despite being told not to. That's how change happens. Bessie Stringfield was one of those people.

Bessie Stringfield was an African-American woman, born Bessie Beatrice White in February (or possibly March) 1911, or maybe 1912 (she wasn't sure), in Edenton, North Carolina.

When she was older, she told people she was born in Kingston, Jamaica, to a black Jamaican man and a white Dutch woman. That became the story most people told about her for years, and many biographies of Stringfield still say that today. (Researchers are pretty sure the former story is the true one.)

Bessie's family moved to Boston when she was young. In her teens she became obsessed with motorcycles. She got her first, a 1928 Indian Scout, when she was just 16 or so, and quickly taught herself to ride. Within a few years, she had moved on to a Harley-Davidson motorcycle, the first of 27 she would own in her lifetime.

In 1930, Bessie hit the road, setting out from Boston on her Harley. Traveling mostly on dirt roads—there were no interstate highways at the time—she eventually drove all the way across the United States, becoming the first black woman to make a solo motorcycle trip across the continent. She repeated the feat several more times over the next decade, performing motorcycle stunts in circuses for food, lodging, and whatever pay she could get along the way. Eventually, she rode motorcycles in every one of the lower 48 states.

Those rides included solo trips through the Deep South. "If you had black skin, you couldn't get a place to stay," she later said of her trips through the Jim Crow South. "I knew the Lord would take care of me and He did. If I found black folks, I'd stay with them. If not, I'd sleep at filling stations on my motorcycle."

During World War II, Bessie worked for the U.S. Army as a civilian mail courier, spending four years carrying mail in the saddlebags of her Harleys between army bases all over the United States.

Stringfield claimed to have married and divorced six times. She kept the last name of her third husband, Arthur Stringfield. (He asked her to because he thought it would make him famous.)

In the 1950s, she moved to Miami, Florida, where she founded the Iron Horse Motorcycle Club. She spent the following decades working as a maid and a nursing assistant, but continued to ride her motorcycle all over town, performing stunts at circuses and fairs, and riding in races. Over the years she became known as "the Motorcycle Queen of Miami." Bessie continued riding until her late 70s. "Years ago the doctor wanted to stop me from riding," she told a reporter. "I told him if I don't ride, I won't live long. And so I never did quit."

Bessie Stringfield died in Opa-locka, Florida, in 1993, at the age of 82 (or thereabouts).

In 2000, the American Motorcyclist Association created the Bessie Stringfield Memorial Award for outstanding achievements by female motorcyclists. In 2002, Bessie was inducted into the Motorcycle Hall of Fame.

In June 2014, a group of six female motorcyclists in Gulfport, Mississippi, made a group ride from Gulfport to Shreveport, Louisiana. The 376-mile day trip was the inaugural Bessie Stringfield All Female Ride. It has taken place every June since then, and the numbers—of miles and riders—have grown every year. The 2019 event went from Washington, D.C., to Oakland, California (roughly 2,800 miles). More than 100 female riders made the 10-day trip. (Want to be in the next one? Ladies only. Google "Bessie Stringfield All Female Ride" and find out how you can make female motorcycle history yourself.)

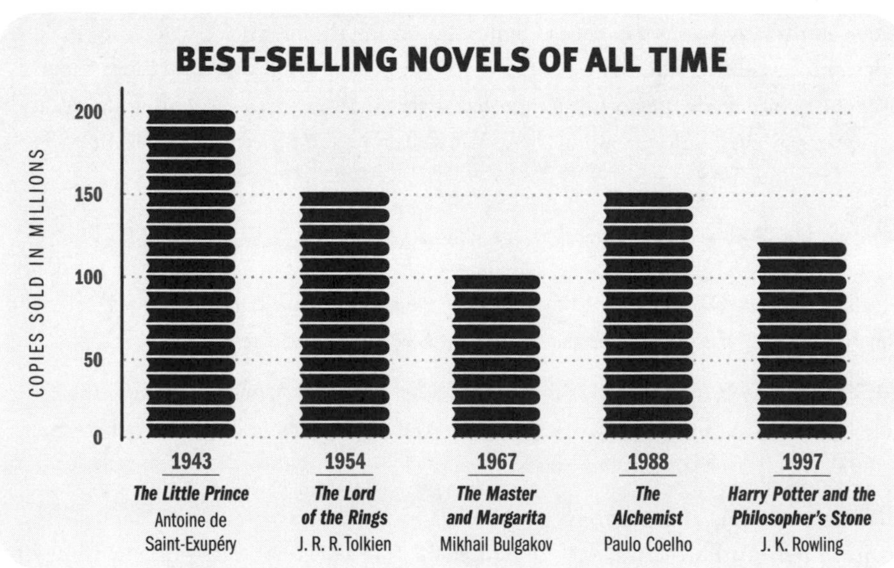

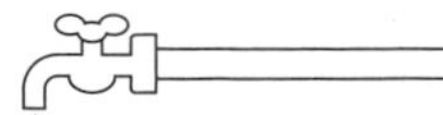

DRUNK DURING PROHIBITION

From 1920 to 1933, the 18th Amendment to the U.S. Constitution banned the "manufacture, sale, and transportation" of alcohol. But it wasn't illegal to drink booze. Here's how people got around the law during Prohibition.

Save It for a Rainy Day

Prohibition went into effect in January 1920. Any commercial beer, wine, or hard spirits people still had in their homes were perfectly legal for private consumption. Those who thought ahead—and had the means—stockpiled liquor. The late 1910s saw a boom in the construction of wine cellars, and some wealthy individuals reportedly bought out the entire stock of liquor stores that were about to go out of business.

Move to Maryland

Prohibition was a series of federal laws, but the government left much of the enforcement up to the individual states. Tracking and preventing the transport and sale of illegal alcohol was a costly, complicated endeavor, and some states just didn't have the budget to fight booze...so they didn't. Maryland was particularly lax about upholding the law, and as Prohibition dragged on into the 1920s, law enforcement in other states slowly got less and less vigilant.

Doctor's Orders

Alcohol wasn't completely banned under Prohibition—like most laws, there were some loopholes that could be exploited. The pharmaceutical industry was still in its infancy, and small doses of alcohol were used to treat an array of minor maladies, such as toothaches, colic, colds, and flus. Drug stores could sell spirits for "medicinal reasons" to anyone who produced a prescription from their doctor. There was a limit, however: You couldn't buy more than one pint of hard liquor every 10 days in this manner. (Sales of "medical" booze helped turn Walgreens into a national chain. At the beginning of Prohibition, the pharmacy chain had 20 stores. By the end of the decade, booze sales had fueled the company's growth to 500 locations.)

Let's Go to the Malt

The nation's biggest breweries faced major economic hardship with the advent of Prohibition, so they changed gears to stay afloat. Coors utilized clay deposits near its Colorado headquarters to start a ceramics division, Anheuser-Busch made ice cream and a beerlike malt beverage called Bevo, and Pabst made cheese. Many also produced a beer derivative—the manufacture and sale of which fell into a legal gray area—called malt syrup. It's concentrated beer flavoring, and when water, yeast, sugar, and time are added, fermentation happens and the whole concoction turns alcoholic.

Wine Not?

Commercial vineyards also faced economic doom under Prohibition. Taking a cue from the beer industry's malt syrup idea, many sold "wine bricks." According to federal law, grapes could be grown and sold for anything other than use in the production of alcohol. But there was a loophole: If a grape grower explicitly stated on their products' packaging (in the form of a disclaimer) that the grapes were *not* to be used to make wine, they couldn't be held legally accountable for how the consumer used it. So vineyards sold wine bricks. With names like Vine-Glo and Vino Sano, the bricks consisted of concentrated and dried grape juice. When mixed with water to become juice, and then left for a few weeks to ferment, it became wine. Amazingly, wine bricks came with instructions directing buyers exactly how to make the wine, but phrased it in a way that told the consumer what they absolutely should *not* do with the wine brick. For example, they should *not* dissolve the brick in a large container filled with a gallon of water, and they should *not* leave that concoction in a cool place for 21 days, because if they did, it would turn into—gasp!—wine.

* * *

I GOT TRADED FOR A RABBIT!

That's what happened to veteran *Monday Night Football* play-by-play man Al Michaels in 2006. ESPN had secured the rights to *MNF* from ABC; both ESPN and ABC are owned by Disney. ESPN would take over Monday nights, while NBC would take over Sunday nights, which EPSN had been doing. In the shake-up, Michaels wanted to go to NBC, but Disney CEO Bob Iger wanted something in return. NBC owns Universal Studios, which still owned the rights to Oswald the Lucky Rabbit, co-created by Walt Disney in 1927. After Disney lost the rabbit's rights to Universal, he redrew the same character as a mouse and named him Mickey. But the company that the mouse built wanted to get the rabbit back, so a deal was struck. When asked about being traded for a rabbit, Michaels responded, "It's hysterical." (Strangely, he wasn't laughing.)

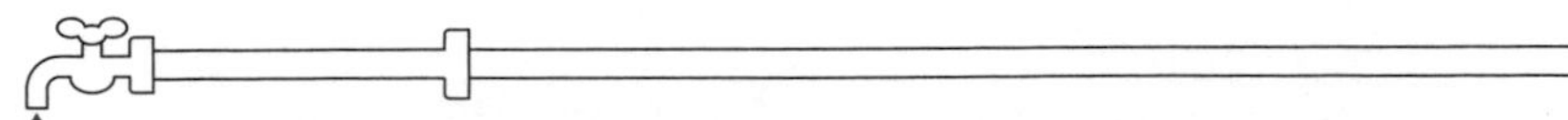

A 1967 Florida law allows Walt Disney World to build its own nuclear power plant. (So far they haven't.)

VEGAN OR NOT VEGAN?

Vegans are more hardcore than vegetarians. It's not just meat that they eschew—they won't eat anything that has milk, eggs, or any animal product in it. But today's processed foods combine so many different ingredients, it can be tricky to know what is and isn't vegan-friendly. Here are some foods that are surprisingly vegan...and some that are surprisingly not.

VEGAN

Oreos
They have a "creme" filling, not a "cream" filling. Translation: there are no dairy products in them.

Hershey's Chocolate syrup
It's not "milk chocolate" so there's no milk in there—just cocoa, sugar, and water.

Fritos
They're made from just three things: corn, corn oil, and salt.

Ritz Crackers
They get their distinctive buttery taste from various vegetable oils...not butter.

Pop Tarts
Unfrosted ones are free of animal products. (The ones *with* frosting have some milk products.)

Pillsbury refrigerated crescent rolls
The ones that come in the narrow cylinder you have to whack open? They may be butter-flavored, but they're made with soybean and palm oils.

Sour Patch Kids
Most gummy candies are made with gelatin, which is derived from the boiled hooves of cows. Sour Patch Kids (and their cousins, Swedish Fish) get their gummy texture from cornstarch, not gelatin.

Nutter Butters
The package boasts that they're made with "real peanut butter," which means that the filling is made almost entirely out of peanuts.

Spicy Sweet Chili Doritos
The only vegan Doritos flavor.

Bagels
Traditionally, this "bread" is made without milk or eggs. (Well, except egg bagels.)

Instant Pudding
Jell-O gelatin contains gelatin, of course, but Jell-O pudding doesn't. What makes it thick is not gelatin or dairy products—it's tetrasodium pyrophosphate and disodium phosphate. (Yum!)

NOT VEGAN

Worcestershire sauce
It gets its distinctive flavor, in part, from anchovies.

Anything with red food coloring
If it's labeled as cochineal, E120, or red #4, the food dye is made from crushed beetles. It's used to color a variety of candies and juices.

Altoids
They contain gelatin.

Peanuts
Mass-produced, shelled kinds are coated with gelatin to help the salt stick.

Bananas
If you were to grow them yourself in your backyard, they're vegan, but not if you buy them at a store. Commercially available bananas are commonly sprayed with *chitosan*, a chemical that kills bacteria and allows bananas to last longer in transit and on shelves. Chitosan is made from crab and shrimp shells.

Nondairy creamer
Ironically (and illogically), nondairy creamers often contain a trace amount of casein, which is a dairy product.

Beer
To keep bottled beer free of sediment, brewers may use gelatin, egg whites, casein (a dairy protein), or isinglass...which is made from fish bladders.

Canned vegetable soup
Many varieties of soup, such as Campbell's Old Fashioned Vegetable, have a base made from beef stock.

Figs
How can a fruit have animal products? Well, they do if you consider insects animals. Wasps lay eggs inside figs, but then get trapped inside the sticky, growing fruit, where they die and then decompose and are absorbed into the fig through a special enzyme. So when you eat a fig, you may also be eating the remains of a wasp.

Fortified orange juice
Cartons of juice boasting of additional vitamins usually offer an extra dose of vitamin D3. The kind used in juices is made from fish oils or lanolin, a waxy compound naturally found in the wool of sheep.

* * *

OOPS!

One morning in April 2018, commuters on busy Interstate 5 near Tacoma, Washington, were insulted by an electronic highway sign (usually reserved for traffic alerts) that read "U SUCK." The mishap was blamed on a "training error."

California's swimming pools and hot tubs use more energy in a year than the entire nation of Jamaica.

FOUND WITH A METAL DETECTOR

Most people who pursue metal detecting as a hobby find more trash than treasure, but every once in a while somebody gets really lucky.

METAL DETECTORIST: Michael DeMar, a 20-year-old scuba diver

THE FIND: DeMar was brand new to treasure hunting when he went diving with a metal detector in the ocean 30 miles west of Key West, Florida, in 2008. He was searching the sandy ocean floor in 18 feet of water when his detector started beeping. In previous dives, this always meant he'd found some metallic trash, such as a beer can, and that's what he expected to find this time as well. And after sifting through about three feet of sand he found a beverage container, all right, but not a beer can: it was a solid gold chalice, engraved with lions, castles, a family crest, and other decorations. The chalice is believed to be from the *Santa Margarita,* which sank in a storm off of the Florida Keys in 1622. Millions of dollars of treasure have been salvaged from the wreck since it was discovered in 1980, but the chalice is the most valuable item to be recovered in decades. Centuries of storm activity had moved it and other debris a considerable distance from the site of the shipwreck, which is why it remained undiscovered until DeMar came swimming by.

AFTERMATH: In 2015, the chalice sold at auction for $413,000. Because DeMar was employed by a salvage company when he made his discovery, it's not clear how much of the money, if any, went to him.

METAL DETECTORIST: Kevin Hillier, an Australian man who was living in a bus in a campground with his wife and four children in 1980

THE FIND: The Hilliers' vagabond bus trip around Australia started out as a fun travel adventure, but their situation turned desperate when Kevin injured his back and was unable to work. As he recovered from his injury, his doctor told him to take up metal detecting, saying that the exercise would strengthen his back.

Hillier was doing just that in the Kingower State Forest in southeastern Australia in September 1980 when his metal detector started chirping. He dug about a foot down into the soil and uncovered the tip of a gold nugget. "I thought, 'Hey, it looks like a

He dug about a foot down into the soil and uncovered the tip of a gold nugget. "I thought, 'Hey, it looks like a 50-ouncer,' but it just kept getting bigger."

50-ouncer,' but it just kept getting bigger," he told Australia's *Weekly Times* in 2010. After more than two hours of digging, he finally uncovered the entire thing: It was a hand-shaped nugget weighing almost 60 pounds. Forty years later, the "Hand of Faith" nugget remains the largest gold nugget ever found by a metal detector, and the largest nugget that remains intact today.

AFTERMATH: The Hilliers sold the Hand of Faith to the Golden Nugget Casino in Las Vegas for $1 million. They used the money to buy a house in Perth, a new car, a trip to Holland, and other goodies. They also staked a gold mining claim in the area where they found their nugget, then cleared the site with a bulldozer. So did they get rich twice? Nope: "We found a few 20-gram (0.7-ounce) nuggets," Hillier says, "but otherwise, not a thing."

IN THE KNOW

How do metal detectors work? They find metal objects buried in the ground using a process similar to radar. A coil at the end of the detector transmits an electromagnetic field into the ground. If this field strikes a metal object, it becomes energized and reflects back its own electromagnetic field, which is detected by a receiving coil.

METAL DETECTORIST: Terry Herbert, 54, a British man living near the village of Hammerwich, Staffordshire, England

THE FIND: In July 2009, Herbert was unemployed. So he had plenty of time to pursue his hobby of metal detecting, using a secondhand detector he bought at a "car boot sale" for about $2.50. He asked a farmer he knew, Fred Johnson, if he could search Johnson's freshly plowed field for treasure. Johnson reluctantly agreed, on condition that Herbert look for a wrench that Johnson believed he'd lost somewhere in the field.

Herbert never did find Johnson's wrench, but after walking about 80 yards into the field, he got a signal and started digging. He had to dig about 12 feet down before he found the first object: a gold pin. He kept at it, and after five days of digging he found 244 gold objects, most of them military related. He and Johnson reported the find to the government, which obtained Johnson's permission to excavate the area further. By the time the excavation was complete, more than 3,500 gold, silver, and jeweled items dating back to the sixth and seventh centuries had been recovered from the field. To date, the "Staffordshire Hoard" remains the single largest collection of Anglo-Saxon gold and silver objects ever discovered.

AFTERMATH: The find was appraised by the British government to be worth £3.285 million, or about $4.4 million. British law gives museums the right to acquire found treasure, but only if they pay the finders a cash reward equal to the appraised value of the treasure. When two museums pooled their resources to buy the Staffordshire Hoard, Herbert and Johnson each walked away with more than

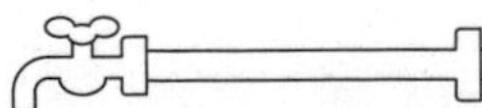

$2 million in cash. The treasure made them rich...but ruined their friendship. "I think Fred wanted all of the money and is now resentful he has had to share it. I'm not sure there is any way we can patch things up," Herbert told the *Sunday Mercury* newspaper in 2011. "Sometimes I wish we'd never found that hoard."

METAL DETECTORISTS: Reg Mead and Richard Miles, two treasure hunters who began searching for coins on the British island of Jersey in the 1980s

THE FIND: If Terry Herbert thought he had problems with Fred Johnson, they were nothing compared to the trouble that Mead and Miles had with their farmer (unnamed in news reports), who only let them search his field one day each year, right after he'd harvested his crops. But Mead and Miles were persistent: They had heard stories of ancient coins being discovered on the land, and they suspected there were more to be found. They returned one day each year for more than 30 years, never finding much of anything until 2012. That year they dug up one coin, and then another, and then another. Digging deeper, they found a mass of fused-together coins six feet long, eight inches thick, and weighing about 1,500 pounds. The coins are Celtic in origin and are believed to have been buried around 50 BC, probably to protect them from invading Romans. (It worked!) The "Grouville Hoard," as it's become known, is the largest treasure hoard ever found on Jersey, and six times larger than the next largest Celtic cache found anywhere on earth.

AFTERMATH: It took preservationists nearly three years to separate the more than 68,000 fused-together gold and silver coins. Estimated value: about $13 million—though it's not clear how much Mead, Miles, and the landowner got, or how they split the money.

METAL DETECTORIST: Gordon Graham, 41, of Edinburgh, Scotland, who went hunting for treasure on the Isle of Man in 2018

THE FIND: Graham was working his way through a field in the north of the island when the detector sounded. He started digging and soon found a gold-gilded silver ring engraved with geometric shapes. He wasn't sure how old it was, so he took some pictures and posted them online to see if anyone could tell him about the ring. "An expert identified it as a medieval iconographic ring," he told the BBC. "That was a game changer, and I informed the landowner and the Manx museum straightaway."

AFTERMATH: The ring has been dated to the 1400s and declared a treasure, which means that Graham will split a reward with the landowner for finding it. But Graham says it isn't the money that interests him: "I don't do it to find gold or get rich. I do it to find something I can show to the Manx people and have in the museum. It's a fantastic thing to find."

ACHIN' FOR BACON

Remember that fad a few years ago where bacon was in everything, and millions of people proudly declared it their favorite food? The world embraced bacon as it never had...which is precisely how the National Pork Board engineered it.

MMMM...BACON

The Internet had already been around for a few decades when its popularity exploded in the mid-2000s. That's when social media networking sites like MySpace, Facebook, and Twitter took off, and people started to share their thoughts and opinions on everything. Along with another popular form of communication, blogging, they became new ways for fads to spread.

In Internet lingo, when everybody starts talking about, joking about, and posting about one thing until everybody's sick of it, it's called a "meme," and between 2007 and 2010, that's what happened with bacon. A few people mentioned how much they loved bacon—even though bacon had been part of Western diets for centuries—and before long, every social media feed and food blog was full of people expressing their love for it. Companies took notice and fueled the craze even more, offering up a slew of bacon-flavored and bacon-oriented products: bacon cupcakes, bacon chocolate bars, bacon-infused vodka, bacon lip balm, bacon-flavored soda, bandages made to look like little strips of bacon, T-shirts with bacon-based slogans on them, fast-food items with as much bacon stuffed into them as possible, and many more.

It seemed like a joyous, organic thing, these millions of people bonding over their love of this good old-fashioned food staple. But in reality, they were unwittingly doing the bidding of the pork industry.

SIZZLING

Conventional wisdom about what foods are or are not healthy always seems to be in flux. Nowadays, scientists say that sugar is a leading cause of obesity and heart disease. But in the 1980s, nutrition experts held that eating saturated fat and cholesterol was what made people overweight and unhealthy. Thousands of "lite" or "low-fat" versions of products flooded grocery stores, catering to health-conscious consumers. People also avoided fatty foods. Butter sales suffered (replaced by cholesterol-free margarine) and so did sales of bacon, which is made from smoked and salted pork belly and is about two-thirds fat. By the end of the 1980s, bacon sales in grocery stores had dropped by 40 percent. Pork producers had to adapt. Sales of low-fat skinless chicken breasts were skyrocketing, so the National Pork Board, an Iowa-based trade association, launched a public awareness campaign to inform Americans that pork tenderloin was just as healthy as chicken. The tagline of the advertisements: "Pork: The Other White Meat."

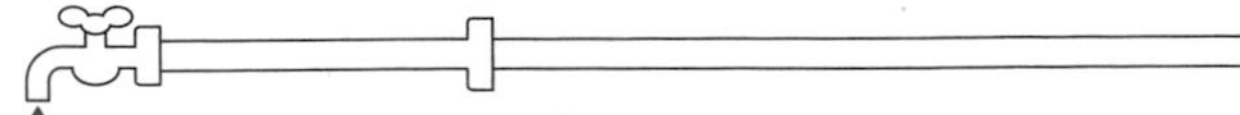

Zapoy is a Russian word that means "two or more days of continuous drunkenness."

The campaign was successful, and the sales of low-fat pork products (particularly tenderloin) supplanted the income lost by declining interest in bacon. That created another problem for pork producers: They could easily sell the lean parts of the pig wholesale at a profit, but the rest of the animal—including pork bellies—was far less desirable. Warehouses across the Midwest sat full of unwanted, unsold bellies, and the excess supply caused the price to drop to as low as 19 cents a pound, a fraction of what they cost just a few years before. The Pork Board asked for and received a government bailout—pork packagers got massive tax breaks if they exported the inexpensive pork bellies to the former Soviet Union. Producers had to keep raising pigs to meet the demand for lean pork, even breeding animals with smaller bellies and larger, meatier tenderloins. But that still meant a lot of unused pork bellies.

THINK FAST

Fast-food chains of the early 1990s also responded to the low-fat food trend, and offered "healthy" burgers. But Pork Board research showed that while consumers were avoiding bacon in grocery stores, they were much more likely to eat it while dining out, because restaurant eating is all about indulgence and treating yourself to things you wouldn't eat every day.

That's what Hardee's president Bob Autry told National Pork Board marketing director Larry Cizek during a 1991 fast-food industry convention. Cizek lamented the difficulty of pitching bacon to restaurants, because executives were convinced customers wanted healthier options. "Everyone says that you have to have the lean stuff on your menu," Autry reportedly told Cizek, "but I only sell three, four lean sandwiches a day" per location. When Cizek told Autry about the abundance of pork bellies that were readily available for pennies on the dollar, Autry proclaimed, "I'm gonna come up with a sandwich with grease dropping down their chin and we'll see what they say."

CITY BY THE BACON

One reason those extra-lean "healthy option" sandwiches were failing: they tasted terrible. After the 1993 *E. coli* outbreak at several Jack in the Box restaurants across five western states, many burger restaurants started cooking their products to extra well-done as a matter of course. While that destroys any deadly germs, it also kills flavor. But burgers made with bacon—even too-done burgers—tasted better, because the bacon added fat. It also added profits. A 20-cent slice of bacon could add 50 cents to the price of a burger—a very good deal for the restaurants.

One chain—Hardee's—was slightly ahead of the curve. In 1992, it debuted its Frisco Burger, consisting of a quarter-pound beef patty, Swiss cheese, sliced tomatoes, and four slices of bacon on sourdough bread (hence the name—San Francisco is famous for its sourdough). Autry's hunch was right—customers uttered a resounding "yes" to the sandwich that caused grease to drop down their chins. It led to a massive sales surge for

Barack Obama thinks snowmen are creepy.
"There's a whole kind of Chucky element to them," he told *People* magazine in 2016.

the fast-food chain, and the Frisco Burger became one of Hardee's top menu items.

Yet despite that success, rival fast-food chains were hesitant to embrace bacon. Burger King and Jack in the Box tentatively put bacon cheeseburgers on their menus as "limited time only" offerings. Reason: bacon is messy. Every Hardee's cooked its own bacon for the Frisco, which led to smoke-filled kitchens and clogged grease traps. While Hardee's didn't mind because sales were brisk, bacon burgers at other places didn't sell well enough to justify dealing with all the smoke and grease.

ANOTHER SLICE

But the National Pork Board wasn't going to take no for an answer—there was money to be made and a ton of pork bellies going to waste. Figuring that fast-food chains would reconsider if the bacon were easier to serve, the Pork Board paid meat companies to develop precooked bacon that could simply be reheated in a microwave. Hormel and Swift came up with microwavable bacon strips; Chicago meatpackers Wilson Foods and OSI Group (at the behest of McDonald's) created bacon discs to fit more easily on top of a hamburger.

Meanwhile, the Pork Board continued to lobby fast-food places to develop bacon-based foods, even paying the costs of recipe development. (They were responsible for a Burger King sandwich comprised of a deep-fried pork patty topped with bacon.) After attempts at menu items such as bacon balls and deep-fried bacon fell apart, the Pork Board decided to keep it simple: In the late 1990s, it focused on getting restaurants to put bacon (precooked) on a cheeseburger, which led directly to the McDonald's Bacon Double Cheeseburger and the Quarter Pounder BLT.

CAN'T...STOP...EATING

By the mid-2000s, nearly every major fast-food chain offered at least one item that featured bacon. Some examples: Burger King's Enormous Omelet Sandwich, Wendy's Baconator, Taco Bell's Bacon Club Chalupa, and Jack in the Box's Bacon Shake—a bacon-flavored milkshake. Hardee's discontinued its Frisco Burger in 2003 in favor of a line of extra-large, bacon-topped Thickburgers. Customer outcry was so intense that they brought back the Frisco in 2005.

The National Pork Board's decades-long drive to capture the hearts of Americans with bacon had worked. Pork bellies cost under 30 cents a pound in 1989. As baconmania gained speed in 2006, the price rose to $1 a pound, wholesale. By 2010, America's seemingly insatiable appetite for bacon had driven the wholesale price to $1.40 a pound and the retail price, on average, to $5.75—about double what it was a decade earlier.

But the well-engineered bacon craze isn't really a fad. Fads, by their very nature, burn brightly and then die. Bacon sales have remained hot and crispy. Bacon is now a $4 billion industry with an average annual sales growth of 10 percent.

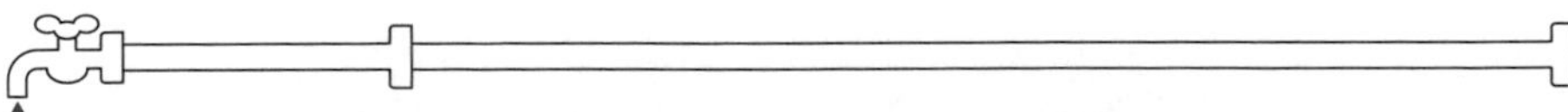

WHAT THE FAKE?

Let these weird news stories be a warning to always keep your BS detector finely tuned.

DEAD TO RIGHTS

The Ruse: In August 2012, a well-dressed 58-year-old man walked into the Wadlow Rozanek Funeral Home in Lincoln, Nebraska, and introduced himself as "Terry Kurtzhals—Funeral Director." He explained to staffer Linda Hubsch that he was there on the behalf of the family of a deceased 34-year-old woman, who wanted him to retrieve two diamond engagement rings. Suspicious, Hubsch told Kurtzhals he'd have to wait until the owner of Wadlow's arrived. Kurtzhals quickly grew impatient and demanded she hand over the rings. "He wouldn't stop badgering me," Hubsch said. "Funeral owners just don't act like that."

The Reveal: The owner called the police, and Kurtzhals was later arrested. According to reports, he *had* been a licensed mortician, but his license was revoked back in 1996 for "mishandling clients' money." It turned out that he'd been engaged to the deceased woman, and he gave her those two rings—worth about $500—prior to her death. The ruse was his plan to get them back.

Outcome: A few months later, Kurtzhals was arrested again for voting illegally in the 2012 presidential election. He'd been in prison for felony possession of burglary tools, making him ineligible to vote. The charge for impersonating a funeral director was only a misdemeanor, but voting illegally was a felony that landed Kurtzhals a 2½-year prison sentence. He was reportedly picked up by police after an acquaintance saw him wearing a sticker that said "I Voted Today!"

HARD TO SWALLOW

The Ruse: In 2018, a performance artist named Douglas Bevans was selling an "organic elixir" at a street festival in Vancouver, British Columbia. The clear juice was professionally packaged in one-liter bottles with shiny silver caps and labeled "Hot Dog Water." And there was a boiled hot dog floating in each bottle. Bevans touted it as a "gluten-free, Keto diet–compatible, post-workout source of sodium and electrolytes." Each bottle cost $37.99. (Also for sale: "Hot Dog Water Breath Freshener.")

The Reveal: Most customers believed that the Hot Dog Water was an actual product. It wasn't—Bevans called it a "social experiment," to see if people could be duped into believing a *hot dog floating in water* was a health drink...and pay nearly $40 for it.

Outcome: After selling more than 60 bottles of Hot Dog Water, Bevans offered this friendly advice: "Next time you're in the grocery aisle, and you've got some fancy-sounding, sciency-blingy product, take a moment to ask yourself, 'Is this hot dog water?' "

IN THE FLESH

The Ruse: Touted as "one of Russia's most advanced robots" by state-run TV channel Russia-24, Boris the Robot took the stage at the annual Proyektoria youth technology forum in 2018. But something about the white plastic android seemed off. For one, his robotic voice ("I know mathematics well, but I also want to learn to draw and write music") was coming from a loudspeaker, yet he wasn't speaking into a microphone like everyone else on stage. Also, Boris had blinking lights for eyes, but no visible sensors (which is how robots actually see). At one point, the host said, "Robot Boris has already learned to dance, and he's not that bad!" Yes, he was. Weirdest of all, a photograph of Boris that was posted on social media shows a flash of human neck beneath the plastic. How did that get there?

The Reveal: Shortly after footage of the clumsy robot with a human neck went viral, Russia-24 removed all mention of Boris from its YouTube channel. Then came reports that not only was Boris just a costumed actor in a robot suit, it was a slightly modified "Alyosha the Robot" costume that can be purchased online for about $3,500.

Outcome: After many international press outlets ran stories about Boris, Russia-24 issued a statement saying it was only trying to inspire the "future intellectual leaders of Russia."

FAT CHANCE

The Ruse: A young bride-to-be, identified only as "Penny," decided to fatten up her bridesmaids, who happened to be her two sisters. Describing herself as a "Jan Brady" (a middle child who is often overlooked), Penny was obsessed with what her wedding photos would look like. "My sisters are gorgeous," she later said. "I don't want to be reminded until my last day on Earth that I was the plain sister." So every morning, for the month leading up to the wedding, she made "weight-loss smoothies" for her sisters...but they weren't really diet drinks—they were loaded with weight gain protein powder. Penny added more and more of the powder the closer the big day got, until she was adding three times the recommended amount daily.

The Reveal: After the wedding, Penny shared her ruse with the lifestyle website Whimn, bragging, "My sisters had to have their dresses altered to accommodate their thickening waistlines!" She said she also talked her pale-skinned siblings into wearing "fun" neon yellow gowns that actually made them look "slightly ill."

Outcome: The sisters have since lost the weight, she said, but they still don't know what happened. "Sometimes they ask me to make those delicious smoothies I used to make, but I tell them the weight-loss shake has been discontinued. I make them toast instead." Was it worth it? "I sometimes feel a twinge of guilt that I'm standing there glowing and gorgeous in my bridal gown, and my sisters are looking washed out and chubby. But mostly I feel happy."

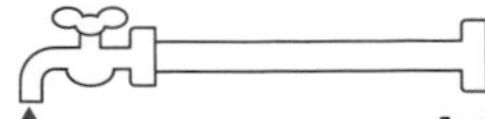

In 2019, Macaulay Culkin changed his middle name from Carson to Macaulay Culkin, making his name Macaulay Macaulay Culkin Culkin.

FABULOUS FART FACTS

It's not just a bunch of hot air–these trivia tidbits are all true.

- **The part of the fart that lends its distinctive noxious odor is hydrogen sulfide—which comprises just 1 percent of the average toot.**
- Want to know how bad your farts are? Researchers at Laurentian University in Ontario have developed a fart meter–an electronic sensor that can measure the level of hydrogen sulfide in a given area.
- **Herring communicate through a process called FRT (pronounced "fart"). It stands for "fast repetitive tick" and involves expelling bubbles out of their butts, which creates a high-pitched "pop" that only other herring can hear.**
- It's disgusting, but effective: For centuries, maggots have been used to help open wounds heal. There's scientific merit to the idea. Researchers in Singapore discovered a compound in maggot flatulence that kills aggressive bacteria.
- **Deep-sea divers can't fart. The water pressure is so intense below 33 feet that the stomach is unable to form and pass gas bubbles.**
- The Yanomami people, who reside in the rainforests of Brazil and Venezuela, greet each other by farting.
- **People are naturally more flatulent on airplanes. Reason: the reduction in air pressure in a plane causes gases to expand—including the ones in passengers' digestive systems—and then escape. Farts may increase by up to 30 percent during a flight.**
- Farts travel at a speed of about 10 feet per second, which works out to about 7 miles per hour. But individual fart molecules move a lot faster. They diffuse at a rate of about 800 feet per second, or 545 mph.
- **The average person farts 14 times a day. With a worldwide population of about 7.5 billion, that's 105 billion farts, worldwide, every day. And since a fart consists of about half a quart of gas, that works out to 55 billion gallons of human farts added to the atmosphere daily.**
- If that seems like a lot, it's nothing compared to what termites are putting out there. Eating all that wood leads to a lot of gas–scientists estimate that these tiny bugs collectively expel 77 billion gallons of farts each day.
- **About 2,000 years ago, a small religion called Manichaeism spread throughout the Middle East and Asia, which held that farts release "divine light" out of the body.**

GOING BATTY

Bats are everywhere—with 1,300 species, they make up about 25 percent of all mammal species on Earth. They commonly hang out in caves, hide out in mines, and cover their ears in belfries (a fancy name for bell tower) all over the world.

Sound Familiar?

In 2016, researchers at Tel Aviv University in Israel published the results of a study in which they analyzed 15,000 individual bat calls made by 22 captive Egyptian fruit bats and attempted to decipher what the bats were saying. They did this by recording audio and video of the bat colony for 75 days, then they isolated the 15,000 calls from the footage and analyzed them using software that divided the calls into categories. The researchers then compared the calls with the corresponding video of the bats to see if they could match the calls with the behavior being observed. The researchers were able to classify 60 percent, or about 9,000 of the calls, into four categories: 1) arguing over food; 2) arguing over who they're sleeping next to in the cluster; 3) males making unwanted sexual advances; and 4) individual bats complaining when another bat is sitting too close to them. "We have shown that a big bulk of bat vocalizations that previously were thought to all mean the same thing, something like 'get out of here!' actually contain a lot of information," the study's author, neuro-ecologist Yossi Yovel, told the *Guardian* newspaper in 2016.

Howdy, Neighbor!

Since 1980, a large and growing colony of migrating Mexican free-tailed bats have made the Ann W. Richards Congress Avenue Bridge in Austin, Texas, their springtime home. When the colonizers first took up residence in crevices beneath the bridge, some residents were unhappy. But opposition faded as awareness grew that these animals aren't pests, they're *pest control:* The colony, which has grown to an estimated 1.5 million bats, eats an estimated 20,000 pounds of insects every night. It is believed to be the largest urban bat colony in the world. Every spring, the bats migrate northward to Austin, where the females give birth to pups—one pup per mama bat. Warm air gets trapped in the crevices beneath the bridge, making them perfect nurseries for the hairless pups. When it's time to fly, free-tailed bats can zoom two miles into the atmosphere and fly at up to 60 mph as they hunt bugs. Not only have Austinites embraced their bats, they've built a bat observation center beside the bridge. Bonus: the bats make money. More than 100,000 people come to watch the bats spiral into the sky each summer evening, generating an estimated $10 million for the local economy each year.

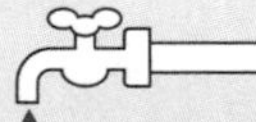

The volume at a Deep Purple concert in 1972 was so loud (117 decibels, about as loud as a thunderclap)...

Trouble in Paradise

For nine weeks every summer, the 750-acre Chautauqua Institute in southwestern New York state fills with visitors enjoying programs in the arts, religion, and education. Until recently, as twilight shimmered across Lake Chautauqua, as many as 10,000 little brown bats swirled out of chimneys and emerged from eaves, swooping down to the shore for their evening bug-feast. The lakeside community loved its bats. Not only were they entertaining, they kept the grounds virtually mosquito-free. The institute adopted the slogan "Chautauqua is Bats." Bat hats, bat T-shirts, bat tote bags, mugs, and even bat jewelry can be purchased in Chautauqua's quaint shops.

The little brown bats that once filled Chautauqua's evenings with the whisper of wings were gobbling down an estimated 500 million bugs each summer season. Not anymore: since 2006, Chautauqua has become nearly batless. The culprit: *Pseudogymnoascus destructans,* better known as "white nose syndrome."

White nose syndrome is caused by a fungus that thrives in cold, dark places like the caves and mines in which bats hibernate. As the bats sleep, the fungus grows, covering their still bodies, growing along their wings and over their muzzles. It's believed that the fungus awakens the bats from hibernation repeatedly during the cold winter months, causing them to use up their stores of fat before winter is over, starving them to death. The fungus probably came from Europe or Asia, brought by humans or by bats stowing away aboard ships. Dr. Jeremy Coleman of the U.S. Fish and Wildlife Service calls the bat die-off "the greatest disease-driven decline of wildlife populations ever documented." To date, no cure for the disease has been found.

Food for Thought

Because bats eat bugs, they're good for farmers: Bugs eaten by bats can't eat crops. It turns out farmers aren't the only ones who can benefit: so can librarians and book lovers. The Biblioteca Joanina, a library at the University of Coimbra in Portugal, has its own colony of bats that feast on insects that might otherwise destroy its priceless collection of 250,000 books dating to the 16th, 17th, and 18th centuries. During the day, the bats roost behind the magnificent rococo bookcases. When the library workers close up for the evening, they cover the bookcases and other furniture with animal skins, then turn off the lights. The bats come out and feast on insects all night; at sunrise they return to their roosts. When the librarians return in the morning, they remove the animal skins and mop up the guano that the bats have deposited on every uncovered surface, then open for the day. It may sound crazy to the uninitiated, but the system has kept the irreplaceable books safe from infestation for hundreds of years. The library at the Palace of Mafra, also in Portugal, has its own protective colony of bats. They may be the only two libraries in the world that do.

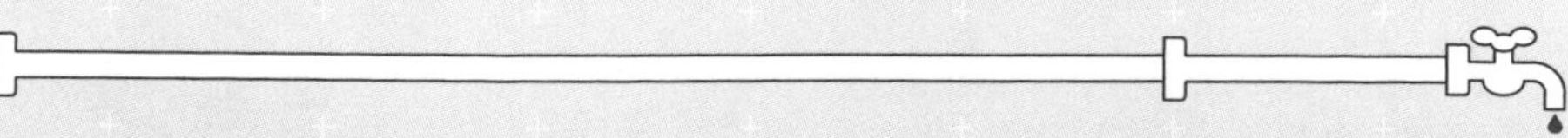

...that three people standing near the speakers passed out.

THE SUE ME, SUE YOU BLUES

Rock 'n' roll music is all about having a good time, sticking it to the establishment, and, apparently, filing lawsuits against your former friends, bandmates, and associates.

COME JAIL AWAY

BACKGROUND: After enjoying its heyday in the 1970s and early '80s, Styx broke up in 1983. Guitarist Tommy Shaw and lead singer Dennis DeYoung were at odds over the future of the band—Shaw favored the harder rock of Styx songs like "Renegade" and "Come Sail Away" while DeYoung preferred the soft rock of hits like "Babe" and "Lady." The two put their differences aside and reunited Styx in 1989, broke up again in 1995, then got back together once again in 1999 to record the album *Brave New World.* The next year, to promote the album (which wasn't selling very well), Shaw proposed a concert tour. DeYoung asked if that could be delayed because of his health issues—he claimed to have a mysterious (and not officially diagnosed) medical condition that made him extremely sensitive to light and sound, both of which are plentiful at rock concerts. Shaw declined the request, and Styx went out on tour anyway...with new lead singer Lawrence Gowan.

LAWSUIT: DeYoung sued Styx, claiming that to tour without him violated a legal agreement the band made in 1990 calling for all major band decisions to be approved by every member of the group. Charging that the tour damaged his name and reputation (and didn't give paying audiences what they really wanted—him), DeYoung sued for what would have been his share of tour proceeds.

By 2000, DeYoung's medical condition disappeared (miraculously) and he embarked on a solo tour. That's when the band he left behind countersued, because DeYoung was marketing himself as "the voice of Styx." That, the suit alleged, implied that DeYoung was still a member of Styx, which he wasn't, and that the rest of Styx approved the solo tour, which they hadn't.

VERDICT: DeYoung and Styx reached an agreement that allowed the former lead singer to bill himself as "formerly of Styx" or "performing the music of Styx" but never "the voice of Styx."

SOUNDS "CREEP"Y

BACKGROUND: In 2017, singer Lana Del Rey released her fifth album, *Lust for Life.* It ends with the dreamy ballad "Get Free," co-written by the singer. It wasn't a single, but the album was a #1 chart-topper, so even a deep album cut can garner attention, and that's what "Get Free" got from the members of Radiohead. They noticed that Del Rey's

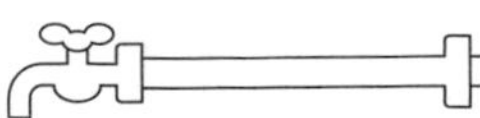

song had the exact same melody and chord progression as their 1993 hit, "Creep."

LAWSUIT: In January 2018, Del Rey revealed that Radiohead was taking legal action against her and that, on the advice of her attorneys, she'd offered Radiohead 40 percent of the "Get Free" songwriting royalties. But she claimed the band turned it down, demanding the full 100 percent.

VERDICT: After dropping the song from her set list for two months, Del Rey sang "Get Free" in concert once again in March 2018, telling the crowd, "Now that my lawsuit's over, I guess I can sing that song anytime I want, right?" The terms of a settlement—if there was one—were not disclosed, but the official songwriting credits were never updated, so it appears that either Del Rey quietly won the case, or it was withdrawn before it went in front of a judge.

That might be because Radiohead's claim on the melody and chord progression of "Creep" are shaky to begin with. After the song hit big in 1993, the band was sued by Rondor Music, publisher for the Hollies, which alleged that "Creep" lifted heavily from their 1972 hit "The Air That I Breathe." Rondor won that suit, and songwriters Albert Hammond and Mike Hazlewood were added to the credits of "Creep" and still receive royalties whenever that song is played.

CRÜE AND UNUSUAL PUNISHMENT

BACKGROUND: Have you ever heard of New York–based hard rock duo the Raskins? Probably not, and few people had when the group—fronted by identical twins Logan and Roger Raskin—won a plum spot opening for 1980s heavy-metal band Mötley Crüe on its 2014 reunion tour. How'd they get the gig? They bought their way in. The Raskins (sons of wealthy Broadway performers) paid Mötley Crüe $1 million to tour with them. It didn't gain the band much exposure, as the Raskins played to mostly half-empty rooms and arenas.

LAWSUIT: The Raskins sued Mötley Crüe and management company Artist Group International in November 2016, claiming that the band and its associates actively sabotaged them. The duo says that the reason they played to such small crowds was because Mötley Crüe's manager wouldn't open arenas in time to let fans in, that their sound mix was routinely tampered with or turned off mid-song, and they were victims of other "assorted acts of...harmful conduct," including not being given dressing rooms and not being allowed to sell Raskins merchandise after shows. But that's nothing compared to the worst indignity they faced. During a show in Darien, Connecticut, the Raskins' set was interrupted when the Crüe road crew ran onstage wearing gorilla masks and sprayed squirt guns at the duo that were reportedly filled with urine.

VERDICT: The suit was quietly settled out of court.

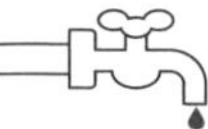

SUCH A KNIGHT

BACKGROUND: After playing in a series of Michigan-based bands that went nowhere, Mark Farner and Don Brewer formed Grand Funk Railroad in 1969. To ensure their success, they hired Terry Knight to be their manager. Knight had once been the singer in a band with Farner and Brewer called the Pack, but had switched to the business side of music. Good move. Knight helped turn Grand Funk (they later dropped the "Railroad") into one of the most popular bands on the planet. He landed them a debut gig at the massive Atlanta International Pop Festival in the summer of '69, where they were discovered by Capitol Records. Knight dictated every aspect of Grand Funk's career. He managed them, produced their albums, co-wrote their songs, designed album covers, handled all their interviews and promotions, and more. On paper, it all worked: By the end of 1971, scarcely two years after forming, Grand Funk had six gold records and had sold out Shea Stadium in 72 hours—a feat not even accomplished by the Beatles.

By early 1972, Farner and Brewer figured something was off. They were generating a lot of revenue, but were each being paid only $200 a week by Knight's company, GFR Enterprises. A look at the books revealed that the band was actually signed to Knight's firm, which is who had the deal with Capitol. Legally, Knight could do whatever he wanted with the band's money, so he assigned them 6 percent of album profits (split between the three members of the band), while he earned 16 percent, in addition to his standard manager cut of 10 percent, plus whatever he was pulling in as the CEO of GFR Enterprises. Brewer hired music industry lawyer John Eastman (who'd helped his brother-in-law, Paul McCartney, dissolve the Beatles), and together they fired Knight.

LAWSUIT: In March 1972, Knight sued Eastman, alleging illegal interference with his contractual agreements. A week later, he sued the band for breach of contract, asking for a total of $57 million in damages. (In announcing his suit to the media, Knight pointed out that the band's contract was set to expire just three months later—they could've just waited it out.) The band countersued for $8 million, alleging fraud and financial abuses. Knight then filed *more* lawsuits—more than two dozen of them—for everything from trademark infringement to incorrect royalty payments. Before a show in December 1972, Knight confronted the band, holding a court order that permitted him to seize their guitars and amps, against the money he was owed. (He let Grand Funk play the show...and *then* he took the gear.)

VERDICT: In February 1974, all of the various suits were settled. The band was allowed sole ownership of the name Grand Funk...while Knight got millions, including publishing rights to the band's songs.

Old French custom: If a man rejected a woman's marriage proposal on Leap Day, he had to buy her 12 pairs of gloves.

DEATH IN THE NEWS

Death is never funny...except when it is.

YOU CAN'T HAVE DEATH ON HALLOWEEN

In 2016, 18-year-old Cole Wohle of Francestown, New Hampshire, passed away from a heart ailment. When Halloween 2019 rolled around, his parents wanted "to honor our son's sense of humor" by decorating his gravesite in a spooky way. So Rob and Christina Wohle set up a display at the Francestown Cemetery which included a fake skeleton rising up out of the ground in front of Cole's tombstone, and wearing a cowboy hat. (Cole Wohle was a rodeo rider.) The Francestown Cemetery Commission was so appalled that they dismantled the display without telling the Wohles. The family put the skeleton back...and the commission removed it again. Then the Wohles put it back again. And the cemetery removed it for a third time. "It was just something to remember him by and to help bring a smile, because it's always tears and sadness when we come down here," Rob Wohle said. "And [Cole] would like to see a smile on our faces."

TOO MANY SPIRITS

Are cemeteries haunted? Some visitors to Kingston Cemetery in the English city of Portsmouth certainly thought so. One day in 2014, people visiting the graves of loved ones encountered a male figure throwing his arms up in the air and (according to reports) shouting "Woooooo." Police don't usually investigate ghost sightings, but they investigated this one. The "ghost" was 24-year-old Anthony Stallard. Having been out drinking with his friends, Stallard and the group played a game of soccer in the cemetery, and then Stallard got the idea to pretend to be a ghost. He pled guilty to charges of engaging in "behavior likely to cause distress" and was fined £35 ($45) along with £40 ($53) in court fees.

OUTSOURCING

Tan Youhui is a real estate developer in Guangxi, China. In 2013, a rival mogul, identified in reports only as "Wei," sued Tan. Tan's response: he hired a hit man to murder Wei. He paid contract killer Xi Guangan the equivalent of $280,000 for the job, but instead of carrying out the murder, Xi outsourced it to another hit man, Mo Tianxiang. Xi paid Mo half of what he'd been paid by Tan ($140,000)...but then Mo didn't kill the guy—instead he found a *third* hit man. Yang Kangsheng received the equivalent of $38,000, with the promise of another $71,000 when the murder was complete. Yang couldn't go through with the killing either, and, yes, he hired yet another hit man, Yang Guangsheng, to whom he gave $28,000 and a bonus of $71,000 if he actually went through with it. He didn't, of course: he outsourced it to hit man #5, Ling Xiansi, who was offered a mere $14,000 to kill Wei. Ling got nervous at the last minute and approached Wei, explained the situation, and together they staged the hit, and took fake photos that got sent through the various hit men and back to Tan, six months after he first ordered the killing. Wei then reported everything to the police. Tan Youhui received a five-year prison sentence; the other "hit men" got between two and four years.

THE LAST LAUGH

Dublin man Shay Bradley passed away in October 2019. As his coffin was lowered into the ground, and as a small band of bagpipers played traditional Irish music, the mourning friends and family heard muffled cries of "Hello? Hello? Hello? Let me out!" that sounded like they were coming from inside the coffin. And then they heard knocking. "Where the f*** am I?" Bradley shouted. "Let me out, it's f***ing dark in here!" But nobody rushed to get Bradley out of the ground. They all started laughing–they'd been pranked by the deceased...from beyond the grave. Bradley, an inveterate prankster, had been terminally ill for about a year before his death, leaving him plenty of time to stage one last bit at his own funeral. When he first fell ill and knew he wouldn't last much longer, Bradley had his daughter record him from "inside" the coffin, and asked her to make sure it got played as he was being lowered into his grave.

Family heard muffled cries of "Hello? Hello? Hello? Let me out!" coming from inside the coffin.

THAT'S LIFE

Back in 1997, Benjamin Schreiber was convicted of murder and sentenced to life in prison at the Iowa State Penitentiary. In 2015, he became severely ill, developing kidney stones that turned to a case of sepsis, which caused his heart to stop. Doctors performed emergency surgery and brought Schreiber back to life. Good news? Schreiber thought so. He filed a lawsuit asking to be released from prison. Reason: he argued that because he had technically died, his life sentence had been served in full. His court filing claims that he was sentenced to life in prison, and not "life plus one day." The Iowa Court of Appeals threw out the case, with a judge stating that since Schreiber was able to file the suit, he was still legally alive, and thus quite able to continue serving out his sentence.

* * *

"The bad news is time flies. The good news is you're the pilot." –**Michael Altshuler**

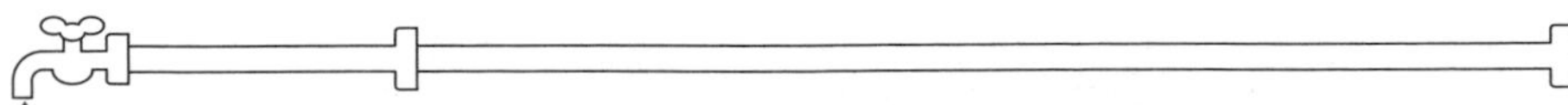

Iran allows its citizens to sell their kidneys for profit. It's the only country in the world that does.

CANON, BLIMY, AND ZEF

Every year, the Social Security Administration releases a list of the top 10 baby names for that year. What gets much less attention are the names at the bottom of the list.

MIKE DROP

Michael Shackleford was an actuary (someone who analyzes statistical information) with the Social Security Administration in the 1990s. He and his wife were expecting a baby daughter, due in August 1997, and they were trying to think of a good name for her. Michael was adamant that they pick a name that wasn't very popular. Why? Because his name was Michael, one of the most popular boys' names in the United States during the second half of the 20th century. Everywhere he went, from childhood into adulthood to the present day, there were always other Michaels around. Shackleford found that annoying.

"You'll be in waiting rooms and someone will call 'Mike' and two or three people will stand up. In the classroom, the teacher will call 'Mike' and you'll always have to say, 'which one?' And in the office, there will be other Mikes and you will always be identified as 'Mike S.' or by your last name. So it's very impersonal to have a popular name," he told NPR in 1997.

As an actuary with the Social Security Administration, he had access to an enormous database that contained the names of every American born after 1879 who'd ever applied for a Social Security card. That put him in a better position than most people to find a name for his daughter that he and his wife liked, but that wasn't too popular.

GOING PUBLIC

Shackleford wrote a quick software program that compared the frequency of "given" names (first names) for every Social Security applicant, sorted by year of birth. He ran the program...and just as he'd expected, Michael proved to be very popular. Perhaps even more popular than he realized: It was the #1 most selected boy's name every year from 1954 to 1998, except for 1960, 1961, and 1963, when David nudged it into second place. So what name did Shackleford and his wife pick for their daughter? Melanie, the 127th most popular girl's name in 1997.

In 1998, the Social Security Administration published Shackleford's research in a paper titled *Actuarial Note #139: Name Distributions in the Social Security Area, August 1997*. That, in turn, led to the creation of the administration's Popular Baby Names website, which makes headlines every year with a new list of Top 10 Most Popular Baby Names.

LOW FIVES

What interests Uncle John (perhaps because the name John is also very common) are the names that are the very *least* popular in a given year. For privacy reasons, the Social Security Administration's list of baby names stops at a minimum of five names: If four or fewer babies in the entire United States were given a particular name in a given year, that name is left off the list. But there are plenty of names that were used only five times, and those names make for some interesting reading. Here are some of our favorites:

1880

BOYS:	GIRLS:
Arvid	Ula
Spurgeon	Texas
Roswell	Pinkey
Nimrod	Omie
Harl	Dosha

1893

BOYS:	GIRLS:
Pomp	Medie
Hobert	Dagny
Ancil	Gordon
Mahlon	Thursa
Simmie	Lealer

1900

BOYS:	GIRLS:
Bubber	Algie
Doris	Zonie
Ott	Ferrol
Wert	Modie
Pet	Ota

1917

BOYS:	GIRLS:
Bunion	Etola
Idus	Albirtha
Abelardo	Opaline
Od	Snoda
Lafe	Boots

1930

BOYS:	GIRLS:
Ramona	Lanta
Ottice	Eltra
Burr	Willodeen
Parvin	Bacilia
Mervel	Ebba

1944

BOYS:	GIRLS:
Dink	Mliss
Dud	Ree
Add	Izella
Goree	Zerline
Omega	Kenny

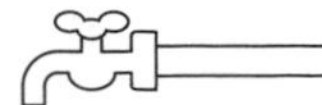

1957

BOYS:	GIRLS:
Esco	Romanita
Anothy	Oweda
Lige	Monet
Corley	Zippora
Irl	Bert

1965

BOYS:	GIRLS:
Heidi	Elfida
Atul	Cozy
Colonel	Afton
Gy	Donza
Je	Gudelia

1978

BOYS:	GIRLS:
Roozbeh	Earlean
Namath	Cayenne
Yaron	Anona
Shunta	Hye
Pleas	Erum

1986

BOYS:	GIRLS:
Travious	Ita
Zef	Canon
Ryo	Blimy
Uber	Vlora
Seville	Eiman

1992

BOYS:	GIRLS:
In	Floyd
Adedayo	Blenda
Gardy	Jazzi
Matrix	Aqua
France	Gisem

2005

BOYS:	GIRLS:
Dinero	Copper
Rocket	Liczy
Jedi	Aleidy ("A lady")
Aero	Desta
Manson	Jla

2018

BOYS:	GIRLS:
Henos	Diti
Dasiah	Icey
Jefe	Ansha
Aagam	Ecclesia
Moti	Fizza

Technically, a polygraph detects autonomic arousal (elevated pulse, blood pressure, breathing, etc.), not lies.

AMAZING LUCK

Do things happen for a reason...or simply by chance? Something to ponder as you read these true stories of amazing luck—both good and bad.

CRUSHED

It was one of those accidents that you just couldn't believe anyone could survive, much less walk away from. A rancher named Kaleb Whitby, 27, was driving his Chevy Silverado on an Oregon highway just before dawn in January 2015. The ride was cold, dark, and foggy. Whitby was listening to a book when all of a sudden the semi-truck in front of him hit a patch of black ice and started sliding out of control. Then Whitby hit the ice and started sliding. He slammed right into the back of the truck, and both vehicles slid to a stop. His airbag hadn't deployed, but the 250-pound former bodybuilder seemed okay. As he was assessing the situation, he looked back and saw two headlights coming right for him. He closed his eyes and braced for a second impact. "It was loud, and it was hard," he later told *Oregon Live.* The other vehicle was another semi truck; it crushed the Silverado, and all three vehicles slid down the highway in a twisted mess. That was the final accident of a predawn pileup that involved 20 vehicles.

Seeing Whitby's truck crushed between the two trailers, no one could believe that he was alive and responsive, but he was. One of the truckers snapped a phone pic of Whitby's face peeking out through the wreckage. It went viral. Not willing to wait for the "jaws of life," he managed to cut himself out of his seatbelt with a pocketknife. Then, with some help from the other accident victims, he shimmied out through the bottom of his mangled truck and crawled out of the tiny gap between the two trailers. Aside from a few bruises and a black eye, he was fine. A devoutly religious man, Whitby said the accident didn't change him too much. "I make sure to say thank you more often," he said.

IN THE KNOW

Experts say: If you've been involved in a pileup accident, remain in your vehicle unless you're sure it's safe to get out. Why? Odds are you won't be the last collision, so the most protection you'll have is inside your car, with your seat belt on. If you must escape to safety, move as fast as you can, but don't take your eyes off the road, not even for a second.

BEST-LAID PLANS

Proving the proverb that "Man plans and God laughs," Luke Metcalfe planned to take his girlfriend Lauren Dodds to Cuba so he could propose to her...in September 2017 as Hurricane Irma, one of the strongest storms in recorded history, was ravaging its

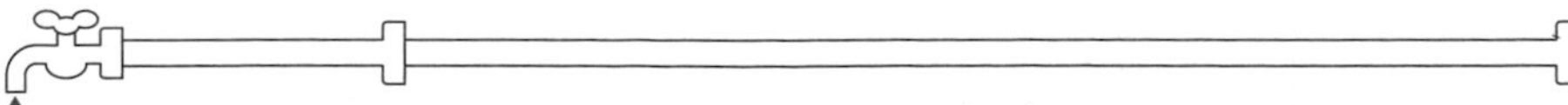

way through the Caribbean. Metcalfe's trip was canceled when the Santa Maria resort he'd booked was wiped out by the storm, so he rebooked the trip for two weeks later in the Dominican Republic...and arrived just before Hurricane Maria made landfall. On the couple's first night at the resort—before Metcalfe had a chance to propose—the hotel was evacuated, and they were taken to a shelter on the mainland to wait out the storm. "It was an absolute nightmare," Metcalfe told the *Sun*, "running around from hotel to hotel with the engagement ring stashed in my shoe." It wasn't until after they returned to the ravaged resort to salvage what was left of their vacation that he finally proposed. She said yes, so Metcalfe booked a wedding package in Cyprus with the same travel agency, Thomas Cook. But the 178-year-old company collapsed in late September—just before the October 2019 wedding...and the trip was canceled. All told, two botched proposals and one canceled wedding cost Metcalfe nearly £20,000 ($25,800). "We are absolutely devastated about our run of bad luck," he said. (The couple put off the wedding for another year. We'll let you know if their luck changed.)

TWO TACOS TO GO

- "I had the window closed because I didn't want pieces of the taco flying around," said Ryan Bishop of his near-miss in 2019. He was driving on a road in Tucson, Arizona, enjoying his taco, when the driver's-side window suddenly shattered. Thinking his car was hit by a rock, he pulled over, got out, and heard several loud pops. Bishop quickly got back in the car, drove to a safe distance, and called 911. That's when he noticed a bullet sitting on his dashboard. And he realized that if his window had been down—as it almost always was—then the bullet probably would have hit him. "I'm pretty sure that taco saved my life." (The police never did locate the shooter.)

- In March 2019, a Florida man was sitting alone in a booth in a Taco Bell when he got up to get some more hot sauce. At that very moment, another Florida man in the parking lot accidentally put his car in reverse and smashed through the restaurant wall...crushing the booth where the other man had just been sitting. No one was hurt.

UNLUCKY STRIKE

On November 30, 1954, Ann Hodges of Sylacauga, Alabama, became the only person in history known to be hit by a meteorite. She was taking a nap on her couch when a nine-pound piece of sky rock—one of several that had broken apart over the town—crashed through the ceiling. It bounced off the radio and then struck her in the thigh. Hodges was lucky that the rock didn't kill her, and also lucky that it hit her in the first place. She became an instant celebrity. But her luck ran out when she tried to sell the famous rock. (Her neighbor, who found a meteorite half that size, sold it for

thousands.) Hodges's landlady, Birdie Guy, claimed sole ownership of the meteorite. So instead of going to the bank, Hodges went to court. The case went on and on until Guy finally gave up, agreeing to sell the meteorite to Hodges for $500. By that time, the lawsuit and all the media attention had taken a toll on Hodges's mental and physical health. She and her husband divorced, and she died in a nursing home (cause: kidney failure) at the age of 52.

THE HOLE STORY

In the spring of 2019, the roads in the Omaha, Nebraska, metropolitan area were dotted with thousands of potholes, a byproduct of an unusually harsh winter. Despite road crews' overtime efforts to repair them all, it was taking a while, and commuters were growing impatient. Those were the conditions that set up this bit of amazing luck. Omaha first responders were transporting a 59-year-old patient when his heart started beating at an "abnormally high rate." Unable to get it to slow down, the paramedics had to get him to the hospital—stat! All of a sudden, the ambulance driver drove into a large pothole that road workers hadn't gotten to yet. According to news reports, "The jolt returned the patient's heart rate to normal."

HANNAH AND HER KITTY

In 2016, Spunky the kitten was adopted by 12-year-old Hannah Roundtree. They were best friends...until Hannah's family went on vacation and Spunky wandered away from their Roseburg, Oregon, home. Three years later, a stray cat living five miles away in another town was brought to a shelter in Roseburg. Staffers named him Bear and put him up for adoption. Three months passed without the cat finding a home, but then a couple dealing with a mouse infestation adopted Bear. Turns out, he wasn't much of a mouser, so the couple brought him back to the shelter. That wasn't good news for a cat that was no longer a kitten and couldn't catch mice. He was looking at a life of being a shelter cat. Then, just before Christmas, a new volunteer arrived at the shelter: 15-year-old Hannah Roundtree. On her second day, she walked to an outdoor enclosure and asked, "Is that my cat? It literally looks so much like Spunky." The markings matched up to old photos, verifying that it was indeed Spunky, and the two were reunited. It turned out that the kitten's disappearance had affected Hannah so much that, after months and months of searching for him with no results, she decided to dedicate her life to helping animals. As soon as she was old enough, she started volunteering at the shelter...where Spunky was waiting for her. "Where were you for those three years?" Hannah asked him. "We may never know."

* * *

"I'm such a bad housekeeper, people wipe their feet before they leave."

—**Joan Rivers**

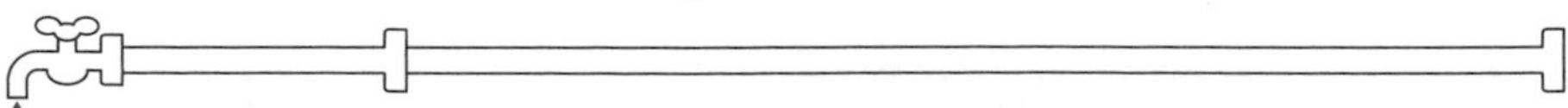

FOR CONVENIENCE' SAKE

People are always on the go these days. One result: any product that saves us time has a potential market. These popular convenience foods may seem like no-brainers, but somebody actually had to invent them.

PRESLICED APPLES

Eating more fruits and vegetables may be a good dietary choice, but for a lot of kids—and parents—it's a tough sell, unless they could be made more convenient. Take presliced apples, for example. Today they're very popular, available in grocery stores and as a fun option in kids' meals in fast-food restaurants. But the concept wouldn't be possible without food additives, because cut apples quickly turn an unappetizing brown, as anyone who has ever sliced one at home knows. Presliced fruit has only been commercially available for about 20 years, and that's thanks to USDA research chemist Attila Pavlath. In 1986, Pavlath led a team trying to figure out how to preserve freshly cut fruit. Pavlath discovered that calcium salts protect apple flesh from oxidation without affecting its color, texture, or taste. It worked even more effectively when combined with vitamin C. Apple slices sprayed with or dipped in Pavlath's concoction can go a full 21 days without discoloring. By 2013, the chemical introduced in 2000 had generated annual cut fruit sales of $475 million.

LUNCHABLES

In 1985, the Oscar Mayer company was experiencing a slump in sales of its processed and sliced lunch meats, primarily bologna. The company did some market research and discovered that the main reason for the slump was that fewer moms were packing lunches for their kids. By the mid-1980s, households with two working parents were becoming the norm, and the moms who had traditionally done the lunch packing were now sending their kids to school with lunch money because it was way easier and less time-consuming. This gave Oscar Mayer executive Bob Drane the idea of making lunch meat more viable by making it more convenient. First he came up with the concept of Oscar Mayer–branded ready-made sandwiches, but that idea was dead on arrival, because the bread would get stale or moldy too quickly. So Drane replaced the bread with crackers. Packaged to look like a TV dinner, all the new product needed was a name. After rejecting On-Trays, Crackerwiches, and Fun Mealz, Drane and his team decided on Lunchables, and introduced it (in Seattle) in 1988. It was an instant hit, selling $300 million worth to time-constrained parents who wanted to send their kids to school with a meal "made" at home. Today, the Lunchables brand offers dozens more options than just bologna, and since the product was launched, sales have exceeded $1.5 billion.

GO-GURT

While working for General Mills in the late 1980s, food scientist Stephen Kaufman was looking through a women's magazine and came across a sample packet of shampoo—a sealed package of white goo. It reminded him of yogurt, and made him wonder if that product could be made and sold in little tubes—no spoon required for kids or commuters. When he presented the idea to his colleagues at General Mills, opinions were mixed—the marketing department thought it was a great idea, but the engineering department didn't think there was any way to make cost-effective yogurt tubes that didn't tear or leak. So Kaufman rented a personal-care product pouch maker, which is normally used to make magazine samples and hotel-size soaps and shampoos. With it, he made 500 pounds of tubed yogurt, and convinced the engineers that his idea would work. General Mills finally brought the product to market in 1998 under the name Go-Gurt. Today, about 1 billion tubes of the stuff sell each year.

BAGGED SALAD

In 1989, Del Monte devised a way to sell pineapples that were bruised, misshapen, or otherwise unattractive: It skinned them, cut them into spears and chunks, and sold them in airtight bags, which they shipped from the packaging plant in Hawaii via airmail to U.S. food distributors on the mainland. In northern California, where the majority of lettuce and salad greens are raised, big produce companies were thus inspired to bag up their stock. A company called Fresh Express figured out a way to sell lettuce that was chopped into bite-size pieces—they developed a type of plastic incorporating "oxygen transfer rate" technology. Microscopic holes in the bag allowed for the free exchange of gases, which helped extend the lettuce's shelf life and prevent immediate oxidization. Another produce distributor, Transfresh, added to the salad bag technology with a process called nitrogen flushing, in which that gas is added to the bags, slowing aging. Combined, those two concepts add five days to a bag of lettuce's shelf life. It was all a very successful endeavor for produce packagers. By 2017, 4 billion pounds of head lettuce sold annually in the U.S., versus about 3.9 billion pounds of bagged, chopped lettuce.

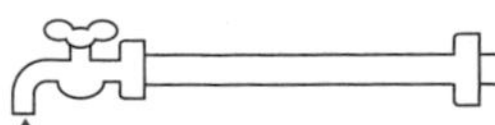

FOUNDING FATHERS: COLLEGE EDITION

You know the names—now learn about the people behind them.

EZRA CORNELL

Story: Cornell was born in 1807, in what is now the Bronx, New York. A carpenter by trade, he settled in Ithaca in central New York at the age of 21. In the 1840s, he began working as a mechanic and technician for Samuel Morse, inventor of the telegraph. He worked with Morse, and later, with Morse's partners, to expand the nation's network of telegraph lines, and in 1851, he founded the Western Union Company, which eventually made him a millionaire. In 1864, by this time a New York state senator, he began thinking of ways to use his fortune, writing, "My greatest care now is how to spend this large income to do the greatest good to those who are properly dependent on me, to the poor and to posterity." With that in mind he founded Ithaca's first public library in 1864, and the following year, with the aid of fellow state senator Andrew White, founded Cornell University, which officially opened three years later, in 1868. Cornell donated his own land (a farm) for the university, and provided a $500,000 endowment from his personal fortune. Cornell died in 1874, but his family is still connected to Cornell University. According to the school's charter, "The eldest lineal descendant of Ezra Cornell shall be a trustee for his or her life." Currently, that trustee is Ezra Cornell's great-great-great grandson, Ezra Cornell.

Notable Alumni: Bill Nye the Science Guy, writer Toni Morrison, Supreme Court Justice Ruth Bader Ginsburg, NHL Hall of Fame goalie and Canadian politician Ken Dryden, actor Christopher Reeve, and Surgeon General C. Everett Koop

WILLIAM III AND MARY II

Story: The College of William & Mary was founded in 1693, in what was then the British Colony of Virginia, and what is today the Commonwealth of Virginia, making it one of nine colonial colleges formed before the American Revolution and the second-oldest institution of higher education in the United States, after Harvard University. The college's founding was the direct result of a royal charter from William III, king of England, Scotland, and Ireland, and his wife, co-sovereign, and cousin, Queen Mary II. The charter was granted at the appeal of some of the colony's most esteemed residents, particularly James Blair, a Scottish-born clergyman and the colony's highest-ranking representative of the Anglican Church. Blair was the college's first president, a position he held until his death 54 years later. Mary died in

1694 at the age of 32; William died in 1702, aged 51. They are buried side by side in Westminster Abbey.

Notable alumni: U.S. presidents George Washington, Thomas Jefferson, former FBI director James Comey, comedians Patton Oswalt and Jon Stewart, Pittsburgh Steelers coach Mike Tomlin, and actors Scott Glenn and Glenn Close

OLIVER OTIS HOWARD

Story: The Howard Normal and Theological Institute for the Education of Teachers and Preachers opened on March 2, 1867. It began as a school for African American men who wanted to become ministers, and was named for its founder, Oliver Otis Howard, a white U.S. Army general (he lost his right arm in the Civil War) and evangelical Christian preacher. After the Civil War, Howard headed the Freedman's Bureau, a federal agency dedicated to helping freed slaves integrate into the new American society. The Freedman's Bureau was closed in 1872, its funding killed by Southern Democrats in Congress. But Howard University, as the school quickly became known, continued to grow, with a broader curriculum and an expanded student body, designed to include students of all religions and both sexes.

Notable Alumni: Nobel Prize–winning author Toni Morrison, Supreme Court Justice Thurgood Marshall, U.S. Representative Elijah Cummings, musicians Roberta Flack and Sean "Puffy" Combs, and actors Chadwick Boseman and Isaiah Washington

MATTHEW VASSAR

Story: In the 1840s, Lydia Booth, a teacher and the headmistress of a girl's school in Poughkeepsie, New York, began to pester her wealthy uncle to use his fortune to open a college for women. Her uncle was Matthew Vassar, the English-born son of a poor farming family who had received almost no formal education, but who had amassed an enormous fortune as a beer baron. He was the founder and owner of Poughkeepsie's M. Vassar & Co., one of the country's most successful breweries at the time. Booth died in 1854, but Vassar would later write that it was his schoolteacher niece who gave him the idea to use his fortune to found Vassar Female College in 1861. It was just the second degree-granting women's college in the United States. (Vassar later insisted the word "Female" be removed from the name because he thought the school might admit men someday. He was right. Vassar College became coeducational in 1969.) Vassar donated $408,000—about $10 million in today's dollars—to open the school, and also donated the land, about 200 acres, on which it would be built. The college opened its doors in 1865, and remains one of the most respected schools in the country today.

Notable Alumni: computer pioneer Grace Hopper; actors Lisa Kudrow, Anne Hathaway, and Meryl Streep; Jacqueline Kennedy Onassis; and chef Anthony Bourdain

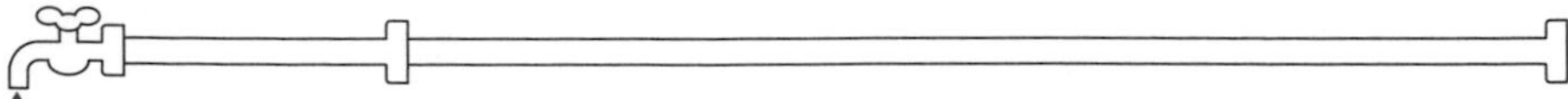

THE QUEEN BEE

If Margaret Vinci Heldt had never been born, what kind of hairstyle would Marge Simpson have today? Maybe it's better to not even think about it.

HAT TRICK

Margaret Vinci Heldt was a Chicago beauty salon owner and one of the top hairstylists in the country in the 1950s and '60s. And she was a regular contributor to *Modern Beauty Shop*, a beauty industry trade journal. Early in 1960, the editors of the journal asked her to come up with a completely new hairstyle for the new decade. "They said, 'Margaret, hairstyling has gone dead, there's nothing exciting,' " Heldt recalled in 2014. " 'We have the pageboy, the flip, the upsweep like the French twist, but nothing is happening around the top of the head.' " The journal scheduled a photo shoot with a fashion model so that it could take pictures of whatever Heldt came up with.

That night after her family went to bed, Heldt pulled out a mannequin head (with hair) and started trying out ideas. She thought of a hat she owned—a small black cap, or "fez," that had kind of a gumdrop shape to it. It was a style that First Lady Jackie Kennedy had made popular. "I really loved it," she told *Modern Beauty Shop* (renamed *Modern Salon*) in 2012. "I'd always thought, 'Someday I'm going to invent a hairstyle that's going to fit right under that little hat.' Then, I realized, that's exactly what I should do for the photo shoot!"

"I'd always thought, 'Someday I'm going to invent a hairstyle that's going to fit right under that little hat.'"

Heldt "teased" (back-combed) the hair to create a mound on the top of the mannequin's head. Then she swirled some hair around the mound to give it a cleaner look, and secured everything in place with some hairpins and lots of hairspray. When she finished, she had a short, wide cone of hair that barely fit under the hat—just the way she wanted it.

CREATING A BUZZ

A few days later, Heldt went to the photo shoot and re-created the cone of hair on the fashion model's head. As she finished up, she thought the hairstyle needed a little something extra. So she pulled a little black butterfly decoration off of the black hat and attached it to the cone of hair. She hadn't come up with a name for the hairstyle yet, and now she wouldn't need to: "The editor said, 'Margaret! That looks just like a beehive. Could we call it a beehive?' I said, 'You can call it whatever you want!' And so the beehive was born."

PICTURE PERFECT

The beehive made its public debut in the February 1960 issue of *Modern Beauty Shop*, in an article illustrated with pictures from the photo shoot. The magazine described the hairdo as having a "wrap-around crown movement, softly draped bangs, and ear-hugging side patterns." As Heldt originally conceived it, the first beehive was quite small—shaped more like a soft-serve ice-cream cone than the huge towers of hair that people would soon come to associate with the hairstyle. In fact, if you didn't know what you were looking at, you might have trouble recognizing the first beehive as a beehive.

Heldt's original design had a certain elegance all its own, and it caught on quickly. Audrey Hepburn wore one in *Breakfast at Tiffany's* (1961), and so did all three members of the Ronettes, one of the most popular girl groups of the early 1960s. Barbra Streisand wasn't far behind, and neither were singers Aretha Franklin and Dusty Springfield. And as more celebrities wore the hairstyle, their female fans clamored for the look as well. "It was an instant hit," Heldt remembered. "It made people feel taller, and more elegant, refined, and glamorous."

LOW MAINTENANCE

In an odd way, the beehive was a practical hairstyle for the way many women lived in those days: They went to the beauty parlor once a week to have their hair washed and set. Then they didn't wash their hair during the rest of the week, and when they bathed they wore shower caps.

Because a beehive piled the hair on top of the head instead of distributing it around the sides, a woman could sleep with her head on a pillow and not mess up her hairdo too much. She just wrapped a scarf around her hair before going to bed, and in the morning removed the scarf and combed the beehive a bit to work it back into shape. These women valued a hairstyle that they didn't need to redo from scratch every morning. That was how Heldt liked it: She didn't want her customers—or their husbands—touching her work any more than was necessary. "I used to tell my clients, 'I don't care what your husband does from the neck down, but I don't want them to touch you from the neck up.' "

BLASTOFF

Heldt believed that the beehive looked best when it was proportioned such that a woman's head was two-thirds "face" and one-third "hive." But as the look caught on, beehives got taller and taller. The ratio flipped to one-third "face" and two-thirds "hive," and kept right on going from there. "They just kept rolling it up and up," she complained to the *Chicago Daily Herald* in 2000.

Beehives went from being an elegant look that complemented a woman's features to one that called so much attention to itself that it was difficult to notice or appreciate the face peeking out from beneath the pile of hair. For a lot of people, that was part of the fun, but Heldt hated the big beehives; she called them "hornets' nests." (She didn't think much of beehives that were too small, either; she called

Would-be presidential assassin John Hinckley Jr. received royalties from a song that the 1982 pop group Devo based on one of his poems.

them "anthills.") Another popular name for the big beehives: "B-52s," because they reminded people of the U.S. Air Force bomber's big nose.

SPLASHDOWN

As the 1960s progressed, the beehive fad ran its course, eventually falling victim to changing fashions and changing times. As more women worked outside the home, few of them had time for 2½ hour trips to the salon. Hairstyles became simpler, more natural, and more flowing—the kinds of styles that women could do themselves at home, preferably without shellacking their hair in place with huge quantities of hairspray.

By the early 1970s, the beehive look was, in the minds of a lot of people, completely passé. It was something that hip youngsters made fun of. In Athens, Georgia, two young women named Kate Pierson and Cindy Wilson used to buy beehive wigs at thrift shops; then they and their friends would get dressed up and try to crash parties thrown by squares so that they could drink free beer. Later on, when Pierson and Wilson started a band with Wilson's brother Ricky and their friends Fred Schneider and Keith Strickland, they kept the wigs as part of their onstage look, and named their band the B-52's. In the process, of course, they helped to make the beehive hip again.

STILL BUZZING

Heldt lived long enough to watch the hairstyle she created cycle in and out of fashion more than once. "Every time [the beehive] would resurrect again," her son William told the *Chicago Tribune*, "somebody would be wearing it, and she would call me and say, 'It's starting again! They're calling me again!" Heldt kept styling hair until 1998, when she retired on her 80th birthday after 63 years on her feet. She still had the little black felt hat that started it all, and she happily brought it and the original mannequin head—still sporting a beehive—out to show to visitors or journalists whenever they came to see her. "Everybody looks good in that style," she'd tell them, "everybody." She passed away in 2016 at the age of 98. Today the black hat that inspired the beehive—and the mannequin head Heldt used to invent it—are both on display at the Chicago History Museum.

* * *

SAY THESE TONGUE TWISTERS THREE TIMES FAST!

Toy boat
Prepaid plan
She sees cheese

Cheap sheep soup
Baboon bamboo
Specific Pacific

Selfish shellfish
Sixth sick sheep
Purple paper people

MOUTHING OFF

ALWAYS &...

Comedian Amy Poehler offered this bit of advice: "Limit your 'always' and your 'nevers.'" Notice she said "limit" and not "completely eliminate." You always should never do that.

"ALWAYS DRINK UPSTREAM FROM THE HERD."

—Will Rogers

"Always remember that striving and struggling precede success, even in the dictionary."

—Sarah Ban Breathnach

"ALWAYS DESIRE TO LEARN SOMETHING USEFUL."

—Sophocles

"Always wear a smile because you never know who is watching."

—Gracie Gold

"Always let life be wild. Forever have life be interesting."

—A. D. Posey

"It is always wise to look ahead, but difficult to look further than you can see."

—Winston Churchill

"Always remember that you are absolutely unique. Just like everyone else."

—Margaret Mead

"YOU CAN ALWAYS, ALWAYS GIVE SOMETHING, EVEN IF IT IS ONLY KINDNESS!"

—Anne Frank

"Always have an attitude of gratitude."

—Sterling K. Brown

...NEVER

"Never be fearful about what you are doing when it is right."

—Rosa Parks

"Never use exclamation points in writing. It is like laughing at your own joke."

—Mark Twain

"Never get married. That's probably the best advice I could give myself."

—Britney Spears

"NEVER MISS A GOOD CHANCE TO SHUT UP."

—Will Rogers

"Never limit yourself because of others' limited imagination; never limit others because of your own limited imagination."

—Mae Jemison

"Never get into a wrestling match with a pig. You both get dirty, and the pig likes it."

—John McCain

"NEVER GIVE ADVICE UNLESS YOU HAVE WALKED THE WALK, BECAUSE ANYBODY CAN TALK THE TALK."

—Valencia Mackie

"NEVER RUIN AN APOLOGY WITH AN EXCUSE."

—Benjamin Franklin

"Never order barbecue in a place that also serves quiche."

—Lewis Grizzard

"Never bend your head. Always hold it high. Look the world straight in the eye."

—Helen Keller

THE ORIGIN OF CHEWBACCA: FINDING HIS VOICE

In the final episode of our Wookiee trilogy, we learn how Chewie learned to roar...and then what happened when that roar hit the big screen. *(Part II is on page 236.)*

THE FINAL PIECE

Sound designer Ben Burtt's challenge with finding the voice of Chewbacca: how do you invent and record a language that an intelligent animal would speak, if he could only speak in grunts, whines, and growls? Making matters worse, recalled Burtt: "Chewie didn't have articulated lips. He could basically open and close his mouth." They'd decided that the alien's entire vocal range would be made up of various earthly animal sounds that Burtt would record and then splice together. It was Lucas who suggested starting with bears, because they make their noises from the backs of their throats—just like Chewbacca. So Burtt spent a lot of time at the Happy Hollow Zoo in San Jose with a black bear named Tarik. He also recorded lions, camels, rabbits, tigers, badgers...and walruses. "One time I went to Marineland down in Long Beach to record a walrus," he said. "Its pool had been drained for cleaning—the walrus was stranded at the bottom, moaning—and that was the sound!"

Without any actual words for Chewie to speak, Burtt sorted the utterances by the emotion they conveyed—agreeable, affectionate, sad, angry, etc.—and then he "cut those together to get a sense of speech out of Chewie." After much trial and error, and many long conversations with Lucas, Burtt finally had a library of Chewbacca vocalizations they could add during postproduction. (For the record, the language Chewie speaks is called Shyriiwook.)

Lucas was so adamant that this effect and the hundreds of others had to blend together seamlessly that the movie's release date had to be pushed back six months. Fox executives were very concerned, but as it turned out, all that attention to detail was worth it. *Star Wars* broke box-office records after it opened in the summer of 1977, and it's still going strong today.

BEHIND BLUE EYES

One detail that most viewers may not have noticed: Mayhew's blue eyes—they're the only part of the actor you can see. Unlike similar monster masks, there were no

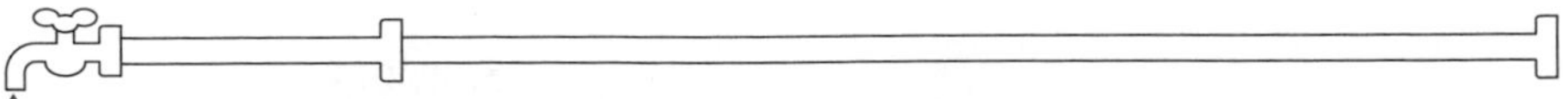

contact lenses or other effects added in postproduction, only dark makeup around each eye to hide his skin. That barely noticeable detail went a long way to showing Chewie's "humanity." And, according to Richard Newby in *The Hollywood Reporter,* it's this relatability that audiences are drawn to:

> Chewbacca, largely through the expression of Mayhew's eyes and body language, became our emotional lens. Regardless of language barriers, age or familiarity with Lucas' sci-fi saga, Chewbacca showed us what to feel across these films, with larger-than-life gestures harkening back to film's silent era, and a subtle expressiveness that gave him the same range as *Star Wars'* human characters.

PETER AND THE WOOKIEE

After the original trilogy ended with 1983's *Return of the Jedi,* Mayhew went back to England to live a quiet life—always willing to don the Chewie mask if asked. Over the next 20 years, he had a handful of acting parts outside of *Star Wars,* but very few chances to play the part he cherished most. No longer physically able to perform his duties as an orderly, he started selling furniture. A big boost came at the 1997 MTV Music Video Awards show, when Chewbacca was given a Lifetime Achievement Award. The backstory: ever since *Star Wars* came out, fans had complained that when Princess Leia (Carrie Fisher) gave a medal to each of the heroes, she left out Chewbacca. So it was fitting that Fisher was on hand to finally give the Wookiee his award. It was the first time Mayhew had put on the costume in 13 years. "I got the only standing ovation of the night," he boasted.

When the prequel trilogy was announced, Mayhew wondered if Chewbacca would be a part of it. The first two movies came and went without his character, and he knew that if he was to put the costume back on, it would have to be soon. Nearing his mid-50s, it was getting harder for Mayhew to walk, much less run. Being over seven feet tall was difficult for him as a young man, and it grew even more so as he aged. "When I go to restaurants I can never get my legs under a table," he said at the time. "I bump my head in planes. People who sit behind me in the theater hate me. But I have given up apologizing to the world."

Knowing that he could live comfortably on the fees he earned signing autographs at conventions, Mayhew decided to dedicate the rest of his life to *Star Wars,* becoming, as he called it, a "Chewbacca Ambassador." He got married and moved to Texas in 1999 and attended upward of 20 conventions per year. He truly loved meeting fans and was known to chime in on Reddit *Star Wars* discussions from time to time. In addition to founding the Peter Mayhew Foundation, "devoted to the alleviation of disease, pain, suffering and the financial toll brought on by life's traumatic events," Mayhew wrote two children's books—one about being different, and one about standing up to bullies.

RETURN OF THE WOOKIEE

In the early 2000s, George Lucas decided to bring Chewie back for the third prequel, *Revenge of the Sith.* Even though Mayhew was pushing 60, he signed on. Otherwise, Lucas might not have even included the Wookiee, saying at the time, "Peter Mayhew *is* Chewbacca. He's very unique the way he has created the character, and the way he walks, and the way he tilts his head, the way he uses his eyes. You can't put anybody else in the suit."

One problem: there was no suit to put Mayhew in; the only remaining original Chewbacca costume had been altered for another Wookiee character in 1999's *The Phantom Menace.* So they were forced to start from scratch. "Chewbacca has to look like Chewbacca," said creature designer Dave Elsey. "Nobody wants to do a character from *Star Wars* and get it wrong, especially one that's so cherished by so many people." With a pivotal scene taking place on Chewie's home world, the effects artists designed and built seven Wookiees. (Dozens more Wookiees were added using CGI.)

For the new Chewbacca, designers mostly stuck with the original 1970s techniques, but were much more concerned with Mayhew's comfort level than Stuart Freeborn had been. The updated suit came with a cooling system and remote-controlled servos to give Chewie more nuanced jaw movements. And the fur was mostly synthetic, making it lighter.

CHEWBACCA AWAKENS

Star Wars outlasted Lucas's involvement with the franchise. After Disney took over in 2012, they hired writer-director J. J. Abrams to oversee the final three films. Abrams knew right away that fans were going to want to see Han and Chewie reunite on the *Millennium Falcon,* so he called up Mayhew and said coyly, "There's a little thing I'd like you to do for me." Now close to 70, Mayhew was excited to bring Chewbacca back for *The Force Awakens,* but he told Abrams that he'd spent the previous few years in a wheelchair and had just undergone double knee replacement surgery. "I can do most things, but the only thing I can't really do is walk. But I can do the facial expressions and everything else like that for Chewie."

Abrams agreed to use Mayhew for the scenes where the Wookiee is on the *Falcon,* but they'd need someone else to handle all the action scenes. It was time to find a new Chewbacca.

PASSING THE BOWCASTER

"I was told to send in an audition tape of me doing a caveman impression," said Joonas Suotamo, a Finnish former professional basketball player who answered a worldwide casting call for an actor who topped seven feet. He didn't even know what

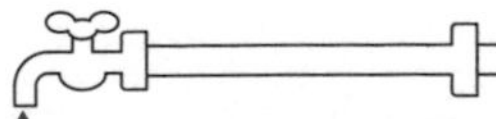

Spider-Man creator Stan Lee's first writing job: producing "advance obituaries" for celebrities who weren't dead yet for the Associated Press.

movie it was for when he auditioned, and when he found out it was for the new *Star Wars*, it wasn't until after he signed a contract that Abrams informed him he'd be taking over the role of Chewbacca.

Suotamo wasn't ideal for the part, being several inches shorter than Mayhew at 6' 11", but the Penn State Film School graduate had something Mayhew didn't have: acting experience. "I loved doing theater in high school," he said. "I just didn't believe my chances to get any acting part were possible because of my size, so I studied more behind the camera." He was selling insurance in Finland when he auditioned in 2013. Once cast, Suotamo had a lot more sources to draw from than Mayhew did back in 1976—including all the films and Mayhew himself, whose new title was "Chewbacca Consultant."

"Joonas learned very, very quickly," said Mayhew. "He had seen Chewie as a hero for him, and he's almost as big as I am. By the time he got the costume on, there was not that much difference between us." (Suotamo got a boost from the two-inch heels inside his Chewbacca feet/boots.) After fully taking over the role in 2017's *The Last Jedi*, Suotamo assured fans that the Wookiee is in good hands, saying, "I now have a pretty good idea of what Chewie would do in any situation. It's a very specific character. That's part of why he's so lovable."

THE BIG TEDDY BEAR

Peter Mayhew underwent spinal surgery in 2018 to increase his mobility, but died of a heart attack a year later. He was 74. As the news of his death spread, celebrities and fans from all walks of life started paying their respects. "Thank you Peter for inspiring generations of explorers," tweeted NASA astronaut Nick Hague from the International Space Station.

"What was so remarkable about Peter," said Mark Hamill, "was his spirit. His gentleness was so close to what a Wookiee is. He just radiated happiness and warmth. We hit it off immediately and stayed friends for over 40 years." Harrison Ford also said he and Mayhew remained friends and praised the way he "invested his soul in the character." George Lucas wrote, "Peter was a wonderful man. He was the closest any human being could be to a Wookiee: big heart, gentle nature—and I learned to always let him win."

But Mayhew always knew that it was Chewbacca—not the people who created him or the man who played him—that fans adored. And he knew why: "My character is a teddy bear, basically. How many people had a teddy bear or a security blanket as a youngster? And that's what Chewie is, he looks after everybody."

For more exciting adventures of the galaxy's most famous Wookiee, set the Falcon's *navicomputer for page 388 and then...punch it, Chewie!*

UNCLE JOHN'S PAGE OF LISTS

More top tidbits from our bottomless files.

President Franklin D. Roosevelt's 4 Freedoms (1941)

1. Freedom of speech and expression
2. Freedom of worship
3. Freedom from want
4. Freedom from fear

5 Basic Soil Components

1. Minerals (45–49% of soil volume)
2. Water (2–50%)
3. Organic matter (1–5%)
4. Air and other gases (2–50%)
5. Microorganisms (less than 1%)

9 Original Ty Beanie Babies (1993)

1. Legs the Frog
2. Squealer the Pig
3. Spot the Dog
4. Flash the Dolphin
5. Splash the Orca
6. Chocolate the Moose
7. Patti the Platypus
8. Brownie the Bear
9. Pinchers the Lobster

20 Native American Words

1. Alabama: "clears the thicket" (Choctaw)
2. Alaska: "mainland" (Aleut)
3. Arizona: "small springs" (O'odham)
4. Connecticut: "at the long tidal river" (Algonquin)
5. Illinois: "many men" (Algonquin)
6. Kansas: "people of the south wind" (Siouan)
7. Kentucky: "on the meadow" (Iroquoian)
8. Massachusetts: "at the great hill" (Algonquin)
9. Michigan: "large lake" (Algonquin)
10. Minnesota: "white water" (Siouan)
11. Mississippi: "big river" (Algonquin)
12. Missouri: "people of the large canoes" (Algonquin)
13. Nebraska: "flat water" (Siouan)
14. Ohio: "good river" (Iroquoian)
15. North and South Dakota: "friendly" (Siouan)
16. Oklahoma: "red people" (Choctaw)
17. Texas: "allies" (Caddo)
18. Utah: "high" (Athabaskan)
19. Wisconsin: "it lies red" (Algonquin)
20. Wyoming: "at the big river flat" (Algonquin)

9 Movies with a Scientist Main Character

1. *Raiders of the Lost Ark:* archaeologist
2. *I Am Legend:* virologist
3. *Jurassic Park:* paleontologist
4. *Arrival:* linguist
5. *Contact:* astrophysicist
6. *Dr. Strangelove:* nuclear physicist
7. *Gorillas in the Mist:* primatologist
8. *The Martian:* botanist
9. *A Beautiful Mind:* mathematician

BATHROOM NEWS

Bits and pieces of bathroom trivia we've flushed out in recent years.

ROAD RUNNER

In June 2019, the Royal Canadian Mounted Police pulled over a speeding Camaro after clocking it doing 170 kilometers per hour in a 100 kph zone. (That's about 105 mph in a 60 mph zone.) What excuse did the driver, an unnamed 16-year-old boy with a brand-new driver's license, have for driving so fast? "He had too many hot wings and needed a bathroom," the police noted in their report. So...did the kid beat the rap? Nope—he was slapped with a $966 fine for speeding, plus an additional $203 for not being accompanied by a "supervising driver" as Manitoba law requires for new drivers. "Absolutely #noexcuses for that kind of speed," the Mounties tweeted after the incident.

CORNERED

In April 2019, the Washington County, Oregon, Sheriff's Office received a 911 call from two house sitters who said they'd trapped a burglar in the bathroom after returning home from walking the dog. They said they could hear the burglar "rustling" around inside the bathroom, and they could see shadows moving under the door. Sheriff's deputies raced to the scene, entered the home, and with guns drawn and a police dog at the ready, ordered the burglar, still rustling around, to come out of the bathroom with his hands up. The burglar did not come out. Finally, a sheriff's deputy opened the bathroom door and rushed in to confront the "burglar"...who turned out to be a Roomba robotic vacuum. "We breached the bathroom door and encountered a very thorough vacuuming job," said a spokesperson for the Sheriff's Office. "Every call is unique, and this was a fun one."

BOMBS AWAY!

In February 2019, a staff member at a Wichita, Kansas, Home Depot called 911 to report an emergency. "We just had a customer here who made what may have been a bomb threat," the caller told the 911 operator. "He said, 'Somebody told me there's a bomb in here and you need to leave the building.' He said it three times." The police went to Home Depot to investigate, and quickly determined that the "bomber" was actually a customer who had really needed to go to the bathroom. As a courtesy, he had warned other people in the restroom that he was probably going to stink up the joint, and that now would be a good time for them to leave. "You all need to get out of here," he'd warned, "because I'm fixin' to blow it up."

OFF THE WALL

In May 2018, a maintenance worker at the Core Shopping Centre in Calgary, Alberta, was sent to the fourth-floor women's restroom to fix a toilet that wouldn't flush. When the worker removed a panel behind the toilet to gain access to the plumbing, he discovered the dead body of a man in his 20s wedged inside the wall. An investigation later concluded that the man had entered the women's restroom three days earlier. "Based on evidence at the scene, officers believe the victim then climbed inside the wall through the vent opening, where he became stuck and later died," the investigators noted in their report. An autopsy ruled the death accidental; police were never able to determine why the man had climbed into the wall in the first place.

FACE OFF

So who's the vandal in this case? That depends on your politics. In February 2019, someone removed a giant decal that had been plastered over the entire "peeing surface" of the men's room urinal of the Dubliner Irish Bar & Restaurant in Methven, New Zealand. What was printed on the decal? An enlarged black-and-white photo of Donald Trump grimacing as he points with his right index finger. (Proprietor Gary Manning is not a fan of America's 45th president.)

The crumpled decal was later found in the men's room trash can. "I've got to try to straighten it out tonight and put it back up, and get him on for a second term," Manning told the *New Zealand Herald*. Manning says he has an idea of who it was that de-faced—literally—his presidential pissoir. "There were two elderly Americans in last night," he told the *Herald*. "They were the only Americans in the pub. I'm not saying it was definitely them...[but] my chef saw one of them outside the toilet looking around suspiciously. It was only in hindsight that he realized he was [the lookout] for the other guy who was doing the damage."

ACT OF GOD

In August 2019, a Port Charlotte, Florida, woman named Marylou Ward was at home with her husband and their three dogs when they saw a lightning flash and heard what Ward described as "the loudest noise I've ever heard." The lightning had struck the ground outside, scoring a direct hit on the lid of their septic tank and igniting the methane gas built up inside the tank. The resulting fireball traveled along the sewer pipe into their home, blowing up the toilet and shattering it into hundreds of pieces, some of which ripped through the bathroom walls like shrapnel. Jordan Hagadorn, the plumber who was called to assess the damage, says neither he nor his father, a plumber for 40 years, have ever seen or heard of anything like it. "This is probably a first in toilet history," he told reporters.

"I'm just glad no one was on the toilet. That's the main thing," Marylou Ward said.

Why do TV shows say they're "taped in front of a live studio audience"?
To brag that they don't use a laugh track.

CATS & DOGS

True stories of dogs and cats at their best and worst. Mostly worst.

Good Dog! A fire destroyed Christine Marr's home in South Haven, Michigan, in March 2017, and her family narrowly escaped. Their dog, Chloe, was rescued by firefighters (they used an improvised oxygen mask to revive the pooch), but their cat, Ringer, didn't make it out. Firefighters looked for her inside the home, and the family searched the surrounding area, but the cat didn't turn up. Two months later, Marr was ready to start rebuilding, so she and Chloe drove to the condemned structure to meet a contractor. It was their first time back. From the moment they went inside, the dog was fixated on a particular spot underneath the floor—so much so that Marr asked the contractor to pull out the floorboards. Sure enough, there was a hole underneath the house that Ringer had been trapped in for 60 days. He was less than half his weight and severely dehydrated, but thanks to Chloe, he was reunited with his family and was expected to make a full recovery. "This cat's a miracle," said Marr. "I think he used more than just nine lives."

Bad Kitty! Early one morning in 2019, Emma Rhodes of Canberra, Australia, was awakened by her smoke alarm. She, her partner, and her three-year-old daughter had to make their way through thick, black smoke to get outside. Fortunately, firefighters were able to extinguish the blaze before it spread. A brief investigation determined the cause of the fire: their black cat Belle. While everyone else was asleep, he jumped up onto the counter and knocked a box of cling wrap onto the touch-sensitive stove... which starts automatically when something is placed on it. Firefighters point out that it's a good idea to lock touch-sensitive stoves at night (especially if you have a disobedient cat).

Good Dogs! A man was riding his bike on a path near the Potomac River in Maryland when all of a sudden two loose dogs, their leashes still attached, ran up and started barking at him. After determining that they weren't dangerous, the cyclist noticed a faint call for help from the woods down by the river. He followed the two excited dogs 50 yards through thick underbrush until he found their owner—an 87-year-old man—stuck in the mud up to his knees in 110-degree heat. The old man explained that they'd been playing fetch and he was retrieving the stick from the mud when he got stuck...more than an hour earlier. No one had heard his calls for help, so the dogs took matters into their own paws. It was difficult for rescuers to reach the man and free him, but they finally managed to get him to safety. But without his dogs' assistance, who knows how long—or if—he would have survived.

Priorities: In Japan, more paper is used for comic books than for toilet paper.

Bad Kitty! Remember the scene in *Alien* where a newly hatched alien-thing wraps itself around an astronaut's face? That kind of happened to a man from Thailand, except that instead of an alien, it was his cat, Achi. The man was having trouble breathing at night, so he installed a camera to find out why. In the footage, you can see him sleeping peacefully on his back...while Achi slowly scoots his way upward until he's enveloped his owner's face, including the nose and mouth. Then Achi falls asleep. Was the cat owner angry? Hardly. "I feel very much in love with him that he loves me like this."

Bad Kitty! "Please. Come meet him. And take him home. Please." That was the final line of a desperate Facebook plea posted by Friends for Life Animal Shelter in Houston, Texas, after they discovered who was letting all the cats out. Who? It was Quilty. Surveillance video showed the six-year-old housecat, who was kept with several old cats in the "senior room," leap up and grab hold of the door handle, and then swing until the door opens, letting all the other cats run free. (At Quilty's previous home, it was his job to let the dog out.) So the shelter begged someone to adopt "a clever cat that gets along with dogs but does not get along with closed doors." Good news: the post received 19,000 shares, and Quilty got adopted by a man who reported that he "sleeps under my covers like a dog."

Good Kitty! In November 2019, Diana Lorena Álvarez was working at her office in Bogotá, Colombia, when she noticed that her one-year-old son, Samuel León, had escaped from his crib and was sitting on the floor next to their one-year-old Siamese cat, Gatubela. The name means "Catwoman," which is fitting for this feline hero. Álvarez checked the office's CCTV footage to find out how her son had done it. Answer: he simply climbed out. But it was what happened next that made Gatubela a hero. After getting out of the crib, Samuel León crawled over to the top of a long flight of stairs. The Siamese cat watched intently as the baby got closer to the edge. Then, just as Samuel León was about to plunge down the stairs, Gatubela leapt from a chair and flew across the room, landing directly between the boy and the steps. Then she literally wrestled him away from the precipice and dragged him to safety. "Watching the footage, I felt really surprised...and lucky," said Álvarez, who credits Gatubela with saving her baby's life.

Badass Kitty! In 2017, birdwatchers in Laguna Vista, Texas, spotted a "massive rattlesnake" next to a walking trail. Lying just a few feet away was a regular-sized housecat. It was facing the venomous serpent, which was coiled, rattling, and ready to strike. When police and animal wranglers arrived later that afternoon, the two animals were still in the same positions. An officer snapped a photo of the standoff (which went viral) before wranglers shooed the cat away and safely removed the

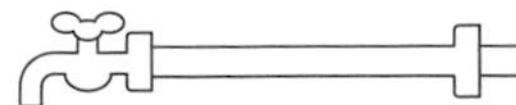

Had the War of 1812 not ended when it did, the New England states might have seceded from the Union over it. (They opposed the war.)

rattlesnake, which, based on a photo on the department's Facebook page, appears to be at least eight feet long. In a post titled "The Fearless Laguna Vista Cat," officers warned people not to treat rattlesnakes as nonchalantly as that cat had: "If you bother them, they will probably bite you. Stay away from them."

Bad Dog! In November 2019, a Florida man driving his Mercury Sable took a wrong turn and ended up on a dead-end cul-de-sac. He got out of the car and closed the door...which locked. Still in the car was Max, his black Lab, who got so excited that he hit the shifter and put the car in reverse. It started going around in circles—backward—and the only way to get in was to manually punch in the code on the door. An agile police officer was finally able to do that and stop the car...after it had been "doing donuts" for more than an hour. Max jumped right out, wagging his tail, as if nothing odd had occurred. No one was injured, but a neighbor reported that the Sable "took out a mailbox and a garbage can."

Bad Dog! The 34 homemade gingerbread cookies might have passed through Marley without too much fuss, but the ribbons that were tied around the cookies presented a real problem for the seven-year-old Lab. Marley's owner, Rachael Bulmer of Dorset, England, knew it was bad when she noticed the cookies missing from the kitchen table in December 2019; Marley had done this before. "But this time," she told the *Independent*, "he started acting strangely and looked like he was going into shock. He was violently sick and brought up some of the ribbon."

Marley was rushed to a veterinarian, who told Bulmer not to get her hopes up. "We were preparing to say goodbye to him." After four hours and two operations, veterinarians had successfully removed what was left of the 34 ribbons...along with several undigested bones that had been inside Marley for who knows how long. He had to spend four days in intensive care before he got to go home for the holidays, and Bulmer learned a valuable lesson about Marley's abilities: "I thought I'd left the biscuits safely out of reach."

Bad Kitty! In 2019, a toy store worker in Thailand received a monumental task a week ahead of a New Year's Eve party: put together a life-size LEGO model of Doraemon, a popular Japanese manga character described as a "cat robot from the 22nd century." The dutiful worker spent every workday that week painstakingly placing all 2,432 plastic bricks in place, unaware that he was being watched...by a kitten. On New Year's Eve, the proud worker placed the final brick and took a photo of his masterpiece. A moment later he snapped another photo showing the model all over the floor in thousands of pieces, with the adorable ginger kitten (we're talking kitten-poster-adorable) lying on his back in the wreckage with his little paws sticking up. The man posted the before-and-after photos to Facebook with the caption: "I will kill you."

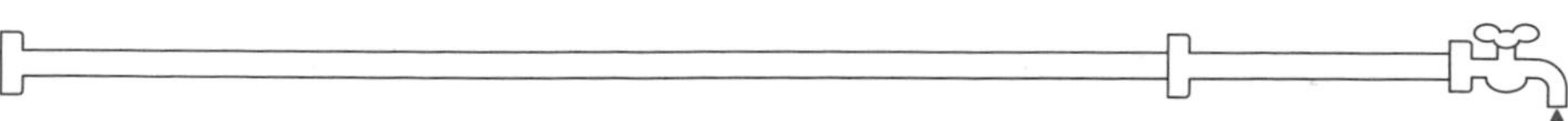

Starfish eat by sticking their stomach out of their mouth and eating their prey's digestive organs.

BETTER LIVING THROUGH ROBOTS?

These recent advances in robotics and artificial intelligence—some silly, some serious—will either make our lives easier...or make us that much easier to conquer.

ROLL-BOT

Problem: What's the worst thing that can happen in the bathroom (other than running out of quality reading material)? Running out of toilet paper, of course.

Solution: RollBot is a cute little automaton on two wheels with a cylinder on top that holds a roll of emergency TP. Activated by an app on your smartphone, RollBot will always be on the ready to rescue you in your time of need. Unlike some of these other robots, this one isn't a prototype built by a student or hobbyist. RollBot was unveiled at the 2020 Consumer Electronics Show in Las Vegas by none other than Charmin. Despite consumer interest, the toilet paper company says it has no plans to offer the RollBot for sale. (Too bad.)

PASS-THE-BUTTER-BOT

Problem: There's a delicious dinner roll on your plate, but the butter is way over on the other side of the table. What if there's no one there to pass it to you? (Or they simply don't want to?)

Solution: You'll need a butter-passing robot. Not available in stores, there is at least one prototype of such a robot—made by someone who goes by the online name of "andredotcom," who used 3-D printed materials and the guts of a radio-controlled toy car to build his invention. Before you sit down to eat, you strategically place the robot on the far side of the butter dish. When you're ready for some butter, use an app on your smartphone to order the robot to push it across the table to you. Andredotcom said he was inspired by a 2014 episode of the Cartoon Network's *Rick and Morty*, in which mad scientist Rick builds a robot that can do only two things: slide a butter dish across a table, and vocally lament that all it can do is pass the butter.

VACATION-BOT

Problem: Going on vacation can be a big pain. You spend a fortune to sit in a cramped, germy airplane just to go to a faraway place full of snakes, uncomfortable beds, and other scary things. What if you could travel without ever leaving your house?

Solution: In 2019, Japanese airline All Nippon Airways announced plans to introduce a fleet of 1,000 "telepresence" robots, collectively called Newme, that will do the traveling for you. Resembling a rolling parking meter with a tablet for a head,

each robot comes equipped with a screen that displays a live feed of your face while a high-resolution camera and sensors act as your eyes and ears. You can tell your Newme where to go, use it to take photos and interact with people, and yell, "Put me down!" over and over when a local runs away with you.

CHEF-BOT

Problem: Really, who has the time to cook an entire meal anymore?

Solution: "Imagine someone like Gordon Ramsay or Jamie Oliver cooking for you in your kitchen. Imagine dishes from top Michelin restaurants cooked in front of you to the highest standard, not in your kitchen, but by your kitchen." So read a 2015 press release from the London-based firm Moley Robotics. Their robotic kitchen will prepare the meal, plate the food, and then clean the dishes afterward. The contraption consists of two hydraulic arms (with hands) that glide back and forth over your counter and stovetops, adding ingredients, stirring, and cooking. To get this level of realism, a professional chef's movements were filmed with a 3-D camera, and then uploaded to a computer that can store thousands of recipes. All you have to do is provide the ingredients. And if you think this robot is too good to be true, think again. "Our dream," said Moley CEO Mark Oleynik in 2018, " is to bring the cost down to a point where it is affordable for the middle class."

FACE-BOT

Problem: It's estimated that by 2050, the worldwide population of 85-year-olds will be three times what is today. What if there aren't enough young people to care for them? They'll need robots, of course. But today's interpersonal robots are, in a word, creepy. The elderly of tomorrow will require something a bit more personable.

Solution: In October 2019, a British engineering company called Geomiq made a casting call like none before: They're looking for someone with a "kind and friendly" appearance to become the face of hundreds of thousands of helper/companion robots that will look and talk just like a real person. The project, funded anonymously by "venture capitalists in China," reportedly costs billions. Geomiq is offering a licensing fee of £100,000 (about $130,000) for the winning face.

RO-BUTT

Problem: If you keep your smartphone in your back pocket, don't you risk destroying your phone every time you sit down? How do phone companies test their products to prevent this from happening?

Solution: South Korean electronics giant Samsung tackled the problem by inventing a robotic butt. Shaped exactly like a human rear end (and clad in jeans for a more realistic simulation), company engineers lower the robot onto phone prototypes to see if they bend, break...or crack.

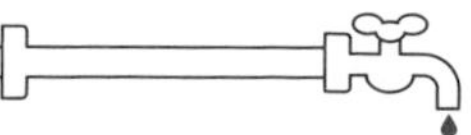

... a year after the publication of Agatha Christie's *Murder on the Orient Express.*

THE 9/11 BOATLIFT

The attack on the World Trade Center on September 11, 2001, left hundreds of thousands of people stranded in lower Manhattan. Here's the story of the people who came to their rescue.

NO MOVIE

The morning of September 11, 2001, started out like any other late summer day for Vincent Ardolino, the captain of a 120-foot charter boat called the *Amberjack V.* He was at home in Brooklyn, New York, flipping through the TV channels when he came to a channel that showed a tall building on fire. For a second he thought he was watching *The Towering Inferno,* a 1974 movie about a fire in a San Francisco skyscraper. Then he realized the building was one of the twin towers of the World Trade Center in New York.

Ardolino and his wife sat watching the news coverage in disbelief. Then he noticed that some of the New York Harbor ferries had started evacuating people from the island. "I said, 'Fine, we could do the same thing. I can take people on my boat, get in there, take them where they have to go,' " Ardolino recounted in an interview.

"But what if they're attacked again?" his wife asked him.

"I said, 'Well then that's something I'll have to live with.' " He raced to the *Amberjack V* and was soon underway to lower Manhattan.

STRANDED

Just 17 minutes after American Airlines Flight 11 struck the North Tower of the World Trade Center, United Airlines Flight 175 crashed into the South Tower. From that point on, it was clear that whatever this was, it was no accident—New York City was under attack. Local, state, and federal officials acted quickly to close the bridges, tunnels, subway, and bus lines to thwart any other terrorist attacks that might still be in the works. For the hundreds of thousands of people living and working in lower Manhattan, this meant that their only means of escape was on foot. People north of the World Trade Center could make their way uptown; people to the east could walk across the Brooklyn Bridge, which remained open to pedestrians leaving Manhattan. But for the hundreds of thousands of people who fled west or south, they soon came to the water's edge and could go no farther.

For the hundreds of thousands of people living and working in lower Manhattan, this meant that their only means of escape was on foot.

FROM BAD TO WORSE

Some of the boats on the Hudson River, the East River, and in New York Harbor had the presence of mind to head for lower Manhattan as soon as the first tower was hit. City ferries and harbor tugboats were among the first to arrive and they immediately began taking people off the island. And for more than an hour, the evacuations were orderly: People made their way calmly to where the boats were loading passengers, climbed aboard, and were taken to safety.

Then at 9:59 a.m., the South Tower collapsed in a tremendous roar, filling lower Manhattan with enormous choking clouds of pulverized concrete, gypsum, and burning debris. In the panic that followed, tens of thousands more New Yorkers, many of them ghostly figures covered in gray dust, emerged from the clouds and stumbled toward the shoreline of lower Manhattan, desperate to escape. Some even jumped into the water and tried to swim to safety.

CALLING ALL BOATS

As the number of people arriving at the shoreline continued to climb, it was clear that a larger effort would be needed to evacuate them. Soon after the South Tower collapsed, Michael Day, a Coast Guard commander aboard the pilot boat *New York*, put out a radio call asking that "All available boats...anyone who wants to help with the evacuation of lower Manhattan, report to Governor's Island," an island just south of Manhattan.

Day wasn't sure how many boats would respond. How many skippers would be willing to head *toward* the danger when no one knew if another attack, perhaps by a ship filled with explosives in New York Harbor, was imminent? But within 15 minutes, more than 100 boats of every description—tugboats, charter boats, party boats, private cabin cruisers, pretty much anything that was on the water that day—began converging on Governor's Island, where they were quickly put to work evacuating people from lower Manhattan.

Larger boats, like the ferries and Ardolino's charter boat, the *Amberjack V*, pulled into the docks and slips, the only places that could accommodate them. Tugboats and other, smaller boats were able to shove right up against the seawall in places like the Battery, a 25-acre public park on the southern tip of Manhattan, where they tied up to a tree or a fencepost or whatever else was available and began loading as many passengers as they could carry. Then they set off for Hoboken, Sandy Hook, Staten Island, and other places, dropped off their passengers, and went back for more, often bringing relief supplies to lower Manhattan on the return trip. In places where the smoke and dust clouds were too thick to see through, the boats used radar to find their way to shore.

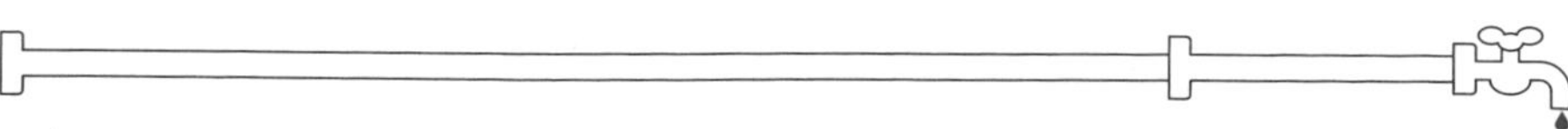

GETTING ORGANIZED

For the first hour or two, the evacuations were pretty haphazard: The boats pulled up, people piled on, and off they went to whatever destination the boat happened to be going to. A person living in Brooklyn, east of Manhattan, might end up on a tugboat bound for New Jersey to the west; someone from New Jersey might end up in Brooklyn. But as time passed, the rescuers became more organized. Aboard the boats, crew members fashioned makeshift signs to let people know where their boats were headed. Onshore, people began lining up according to where they needed to go, then boarded the boats that would take them there.

One retired fireboat, the *John J. Harvey*, began the day by helping in the evacuation, but when city officials realized that a number of water mains had been knocked out when the towers collapsed, it tied up alongside two other fireboats near Ground Zero and began pumping 18,000 gallons of water a minute to the firefighters battling the blazes that had broken out at the site. The boats kept pumping until the water mains were repaired three days later.

LARGER THAN LIFE

The rescues began within minutes of Flight 11 striking the North Tower at 8:46 a.m. and continued until around 5:00 p.m., when the last evacuees were taken off the island. During the evacuation of Dunkirk, France, during World War II, 339,000 British and French soldiers were taken across the English Channel to England in an operation lasting nine days. By comparison, in New York City on 9/11, nearly 500,000 people were transported from lower Manhattan in less than nine hours, making it the largest evacuation by sea in history. (Some estimates place the number of evacuees at 750,000 or even 1 million.) "I've worked on the water for 28 years. I've never seen that many boats come together at one time that fast," Robin Jones, the engineer of the tugboat *Mary Gellatly*, told an interviewer for the documentary *Boatlift*. "One radio call and it just came together just that fast."

* * *

DUDE, WHERE'S MY LEG?

Dion Callaway lost his leg in a skydiving accident...and then lost his prosthetic leg when it flew off in a subsequent skydiving accident. When a worker found the metallic leg—wearing a Nike sneaker—on a pile of sawdust at a lumber yard in Cloverdale, California, he brought it to his boss, Micah Smith, whose first thought was, "Okay, where's the rest?" The rest (Callaway) was frantically looking for his $15,000 leg. A few days later, man and leg were reunited at the Sheriff's office. Callaway said he's really relieved it didn't fall on anyone.

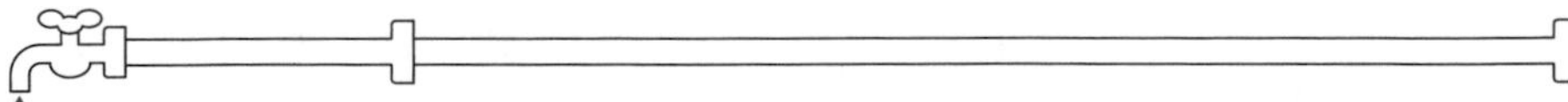

POLICE BLUNDERS

The men and women of law enforcement have a really difficult job, and most of them make it through their entire careers without getting on the news for a boneheaded goof. Not these cops.

Get Out of Jail Free, Pt. 1

"My prayers go out to them," said one sympathetic neighbor, "because that's not right." What's not right? Seeing the man who murdered one of your family members walking down the street when he's supposed to be serving a 20-year sentence for the crime. The blunder occurred in February 2018 after Javoris Hurston was spotted in his Atlanta, Georgia, neighborhood. Relatives of Barry Hawkins, whom Hurston had been convicted of killing, called police to find out why he wasn't serving out his sentence. It turned out that Hurston had been transferred from the Fulton County Jail, where he had been serving the murder sentence, to the DeKalb County Jail, where he was facing assault and battery charges stemming from a separate incident. Due to a bureaucratic snafu, staff at the first jail didn't tell the staff at the second jail that Hurston was a convicted murderer, so after the assault charges were dropped, he was mistakenly released. He'd spent two days in his old neighborhood before the cops caught him and put him back in prison. According to reports, no one at either jail was disciplined.

Get Out of Jail Free, Pt. 2

When staffers at the Mesa County Jail in Colorado released an inmate named Marvin March in June 2018, they made one crucial mistake: It wasn't Marvin March. The real March, 35, was in a holding cell while his own cell underwent renovations. The man who was rehoused in March's cell—James Rynerson, 38—didn't inform the jailors of their error when they told him he was being let go. Instead, Rynerson signed March's name on the release papers, put on March's leather jacket, took his belongings, and left. According to reports, "Neither the deputy who retrieved Rynerson from his cell, nor the booking technician who processed his papers, checked the inmate wristband with Rynerson's name." So Rynerson—who was in jail awaiting trial for menacing, disorderly conduct, and trespassing—walked out a free man. Briefly. When he showed up at home and told his wife the good news an hour later, she immediately drove him back to jail, where he was charged with escape, forgery, criminal impersonation, and theft. A jail spokesperson said they are reviewing their procedures to make sure no other inmates are accidentally released.

Take a Bite Out of Crime

In July 2019, a cop employed by the Marion County (Indiana) Sheriff's Office—identified in press reports as "DJ"—stormed into a McDonald's restaurant and

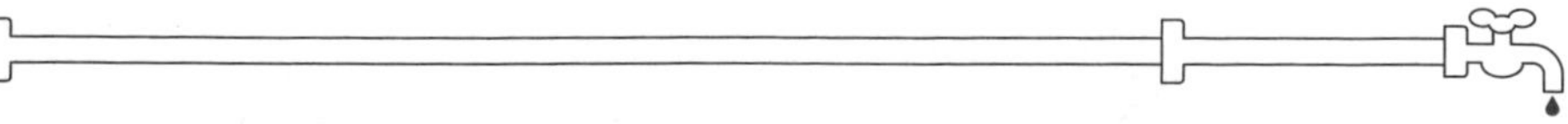

demanded to know why someone there had tampered with his McChicken sandwich. He claimed he'd purchased the sandwich that morning, took it to work and put it in the fridge, and when he went to retrieve it for lunch, found that someone had taken several small bites out of it. According to Officer DJ, "[The manager] offered me some free food I didn't care anything about. I just wanted to find out who the person was and they deal with that person in an appropriate way." All the workers denied tampering with the sandwich. The department launched an investigation and posted their embarrassing findings a few days later: "The [law enforcement] employee took a bite out of the sandwich upon starting his shift...He returned nearly seven hours later having forgotten that he had previously bitten the sandwich. He wrongly concluded that a McDonald's restaurant employee had tampered with his food because he is a law enforcement officer. He has since formally apologized."

A Failure to Communicate

In December 2017, the Tampa Police Department held a press conference announcing the high-profile arrest of a serial killer. At first glance, it looked like a typical presser: The police chief was speaking at the podium while an interpreter used American Sign Language (ASL) to translate for the deaf community. Except that no one understood what the interpreter was signing. "She was standing there twisting her hands back and forth," explained certified ASL instructor Rachelle Settambrino. "Interpreters don't do that." Another expert described the signing as "gibberish." The woman in question, Derlyn Roberts, had informed police that she was the interpreter, and they saw no reason to question her. The Tampa PD apologized for the ruse, and explained that what Roberts did wasn't a crime per se, but more of an "ethical violation." She wasn't charged, and the department promised to vet their interpreters more carefully in the future. (They also offered no explanation for why Roberts did it, except to say that she has been in trouble for fraud in the past.)

Claw Enforcement

In some cases, a moment of levity can cheer up a somber event, but not in this case. In 2019, Royal Canadian Mounted Police in British Columbia were holding a press conference about an unsolved double homicide that had shaken the region. The conference was being livestreamed on Facebook, and while Sgt. Janelle Shoihet was sharing the grisly details about the murders, Facebook's "cat filter" was turned on, giving the uniformed sergeant a set of animated cat ears and long whiskers. As the presentation went on, commenters and tweeters alike alerted the police, who tweeted back that they were having a "technical difficulty" due to an "automatic setting" that no one figured out how to rectify. (They later re-recorded the press conference without the cat filter.)

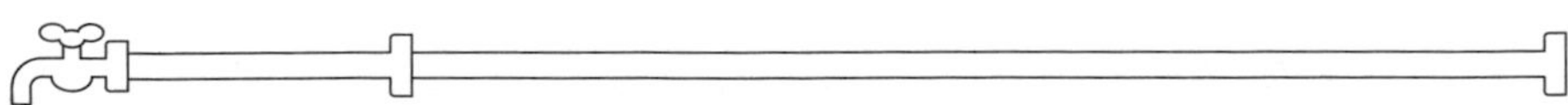

A Dartmouth College study calculated the "most miserable age": 47 years, eight weeks.

THE BIG FIZZLE

Pro sports drafts are risky. Teams select a player and hope that his success in college or high school will carry over to the big leagues. Sometimes it works out—John Elway, LeBron James, and Ken Griffey Jr. were all #1 picks. But other times it doesn't and, in a few cases, the draftees never play a single game.

Player: Clifton McNeely

Story: The Basketball Association of America (which later absorbed the National Basketball League and changed its name to the National Basketball Association, or NBA) held its first draft in 1947. The Pittsburgh Ironmen, by virtue of having the worst record in the league, got the #1 pick, and used it to select Clifton McNeely of Texas Wesleyan University. McNeely was a star for the school in the early 1940s, left to join the Army Air Corps in World War II, and then returned to TWU in 1946. That season, he led all college players in scoring, led his team to a conference championship, and was named an All-American. But McNeely wasn't sure he wanted to play for money, and the BAA was still new and unstable. It didn't matter: The Ironmen wound up folding before the start of the 1947–48 season, by which time McNeely had already decided to skip the pros and become a high school basketball coach.

Bonus fact: In drafting McNeely, Pittsburgh passed on future basketball Hall of Famers Harry "the Horse" Gallatin (played for the Knicks), Andy "Handy Andy" Phillip (Warriors, Pistons, and Celtics), and Jim "the Kangaroo Kid" Pollard (Lakers).

Player: Gene Melchiorre

Story: A star athlete in multiple sports in high school, Melchiorre found his niche as a basketball player while he was in the U.S. Army, playing for the Fort Sheridan Ramblers. When his stint in the military was over, he utilized the G.I. Bill to attend Bradley University, where he played for the Bradley Braves, scoring more points than anyone else on the squad and running up a 119–22 record in four seasons. Melchiorre was expected to go high in the 1951 NBA Draft. And he did—the Baltimore Bullets nabbed him with the #1 pick. But before the start of the 1951–52 season, Melchiorre was found to be complicit in a college basketball point-shaving scandal. NBA president Maurice Podoloff issued lifetime bans to everyone involved, including Melchiorre. Forced to retire from pro basketball before he even got started, Melchiorre returned to his hometown of Highland Park, Illinois, and worked at the post office.

Player: Steve Chilcott

Story: In 1966, only the second year that Major League Baseball used a draft, the

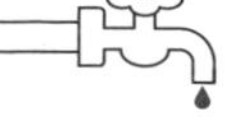

New York Mets earned the #1 pick. The team's selection: an 18-year-old catcher from Southern California named Steve Chilcott, personally scouted by legendary Mets manager Casey Stengel and thought to be baseball's next big thing. As a teenager at Antelope Valley High School, Chilcott was a fast-running power hitter who led his team to three league titles. The Mets signed him to a $75,000 contract—just slightly less money than the $100,000-a-year stars of the era, Mickey Mantle and Willie Mays, commanded. Chilcott's new team assigned him to the minor leagues, and halfway through his second season, he was hitting .290 with 45 runs batted in. That was good enough to make a call-up to the Mets likely...until he dove into second base during a game in 1967 and dislocated his right shoulder. That led to chronic pain and injuries that plagued him for the rest of his career. The Mets parted ways with Chilcott in 1971, and after playing just 24 games for the New York Yankees' farm system, he was cut there, too. He retired from baseball at age 24, having never played a single game in the big leagues. His career over, Chilcott became a firefighter and, later, a contractor.

Bonus fact: Players who were taken later in the draft that the Mets could have selected include Hall of Famer Reggie Jackson and superstar Steve Garvey.

Player: Brien Taylor

Story: Taylor, a pitcher at East Carteret High School in Beaufort, North Carolina, was among the top young players of the 1990s. He had a record of 29–6 and an earned run average of 1.25, struck out 213 batters while walking only 28, all with a pro-quality 99 mph fastball. It was a no-brainer for the New York Yankees to take Taylor with the #1 pick in the 1991 Baseball Draft. They offered him the standard signing bonus at the time: $300,000. But Taylor's agent convinced him to hold out for more—a year earlier, top prospect Todd Van Poppel had secured $1.2 million from the Oakland Athletics. Their hand forced, the Yankees gave Taylor a $1.55 million contract and sent him to its Single-A affiliate, the Fort Lauderdale Yankees, where he struck out an impressive 187 batters in 161 innings pitched. Bumped up to the AA Albany-Colonie Yankees in 1993, Taylor's record was a respectable 13–7 with 150 strikeouts. Then, in 1994, Taylor didn't play at all. When he went home to North Carolina for the holidays in 1993, he got into a fistfight (defending his brother) and suffered two torn muscles in his shoulder that prevented him from throwing a baseball fast or well ever again. Taylor played the 1995 season with the low-level Gulf Coast Yankees, his fastball reduced to 90 mph, which led to a 2–5 record and just 40 innings pitched. He pitched so poorly in 1996 spring training that the Yankees released him entirely. Taylor moved back to North Carolina to work as a UPS handler, then a bricklayer. In 2005, he was arrested for child neglect, and in 2012 he was sentenced to three years in prison after selling crack cocaine to an undercover cop.

Bonus fact: The #13 selection in 1991 was 13-time all-star Manny Ramirez.

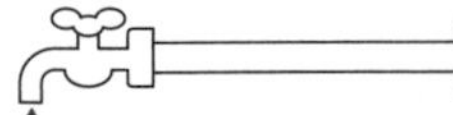

THE ICE (CREAM) AGE

I scream, you scream, we all scream for this timeline about the development of frozen treats over the centuries.

2000 BC Farmers in northern China take animal milk and mix it with softened rice and spices, and then firm up the mixture by packing it in snow. When Chinese nobles hear about it, they send for snow to be brought down from the mountains so that the frozen treat can be made closer to home.

500 BC A popular frozen treat in Persia is grape juice poured over snow—the first snow cone. (Though it had no cone, it really was made from snow.) Within a century, this treat will evolve into a delicacy for royals and nobility, in which iced rose water, vermicelli, saffron, and fruits are mixed together and firmed with ice and snow.

60 BC Roman emperor Nero has ice brought down from surrounding mountains so that he can eat it topped with honey and fruit.

AD 800–900 The modern-day recipe for ice cream takes shape in the Arab world, where cooks make a sweet (nonfrozen) dish in which milk and sugar are the primary ingredients. In population hubs like Baghdad, Damascus, and Cairo, a treat made from milk, cream, sugar, rosewater, dried fruits, and nuts becomes standard fare.

1295 After a 24-year journey in which he travels extensively throughout China, Marco Polo returns to Venice, where he introduces to Europe the idea of freezing milk and other ingredients to make frozen treats.

1565 Bernardo Buontalenti, an artist, party planner, set designer, and official royal architect to the ruling de Medici family of Florence, introduces to the court of Francesco de Medici his culinary concoction similar to Polo's Italian-style ice cream. To milk and sugar he adds cream and egg yolks, making for a much softer and creamier result. He calls it *gelato* ("frozen"), or *crema buontalenti.* He also comes up with a method of freezing the desserts—filling a cold, underground cork-lined room with water, which keeps the product cold.

1686 Italian restaurateur Francesco Procopio opens Café Procope in Paris. Not only is it the first Parisian café, but it's the first place in Europe to offer ice cream for sale. (Café Procope is still in business.)

1776 A London caterer named Philip Lenzi moves to New York City and opens the first ice cream parlor in what will soon be the United States. This marks the first time in America that ice cream can be purchased, instead of being made at home.

1784 George Washington is so beloved in the newly formed United States that his love of ice cream helps popularize the dish. In this year, he buys one of the first commercially available ice cream makers. It consists of two pewter bowls—an inner chamber holds cream, sugar, and other ingredients, which sits inside an outer bowl full of ice and salt. It takes two servants an hour to make ice cream—one holds the outer bowl steady and refills the ice as necessary while the other stirs the ingredients in the inner bowl.

1813 At her husband's second presidential inaugural ball, First Lady Dolley Madison serves strawberry ice cream to the many distinguished guests.

1843 American inventor Nancy Johnson patents the first hand-cranked portable ice cream freezer. Johnson's invention significantly reduces the amount of ice and labor needed to produce a batch of ice cream, making the treat accessible to more people.

1851 Large-scale commercial ice cream production begins in Baltimore when Jacob Fussell uses icehouses to make and store the product.

1874 With soda fountains already common in major cities, Philadelphia fountain operator Robert McCay Green looks for a way to lure customers away from a bigger, nicer store across the street. He strikes on the idea of combining vanilla ice cream with syrup and soda water. The ice cream soda is born.

1892 Chester Platt sells a treat called a "Cherry Sunday" at his Ithaca, New York, soda fountain, Platt & Colt's. A minister comes in every Sunday after services for a dish of vanilla ice cream. One day Platt gets the idea to pour cherry syrup over the ice cream and add a candied cherry on top. Result: the first ice cream Sunday—or sundae.

1897 African American inventor Alfred L. Cralle patents his "Ice Cream Mold and Disher," the first ice cream scoop with a built-in scraper, activated by squeezing the handle, which allows ice cream to be scooped with one hand.

1903 While Italian American ice cream vendor Italo Marchiony has been selling ice cream from a pushcart for almost a decade, it's in this year that he comes up with the idea of serving it in small bowls made out of waffle batter. He patents a waffle iron–like device that makes edible pastry cups.

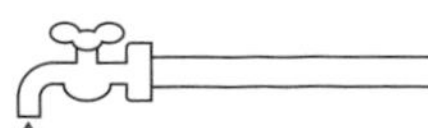

1904 Ice cream is in such huge demand at the St. Louis World's Fair that vendors run out of dishes. Syrian American vendor Ernest Hamwi, ordinarily selling a thin, sweet pastry called zalabia, teams up with ice cream sellers Arnold Fornachou and Charles Menches to roll his product into a funnel shape and fill it with scoops of ice cream. Before long, other pastry vendors are making cones for the fair's more than 50 ice cream vendors, popularizing the notion of the edible ice cream cone.

1920 The Good Humor company goes into business, selling ice cream in a novel way: from a fleet of white trucks outfitted with freezers full of treats. (This is the birth of the "ice cream man.")

1921 Eskimo Pie, the first chocolate-covered ice cream bar, debuts in grocery stores.

1922 Shortly after Steven Poplawski invents the blender, a Walgreens soda jerk named Pop Coulson uses one to add vanilla ice cream to its malted milk, thereby inventing the milkshake.

1925 With a $2,000 bank loan, Howard Deering Johnson opens a neighborhood pharmacy in a section of Quincy, Massachusetts. Realizing that his soda fountain, with its many ice cream treats on offer, is the most successful part of the business, he decides to focus on that. He develops a new recipe for ice cream that contains significantly more fat—making it taste a lot better. Eventually, Johnson creates 28 flavors of ice cream, which propels Howard Johnson's to become a 1,000-location chain of restaurants selling ice cream, hamburgers, and clam rolls. By the 1960s, it's the most franchised restaurant in the United States.

1926 Inventor Clarence Vogt patents the continuous freezer—an industrial method of making ice cream. The machine scrapes a mixture from a drum and pumps in air as it freezes. This makes mass production of ice cream possible, and much more inexpensive than ever before.

1928 Brothers Bruce, I. C., and J. T. Parker improve on the ice cream cone by coating it in chocolate and chopped nuts. They fill it with ice cream and sell the new product under the brand name Drumstick, because one of the Parker's wives thought the concoction resembled a chicken leg.

1938 John "Grandpa" McCullough and his son Alex run a soda fountain in Iowa and invent soft-serve ice cream. They convince their friend Sherb Noble to sell it at his ice cream parlor in Kankakee, Illinois, and it's a wild success—they serve 1,600 customers in just two hours.

...sell a speed-like energy tonic called Peppo.

1940 The McCulloughs and Noble use soft-serve ice cream as the basis for a new concession concept called Dairy Queen. The first of 6,400 stores opens in Joliet, Illinois.

1945 Brothers-in-law Burt Baskin and Irv Robbins open the first Baskin-Robbins ice cream parlor in Glendale, California. It will grow to more than 7,000 locations thanks to its huge menu of choices—the chain promises 31 flavors at any given time, one for every day of the month (and three more than the 28 offered by rival Howard Johnson's).

1976 Reuben and Rose Mattus open the first Häagen-Dazs store, selling premium ice cream in Brooklyn Heights, New York. (First three flavors for sale: chocolate, vanilla, and coffee.) The name is meaningless—they wanted something European-sounding, to denote quality and sophistication, so they made up "Häagen-Dazs."

1978 After taking a correspondence course in ice cream production from Penn State University, childhood friends Ben Cohen and Jerry Greenfield convert a gas station in Burlington, Vermont, into an ice cream store called Ben & Jerry's. Because Cohen has anosmia, he can't smell or taste much of anything, so he develops his ice creams to have a smoother texture and lots of ingredients.

1981 The Country's Best Yogurt, or TCBY, opens its first location in Little Rock, Arkansas. The outlet sells a frozen, lower-fat, ice cream–like product called frozen yogurt. In the health-conscious '80s, it's a huge hit, and within just three years there are more than 1,000 TCBYs across the United States (and eventually more than 1,400 worldwide).

1988 Curt Jones invents Dippin' Dots in New Grand Chain, Illinois. Marketed as "the ice cream of the future," it's BB-sized pellets of flash-frozen ice cream.

2012 Halo Top, a line of lower-calorie ice creams created by a health-conscious attorney named Justin Woolverton, debuts in grocery stores in Los Angeles. Halo Top is made with less sugar and more protein than regular varieties, and has about 25 percent of the calories of normal ice cream. By 2017, it's the best-selling ice cream at grocery stores in the United States.

* * *

"Sometimes you will never know the value of a moment until it becomes a memory."

—Dr. Seuss

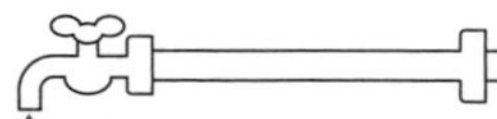

In Ecuador, you can buy ice cream flavored with guinea pig meat.

THEY WERE FIRST... BUT CAME IN LAST

History doesn't always embrace the first instance of an exciting new product or technology. Here are some innovative people and products that got overshadowed by the next guy.

THE FIRST AIRPLANE

On December 17, 1903, Wilbur and Orville Wright decided it was the right time to test out their prototype airplane...and to see if it could fly. On a strip of land outside of Kitty Hawk, North Carolina, each Wright brother took two turns behind the controls and with each test they got a little farther. In the fourth and final flight of the day, Wilbur took the plane 852 feet in a trip that lasted just under a minute. The age of aviation had begun. Except that, technically, it began more than a year earlier when a man on the other side of the world quietly flew *his* plane. Who? A rural New Zealand farmer named Richard Pearse. He was a tinkerer and inventor who enjoyed creating and improving new farm equipment. But he also had an interest in aviation. In 1902, he built a plane, and on March 31 of that year, he took it for a flight of about 1,000 feet. (It ended when he ran into a hedge.) By mid-1903, Pearse had taken five flights of increasing length, with one that continued for more than half a mile. Pearse didn't publicize or announce his achievements, which he considered just more of his tinkering. Result: there are no records of his pre-Wright flights that back up the dates he claimed he took to the skies. But dozens of eyewitnesses saw it and reported their accounts over the next decade. Pearse kept building planes and taking flights until 1911, when he moved to a town surrounded by hills, which made flying much more difficult.

THE FIRST INSTANT COFFEE

Nescafé, which hit stores in 1938, is generally regarded as the first coffee that didn't have to be brewed—consumers just mixed it with hot water and voilà, they had an instant cup of joe. But Nescafé merely perfected the process of making dehydrated powdered coffee. Belgian-American inventor George C. L. Washington figured out how to make coffee powder 20 years earlier, and by 1910 had started the G. Washington Coffee Company to sell it. Washington made a fortune, thanks to a lucrative government contract to provide instant coffee to American troops in World War I. He wasn't as lucky in World War II: The government contract for supplying instant coffee went to Nescafé, which is how that product became a household

name. Washington sold his company in 1943, and the new owners, American Home Products, kept G. Washington Coffee in stores until 1961, by which time it had been overshadowed by Nescafé and other brands. (Washington still wasn't the first instant coffee creator. In 1890, New Zealanders were introduced to Strang's Coffee, an instant coffee drink made possible by the "dry hot-air" process developed by local inventor David Strang.)

THE FIRST VIDEOCASSETTE TAPE

The era of home video began in the mid-1970s, when electronics giants JVC and Sony introduced their versions of the videocassette recorder, or VCR. A "format war" soon developed between JVC's VHS and Sony's BetaMax players and cassettes. JVC ultimately won the war because it licensed its technology to dozens of other electronics companies, flooding the market and diminishing the presence of BetaMax, which Sony kept proprietary. Result: by 1981, VHS had 75 percent of the American video market; Sony continued to make BetaMax players until 2002 and cassettes until 2016, at which point it ceased production. But neither VHS nor BetaMax were the first VCRs. The first one was the U-matic, which was introduced by Sony in 1971. Like VHS and BetaMax, a U-matic cassette consisted of magnetic tape encased in plastic. Unlike those two, tapes wore out quickly, and players could cost in excess of $5,000. And all they could do was record TV shows—no movies were available for rental or purchase.

THE FIRST TRANSFORMING ROBOT TOY

In 1985, a cartoon called *The Transformers* debuted on TV. It was about two warring factions of giant robots from the planet Megatron—the Autobots and the Decepticons—who crash-land on Earth and hide out disguised as ordinary-looking cars, trucks, and household objects. The show was essentially an advertisement for Hasbro's line of Transformers toys: small robots that with a few turns and manipulations could "transform" into cars, trucks, and household objects (and then back again). Kids loved them, but it wasn't Hasbro's idea. Hasbro had partnered with Japanese toy company Takara, which was already selling two similar robot toy lines—Microman (itself based on Hasbro's G.I. Joe action figures) and Diaclone—and rebranded them as Transformers. And Hasbro had competition: In 1983, Tonka (known for its toy metal trucks) had launched GoBots, along with a cartoon called *Challenge of the GoBots*. (The GoBots were based on an existing Japanese toy line called Machine Robot.) Hasbro needed to distinguish itself from the competition, so the company's developers nixed all the Japanese toy names and brought in comic book writers to devise a brand new backstory. It worked: the Autobots and Decepticons netted Hasbro hundreds of millions of

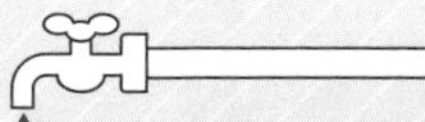

dollars—even spawning a successful live-action film franchise. What happened to the GoBots? Hasbro bought the line from Tonka in 1991 and integrated it into the Transformers universe.

THE FIRST DIGITAL MUSIC PLAYER

As a class-action lawsuit later proved, the major music labels conspired in the 1990s to artificially inflate the price of compact discs. Music fans were forced to pay as much as $16 for a new album. Disgust over that, combined with the rise of high-speed Internet connections, particularly on college campuses, led to the rise of digital music piracy. Any computer could "rip" the tracks off a CD and convert them into small, shareable digital music files. Services like LimeWire and Napster sprang into existence to facilitate music trading—completely free and violating all kinds of copyright and commerce laws. In 2001, Apple struck a huge blow to illegal downloading with the introduction of its industry-sanctioned iTunes Store. For about one dollar per song, music fans could legally purchase digital files. Then they'd listen to them on their brand new Apple iPod, a personal music listening device that cost about $300 and could potentially store thousands of songs. It was like a Walkman for a whole new generation...or an MPMAN F10. That's the name of the very first digital music player, released in 1998—three years before the iPod—by a company called Elger Labs. It cost $250 and could hold a whopping seven songs. Other similar players hit stores in the early 2000s, but none could compete with the high style and marketing genius behind the iPod.

THE FIRST CHOCOLATE SANDWICH COOKIE

The Oreo is as iconic as a cookie can be: two crunchy chocolate disks held together with a creamy white filling. They're marketed with the slogan "Milk's favorite cookie," which is not wrong—about 40 billion individual Oreos are consumed each year. When they first hit grocery stores in 1912, it was an attempt by the National Biscuit Company (Nabisco) to steal sales from a very popular cookie of the time: Sunshine Biscuits' Hydrox. What's a Hydrox cookie? It's two crunchy chocolate disks held together with a creamy white filling, and it was introduced four years earlier. In other words, it's *exactly* the same as an Oreo, so the National Biscuit Company's drive to beat Hydrox was an absolute success. Hydrox cookies are still available, persisting over the decades thanks to one feature that Oreo couldn't claim: They're kosher. However, Nabisco started producing kosher Oreos in 1998, so Hydrox, now a product of Keebler, may eventually crumble.

* * *

"Pioneers get the arrows; settlers take the land." —**Anonymous**

Popcorn king Orville Redenbacher's cause of death: he had a heart attack in his jacuzzi and drowned.

YOU'RE MY INSPIRATION

Here are some more surprising inspirations behind pop culture icons.

PRINCE HANS: This *Frozen* character who turned from love interest to villain was named after fairy tale writer Hans Christian Andersen. Hans's look and mannerisms have a more surprising inspiration: Donny Osmond, whose nephew Hyrum was an animation supervisor. "When Hans walks out from behind the waterfall," explains Osmond, "he closes his eyes and tilts his head while belting a note in the same way I do."

"LAYLA": Derek and the Dominos front man Eric Clapton based the lyrics of this 1971 rock anthem on *Layla and Majnun*, a story by 12th-century Persian poet Nizami Ganjavi, about a lovesick young man who goes insane because he can't have the woman he covets. That story mirrored Clapton's own struggles: He was secretly in love with Pattie Boyd, but she was married to his friend, Beatle George Harrison. "Layla" became one of Clapton's biggest hits and, unlike Majnun and Layla, his love for Pattie was eventually requited. The two were married in 1977. (And divorced in 1989.)

"A TOWEL," wrote Douglas Adams in *The Hitchhiker's Guide to the Galaxy*, "is about the most massively useful thing an interstellar hitchhiker can have." Towels feature so prominently in his seminal science-fiction series, there's even a "Towel Day" every May 25. Why a towel? When Adams was on vacation in Greece, his friends "had to...wait for me every morning because I couldn't find my blessed towel. I came to feel that someone really together...would always know where his towel was."

SHREK: The computer-animated ogre (introduced in William Steig's 1990 children's book) bears an uncanny resemblance to a 1940s French wrestler named Maurice Tillet, aka "the French Angel," who had overly thick bones due to a condition called *acromegaly*. Even though Shrek has the same cone-shaped head and massive chin as Tillet, Dreamworks won't confirm that his look is based on the wrestler.

AQUAMAN: Jason Momoa's Aquaman, introduced in the 2018 movie, is much tougher than the 1980s Super Friends version. Momoa credits that toughness to his love of heavy metal music, explaining: "I'd say Aquaman was probably mostly built out of Tool's 'Ticks and Leeches' and Metallica's 'Kill 'Em All,' if I want to get specific. There's a lot of [Black] Sabbath in there, too." (He also said that his portrayal of Conan the Barbarian was "really heavy Pantera.")

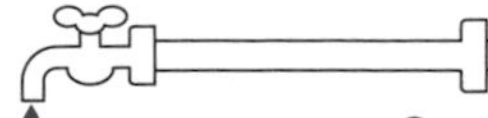

Oscar-winning movie with the longest title: *Deadly Deception: General Electric, Nuclear Weapons, and Our Environment.* (Documentary Short Subject, 1992)

BAD NEWS

Sometimes it seems like there's danger everywhere you look.

ALL WET. When you turn on the faucet, you expect to see clean water, free of dangerous metals and pollutants. But a 2017 investigation by the Environmental Protection Agency found that millions of Americans have been exposed to contaminated drinking water in the past decade. Consider Newark, New Jersey: In 2017, city officials learned that lead was leaching from old pipes into the tap water in some areas. That can be harmful for anyone, but in children it can cause irreversible damage to nerves, hearing, and brain development. Experts found that kids in Newark were twice as likely to suffer lead poisoning as other New Jersey kids.

Watchdog groups blamed city officials for not taking the issue seriously. Even as lead levels were increasing in 2017, Mayor Ras Baraka authorized mailers and robocalls to residents declaring that the water was safe. (He also made an odd pick for the Water Department's director. Though engineers usually hold that position, Baraka promoted a department official who had no college degree and who'd served four years in prison for selling drugs.) After downplaying warnings about the water for more than a year, the city finally issued an emergency declaration to give affected residents water filters to use at home...but it didn't publicize the declaration. Result: many people didn't know whether their water was drinkable, didn't know that boiling it would not make it safer, and didn't know that the city was handing out filters. When 40,000 filters were finally distributed, tests showed they couldn't reliably filter out lead. It wasn't until the federal government threatened penalties that the city started providing bottled water to some residents in 2019. By that time, about 15 percent of Newark's water samples contained *even higher* amounts of lead—more than four times the level at which federal law requires cities to take action. In 2020, Baraka did earn legitimate praise for his plan to replace all of Newark's lead pipes within just a few years, which—if accomplished—would be one of the fastest projects of its kind in the country. Meanwhile, lead levels were still high, and many people used purified water even if officials declared that their tap water was clean—they'd heard that story before.

THAT'S (NOT) THE TICKET. Ticket brokers are agencies that, for a fee, help connect buyers with people reselling event tickets, and many have solid safeguards to protect customers from being ripped off. But resellers still find ways to cheat the system. Example: in late 2015, an L.A. Lakers fan named Jesse Sandler bought four tickets to the last home game of the season for $200 each through the online marketplace StubHub. A month later, Kobe Bryant announced his retirement. Suddenly, tickets to that game were in great demand, and Sandler must've felt like he'd made a slam

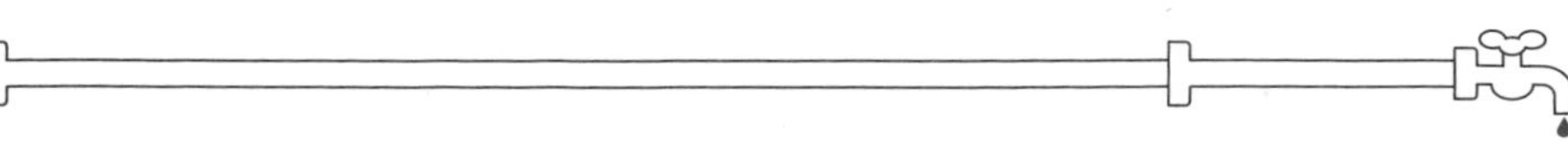

dunk...until he got a message informing him that the seller had canceled his tickets, claiming they'd been "listed incorrectly." In other words, the seller realized the seats could now be sold for much more. Worse, StubHub couldn't offer Sandler replacements because ticket prices had jumped to as much as $2,000 each. StubHub's official policy forbids sellers from canceling tickets and then relisting them at a higher price. Sellers who cancel tickets forfeit 20 percent of the ticket price, but in this case, the seller could pay the fee and still make a huge profit by relisting them.

StubHub eventually offered Sandler a refund plus $250 in vouchers...which together wouldn't cover the cost of even one "new" ticket. So he alerted the press, and *then* StubHub offered up four tickets. Too late. Sandler had already been given better seats by StubHub's competitor, Tickets For Less. (Score!)

WRECKED. Despite the auto industry's efforts to maintain a reputation for producing vehicles that are safe, a disturbing number of manufacturers have knowingly sold cars with defective parts and have even orchestrated cover-ups. General Motors, for example, knew by 2004 that some of its cars contained a faulty ignition switch that randomly shut off while cars were moving. Even so, GM did not initiate a recall until 10 years later, by which time the defect had caused crashes that killed at least 13 people. From 1991 to 2000, some Ford SUVs and pickup trucks were equipped with Firestone tires that shredded at high speeds, sometimes causing rollovers. This resulted in the deaths of at least 119 people and injured thousands more. Although Ford and Firestone settled a lawsuit over the tires in 1992, Ford continued to install them on its SUVs until 2000. More recently, there's the recall of at least 100 *million* defective airbags sold by Takata, a Japanese auto parts company. As early as 2000, the company knew that its airbags sometimes exploded, hurling shrapnel into people's faces. Yet by hiding the evidence and continuing to sell them, Takata was responsible for at least 24 fatalities and 300 injuries. In 2017, the company was fined $1.3 billion, and it filed for bankruptcy. However, the recalls—and deaths—have continued.

TOO MUCH OF A GOOD THING. Sales in the strong coffee industry are up, but have these companies made their products *too* good? It turns out that what makes mornings bearable can also kill you. In a 175-pound person, a lethal dose of caffeine is about 73 cups of coffee. However, let's say it's a high-caffeine brand such as Black Label. You could die from drinking less than eight cups of it. Another brand, Biohazard Coffee, has a whopping 928 milligrams of caffeine per cup, more than five times as much as regular coffee—enough to cause heart palpitations. One reviewer describes Biohazard as "a roundhouse from Chuck Norris followed by Chuck Norris putting on a Scorpion from Mortal Kombat uniform and doing his patented spinning back kick to your brain (going right through your skull) with Christopher Walken screaming, 'Like...uhhhh...finish him!' " Bottoms up.

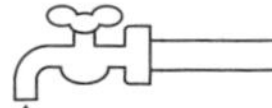

THE RIDDLER

When first I am said, I am very mysterious. But when I am known, it's not that serious. What am I? A riddle! Here are some more. *(Answers are on page 405.)*

1. What tastes better than it smells?

2. If you have three, you have three; if you have two, you have two; but if you have one, you have none. What are they?

3. How much is 6 without S?

4. They say a bird in the hand is worth two in the bush, so if there's a bee in my hand, what's in my eye?

5. You can find one in a pig, two in a gecko, three in an ocelot, and four in a meadowlark. What is it?

6. My walk is a jump. My stand is a sit. My home is below. What am I?

7. How many 3-cent stamps are in a dozen?

8. You can see me toward the end of January and February, in the middle of March and April, but never in May or June. What am I?

9. I touch the earth, I touch the sky. I touch you and you could die. What am I?

10. What is harder to catch the faster you run?

11. One is your ego, the other your window. They sound the same but share not a single letter. What are they?

12. Treasured in the ground, treasured in the chest, treasured in the sky, I am the best of three. What am I?

13. I am two things bound together so tightly you could never pull me apart, but you can hold many of me in your hand and you won't feel a thing. Hold me in your mouth for too long and it will be the last thing you ever do.

14. I am not pants, but I have pockets. I cannot dance, but I have legs. I have no hands, but I have felt. What am I?

15. You can crack me, you can play me, you can tell me, and you can get me or not get me. What am I?

UNCLE JOHN'S STALL OF SHAME

We're always amazed by the creative ways people get into trouble with bathrooms, toilets, toilet paper, etc. To "honor" them, we've created Uncle John's Stall of Shame.

DUBIOUS ACHIEVER: Thomas Porter Wells, 33, of Pittsburgh, Pennsylvania

Achievement: Flushing his grandparents down the pot...in an argument over pot

True Story: In September 2018, Wells asked his mother, Denise Porter, if he could come live with her. Porter agreed...but a few days later kicked him out because "all he wanted to do was smoke marijuana and drink alcohol." That made Wells angry so, according to police, before he moved out, he went into the bedroom where Porter kept her parents' cremated remains in a memorial box, and flushed both of his grandparents' ashes down the toilet. Only later did Porter learn from a relative what her son had done, and when she went to check the ashes, they were indeed missing. In a phone conversation, Wells denied dumping the ashes down the toilet. But as soon as the call was over, he changed his tune, texting his mother, "Yup and soon as you die you'll be going in the same spot where you belong down the sh*tter you b*tch."

Porter reported the incident to police; Wells was arrested and charged with two counts of abusing a corpse and one count of criminal mischief. When he pled guilty to the criminal mischief charge in November 2019, the two counts of abusing a corpse were dropped and he was sentenced to 90 days' probation.

DUBIOUS ACHIEVER: Patrick D. Beeman, 35, of Sheboygan, Wisconsin

Achievement: He never met a toilet he couldn't clog

True Story: In March 2018, someone clogged a toilet in the women's restroom of the community center in Sheboygan's Deland Park, causing it to overflow. The vandalism was accomplished by shoving a clear plastic bottle so far down the toilet that the toilet had to be disassembled in order to remove it. It was the 11th such clogging incident in the women's room at the facility, and each one had involved a clear plastic bottle. When police interviewed the manager of the temp agency that assigned people to work at the community center, the manager reported that one of the workers assigned to the center, Patrick Beeman, had a history of clogging women's toilets at two other workplaces. When the police interviewed Beeman, he initially denied stopping up the commodes, but then admitted to being the culprit

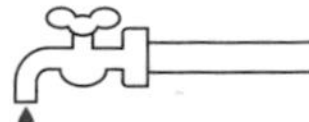

Why did the World Pie-Eating Championship switch from traditional meat-and-potato pies to chicken pies in 2018? Less flatulence.

behind all of the cloggings. "He could not explain this behavior, but simply that he would get very strong urges to do this," the police noted in their report.

In June 2019, Beeman pled guilty to five counts of criminal damage to property and was sentenced to 150 days in jail plus three years' probation, and ordered to pay $5,500 in restitution. He'll also have to complete 100 hours of community service (no word on whether he'll be required to clean restrooms). At the sentencing hearing, he apologized for the harm he'd caused. "I need to make things right and pray for forgiveness every day," he said.

DUBIOUS ACHIEVER: Plumber Richard Mirabile, 44, aka the "Queens Crapper Klepto" who lives in upstate New York

Achievement: Frequenting Queens County restaurants, not to fill up on fast food but to pilfer privy parts

True Story: Police say that on at least eight occasions beginning in November 2018, the plumber entered Queens County fast-food restaurants carrying an empty bag. But instead of walking up to the front counter to order food, security camera video footage shows him running for the restrooms. There he would use a wrench and screwdriver to remove the automatic flushing mechanisms from the toilets and urinals, worth about $250 apiece. In most cases he was in and out within minutes. Surveillance footage showed him carrying the bag—empty when he enters, and filled with the automatic flushers when he exits the restaurant.

Sometimes the devices proved harder to steal: When he tried to filch the flushers from the Wendy's in Ridgewood, he spent what seemed like ages locked in the restroom banging away on the pipes. "I told him, 'Hey, get out of the bathroom, because a lot of people want to use it and you have been in there for like an hour,' and he was like, 'I'm not stealing anything, I'm just using the bathroom,'" manager Lolita Javier told the *New York Post*. "I think he was really high on drugs. He was screaming at us."

Mirabile's luck ran out on December 28, when an employee caught him red-handed in the men's room of the Burger King in Astoria and called the cops. Mirabile was charged with burglary and criminal mischief. At last report, he was lodged at Rikers Island on $25,000 bail

IN THE KNOW

Everyone who's ever used a public restroom has probably wondered why the toilet seats are U-shaped instead of O-shaped. According to the International Association of Plumbing and Mechanical Officials, which includes the seats as part of its Uniform Plumbing Code, the original purpose was hygienic: to make it easier for women to wipe themselves without coming in contact with an unhygienic toilet seat. But the seats are also popular with businesses because they're unlike the kind of toilet seats people have at home, which means people are less likely to steal them.

awaiting trial. Considering that he has 13 prior arrests, if the Queens Crapper Klepto is found guilty of the commode capers, he could end up spending a lot more time...in the can.

DUBIOUS ACHIEVERS: Taxi drivers serving Ashfield, a suburb of Sydney, Australia

Achievement: Dropping off more than just their passengers

True Story: In 2017, shop owners along Hercules Street in Ashfield began noticing a disturbing trend. People were pooping in the alleyway behind their businesses on an almost daily basis. (How did they know the poop was human? The poopers used toilet paper, which they also left behind.) It was only after a shopkeeper caught one, and then another, taxi driver in the act, that it became clear the alleyway had become a popular "dumping ground" for local taxi drivers. The only public restrooms in the area are in the Ashfield train station, and it's only available to people who've purchased a train ticket.

To their credit, local taxi companies are taking the issue seriously and are working to identify which drivers are to blame, by matching the timing of different incidents with GPS data taken from individual taxis. Public pooping is "not in any way, shape, or form in line with our corporate guidelines," said Simon Purssey, head of client services for the 13 CABS taxi firm. "If you've eaten a bad souvlaki and all of a sudden have to pull over, you don't do it on someone's property...This is the first time the taxi industry has had competition [from Uber] in 135 years and we have to be smarter."

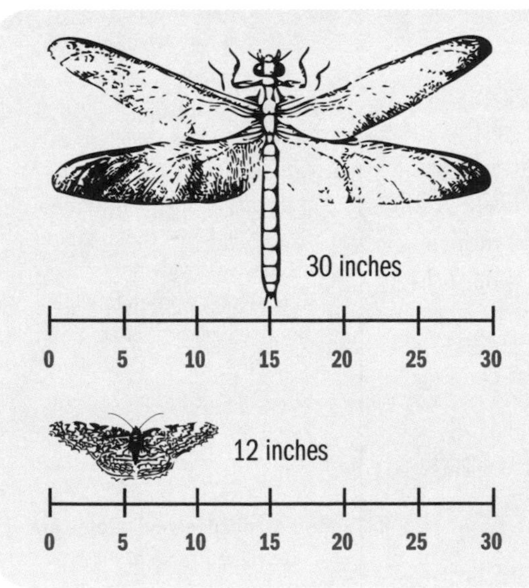

WORLD'S BIGGEST BUGS

Largest ever:
the extinct Meganeuropsis, a 18-inch-long dragonfly with a 30-inch wingspan

Largest living today:
the White Witch moth (Central and South America), with a 12-inch wingspan

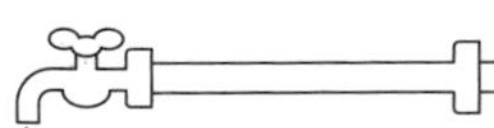

LIFE BEFORE AMAZON

Before the Internet existed, there was nothing quite like getting a big Montgomery Ward or Sears catalog in the mail and drooling over the goodies inside. Here's the story of the catalog that started it all.

THE SALESMAN

In the late 1860s, Aaron Montgomery Ward was a traveling salesman in his mid-20s, working for a dry-goods wholesaler named Wills, Greg & Company. He spent a lot of time in the rural South trying to drum up sales for his company. As he went from town to town, he got an earful from customers who complained that the country stores had very little selection and charged too much for their merchandise. Shopkeepers sold goods on credit, and adjusted prices from one customer to another. If a customer seemed creditworthy, they might—*might*—get a good price, but if not, they certainly didn't. And if the merchandise was shoddy and fell apart soon after purchase, tough luck! Refunds were seldom offered.

As Ward listened to these complaints, he came up with a business idea that he believed would deliver better value to rural customers: selling goods direct by mail from a central distribution center. He figured if he set up operations in Chicago, the nation's railroad hub, he could ship goods all over the country by rail, and customers could pick them up at the nearest train station. The prices would be listed right in the catalog, no haggling would be necessary, and payment would be in cash—no credit would be offered. By buying goods in large quantities and cutting out layers of middlemen who were normally required to transport goods from the city out into the country, he'd save a fortune...and he'd pass the savings on to his customers in the form of lower prices.

MAIL ORDER

Ward thought his idea was a good one, but nobody else did, and he had trouble getting his business off the ground. He lost his initial inventory in the Great Chicago Fire of October 1871, but by August 1872, he'd raised another $1,600 in start-up capital and tried again. This time he mailed out a single-page "catalog" to prospective customers listing 163 items for sale, along with instructions on how to place an order. The business got up and running, but sales were slow and Ward continued to struggle; his two business partners backed out of the venture the following year.

It's a safe bet that those partners lived to regret their decision, because Ward's idea caught on and his business began to grow. People got used to—and even started to enjoy—sending away for things in the mail. Country store owners didn't

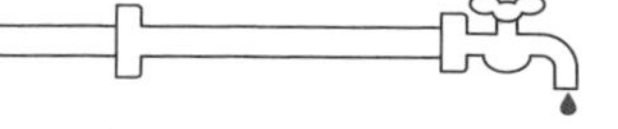

appreciate the competition; some of them demonstrated their frustration by burning Montgomery Ward catalogs in the street. But the customers loved it, and as sales grew so did the selection of goods and the size of the catalogs. By 1875, the catalog sold 65 pages' worth of goods; eight years later, the catalog was 240 pages long and sold 10,000 different items. The free catalogs became so popular—and in that age of limited entertainment opportunities, so much fun to flip through and look at all the merchandise—that they became known as "Wish Books."

GOOD TIMES, BAD TIMES

Ward had few competitors in the mail-order business until 1892, when two businessmen named Richard Sears & Alvah Roebuck launched their own mail-order firm. By 1900, Sears, Roebuck & Company had grown to be even larger than Montgomery Ward, giving customers more variety than Ward had ever intended. But despite the competition, general merchandise catalog companies remained strong into the 1980s.

The golden age of the mail-order catalog is long gone; Montgomery Ward mailed its last catalog in 1985 and went out of business in 2001. Today a small mail-order business owns the name and even distributes catalogs, but it does a fraction of the business that the original Montgomery Ward did in its heyday. Sears shuttered its catalog business in 1993, and by 2020 had closed all but 182 of its 3,500 stores after filing for bankruptcy in 2018. Amazon, an online version of what Montgomery Ward and Sears used to be, is the heart of retailing today.

MEMORY LANE

The old catalogs are still popular with collectors, who love to flip through the pages and look at merchandise that hasn't been sold for decades. If you've got one lying around, hang on to it! It might be valuable. In good condition, the rarest and most sought-after catalogs sell for hundreds of dollars on eBay. Here's a look at some of the merchandise we found in a Montgomery Ward catalog from 1935:

- Complete 9-piece Boy's Cowboy Suit (hat, shirt, chaps, belt, vest, neck kerchief, gun, holster, and lariat), ages 4–14 years: **$1.98**
- Men's Trench Coat: **$2.98**
- Celluloid and Bamboo "Manheim-Type" Slide Rule: **$4.19**
- Men's 3-piece Virgin Wool Worsted Suit: **$16.95**; **$22.50** with Two Pairs of Trousers
- Men's Rayon Boxer Shorts: **23¢**
- 4-piece boy's sailor suit (shirt, pants, undershirt, belt): **98¢**
- Console (free-standing floor model) AM Radio, Long and Short Wave: **$74.50**, or **$7** down and **$7** a month
- Child's "Air-Flow Design Sky King" Tricycle with Electric Headlight and Red and Green Cruising Lights: **$5.79**

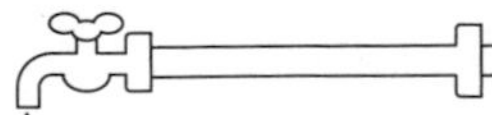

- Iron (gasoline fueled): **$3.89**
- Iron (electric): **$3.75**
- 32-piece Dinner China Set, Pussy Willow Pattern: **$2.98**
- 3-Piece Walnut Bedroom Set (bed, dresser, chest of drawers): **$27.85**
- Ladies' Suede Leather Jacket: **$4.79**
- Tarzan Novels: **63¢** each
- Home Barber Kit with Hand-powered Clippers: **$1.19**
- Big Beautiful Dolls that Cry and Sleep: **95¢**
- Ladies' Dainty 7-Jewel Baguette Wristwatch: **$14.50**
- Betty Boop and Popeye Pocket Watches: **98¢** each
- Mickey Mouse Wristwatch: **$2.69**
- Guitar, 2-in-1 for Spanish or Hawaiian Playing: **$4.98**
- Learn to Play the Guitar at Home, 12 Complete Lessons: **$1.39**
- Tenor Saxophone: **$62.95**
- Castile Shampoo, 1 lb. 2 oz: **9¢**
- Woodbury Facial Soap: 3 bars for **49¢**
- Lucky Tiger Dandruff Remover: **37¢.**
- Cod Liver Oil, 1 pint: **49¢**
- Electric Automatic Washing Machine: **$69.85**
- Hand-powered Washing Machine: **$9.95**
- Ladies' All Wool Swimsuit: **$1.69**
- Noiseless Portable Typewriter: **$67.50**
- Our Most Popular Accordion: **$11.65**
- Imported English Saddle: **$36.95**
- 34-Key Piano Accordion: **$64.95**
- Men's Dress Shirts ("Choice of Any Shirt on This Page!"): **$1.39**
- Electric Console Sewing Machine: **$54.50**
- Speedline Roller Skates with New Dreadnought Wheels: **$1.59**
- Foot-powered Sewing Machine: **$26.50**
- Ladies' All Wool Nubbed Tweed Suit: **$9.98**
- Bolt-Action Rifle: **$9.25**
- Spring Plaid Wallpaper: 10-ft. by 12-ft.: **$2.29**
- Full Porcelain Gasoline Stove and Oven Range: **$54.95**
- Ladies' Hat with Scarf to Match: **49¢**
- Ladies' Corset ("Don't Let Your Figure 'Give Away' Your Age!): **$1.84**
- Child's Bicycle with Electric Horn and Headlight: **$34.95**
- Built-in Recess Bathtub: **$25.95**
- Ladies' Pure Silk Stockings: **44¢** a pair
- Girls' Printed Cotton Dress: **49¢**
- Men's denim overalls: **74¢**
- Ladies' Fine Cotton Dresses, choice of eight styles: **$1.88 each**
- Mantle (table or shelf model) AM Radio, Long and Short Wave: **$30.95**

Day job of Rudolph Hass, who developed the popular Hass avocado: mailman.

SURVIVAL STORIES

Never underestimate the power of the human spirit.

INTO THE WOODS

Mary Byman's fight for her life began as a leisurely stroll to pick berries on a July 2019 afternoon in a rural Manitoba, Canada, forest. The 84-year-old woman and her friend had a system: If either got lost, they would blow a whistle. Byman got lost. She blew her whistle, but her friend was out of earshot. Before she knew it, night was approaching, and she had no idea where the car was parked. So she hunkered down.

The next morning, an official search commenced for an octogenarian "wearing a long-sleeved blue-and-white checked blouse." Rachel Geurts, Byman's granddaughter, joined the search party. "We had drones, we had a helicopter and two planes," she told reporters. "There were dogs, there were horses, there were people on ATVs. They said something like 300 people had come [to help] over the course of three to four days." But they couldn't find Byman, and time was running out. The forest was, as one official described it, "a tangled mass of fallen trees and overgrown ravines." There were also swamps and hidden animal dens. After five days and no sign, Geurts was told there was little chance of finding her grandmother alive.

After five days and no sign, Geurts was told there was little chance of finding her grandmother alive.

That's not to say they gave up hope. A few hours after the search-and-rescue mission had turned into one of search and recovery, one of the searchers fired a gun into the air. Then they heard a faint voice calling out, "Please help me" and started making their way through the dense forest, looking for the source of the calls. Forty minutes later, Byman was found beneath some thick brush. It took another two hours for firefighters to cut a path to get her out of there. It was unclear how long Byman, who was without her medications and had lost her whistle, had been stuck in that spot, or what she had done to survive for a week on her own. But she was found only a mile and a half away from where she got lost. "After trying to deal with them telling you that she's dead," said Geurts, "for her to sort of pop back to life, it's unbelievable. She's obviously made of some strong stuff."

EYE IN THE SKY

Hurricane Michael was expected to hit the Florida Panhandle in October 2018 as the first Category 5 hurricane to make U.S. landfall since 1992. Ernest Gee's rural property was 20 miles inland, so he, his wife, and a friend made the decision to ride out the storm. Good news: they survived. Bad news: downed trees blocked their only escape route. With no power or water, and no way to call loved ones or the

First person to buy a ticket for the first comic book convention in New York in 1964: *Game of Thrones* author George R. R. Martin.

authorities, Gee collected some fallen limbs and spelled out the word "HELP" on his lawn. Three days passed without anyone locating them. Ernest's niece, Amber Gee, had evacuated her home on the coast before the storm hit, so she was safe, but she was worried about her uncle. "I had been seeing this link to [aerial] images [of the destruction] all over Facebook," she told ABC News, "and I decided to check it out." A minute later, she was on the National Oceanic and Atmospheric Administration's website, looking at a recent satellite image that included her uncle's property. It looked abandoned...until she zoomed in and saw the word "HELP" on the lawn. Amber immediately called 911, and rescuers responded, cutting their way through a mess of downed trees, which took hours, until they finally reached Gee and his companions at 2:00 a.m. They were all okay.

STAYING AFLOAT

Kay Longstaff insisted that she fell off the cruise ship. Croatian authorities countered that CCTV footage proves she fell "in a voluntary and determined fashion." According to news reports, the 46-year-old vacationing British flight attendant had been drinking and had a quarrel with her boyfriend. Then she reportedly walked to the stern (rear) of the ship, where she casually started to take off her clothes. Then Longstaff climbed up the railing...and fell (or jumped) overboard. After slamming her cheek on the water, she regained her senses and started treading water. She was 60 miles out to sea without a life jacket or much else on, and night was falling.

Meanwhile, back on the cruise ship, several hours had passed before Longstaff was reported missing. At around 2:00 a.m., the captain rang the alarm bell and announced that he was turning the ship around: "We have a reported jumper and we're now in a search-and-rescue mission." The next morning, nearly ten hours after Longstaff fell (or jumped), the coast guard located her. She was weak and dazed but somehow still barely treading water. She credited her survival to two things: her yoga practice, which kept her fit, and singing, which kept her warm and awake. Unfortunately, the question of whether Longstaff fell or jumped marred her amazing tale of survival. "I just want to go home," she told reporters.

HOUSE BOAT

A *rompong* is a small, wooden raft with a one-person hut built on top. Aldi Adilang had lived and worked on his rompong—located about 75 miles off the coast of Indonesia—since he was 16. Every night, his job was to light the lamp in order to attract fish to the traps below. His only lifelines were a rope anchored to the ocean floor and supplies delivered once a week. By the time he was 18, his rompong had already broken free of its line twice. Both times, he was quickly rescued. But when Adilang's line broke during a summer storm in 2018, the weather was too rough to mount a search. By the time the seas calmed, he was adrift hundreds of miles away with no oar to steer him or motor to propel him. He was presumed lost.

The hut kept Adilang protected from the elements, and he had several weeks' worth of food, water, and fuel for his generator. Now, he just had to hunker down and wait for rescue. "After a week," he later told reporters, "I started to get scared." And frustrated, too, as ship after ship passed by but failed to see him waving his blanket from the tiny raft. One ship's captain said by walkie-talkie that he would turn around...but never did. "There were times when I was crying and thinking about killing myself," Adilang admitted.

After more than a month passed, the rains had stopped and the castaway's supply of fuel and fresh water ran out. He drank seawater that he filtered through his T-shirt (not recommended) and lit fires from whatever wood he could spare from the rompong. He had to fish for tuna from the boat because of all the sharks swimming around. To pass the time, he sang gospel songs, read from his Bible, and marked off each day on a calendar. On day 49, Adilang saw a passing ship and waved his flag while repeating into his walkie-talkie the only English word he knew: "Help!" The ship kept going, and once again the teen's hopes of rescue seemed dashed. But then the ship, the MV *Arpeggio* out of Panama, turned around and Adilang was finally rescued! He was severely dehydrated but otherwise in surprisingly good shape after spending nearly two months alone on the open ocean. He'd almost made it to Japan, several thousand miles away from home.

SHUT IN

In September 2018, a three-alarm fire tore through a public housing senior apartment building in Washington, D.C. Firefighters went door to door to get everyone out, but the walls and roof began to cave in, so they had to flee the building. Outside, there was some confusion as to whether all the residents had escaped. Someone from the property management company checked an occupancy list and said that everyone was accounted for. But there were *two* different lists, and doubts lingered.

After the fire was extinguished, the building was condemned and the entrance was sealed. Five days later, after structural engineers had deemed the area safe enough to conduct a search, police went in with rescue dogs. They knew that if they found anyone, more than likely it would be a body. Then, on the second floor, the searchers heard someone yelling from an apartment. It took ten minutes and some heavy equipment to get through the swollen, waterlogged door. Inside was a 74-year-old man who'd been stuck in there for nearly a week without any power or running water. He rationed a few bottles of water to stay hydrated, and nibbled on what little food he had. "For somebody that's been in that situation for as long as him," said structural engineer Allyn Kilsheimer, "he seemed incredibly in good shape." The survivor was taken to the hospital with minor injuries. "Very lucky man," observed Kilsheimer.

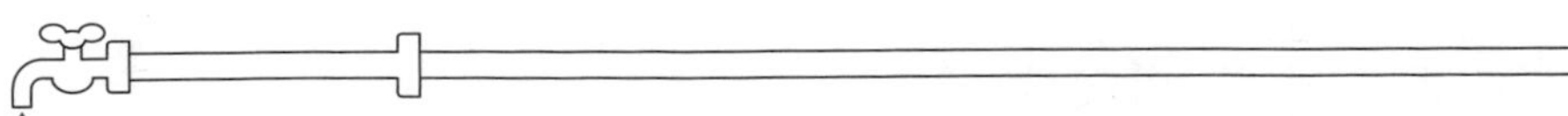

"HERE IT IS, BAM!"

The music business is littered with the corpses of short-lived careers—acts that had one big success on the pop chart...and couldn't duplicate it. But it wasn't for a lack of trying. Can you match the one-hit wonder to their feeble follow-up? Answers are on page 405.

1) Carl Douglas, "Kung Fu Fighting" (1974)
2) Tag Team, "Whoomp! (There It Is)" (1993)
3) Jan Hammer, "Miami Vice Theme" (1985)
4) Larry Verne, "Mr. Custer" (1960)
5) Rick Dees, "Disco Duck" (1976)
6) Taco, "Puttin' on the Ritz" (1982)
7) Sugarhill Gang, "Rapper's Delight" (1979)
8) Bobbie Gentry, "Ode to Billie Joe" (1967)
9) The Buggles, "Video Killed the Radio Star" (1979)
10) Kyu Sakamoto, "Sukiyaki" (1963)
11) Buckner and Garcia, "Pac-Man Fever" (1982)
12) Starland Vocal Band, "Afternoon Delight" (1976)
13) Toni Basil, "Mickey" (1982)
14) Barry McGuire, "Eve of Destruction" (1965)
15) Nena, "99 Luftballons" (1983)
16) Right Said Fred, "I'm Too Sexy" (1991)
17) Patrick Swayze, "She's Like the Wind" (1987)
18) Los Del Río, "Macarena" (1993)
19) Napoleon XIV, "They're Coming to Take Me Away, Ha-Haaa!" (1966)
20) James Blunt, "You're Beautiful" (2005)

a. "Macarena Christmas"
b. "China Nights"
c. "Rapper's Reprise (Jam Jam)"
d. "I Saw an Angel Die"
e. "California Day"
f. "Doin' the Napoleon"
g. "Don't Talk Just Kiss"
h. "Dis-Gorilla"
i. "Leuchtturm"
j. "Do the Donkey Kong"
k. "Here It Is, Bam!"
l. "Mister Livingston"
m. "Singin' in the Rain"
n. "Living in the Plastic Age"
o. "Crockett's Theme"
p. "Goodbye My Lover"
q. "Child of Our Times"
r. "Nobody"
s. "Raising Heaven (in Hell Tonight)"
t. "Dance the Kung Fu"

Before Jim Carrey was cast as the Grinch in 1999, Eddie Murphy and Jack Nicholson were considered for the part.

APARKALYPSE NOW, PART II

The esteemed philosopher Yogi Berra once said, "Nobody goes there anymore, it's too crowded." He was referring to a restaurant, but the same could be said about America's national parks and outdoor recreation areas. The busiest ones can look like something out of a Mad Max movie. And the collateral damage is spreading. *(Part I is on page 197.)*

GROUND ZEROES

Almost every outdoor tourist destination in the United States started seeing massive crowds in the 2010s, and some spots really got hit hard. "Over a period of four months," reported the *Guardian* in 2018, "[we] dispatched writers across the American West to examine how overcrowding is playing out at ground level. We found a brewing crisis: 2-mile-long 'bison jams' in Yellowstone, fistfights in parking lots at Glacier, a small Colorado town overrun by millions of visitors." It doesn't even need to be a national park or a famous landmark. It just needs to go viral.

WHAT'S THAT SMELL?

In late 2009, the *Oregonian*'s online magazine published a seemingly innocent article that included "a list of the state's best natural hot springs, which have seen little or no development. All you need to enjoy them is plenty of water, a good map, clear roads, and careful directions." Then came links to the directions, then came the copycat articles, and the copycats of the copycat articles, and then shares of those copycat articles. Result: the hot springs were inundated by so many weekend warriors that some have had to build parking areas and charge entrance fees. Hit especially hard was Umpqua Hot Springs, a four-hour drive south of Portland in the Cascade mountains. In the past, you would have needed a map just to find the trailhead, and then a trail book to find the pools. Now you simply enter the location into your phone and follow the directions.

Umpqua Hot Springs got so overrun with visitors that in 2016, the area was closed to overnight camping. Reason: according to the *Oregonian,* campers were dumping their trash on the ground, removing trees, and "leaving behind incredible amounts of human waste." When the same thing happened at Conundrum Hot Springs in the Colorado Rockies after it became popular online in 2018, the U.S. Forest Service had to institute a paid permit system and a "human waste awareness campaign."

#POPPYNIGHTMARE

In March 2019, Southern California's poppy "superbloom" exploded on social media, enticing the hordes to hop in their cars and head to Lake Elsinore, about 90 minutes

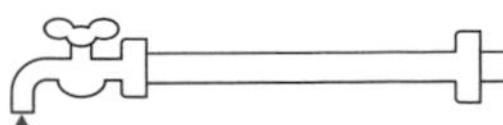

south of Los Angeles. Over the weekend of the peak bloom, the city of 66,000 was getting 50,000 visitors per day, causing traffic jams, car accidents, and mad dashes to find parking spots so that they could catch the shuttles to Walker Canyon, where the delicate orange flowers were blanketing the steep slopes. The Palm Springs *Desert Sun* dispatched this harrowing report from the scene:

> "Wildflower-seekers slid and fell down the side of Walker Canyon that was never meant to be hiked on, though some managed to do so anyways—even in very chic wedge heels. Families and Instagram-influencer wannabes alike attempted feats of free-climbing and scrambling as large boulders toppled down behind them as every step kicked more rocks loose, threatening to squish children or seniors who couldn't lunge out of the way fast enough."

Local officials used the city's Facebook page to issue pleas for people to turn around: "Our city is not made for Disneyland size crowds!" On Sunday, they finally had no choice but to initiate #PoppyShutdown (also using the hashtags #PoppyNightmare and #IsItOverYet). The shuttle service was canceled, and the canyon was closed to the public until the poppies faded and no one cared anymore.

But it didn't end there. In the middle of the *Desert Sun* story was this embedded ad: "Best Spring Destinations to See Flowers Bloom, from Arizona to Japan." Clickbait articles like that and the social media shares they generate have caused an invasion of public (and sometimes private) flower farms all over the world. In July 2019, the owners of a lavender farm near Milton, Ontario, took their complaints about selfie-seekers to CTV News: "We love it when they sit next to the lavender and carefully respect the lavender, but you'll find people lie in the lavender and crush it. Once it's crushed, we can't harvest it." He added that when he asks people to step out of the lavender, many refuse, saying, "Hey, I paid to come in here."

PARKS AND WRECK

More people brings more rule breakers—from selfie-seeking influencers (and wannabe influencers), to landscape and wildlife photographers focused on getting the perfect shot, to stereotypical "city folk" who don't see the harm in petting the wildlife. So it's not surprising that the 2010s saw an unprecedented number of people getting injured or even killed at national parks.

- From 2008 to 2017, Yellowstone National Park in Wyoming recorded "a 90-percent increase in vehicle accidents, a 60-percent bump in ambulance calls, and a 130-percent rise in searches and rescues." In 2016, a 13-year-old boy received serious burns after his father, who was carrying him off-trail, slipped and fell into a hot spring. A few days later, a 23-year-old man was killed in a hot spring after he left the boardwalk at Norris Geyser.

In Denmark, it's illegal to burn any country's flag...except Denmark's.

- At the Grand Canyon, over a period of three weeks in March 2019, there were four separate incidents of visitors who fell to their deaths. (At least two were attempting selfies.)
- In February 2019, a 56-year-old California woman ignored closure signs at Yosemite's Mist Trail, which was cordoned off due to icy conditions. She was struck by falling rocks and ice, and died. The previous summer on that same trail, a teenager visiting from Israel attempted to duplicate a popular "hanging from a rock" selfie. Despite warnings from other visitors not to, and heroic efforts to save him, he fell to his death. That wasn't long after a married couple—the wife was a popular Instagram travel blogger—fell to their deaths off another Yosemite cliff. All that was left was their camera on a tripod.

There's a selfie epidemic taking place in national parks. As Michael Ghiglieri, coauthor of *Off the Wall: Death in Yosemite,* told the *Los Angeles Daily News,* "In the old days people went out to have an experience. Now they go out to record that they had that experience."

IT ONLY TAKES ONE

Higher attendance has also led to more willful destruction of some of the NPS's most sensitive areas, where stepping off the trail or going off-road—even by just a few feet—can potentially cause damage. Doing donuts in a 4x4 can cause carnage:

- In July 2018, a visitor at Oregon's Crater Lake National Park took a joyride across the Pumice Desert—a large wildflower meadow on top of a thick layer of volcanic ash. According to news reports, the car left ruts a foot deep and destroyed a wide swath of plant life, including at least 15 native species. The man had to pay $60,000 in fines for the damage.
- At Racetrack Playa, where the boulders famously move across a flat desert lake bed in California's Death Valley National Park, there are numerous "No Motor Vehicles Allowed" signs. But that didn't stop an unknown person (or persons) from leaving 15 miles of tire tracks across the surface in 2016. That's not the only time someone has done this to Racetrack Playa. (Maybe they should change the name.) The high cost to build a barrier around the remote area—which can only be accessed via a 27-mile dirt road—means it will remain unprotected.
- In 2016, a crew of YouTube influencers from Vancouver, B.C.—members of a group called "High on Life"—drove their bright blue RV past closure signs and water-skied across Utah's Bonneville Salt Flats, causing extensive damage. The young men were also caught on video—taken by witnesses *and* themselves—stomping all over Yellowstone's delicate Grand Prismatic Spring, riding their bikes

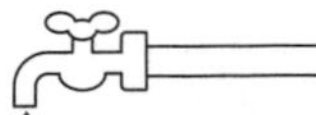

off-trail at Death Valley, and illegally using a drone in Colorado's Mesa Verde National Park. Two of them spent a week in jail, and all had to pay hefty fines.

LEAVING THEIR MARK

Of course, not everyone who harms nature does it with malice. Take the two (now former) Boy Scout leaders in Utah's Goblin Valley State Park who posted a video of themselves toppling a hoodoo—a giant, 170-million-year-old rock formation. The men argued in court that they did it to "prevent the rock from hurting anyone," but later acknowledged that if they really thought it was a danger, they should have notified a ranger.

Fortunately, they didn't have millions of impressionable Instagram followers, like Vanessa Hudgens did when she carved a heart with "Austin + Vanessa" onto a rock in the Coconino National Forest outside Sedona, Arizona, on Valentine's Day 2016. In doing so, she broke federal law for defacing a natural feature and was fined $1,000 by the U.S. Forest Service. "I'm such an earth person, I love Mother Nature," the former Disney star said in her defense on the radio show *Sway in the Morning.* "Literally, I took a piece of rock and wrote on the rock, so it's the type of thing where it's chalk. If you rub it, it comes off, so I knew that, like, with the first rain it would go away." That might sound reasonable, but it isn't. Scratch-marks can take decades or more to disappear; in fact, some ancient petroglyphs were made the exact same way. And as Coconino National Forest Public Affairs Officer Brady Smith pointed out to *US Weekly,* "We have found that when one person carves something, it encourages others to carve." Especially when that person posts a selfie with the carving to her 10 million-plus Instagram followers. That can lead to stories like these:

- In 2014, a 21-year-old New York woman used permanent acrylics and markers to paint weird faces at iconic spots in seven national parks in the West. Then she posted selfies with the images onto her Facebook and Tumblr pages. (She got two years' probation.)
- In 2019, a young couple posted Instagram selfies of their freshly carved initials ("B+X") at Council Overhang, a 425-million-year-old rock formation and sacred Native American site in Illinois's Starved Rock State Park. At last report, they were still at large.

KEEP OFF THE BISON

Increased human presence has also wreaked havoc on the animals, especially at Yellowstone. Every visitor is warned at the entrance, in the visitors' guide, and on signs throughout the park *not* to approach the animals. But many do it anyway:

- "According to witnesses," said an NPS report, "a group of approximately

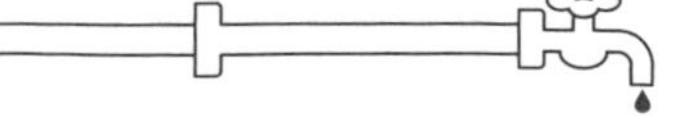

50 people were within 5–10 feet of the bison for at least 20 minutes before eventually causing the bison to charge the group." A disturbing 12-second video shows what happened next. Two adults run one way, leaving a 9-year-old Florida girl to fend for herself. Right after she turns to run, the charging, 1,000-pound bison head-butts her from behind, throwing her several feet through the air like a rag doll. (She survived.)

- In May 2016, two Yellowstone tourists, described in reports as a "father and son from another country," drove to a ranger station with a bison calf in their back seat and said they rescued it from a field because it looked too cold. The calf was later rejected by its herd and had to be euthanized. The dad got a ticket.

Similar reports from Yellowstone include a man who teased and then lunged at a bison, a woman who was injured after trying to take a selfie with a bison, and many more. "We're exceeding [our] capacity," said former Yellowstone superintendent Dan Wenk. "Our own species is having the greatest impact on the park."

HERD MENTALITY

Another problem: people are trying to beat the crowds by going farther out into nature. In many remote areas, that's been bad news for nature. And it's been especially bad for the Vail elk herd, which inhabits a wilderness area in the Rocky Mountains near Vail, Colorado. In 2009, biologists flew above the herd and counted more than 1,000 elk roaming through the snowy terrain. Ten years later, biologists flew over the same herd and counted only 53. Instead of animal tracks, they saw ski tracks.

Until recently, many of these trails were considered "backcountry." Now, some of them see up to 500 hikers a day—and the elk must contend with hikers, bikers, backpackers, school field trips, photography workshops, and in many places Jeeps, all-terrain vehicles, and motorcycles. Thanks to improved mapping technology and more cell phone towers, people are making it farther into the wilderness than ever before, even in the winter, which brings a steady stream of snowmobiles and cross-country skiers.

Elk are so vulnerable because they are easily spooked—especially pregnant or nursing females. Whenever people enter their habitat, the skittish elk scatter and run away. When this happens every day and night (even "night hiking" is now a fad), the females can either become separated from their young—which are left vulnerable to predators and the elements—or the females become so stressed that they stop producing milk.

And the elks' decline isn't just happening in Colorado; similar elk populations are under siege at Point Reyes National Seashore, just north of San Francisco, and at several other remote areas once known for their solitude. Colorado Parks and

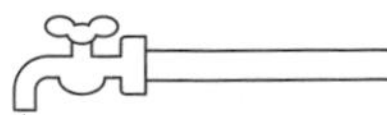

Wildlife's district wildlife manager Devin Duval warns that if trail expansion into critical elk habitat continues, "it will be a biological desert."

LOUD NOISES!

"After visiting Monument Valley about 12 years ago, I was looking forward to showing it to my family," began a 1-star TripAdvisor review. "While the sites were still incredibly beautiful, the peaceful desert silence I remember from years ago is now marred by the sounds of tour buses and hundreds of tourists."

To find out exactly how loud it's gotten in protected areas, researchers at the NPS and Colorado State University made recordings at 492 sites across the country in 2017. Their findings, as reported by *Science* magazine: "Noise pollution from humans has doubled sound levels in more than half of all protected areas in the United States—from local nature reserves to national parks—and it has made some places 10 times louder." This does more than mar the human experience. It can negatively impact animals that rely on hearing to hunt, or to hide from hunters, or to find a mate.

WORST-CASE SCENARIOS

What's the worst that can happen? The damage suffered by California's Joshua Tree National Park during a partial government shutdown in January 2019 illustrates what could transpire if the NPS loses the ability to protect these sensitive areas. When staffers returned to a campground that had been closed for only *one week*, they discovered that hundreds of people had camped there anyway. According to the *Los Angeles Times*, they also discovered "24 miles of unauthorized trails carved into the desert landscape by off-road vehicles, along with some of the park's namesake trees toppled." Not just Joshua trees—dozens of juniper and acacias were chopped down and burned in more than 100 illegal firepits. Park officials said some of the more sensitive areas could take centuries to recover.

"Park and recreation funding has been slow to recover since the end of the recession," reported the National Recreation and Parks Association in 2018. The decade ended with a backlog of $11 billion for crucial maintenance to park trails and roads, while the NPS was facing even steeper budget cuts. Entrance fees were raised to $35 per vehicle, but it will take more than that to keep the parks maintained. One extreme example is the busy toilet at the top of Zion's Angels Landing trail: It costs $20,000 per year to empty by helicopter. Not all park toilets are that expensive, but there are thousands upon thousands of them filling up faster than ever before. And when the toilet lines get too long, nature becomes the toilet.

To find out how we can all enjoy the outdoors without soiling it for future generations, tread lightly over to page 382.

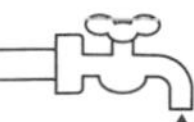

Pros and cons: Citizens of Monaco pay no taxes but are not allowed to step foot in the country's casinos (unless they work there).

IT'S A WEIRD, WEIRD WORLD

Is it just us, or is the world getting weirder?

A CLEAN GETAWAY

In May 2019, Nate Roman, 44, of Marlboro, Massachusetts, arrived home and noticed immediately that something wasn't right. After looking around the house, he called the police. What was wrong? The place was too clean. "You could smell the cleaning chemicals," he told reporters, and the house was spotless. "My son's room has never looked better," he said. The cops were just as dumbfounded as Roman was. Their theory: a professional cleaning service went to the wrong address, and got in through the unlocked back door. That would explain the toilet paper origami roses that Roman found in his bathroom. He admitted that the experience was unsettling... but he was so impressed with the work that he'd like to know how much the intruders would charge to do it again.

TV ON THE DOORSTEP

In a scene that one bewildered cop described as "very *Twilight Zone*," 50 residents in rural Virginia awoke one morning in July 2019 to find a television set sitting on their doorstep facing the front door. These weren't late-model flat-screens—they were old-style tube televisions. Whoever left the odd gifts is a mystery, but according to security footage, there were at least two of them; both were wearing jumpsuits, and both had TVs over their heads to hide their identities. According to police officer Matt Pecka, "We determined there was no credible threat to residents and that this was strictly an inconvenience." As of last report, police have no leads, and because no actual crime was committed, they said they won't be investigating further.

MANSTER

Proving that sometimes the scariest monsters can come from real life, in 2019, a new foe was added to the role-playing game *Dungeons & Dragons*: "Florida Man." Based on the popular meme that celebrates weird criminals from the Sunshine State, this monster was introduced on the Twitter account RPGSite as yet another way for Dungeon Masters to terrorize players. According to comicbook.com, Florida Man is "presented as an agent of chaos, with the ability to spontaneously toss either unsecured objects or creatures at opponents. If there's not an unsecured object nearby, the Florida Man can then pull out a small alligator from its biomass and toss it at enemies instead." Warning to *D&D* devotees: be careful using magic to defeat Florida Man, "as he can turn players into chickens."

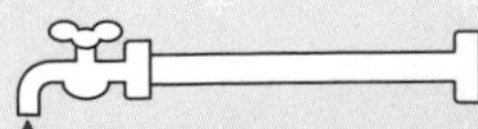

KFC founder Colonel Sanders also practiced law and obstetrics, even though he wasn't licensed to do either.

BIG BROTHER IS WATCHING

Mark "Iceman" Fellows was a man of many talents—a competitive runner and cyclist... who moonlighted as a mob hit man. He was the leading suspect in a 2015 murder, but police had no evidence, and potential witnesses were afraid to come forward. In 2018, an astute investigator was looking at a photo of Fellows competing in the Great Manchester 10K that took place about two months before the murder. Fellows was wearing a Garmin Forerunner watch that runners use to track their race times. Police seized the watch, which, thanks to its GPS tracker, put Fellows at the scene of not only one mob hit but two. He was convicted of both murders and sentenced to life in prison.

LAUGH OUT LOUD

Art and technology came together aboard the International Space Station (ISS) in 2016. Israeli artist Eyal Gever launched a contest in which more than 100,000 entrants used an app to record themselves laughing. Then Gever, teaming with a 3-D printing company from California, selected the best laugh and converted the sound waves into a "3-D visualization" that was printed on the ISS. The resulting work of art, called a "laugh star" (it looks like a cross between a star and a donut), is the first sculpture ever created in zero gravity.

MAID-OF-HONORSAURUS

In 2019, Christina Meador was asked to be maid of honor at her sister Deana Adams's wedding in Nebraska. Knowing that Meador wasn't happy about the idea of wearing a formal dress, Adams told her she could wear whatever she wanted. "I was trying to think of something that I would be willing to wear more than once," Meador told the *Daily Mail*, "and if I'm spending more than $50, I want it to be a dinosaur costume, because they're fantastic and I've always wanted one." So, with the bride's blessing, Meador attended the ceremony wearing a seven-foot-tall, inflatable Tyrannosaurus rex costume. Despite barely being able to see—and taking some criticism on social media—Meador said, "I regret nothing."

PETE THE PHOTOGRAPHER

In October 2019, the London Zoo announced that, for the first time in history, a plant has snapped its own selfie. The plant—a maidenhair fern named Pete—deposits biomatter into the soil. After microbes eat the biomatter, they release energy that slowly charges a super-capacitor. Once it has enough power, it activates a camera pointed at the plant. The resulting photograph, best described as a "blurry picture of some leaves," is the only photo ever taken by a plant. According to researchers, this tech could be used to keep remote field cameras charged, even in the shade. (Pete couldn't be reached for comment.)

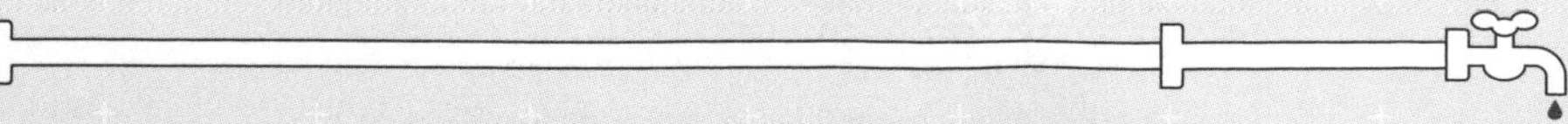

According to the Dead Sea Scrolls, Goliath was 6'9" tall.

INDIANS, MONSTERS, AND APPROPRIATION

When Uncle John was a kid, he played "Cowboys and Indians." That game hasn't aged well—mainly because the Indians were usually the bad guys. These days, as we learn more about indigenous cultures (properly referred to as American Indians in the United States, and First Peoples in Canada), it becomes obvious that negative portrayals in games aren't the only way a culture can be co-opted.

GATHER 'ROUND THE FIRE

Every culture has its own rich mythology. In modern times, the larger-than-life characters that were born out of these myths mainly serve as distractions from the daily grind. But for many American Indians (a term that most Indians prefer to Native Americans), legends play a sacred role, as they have for thousands of years. It's no secret that following the Europeans' arrival in the New World, most native peoples were driven from their ancestral lands and later forced onto reservations, where they were often forbidden to speak their own languages. But that didn't stop many of their myths and legends from being co-opted by their conquerors.

Known today as "cultural appropriation," the practice goes back to ancient times. For example, the Romans conquered the Greeks and appropriated their gods: Zeus became Jupiter, Aphrodite became Venus, and so on. But the Romans considered the Greeks to be superior, which is not how most Europeans viewed Indians. Over time, it became an accepted fact that members of a dominant society could appropriate aspects of a minority culture—music, art, religion, fashion, sports, stories, language, etc.—and use them in any way they choose, the grown-up equivalent of playing "Cowboys and Indians."

In fact, that's what happened to one of the most famous indigenous legends of them all.

SASQ'ETS

When it comes to American Indians and First Peoples, it can be difficult to trace a mythical monster's origin back to a single tribe or nation. In many cases, the stories were passed between neighboring cultures that spoke different languages, few of which were written down. (Today, most of those languages are gone or critically endangered.)

But one legend—that of a mystical race of tall, hairy Indians called *Sasq'ets* (pronounced sess-kah-uts) was first attributed to the Chehalis Band that lived along the Harrison River in southern British Columbia. Now known as the Sts'ailes First Nation, they speak a language called Halq'eméylem, but they're part of a larger

language group known as the Salish (specifically the Coast Salish), who shared common words for trading and negotiating...and for sharing stories. Other tribes in southern British Columbia and western Washington called these mystical beings similar-sounding names like *Sésquac* and *Sas-ket*, which mean "wild man" or "hairy man." You probably know them better as the Sasquatch.

WHAT'S IN A NAME?

"Sasquatch," it turns out, isn't even an Indian word (nor is "Indian"). It was coined in 1929 by a white teacher named John Burns, who was the "Indian agent" on the Chehalis Reservation in Harrison Hot Springs, 80 miles east of Vancouver. Burns collected stories of these "wild men of the forest," combining the similar names to come up with the amalgamation "Sasquatch." Over the next 25 years, Burns wrote more than 50 articles about Sasquatch in *Maclean's* magazine, pushing the narrative that it was no myth:

> "I am convinced...the Sasquatch do still inhabit the inaccessible interior of British Columbia. Only by sheer luck, however, is a white man likely to sight one of them because, like wild animals, they instinctively avoid all contact with civilization and in that rocky country it is impossible to track them down. I still live in hope of someday surprising a Sasquatch, and when that happens, to have a camera handy."

A NEW LOOK

When you think of Sasquatch, you probably picture an apelike creature covered in thick, brown fur that speaks in grunts, growls, and howls. That's a far cry from the beings that the Salish people originally described to Burns. They described the Sasq'ets as a tribe of humans, not beasts, who are covered in hair, not fur. Most were very tall, and they were naked. The Chehalis described them as a secretive tribe with its own language, who are almost always seen just one at a time. In many of the legends, they have the ability to pass between this world and the spirit world.

But as Burns's articles gained popularity, there were a growing number of "eyewitness" reports, and the creature's features began to change. In 1955, a highway worker named William Roe claimed he was hiking alone in the remote mountains of eastern British Columbia when he spotted what he first mistook for a grizzly bear crouching on the ground, eating berries. "The shape of this creature's head somewhat resembled a Negro's," he wrote in a sworn affidavit in 1957, adding, "The head was higher at the back than at the front. The nose was broad and flat. The lips and chin protruded farther than its nose...Its arms were much thicker than a man's arms, and longer, reaching almost to its knees. I had heard stories of the Sasquatch, the giant hairy Indians that live in the legends of British Columbia Indians. Maybe this was a Sasquatch, I told myself." After Roe described it as apelike, nearly every subsequent

Ever say a word over and over until it sounds weird and meaningless? That's called *semantic satiation*.

eyewitness account painted the same basic picture.

A sanctioned "Sasquatch Hunt" held in Harrison Hot Springs in 1958 brought so many people to the region that even John Burns came to "regret that these harmless people of the wilderness are to be hunted with dogs as if they were criminals and if captured, exposed to the gaping and gaze of the curious. They have been referred to as monsters but they have committed no monstrous acts. It appears our veneer civilization does not hesitate to even use monsters for commercial purposes."

He had no idea.

THE BIGFOOTAGE

In 1958, about 1,000 miles to the south, a northern California man named Ray Wallace decided to have some fun with the Sasquatch fad, so he cut out two wooden feet, 16 inches long and seven inches wide...and left some "tracks" around a construction site. (He kept his hoax a secret until his death in 2002, when his family revealed the truth.) That summer, the *Humboldt Times*, which serves northern California's Redwood Coast, published a "fluff piece" for the Sunday edition about some local loggers who reported finding those giant footprints in the forest. They called the creature that left them "Big Foot." The article was so popular that the paper published an entire series of "Bigfoot" stories—mostly tongue-in-cheek, but serious enough to draw even more interest. That brought Bigfoot hunters to the ancient lands of the Yurok Indians, who live along the lower Klamath River and don't even have a Sasquatch-type legend (though other California tribes do). It was in 1967 along Bluff Creek, a tributary of the Klamath, that two rodeo cowboys-turned-Bigfoot-hunters filmed the famous grainy 16mm footage of a mysterious creature (or a man in a suit) briskly walking along a creek bank, supposedly a female Bigfoot that they named "Patty." The 59.5 seconds of blurry footage was one of the most scrutinized pieces of film in history (right up there with the Zapruder film of JFK's assassination), but despite that, Bigfoot's existence wasn't—and still hasn't—been confirmed by the scientific community. That classifies it as a *cryptid*, an animal whose existence is suggested but not proven.

IN SEARCH OF...

By the 1970s, the names Bigfoot and Sasquatch were being used interchangeably, and the creature's habitat expanded to wherever someone said they saw one. The sacred Salish legend joined other cryptids like the Abominable Snowman, the Loch Ness Monster, and Little Green Men on pseudoscience shows like *In Search Of...*, except that because the western United States still had large swaths of unexplored wilderness, people took Bigfoot's existence a lot more seriously. The FBI opened a file on him, and an organization called the North American Wildlife Research Team constructed a 10-foot by 10-foot "Bigfoot Trap" in a southern Oregon forest where some big footprints had been spotted. More proof that Americans became obsessed

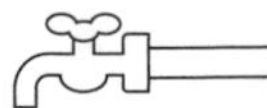

More French soldiers died in World War I than American soldiers died in all U.S. wars combined.

with the big, hairy beast:

- A 1976 two-part episode of *The Six-Million Dollar Man* called "The Secret of Bigfoot" pitted Steve Austin (Lee Majors) against Bigfoot (Andre the Giant). What was "the secret"? That Bigfoot is actually a robot built by aliens.
- "Bigfoot," the monster truck that started the monster truck craze, debuted in 1979.
- In 1987, *Harry and the Hendersons,* a comedy about a friendly Sasquatch that moves in with a suburban family, made $50 million worldwide and spawned a TV series.

Even today, the elusive cryptid is still a staple of such pseudoscience TV shows as *Finding Bigfoot* on Animal Planet and *Expedition Bigfoot* on the Travel Channel. Yet while non-Indians may enjoy searching for the creature and debating its existence, many indigenous people still hold him in the same high spiritual place they always have: "Here in the Northwest, and west of the Rockies generally," said author Gayle Highpine of Idaho's Kootenai Tribe, "Indian people regard Bigfoot with great respect. He is seen as a special kind of being, because of his obvious close relationship with humans. Some elders regard him as standing on the 'border' between animal-style consciousness and human-style consciousness, which gives him a special kind of power."

THE SKINWALKERS

The Sasq'et is just one of many indigenous monsters that have been co-opted by non-indigenous people. Another one is the Navajo Skinwalker. Actual information about the legend is scarce because, for the most part, the Navajo—who have lived in the Southwest for at least 700 years—don't talk about Skinwalkers. What is known is that the Navajo call them *Yee Naaldlooshii,* which translates to "With it, he goes on all fours." Part human, part animal, they roam at night, performing brutal acts of violence. According to legend, the Skinwalkers were once benevolent shamans who were lured to evil by a secret society, and were taught how to "walk in the skin" of any animal just by wearing its pelt. But the legend also says that, by day, a Skinwalker can look like a regular person, which is why it's still taboo for a Navajo man to wear the pelt of a predator like a wolf or a bear.

The first reported sightings of Skinwalkers among non-Indians occurred in the 1960s. In 1986, a white author named Tony Hillerman co-opted the legend for his crime novel *Skinwalkers,* about two Navajo cops who must solve a murder blamed on the mythical monster. The book was so popular, it spawned a critically acclaimed PBS TV movie, and Skinwalkers have since joined Sasquatch and other Indian legends as creatures that cryptozoologists search for in desolate areas with night-vision goggles.

NO-MAJ MEDICINE MEN

But the Navajo take the legend *very* seriously, and they view Skinwalkers as purely

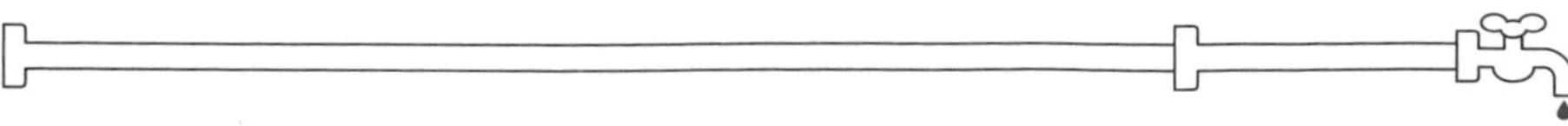

Norwegian delicacy: *smalahove*—boiled, salted, dried sheep's head (with the brain removed).

evil. That's why J. K. Rowling received so much criticism in 2016 for her sympathetic portrayal of Skinwalkers on the *Pottermore* website, her highly anticipated expansion of Harry Potter's wizarding world. In the chapter "History of Magic in North America," Rowling wrote that "Native American skin-walkers" were actually "evil witches and wizards" who "assumed animal forms to escape persecution" by "No-Maj medicine men, who were sometimes faking magical powers themselves."

Among the complaints Rowling received—on her own Twitter feed, and in numerous opinion pieces—was that she replaced "Navajo" with the blanket term "Native American." But that wasn't the biggest issue. In an open letter to Rowling, Dr. Adrienne Keene, a member of the Cherokee Nation of Oklahoma and founder of the blog *Native Appropriations*, wrote that *Pottermore* is yet another in a long line of narratives that have helped to paint *all* Indians as fictional characters:

> "Think about Peter Pan, where Neverland has mermaids, pirates...and Indians. Or on Halloween, children dress up as monsters, zombies, princesses, Disney characters...and Indians. Beyond the positioning as 'not real,' there is also a pervasive and problematic narrative wherein Native peoples are always 'mystical' and 'magical' and 'spiritual'—able to talk to animals, conjure spirits, perform magic, heal with 'medicine' and destroy with 'curses.' Think about Grandmother Willow in *Pocahontas*, or Tonto talking to his bird and horse in *The Lone Ranger*, or the wolfpack in *Twilight*...or any other number of examples."

At the worst, wrote Keene, these kinds of portrayals make it much harder for Native Americans to be taken seriously when trying to advocate for themselves. "We are fighting every day for the protection of our sacred sites from being destroyed. If Indigenous spirituality becomes conflated with fantasy 'magic'—how can we expect lawmakers and the public to be allies in the protection of these spaces?" (She also points out that it wasn't until 1978 that Indians were legally allowed to practice their religion openly.)

THE VANISHING INDIAN

As Leanne Howe, a Choctaw Nation citizen and editor of *Seeing Red—Hollywood's Pixeled Skins*, summed it up to *National Geographic* in 2016: "The vanishing American Indian is in art, it's in stories—we're the so-called Last of the Mohicans. We exist in the minds of mainstream America as dead and forgotten because the white Americans won the American West."

But Indians are very much alive and worth remembering. If you're interested in learning about their cultures, myths, and legends, there are a multitude of books, films, and websites created by Native Americans and the First Peoples of Canada. That's where you'll find the *real* stories—which are just as fascinating as anything Hollywood could create.

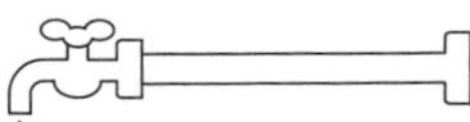

Diamonds were first discovered in India in the 4th century BC, and then not again until Brazil in 1725.

A CANDY IS BORN

If you were a kid in the late 1970s, you probably remember the first time you tried this strange new candy. Here's the even stranger story of how it came to be.

SOMETHING TO DRINK

In 1953, the General Foods Corporation, makers of Grape Nuts Cereal, Maxwell House Coffee, Log Cabin Pancake Syrup, Jell-O gelatin, and more than 70 other food products, purchased the Kool-Aid Company and added the line of powdered drink mixes to its stable of brands. Kool-Aid was highly profitable and a leader in its category, but it didn't make anywhere near the kind of money that Coca-Cola and Pepsi made selling carbonated soft drinks. General Foods thought that if it could figure out a way to add carbonation to Kool-Aid, it could make a fortune selling instant soft drink mix.

The company put one of its best food scientists on the case: William Mitchell, who had been with the company since 1941. Mitchell had gotten his start with the photographic film company Eastman Kodak in 1939, when it was working to bring color film to the market. But after helping to design a process for developing the color green, he became so wary of working with the hazardous chemicals used to make and develop film that he jumped ship and went to work for General Foods.

ON THE ROCKS

One of Mitchell's first attempts at carbonating Kool-Aid was to try to create carbonated ice. He envisioned carbonated ice cubes being sold in a grocer's freezer, almost like ice cream, maybe with pouches of Kool-Aid already attached. The consumer would buy the ice cubes and keep them in the freezer until they wanted to make some Kool-Aid. They'd make it just as they always had (pour a pouch of unsweetened Kool-Aid mix into a pitcher of water, add sugar, and stir), and then drop in the carbonated ice cubes. Voilà! Instant soda for a fraction of what Coke or Pepsi cost.

The funny thing is that Mitchell actually solved the carbonated Kool-Aid problem in his first attempt. He really did figure out a way to pack so much carbon dioxide into a few ice cubes that dropping them into a pitcher of Kool-Aid turned it into carbonated soda. So why don't we drink Kool-Aid brand ice-cube soda today? The problem was that in the 1950s, many grocers were in the habit of turning up the thermostats on their freezers at the end of the day to save on electricity overnight. Not above the freezing point (32°F), but close to it. That was fine for most frozen foods, but when the temperature of carbonated ice rose above 14°F, the carbon dioxide escaped, and the ice went flat.

General Foods learned all this the hard way when it test-marketed Soda Burst, its first carbonated ice product. Soda Burst was a chunk of carbonated ice covered in frozen chocolate syrup: When you dropped it into a glass of water or milk, it Alka-Seltzered itself into a carbonated chocolate soda right before your eyes. At least that's what it was supposed to do. So many Soda Bursts went flat when the grocers' freezers warmed up overnight that the company abandoned the idea of selling carbonated ice products entirely.

SWEETENING THE DEAL

The next thing Mitchell tried was to add carbon dioxide to a sugar mixture. In those days, Kool-Aid was sold only in unsweetened form; you had to add the sugar yourself. (Kool-Aid mix with the sugar already added wasn't introduced until 1963.) Mitchell figured that if you couldn't get the carbonation when you added ice cubes to Kool-Aid, maybe you could get it when you added the sugar. And if the carbonated sugar also contained Kool-Aid's coloring and flavoring, you'd have a product that was even more convenient than unsweetened Kool-Aid. You'd just pour the powder into a pitcher of water, stir, and you had instant soda. No added sugar required.

But it did have one interesting quality: When he popped some of the mixture into his mouth, it popped right back at him.

Though he experimented with one formula after another, finally settling on a formula that used sorbitol, a form of hydrogenated sugar, Mitchell only managed to get about an eighth as much carbon dioxide into the sugar as he'd gotten into the ice cubes—not nearly enough to turn a glass of water into a carbonated drink. The result was very bland. But it did have one interesting quality: When he popped some of the mixture into his mouth, it popped right back at him.

AN ACQUIRED TASTE

Mitchell completed the first batch of his carbonated sugar mixture in October 1956. He liked how it popped in his mouth, and he thought it might make an interesting candy. He gave a big chunk of it to his secretary without telling her what it was or what to expect. When it popped in her mouth, she spit it out, and it made another loud POP! when it hit the floor. She was not a fan, but Mitchell thought his kids might like it, so he made a special batch for them, flavored it with pineapple (the only flavor on hand), and brought it home. Kids being kids, they loved it.

Mitchell's bosses at General Foods were not as impressed. They didn't know what to make of the stuff, and they weren't in the candy business, so they did nothing with Mitchell's invention. That was the way things remained for nearly 20 years. On his

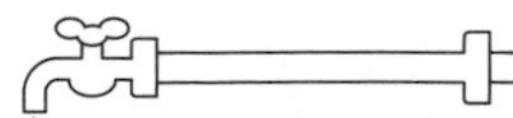

The city of Amsterdam has an unofficial "night mayor" who keeps the peace between residents and revelers.

own, Mitchell would whip up small batches of the candy, which he called "Popping Candy" or "Atomic Candy," for his kids, for office parties, and to keep on hand at work to dazzle visitors when they toured his lab. But General Foods never gave a thought to marketing it.

'NEFF SAID

Then in the early 1970s, Herman Neff, the head of Hostess, General Foods' Canadian snack food division, paid a visit to Mitchell's lab and got a taste of the popping candy. He was so impressed that when he returned to Canada, he authorized spending $500,000 to build a carbonated candy factory in the basement of a snack food plant in Cambridge, Ontario, so that he could introduce the candy to the Canadian market. Not as a product for sale—he wanted to use it as a promotional item to give away free to customers when they bought his division's potato chips, pretzels, and other snacks.

But first he wanted to give the product a better name. Popping Candy was kind of a dull name, and Atomic Candy didn't appeal to him either. So he went to his son's elementary school classroom and wrote several possible names on the board: Exploding Treats, Pop and Snap, Vesuvius, and...Pop Rocks. Then, according to food historian Marv Rudolph, "he gave each student an unlabeled, white pouch of candy, asked them to sample it, and then asked them to pick from the list of names the product they just ate. The unanimous consensus was Pop Rocks."

CHASE SCENE

In 1974, Neff's basement candy factory was completed, and he began giving away free half-ounce pouches of Pop Rocks with every bag of snack food purchased. The flavors available were orange, cherry, and grape. When you were a kid, did you ever chase after an ice cream truck when it came to your neighborhood? What about a potato chip truck—did you ever chase one of those? As soon as the kids around Cambridge, Ontario, came to associate their free Pop Rocks with potato chips, they began running after the trucks and begging the drivers for more Pop Rocks. When word of this spread back to General Foods headquarters in White Plains, New York, the company realized that it might have a hit on its hands. General Foods had been in business in one form or another since 1895, but this may have been the first time that mobs of children had ever chased after the company's delivery trucks begging for more of a product.

General Foods test-marketed Pop Rocks in Ontario and in Yuma, Arizona, and again the results were spectacular: The product testers reported a higher level of enthusiasm for Pop Rocks than for any other product they had ever tested on children. That was all General Foods needed to hear; after nearly 20 years of ignoring Mitchell's invention, it made plans to enter the highly competitive U.S. candy market in a big way by introducing one carbonated product after another. First they'd roll out

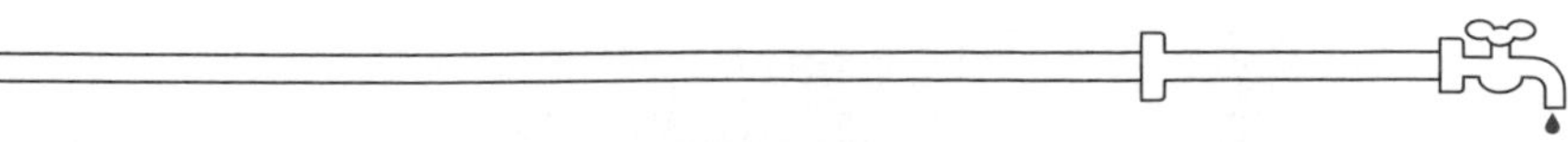

Pop Rocks, then a product called Space Dust, made from powdered Pop Rocks material, a byproduct of the production process. The powder fizzed because it was too small to pop. (The name Space Dust was later changed to Cosmic Candy when the company realized that Space Dust sounded like a drug reference.) These products would be followed by carbonated chewing gum, carbonated mints, and carbonated chocolate. General Foods expected to make about $100 million a year selling Pop Rocks alone, with a lot more money pouring in once the other products hit the market.

...NOT SO FAST

It took until 1976 to scale up production for the entire U.S. market, and then Pop Rocks was rolled out regionally, starting with the Midwestern states. In another sign of how much interest there was in the candy, General Foods had a problem with independent distributors "bootlegging" Pop Rocks, shipping them to parts of the country where the candy hadn't been introduced yet and selling them at inflated prices: $1.00 a pouch (or more) instead of the 20¢ retail price.

But almost as quickly as Pop Rocks rolled out around the country, the product came to be dogged by an urban legend, vague at first, then more specific, claiming that the product had killed a kid after he washed down two or three pouches of Pop Rocks with a bottle of soda, causing his stomach to explode. By 1978, the legend had coalesced around child actor John Gilchrist, who played "Mikey," the youngest brother in a popular Life Cereal commercial that had been running on TV since 1971. In the ad, Mikey is a picky eater who "hates everything" until his two brothers slide a bowl of Life Cereal in front of him, which he eats. "He likes it! Hey Mikey!"

Now, rumor had it, the adorable kid was dead, blown up by Pop Rocks. It's possible that the urban legend started out as a pun—Mikey lost his life. (Get it? Life!) But moms and dads didn't know that, and soon the telephone switchboard at General Foods' corporate headquarters was deluged by calls from concerned parents demanding to know if the stories were true. (The only real Pop Rocks casualty, Marv Rudolph writes in his book, *Pop Rocks: The Inside Story of America's Revolutionary Candy*, was a "tractor-trailer load of Pop Rocks, which inadvertently was left to heat up in the sun outside Kansas City, Missouri. The sides of the trailer literally blew out when the eighty thousand pouches in the shipment all 'pillowed' together," causing the Pop Rocks to overheat and release their carbon dioxide gas.)

DAMAGE CONTROL

For more than a year, General Foods ignored the urban legend, hoping it would fade away. And the strategy seemed to work: In 1978, the company sold 500 million pouches of Pop Rocks—or about 2.2 pouches for every man, woman, and child in America. But in the beginning of 1979, sales dipped sharply, prompting General

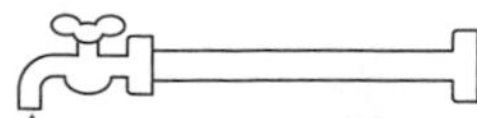

Foods to launch a PR campaign to combat the rumors. They got the FDA to release a statement saying that the candy was safe, and they issued public letters to parents, retailers, and school principals assuring them that the candy was harmless. The company spent hundreds of thousands of dollars on newspaper ads to get its message out, and sent Bill Mitchell on a speaking tour in an attempt to allay the public's fear.

One thing that might have killed the story once and for all would have been for General Foods to film a Pop Rocks commercial starring John Gilchrist, the actor who played "Mikey" in the Life Cereal ad. General Foods wanted to do it, and Gilchrist, now a happy, healthy unexploded teenager, was also willing. The only problem: the Life Cereal ad was still on TV, and Gilchrist and his two brothers, who also appeared in the ad, were still being paid handsome residuals. When Quaker Oats, owners of Life Cereal, learned that he was thinking about doing a Pop Rocks commercial, they threatened to pull the Life Cereal ad off the air. Rather than risk losing his and his brothers' residual income, Gilchrist backed out of the Pop Rocks ad.

FLAT

As 1979 progressed, General Foods' warehouses began filling up with unsold and returned cases of Pop Rocks. This was partially due to the urban legend, but part of it was also due to the fact that General Foods, brand new to the candy business, never really understood what kind of product Pop Rocks was. They thought it was something like chewing gum or a chocolate bar: Once kids were introduced to it, they'd keep eating it forever. But they were wrong. Pop Rocks was a novelty—one, it turned out, that wore off pretty quickly. How many times does a person need to experience the sensation of candy popping in their mouth? Kids all over America tried Pop Rocks maybe half a dozen times (that's about as many times as Uncle John did), and then they moved on. The product never really caught on with adults at all.

As sales continued to fall, General Foods began winding down production; then in 1982, execs shut down that business entirely. They'd sold several hundred million packets of Pop Rocks by then, but they'd spent so much money building up what they thought would be a permanent business that they actually lost between $30–40 million doing it.

IN THE KNOW

Another odd fizzing product: Pepsi-flavored Cheetos, introduced in Japan in 2013. They had a limited run and were followed by Mountain Dew–flavored Cheetos. So are fizzy Cheetos coming to the United States? According to a Frito-Lay spokesperson, "No."

STILL POPPING

In the late 1980s, General Foods licensed its Pop Rock patents and trademarks to a new company, Carbonated Candy Ventures...which struggled for a few years and then went out of business in 1992. Later that same year, a

In 1997, Nintendo offered to buy "gaming gloves" for anyone who injured themselves playing their systems.

Spanish company called Zeta Espacial S.A. bought the company's assets and resumed production of Pop Rocks, and it is still making the candy today. Ironically, the brand has outlasted General Foods itself: The company was acquired by cigarette maker Philip Morris in 1985, which later bought Kraft, Inc., and merged the two businesses to create Kraft General Foods. The company was renamed Kraft Foods in 1990.

Sales of carbonated candy are way down from their heyday in the late 1970s, but selection is better than ever. Today Zeta Espacial sells Pop Rocks in regular and "extreme sour" flavors, as well as Pop Rocks Bubble Gum. If those don't float your boat, you can buy Pop Boom Popping Candy, Kandy Ka-Boom, Popping Pebbles, Super Pebble Pops, Sour Pebble Pops, Circus Fleas Pops, Stardust Space Rocks, or 7-Eleven Slurpee Shocks, to name just a few of Pop Rocks' competitors. 7-Eleven sells its own line of popping candy bars, and so does Cadbury, and so do other chocolate companies. Even if you weren't around for the first Pop Rocks craze in the 1970s, don't worry: It's not too late to give the strange candy a try.

William Mitchell made many more contributions to the American food palate. That story is on page 391.

* * *

SIGNS OF THE TIMES

Seen near a bus stop:
Slow Kids On Road
With No Shoulders

Seen on a gate at the end of a street:
This gate must be open or closed at all times.

Seen at a state park:
Red Squirrels
Drive Slowly

Seen at a resort:
Please be aware that the balcony is not at ground level.

Seen at a public park:
People Are Eating
Children In This Area

Seen in a Japanese restroom:
Please urinate with precision and elegance.

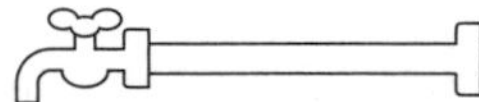

UNLIKELY BUT LUCKY STORIES

Want to be an actor in hit movies and TV shows? It's easy–take some acting classes, move to Hollywood, rehearse hard before that big audition, and then nail that audition. Or, you could go about it in an entirely different way that involves a fair amount of kismet, luck, or things not going the way anybody originally intended.

Johnny Depp was a musician playing in a Miramar, Florida, band called the Kids. In 1983, the group moved to Los Angeles, where Depp met and married his bandmate's sister, a movie makeup artist named Lori Anne Allison. She introduced her husband to actor Nicolas Cage, who suggested Depp get into acting. Depp thought small acting gigs could be a good way to pay the bills while waiting for the Kids to get a record deal. To get an idea of what the life of an actor was like, he accompanied his friend, former teen star Jackie Earle Haley (*The Bad News Bears*) to an audition for Wes Craven's horror movie *A Nightmare on Elm Street*. Depp didn't plan on auditioning, but Craven spotted him and asked him to...and he landed the lead role of Glen Lantz, Freddy Krueger's third victim.

CBS's 1990–95 hit *Northern Exposure* took place in a tiny town in Alaska, a place with a substantial Native American population. The show was one of the first and few TV shows to prominently feature Native American performers, notably Elaine Miles as Marilyn Whirlwind, the nearly silent, inscrutable receptionist for town doctor Joel Fleischman (Rob Morrow). It was Miles's very first screen-acting work, and she didn't even plan to go for it. Her mother, Armenia Miles, thought it would be fun to go to an open audition in Seattle for the show that was specifically looking for local Native American performers. So Elaine drove her mother there...and a casting agent who noticed her sitting in the waiting room asked her to read for the part of Marilyn. (Armenia Miles won a part in the show too—a small, recurring role as Marilyn's mother.)

In 2019, Mexican director Alfonso Cuarón won his second Best Director Oscar for *Roma*, an extremely personal, semiautobiographical film about a family in 1970s Mexico City. The story is told primarily through the

eyes of Cleo, an indigenous woman who works as a live-in maid for a wealthy family. Actress Yalitza Aparicio earned an Academy Award nomination for Best Actress for her work as Cleo, a remarkable feat considering *Roma* was the first time she'd ever acted. Just before the film began shooting, she'd earned a degree in early childhood education. Her sister, Edith, was the actress in the family, and had landed an audition for Cuarón. But when Edith became pregnant, she backed out and suggested her younger sister go on the call instead. Aparicio apparently nailed the audition, because Cuarón personally offered her the role of Cleo...which she didn't accept right away. "She says, 'Well, I think I can do it,'" Cuarón told the *New York Times*. "I have nothing better to do."

When David Crane and Marta Kauffman wrote the pilot for the show that would become *Friends* in 1993, they created certain characters with specific actors in mind. The role of sad-sack paleontologist Ross Geller was written just for David Schwimmer (who took the part), and the role of his sister, Monica, was tailor-made for comedian Janeane Garofalo. She was offered the part, but turned it down for a bigger gig: joining the cast of *Saturday Night Live*. But Courteney Cox *really* wanted to play Monica. She'd read the pilot script because she was offered the role of Rachel Green...which Crane and Kauffman wrote just for her. Cox auditioned, impressed the writers with her Monica, and got the part. The role of Rachel went to Jennifer Aniston, who, ironically, picked *Friends* over a chance to audition for *Saturday Night Live*.

The hangdog-faced character actor Abe Vigoda is best known for two roles: as gangster Sal Tessio in *The Godfather*, and as police detective Phil Fish on the TV sitcom *Barney Miller*. Vigoda came to both roles in decidedly nontraditional ways. For *The Godfather*, he beat out dozens of other actors at an open audition held by director Francis Ford Coppola specifically for struggling actors who, like Vigoda, didn't have agents. About five years later, Vigoda was living in Los Angeles, and he kept in shape by jogging about five miles every day. One morning he'd just returned from a run when he got a call from his agent (he had one by that point) telling him to go *immediately* to an audition for a supporting role on a new police sitcom. The producers knew Vigoda from *The Godfather* and had asked for him specifically—but they needed to see him right that minute. The agent told Vigoda that he didn't even have time to shower or change out of his running shorts, so he drove to the audition and met with producers who told him he looked "tired"...and gave him the role of Fish.

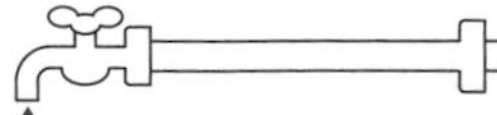

SILLY WORLD RECORDS

More people trying any odd way they can think of to make their mark.

WORLD RECORD: Most people wearing plaid

DETAILS: In November 2015, Georgia-Pacific, which owns the Brawny paper towel brand, challenged Atlanta Falcons fans to come to a game at the Georgia Dome dressed in the same red-and-black plaid outfit the Brawny Man wears. More than 1,100 plaid-wearing people showed up, setting the first officially recognized world record in this category.

That record didn't sit well with the people of Kenora, Ontario, a region known for red-and-black plaid lumberjack shirts, sometimes called "Kenora dinner jackets." After years of planning, in July 2019, the town put on a "PLAIDurday" celebration. According to the rules, to be officially counted for the world record, "Each person needs to be wearing two (2) pieces of plaid. One piece must be a top or bottom (shirt, pants, dress, skirt, hoodie, etc.), and the other can be an accessory like a hat, scarf, toque, tie, etc. (as long as it's made of cloth)." As the checkered record breakers began gathering at the Kenora Harbourfront that morning, Mayor Dan Reynard told the *Miner & News,* "We're not just going to win, we're going to smash the record!" He was right. Final tally: 1,359 people wearing plaid. Your move, Atlanta.

WORLD RECORD: Most pairs of underpants put on in one minute

DETAILS: Some people take their silly world records seriously, perhaps no one more than Cherry Yoshitake, a Japanese comedian and game show host who goes by the name "Mr. Cherry." He claims to hold the most world records in Japan—21. A stalwart on the Guinness-themed British kids' show *Officially Amazing,* Mr. Cherry performed the underwear stunt at a Japanese shopping mall in front of a cheering crowd. When the minute was up, he had pulled on 36 pairs of underpants. (There's also a team category, in which one person puts underpants on the other person.) A few other Mr. Cherry records: most shuttlecocks caught with chopsticks in one minute (23), and most whoopee cushions sat on in 30 seconds (52).

There are other underpants-putter-onners out there. An Italian man named Silvio Sabba—who holds the most world records in Italy—owns the record for most pairs of underpants put on in 30 seconds. Taking a more athletic approach than Mr. Cherry, Sabba holds each pair of underpants waist high and literally jumps into them. His 30-second record: 13 pairs. In November 2019, the record was again broken. Toshiaki Kasuga of Japan managed to put on 17 pairs. (Uncle John's personal record: 1.)

Sting wrote "Every Breath You Take" on the same desk that Ian Fleming used to type out James Bond novels on his gold-plated typewriter.

WORLD RECORD: Most walnuts crushed by a butt in one minute

DETAILS: To attempt this record, you have to master the art of sitting on a walnut with enough force to break it... without breaking your tailbone. Then see how many you can break in 30 seconds. Japan's Mr. Cherry (see the previous entry) originally set this record, only to be outdone by Spain's Juan Carlos Diez Soto. In 2009, Soto appeared on a *Guinness World Records* TV show in Madrid, and managed to crush 33 walnuts with his butt before collapsing on the floor in agony. Four years later, Tomoharu Shoji of Japan crushed 43 walnuts (and did not collapse in agony).

"The arrow of fate selected my butt," said Mr. Cherry when he attempted to reclaim the record in 2013. Upping his game, Mr. Cherry employed the "crab style" technique, wherein he propped himself up with his feet and palms and crushed 48 walnuts...and the record.

Care to try any of these yourself? Check with Guinness first, because some—or all—of them may have already been beaten by the time you're reading this. And chances are someone will be vying for your record the moment you set it.

MORE SILLY WORLD RECORDS

- Largest collection of teddy bears: 8,026 by Jackie Miley of Rapid City, South Dakota.
- Most rolls of toilet paper balanced on the head (a person's head, that is): 12, by Josh Horton of California, who stacked 12 rolls on top of his dome and kept them balanced for 30 seconds.
- Most people dressed as Spider-Man: 547 in Stockholm, Sweden, beating the previous record of 438 set in Sydney, Australia.
- Fastest 100 meters in an office chair: Andre Ortolf of Augsburg, Germany: 31.92 seconds.

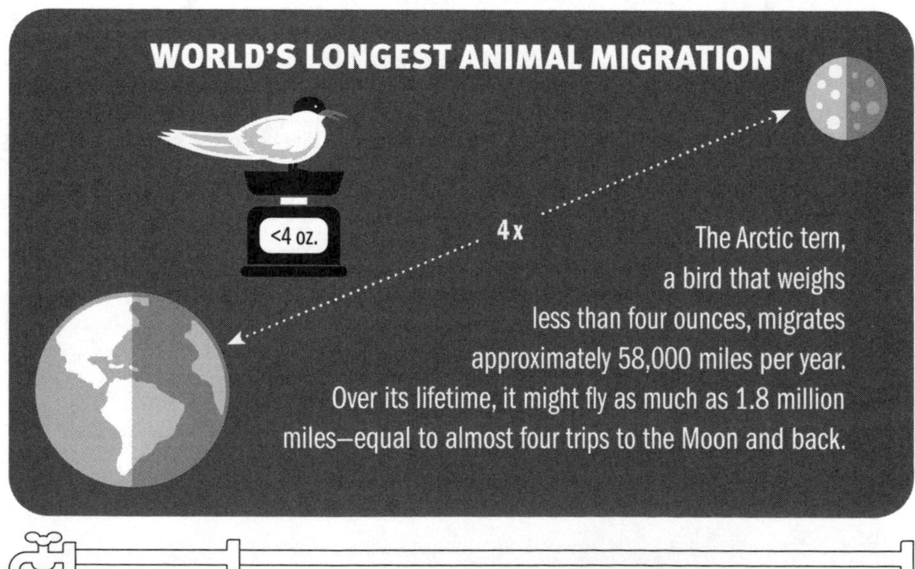

Q. Can you name the country with the most Summer Olympic medals per capita? A. Finland.

STRANGE CRIME

Another head-scratching edition of crimes so odd that you almost feel sorry for the crooks. Almost.

Bad Taste

"You kind of laugh about it afterwards because, technically, he didn't harm anybody, he didn't break anything," said Sylvia Dungan of Salinas, California. She was referring to a suspect identified as Roberto Arroyo, 33, who was captured on a surveillance camera licking the family's doorbell for roughly three hours late at night in January 2019. (He also relieved himself in the front yard.) At last report, Arroyo was still at large. The family bleached their doorbell.

Son of a Gun

In May 2019, Keith Tilton took his 39-year-old son Joseph to a Lewiston, Maine, bank to cash a check. Keith waited in the car, and Joseph returned a few minutes later with $620 in cash. The father noticed that his son was acting a bit oddly, but Joseph was going through a rough time, so Keith didn't think much more of it. After he dropped his son off in another part of town, Keith was driving past the bank on his way home when he noticed several police cars in the parking lot, one of which sped out and pulled him over. It turned out Keith's car matched the description of a getaway vehicle used in a bank robbery...that his son had committed. Joseph was later arrested; Keith, who had no idea what had transpired, wasn't charged.

Disappearing Act

Someone, for some reason, stole a bouncy house from the Cincinnati Circus Company in July 2019. A few weeks later, either the same or different thieves made off with another one of the circus's assets—a black trailer containing $10,000 worth of various sideshow equipment, including a coffin, an electric chair, and a bed of nails. It's unclear whether the thief actually meant to steal those items; whoever it was just hooked their vehicle up to the trailer (it was parked on private property) and vanished into the night. But whatever the motive, the strange burglary took a big chunk out of the circus company's budget. A spokesperson told local news stations that they didn't care why the stuff was stolen, but they really needed it back. At last report, there were no suspects.

Original name of the Subway chain: Pete's Subway.

HOW TO MAKE A RAINBOW

And now for three fun home science demonstrations that will have you seeing colors.

OPTICAL ILLUSIONS

Light is a form of energy made up of different wavelengths; the wavelengths that are visible to the human eye are referred to as "the colors of the spectrum." When all these visible wavelengths of color are combined, the result is pure white light. But wait a minute—if that's the case, then how come when you combine all the colors of paint, it turns black? Because of light's *additive* and *subtractive* qualities. Confused? The following demonstrations will shed a little light on the matter (literally).

Note: If you're a kid, you'll need an adult to assist you with these experiments. If you're an adult, these might be more fun with a kid around.

Experiment #1: A Tall Glass of Rainbow

OBJECTIVE: To split direct sunlight into the colors of the spectrum

WHAT YOU'LL NEED:

- A glass of water (preferably a clear, smooth glass)
- Sunlight or a bright, white flashlight
- A white surface or a white piece of paper to make the rainbow appear brighter

WHAT TO DO: You'll have to time this experiment for when the Sun is shining in through a window onto a horizontal surface like a table or countertop. When the light is just right...

1. Place the glass of water in the sunlight. You might have to move it around until the rainbow appears next to it on the table. Use the piece of paper if necessary.
2. Carefully position the glass half off the table, and the rainbow will appear on the floor.
3. If you're using a flashlight, place the glass on a white surface. Aim the flashlight at the glass from a few inches away, moving it around until a rainbow appears.

THE SCIENCE EXPLAINED: *Additive light* refers to all colors of the spectrum combining into white light. This activity shows that process in reverse. When the white sunlight passes through the glass, the wavelengths split into colors of the

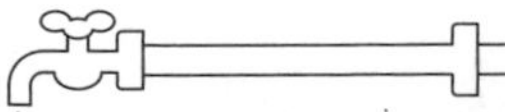

spectrum (also known as Roy G. Biv, an acronym for "red, orange, yellow, green, blue, indigo, violet"). The glass acts as a prism—which can be any transparent object that disperses light rays.

Three factors are at work here: refraction, dispersion, and reflection. When light rays move from one density to another—in this case, from air to water—they are refracted, or bent. Different wavelengths bend at different angles, dispersing the light rays into the aforementioned Roy G. Biv. That's how it works with any prism. In the case of a rainbow, the prisms are all the water droplets in the air. The dispersed light rays are reflected off the sides of the water droplets, and that appears to us as a rainbow arc with red on the outside and violet on the inside. In order to see a rainbow, the Sun must be directly behind you, shining unencumbered onto raindrops directly in front of you. That's why every rainbow is unique to the person viewing it...and why it seems to follow you in the car.

Experiment #2: Walking Water

OBJECTIVE: To utilize capillary action and color blending to make a liquid rainbow on your table

WHAT YOU'LL NEED:

- 7 clear plastic cups. You can also use drinking glasses or Mason jars—anything you can see through. They should all be the same size.
- Paper towels; the more absorbent, the better.
- Liquid food coloring—red, yellow, and blue—that dissolves in water
- Scissors (which you will most likely need to cut the paper towels)
- A spoon or a stirring stick

WHAT TO DO:

1. Do this experiment on a surface that can stay undisturbed for several hours.
2. Place the 7 cups right next to each other in a semicircle.
3. Fill every other cup with water, nearly to the top, and all to the same level. Cups 1, 3, 5, and 7 should have water; cups 2, 4, and 6 should be empty.
4. Put a few drops of red food coloring in the two outside cups (1 and 7), blue food coloring in cup 3, and yellow food coloring in cup 5. Stir each one gently until the color is even, making sure to wipe off the stirrer between stirrings to keep the primary colors intact.
5. Fold 6 paper towels into long strips less than 1 inch wide. Now bend

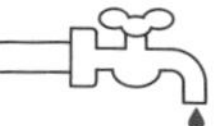

...which Springsteen recovered after the Ramones turned it down.

each strip in half, forming a V shape. Each "leg" should be about the height of the cup. If they're much longer than that, use the scissors to cut them down to size.

6. Carefully place one end of a paper towel strip into the first cup with the red water, and the other end into the empty cup next to it. Take the second paper towel, and place one end into the same empty cup and the other into the third cup with the blue water. Put the next paper towel into the third cup, making a "bridge" to the fourth, and so on until you've used all 6 paper towels.
7. Wait. It can take several hours for this reaction to be completed, depending on the paper towel's absorption power. If you're so inclined, record a time-lapse video on your phone. You *should* have seven cups half-full of water. The three primary colors—red, yellow, and blue—are still in their cups, but they've combined to create secondary colors between them—orange, green, and purple.

THE SCIENCE EXPLAINED: How does the clear water become colored? A chemical reaction is taking place between the water molecules and the polarized ions in the food coloring. Simply put, the food coloring is made of tiny solids called *pigments.* Upon entering the water, the pigments begin to dissolve and break up; the free-floating color molecules bond with oppositely charged water molecules until a new equilibrium is reached and the water in the cup is a solid color—in this case red, yellow, and blue.

How did the water seemingly defy gravity to get from one cup to another? By *capillary action,* that's how. Within the paper towel are tiny cellulose fibers that have tiny openings. Water molecules are polar—they have both positive and negative ions—which means they are attracted to polarized molecules in the cellulose. That's what pulls the water molecules up. Those water molecules are also attracted to each other—it's called *cohesion*—which is why raindrops form little globules. This creates *surface tension* that bonds the water molecules together as they are drawn through the paper towel. (Capillary action is also how plants and trees are able to "drink" water from the ground.)

This is considered subtractive color blending because we're dealing with matter, not light. Light waves are a type of energy, and when they enter a molecule, most of those light rays are absorbed as energy. The light rays that aren't absorbed reflect the color that we can see. So that red water only appears red because all the other colors were absorbed. The more colors you add, the more colors get absorbed—or subtracted—and the fewer get reflected back. When all the colors are absorbed, the water turns black.

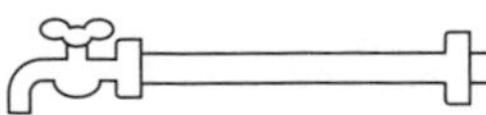

Experiment #3: The Psychedelic Plate

OBJECTIVE: To demonstrate surface tension and color blending, and learn how soap works

WHAT YOU'LL NEED:

- A deep, white plate. A saucer or Frisbee will also do.
- 2-percent or whole milk. Skim milk or a nondairy substitute won't work.
- Liquid food coloring. The more, the better.
- Liquid dish soap (like Dawn)
- Cotton swabs or toothpicks

WHAT TO DO:

1. Carefully pour some milk onto the plate so it covers the entire surface less than ¼ inch deep.
2. Once the surface is calm, add one drop of each food coloring no farther than one inch from the center. Try not to let the drops touch each other.
3. Use the toothpick or cotton swab to collect a very small glob of dish soap.
4. Slowly place the glob of soap into the center of the plate and hold it there.
5. Try not to freak out as the solution erupts into a maelstrom of psychedelic swirling.

THE SCIENCE EXPLAINED: Whole milk is a solution of mostly water with trace amounts of proteins and vitamins, along with tiny globules of oils, collectively referred to as fat. Fat molecules are *nonpolar,* meaning they have no charge and are therefore not attracted to polar molecules in water, so they don't dissolve. That's why oil and water don't mix. Fat molecules do, however, cling to surfaces. That's why washing with water alone doesn't always remove the oils. The soap's molecules are nonpolar, and they're attracted to the nonpolar fat molecules, so much so that they twist and contort them and even break them up in order to make new bonds. On a dirty plate or dirty hands, the soap molecules bond with and then break up fatty deposits so they can be washed away in the water. This reaction would still take place without the food coloring—it just makes it easy to see. Once the soap has bonded with all the fat molecules, a new equilibrium has been reached and the swirling stops. (Too bad there's no chemical reaction that will magically clean up the mess.)

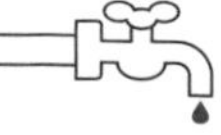

World's largest covered market: Iran's Bazaar of Tabriz, which is about the size of 50 football fields.

VIDEO GAME URBAN LEGENDS

Urban legends can spring from anywhere...but from video games? Sure They've been part of the culture and a major source of entertainment for more than 40 years now, and they've generated their own folklore—most of it a lot creepier than four ghosts chasing a little yellow dot-eating pie man.

Legend: In 2000, at the peak of the Sony PlayStation 2 game console's success, Iraqi dictator Saddam Hussein purchased about 4,000 units and had them sent to his secret weapons-building facilities. The reason: each PlayStation ran on a then-powerful 32-bit processor unit. Bundle enough of them together—say, 4,000 of them—and a bad guy could build a supercomputer that could be used as a guided missile system.

Truth: It's two accurate news stories conflated to create one false urban legend. Around 2000, Hussein was still in power and was viewed as a major threat—after all, the U.S. government invaded the country in 2002 on the assertion that Hussein had stockpiled "weapons of mass destruction." That was a real fear at the time. Coupled with an odd-but-true news item about how it was cheaper to buy a PlayStation 2 than it was to buy a 32-bit CPU chip, the existence of a PlayStation-powered missile system became an online rumor, then a legend, then something Hussein was supposedly really doing. He wasn't.

Legend: The 2008 game *Fallout 3*—in which players wander around what's left of Washington, D.C., after a nuclear apocalypse—contained several eerie but accurate predictions of the future.

Truth: The end-of-the-world nuclear disaster in *Fallout 3* occurs in 2077, so there's still no telling whether or not *that* prediction is true. But there's a creepy radio station that plays throughout the game. A voice delivers numbers, and then some words in Morse code. Some of those numbers can be translated into dates...and more than one revealed a creepy coincidence. Among them: "1-2-5-5-2-8-2-0-1-0. What you talkin' bout? You will be missed." That sounds like an allusion to the death of Gary Coleman, who uttered that catchphrase on the 1980s sitcom *Diff'rent Strokes*. Oddly, he died at around 12:05 on May 28, 2010...or 1-2-5-5-2-8-2-0-1-0. Another message reads: "9-4-5-4-2-0-2-0-1-0. Accident in Gulf, several dead." The Deepwater Horizon oil spill occurred in the Gulf of Mexico on April 20, 2010, or rather 4-2-0-2-0-1-0. Only those two messages line up with real events, however. The

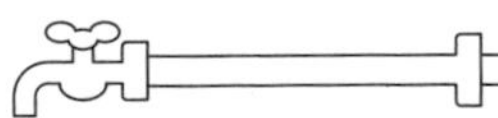

Star Wars creator George Lucas's earliest name for Yoda was "Buffy."

rest didn't come true, including the March 2014 death of Queen Elizabeth II.

Legend: "You are in a dark room. Moonlight shines through the window." That's how *Pale Luna* began. Like most "text-based" games popular in the 1980s, rather than controlling a character in a graphic world, players had to read instructions and type in what they wanted to do. In *Pale Luna,* players had to make their way through a door and then head either east, west, north, or south. But no matter which direction players chose, they would invariably be led in circles before finally receiving this message: "Pale Luna smiles wide." It was baffling and, ultimately, impossible, although one player named Michael Nevins reportedly kept at it and finished the game. The reward: a series of mysterious coordinates. The player located them on a map, which led to a spot in California. He went there, to a remote section of woods...where he found the remains of a missing girl named Karen Paulsen, who'd disappeared a year prior.

Truth: The entire tale was a ghost story spread around the Internet—a genre of short-story writing called "creepypasta." There was never a game called *Pale Luna,* and no murder victim named Karen Paulsen.

IN THE KNOW

Two of the worst gaming system flops of all time:

- **LaserActive (1993):** Not only could this play games with sophisticated graphics, it could also play Laserdisc movies, CDs, karaoke discs, and Sega Genesis cartridges. But to do that, consumers had to buy modules that cost $350–650 each—on top of the LaserActive base price of $970. Only 10,000 units sold in the United States.
- **Gizmondo (2005):** Tiger Telematics spent millions promoting the introduction of this portable, handheld gaming system. Then, before it was released, the company announced an improved widescreen version with a digital camera, GPS, and software that allowed users to text. Result: most buyers decided to wait for the new model, and only 25,000 Gizmondos were sold. The widescreen version never came out, and within a year Tiger Telematics went bankrupt.

Legend: In 1989, a game for the Nintendo Entertainment System called *Taboo: The Sixth Sense* was released. Marketed as a party game (with dual warnings to "use at your own risk" and "not for children under 14"), it was little more than a digital deck of fortune-telling tarot cards. However, it would occasionally predict how a player was going to die. Then a few kids (who didn't heed the 14-and-over-only warning) started dying in the exact same manner as the game predicted. Fearful of bad publicity and more deaths, Nintendo banned the game.

Truth: Nintendo did pull the game from stores...because it sold extremely poorly—not because of any creepy death predictions that came true.

MOUTHING OFF

BAD HAIR DAYS

Famous folks lament about the dead skin cells that grow out of follicles in their dermis.

"Some of the worst mistakes in my life were haircuts."

—Jim Morrison

"IT'S HARD TO HAVE A BAD HAIR DAY WHEN YOU'RE FAMOUS."

—Marion Jones, Olympic athlete

"Love is telling someone their hair extensions are showing."

—Natasha Leggero

"There are no bad haircuts in cyberspace."

—Dave Barry

"A man's main job is to protect his woman from her desire to 'get bangs' every other month."

—Dax Shepard

"If I have a bad hair day, I just think, Well, it will be an OK hair day tomorrow."

—Mitt Romney

"I HAVE LITTLE HAIR BECAUSE MY BRAIN IS SO BIG IT PUSHES THE HAIR OUT."

—Silvio Berlusconi, Italian prime minister

"I GOT MY HAIR HIGHLIGHTED BECAUSE I FELT THAT SOME STRANDS WERE MORE IMPORTANT THAN OTHERS."

—Mitch Hedberg

"People always ask me how long it takes to do my hair. I don't know, I'm never there."

—Dolly Parton

SPECIAL UNDERWEAR

Here's a look at some underwear with a little something extra.

SWAMPBUTT BRIEFS

What They Are: The first underpants "designed specifically for men who sweat a great deal, particularly below the waist," a phenomenon known as "swamp a**" or "monkey butt"

How They Work: The briefs look like ordinary lightweight cotton briefs, but they're made from a blend of 93 percent cotton and 7 percent Lycra. So instead of just soaking up sweat like cotton briefs do, the Lycra helps the fabric "draw moisture away from the skin and allow for greater air-flow around the fabric," speeding evaporation. And for greater comfort, the seams are sewn facing outward, giving the skivvies the appearance that they are being worn inside out.

Bonus: "We guarantee," says the company, "that every pair of SwampButt Underwear we sell has never been worn before."

MODIBODI BREASTFEEDING SINGLET

What It Is: An undergarment specially designed to absorb breast milk "leakage"

How It Works: When a mother is lactating, it's not uncommon for her breasts to secrete milk even when she isn't breastfeeding her baby. (Sometimes even hearing the sound of a baby, or thinking about breastfeeding, is enough to stimulate the release of droplets of milk.) The Modibodi "singlet" (part sleeveless shirt, part bra) incorporates breast cups made with three layers of fabric. The first layer, which touches the skin, wicks any breast milk away from the skin and into a second, middle layer of absorbent material. A third, outer layer of waterproof fabric prevents the breast milk from leaking through to whatever garment the mother is wearing on top of the singlet. The singlet can absorb as much as two teaspoons of breast milk in each cup.

UPSPRING C-PANTIES

What They Are: Panties designed to help women recover from cesarean sections

How They Work: The panties are made from a stretchy fabric that provides gentle compression that "reduces swelling, plus supports tissue that has been weakened from surgery," and "supports your body's return to its pre-pregnancy shape," Upspring says.

The garment also incorporates a panel of medical-grade silicone over the incision area that helps to reduce itching, speed healing, and minimize the appearance and size of the C-section scar. Because the high waistline of the panty rises to just an inch or two below the wearer's breasts, there's no danger of discomfort caused by a low waistline rubbing against the incision area. "C-Panties can also speed recovery and increase comfort after other abdominal surgeries," says the company.

SAFE SHORTS

What They Are: Underwear engineered to protect the wearer against sexual assault

How They Work: Created by German designer Sandra Seilz, who once fought off three attackers while jogging, the shorts, which look like spandex biking shorts, are made of a material that is very difficult to tear or cut through. They are secured around the waist by drawstrings that are also difficult to cut through, and the drawstrings are in turn secured by a combination lock that prevents the drawstrings from being untied without the wearer's consent. And there's an alarm attached. If it detects that the shorts are being tampered with, it emits a 130-decibel screech (as loud as a military jet taking off from an aircraft carrier). The wearer can also trigger the alarm manually, by tugging sharply on the drawstrings. Seilz says she was inspired to create Safe Shorts following a string of sexual assaults that took place during New Year's Eve celebrations in Cologne in 2015. "Safe Shorts provide triple protection against sexual assaults," she says, "and we're very proud of them."

If it detects that the shorts are being tampered with, it emits a 130-decibel screech.

DANIEAL BOXER SHORTS

What They Are: Boxer shorts...with built-in pockets

How They Work: Inventor Danieal Cormier, 20, was sitting around in his boxers one day at his home in Quispamsis, New Brunswick, Canada, when the idea struck him. "I kept doing the hand motion to put my cellphone in my pocket, but my underwear didn't have any," he told the CBC in 2014. "So that's when it kind of sparked in my head, 'Why doesn't underwear come with pockets?' " When he couldn't find any pocketed boxer shorts online, he bought a sewing machine, taught himself to use it, and began making boxers, using his own taken-apart underpants as a template. Today he sells the pocketed boxers and briefs online. Some of his best customers are diabetics, who use the pockets for insulin pumps, and travelers, who carry their passports and wallets in their underwear to deter pickpockets.

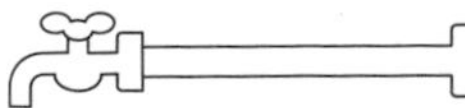

Largest volcano on Earth: Tamu Massif, at the bottom of the Pacific Ocean. It's about as big as the state of New Mexico.

DUSTBIN OF HISTORY: THE ABERNATHY BOYS

How old were you when you first left home and traveled on your own? 18? Here's the true story of Temple and Louis Abernathy, who were mere boys in the early 1900s when they set off on horseback to ride from Oklahoma to New York City.

KIDS ON THE ROAD

In 1910, Louis and Temple Abernathy, the sons of a U.S. marshall in Oklahoma known as Catch 'Em Alive Jack (see page 139), learned their father was going to New York to greet his friend, former president Theodore Roosevelt, who was returning from a yearlong trip to Africa and Europe. The boys asked their father if they could go to New York too. When Jack asked how they planned to pay for their train tickets, the boys responded that their tickets were "out in the barn, eatin' hay." Ten-year-old Louis and six-year-old Temple wanted to ride from Oklahoma to New York City on *horseback*, not take the train.

Traversing a dozen states by car, let alone on horseback, was a perilous journey in those days, one that many adults would not have dared to undertake. This certainly wasn't the first time that young boys asked for permission to make such an audacious trip, but it may well have been the first time a father said *yes*. Abernathy, a widower, was raising his boys alone. The old man was tough: catch-wild-wolves-with-your-bare-hands tough, and he wasn't about to let his boys become softies. In 1909, he let them ride their horses from Oklahoma to Santa Fe, New Mexico. Now, after talking with the boys about how to best make the trip to New York, he gave his consent. The boys agreed not to ride on Sundays or carry more than $5 cash. Carrying cash would have been dangerous, so the boys would pay their expenses using money that their father deposited for them in a checking account.

AND THEY'RE OFF

The brothers left home on April 5, 1910. Louis set off on Sam Bass, an Arabian horse his father used on hunts. Temple rode his pony, Geronimo, even though the boy was too small to mount the pony on his own. Rather than ask for help, Temple would lead Geronimo to a stump or bench, climb that first, and then mount the pony. To dismount, he slid down Geronimo's front leg. They packed oats for Sam Bass and Geronimo and bacon, onions, and bread for themselves.

The brothers soon arrived at a Comanche Indian reservation in Oklahoma and spent a night with their father's friend, the famous Comanche war chief Quanah

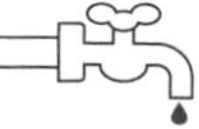

Parker. They also stopped in Oklahoma City for a few days to see their dad...and then they set off again. Back on the trail, one night they arrived at a lone farmhouse and requested a place to sleep. When the woman, suspicious, asked the boys if they had run away from home, they handed her a letter signed by their father. It turns out the woman had read about their trip in the local newspaper, and once she knew who they were, she welcomed them in.

Unfortunately, the boys hadn't even left Oklahoma when Geronimo became lame and had to be left behind with a rancher named Wylie Haynes who agreed to keep Geronimo on his land. For a replacement, Temple chose a wild bronco and managed to tame it. After bargaining a price, he named it Wylie Haynes after the rancher.

HOME ON THE RANGE

Every morning, the youngsters woke at 6:00 a.m., ate a simple breakfast, and started off again. At lunchtime, Louis looked after the horses while the kindergarten-aged Temple cut branches from a mesquite bush, started a small fire, and fried bacon for them. Each day, they rode 40 to 50 miles. If they couldn't find lodging at night, they brought out their bedrolls and slept on the range. They navigated by the Sun and maps (paper ones!) that they bought in each state.

Dubbed "the little cowboys from Oklahoma" by newspapers all over the country who eagerly followed their trip, the boys were greeted as celebrities in many places when they rode into town. There were bands, dinner parties, and tours of the cities' attractions. The brothers rode in a fire truck on an emergency call, got fingerprinted at a police station, and were awakened by a hotel manager to watch Halley's Comet travel across the sky.

In Joplin, Missouri, they spent a few days touring a zinc mine and watching moving picture shows. Then a blizzard struck as they rode through a remote area of the state. The boys could hardly see through the falling snow and were so cold that they walked rather than ride their horses in an attempt to keep warm. They made it through the blizzard and in late April they arrived in St. Louis, where they were treated to the opera, a ride in the mayor's car, and a room at the famed Hotel Jefferson. Temple was too short to reach the hotel registration book, so an employee signed his name for him.

On May 9, after being on the road a little more than a month, they got to Cincinnati, Ohio. There they visited the Cincinnati Zoo and then continued on to Dayton, where Wilbur Wright showed them his airplane factory. Though Wright offered to take the kids on a flight, they feared their dad wouldn't approve, and declined.

TROUBLE ON THE HORIZON

On the next stretch of the trip, the Abernathy boys faced new dangers. First, Temple fell into delirium and passed out on his horse. When Louis found a doctor, he learned his

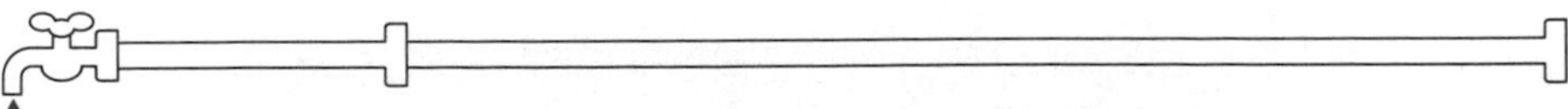

brother had a temperature of 103 degrees and had developed bronchitis. Temple was told to rest, and after a couple of harrowing nights they were ready to leave Ohio.

Next, outside Wheeling, West Virginia, the boys confronted a new problem. They had promised their dad they wouldn't cross a river or stream alone if they couldn't see the bottom. Five miles from the nearest house, they came upon a swift, muddy stream. They waited for someone to come along to help, but no one did. The boys had seen their dad ride Sam Bass across the rushing Red River, and Louis finally decided to try to cross. Louis put Temple on Sam Bass, then mounted Wylie Haynes and started to cross the stream. But Wylie Haynes suddenly plunged underwater and was swept downriver with Louis on his back. Temple frantically crossed to the other side, then ran alongside them on the bank, calling to his brother. That's when the kids spotted dangerous boulders in the fast-moving water ahead. Louis prepared to ditch the horse, sure they would both be dashed against the rocks. Just then, the horse found its footing. It stood and carefully carried Louis to the river's edge.

Besides the often-treacherous weather, the dirt roads they traveled on turned into muddy swamps after heavy rain. At one point, Louis fell and seriously injured his leg. At another, the boys' supplies were stolen. In some places the local kids threatened them. "Many followers of our exploits complained that we were too young to be making such dangerous trips," Temple recounted years later. "Some folks were aghast that two boys were allowed to ride anywhere near that far alone."

Among the concerned bystanders were some women who recognized the boys' dad on a train. They threatened to haul him off the train and hang him on the spot for endangering his kids' lives. Abernathy was unmoved. "We've brought them up to take care of themselves," he'd say. "We never bother about them. Why should we?"

MAKING HEADLINES

In late May, the boys arrived in Washington, D.C., and trotted down Pennsylvania Avenue. Wearing their signature cowboy boots and hats, the kids were honored guests in the U.S. Capitol. On May 31, they met President William Howard Taft, who Louis didn't like as well as Theodore Roosevelt. He explained, "When we go to see 'Teddy,' he sits down on the floor and plays with us, but Mr. Taft didn't do that." At the offices of the *Washington Post*, Temple was most impressed by the teletype machine. He recalled, "I watched it type out baseball scores and thought it was as magical as pink rabbits out of a hat in Arcadia, Oklahoma."

When a reporter asked Temple if he wanted to become a mounted police officer, Temple said no, he'd like to be a hotel clerk. "Temp Admires Hotel Clerks," read the headline of a subsequent story in the *Los Angeles Times*. Another correspondent wrote, "The Abernathy boys are beating all records for juvenile fame...They couldn't have become better known if they had got themselves kidnapped and ransomed."

The two NFL teams playing in a given Super Bowl will produce 11 gallons of sweat by the time the game is over.

After D.C., Louis and Temple rode to Philadelphia, where a veterinarian fixed up their horses, and then on through New Jersey, where a crowd of young boys followed behind the pair, "galloping" on their wooden hobby horses.

THE BIG APPLE

Finally, after traveling about 2,000 miles over more than two months, the boys rode into New York City on June 11. The child celebrities were accosted by crowds who yelled their names, grabbed at them, and plucked hairs from their horses' tails as mementos. So many women smooched them that the *New York Times* reported, "Abernathy Boys Put Ban on Kissing."

Theodore Roosevelt arrived in New York a week later, on June 18; by then Jack Abernathy was in town as well. When Roosevelt disembarked his ship and saw Jack and his boys were there to greet him, he clasped Abernathy's hand and asked, "Jack, old friend, how are you?" Then Roosevelt turned to the boys. According to Temple, "The high point of the whole trip was the smile he gave us at that moment. 'You made a long ride to come see me,' he said to [Louis] and me. 'Bless you.'"

The youngsters joined Roosevelt in a ticker-tape parade attended by more than a million people. Sitting in khaki suits on silver-trimmed saddles, the brothers rode with Spanish War cavalry veterans behind Roosevelt's car. All down Fifth Avenue, they were cheered, filmed, and photographed. At the end, the president gave Temple a huge teddy bear (the stuffed bears get their name from *Teddy* Roosevelt). "I want to see you brave and manly, and I also want to see you gentle and tender," Roosevelt told the brothers. "Alike for the nation and the individual, the one indispensable requisite is character." The boys remembered his words for the rest of their lives.

HOMEWARD BOUND

In July, the Abernathy boys departed New York, but this time, they put their horses on a train home. They'd return in a red 1910 Brush Runabout car with a one-cylinder, six-horsepower engine, about as powerful as a modern push lawn mower. A few days earlier, when the boys asked their father if they could drive themselves all the way back to Oklahoma, Jack Abernathy agreed...on one condition: He gave them one day to find a car that Abernathy thought they'd be able to handle by themselves. When the boys found the Runabout, Abernathy gave his consent. Price: $485, and the salesman promised he'd buy the car back if it broke down on the way home.

After a few hours of lessons, 10-year-old Louis took the wheel. "In thirty minutes, I had it minding me just like I had always been its boss," he claimed in his book *Meeting Roosevelt*. He drove it down Broadway and "never ran over anyone or had any trouble at all." Temple had planned to help with the driving but he was too short, so he rode along as passenger. Jack Abernathy followed in a bigger car with a mechanic

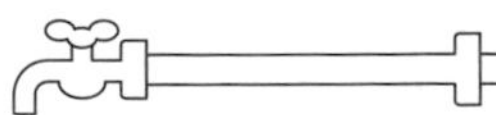

The dessert baklava is based on "placenta cake," an ancient Roman treat made with layered dough, cheese, honey, and bay leaves.

who doubled as a chauffeur—unlike his 10-year-old son, he didn't know how to drive.

On the trip, the family detoured to Detroit for a tour of the Brush auto factory. The boys became spokespeople for Brush and appeared in ads that bragged the car could be easily operated by anyone, even a child. There was no mention that in Poughkeepsie, New York, Temple stepped in front of the car his brother was driving and got run over, narrowly escaping serious injury. Another challenge on their journey was the lack of paved roads, forcing the boys to drive on muddy dirt paths they called "gumbo." In Kansas, construction workers laid wood beams to let them precariously cross a washed-out bridge. Meanwhile, the heat and humidity were insufferable. Despite these perils, the brothers averaged more than 100 miles per day. Their 2,512-mile return to Oklahoma City took only 23 days.

FURTHER EXPLOITS

Capitalizing on their fame, the brothers made film industry connections through another of their father's famous friends, Thomas Edison, who invented the motion picture camera and had his own movie studio. Catch 'Em Alive Jack had already been filmed on a wolf hunt; now his sons starred in their own silent Western called *Abernathy Kids to the Rescue* (1910). The boys also got paid for further adventures. In one election stunt, Louis was hired to ride an elephant, and Temple a donkey. They attempted to plod along from New York to D.C., but they were forced to end their journey when the *elephant*, not the boys, became too exhausted to continue.

For a few weeks, the brothers toured the vaudeville circuit. Then in 1911, they accepted a challenge to ride horseback across the entire country, from New York to San Francisco. If the boys, now eleven and seven, made it to San Francisco in 60 days, they'd win $10,000—the equivalent of more than $272,000 today, and twice what their father made in a year. If they took longer, they'd win nothing; no eating or sleeping indoors allowed. The boys straggled into San Francisco after 62 days and got nothing, but they set a record for the shortest coast-to-coast trip by horse.

After that, the boys made one more cross-country trip, this time by motorcycle, a trip sponsored by the Indian Motorcycle Company. Then, the worst kind of tragedy struck: The boys grew up. Louis became a lawyer and judge, and Temple worked in the Texas oil industry. Louis passed away at the age of 79 in Austin, Texas, in 1979; Temple was 82 when he died in Teague, Texas, in 1986. The story of their extraordinary childhood adventures is largely forgotten today, except in their hometown of Frederick, Oklahoma, which has an Abernathy Day festival in June of each year, and a statue of the boys in the courthouse square. The brothers are also the subject of an exhibit in the town's pioneer museum. Their father liked to say that his boys "got all their good points from their mother." But it seems a bit of Catch 'Em Alive Jack rubbed off on them as well.

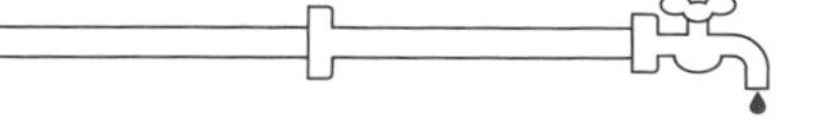

APARKALYPSE NOW, PART III

If you read Part I about how America's national parks got so overcrowded (page 197) and the mayhem that ensued (page 344), then it might seem like our most treasured outdoor destinations have been ruined forever. That's far from the case.

THE SEVEN PRINCIPLES

The U.S. Forest Service introduced Smokey Bear in 1944 as the mascot for its Wildfire Prevention Campaign. Woodsy Owl debuted in 1971 as the mascot for the children's Conservation Education Program. Maybe if the Forest Service's Leave No Trace Center for Outdoor Ethics (LNT), launched in Colorado in 1987, had a similar mascot, more people would know about the "Seven Principles of Leave No Trace." They are: "1) Plan ahead and prepare, 2) travel and camp on durable surfaces, 3) dispose of waste properly, 4) leave what you find, 5) minimize campfire impacts, 6) respect wildlife, and 7) be considerate of other visitors."

IN THE KNOW

The NPS's largest park is Alaska's Wrangell–St. Elias National Park and Preserve at 13.2 million acres (that's nearly two Rhode Islands). It also has the most elevation gain: 18,008 feet from sea level at the Gulf of Alaska to the summit of Mt. St. Elias, the second highest spot in the U.S.

LNT first published the list in 1999, but the seed for Leave No Trace was planted in the 1970s during the early days of the modern environmental movement. Back then, more Americans than ever before were going hiking and backpacking, but there was a prevailing "live off the land" mentality that made it seem like no big deal to pitch your tent wherever you liked and cut down trees for firewood. The Seven Principles were the culmination of decades of the LNT's research team drawing from "the latest insights from biologists, land managers, and other leaders in outdoor education."

THE DAY HIKER'S GUIDE TO THE GREAT OUTDOORS

Because the original Seven Principles dealt mainly with the backcountry, LNT later issued a "front-country" version for day hikers and car campers. They are: "1) Know before you go, 2) stick to trails and camp overnight right, 3) trash your trash and pick up poop, 4) leave it as you find it, 5) be careful with fire, 6) keep wildlife wild, and 7) share our trails and manage your pet." You can read more about these on LNT's website. Some pointers:

- **Don't Feed Wildlife:** Approaching and feeding an animal can alter its behavior, making it more likely to approach other people. As rangers often say, "A fed bear is a dead bear." Even throwing food scraps can cause harm. Although banana peels are technically biodegradable, they can take a long time to degrade. When eaten, scraps can alter an animal's organs so it can't digest its own food.
- **Don't Cut Switchbacks:** Trails that traverse steep slopes are zigzag-shaped for two reasons: to make the hike less strenuous, and—more importantly—to help maintain the integrity of the slope. But taking shortcuts, in addition to ruining the aesthetics, destroys vegetation and increases erosion.
- **Don't Pick Wildflowers:** The U.S. Forest Service strictly forbids removing any plant life from public lands. Why? "A critical chain of events is triggered for years to come once wildflowers are lost...Some pollinators depend on just one species of plant and die once their habitat has been destroyed." They add that it's not even worth it: "Wildflowers are fragile and many wilt and perish soon after being picked."
- **Tag Responsibly:** When it comes to sharing locations, LNT "encourages outdoor enthusiasts to stop and think about their actions and the potential consequences of posting pictures, GPS data, detailed maps, etc." It's also important for the more experienced enthusiasts, especially photographers, to set a good example by not going out of bounds just to get a better shot.

KNOW BEFORE YOU GO

And finally, we at the BRI wouldn't be doing our job if we didn't take this opportunity to tell you how to sh*t in the woods, Leave No Trace–style: Rule 1: Take it out with you in a bag. That's it.

However, if you are in the backcountry and you have no choice but to leave it out there, the experts recommend that you find a spot at least 200 feet from a water source, dig a hole eight inches deep, do your business, cover up your business, seal your toilet paper in a plastic bag, and at least take *that* out with you. And don't under any circumstances do this (as reported by LNT): "Zion's delicate desert ecosystem has been battered by tourists, some of whom wash diapers in the Virgin River."

Hopefully this all won't deter you from enjoying nature yourself. There are so many special places in the American West and elsewhere, with room enough for everyone to have fun—as long as you do some research before you head out and maintain a keen awareness of your surroundings while you're out there.

WHO IS COWBOY BOB?

If you're a fan of heist films, here's the true story of a bank robber the FBI nicknamed "Cowboy Bob." It may be coming soon to a theater near you.

★ THE PROFESSIONAL

In May 1991, a bearded man wearing dark sunglasses, a leather jacket, and a 10-gallon cowboy hat walked into the American Federal Bank in Irving, Texas. He waited his turn in line, and then walked up to the teller window. Without uttering a word, he handed the bank teller a note. "This is a bank robbery," the note read. "Give me your money. No marked bills or dye packs." (Dye packs are anti-theft devices hidden in stacks of bills that explode as soon as the robber leaves the bank. The explosion sprays the bills with a bright, indelible dye that makes spending the money impossible.)

The teller did as the note instructed and handed over the money in the cash drawer. The bank robber flexed each stack of bills to be sure there were no dye packs hidden inside, then he put the money in his bag and walked calmly out of the bank. He was in and out in less than 60 seconds and did not attract the attention of anyone other than the teller who received the note. No one saw the getaway car.

The FBI agent assigned to the case was a man named Steve Powell, who worked out of the bureau's Dallas office. After interviewing the bank staff and reviewing the security camera footage, Powell felt certain that the bank robber, whom he nicknamed "Cowboy Bob," was a professional criminal. Reason: Cowboy Bob did everything right. He was calm, not fidgety; he never spoke; and he wore gloves, so there were no fingerprints to tie him to the crime scene. What's more, he kept his head down and never looked directly at the security cameras. Between Cowboy Bob's mustache and beard (which Powell suspected were fake), his dark sunglasses, and the 10-gallon hat he wore, nearly all of the man's face was concealed from view.

With no voice, no fingerprints, and no clear idea of what Cowboy Bob looked like, Powell had almost nothing to go on. All he knew was that Cowboy Bob appeared to be about 5'9" tall, Caucasian, a bit paunchy, and there was gray in his hair, so he was probably in his mid- to late 40s. He could have been anyone.

★ REPEAT OFFENDER

Powell suspected that Cowboy Bob would strike again, and he was right: Seven months later in December 1991, someone matching Cowboy Bob's description and modus operandi struck the Savings of America bank, also in Irving, and made off with $1,258. This time a witness saw the getaway car, a brown 1975 Pontiac Grand Prix, and took down the license plate number. But the license plate didn't belong to a Pontiac—it belonged to a Chevrolet. When Powell went to the home of the Chevrolet

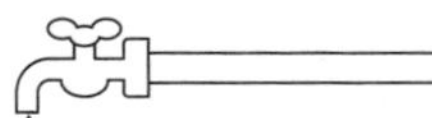

owner, the car's license plate was missing. It had been stolen earlier that day (no doubt by Cowboy Bob) so that it could be used in the bank robbery. Once again, what few leads Powell had were dead ends.

In January 1992, Cowboy Bob robbed the Texas Heritage Bank in Garland, Texas, this time getting away with about $3,000. Then in May he robbed the Nation's Bank in Mesquite, Texas, and took $5,317. When the teller tried to hand him a stack of bills containing a dye pack, Cowboy Bob calmly handed it back; then he walked out of the bank with the rest of the money and disappeared.

★ TWO-FER

Eight months later, Cowboy Bob struck again: In September 1992, he robbed the First Gibraltar Bank in Mesquite and made off with $1,772. Someone did get a look at the getaway car—it was the same brown Pontiac Grand Prix—and took down the license plate number. But just as before, the license plate had been stolen earlier that day.

Later that same afternoon, Cowboy Bob robbed another bank in Mesquite—First Interstate. It was the first time he'd robbed two banks in one day, and it was his biggest haul yet: $13,706. Once again, someone saw the Pontiac Grand Prix and wrote down the license plate number, and it was a different number than had been reported in the first robbery that day.

Powell naturally assumed that Cowboy Bob had stolen two license plates, one for each bank robbery...until he ran the plate and it came back for a brown 1975 Pontiac Grand Prix owned by a man named Pete Tallas. Powell tracked him down at his work, but Tallas denied that he was Cowboy Bob or that he even had the Grand Prix in his possession. He explained that he'd given the Grand Prix to his sister Peggy Jo, who lived with their mother, Helen Tallas. Peggy Jo was unmarried, so Agent Powell figured she must have gotten romantically involved with whoever Cowboy Bob was, and that with or without her knowledge, he was using her car in the bank robberies.

★ THE PLOT THICKENS

Powell and other FBI agents raced to Peggy Jo's apartment. The brown Grand Prix was parked outside, and a short time later a middle-aged woman who turned out to be Peggy Jo walked up to the car and drove off. The FBI agents waited until she was well out of view of the apartment before they pulled her over. If Cowboy Bob was still in the apartment, they didn't want him to know that they were outside.

Peggy Jo denied knowing anything about any bank robberies. She said she'd used the car earlier that day to buy fertilizer, and when the agents checked her trunk, the bag of fertilizer was there. When Powell asked if the agents could search her apartment, she consented.

Helen Tallas was alone in the apartment; Cowboy Bob was nowhere to be found. But when FBI agents searched Peggy Jo's bedroom, they found a styrofoam mannequin's head on a shelf in the closet. Pinned to the head was a fake beard that closely resembled the beard worn by Cowboy Bob in the bank surveillance tapes. They also found Cowboy Bob's leather jacket, his 10-gallon hat, and a pair of men's cowboy boots. But no Cowboy Bob. Had he spotted the FBI agents and made his escape?

★ A LIKELY STORY

Powell pressed Peggy Jo to give him Cowboy Bob's identity and to tell them where they could find him. "I said, 'Now come on, who's been with you? Where is he?' " Powell remembered.

"There is nobody else," Peggy Jo insisted. She stuck to her story even after agents found the money from both of that day's bank robberies hidden under her bed. Powell was certain that Peggy Jo was lying to protect a man in her life...until he noticed faint spots of glue above her upper lip, which could have been used to attach a false mustache. Then he noticed some gray material on Peggy Jo's hair that was flaking off and landing on her shoulders. "At that moment it clicked for me," he told NBC News in 2005. Cowboy Bob wasn't a man—Cowboy Bob was Peggy Jo Tallas. "I asked her to step out of the vehicle [and told her] that she was under arrest for bank robbery."

It's not clear what happened in Peggy Jo's life in the early 1990s that caused her to start robbing banks at the age of 47. Did she do it for the thrill, perhaps as part of a midlife crisis? Her favorite movie was the 1969 film *Butch Cassidy and the Sundance Kid*, starring Paul Newman and Robert Redford as the famous Wild West train and bank robbers. She'd seen it dozens of times. Or was the money her primary motivation? And how did she get so good at it? Were there other, earlier robberies that the FBI didn't know about, or did Peggy Jo learn her "trade" by devouring heist movies and true-crime paperbacks? Some of these questions might have been answered had the case ever gone to trial, but it never did: In 1992, Peggy Jo pled guilty to bank robbery and was sentenced to 33 months in prison.

★ DO OR DIE

Peggy Jo served her time without incident and was released from prison in 1996. She moved back in with her mother and cared for her until Helen passed away in 2002. Two years later, Peggy Jo bought a used motor home, telling friends that she wanted to drive it to Mexico and live on the beach. She sold her car, moved out of her apartment, and hit the road in the RV.

It wasn't clear to friends and family how she was going to pay for her new lifestyle, though. Then in October 2004, someone described as an old man wearing a floppy hat, baggy clothes, gloves, and a glued-on mustache walked into the Guaranty Bank in Tyler, Texas, and told a teller, "All your money. No bait bills. No blow-up money," in a voice that the teller thought "sounded a bit feminine." About a minute later the "old man" walked back out again with a bagful of the bank's cash—how much was taken

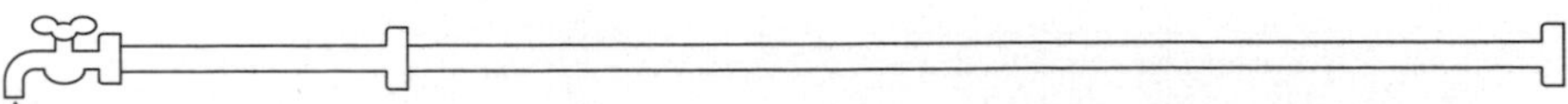

The Japanese word for raccoon is *araiguma*, which translates to "washing bear."

was never disclosed.

That bank heist was not linked to Peggy Jo at the time, but seven months later, on May 5, 2005, she walked into the same bank dressed in dark women's clothing, a floppy hat, and oversized sunglasses. Rather than handing the teller a note, she spoke to the teller and told them to hand over the money in the cash drawer. The teller complied. And this time, instead of inspecting the bills to make sure there were no dye packs as she had in previous robberies, Peggy Jo let the teller put the money into the bag.

★ RED ALERT

Seconds later, Peggy Jo walked out of the bank with $11,241 in cash. She didn't get far: As soon as she stepped out of the door, a dye pack hidden in the money exploded, spraying her and the money with red dye. Peggy Jo ran to her motor home to get away, but the bag of money trailed clouds of bright red smoke behind her as she ran. Some people driving by saw the smoke, and correctly assumed that she was a bank robber and called the police. When Peggy Jo sped off in her RV, they followed her, giving directions to the police over the phone as they gave chase.

A few minutes later, the police cornered the RV in a residential neighborhood. After a standoff that lasted several minutes, Peggy Jo poked her head out of the RV and told the police, "You're going to have to kill me." The officers pleaded with her to surrender peacefully, but she stepped out of the vehicle brandishing what appeared to be a handgun. When she lowered it in the direction of the officers, they opened fire. She was struck by four bullets and died at the scene. The gun turned out to be a toy pistol; a loaded .357 Magnum handgun inside the RV had not been touched.

★ THE CALL

Peggy Jo Tallas was anything but a typical bank robber. Fewer than 5 percent of bank robberies in the United States are committed by women, and almost never by women in their mid-40s—and in the case of Peggy Jo's last robbery, at the age of 60. Perhaps because of this, Steve Powell, the FBI agent assigned to her case in the 1990s, viewed her more sympathetically than he did other bank robbers he'd chased. By the time of Peggy Jo's final bank heist, he had retired, but he still received a message on his answering machine from an FBI agent telling him that he had some bad news to report about Cowboy Bob. When Powell called back, he said to the agent, "Say it ain't so."

Peggy Jo shied away from publicity and never sought fame for her crimes. She turned down reporters' requests for interviews, and while in prison, she even declined at least one lucrative offer from a true-crime author to collaborate on a book about her life. But she loved *Butch Cassidy and the Sundance Kid*, so what about a movie? Whether she would have approved or not, a film is in the works—in 2017, Searchlight Pictures signed Michael Showalter, director of the 2017 film *The Big Sick*, to direct a "Western/thriller" based on her life. The working title is *The Last Ride of Cowboy Bob.*

As a child, pop star Ariana Grande was hit in the face by hockey pucks while in the stands at two separate games.

THE CHEWBACCA CHRONICLES

We found more fun bits of Wookiee trivia than we could fit into the Chewbacca story (page 304), so we smuggled the surplus over to this page.

Things That Sound Like Chewbacca

Apparently it's very difficult to do a convincing Chewbacca impression. (Don't believe it? Try it.) That makes sense, considering that his "voice" was created by splicing together several different animal sounds. But some *Star Wars* fans have been able to re-create it by using inanimate objects. Here are some odd examples we found on the Internet that bear an uncanny resemblance to the Wookiee's call:

- A wooden chair sliding across a stone floor
- A car driving through a tunnel
- A stuck kitchen drawer being pulled open
- A wall heater turning on
- Old elevator doors opening
- An electric car window opening and closing
- An electric toothbrush with a low battery
- A toilet paper dispenser in a public restroom stall

Bigfoot from Space

In 1967, two men exploring a remote creek in northern California filmed the now-famous blurry footage of a supposed Sasquatch (see page 352) walking briskly past them, sparking off the modern Bigfoot craze. Fifteen years later, in a redwood forest only a few miles from that original sighting, a movie crew was filming *Return of the Jedi.* Just to be safe, while Peter Mayhew was in his Chewbacca costume, he was accompanied by bodyguards wearing bright orange vests...on the off chance that a hunter would mistake the Wookiee for Bigfoot.

The Chewbacca Defense

In 1998, *South Park* used the Wookiee to satirize the O. J. Simpson trial. In the episode, attorney Johnnie Cochran is suing the Chef. "Ladies and gentlemen of this *supposed* jury," he says, "I have one final thing I want you to consider. Ladies and gentlemen, this is Chewbacca. Chewbacca is a Wookiee from the planet Kashyyyk. But Chewbacca lives on the planet Endor. Now think about it; that does not make sense! Why would a Wookiee, an eight-foot-tall Wookiee, want to live on Endor, with

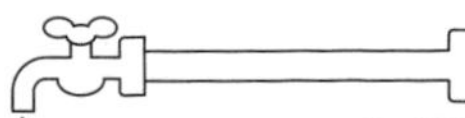

In 1997, scientists at Cornell University made a six-string guitar the size of a single human blood cell. It's played by shooting laser beams at the strings.

a bunch of two-foot-tall Ewoks?" The other attorney says, "Damn it! He's using the Chewbacca defense!"

Cochran continues, "That does not make sense! But more important, you have to ask yourself: What does this have to do with this case? Nothing. Ladies and gentlemen, it has nothing to do with this case! It does not make sense! Look at me. I'm a lawyer defending a major record company, and I'm talkin' about Chewbacca! Does that make sense? Ladies and gentlemen, I am not making any sense! None of this makes sense! And so you have to remember, when you're in that jury room deliberatin' and conjugatin' the Emancipation Proclamation, does it make sense? No! Ladies and gentlemen of this supposed jury, it does not make sense! If Chewbacca lives on Endor, you must acquit! The defense rests."

Although Cochran's argument has nothing to do with the case, he wins...much like the way he won the Simpson trial by getting the jury to ignore overwhelming evidence and focus only on the questionable size of one glove. (And for the record, Chewbacca never lived on Endor; he was just visiting.)

Head Games

At a Profiles in History auction in 2012, a Chewbacca head that had been used in the original *Star Wars* trilogy sold to a private collector for $172,200.

That's No Cane

In 2013, Peter Mayhew, then 69, was going through security at Denver International Airport when he was stopped by TSA agents. Reason: they were suspicious of his cane, which was much heavier than a regular cane and looked a lot like a lightsaber from *Star Wars*. The 7' 3" Mayhew explained that he needed a sturdy cane, and that it looked like a lightsaber because he is Chewbacca. He was briefly detained while they made sure his laser sword was not operational. During the holdup, Mayhew took the opportunity to send out a tweet to his 25,000 Twitter followers: "@AmericanAir won't allow me through the airport with me cane!" Mayhew's faithful fans inundated the airline's Twitter page with cries of "Let Chewbacca fly!" Less than five minutes later, Mayhew was on his way (but American denied it had anything to do with the tweets).

IN THE KNOW

Ever heard of a Wookiee Cookie? No, it's not something you might step in on a Kashyyyk forest floor. It's one of 29 recipes in *The Star Wars Cookbook: Wookiee Cookies and Other Galactic Recipes*, by Robin Davis. In addition to the chewy (Chewie?) chocolate snacks, there are recipes for "Boba Fett-uccine," "Greedo's Burritos," "Han-burgers," "Jabba Jiggle," and "Obi-Wan Kebobs."

Wookiee Talk

According to Wookieepedia, the online *Star Wars* encyclopedia, Chewbacca's language is

called Shyriiwook, which translates to "Tongue of the Tree People." (It's said that Shyriiwook has more than 150 words for "wood.") Here are a few phrases from the *Star Wars Galactic Phrase Book & Travel Guide* by Ben Burtt, the man who came up with Chewie's voice:

- *Wyaaaaaa. Ruh ruh.* ("Hello. How are you?")
- *Huwaa muaa mumwa.* ("Can I buy you a drink?")
- *Roooarrgh ur roo.* ("I have a bad feeling about this.")
- *Wua ga ma uma ahuma ooma.* ("I think my arm has been pulled out of the socket.")
- *Wooo hwa hwa?* ("Nice weather, eh?")

Death of a Wookiee

Q: How do you upset an entire legion of *Star Wars* fans?

A: Kill Chewbacca.

That's exactly what George Lucas allowed to happen in a novel from the *Star Wars* EU (Expanded Universe)—the collection of licensed *Star Wars* spin-off material in books, comics, video games, and other media that is considered canon (elements of the story that, together, are accepted as part of the official version of the story). That means that if a character dies in an EU book or TV show, that character is dead in every other incarnation, even the movies. In 1999, with interest in the *Star Wars* EU starting to wane, editors from Del Rey Books sent George Lucas a letter asking if they could kill off a major character (reportedly, their number-one wish was Luke Skywalker). Lucas sent back a letter with a list of characters they could *not* kill. Skywalker was on that list...but Chewbacca wasn't.

So in October 1999, the New Jedi Order novel *Vector Prime* was published. In a pivotal scene, Chewbacca gets stranded on a planet...that gets crushed by its own moon. He does not survive. The novel, which even had its own TV commercial, made the *New York Times* best-seller list. Suffice it to say there was a great disturbance in the Force when news of the Wookiee's demise spread. Some radio stations were even falsely reporting that Chewbacca's portrayer, Peter Mayhew, had died (he hadn't). After Disney took over the franchise in 2012, it scrapped every last EU storyline from the canon...and Chewbacca came back to life.

* * *

"You're not a star until they can spell your name in Karachi."

—Humphrey Bogart

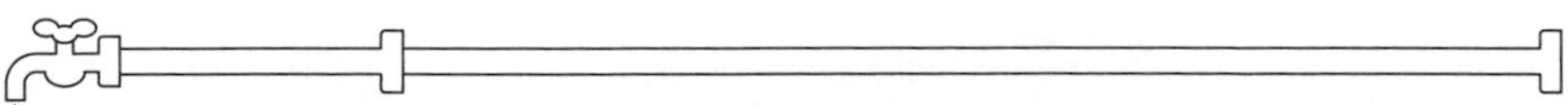

Put together, all the parking spaces in the U.S. take up more space than the entire nation of Israel.

WILLIAM MITCHELL'S HITS AND MISSES

On page 357, we told you the story of how food chemist William Mitchell sparked one of the biggest candy fads of the 1970s. That's not his only claim to fame.

HIT: Tang Instant Breakfast Drink (1957)

Description: Tang wasn't much more than Kool-Aid reformulated and reimagined so that it could be passed off as a healthy breakfast drink. General Foods marketed it as an instant, powdered orange juice substitute "you don't squeeze, unfreeze, or refrigerate...packed with more vitamin C and A than any orange juice you can buy." Tang was 94 percent sugar by weight.

Details: Mitchell came up with the formulation for the drink mix, which included a "dry flavor and aroma enhancer" he invented that helped give Tang its characteristic tangy flavor and smell.

Even in those more innocent days of the late 1950s and early 1960s, not many parents saw Tang as a credible substitute for orange juice. Sales languished...until the United States got ready to go to the Moon, and then only by chance. NASA's Gemini spaceflight program, which lasted from 1961 to 1966, used a life-support module that produced drinking water, but it employed a chemical reaction that gave the water an off taste, which the astronauts didn't like. So NASA sent them into space with vacuum-sealed bags of Tang. When they wanted a drink, they used a needle to squirt water into the bag, squished the bag to mix it, then inserted a straw and drank—the zero-gravity equivalent of a juice box.

The NASA connection proved to be quite a marketing hook for General Foods, which used TV and print advertising campaigns to capitalize on Tang's association with the space race. If Tang was good enough for the astronauts, many parents now concluded, it must be good enough for their kids. That kind of thinking helped turn Tang into one of the top-selling instant breakfast drinks of the 1960s and '70s...even though it never really did win the hearts of the astronauts. As Buzz Aldrin, the second man to walk on the Moon, put it, "Tang sucks."

MISS: "Dessert-on-the-Stick" instant powdered dessert mix (1969)

Description: Dessert-on-the-Stick was Mitchell's kid-friendly alternative to messy popsicles and ice cream bars. "While these products have been widely accepted...one

major disadvantage is that the product must be eaten in the frozen state; otherwise, it will not remain firmly attached to the stick. This characteristic makes the product somewhat undesirable as a treat for young children who invariably prolong the consumption of it until it falls off the stick and onto their clothing, a rug, etc.," he wrote in his patent application.

Details: Previous attempts to create an instant powdered dessert mix used either gelatin or starch as the main ingredient. But when gelatin was prepared with cold milk or water, the result was a "rubbery, grainy texture which does not dissolve easily in the mouth," Mitchell wrote. Starch-based desserts made with cold milk or water did not gel well and had a slimy texture. What Mitchell did was find a way to combine gelatin and starch powders (he used potato starch) in such a way that "all the desired properties of starch and gelatin are retained." Bonus: "The pudding has a tendency to remain firmly attached to the stick." As delicious as it sounds, half-gelatin, half–potato starch Dessert-on-the-Stick somehow never caught on.

HIT: Cool Whip Dessert Topping (1967)

Description: As you probably already know, Cool Whip is a ready-made, hassle-free substitute for real whipped cream.

Details: Making whipped cream from scratch requires time, skill, and—for people who didn't own electric mixers in the mid-1960s—physical labor. Whipped cream is also perishable, and it doesn't hold its shape for long, so you can't make it in advance.

The dessert topping that Mitchell came up with—whose main ingredients are water, hydrogenated vegetable oil, high-fructose corn syrup, and regular corn syrup—had none of these drawbacks. It was sold pre-whipped and could be stored in the freezer for months on end. Once opened, it could be stored in the refrigerator for up to two weeks, and it held its shape seemingly forever, even at room temperature. And unlike dairy products such as whipping cream, it could be distributed frozen. That meant that Cool Whip could be manufactured in a single giant factory in Avon, New York, and distributed nationwide. (Dairy products are produced regionally because they don't last long enough to be shipped long distances.) More than 50 years after Mitchell invented Cool Whip, it remains the best-selling brand of whipped topping in the United States.

MISS: Powdered Alcohol (1976)

Description: Powdered Alcohol was Kool-Aid for grown-ups. When the dry powder was mixed with water, the result was a clear, flavorless alcohol similar to vodka.

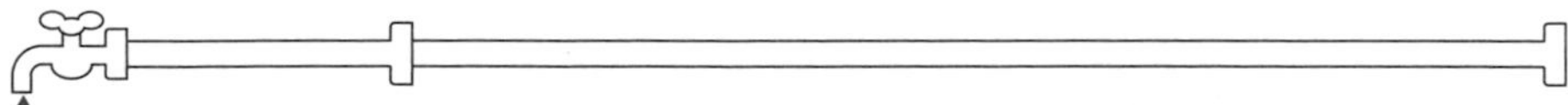

Details: Mitchell's formula for powdered booze wasn't the first, but it was the first that was actually pleasant to drink. Earlier versions used too much carbohydrate material as a powder "fixative," and didn't dissolve easily or well in cold water. The result was "either undesirably sweet...or cloudy appearing beverages...with too high viscosity [and] poor appearance and texture," he wrote in his patent application. The formula that Mitchell came up with solved these problems by using "certain carbohydrate materials, [that]...will readily dissolve in cold water to form low-viscosity, clear, colorless alcoholic solutions." Why he wasn't awarded the Nobel Prize for Chemistry for this important work is a mystery.

General Foods wasn't in the alcohol business, so it's no surprise that the company never tried to capitalize on Mitchell's instant vodka. If they had, they probably would have regretted it: When Lipsmark LLC, an Arizona company, tried to bring its own version of "Palcohol" (short for powdered alcohol) to market in 2014, 29 out of 50 U.S. states banned it at least temporarily amid fears that drinkers might abuse the product, perhaps by snorting it. Powdered alcohol is legal, however, in Germany, the Netherlands, and Japan.

HIT: Rice Milk (1988)

Description: If you've read this far, smug with satisfaction that you would never, *ever* allow Tang, Cool Whip, Pop Rocks, or any of Mitchell's other culinary monstrosities to pass your lips, brace yourself. Rice Dream brand rice milk is another one of his creations. (Well, co-creations.)

Details: Mitchell retired from General Foods in 1976, but he never stopped inventing. When his daughter Cheryl got her PhD in chemistry and went into business for herself in 1980, the two of them worked together on various projects. In March 1988, they applied for two patents for rice products that were manufactured using very similar processes: When the rice fiber was removed during processing, the result was "rice syrup sweetener." When the fiber was left in, the result was a "nutritional rice milk product" that, unlike other kinds of rice milk on the market, had a nutritional value similar to whole-grain rice and yet was "characterized by absence of a rice flavor." Today that product, sold under the brand name Rice Dream, is the top-selling rice beverage in the United States.

William Mitchell passed away in 2004 at the age of 92, but Cheryl Mitchell has continued to innovate. If you're a fan of soy, almond, walnut, cashew, peanut, hazelnut, oat, or other nondairy milks, especially if they're high in protein and low in oils, stabilizers, thickeners, and other additives, there's a very good chance you are drinking a milk made using a process she developed. Bon appétit!

DUMB CROOKS

More proof that crime doesn't pay.

WHEN YOUR GETAWAY GOES AWAY

In 2015, a 25-year-old man named Che Hearn drove to a Walmart Superstore in Round Lake Beach, Illinois, where he placed some electronics in his cart and then tried to leave without paying for them. Confronted by employees, Hearn ran away empty-handed, but when he went to look for his car, it wasn't there. Where could it have gone? Apparently Hearn was behind on his car payments (which might explain the shoplifting), and he'd been followed to the Walmart by a repossession company. While he was botching his crime, they were towing away his car. Police later caught up to Hearn...on foot.

ORDER TO GO

At around 3:00 a.m. one night in May 2019, someone stole a food truck from outside a bar in Mount Pleasant, Michigan. Staffers went outside and heard a crash and then loud screeching sounds. A block away, a patrolman saw the food truck dragging a large grill on its side; sparks were everywhere. They arrested the driver, 21-year-old Zachary Jenkins, who reportedly failed every sobriety test he was given—even answering "12" after being told to "pick a number between 13 and 15." When asked why he decided to steal a food truck, Jenkins said, "I'm a dumbass."

CRIMINAL, PUNCH THYSELF

A 29-year-old man named Brandon Killian was arrested after taking part in a violent assault on another man in Shawnee, Oklahoma, in 2019. In the interrogation room, Killian claimed that the other guy started the fight, and that he was actually the victim. "This side of my face hurts," he told the police, "right here, where I was first socked." Killian was unaware that the fight had been recorded on video by an onlooker. He was also unaware that the interrogation room had a surveillance camera. When the officer stepped out of the room to get a camera to photograph Killian's alleged injuries, Killian proceeded to punch himself in the face several times, hoping to make it look like self-defense. Result: "preparing false evidence" (namely, his face) was added to his litany of charges. He got 18 years.

About 1 in every 7 Google searches is for something that's never been googled before.

FILM FIRST: *SKY CAPTAIN*

Here's a story from Hollywood's "dustbin of history"–about the men who made a movie that seemingly offered a glimpse of future filmmaking, and who captured the world's attention...for a brief moment, at least.

GORGEOUS, GEORGE

When he was making his *Star Wars* prequels in the late 1990s and early 2000s, George Lucas proclaimed that he'd like to someday make a movie entirely with computers–settings, characters, everything. He had to settle for placing real human actors like Natalie Portman and Ewan McGregor alongside CGI alien Jar Jar Binks. But in 2004, two novice moviemakers, brothers Kerry and Kevin Conran, took the cinematic world a little closer to Lucas's goal when their first film, a retro, World War II action-adventure called *Sky Captain and the World of Tomorrow,* opened in thousands of theaters across the country. Unlike the *Star Wars* movies, which filmed in the deserts of Tunisia and other locations, *Sky Captain* was filmed entirely on a set lined with blue walls. With a relatively cheap computer and some software, the Conrans showed that even the little guy could make a movie that looked like an expensive Hollywood blockbuster.

In the end, the Conrans' methods were adopted by the big studios to make big movies even bigger...while the Conrans completely disappeared from the film industry they helped revolutionize.

BROTHER ACT

In the 1980s, Kerry Conran was accepted into the filmmaking program at the prestigious California Institute of the Arts, but he wound up hanging around the animation department. He was intrigued with how the artists could create whatever they wanted from scratch. "If you wanted something gigantic, they could do it, just draw it," he told the *New York Times* in 2004. Inspired, Conran got to work on a student film called *That Darn Bear,* an innovative work that combined live-action footage with animated characters. He never finished it, though–in 1988, after he'd been working on the movie for three years, *Who Framed Roger Rabbit* hit theaters and it did exactly what Conran had sought to do, making *That Darn Bear* instantly outdated.

Discouraged, Conran quit filmmaking and went to work in tech support and software design. But in 1993, he found creative inspiration again in the lifelike CGI dinosaurs of *Jurassic Park.* When he saw the movie's giant creatures, all of which had been rendered with computers, Conran realized there was no limit on what he could do. "What does it cost to hit the 'scale' button and make something enormous? Nothing," he said.

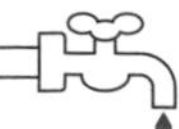

He teamed up with his brother Kevin, a freelance advertising illustrator, and they decided to make a film—all by themselves. They both liked old movies, particularly Saturday-afternoon serials from the 1940s, so at Kerry's suggestion, they planned out a feature-length homage to those serials. The plot: a cocky fighter pilot and a plucky reporter team up to track down the evil villain who's sending out armies of giant flying robots to terrorize Earth's cities. Using one Mac IIci computer, the Conrans got to work, creating every individual item in every individual frame with software. And after four years of work, they had amassed six minutes of footage.

HOORAY FOR HOLLYWOOD

By that time it was 1998, five years into the Conrans' quest to make a movie entirely at home. That's when a friend of Kevin Conran's wife, a movie producer named Marsha Oglesby, came over for dinner one night. The conversation turned to filmmaking, and Oglesby really wanted to see this cool, six-minute film the brothers had so painstakingly crafted. At first Kerry hesitated to show her the unfinished product, but he finally relented...and Oglesby loved it. She sent it to the biggest name in Hollywood she knew: Jon Avnet, producer of films such as *Fried Green Tomatoes* and *Risky Business.* He asked to see the screenplay, which he read and loved, and then sent to an actor he had in mind for the lead role—Jude Law, who liked the project, too. With big stars on board (Angelina Jolie agreed to play one-eyed Royal Navy commander Franky Cook, and Gwyneth Paltrow took the role of ace reporter Polly Perkins), and with Avnet's company investing over $70 million in the film, production got underway in 2002.

SAVE THE DATE

Despite the Conrans being complete novices, the production went relatively smoothly, with no major clashes or technical difficulties—until Avnet successfully pitched *Sky Captain* to Paramount Pictures, which would distribute the movie upon its release. Paramount insisted they move the planned release date of March 2005 to September 17, 2004. In other words, the Conrans would have six *fewer* months to complete the film's extensive special effects. To make the deadline, they hired 13 different companies around the world to process the special effects for *Sky Captain* simultaneously. (That's now commonly done on big blockbusters, but at the time, it was standard practice in Hollywood to hire just one special-effects company per movie.)

The release date move showed the studio's confidence in the movie, and its late summer release date positioned it as a blockbuster in the making, alongside other big hits of 2004 like *The Day After Tomorrow* and *Spider-Man 2.* Movie blogs and magazines provided endless press, calling the film "revolutionary" for its technical innovations and unique look. The trailer hit theaters in mid-2004, featuring a

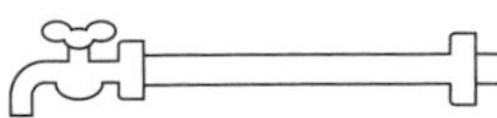

First major third party in the U.S.: The Know Nothings (1855–1860).

stylized, retro black-and-white New York under attack by huge flying robots. It also showed brief glimpses of dazzling imagery: military bases atop clouds, and World War II planes dogfighting around skyscrapers.

BLOWN OUT OF THE SKY

In September 2004, *Sky Captain and the World of Tomorrow* opened in more than 3,100 theaters in the United States and Canada. The prerelease hype was very effective, and the film grossed $15.5 million in its first weekend, enough to make it the #1 movie in the country. Critics praised it, too. Roger Ebert called *Sky Captain* "a film that escapes from the imagination directly onto the screen." But audiences disagreed. Once the film opened, word of mouth supplanted studio hype and critical praise, and moviegoers stayed away. In its second weekend, *Sky Captain* earned $6 million, and in its third, just $3 million. After about a month, it quietly disappeared from theaters altogether.

Why didn't the public like it? Ironically, according to Hollywood analysts, it was for exactly the reasons the Conrans made it in the first place: *Sky Captain* was a black-and-white, old-fashioned movie that seemed like a corny throwback to films of the 1940s.

INTO THE DUSTBIN

When all was said and done, *Sky Captain and the World of Tomorrow* grossed $37 million in the United States, just over half of its high production budget. In other words, it was a bomb. And what happens to filmmakers—especially unproven newbies—whose movies bomb? They don't get to make more movies.

After production was finished and while prerelease buzz was growing, Kerry and Kevin Conran lined up their next film: *John Carter of Mars*, an adaptation of Edgar Rice Burroughs's classic sci-fi novel *A Princess of Mars*. They made a special effects–heavy short film as they'd done for *Sky Captain*, with Martians and a Martian landscape, and Paramount was on board. But when *Sky Captain* bombed, Paramount started to drag its feet on making another expensive movie with the Conrans at the helm. (Ultimately, the company's rights to the book expired, and the Burroughs estate sold the rights to Disney, which did make *John Carter*—and it was an even costlier bomb than *Sky Captain*.) There were also plans for a Japanese-made *Sky Captain* TV show, but those fell apart too.

Neither Kerry nor Kevin Conran ever headed up a major motion picture again. In 2012, Kerry directed a short film called *Gumdrop*, and subsequently gave up filmmaking for good. Kevin found work as a production designer in animation, working on the teams that made *Bee Movie* and *Monsters vs. Aliens*. They never accomplished what they set out to do—make it possible for anyone with a computer to produce a big movie. Instead, they made it possible for big studios to make bigger movies for less money. But they were true innovators, and they did give shape to a kind of moviemaking that's now considered standard. Despite that, the Conrans felt like losers. As Kerry told a reporter for the *New York Times*, "I am basically an amorphous blob of nothing."

"WE ARE ALL IN SPACE"

If you happen to be reading this in the distant future, then you probably already know what it's like to go to space. But when this Bathroom Reader *was written in the early 21st century, only about 600 humans—out of the billions who ever lived—had gotten the opportunity to leave Earth's atmosphere. And all of those early spacefarers came back...different. Here's a look at what space travel does to a person's outlook... and what a lot more of it could do for our planet.*

THE OVERVIEW EFFECT

Do you remember the first time you gazed out of an airplane window? No picture or movie could have prepared you for the actual experience of witnessing the trees, roads, and buildings shrink beneath you. Whether you realized it or not, your worldview was expanded that day. Now imagine what it would be like to look out of a spaceship window and see your entire planet.

In the 1970s, a self-described "space philosopher" named Frank White was on an airplane staring out his window, thinking about this very thing, when he came up with the concept that led to his 1987 book *The Overview Effect: Space Exploration and Human Evolution.* After interviewing 29 space travelers, White describes the Overview Effect as a sense of euphoria that leads to a "cosmic connection" shared by everyone who has seen the Earth from space. It doesn't matter whether they're astronauts, cosmonauts, taikonauts (Chinese astronauts), or space tourists, or what country they're from. "They have the feeling that the Earth itself is a whole system," White says, "and we're just a part of it."

Aside from simply being fascinating, the implications of this are profound. White and many others have suggested that if a lot more people got to experience the Overview Effect, we could finally achieve world peace. "How would everything change if we began to think of ourselves as a seven billion member team, a crew on a spacecraft?" There are plans underway—from White and others in the growing "space citizenship" movement—for that vision to become a reality. (More on those plans later.) In the meantime, if you want to know what it's really like to travel in space or walk on the Moon, there's no one more qualified to describe it than those who have already been there.

YURI'S VIEW

The Space Age officially began in 1957 when the USSR launched the unmanned *Sputnik 1* satellite. The first *human* spaceflight, which took place four years later,

A road in Calgary, Alberta, is called "Vaseline Alley" because empty jars of petroleum jelly keep showing up there. (Nobody knows why.)

was as much for bragging rights as anything else—at least for the countries vying for technological supremacy during the Cold War. All Yuri Gagarin wanted to do was fly, and the 27-year-old test pilot beat out 200 other applicants to become the Soviet Union's first cosmonaut. Four days after his historic flight on April 12, 1961—in which he completed one Earth orbit in a little less than two hours and became a national hero—Gagarin said in a speech at the Kremlin, "I completed this flight in the name of our Fatherland, in the name of the great Soviet people, and the communist party of the Soviet Union."

At least that's what he said in front of Soviet leader Nikita Khrushchev. When Gagarin gave a magazine interview only two months later, he had a much more worldly view, saying our planet is "blue, without boundaries, all countries unite." He died during a test flight two years later.

He gave humanity its first eyewitness description of what our planet looks like from orbit.

In 2013, Gagarin's daughter Elena Gagarina said she could remember from her childhood how much her father "desperately wanted to fly in space again. He'd enjoyed that first flight, but it was over so quickly!" That illustrates another aspect of experiencing the Overview Effect: You can't shake it.

Gagarin's historic mission did more than just prove, once and for all, that a person can indeed survive a spaceflight (there were doubts)—he gave humanity its first eyewitness description of what our planet looks like from orbit:

> "What beauty...The clouds which cover the Earth's surface are very visible, and their shadow on the Earth can be seen distinctly. The color of the sky is completely black. The stars on this black background seem to be somewhat brighter and clearer. The Earth is surrounded by a characteristic blue halo... particularly visible at the horizon. From a light-blue coloring, the sky blends into a beautiful deep blue, then dark blue, violet, and finally complete black."

MORE OVERVIEWPOINTS

The Overview Effect has had a similar effect on just about everyone who has traveled to space, but each in their own unique way. Here's what these spacefarers had to say about their out-of-this-world experiences, along with a few details about what made them tick.

SPACEFARER: Nicole Stott, NASA astronaut

OVERVIEW EFFECT: *"You really realize very quickly that we, and our planet, are small. We're not that far away from each other. We all share the same 'planet in space.' When you take the time to think about it, that 'we're all in space' part is pretty compelling."*

DETAILS: In the first half-century of spaceflight, it wasn't too difficult to be the first to do something. For example, in 2011, Stott became the first painter in space to use watercolors. (That painting is now in the Smithsonian.) Known as the "Artistic Astronaut" during her 27 years with NASA, Stott flew twice on the space shuttle *Discovery* to the International Space Station (ISS). "Going to space gave me the opportunity to separate from our planet," she said, "but in doing so it allowed me to feel more connected to it than I ever had on its surface...I carry that with me all the time now."

SPACEFARER: Neil Armstrong, NASA astronaut

OVERVIEW EFFECT: *"I remember on the trip home on* Apollo 11 *it suddenly struck me that that tiny pea, pretty and blue, was the Earth. I put up my thumb and shut one eye, and my thumb blotted out the planet Earth. I didn't feel like a giant. I felt very, very small."*

DETAILS: That was on Armstrong's trip home in July 1969, after he became the first person to set foot on the Moon. Although he trained as a test pilot, Armstrong was an aeronautical engineer by trade, and a self-proclaimed "space nerd" at heart. Though he seldom gave interviews, he did say in 1970 that he fully expected a permanently manned Moon base by the year 2000.

Decades later, as it became evident that politics were getting in the way of space exploration, Armstrong testified before the U.S. House of Representatives' Science and Technology Committee in 2010: "Some question why Americans should return to the Moon. 'After all,' they say, 'we have already been there.' I find that mystifying. It would be as if 16th-century monarchs proclaimed that 'we need not go to the New World, we have already been there.' Or as if President Thomas Jefferson announced in 1803 that Americans 'need not go west of the Mississippi, the Lewis and Clark expedition has already been there.' Americans have visited and examined six locations on Luna, varying in size from a suburban lot to a small township. That leaves more than 14 million square miles yet to explore."

SPACEFARER: Valentina Tereshkova, Russian cosmonaut

OVERVIEW EFFECT: *"Once you've been in space, you appreciate how small and fragile the Earth is."*

DETAILS: Unlike American astronauts, who until the late 1970s were required to be fighter pilots, the only qualification for a Russian cosmonaut was to be a parachutist. That opened the door for women to apply. Tereshkova beat out more than 400 other applicants, and on June 16, 1963, she became the first woman in space, orbiting Earth 48 times over three days (without a toothbrush). Twenty-six years old at the time, she still holds the record as the youngest woman in space, and she's the only woman to go up there by herself. Tereshkova went on to attain the rank of major

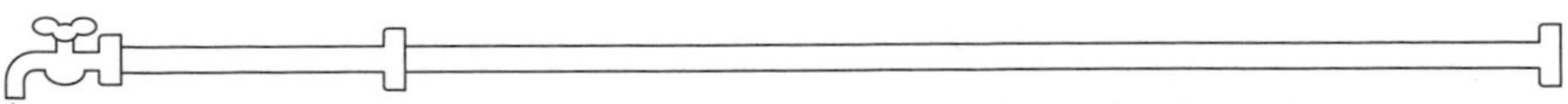

The Bloody Mary drink was originally called the Bucket of Blood.

general in the Soviet Union, another first-and-only for a woman.

SPACEFARER: Sally Ride, NASA astronaut

OVERVIEW EFFECT: *"The view of Earth is absolutely spectacular, and the feeling of looking back and seeing your planet as a planet is just an amazing feeling. It's a totally different perspective, and it makes you appreciate, actually, how fragile our existence is."*

DETAILS: When NASA made the switch from command modules to space shuttles, scientists could finally be astronauts. Ride, a physicist, was one of six women accepted in the first group, and was later selected for a 1983 *Challenger* mission. Admitting that she "felt a special responsibility to be the first American woman in space," Ride's historic flight took place nearly 20 years to the day after Valentina Tereshkova's. "I'm sure it was the most fun that I'll ever have in my life," Ride said afterward. She got to fly to space one more time, in 1987, before retiring from NASA and returning to academia. But she said a part of her would always remain on that orbiter.

SPACEFARER: William Anders, NASA astronaut

OVERVIEW EFFECT: *"We came all this way to explore the Moon, and the most important thing is that we discovered the Earth."*

DETAILS: Before NASA put men on the Moon, they flew men around it. On Christmas Eve in 1968, *Apollo 8* astronaut William Anders was completing a Moon orbit when he saw a glowing blue orb rise into view beyond the cratered Lunar surface, and decided to photograph it. "Oh my God!" he said. "Look at that picture over there! There's the Earth coming up. Wow, that's pretty."

"Hey, don't take that," joked crewmate Frank Borman. "It's not scheduled."

Anders laughed and asked Commander Jim Lovell, "You got a color film, Jim? Hand me that roll of color quick, would you..."

Lovell replied, "Oh man, that's great!"

Then Anders snapped what is arguably the most important photograph ever made. Called *Earthrise,* it marked the first time that the people of Earth were able to see their home planet as a small dot in space. According to *National Geographic,* "That photo...is often credited with helping to launch the environmental movement."

SPACEFARER: Mae Jemison, NASA astronaut

OVERVIEW EFFECT: *"Once I got into space, I was feeling very comfortable in the universe. I felt like I had a right to be anywhere in this universe, that I belonged here as much as any speck of stardust, any comet, any planet."*

DETAILS: Jemison, a former Peace Corps doctor, became the first African American woman in space as mission specialist on a 1992 *Endeavour* flight. A huge *Star Trek* fan, Jemison began each shift by informing Mission Control, "Hailing frequencies open."

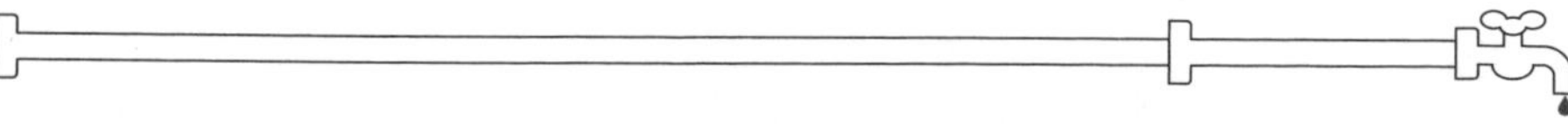

After her historic flight, she asked (begged) to be on an episode of *Star Trek: The Next Generation*, and was given the bit part of Lieutenant Palmer, a transporter room operator. She's also one of a handful of people alive to have been inducted into both the National Women's Hall of Fame and the International Space Hall of Fame. Today, Jemison is actively working to make the utopian future laid out in *Star Trek* a reality. She serves as principal of 100 Year Starship (a joint venture of NASA and the Defense Advanced Research Projects Agency). Launched in 2011, the project's mission is "to make the capability of human travel beyond our solar system a reality within the next 100 years."

SPACEFARER: Gennady Padalka, Russian cosmonaut

OVERVIEW EFFECT: *"Climate change, ecological problems, I don't consider them to be the main problems for the Earth. The bigger problem is people conflicting with each other...But if you take astronauts and cosmonauts, we work together in a very restricted space together, Americans and Russians and Canadians and Japanese. We speak a common language. We understand each other. Why can't the same approach be applied to Earth?"*

DETAILS: That quote comes from a 2019 *National Geographic* interview, in which Padalka described how spending more time in space than any other human in history—879 days and counting—has affected him. He was surprisingly down to Earth, so to speak, starting off the interview by stating that he's "not philosophical." But then he got philosophical, especially when asked if he cares more about the planet after seeing it from far away: "This is probably my best discovery, that the people of different nations, from different countries, under very severe conditions, can work very successfully, can be friendly all the time, understand each other, though their situations are sometimes really stressful. But there's something wrong in the fact that only such difficulties as I've just mentioned unite people. This is wrong. There should be something else."

"This is probably my best discovery, that the people of different nations, from different countries, under very severe conditions, can work very successfully, can be friendly all the time, understand each other, though their situations are sometimes really stressful."

SPACEFARER: Liu Yang, Chinese taikonaut

OVERVIEW EFFECT: *"Though I had been prepared, I was deeply astonished. I could hardly describe how beautiful and miraculous the Earth is. The beauty of our planet is quite beyond words. I couldn't help shouting: 'Look, the Earth is round, indeed'...I felt like a free fish swimming in the ocean of space."*

DETAILS: In 2012, the crew of *Shenzhou 9* ("Divine Vessel 9") docked with China's

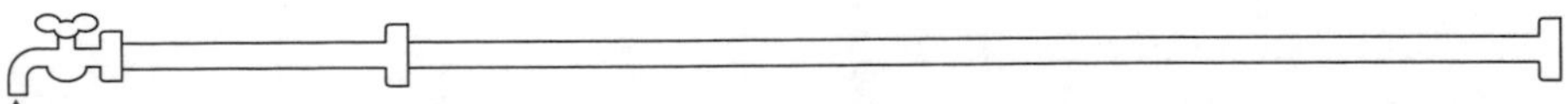

first space station, *Tiangong-1* ("Celestial Palace 1"). Onboard the school bus–sized station was 33-year-old Liu, the first Chinese woman to go into space. Even though the ISS was also in orbit, there was no rendezvous. "I think we all sensed being in space with other astronauts in orbit," she later said in a press conference. Liu expressed pride on behalf of the Chinese government but added that the future of space travel will require international cooperation. "The Chinese have the saying, 'When all the people collect the wood, you will make a great fire.' "

SPACEFARER: Alexei Leonov, Russian cosmonaut

OVERVIEW EFFECT: *"The Earth was small, light blue, and so touchingly alone, our home that must be defended like a holy relic. The Earth was absolutely round. I believe I never knew what the word 'round' meant until I saw Earth from space."*

DETAILS: If you want to see what effect being the first human to perform an EVA (extravehicular activity—an activity performed outside the spacecraft) had on Alexei Leonov, go online and look at his paintings. They're brightly colored earthscapes and spacescapes, along with detailed depictions of his historic space walk. On the March 1965 mission aboard *Voskhod 2,* Leonov brought along paper and a set of colored pencils. Though he could barely move in his bulky space suit, he became the first person to draw a picture in space. It was, fittingly, a sunrise—which, in Russian, is *voskhod.*

Artwork aside, Leonov's historic space walk nearly killed him. It was all going well—"I felt like a seagull with its wings outstretched, soaring high above the Earth"—until it was time to go back in. By that point, his space suit had become so pressurized that he couldn't use his hands to open the outside airlock. He actually had to let some of the oxygen out...in space. And then there was a malfunction on reentry that dropped him and his copilot 600 miles off course. They spent two cold days in the mountains before being rescued. But Leonov came home a national hero, and he continued painting until he died in 2019 at the age of 85.

SPACEFARER: Peggy Whitson, NASA astronaut

OVERVIEW EFFECT: *"You see billions and billions of stars and recognize that you know some of those have planets, too, and maybe there's life out there, and this is just one of billions of galaxies...and so it gives you this huge perspective of how far we potentially have to go for real exploration."*

DETAILS: Here's a slightly less profound Peggy Whitson quote: "Gravity sucks." She should know, having spent a record 665 days in orbit (cumulative)—the most, not only for a woman, but for any American. Whitson, who made her third flight at 57, is also the oldest woman to have gone to space. She said that coming back was always the hardest part. "It's a big challenge just readapting to feeling heavy again, you know?

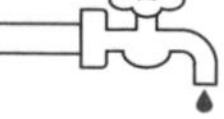

Even my arm feels heavy. My legs feel heavy." Whitson hopes that one day, everyone will get the chance to experience the sensation of weightlessness. "Zero gravity is such an alien environment—completely different from everything we've grown up with every single day of our lives. And it's incomprehensible how much better it was than I anticipated it would be."

SPACEFARER: Kalpana Chawla, NASA astronaut

OVERVIEW EFFECT: *"One day I was in the flight deck looking from the overhead windows outside. It was starting to get dim outside, so you start to see your own reflection...I could then see my reflection in the window, and in the retina of my eye the whole Earth and the sky could be seen reflected."*

DETAILS: Chawla, the first woman of Indian descent to go to space, had that experience on her second *Columbia* mission...which was also to be her last. There were 135 STS (Space Transportation System) missions during NASA's 30-year space shuttle program. All but two were successful. On January 28, 1986, the *Challenger* mission STS-51-L ended 73 seconds after launch when the shuttle's external fuel tank exploded, destroying the shuttle. And on February 1, 2003, the *Columbia*—with Chawla aboard—disintegrated as it reentered the Earth's atmosphere. The shuttle's left wing had been damaged during launch. That exposed the wing's internal structure and, in the extreme heat of reentry, caused the wing to fail and the shuttle to break apart. The two accidents claimed the lives of all 14 crew members.

EPILOGUE

As Sally Ride once said, "I've discovered that half the people would love to go into space and there's no need to explain it to them. The other half can't understand and I couldn't explain it to them." But if you do want to take your own star trek, there might yet be hope. In July 2019, two astro-advocacy groups—the Space for Humanity and the Overview Institute—teamed up to announce a challenge to send 10,000 "citizen astronauts" into space over the next decade. (The organizers said they're in talks with private aerospace companies to create a low-cost space tourist transport system.) If you think you have the right stuff, they're accepting applications. The only two requirements are that you can speak English and that you're 18 years or older. If accepted, your mission is simple: Go to space, look out the window and experience the Overview Effect, and then come back and tell people about it.

But be warned: One flight won't be enough for you. In the words of the fourth person in space, Russian cosmonaut Gherman Titov, who orbited planet Earth 17 times in August 1961, "It's a pity I flew only once. A spaceflight is like a drug—once you experience it, you can't think of anything else."

ANSWERS

WELCOME TO LJUBLJANA *(Answers for page 156)*

1. h; **2.** l; **3.** d; **4.** q; **5.** g; **6.** a; **7.** n; **8.** j; **9.** w; **10.** p; **11.** u; **12.** c; **13.** y; **14.** m; **15.** v; **16.** k; **17.** x; **18.** i; **19.** s; **20.** b; **21.** o; **22.** t; **23.** f; **24.** e; **25.** z; **26.** r.

BRAINTEASERS *(Answers for page 212)*

Palindromic Minute. The shortest: the times 9:59 and 10:01 have only two minutes between them. The longest: from 1:01 to 12:21 is 11 hours and 20 minutes.

One Talented Word. The word is "NOON." It's a palindrome, so it reads the same forward and backward, but it also reads the same right side up and upside down.

Speaking of Time. A quarter to two.

Riding the Bus. 23. The question began with "passengers" but ended asking, "how many people," so you have to include the bus driver.

Where the Wind Blows. There were only two apples on the trees, and the wind blew only one of them onto the ground. That makes both of these plural phrases "apples on the trees" and "apples on the ground" false.

Refreshing Murder Mystery. The poison was in the ice cubes, so the thirsty guy drank his before the ice melted, unlike the slower drinker.

The Adding Times. 1 + 2 + 3 = 6; 1 × 2 × 3 = 6.

Exact Change. 5 cents. Most people would quickly answer: 10 cents. But the question says it's a "dollar more" and $1.00 is only 90 cents more than 10 cents, whereas $1.05 is $1.00 more than 5 cents, and both of them add up to $1.10.

To the Nines. The first answer is...none. You will not be writing the "number 9" at all when you start at "number 900." But disregarding that nerdy technicality, the answer is 120. In the hundreds place, you'll write "9" 100 times; in the tens place, you'll write "9" 10 times; and in the ones place, you'll write "9" 10 times, which adds up to 120.

Tech Talk. Because "brayed coin" is an anagram for "binary code."

Out to Sea. The two soldiers are standing on opposite sides of a ship...facing each other. (And no, they're not at the North or South Pole—both of which are landlocked.)

Roll Call. Tina. The first two letters of each name follow the musical scale: do re mi fa so la ti.

THE RIDDLER *(Answers for page 333)*

1. Your tongue.

2. Choices.

3. 9. Delete the 'S' and SIX becomes IX in Roman numerals.

4. Beauty. It's a play on the common phrase "Beauty is in the eye of the beholder." (In this case, a bee-holder.)

5. Vowels.

6. A kangaroo, which lives in Australia.

7. 12. (Did you say 4?)

8. The letter r.

9. Lightning.

10. Your breath.

11. "I" and "eye."

12. Gold. In the ground it is dug for treasure; in the chest is a heart of gold; a golden sky is also treasured, and a gold medal is the best of the three medals.

13. Oxygen (O_2).

14. A pool table.

15. A joke.

THE ONE-HIT WONDER QUIZ *(Answers for page 343)*

1. t; **2.** k; **3.** o; **4.** l; **5.** h; **6.** m; **7.** c; **8.** d; **9.** n; **10.** b; **11.** j; **12.** e; **13.** r; **14.** q; **15.** i; **16.** g; **17.** s; **18.** a; **19.** f; **20.** p.

...broccoli, coffee with cream, and red wine." She lived to be 38.

- ❒ Uncle John's Bathroom Reader Plunges into the Presidency
- ❒ Uncle John's Bathroom Reader Plunges into the Universe
- ❒ Uncle John's Bathroom Reader Quintessential Collection of Notable Quotables
- ❒ Uncle John's Bathroom Reader Salutes the Armed Forces
- ❒ Uncle John's Bathroom Reader Shoots and Scores
- ❒ Uncle John's Bathroom Reader Sports Spectacular
- ❒ Uncle John's Bathroom Reader Takes a Swing at Baseball
- ❒ Uncle John's Bathroom Reader Tales to Inspire
- ❒ Uncle John's Bathroom Reader Tees Off on Golf
- ❒ Uncle John's Bathroom Reader The World's Gone Crazy
- ❒ Uncle John's Bathroom Reader Tunes into TV
- ❒ Uncle John's Bathroom Reader Vroom!
- ❒ Uncle John's Bathroom Reader Weird Canada
- ❒ Uncle John's Bathroom Reader Weird Inventions
- ❒ Uncle John's Bathroom Reader WISE UP!
- ❒ Uncle John's Bathroom Reader Wonderful World of Odd
- ❒ Uncle John's Bathroom Reader Zipper Accidents
- ❒ Uncle John's Book of Fun
- ❒ Uncle John's Canoramic Bathroom Reader
- ❒ Uncle John's Certified Organic Bathroom Reader
- ❒ Uncle John's Colossal Collection of Quotable Quotes
- ❒ Uncle John's Creature Feature Bathroom Reader For Kids Only!
- ❒ Uncle John's Curiously Compelling Bathroom Reader
- ❒ Uncle John's Did You Know...? Bathroom Reader For Kids Only!
- ❒ Uncle John's Do-It-Yourself Diary for Infomaniacs Only
- ❒ Uncle John's Do-It-Yourself Journal for Infomaniacs Only
- ❒ Uncle John's Electrifying Bathroom Reader For Kids Only!
- ❒ Uncle John's Electrifying Bathroom Reader For Kids Only! Collectible Edition
- ❒ Uncle John's Endlessly Engrossing Bathroom Reader
- ❒ Uncle John's Factastic Bathroom Reader
- ❒ Uncle John's Facts to Annoy Your Teacher Bathroom Reader For Kids Only!
- ❒ Uncle John's Fast-Acting Long-Lasting Bathroom Reader
- ❒ Uncle John's Fully Loaded 25th Anniversary Bathroom Reader
- ❒ Uncle John's Giant 10th Anniversary Bathroom Reader
- ❒ Uncle John's Gigantic Bathroom Reader
- ❒ Uncle John's Great Big Bathroom Reader
- ❒ Uncle John's Greatest Know on Earth Bathroom Reader
- ❒ Uncle John's Haunted Outhouse Bathroom Reader For Kids Only!
- ❒ Uncle John's Heavy Duty Bathroom Reader
- ❒ Uncle John's How to Toilet Train Your Cat
- ❒ Uncle John's InfoMania Bathroom Reader For Kids Only!
- ❒ Uncle John's Legendary Lost Bathroom Reader
- ❒ Uncle John's Lists That Make You Go Hmmm...
- ❒ Uncle John's New & Improved Briefs
- ❒ Uncle John's New & Improved Funniest Ever
- ❒ Uncle John's Old Faithful 30th Anniversary Bathroom Reader
- ❒ Uncle John's Perpetually Pleasing Bathroom Reader
- ❒ Uncle John's Political Briefs
- ❒ Uncle John's Presents: Book of the Dumb
- ❒ Uncle John's Presents: Book of the Dumb 2
- ❒ Uncle John's Presents: Mom's Bathtub Reader
- ❒ Uncle John's Presents the Ultimate Challenge Trivia Quiz
- ❒ Uncle John's Robotica Bathroom Reader
- ❒ Uncle John's Slightly Irregular Bathroom Reader
- ❒ Uncle John's Smell-O-Scopic Bathroom Reader For Kids Only!
- ❒ Uncle John's Supremely Satisfying Bathroom Reader
- ❒ Uncle John's The Enchanted Toilet Bathroom Reader For Kids Only!
- ❒ Uncle John's Top Secret Bathroom Reader For Kids Only!
- ❒ Uncle John's Top Secret Bathroom Reader For Kids Only! Collectible Edition
- ❒ Uncle John's Totally Quacked Bathroom Reader For Kids Only!
- ❒ Uncle John's Triumphant 20th Anniversary Bathroom Reader
- ❒ Uncle John's True Crime
- ❒ Uncle John's Truth, Trivia, and the Pursuit of Factiness Bathroom Reader
- ❒ Uncle John's 24-Karat Gold Bathroom Reader
- ❒ Uncle John's Ultimate Bathroom Reader
- ❒ Uncle John's Uncanny Bathroom Reader
- ❒ Uncle John's Unsinkable Bathroom Reader
- ❒ Uncle John's Unstoppable Bathroom Reader
- ❒ Uncle John's Weird Weird World
- ❒ Uncle John's Weird Weird World: Epic
- ❒ The Wackiest Joke Book Ever!
- ❒ The Wackiest Joke Book That'll Knock-Knock You Over!
- ❒ Who Knew?
- ❒ Who Knew? Women in History

THE LAST PAGE

FELLOW BATHROOM READERS:
The fight for good bathroom reading should never be taken loosely—we must do our duty and sit firmly for what we believe in, even while the rest of the world is taking potshots at us.

We'll be brief. Now that we've proven we're not simply a flush-in-the-pan, we invite you to take the plunge: Sit Down and Be Counted! To find out what the BRI is up to, visit us at *www.portablepress.com* and take a peek!

GET CONNECTED

Find us online to sign up for our e-mail list, enter exciting giveaways, hear about new releases, and more!

Website: www.portablepress.com

Facebook: www.facebook.com/portablepress

Pinterest: www.pinterest.com/portablepress

Twitter: @Portablepress

Well, we're out of space, and when you've gotta go, you've gotta go. Tanks for all your support. Hope to hear from you soon.

Meanwhile, remember...

Keep on flushin'!